TOMS, COONS, MULATTOES, MAMMIES, AND BUCKS

TOMS, COONS, MULATTOES, MAMMIES, AND BUCKS

An Interpretive History of Blacks in American Films, Updated and Expanded 5th Edition

Donald Bogle

BLOOMSBURY ACADEMIC

LONDON • NEW YORK • OXFORD • NEW DELHI • SYDNEY

BLOOMSBURY ACADEMIC
Bloomsbury Publishing Plc
50 Bedford Square, London, WC1B 3DP, UK
1385 Broadway, New York, NY 10018, USA
29 Earlsfort Terrace, Dublin 2, Ireland

BLOOMSBURY, BLOOMSBURY ACADEMIC and the Diana logo are trademarks of
Bloomsbury Publishing Plc

First published 2016
Reprinted by Bloomsbury Academic 2022

Cover Images:
Dorothy Dandridge © 20th Century Fox /The Kobal Collection / Powolny, Frank
Django Unchained (2012) © Columbia Pictures / The Kobal Collection
The Littlest Rebel (1935) © 20th Century Fox / The Kobal Collection
The Help (2011) © Dreamworks Pictures / The Kobal Collection
12 Years A Slave (2013) © Regency Enterprises / The Kobal Collection
Cabin In The Sky (1943) © MGM / The Kobal Collection
Dreamgirls (2006) © Dreamworks / The Kobal Collection / James, David
Shaft (1971) © MGM / The Kobal Collection
Gone With The Wind (1939) © Selznick/MGM / The Kobal Collection
Training Day (2001) © Outlaw/Warner Bros / The Kobal Collection / Zuckerman, Robert
The Defiant Ones (1958) © United Artists / The Kobal Collection

For legal purposes the Acknowledgements on p.v constitute an extension
of this copyright page.

Bloomsbury Publishing Plc does not have any control over, or responsibility for, any
third-party websites referred to or in this book. All internet addresses given in this
book were correct at the time of going to press. The author and publisher regret any
inconvenience caused if addresses have changed or sites have ceased to exist, but
can accept no responsibility for any such changes.

A catalogue record for this book is available from the British Library.

A catalog record for this book is available from the Library of Congress.

ISBN: PB: 9780826429537

Typeset by RefineCatch Limited, Bungay, Suffolk

To find out more about our authors and books visit www.bloomsbury.com
and sign up for our newsletters.

Acknowledgment is made as follows for the use of photographs:

The Bettman Archive, Inc.: page 58, bottom; page 91; page 153, bottom. Alfred "Slick" Chester: page 106, bottom. Cinema 5, Ltd.: page 203, top. Copyright by Columbia Pictures Industries Inc.: page 163; page 173, bottom; page 177, bottom; page 197, bottom. Copyright © 1967 by Columbia Pictures Corporation: page 218. Copyright © 1970 by Columbia Pictures Corporation: page 228, bottom. Ken Freeman: page 106, top; page 112, bottom. Hal Roach Productions, Inc.: page 22. Louis de Rochement: page 149. Metro-Goldwyn-Mayer, Inc.: page 32, top; page 30, top; page 177, top; page 221. Copyright © 1969 Theatre Guild Films: page 228, top. Lorenzo Tucker: page 104; page 112, top; page 112, top and bottom; Twentieth Century-Fox Film Corporation: page 40, bottom; page 49, top and bottom; page 51; page 87, bottom; page 130, bottom; page 153, top; page 167; page 170, top and bottom; page 233, top. Universal Pictures: page 5; page 58, top. Melvin Van Peebles and Friedmen-Abeles: page 237, bottom. Movie Star News: page 55. The Museum of Modern Art/Film Still Archive: page 87, top; most stills pages 230–426. Photographs from Chapter Eleven are from Photofest. Other photographs are from the author's collection.

Frontispiece: Louise Beavers in "Imitation of Life" (Courtesy Universal Pictures)

To my mother
to papa g.
to jeanne & janet & bettina
to dodson & dawson
&
to three terrific bogles:
roger & jerry & jay

CONTENTS

10 THE 1990s: NEW STARS, NEW FILMMAKERS, AND A NEW AFRICAN AMERICAN CINEMA   293

ILLUSTRATIONS

PREFACE TO THE FIFTH EDITION

This new fifth revised edition of *Toms, Coons, Mulattoes, Mammies, and Bucks: An Interpretive History of Blacks in American Films* now takes the history of African Americans in the movies into the early decades of the twenty-first century. Writing this update has admittedly been a challenging and sometimes daunting experience. The previous edition ended with the new African American cinema and stars of the 1990s and the first year of the new millennium. Little did I know then that so much would happen in the new decades of the new century when American movies would once again undergo such significant changes.

This new edition continues the examination of the images of African Americans in the movies and, just as important, the often remarkable work of African American actors, actresses, and filmmakers who have contributed so much to the tone and texture of American cinema. Once again, I have looked at the response of the audience, especially African American moviegoers, to certain key movies and star personas. Sometimes the most important films have not been those that the critics praised but rather those in which moviegoers found cultural signs and symbols—as well as an exploration of issues and themes *and* entertaining, provocative performances and concepts—with which they could identify. Often enough, very popular films have spoken to moviegoers in a far more personal way than we might have imagined. Yet other times, some of those same films have moviegoers feeling frustrated—not so much just by what they said as by what they *didn't* say. Throughout the writing of this edition, I was struck by the new opportunities that sprang up for African Americans in the movie industry, perhaps best exemplified by the number of Oscar winners and nominees during the early part of the new century. But I was also struck by another fact: the movie industry, in certain respects, remained the same. While audiences were excited by the work and points-of-view of black filmmakers, who were finally coming to greater prominence, there still weren't nearly enough. At the same time, some very old images continued to thrive into the new millennium. That made it all the more enlightening to see the manner in which skilled performers worked their way around hack misconceptions and managed to infuse their performances with insights and rich observations. That may explain why African American moviegoers still were more affected (as were white audiences) by who starred in a picture. Because of the nature of this type of historical overview, there has not been enough space to discuss certain movies in the detail I would prefer, especially such films as Oscar Micheaux's *Within Our Gates, Devil in a Blue Dress, Belle, Selma*, and independent filmmaker Barry Jenkins' *Medicine for Melancholy*. A number of films are discussed in the sections covering the careers of the performers who starred in them. In this edition, dates are given for articles about such performers as Angela Bassett and Chris Rock, discussing the film industry but not for reviews of individual films, which can be easily checked. Some changes—but no major ones—have been made in the original text. I did add comments about a rediscovered film from 1913 starring Bert Williams. For me, the first edition of *Toms, Coons, Mulattoes, Mammies, and Bucks* was as much a statement on my own evolving aesthetic and perspective as it was on the history and contributions of African Americans in American cinema.

There are many people to thank for their help while I researched and wrote the material for this edition as well as earlier ones. As I've indicated before, both Cicely Tyson and Morgan Freeman, with whom I conducted public interviews some years ago for the D.C. International Film Festival, provided insights not only into their work and careers but also on the effect of screen images in their own lives. Freeman also provided a dazzler of a surprise. Shortly before we entered the auditorium for his interview, he spoke perceptively of such actors as Mantan Moreland, Stepin Fetchit, and apparently a favorite, Dorothy Dandridge. (She's my favorite too!) He also did a flat-out brilliant impersonation of Fetchit that captured the essence of Fetchit's timing and the core of his lazybones persona. On another occasion some years ago, after I had taped a television program on which Samuel L. Jackson was also a guest, Jackson spoke with admiration of Freeman, stating he aspired to be the type of fine character actor that Freeman had become. It's doubtful if either Jackson or Freeman realized, at the start of their careers, that they would emerge as world-famous movie stars. Nonetheless, actors such as Freeman, Tyson, and Jackson all brought into sharp focus something I've always been aware of: that extraordinary link between African American performers past and past.

Also providing me with insights was Spike Lee during a recent onstage interview I conducted with him at the Turner Classic Movies annual film festival in Los Angeles. Previously, the same was true of my experience with directors Charles Burnett, Wendell Harris, and Neema Barnette as they informally discussed their work during a break at a symposium in Hartford, Connecticut. Hearing filmmakers discuss the pressures and attitudes (racial, cultural) within the entertainment industry is always a stimulating, enlightening experience.

Before beginning work on the previous fourth edition update, I also had a unique, telling experience when the film rights to my book *Dorothy Dandridge: A*

Biography were optioned for a movie to star Whitney Houston. I had numerous meetings and discussions about the movie version in both New York and Los Angeles. Years before I had come to know much about the inner workings of the movie industry when I worked for film director Otto Preminger toward the end of his illustrious career. Since then I naturally had been exposed to changes within the industry. But with the Dandridge film project, I saw in boldface many of the then new attitudes of Hollywood at the tail end of the twentieth century, and I also saw up close the struggles of the New Black Hollywood to do unusual projects for the big screen. In the end, Houston did not star in the Dandridge film, which is a story unto itself. But much of what I observed at that time about the industry and the audience has made its way in some subtle and some obvious comments in both the fourth and now fifth editions.

Finally, there have been my remarkable friends and associates who have provided great assistance and been far more helpful with this edition than they realize. Foremost, I have to express my appreciation to my former researcher, now a director, Phil Bertelsen, who was excellent at gathering information I needed and also in coming up with additional material I had not requested. David Aglow has also researched for important material for me. Jerald Silverhardt has come to the rescue on numerous occasions when I have put in a call to the West Coast to check on some detail or matter about contemporary films and film production. Emery Wimbish and Grace Frankowsky have always been encouraging and inspiring. Bruce Goldstein of New York's Film Forum has also been helpful. It has also always been a terrific experience to talk to my dear friend producer Debra Martin Chase about actors and their careers as well as the daily workings of the contemporary Black Hollywood. My appreciation is also extended to Gloria Hopkins Buck, Pat Faison, Mary Sue Price, and Jane Rappaport of the Newark Black Film Festival, and to the memory of the late Clement Price as well as to Warrington Hudlin of the Museum of the Moving Image, and Todd Hoellerman of K2 Pictures. The great drama coach and acting teacher Janet Alhanti, who also resides in Los Angeles, has always been insightful. Best of all, I want to thank such friends at Turner Classic Movies as Darcy Hettrich, Dori Stegman, and of course, the astute host of TCM, Robert Osborne. Most of all, I have to thank my great friend Charlie Tabesh, the Vice President of Programming at TCM, who has helped me track down rare films to screen—and with whom it is always a pleasure and insightful to discuss film history as well as politics and current events. Charlie is just the best!

My gratitude also goes to Sarah Orrick, Carol Scott Leonard, Marie Dutton Brown, Ronald Mason, Deesha Hill, Martin Radburd, Jeanne Bogle Charleston, Janet Bogle Schenck and her husband Jerry Schenck, Jacqueline Bogle Mosley, Robert W. Bogle, Roslynne Bogle, Roger Bogle, Gerald Grant Bogle, Jay Bogle, Robert Bogle Jr., Luellen Fletcher, Fred Charleston, Fred Charleston Jr., Lori Stimpson Guile, Ayana Charleston, Hassan Charleston, Denise Charleston,

Catherine Nelson, Jeanne Franz, Clerio Demoraes, Allison Samuels, formerly of *Newsweek* and *The Daily Beast*, Joerg Klebe of German Educational Television, Rigmor Newman, Robert Katz, Jeanne Moutoussamy Ashe, Susan Peterson, Tink Peterson, Linda Doll Tarrant, Steve Morris, Brett Haber, Barbara Reynolds, Herma Ross, Aminata Diabate, Alan Sukoenig, Hiroko Hatanaka, Peg Henehan, Doug Rossini, Nels Johnson, dear Sally Placksin, and naturally, Bettina Batchleor and the fantastic Marian Etoile Watson. Thanks also to the Lagow family: Barbara, Ellen, and James. And, of course, I want to thank dear Mariska Bogle, who sometimes griped but nonetheless sweetly adjusted her schedule on so many occasions to help update my filing system on performers and productions. Special thanks go to my former editor Elisabeth Dyssegaard, to my good friends Enrico Pellegrini and Katrina Pavlovs, to my colleagues at the University of Pennsylvania Gale Garrison and Carol Davis as well as to a number of my former students at both the University of Pennsylvania and at New York University's Tisch School of the Arts, and my round table of former Penn students with whom I frequently have lunch to catch up on films and television: Gigi Kwon, Raj Gopal, Jake Stock, and Nadine Zylberberg. Special thanks also go to my former students Marcel Salas, Kyle Webster, Judith Osborne, Wesley Barrow, Robin Williams, and of course, to my former graduate assistant at Tisch Mia Kai Moody and to Laurence Coman. My gratitude also goes to darling Yemaya Bogle.

Finally, my great appreciation and gratitude are extended foremost to my former editor Evander Lomke, who saw me through the previous updates of the book with great insights and expertise and who graciously provided comments for this edition; to Mary Al-Sayed who skillfully guided the book through production, Merv Honeywood, Ellen Conlon and Michelle Chen who also contributed much while the book was in production; and to my current editor Katie Gallof, who (considering my extended deadlines) has been not only helpful, encouraging, and supportive but extraordinarily patient.

INTRODUCTION

When I was a wide-eyed, pint-sized kid growing up in Pennsylvania and still believing in ideals and dreams, I decided one gloomy rainy afternoon to run away from home and go to live at the movies. By chance, the movie I went to "live at" was something called *Carmen Jones*. In no conceivable way has my life been the same since.

Carmen Jones was the first black film I had seen, and as I sat intoxicated by Dorothy Dandridge's lush beauty and invigorated by the dazzling enthusiasm the cast displayed for its work, I realized the film and the actors were unlike any I had ever viewed before. It was more than the fact that these were black faces on the silver screen. I was also affected and moved because these were immensely talented and dynamic people, more colorful, more unpredictable, and more outrageous than most other actors appearing in American films. *Carmen Jones* proved to be a source of inspiration. Thereafter for the duration of my childhood in the late 1950s and throughout adolescence in the 1960s, I found myself always on the look-out in movies and on television for black faces. From the old films on the tube, I caught glimpses of a variety of performers with such "bizarre" names as Stepin, Hattie, Butterfly, Bojangles, Rochester, and Lena. At the local movie houses, I had brief introductions to Sidney Poitier, Ruby Dee, and Ossie Davis. As I silently watched, I compared and contrasted the black actors not only with white performers but with one another. To my surprise and delight, the old-timers came off exceptionally well. They seemed outfitted with a charm, a spontaneity, and an individuality that a number of more modern performers lacked. As my interest in the old-timers mounted, I longed for more information about them. How many pictures had Stepin Fetchit made? Had Hattie McDaniel ever played a *submissive* servant? Was there a movie in which Bojangles did not dance?

Seldom was I able to find answers to my questions. There was not one reference work in the library that I could go to for information. But perhaps more disappointing was the apathy of others about all black actors, old and new. Among my schoolmates, there was hardly any concern about a black face—other than Sidney Poitier's—and if one dared mention a Fetchit or a Rochester, he was soon informed that these people were "villains," "betrayers," nothing more than toms and handkerchief heads. Eventually in this age of great conformity, I learned to keep my mouth shut about any black actor I really did care about. But when alone I still responded to and ultimately came to love the performances of certain black actors.

That love continued through high school, through college, through graduate school, right on up to the beginning of my professional life. Subconsciously, I think I was writing a history of movie blacks in my head. Then two "traumatic" experiences not only heightened my interest in blacks in American movies but served better than anything else as catalysts for the writing of this book.

The first experience occurred in the plush office of film director Otto Preminger, where I was employed as a story editor. One day in the middle of an interoffice debate, I was asked who had played the character Sam in the 1942 movie *Casablanca*. Preminger was certain a black actor had performed the role. But I self-righteously declared that Hoagy Carmichael had played the part. To my everlasting chagrin, I learned that Dooley Wilson, an obscure black actor, was the performer in the picture. Afterward I felt pitifully inadequate for not knowing something that was a part of my own cultural heritage.

My second traumatic experience occurred shortly afterwards while I was a staff writer for *Ebony* in Chicago. Having recently seen the reissued *Gone with the Wind*, I suggested to the managing editors of the magazine that we do a feature story on Butterfly McQueen, who portrayed Prissy. There was a renewed interest in her career because of the film. She was a nostalgic favorite for older readers, I assumed, and I had hoped that an article on McQueen might serve as a kick-off for a series on other forgotten black performers. To my surprise, I heard the *Ebony* editors sounding off like my former grade-school classmates. They dismissed the old-time actors as toms and mammies and spoke of them with boredom, disgust, contempt, and even condescension—as if our bright new movies with their bright new black actors had arrived at something called cinematic integrity!

The attitude of the *Ebony* editors, however, simply pointed out the sad state of black film history in America. There was no history. And it seemed to me that a number of talented people were dismissed or ignored or even vilified because no one knew anything about the nature of their work and the conditions under which they performed. No, I thought. The past had to be contended with. It had to be defined, recorded, reasoned with, and interpreted. And I felt it my task to do so.

Once I decided to write the book, I returned to New York City, where I began an intense and alternately gratifying and frustrating period of research. I watched film after film at almost any place I could—at the Museum of Modern Art, at the Jewish Museum, at the Studio Museum in Harlem, at the Library of Congress, at the homes of friends, at rundown theaters on Forty-second Street, and often in my apartment in front of the friendly tube. My great ambition was to see every motion picture in which a black had ever worked. But that obviously proved impossible. Those black films I was unable to see I read about, going through albums of pictures and clippings at the Schomburg Center for Research in Black Culture, through personal scrapbooks of black personalities at their homes, and through reams of old yellowed newspaper movie reviews. At one point, I seated myself at the library and went through every copy of *Ebony* ever published to track down information on films and actors.

When I checked into what had been written on the subject, I found only one formal piece of work, by an Englishman, Peter Noble. Written in the 1940s, Noble's *The Negro in Films* proved informative. Yet, many of my questions were left unanswered. He deplored—rightfully—the stereotyping of Negroes in American movies. But I wanted comments and analysis on what certain black actors accomplished with even demeaning stereotyped roles. For me, it was not enough to dismiss Hattie McDaniel and Butterfly McQueen as mere mammy and pickaninny. Anyone who had seen them in *Gone with the Wind* and left the theater with no more than that impression really missed or ignored the strength of the performances, and at the same time denied black America a certain cultural heritage. In the opening sections of the book, I have had to cover much of the same historical territory as Noble. But what we have each gotten from the experience of African Americans in American cinema has been vastly different. From my point of view, the history of blacks in American films is one in which actors have elevated *kitsch* or trash and brought to it arty qualities if not pure art itself. Indeed, the thesis of my book is that many black actors—from Stepin Fetchit to Louise Beavers to Sidney Poitier to Jim Brown and Whoopi Goldberg—have played—at some time or another—stereotyped roles. But the essence of black film history is not found in the stereotyped role but in what certain talented actors have done with the stereotype.

My final source of information was the personal interview. Many African American actors refused to talk to me, perhaps out of some fear that I might demean them even more than their old films had. Some of the newer ones were remote and difficult. One older actress, a particular favorite, promised an interview only if I paid her a thousand dollars. Another prominent actor/singer refused to see me but requested that I send him galleys of my book before publication. However, those who consented to interviews, formal or informal, were most helpful. In Hollywood Mantan Moreland was lively and full of fun as he reminisced on his early movie roles. Clarence Muse proved a bit cantankerous when I visited him at his California ranch, but he was nonetheless informative as he discussed his career in the 1930s and 1940s. Sidney Poitier, standing tall and sleek at Kennedy Airport, was so gracious, polite, and charming during the few minutes that I talked with him, that I was ready to forgive him for all his recent bad movies. Behind his massive marble desk in Manhattan, Otto Preminger sat like a monarch as he casually discussed his two all-black films and provided capsule analyses of black actors he had worked with. At a Manhattan restaurant Robert Hooks was first guarded, then thoroughly at ease as he reviewed his roles in *Hurry Sundown* and *Last of the Mobile Hot Shots*. King Vidor was extremely helpful as we talked in his office in Beverly Hills and later as we lunched at the Farmers Market. An enormous treat for me was a special cocktail party arranged by Lorenzo Tucker, who appeared in black-cast race movies and had been called "the black Valentino." At Tucker's party, I came face to face with such race movie stars as "the sepia Mae West," "the colored Cagney," and many others. And I learned not only about their careers but about those of others who had worked in race movies. One important black actor ended his days as a redcap. Another became a notorious Harlem pool-shark. Some became hustlers of all sorts. At least two vivacious leading ladies ended up as domestic workers. Other African American performers drifted into alcoholism, drugs, or bitter self-recrimination.

For me, the most exciting and at the same time depressing interview was a startling, delirious eight-hour chat with Vivian Dandridge, the sister of Dorothy. From Vivian, there emerged the clearest, most articulate definition of black movie stardom (and its differences from white stardom) that I had ever heard. The embarrassments, the humiliations, the affronts her sister endured were distressing. Dorothy's final self-destructive bent was clearly an outgrowth of her experiences as a black woman in a white movie colony.

Once the research was completed, I gathered my material and tried fitting it into some order. As I did so, I saw emerging something more than history. Having come of age at a time when it has been almost impossible to keep politics and aesthetics apart, I felt compelled to interpret the past from my own point of view, that of a black looking at other blacks in motion pictures, that of a black under twenty-five reviewing the work of his cultural ancestors. When I saw *The Birth of a Nation* with a black audience that openly cheered for the black villains to defeat the white heroes, or when I viewed *The Emperor Jones* with a young black audience that openly admitted it was there simply to "understand" the legendary Robeson whom their parents had worshiped, I knew I was seeing reactions far different from those that initially greeted these films and other black movies. I was also aware, while sitting in a Times Square theater one afternoon and listening to black teenagers howling and deriding Juano Hernandez's weathered janitor character in *They Call Me MISTER Tibbs*, that somehow or other I had to make them understand what this man had been like in the early 1950s. These teenagers had to see that without an actor like Hernandez in the 1950s, there might never have been a *They Call Me MISTER Tibbs*. What I have tried to do is put black films and black personalities in their proper historical perspective, at the same time trying to say what these films and actors mean to us today.

Another problem for me in writing the book was deciding whom to include or exclude. Had it not been that the critics of their time were so impressed by performers Hazel Scott and Clarence Muse, I might have referred to them only in passing. Instead I included them and am now glad I did. At the same time, I would have preferred spending more time discussing Hernandez and James Edwards and less on Sidney Poitier. But it was obvious to me that Poitier is such an important figure in the history of black films and black performers that he demanded extensive coverage. In short, I have forced myself to be objective on certain historical matters. I should say also that this book deals primarily with African Americans in Hollywood films. There is one general chapter on the independent film companies (operating outside of Hollywood) which produced black-cast race movies exclusively for ghetto theaters in the 1930s and 1940s, but because information on the independents is still in such disarray, I have limited my comments on the independents and have not always given dates for the films. But I felt it essential that something be said about this vast area of film history that has gone for years without any recognition.

A third problem centered on the personal lives of certain actors. One cannot discuss the careers of Fetchit or Dandridge or Richard Pryor or Whitney Houston without some reference to their off-screen lives. For the most part, I have dealt with the lives of the early black performers because theirs usually ended up so tragically, or so desperately unfulfilled, with Hollywood often contributing to their tragedies. In dealing with many latter-day actors, however, I have not gone into their personal lives. The work of such professionals as Ruby Dee or Ivan Dixon or Angela Bassett or Morgan Freeman is clearly less closely linked to their private lives.

A final problem was simply one of language. Certain performers such as the Lena Horne of the 1940s or the Hazel Scott of the 1940s were clearly bourgeois *Negro* creations. Others, like the tough and uncompromising Hattie McDaniel, were always outspokenly *black* personalities. Generally, I have used *colored*, *Negro*, *black*, and *African American* discriminately and in their proper historical context.

All the problems connected with writing the book weighed on me heavily, but as I worked I saw my perspective changing. Ultimately, my study of African Americans in American movies has become not only a discussion of actors and pictures but a statement on the development of my own consciousness. The energies, the tensions, the study and analysis, the concerns, and then the summation that I initially poured into this book occurred during a clearly circumscribed time in my life. I was not much out of my teens, and I wrote on problems and difficulties as well as pleasures that certain films and personalities raised for me. At this point, I can say with candor and relief that the book has succeeded for me. I see blacks in films differently, with a new awareness and an altered sensitivity. I have been liberated, and I think some kind of general position on African Americans in the movies has taken shape at a time when it is badly needed.

Of course, no book is ever written without the help of others. Along the way to completing any manuscript, almost every author encounters friends and adversaries who motivate or discourage him, who inspire or deflate him, who tell him their problems or listen to his. In the end, these people all influence his work, even if it is just the fact that they delay his getting it done.

Nevertheless it is a pleasure to thank those who helped me in this venture. My thanks go to Arlene Donovan of Creative Management Associates who encouraged me to pursue this project at the very beginning. Later during the research period and for three-quarters of the writing span, Eileen Lottman was most considerate, helpful, and a great ego booster. During the editing and rewriting process, Bob Silverstein stood by with astounding degrees of patience and insight to offer pertinent comments on my work. My gratitude is also extended to Nora Sutton and Vivienne Seraque of Bantam Books, to Regina Cornwell and Melinda Ward of the Museum of Modern Art, to Pearl Bowser during her stint at the Jewish Museum, to Patrick Sheehan of the Library of Congress, to Douglas Barone and Jeffrey Conrad of Doubleday and Company, and to Alice West, Mary Sampson, Reubenia Frazier, and dear Octavia Glasgow. Final special thanks go to Steven Morris of *Ebony*, Daniel Dawson of the Studio Museum, Vivian Dandridge, and last, the most patient of all, Marc Jaffe.

1 BLACK BEGINNINGS: FROM *UNCLE TOM'S CABIN* TO *THE BIRTH OF A NATION*

In the beginning, there was an Uncle Tom. A former mechanic photographed him in a motion picture that ran no longer than twelve minutes. And a new dimension was added to American movies.

The year was 1903. The mechanic-turned-movie-director was Edwin S. Porter. The twelve-minute motion picture was *Uncle Tom's Cabin*. And the new dimension was Uncle Tom himself. He was the American movies' first black character. The great paradox was that in actuality Tom was not black at all. Instead he was portrayed by a nameless, slightly overweight white actor made up in blackface. But the use of whites in black roles was then a common practice, a tradition carried over from the stage and maintained during the early days of silent films. Still, the first Negro character had arrived in films, and he had done so at a time when the motion-picture industry itself was virtually nonexistent. The movies were without stars or studios or sound. There were no great directors or writers. And the community of Hollywood had not yet come into being.

After the tom's debut, there appeared a variety of black presences bearing the fanciful names of the coon, the tragic mulatto, the mammy, and the brutal black buck. All were character types used for the same effect: to entertain by stressing Negro inferiority. Fun was poked at the American Negro by presenting him as either a nitwit or a childlike lackey. None of the types was meant to do great harm, although at various times individual ones did. All were merely filmic reproductions of black stereotypes that had existed since the days of slavery and were already popularized in American life and arts. The movies, which catered to public tastes, borrowed profusely from all the other popular art forms. Whenever dealing with black characters, they simply adapted the old familiar stereotypes, often further distorting them.

In the early days when most important black characters were still portrayed by white actors in blackface, there was nothing but the old character types. They sat like square boxes on a shelf. A white actor walked by, selected a box, and used it as a base for a very square, rigidly defined performance. Later, when real black actors played the roles and found themselves wedged into these categories, the history became one of actors battling against the types to create rich, stimulating, diverse characters. At various points the tom, the coon, the tragic mulatto, the mammy, and the brutal black buck were brought to life respectively by Bill "Bojangles" Robinson, Stepin Fetchit, Nina Mae McKinney, Hattie McDaniel, and Walter Long (actually a white actor who portrayed a black villain in *The Birth of a Nation*), and later "modernized" by such performers as Sidney Poitier, Sammy Davis, Jr., Dorothy Dandridge, Ethel Waters, and Jim Brown. Later such performers as Richard Pryor, Eddie Murphy, Lonette McKee, Whoopi Goldberg, and Danny Glover also found themselves struggling to turn old stereotypes inside out. Often it seemed as if the mark of the actor was the manner in which he individualized the mythic type or towered above it. The types were to prove deadly for some actors and inconsequential for others. But try as any actor may to forget the typecasting, the familiar types have most always been present in American black movies. The early silent period of motion pictures remains important, not because there were any great black performances—there weren't—but because the five basic types—the boxes sitting on the shelf—that were to dominate black characters for the next half century were first introduced then.

The Tom

Porter's tom was the first in a long line of socially acceptable Good Negro characters. Always as toms are chased, harassed, hounded, flogged, enslaved, and insulted, they keep the faith, n'er turn against their white massas, and remain hearty, submissive, stoic, generous, selfless, and oh-so-very kind. Thus they endear themselves to white audiences and emerge as heroes of sorts.

Two early toms appeared in the shorts *Confederate Spy* (c. 1910) and *For Massa's Sake* (1911). In the former, dear old Uncle Daniel is a Negro spy for the South. He dies before a Northern firing squad, but he is content, happy that he "did it for massa's sake and little massa." In *For Massa's Sake* a former slave is so attached to his erstwhile master that he sells himself back into slavery to help the master through a period of financial difficulties.

During the silent period, there were also remakes of the Harriet Beecher Stowe novel in which the tale of the good Christian slave was again made the meat of

James B. Lowe, the star of 1927's *Uncle Tom's Cabin* and the first black actor to be ballyhooed by his studio.

melodrama. The first remakes in 1909 and 1913 had little in style or treatment to distinguish them. But a fourth version, directed by William Robert Daly in 1914, distinguished itself and the tom tradition by starring the Negro stage actor Sam Lucas in the title role. Lucas became the first black man to play a leading role in a movie. Later in 1927, when Universal Pictures filmed *Uncle Tom's Cabin*, the handsome Negro actor James B. Lowe was signed for the leading role. Harry Pollard directed the Universal feature. Twelve years earlier, Pollard had filmed a version of the Stowe classic in which he portrayed the Christian slave in blackface. But for this new venture Negro Lowe was selected to fit in with the "realistic" demands of the times. Congratulating itself on its liberalism, Universal sent out press releases about its good colored star:

> James B. Lowe has made history. A history that reflects only credit to the Negro race, not only because he has given the "Uncle Tom" character a new slant, but because of his exemplary conduct with the Universal company. They look upon Lowe at the Universal Studio as a living black god. . . . Of the directors, critics, artists, and actors who have seen James Lowe work at the studio there are none who will not say he is the most suited of all men for the part of "Tom." Those who are religious say that a heavenly power brought him to Universal and all predict a most marvelous future and worldwide reputation for James B. Lowe.

Although a "heavenly power" may have been with actor Lowe, it didn't have a great effect on the way his character was written. Tom still came off as a good-hearted soul, furnished with new color but no new sentiments. The fierce brutalities and heartbreaking, tragic realities of the slave system that Harriet Beecher Stowe had so passionately written about were softened here. Yet the handsome Lowe played his role thoughtfully with a sensitivity and dignity that make the character human. So affecting was Lowe that he was sent to England on a promotional tour to ballyhoo the picture, thus becoming one of the first black actors to be publicized by his studio. Sadly, afterward Lowe disappeared from the scene. Curiously, in 1958 this version of *Uncle Tom's Cabin*, although silent, was reissued with an added prologue by Raymond Massey. Because it arrived just when the sit-ins were about to erupt in the South, many wondered if by reissuing the film Universal Studios hoped to remind audiences of a less turbulent or heated form of resistance.

The Coon

Although tom was to outdistance every other type and dominate American hearth and home, he had serious competition from a group of coons. They appeared in a series of black films presenting the Negro as an amusement object and black buffoon. They lacked the single-mindedness of tom. There were the pure coon and two variants of his type: the pickaninny and the uncle remus.

The pickaninny was the first of the coon types to make its screen debut. It gave the Negro child actor his place in the black pantheon. Generally, he was a harmless, little screwball creation whose eyes popped, whose hair stood on end with the least excitement, and whose antics were pleasant and diverting. Thomas Alva Edison proved to be a pioneer in the exploitation and exploration of this type when he presented *Ten Pickaninnies* in 1904, a forerunner of the Hal Roach *Our Gang* series. During his camera experiments in 1893, Edison had photographed some blacks as "interesting side effects." In *Ten Pickaninnies*, the side effects moved to the forefront of the action as a group of nameless Negro children romped and ran about while being referred to as snowballs, cherubs, coons, bad chillun, inky kids, smoky kids, black lambs, cute ebonies, and chubbie ebonies. In due time, the pickaninnies were to be called by other names. In the 1920s and the 1930s, such child actors as Sunshine Sammy, Farina, Stymie, and Buckwheat picked up the pickaninny mantle and carried it to new summits. In all the versions of *Uncle Tom's Cabin*, the slave child Topsy was presented as a lively pickaninny, used solely for comic relief. When the 1927 version of *Uncle Tom's Cabin* opened, the character was singled out by one critic who wrote: "Topsy is played by Mona Ray, a wonderfully bright youngster who seems to have the comedy of her part in extraordinary fashion . . . her eyes roll back and forth in alarm. She also evinces no liking for her plight when she is found by Miss Ophelia while dabbing powder on her ebony countenance." In her day, the character Topsy was clownish and droll and became such a film favorite that she starred in *Topsy and Eva* (1927), in which her far-fetched meanderings and her pickaninnying won mass audience approval.

Shortly after Edison introduced the pickaninny in 1904, the pure coon made its way onto the screen in *Wooing and Wedding of a Coon* (1905). This short depicted a honeymooning black couple as stumbling and stuttering idiots. Later the coon appeared in *The Masher* (1907), which was about a self-styled white ladies' man who is rebuffed by all the women he pursues. When he meets a mysterious veiled woman who responds to his passes, the hero thinks he has arrived at his blue heaven. And so finding success, he removes the veil only to discover that his mystery lady love is *colored!* Without further ado, he takes off. He may have been looking for a blue heaven, but he certainly did not want a black one.

Before its death, the coon developed into the most blatantly degrading of all black stereotypes. The pure coons emerged as no-account roustabouts, those unreliable, crazy, lazy, subhuman creatures good for nothing more than eating watermelons, stealing chickens, shooting crap, or butchering the English language. A character named Rastus was just such a figure.

How Rastus Got His Turkey (c. 1910) was the first of a series of slapstick comedies centering on the antics of a Negro called Rastus. Here Rastus tries to steal a turkey for his Thanksgiving dinner. Next came *Rastus in Zululand*, about a darky who dreams of going to Zululand in the heart of Africa. There he wins the affections of the chief's daughter. He is willing to flirt with the girl, but when asked to marry her, in true unreliable, no-account fashion, he refuses, expressing a wish for death rather than matrimony. The savage chief (from the beginning, all Africans are savages) nearly grants that wish, too. *Rastus and Chicken, Pickaninnies and Watermelon*, and *Chicken Thief* were other shorts in the series, all appearing during 1910 and 1911. In some respects, this series and its central character simply paved the way for Stepin Fetchit's coon characters.

The final member of the coon triumvirate is the uncle remus. Harmless and congenial, he is a first cousin to the tom, yet he distinguishes himself by his quaint, naive, and comic philosophizing. During the silent period he was only hinted at. He did not come into full flower until the 1930s and 1940s with films such as *The Green Pastures* (1936) and *Song of the South* (1946). Remus's mirth, like tom's contentment and the coon's antics, has always been used to indicate the black man's satisfaction with the system and his place in it.

The Tragic Mulatto

The third figure of the black pantheon and the one that proved itself a moviemaker's darling is the tragic mulatto. One of the type's earliest appearances was in *The Debt* (1912), a two-reeler about the Old South. A white man's wife and his black mistress bear him children at the same time. Growing up together, the white son and the mulatto daughter fall in love and decide to marry, only to have their relationship revealed to them at the crucial moment. Their lives are thus ruined not only because they are brother and sister but also—and here was the catch—because the girl has a drop of black blood!

In Humanity's Cause, In Slavery Days, and *The Octoroon*, all made around 1913, explored the plight of a fair-skinned mulatto attempting to pass for white. Usually the mulatto is made likable—even sympathetic (because of her white blood, no doubt)—and the audience believes that the girl's life could have been productive and happy had she not been a "victim of divided racial inheritance."

The Mammy

Mammy, the fourth black type, is so closely related to the comic coons that she is usually relegated to their ranks. Mammy is distinguished, however, by her sex and her fierce independence. She is usually big, fat, and cantankerous. She made her debut around 1914 when audiences were treated to a blackface version of *Lysistrata*.

The comedy, titled *Coon Town Suffragettes*, dealt with a group of bossy mammy washerwomen who organize a militant movement to keep their good-for-nothing husbands at home. Aristophanes would no doubt have risen from his grave with righteous indignation. But the militancy of the washerwomen served as a primer for the mammy roles Hattie McDaniel was to perfect in the 1930s.

Mammy's offshoot is the aunt jemima, sometimes derogatorily referred to as a "handkerchief head." Often aunt jemimas are toms blessed with religion or mammies who wedge themselves into the dominant white culture. Generally they are sweet, jolly, and good-tempered—a bit more polite than mammy and certainly never as headstrong. The maids in the Mae West films of the 1930s fit snugly into this category.

The Brutal Black Buck and *The Birth of a Nation*

D. W. Griffith's *The Birth of a Nation* (1915) was the motion picture to introduce the final mythic type, the brutal black buck. This extraordinary, multidimensional movie was also the first feature film to deal with a black theme and at the same time to articulate fully the entire pantheon of stereotypes. Griffith presented all the types with such frightening force and power that his film touched off a wave of controversy and was denounced as the most slanderous anti-Negro movie ever released.

In almost every way, *The Birth of a Nation* was a stupendous undertaking, unlike any film that had preceded it. Up to then American movies had been two- or three-reel affairs, shorts running no longer than ten or fifteen minutes, crudely and casually filmed. But *The Birth of a Nation* was rehearsed for six weeks, filmed in nine, later edited in three months, and finally released as a record-breaking hundred-thousand-dollar spectacle, twelve reels in length and over three hours in running time. It altered the entire course and concept of American moviemaking, developing the close-up, cross-cutting, rapid-fire editing, the iris, the split-screen shot, and realistic and impressionistic lighting. Creating sequences and images yet to be surpassed, the film's magnitude and epic grandeur swept audiences off their feet. At a private White House screening President Woodrow Wilson reportedly exclaimed, "It's like writing history with lightning!" *The Birth of a Nation*, however, not only vividly re-created history, but revealed its director's philosophical concept of the universe and his personal racial bigotry. For D. W. Griffith there was a moral order at work in the universe. If that order were ever thrown out of whack, he believed chaos would ensue. Griffith's thesis was sound, relatively exciting, and even classic in a purely Shakespearean sense. But in articulating his thesis, Griffith seemed to be saying that things were in order only when whites were in control and when the American Negro was kept in his place. In the end, Griffith's "lofty" statement—and the film's subject matter—transformed *The Birth of a Nation* into a hotly debated and bitterly cursed motion picture.

It told the story of the Old South, the Civil War, the Reconstruction period, and the emergence of the Ku Klux Klan. Basing his film on Thomas Dixon's novel *The Clansman* (also the original title of the film), Griffith focused on a good, decent "little" family, the Camerons of Piedmont, South Carolina. Before the war, the family lives in an idyllic "quaintly way that is to be no more." Dr. Cameron and his sons are gentle, benevolent "fathers" to their childlike servants. The slaves themselves could be no happier. In the fields they contentedly pick cotton. In their quarters they dance and perform for their master. In the Big House Mammy joyously goes about her chores. All is in order. Everyone knows his or her place. Then the Civil War breaks out, and the old order cracks.

The war years take their toll. In Piedmont, the Cameron family is terrorized by a troop of Negro raiders, and the South, represented by the Cameron family, endures ruin and devastation. Then comes the Reconstruction. Carpetbaggers and uppity "niggers" from the North move into Piedmont, exploiting and corrupting the former slaves, unleashing the sadism and bestiality innate in the Negro, turning the once congenial darkies into renegades and using them to "crush the white South under the hell of the black South." The old slaves have quit work. Black Union soldiers are on the street, shoving whites off the sidewalk. The former slaves take over the political polls and disenfranchise the whites. A black political victory culminates in a frenzied street celebration as jubilant blacks rejoice. Later they conduct a black Congressional session, itself a mockery of Old South ideals in which the freed Negro legislators are depicted as lustful, arrogant, and idiotic. One bites on a chicken leg. Another sneaks a drink from a liquor bottle. Another removes his shoe and props his bare foot onto his desk. The stench created by the barefoot Congressman becomes so foul that the speaker of the house passes a rule that everyone must wear shoes during legislative meetings! Other rulings are also made. A title card reads: "It is moved and carried that all whites must salute negro officers on the streets." Another title card proclaims: "The helpless white minority." Still another announces: "Passage of a bill, providing for the intermarriage of blacks and whites." Matters in *The Birth of a Nation* reach a heady climax later when the renegade black Gus sets out to rape the younger Cameron daughter. Rather than submit, the Pet Sister flees from him and throws herself from a cliff—into the "opal gates of death." Then the mulatto Silas Lynch attempts to force the white Elsie Stoneman to marry him. Finally, when all looks hopelessly lost, there emerges a group of good, upright Southern white men, members of an "invisible empire," who, while wearing white sheets and hoods, battle the blacks in a direct confrontation. Led by Ben Cameron in a rousing stampede, they defeat the black

Scenes from D. W. Griffith's *The Birth of a Nation*, the most controversial Civil War/Reconstruction Era drama ever released in America. ABOVE: the blacks take over the voting polls from the defeated Southern whites. BELOW: white actors in blackface portray Mammy and the "uppity nigger from de No'" (1915).

rebels! Defenders of white womanhood, white honor, and white glory, they restore to the South everything it has lost, including its white supremacy. Thus we have the birth of a nation. And the birth of the Ku Klux Klan.

The plot machinations of the Griffith epic may today resound with melodramatic absurdities, but the action, the actors, and the direction did not. The final ride of the Klan was an impressive piece of film propaganda, superbly lit and edited. Indeed it was so stirring that audiences screamed in delight, cheering for the white heroes and booing, hissing, and cursing the black villains. *The Birth of a Nation* remains significant not only because of its artistry but also because of its wide-ranging influence. One can detect in this single film the trends and sentiments that were to run through many films with black characters made for a long time afterwards. Later filmmakers were to pick up Griffith's ideas—his very images—but were to keep them "nicely" toned down in order not to offend audiences.

Griffith used three varieties of blacks. The first were the "faithful souls," a mammy and an uncle tom, who remain with the Cameron family throughout and staunchly defend them from the rebels. By means of these characters, as well as the slaves seen dancing and clowning in their quarters, director Griffith propagated the myth of slave contentment and made it appear as if slavery had elevated the Negro from his bestial instincts. At heart, Griffith's "faithful souls" were shameless representations of the Negro as Child or the Negro as a naive figure, incapable of comprehending the social dynamic of the world in which he or she lives. But these characters were to turn up in scores of other Civil War epics, and they were to leave their mark on the characterizations of Clarence Muse in *Huckleberry Finn* (1931) and of Bill Robinson in *The Little Colonel* (1935) and *The Littlest Rebel* (1935).

Griffith's second variety were the brutal black bucks. Just as the coon stereotype could be broken into subgroups, the brutal black buck type could likewise be divided into two categories: the black brutes and the black bucks. Differences between the two are minimal. The black brute was a barbaric black out to raise havoc. Audiences could assume that his physical violence served as an outlet for a man who was sexually repressed. In *The Birth of a Nation*, the black brutes, subhuman and feral, are the nameless characters setting out on a rampage full of black rage. They flog the Camerons' faithful servant. They shove and assault white men of the town. They flaunt placards demanding "equal marriage." These characters figured in the depiction of black Union soldiers. Their film descendants were to appear years later as the rebellious slaves of *So Red the Rose* (1935) and as the militants of *Putney Swope* (1969).

But it was the pure black bucks that were Griffith's most disturbing archetypal figures. Bucks are always big, baaddddd niggers, oversexed and savage, violent and frenzied as they lust for white flesh. No greater sin hath any black man. Both Lynch, the mulatto, and Gus, the renegade, fall into this category. Among other things, these two characters revealed the tie between sex and racism in America. Griffith played on the myth of the Negro's high-powered sexuality, then articulated the great white fear that every black man longs for a white woman. Underlying the fear was the assumption that the white woman was the ultimate in female desirability, herself a symbol of white pride, power, and beauty. Consequently, when Lillian Gish, the frailest, purest of all screen heroines, was attacked by the character Lynch—when he put his big black arms around this pale blond beauty—audiences literally panicked. Here was the classic battle of good and evil, innocence and corruption. It was a master stroke and a brilliant use of contrast, one that drew its audience into the film emotionally.* But in uncovering the attraction of black to white, Griffith failed to reveal the political implications. Traditionally, certain black males may have been drawn to white women because these women are power symbols, an ideal of the oppressor. But Griffith attributed the attraction to an animalism innate in the Negro male. Thus the black bucks of the film are psychopaths, one always panting and salivating, the other forever stiffening his body as if the mere presence of a white woman in the same room could sexually arouse him. Griffith played hard on the bestiality of his black villainous bucks and used it to arouse hatred.

Closely aligned to the bucks and brutes of *The Birth of a Nation* is the mulatto character, Lydia. She is presented as the mistress of the white abolitionist carpetbagger, Senator Stoneman. Through Lydia, Griffith explored the possibilities of the dark, sinister half-breed as a tragic leading lady. Although merely a supporting character, Lydia is the only black role to suggest even remotely genuine mental anguish. She hates whites. She refuses to be treated as an inferior. She wants power. Throughout, she anguishes over her predicament as a black woman in a hostile white world.

Lydia is also the film's only passionate female. Griffith was the first important movie director to divide his black women into categories based on their individual colors. Both Lydia and Mammy are played by white actresses in blackface. But Mammy is darker. She is representative of the all-black woman, overweight, middle-aged, and so dark, so thoroughly black, that it is preposterous even to suggest that she be a sex object. Instead she was desexed. This tradition of the desexed, overweight, dowdy *dark* black woman continued in films throughout the 1930s and 1940s. Vestiges of it popped up as late as the 1960s with Claudia McNeil in *A Raisin in the Sun* (1961) and Beah Richards in *Hurry Sundown* (1967). A dark black actress was

---

* Lillian Gish's comments in the January 1937 issue of *Stage* verify the fact that Griffith was well aware of this contrast and that he used it to arouse his audience. Said Gish: "At first I was not cast to play in *The Clansman*. My sister and I had been the last to join the company and we naturally supposed . . . that the main assignments would go to the older members. But one day while we were rehearsing the scene where the colored man picks up the Northern girl gorilla-fashion, my hair, which was very blond, fell far below my waist and Griffith, seeing the contrast in the two figures, assigned me to play Elsie Stoneman (who was to have been Mae Marsh)."

considered for no role but that of a mammy or an aunt jemima. On the other hand, the part-black woman—the light-skinned Negress—was given a chance at lead parts and was graced with a modicum of sex appeal. The desirable black women who appeared afterwards in movies often were the "cinnamon-colored gals" with Caucasian features. The mulatto came closest to the white ideal. Whether conscious or not, Griffith's division of the black woman into color categories survived in movies the way many set values continue long after they are discredited. In fact, it was said in 1958 and 1970 that one reason why such actresses as Eartha Kitt in *Anna Lucasta* and Lola Falana in *The Liberation of L. B. Jones* failed to emerge as important screen love goddesses was that they were too brown-skinned or too dark.

Influential and detrimental as the Griffith blacks were to be for later generations, they were not meekly accepted in 1915. *The Birth of a Nation*'s blackfaced baddies aroused a rash of hostilities. At the film's New York première, the NAACP picketed the theater, calling the movie racist propaganda. Later, the Chicago and Boston branches of the NAACP led massive demonstrations against its presentation. Other civil rights and religious organizations were quick to protest. Race riots broke out in a number of cities. Newspaper editorials and speeches censured the film. Black critics such as Laurence Reddick said it glorified the Ku Klux Klan, and Reddick added that the film's immense success was at least one factor contributing to the great and growing popularity the organization enjoyed during this period. In the South, the film was often advertised as calculated to "work audiences into a frenzy . . . it will make you hate." The film "did more than any other single thing to nurture and promote the myth of black domination and debauchery during Reconstruction," wrote African American historian John Hope Franklin in *From Slavery to Freedom*. "Lynchings and other forms of violence increased." Ultimately, *The Birth of a Nation* was banned in five states and nineteen cities.

The anger and fury did not die in 1915 either. The film was reissued at regular intervals in later years. At each reopening, outraged moviegoers, both black and white, vehemently opposed its showing. In 1921, *The Birth of a Nation* was attacked as a part of a "Southern campaign to stimulate the Ku Klux Klan"—which it had already done. The Museum of Modern Art temporarily shelved the picture in 1946. Because of "the potency of its anti-Negro bias . . ." read the Museum's press announcement, "exhibiting it at this time of heightened social tensions cannot be justified." The 1947 revival of the movie by the Dixie Film Exchange was blasted by the Civil Rights Congress, and the NAACP picketed New York's Republic Theatre where it was to be shown. "It brings race hatred to New York City," said NAACP Secretary Walter White, "and we don't want it here." The Progressive Labor Party led demonstrations against the film during the following year. In 1950, there were renewed outcries when word leaked out that a Hollywood company was to remake the movie in sound. The remake plans were quickly aborted, as were the 1959 proposals to present it on television.

Throughout the years, D. W. Griffith defended himself as a mere filmmaker with no political or ideological view in mind. Surprised and apparently genuinely hurt when called a racist, Griffith made speeches across the country, wrote letters to the press, accused the NAACP and its supporters of trying to bring about screen censorship, and even went so far as to issue a pamphlet titled "The Rise and Fall of Free Speech in America," all in an effort to squelch the controversy. As late as 1947, one year before his death and some thirty-two years after the movie's release, D. W. Griffith still maintained that his film was not an attack on the American Negro.

The Birth of a Nation has become one of the highest grossing movies of all time. (The amount it has earned has never been fully tabulated.) Eyeing its profits, a number of Hollywood producers undertook projects with similar anti-Negro themes. *Broken Chains* (c. 1916) and *Free and Equal* (filmed in 1915 but not released until 1925) were prominent imitations. The former failed miserably. The latter's release was held up for some ten years while the producer waited for the furor to cool down. For one thing was certain after *The Birth of a Nation:* the Negro could not be depicted in the guise of an out-and-out villain. This treatment was too touchy and too controversial. Griffith's film had succeeded because of its director's artistry and technical virtuosity, but no studio dared risk it again. Consequently, black males in Hollywood films were cast almost always in comic roles. And thus even the great comic tradition of the Negro in the American film has its roots in the Griffith spectacle. Finally, many of Hollywood's hangups and hesitations in presenting sensual black men on screen resulted, in part, from the reactions to the Griffith spectacle. So strong was his presentation, and so controversial its reception, that movie companies ignored and avoided such a type of black character for fear of raising new hostilities. Not until more than a half century later, when Melvin Van Peebles's *Sweet Sweetback's Baadasssss Song* (1971) appeared, did sexually assertive black males make their way back to the screen. Van Peebles and other black filmmakers reappropriated the old type and used it as a sign of political resistance. Afterwards, when the box-office success of that film indicated that black audiences could accept such a type, the screen was bombarded with an array of buck heroes in such films as *Shaft* (1971), *Super Fly* (1972), *Slaughter* (1972), and *Melinda* (1972).

With *The Birth of a Nation* in 1915, all the major black screen types had been introduced. Literal and unimaginative as some types might now appear, the naive and cinematically untutored audiences of the early part of the century responded to the character types as if they were the real thing.

As far as the audiences were concerned, the toms, the coons, the mulattoes, the mammies, and the bucks embodied all the aspects and facets of the black experience itself. The audience's deep-set prejudice against any "foreigners" accounts for the typing of all minorities in all American films. But no minority was so relentlessly or fiercely typed as the black man. Audiences rejected even subtle modifications of the black caricatures. When Jack Johnson became the first black heavyweight champion of the world in 1908, filmed sequences of him knocking out white Tommy Burns so disturbed the "racial pride" of white America that they were banned for fear of race riots. Thereafter, black boxers in films were invariably defeated by their white opponents. Similarly, when the first film versions of *Uncle Tom's Cabin* were released in the South, advertisements announced that the black characters were portrayed by white actors. Even at this stage, the evolving film industry feared offending its dominant white audience, especially those in the South.

Once the basic mythic types were introduced, a number of things occurred. Specific black themes soon emerged. (The Old South theme proved to be a great favorite.) And the basic types came and went in various guises. Guises long confused many movie viewers. They were (and remain) deceptive, and they have traditionally been used by the film industry to camouflage the familiar types. If a black appeared as a butler, audiences thought of him as merely a servant. What they failed to note was the variety of servants. There were tom servants (faithful and submissive), coon servants (lazy and unreliable), and mammy servants, just to name a few. What has to be remembered is that the servant's uniform was the guise certain types wore during a given period. That way Hollywood would give its audience the same product (the types themselves) but with new packaging (the guise).

With the Griffith spectacle, audiences saw the first of the guises. The brutes, the bucks, and the tragic mulatto all wore the guise of villains. Afterwards, during the 1920s, audiences saw their toms and coons dressed in the guise of plantation jesters. In the 1930s, the types were dressed in servants' uniforms. In the early 1940s, they sported entertainers' costumes. In the late 1940s and the 1950s, they donned the gear of troubled problem people. In the 1960s, they appeared as angry militants. Because the guises were always changing, audiences were sometimes tricked into believing the depictions of the American Negro were altered, too. But at heart beneath the various guises, there lurked the familiar types.

2 INTO THE 1920s: THE JESTERS

An engaging Negro child actor brings authentic black humor to the screen.... A Jewish singer made up in blackface to look like a darky minstrel of old proves the movies can talk.... At Fox Pictures, a gregarious group of perpetually happy-go-lucky plantation hands whoop it up in the screen's first all-singing, all-talking, all-Negro musical.... At MGM, a troupe of contented cotton pickers laugh and cry to the heavens above in the screen's second all-singing, all-talking, all-Negro musical.... And a black love goddess and a black blues singer shake their asses and roll their stomachs, burning holes in movie screens with their raunchy sexuality.

By 1918, the villains had come and gone. And the jester was about to be enshrined. Hollywood's postwar films reflected its postwar spirit of artistic aggressiveness and programmed levity. Its production having more than tripled during the war years, Hollywood emerged as the unchallenged film capital of the world. Energetic, frivolous, audacious, and determined to maintain its position, it set out to captivate audiences the world over. Throughout the era and into the 1920s, the black figure that dominated—replacing Griffith's villains—was the black jester. High-stepping and high-falutin' and crazy as all get-out, the comic Negro was ushered in. But the movies of the period, like the post-World War I era itself, started with a slight identity crisis before it saw the comic light. Consequently, the era began—in 1918—with a whimper and ended—in 1929—with both a crash and a bang.

The whimper was *The Greatest Thing in Life*, a film so far removed from the mainstream that it was hard to believe it was directed by one so much a part of the mainstream as D. W. Griffith. It represented a curious departure from the sentiments expressed in *The Birth of a Nation*. Released in 1918, its theme, says Lillian Gish, was its director's favorite—"the brotherhood of man." In its climactic scene, a white racist Southern officer finds himself sharing a shell hole with a black private. At first there is great hostility. But war makes strange bedfellows—and evidently compatible ones. For when the white officer is hit by an enemy shell, the black soldier rescues him. In doing so, he saves the life of the officer but is critically wounded himself. Dying, he calls for his mother, requesting a last kiss. The injured officer grants that request. He pretends to be the black man's mother and kisses the soldier—on the lips. According to Miss Gish, "It was a dramatic and touching scene, during which audiences sat tense and quiet."

As tense and quiet as audiences may have sat, *The Greatest Thing in Life* was a financial failure. Yet it was one of the few early films to depict blacks heroically. Or even sympathetically. At the same time, the Creel Committee issued a film called *Our Colored Fighters* as an endeavor to reveal the contributions of the American Negro to the war crisis. *Our Hell Fighters*, a one-reeler about the 367th all-Negro Regiment, was also filmed and released for the same purpose. These films, like Griffith's, were government propaganda vehicles, produced at a time when the country was promoting all-inclusive solidarity and brotherhood. Made to rally support for the war effort, they reveal the obvious fact that in critical times the use of movies as propaganda becomes intentional and overt. (During noncritical periods, motion pictures still function as propaganda but in more subtle ways.) The great paradox was that after the war was over the country and the motion picture industry appeared washed of their racial sins and reverted to their old ways. For black actors, the old way was soon indicated when a call was issued to "Make Way for the Jesters!"

During 1922 the first of the *Our Gang* comedy shorts was released. Produced by Hal Roach and dealing with "comedies of child life," the series was one of its studio's most successful creations. It ran into the talkie period and was known for a time as *The Little Rascals*. Featured through its run were a motley collection of black schoolchildren with the cornball names of Farina, Stymie, and Buckwheat.

The careers of all three followed in the wake of Sunshine Sammy, an energetic tot, described as a "lovable little pickaninny" and noted for his ability to widen his eyes to the size of ping-pong balls. Sunshine Sammy costarred with comedian Harold Lloyd in early two-reel comedies. He proved such a popular success that he became one of the highest paid juveniles in early silents. As motion pictures grew up, however, so did this "lovable little pickaninny"—so much so that by 1921 his employer, Hal Roach, was on the lookout for a playmate for Sammy. The playmate eventually became a replacement. Sunshine Sammy's real name was Ernest Morrison.

After a talent hunt was initiated to find a "colored boy with hair long enough to play either a boy or a girl," a studio representative announced he had discovered just such a child, an eighteen-month-old boy named Allen Clayton Hoskins. Once he was signed to a contract, there was a problem of an image and a name. When one executive thought the child so "chubby and agreeable" that he was reminded of breakfast "mush"—hot cereal—the problem was solved. Shortly thereafter the name was lifted from the cereal box and bestowed on the little fellow. Thus was born the one and only Farina!

A first assignment for Farina was to feed pearls to a flock of geese in a Roach short! Each time the geese came near him, the child burst into tears, ruining his director's setups. Later, when viewing the rushes, the director realized what a natural-born crier little Farina was, and henceforth the child was relegated to crying parts in shorts.

In *Our Gang*, Farina's face soon became familiar. Typically dressed up with tightly twisted pickaninny pigtails (they stood straight up whenever he was frightened) and old patched gingham clothes, both of which were to become his trademarks, Farina had a success that paved the way for other young black actors. His sister, Mango, made her movie debut at the age of three months in a 1927 *Our Gang* short. Her career was short-lived, however.

Like Farina, the black children who followed him also had their props. Stymie Beard sported a derby, had a head shaved completely bald, and was occasionally decked out in colorful zoot suits. Buckwheat had the pigtails and the gingham clothes of his predecessor. He also resembled Farina in that no one was sure whether he was a boy or a girl. The sexual ambiguity of the pair remains puzzling.

While all the children were admittedly made up as backwoods pickaninnies, each individualized his performances through his own unique personality. With his husky voice and an arrogantly pleasant way about him, Farina was noted for his common sense and a certain heroic demeanor. Often he came to the rescue of little white damsels in distress. In one episode, he attempts to help a little white girl who has fallen into a puddle of mud, only to be accused by the girl's mother of having pushed her in. Farina, however, has the last laugh when the mother herself tumbles into the mud. While Farina was given to heroics (except when there were ghosts about—at which time he was quick to head for the hills), Stymie was noted for his nonchalance and detached shrewdness. Usually, he saw straight through any sham. One *Our Gang* short centers on a pair of midgets who disguise themselves as infants and set out to rob a charity party being given for the neighborhood children by a group of ritzy society matrons. As the disguised midgets rob the society guests, it is Stymie alone who realizes that somethin' ain't right with dem dere chillun. No one pays any heed to Stymie's warnings, but at the end of the short the jewel thieves are unmasked and Stymie's cool perceptiveness has helped save the day. Possibly Stymie's chief charm was that he always spoke as if his mouth were full of food. He was, too, a master of the double take. Little Buckwheat was the last but certainly not the least of the important black children appearing in the series. With a round chocolate moon face and enormous eyes, Buckwheat always came across as a quiet, odd-ball type, the perfect little dum-dum tag-along.

The *Our Gang* series revolved around a group of lower-middleclass American youngsters making their way through childhood in entertaining ups and downs, ins and outs, as black and white together tried figuring out life and play. Throughout the series the black children spoke in a dialect of the familiar *dats* and *deres* as well

At the height of his career as the late 1920s' best-known pickaninny, Farina takes time out for some soul food.

as the *I is's*, you *is's*, and *we was's*. On more than one occasion, Farina was seen banqueting on a colored man's favorite dishes—fried chicken and watermelon. In these respects, the adventures and life styles of the black children conformed to accepted notions and attitudes of the day. But for the most part the approach to the relationships of the black children with the whites was almost as if there were no such thing as race at all. Indeed, the charming sense of *Our Gang* was that all the children were buffoons, forever in scraps and scrapes, forever plagued by setbacks and sidetracks as they set out to have fun, and everyone had his turn at being outwitted.

The "liberal" treatment of the pint-sized jesters in Roach's *Our Gang* was more an exception than the rule of the day. Black comic characters in other features or series did not fare as well. D. W. Griffith's *One Exciting Night* (1922) featured a ludicrous Negro character named Romeo Washington who finds himself trapped in a haunted house way down in ole Kentucky. Cloaked figures wander about. Arms extend from secret hidden passages. Women scream out in the night. Murders are mysteriously committed. Throughout, Romeo and another darky run through the house like scared chickens. Played by white actor Porter Strong in outrageous blackface, Romeo Washington was pure coon, a crude and racially self-demeaning character. But he delighted audiences, and the Griffith film was a great success. In another Hal Roach series featuring Charlie Chase, one could readily spot a colored maid or butler or bystander whose eyes popped or who ran off scared out of his wits by some Chase antic.

In the Buster Keaton film *Seven Chances* (1925), Keaton will inherit millions if he can find a wife within seven hours. When word spreads of the millionaire-to-be in need of a spouse, practically every eligible female in town pursues him, including a rough-and-ready black mammy. Featured in the same film is a slow-as-molasses colored messenger. Although there were still few roles for blacks in movies, whenever they were used in this period, it was usually in this sort of demeaning manner. What degraded the black comic figures of the day even further and made them appear more grotesque and less individualized was that whites often still played the Negro roles. The acting was always grossly overdone. This tradition, however, fell into decline during the mid-1920s, just about the time of the release of Thomas Ince's *Free and Equal*.

Free and Equal, made in 1915, as we have already seen, was as much an example of a producer's miscalculation as it was a demonstration of how prejudice leads to lunacy. It was removed from the jester tradition of the day in that its black characters were literally that of another period. The film's release was held up by its producer, Thomas Ince, who was waiting for the adverse criticism against *The Birth of a Nation* to simmer down. As it turned out, that cooling-off period took ten years.

Free and Equal finally had its premiere in New York in 1925. Its themes were social equality and intermarriage. A Northern liberal, Judge Lowell, having waged a bet with a Southern colonel that blacks are equal to whites, takes young Alexander Marshall, a Negro, into his home. Once ensconced in the good Northern liberal's house, Marshall hotly pursues the white man's daughter. When it appears as if he has failed to seduce her, he succeeds in raping and strangling the family maid! Marshall is brought to trial and convicted. At the same time, he is exposed as not only having married the judge's daughter but as also having a Negro wife. The judge, who has been writing a lengthy treatise on intermarriage, tosses his document into the fireplace. And in the end, the "perfect" Negro has been revealed as the perfect rogue.

Obviously, *Free and Equal* portrayed the black man again as a villain, and the character Marshall was the familiar brutal black buck type. Vicious as the film was, it bore the defects and absurdities of movies made in 1915. Consequently, in 1925 it was a prodigious failure. "A dramatic catastrophe," said *The New York World*, while *The New York Amsterdam News* called it a "dramatic dud." *The New York Times* added: "The dramatic sequences last night caused outbursts of loud laughter.... No wonder old Judge Lowell chucked his precious book advocating full equality into the fire. It might have been well if Mr. Ince had done the same thing with the film."

Better than any other film of the period, *Free and Equal* demonstrated that the old racial themes and thought patterns would no longer stand up. What was denounced as its gravest anachronism was its use of white actor Jack Richardson in blackface to portray Marshall. "Richardson as a Negro is hopelessly out of date and fails to stir a single spark of conviction," *The New York Amsterdam News* commented, pointing out the success and excitement of Eugene O'Neill's play *All God's Chillun Got Wings*, in which a genuine Negro—Paul Robeson—appeared opposite a white actress. When would the cinema reflect such realism? At this time the film industry found itself face to face with a question it had always evaded.

The blackface tradition had hung on after its "effectiveness" had worn thin. The practice had originated in the days of slavery, when Negroes were not permitted to appear on stage. Troupes of white minstrels blackened themselves with burnt cork better to mock and caricature the plantation slaves they imitated. After the Civil War, freed slaves could form their own minstrel companies, but they too were required to darken themselves with burnt cork. Vaudeville upheld the same tradition. In the early 1900s, the popular Negro comedian Bert Williams appeared and almost always had to darken his already dark face. Even Sammy Davis, Jr., said that he recalled as a vivid childhood memory standing in the wings of a vaudeville theater and being warned by his father not to touch his face—for fear he would smear the burnt cork. The tradition was ridiculous and unnecessary certainly, but it was merely one of any number of ways in which the entertainment world bowed to prejudice.

When the blackface tradition had popped up in early movies, no one gave it a second thought. After *The Birth of a Nation* appeared, the protests against Griffith's use of whites for the important black roles alarmed the film industry. Later, Hollywood countered the continued protests of the newly formed NAACP and other civil rights organizations by gradually casting Negro actors in small roles. Noble Johnson and Caroline Snowden were among the early bit players in such silent films as *The Ten Commandments* (1923), *The Thief of Bagdad* (1924), *Little Robinson Crusoe* (1924), *The Navigator* (1924), *The First Year* (1926), *Topsy and Eva* (1927), *Soft Cushions* (1927), *Noah's Ark* (1929), *The Four Feathers* (1929), and *In Old Kentucky* (1927). Sometimes they portrayed Mexicans and Spaniards or other "foreigners." By the 1920s, the absurdity of the blackface tradition was apparent. What finally killed the practice and simultaneously opened the door for a new realism that virtually demanded real Negroes in Negro roles was the advent of sound. Ironically, the film that at once revealed the power and popularity of the talking motion picture was also the one in which the blackface tradition attained its crowning achievement and its final success. That film was *The Jazz Singer*.

Released by Warner Brothers in 1927, *The Jazz Singer* revolutionized the motion-picture industry. Its routine generations-conflict plot offered little to stir audiences, but when its star, the legendary Jewish entertainer Al Jolson, appeared in burnt cork and belted out a passionate rendition of "Mammy," moviegoers were thrilled actually to hear their idol's voice. Jolson's ever-crooning-swooning darky jester was a classic example of the minstrel tradition at its sentimentalized, corrupt best. But it was a great moment for the movies. The picture launched Jolson's film career, and ever afterward he seemed to pay homage to it by often including a blackface number in subsequent features. But more important, *The Jazz Singer* launched the talking-motion-picture era. The film was an enormous success. As a result, the movie industry experienced a great expansion and underwent a period of profound transition.

For blacks in films, the talkie era proved to be a major breakthrough. In the period 1927 to 1940, the number of Negro parts greatly increased. From the start, Hollywood was aware that talking movies needed sounds—music, rhythm, pizzazz, singing, dancing, clowning. And who, according to American myth, were more rhythmic or more musical than Negroes? No sooner had the talkies come into vogue than two major studios, Fox Pictures and MGM, operating on just such a premise, set out to put all that ole-time natchel rhythm on dazzling display. The end results of their labors were *Hearts in Dixie* and *Hallelujah*.

Hearts in Dixie (1929) was released first. It had originally been conceived as a short vehicle for offering spirituals and some minstrel men highjinks, but had been expanded into a feature. On a Southern plantation, pickaninnies romped and ran. Toms worshiped their master, labored in the fields during the day, and then played during the night. There were scenes of the steamboat *Nellie Bly* going down the river while slaves sang in the fields nearby. There was the mournful collection of darkies crooning "Massa's in the cold, cold ground." Throughout all the picturesque episodes, the blacks of *Hearts in Dixie* were mindlessly contented. Here were characters living in shacks and working from sunrise to sunset, and always, instead of suffering or misery, they seemed to be floating on some euphoric high brought on, one would assume, by cotton fields and spirituals. "The spirit of the Southern Negro a year or so after the Civil War is cleverly captured," wrote the *New York Times* film critic. "It is something restful, a talking and singing picture that is gentle in mood and truthful in its reflection of black men of those days down yonder in the cornfields." One would like to say the *Times* review was written with tongue in cheek, but it wasn't. Once again the perpetually happy-go-lucky Negro was presented to movie audiences—stamped with a seal of Establishment approval!

For the most part, the actors played their roles according to the script. Dressed in rags and tatters and grotesquely made up as simple, unaffected rurals, the performers, mostly recruited from the New York stage, often revealed the art of their theatrical experiences a bit too well. Too broad and emphatic, they tended to overplay. In the film they portrayed plantation workers, but without being aware of it they came across as a group of blackfaced jesters rather than as valid representations of black folk culture. In the end, as the first all-Negro musical, *Hearts in Dixie* pinpointed the problem that was to haunt certain black actors for the next half century: the *blackface fixation*. Directed by whites in scripts authored by whites and then photographed, dressed, and made up by whites, the Negro actor, like the slaves he portrayed, aimed always to please the master figure. To do so, he gives not a performance of his own, not one in which he interprets black life, but one in which he presents for mass consumption black life as seen through the eyes of white artists. The actor becomes a black man in blackface.

Hearts in Dixie may not have been the best of all possible movies, but its group of unknowns was the first all-black cast ever seen on the screen. They introduced an exuberance and vitality that eventually came to be associated with the American movie musical. Most of the dancing sequences were exceptionally good. No doubt the performers were given full reign in these sequences, and many looked as if they were ready to jump from the screen into the lap of the audience, so abundant were their energy and eagerness to please. But the dancers' lack of restraint added excitement to their work, and many of the dance steps themselves were derivative of African tribal dances. Without being inhibited by their choreographer, the black dancers in *Hearts in Dixie* were able to bring a part of the black cultural experience to American movie screens.

Prominent among the cast were Clarence Muse and Mildred Washington. Muse portrayed the good-hearted grandfather Napus. He displayed a rich and stimulating voice, and it was obvious he knew how to use it rhythmically. But his Napus was too submissive, disciplined, and stagey to cause much excitement among movie patrons. Neither Muse nor Washington was able to startle or delight audiences as did a walking, talking, dancing, prancing piece of coon dynamite called Stepin Fetchit. This was one of Fetchit's first important roles. Although he was not quite at the height of his powers, he was still the strongest performer in the picture, and the second half of the movie revolved completely around him. In fact, *Hearts in Dixie* was expanded because Fetchit's work in the first half had proved so good. As the roustabout slave Gummy, Fetchit was an outlandish plantation coon. Many may have objected to his self-demeaning absurdities, but it had to be admitted that this disoriented, baffled clown picked up a slow-moving and patronizing film and carried it to new summits with his free-wheeling nuttiness. *Hearts in Dixie* provided Fetchit with the first in a series of coon jesters and coon servants that he was to develop to enormous popularity in the 1930s.

Hallelujah (1929) was the second of the big spectacles. Director King Vidor had long been interested in filming a story of "real Negro folk culture." Not until the sound period, however, did such a project seem commercially feasible. Even then, Vidor was able to get his picture past certain MGM executives only after he invested his own money in it. Vidor meticulously gathered a cast of New York performers, then shot his movie on location in the swamps and forests of Tennessee and Arkansas. When released, *Hallelujah* ranked well above the films of the period. It remains a landmark in sound films.

Hallelujah took as its theme the age-old problem of a Good Colored Boy going bad and the battle within him between callings of the spirit and temptations of the flesh. The film opens on the idyllic little Johnson farm, where the family—Pappy Johnson, Mammy, their adopted daughter, Missy Rose, their eldest son, Zeke, and their younger boys—energetically gather the cotton harvest. Nearing the last rows, the group bursts into song, singing to the heavens. In the evening, when away from the fields, the family entertains itself with spirituals and lively gospels. Good, gentle folk, the Johnsons are pictured as serene and uncomplicated—as long as baser instincts are kept in check. When these are unleashed, however, trouble's a-brewin'!

In this case, trouble proves to be firmly embodied in a full-bosomed, spicy good-time gal called Chick. When the eldest son, Zeke, journeys to town with brother Spunk to collect the family's earnings for their reapings, he takes one look at Chick, and family and finances are forgotten.

"Yo' is jest what I's got on my mind," he tells her.

"Git outta my way, small change," she replies. "You don't look like Big Money to me!"

So begins their evening. When it ends, Zeke has not only lost the family's money, but has accidently killed his brother Spunk during a barroom brawl

Repenting for his sins, Zeke becomes an itinerant preacher, only to meet up again with Chick. Intrigued by his conversion, she too repents, and in one of the most explicit scenes ever to link the bonds of religious ecstasy with sexual fervor, she is baptized by Zeke. During a revival meeting, the religious-sexual fervor builds until Zeke finally deserts his congregation to chase Chick through the woods.

Chick leads Zeke down a path of degradation and tragedy. In a fit of jealous rage he kills her and her lover. The story ends with a repentant Zeke returning home to the serene, uncomplicated family plantation. There he finds his faithful Mammy and Pappy and Missy Rose, the girl he has always loved. Rejoicing, the quartet sings a spiritual. And thus a Good Colored Boy Gone Bad becomes good again, and life is once more idyllic.

Hallelujah's plot may border on operatic absurdity, but director Vidor was able to capture in music a whole emotional aura. In its best moments, *Hallelujah* proved to be the finest record of black grief and passion to reach a movie screen. Although at times the spirituals of the Dixie Jubilee Choir appeared too slicked up—and geared too much toward the mass audience—they supported demanding and difficult scenes and were quite effective. They managed, as do all great spirituals, to touch some psychic cord in their audience and to communicate not only discontent and disillusionment but also a sense of the supernatural and the sublime.

Hallelujah's view of black life was enthusiastically greeted by the white press. The *New York Times* critic Mordaunt Hall, charmed by the reality Vidor had imparted in his treatment of the Negro, said the film succeeded in presenting the "peculiarly typical religious hysteria of the darkies and their gullibility ... their hankering after salvation, the dread of water in the baptism." *Variety* commended Vidor's direction: "Apparently in the massed ensemble groups, Vidor had a mighty tough job holding that bunch down, yet he held them under remarkable restraint and still brought out the effects desired." Much of the Negro press, however, was less charitable. When *Hallelujah* had simultaneous premieres at the Lafayette Theatre in Harlem and the Embassy in the downtown white area, the black press denounced the racism inherent in the dual opening. Black patrons viewed it as a tactical move by MGM to spare the feelings of "swanky whites" who might not object to watching a screenful of darkies but who most certainly did not want to sit next to any in a theater. Of greater concern to some black critics, though, were the spiritual-singing, crap-shooting characters who were old types even in 1929.

In due time, *Hallelujah* became not only an American classic but the precursor of all-Negro musicals, setting the tone for the treatment of Negro casts and themes. Vidor, himself an idealist, had presented his Negroes in an idealized, isolated world. By having his blacks battle it out among themselves rather than with any white antagonists, he created an unreal universe and consequently divorced himself from real issues confronting blacks and whites in America. Vidor's theme of the good colored boy who meets up with the bad black girl while leaving back home the ever-patient, all-submissive Christian Negress came to serve as the basic plot outline for a number of black spectacles. Indeed individual scenes and sequences from *Hallelujah* have popped up repeatedly in other films. The action in the scene of Chick dying in the arms of Zeke was used by Otto Preminger some twenty years later in *Carmen Jones* when Dorothy Dandridge died in the arms of Harry Belafonte. Vidor's directorial approach, that of the white visitor rather than the black inhabitant, survived too. His blacks were often pawns, used for an expression of his own lyrical view of realism and his own feeling for mood and atmosphere rather than for any comment of their own. *Hallelujah* remains an early Hollywood attempt to deal with the black family, and is directly related to subsequent black family dramas such as *The Learning Tree* (1969) and *Sounder* (1972). King Vidor won an Academy Award nomination as Best Director for his direction of *Hallelujah*.

In most respects, the characters of *Hallelujah* were indeed stereotypes, blacks depicted as either sentimental idealists or highly emotional animals. But it should be said that to the credit of the actors, although many suffered from the blackface fixation, they still invested their characters with energy and a raw urgency. Although the film's vision (its view of life) was firmly controlled by Vidor, the director had the sense and sensitivity to let his actors do certain things their way. Often the actors improvised splendidly. Daniel Haynes played Zeke. Originally, Vidor had wanted Paul Robeson for the lead; the picture was written with him in mind. But when Robeson was unavailable, Vidor selected Haynes, then an understudy in *Show Boat*. Haynes often seemed too saintly to be shooting crap or romping through the woods, but he had a voice large enough to move an entire theater, and it added depth and texture to his performance. William Fountaine portrayed the no-account gambler, Hot Shot. Sporting flashy suits and a derby, Fountaine remains the screen model for Sammy Davis, Jr.'s Sportin' Life in *Porgy and Bess*. A ninety-year-old employee of *The New York Amsterdam News* (and a former slave), Harry Gray, made an impressive screen debut as Pappy, while Victoria Spivey interjected a somber, mystical quality as the sad-eyed, sensitive girl-back-home, Missy Rose. Fannie Belle DeKnight played Mammy. Everett McGarrity presented a very poignant Spunk. For most of the cast, *Hallelujah* was the beginning and ending of their screen careers. Hollywood had not yet found a place for the black performer. Of all the actors in the film, the one to meet with the greatest "success"—and heartache—was its energetic leading lady, Nina Mae McKinney.

Executing sensuous bumps and grinds in the famous cabaret scene in *Hallelujah*, Nina Mae McKinney was the movies' first black whore. Almost every black leading lady in motion pictures, from Lena Horne in *Cabin in the Sky* to Lonette McKee in *Sparkle* in 1976, owes a debt to the playfully sexy moves and maneuvers of McKinney's character Chick.

Born in 1912 in Lancaster, South Carolina, Nina Mae McKinney had come with her family to New York and had just won a role in Lew Leslie's famous *Blackbirds* revue when word leaked out that King Vidor was auditioning performers for *Hallelujah*. Vidor had originally considered Ethel Waters for the role of Chick, and had she played the part her career might have run an entirely different course, but when McKinney was spotted—she was seventeen at the time—Vidor virtually lifted her from the chorus and starred her in the vamp role.

In McKinney's hands and hips, Chick represented the black woman as an exotic sex object, half woman, half child. She was the black woman out of control of her emotions, split in two by her loyalties and her own vulnerabilities. Implied throughout the battle with self was the tragic mulatto theme. Chick was always referred to as "that cinnamon-colored gal" or "high yeller." The white half of her represented the spiritual; the black half, the animalistic.

Nina Mae McKinney emerged as the first recognized black actress of the silver screen. She was the first, too, in the tradition of light-skinned black leading ladies. In *The New York Post*, Richard Watts, Jr., called her "assuredly one of the most beautiful women of our time." King Vidor added that it was McKinney's performance more than any other actor's that helped carry *Hallelujah*. "She's sensational," he said. Even Irving Thalberg proclaimed her one of the greatest discoveries of the age. MGM was so impressed that she was signed to a five-year contract. But in the end, her phenomenal success in *Hallelujah* lead her nowhere. Instead of the screen stardom McKinney had expected, and rightfully so, she was the first black actress to learn (as Dorothy Dandridge discovered thirty years later) that there were no leading roles for black leading ladies. All *Hallelujah* secured for her were minor film roles and a handful of appearances in obscure shorts.

Barely five years after *Hallelujah*, Nina Mae McKinney was forgotten in America. But from Greece, Richard Watts, Jr., reported on a spectacular cabaret performer billed as the Black Garbo. The Black Garbo was none other than McKinney, who was touring Europe, singing in cafés and nightclubs in Paris, London, Budapest, and Dublin. Like Josephine Baker before her, she found European audiences more receptive to her talents. While in England in 1935, she appeared opposite Paul Robeson in Zoltan Korda's *Sanders of the River*. Later she returned to the United States and appeared in a number of independent all-black films. Her last important role was as a razor-totin', high-strung, high-yeller girl in *Pinky* (1949). Though she was effective, the part did little for her career, and it was hard to believe that the stocky, bleary-eyed harridan on screen had once been the bright-eyed, carefree Chick. Nina Mae McKinney died in New York City in 1967.

Nina Mae McKinney's later film work obviously did not live up to her early promise, but much that she experimented with in *Hallelujah*—the hands on the hips, the hard-as-nails brassy voice—became stock in trade for black leading ladies. One merely has to view Dandridge's cafeteria entrance in *Carmen Jones* with her particular type of sensual swagger and her hands-on-hips arrogance to realize that McKinney's techniques were picked up by other actresses. At times

ABOVE: "Yo'se jest what I'se got on my mind," Daniel Haynes (right) exclaims as he catches sight of Nina Mae McKinney in *Hallelujah* (1929), one of the first all-talking, all-singing, all-colored musicals.

LEFT: Nina Mae McKinney, the screen's first black love goddess—and its first black victim as well (1929).

RIGHT: McKinney during the later years of her career when she appeared in independently produced all-black movies.

even Jean Harlow appeared as if she had learned something about rough nightlife heroines from her. Nina Mae McKinney's final contribution to the movies now lay in those she influenced.

St. Louis Blues (1929) was the final black film of the 1920s. It, too, featured a tempestuous female performer. This short, directed by Dudley Murphy and financed by Warner Brothers, starred the legendary Bessie Smith, affording her a one and only chance to sing her blues and sway her hips on film. The Murphy venture spotlighted the anguish and misery the major musicals had avoided. It centers on Bessie as Bessie, a blues singer done wrong by her Man, Jimmy the pimp. Bessie fights for Jimmy and runs rampant on a girl who has an eye for him. But ultimately she finds herself deserted and unhappy. *St. Louis Blues* was marred by its white director's overstatement, but it was distinguished by Bessie Smith's extraordinary ability to express black pain. The film swayed and resounded to her great ache. She remains as well one of most sensual black women ever to have been turned loose in an American movie.

Hearts in Dixie, Hallelujah, and *St. Louis Blues* brought the roaring 1920s to a close. None was successful at the box office. *Hallelujah* was banned by the Southern Theatre Federation. American movie audiences were still unprepared to accept blacks in important leading roles. The commercial failure of these films accounts for the long seven-year interval between them and the next big black spectacle, *The Green Pastures.*

Regardless of the failure of this trio, they showed triumphantly the contributions the black performer could make to the sound era. Each film helped open the door wider. In the next decade, a diverse group of household servants, led by Stepin Fetchit, ripped the door from its hinges and proved that in spite of the stock market crash, a little black humor and a lot of black magic never hurt—at least in the movies. The 1920s may have ended on a crash, but they led the way to the 1930s with a bang.

3 THE 1930s: THE SERVANTS

Sir Stepin Fetchit is a much maligned handyman, flamboyantly shufflin' and stammerin'. . . . Bill "Bojangles" Robinson is a smooth-as-silk butler, calm, cool, and lighthearted as he dances up a staircase with Shirley Temple. . . . Louise Beavers is a jolly but submissive cook, forever on the verge of heartfelt tears as she whips up a batch of pancakes. . . . Eddie "Rochester" Anderson is a bright, brisk, and clever manservant without whom Jack Benny would be lost. . . . Hi-Hat Hattie McDaniel is a big, black, bossy, and beautiful maid who continually forgets her place. . . . Butterfly McQueen is a nervous and panicky housegirl, lettin' it all hang out as she confesses, "Miss Scarlett, I don't know nothin' 'bout birthin' babies." . . . Willie "Sleep 'n' Eat" Best is a dim-witted hireling, terr'fied of just about everything. . . . And Paul Robeson is a lordly Pullman car porter, towering above it all.

They were all there. Everybody's favorites. All those strange, neurotically engrossing personalities who were thought of fondly despite the fact that they tommed or jemimaed their way through scores of bad movies. But it was the 1930s. The toms, coons, mulattoes, mammies, and bucks were no longer dressed as old-style jesters. Instead they had become respectable domestics. Hollywood had found a new place for the Negro—in the kitchens, the laundry rooms, and the pantries. And thus was born the Age of the Negro Servant.

No other period in motion-picture history could boast of more black faces carrying mops and pails or lifting pots and pans than the Depression years. In the movies, as in the streets, it was a time when the only people without job worries were the maids, the butlers, the bootblacks, the bus boys, the elevator men, the cooks, and the custodians. In almost any film of the period, from breezy, light-hearted comedies like *It Happened One Night* (1934) or *Twentieth Century* (1934) to super-deluxe spectacles such as *Gone with the Wind* (1939), a black face was bound to appear. And whether that face was seen for two minutes or three and a half hours, it was invariably there to tidy up the house, cook a meal, or watch over the livery stables.

The black servants of the Hollywood films of the 1930s met the demands of their times. They were used for a number of reasons. With their incredible antics, their unbelievable dialects, and their amazing absurdities, the black servants provided a down-hearted Depression age with buoyancy and jocularity. As they delivered their wisecracks or acted the fool, the servants were a marvelous relief from the harsh financial realities of the day. Not only their joy and zest but their loyalty, too, demonstrated that nothing in life was ever completely hopeless. The servants were always around when the boss needed them. They were always ready to lend a helping hand when times were tough. It was many a down-and-out movie hero or heroine who realized his Negro servant was his only real friend. During this period of bread lines, of fireside chats from President Roosevelt over the radio, of labor problems, of intellectual Leftist activities, and of WPA programs, blacks in films were used to reaffirm for a socially chaotic age a belief in life and the American way of living itself. Indeed, the black servants of the 1930s proved that human beings could and should endure. They seemed to say that even during the worst of times everything could be straightened out as long as people kept their chins up.

With its servant syndrome, or perhaps in spite of it, the 1930s was for individual black performers a Golden Age. Admittedly, the black servants were repeatedly exploited and mistreated, and the black servant performers themselves were often criticized by civil rights organizations for accepting such demeaning roles. But through their black characters, the actors accomplished the almost impossible: they proved single-handedly that the mythic types could be individualized and made, if not into things of beauty, then at least into things of joy. Almost every black actor of the period approached his role with a *joie de vivre* the movies were never to see again. Indeed, the enthusiasm the actors poured into their characters seemed often to parallel their own gratitude that at long last blacks were working in films. Perhaps most significantly, because there were but three important black films in this decade, the era was distinguished by personalities rather than pictures. It was in many respects a crucial, exasperating period because the emphasis fell so squarely on the shoulders of the black actors themselves. Without scripts to aid them and generally without even sympathetic directors or important roles, black actors in American films were compelled to rely on their own ingenuity to create memorable characters.

One can detect among the personalities of the 1930s a world order, a microcosm, in which each black performer had his speciality. Traditionally, American whites have felt one Negro looks like another. That attitude was prevalent in the early years of this decade. But each major black actor of the day managed to reveal some unique quality of voice or personality that audiences immediately responded to. Who could forget Bojangles' urbanity? Or Rochester's cement-mixer voice? Or Louise Beavers' jollity? Or Hattie McDaniel's haughtiness? Eventually, audiences came to hold these personalities in such affectionate regard that they were readily identifiable by their nicknames. The very best black performers played their types but played against them. They built and molded themselves into what film critic Andrew Sarris might call nondirectorial *auteurs*. With their own brand of outrageousness, the blacks created comic worlds all their own in which the servant often outshone the master.

But the distinctive black servants were not the first to arrive. In the early 1930s, once black servants were acceptable, countless black faces roamed in and out of movies. They would enter, say or mumble their bit, then quickly fade from the scene. Langston Hughes once described the standard direction for the Negro actor: "Upon opening the car door for one's white employer in any film, the director would command, 'Jump to ground.... Remove cap.... Open again.... Step back and bow.... Come up smiling.... Now bow again.... Now straighten up and grin!'" And at the beginning of the decade many actors went through just these mechanics without trying to individualize their roles. Their appearances, however brief, were always overblown, flashy, far-out, and farcical. Invariably, just the sight of a black face on screen guaranteed laughs from the audience. In the Marx Brothers' feature *Animal Crackers* (1930), Groucho made a spectacular entrance into a Long Island mansion borne on a stretcher by four African natives. "What! From Africa to here on a dollar eighty-five?" he exclaims, chuckling quizzically. In the Al Jolson starrer *Hallelujah, I'm a Bum* (1933), black actor Edgar Connor portrayed a simple-minded character called Acorn. As two hoboes, Acorn and the white character Bumper finally give up their life of leisure to go to work. Upon receiving their first pay check, Bumper is ecstatic about having money in his pockets. Acorn agrees that having cash is fine; his only complaint is that one has to waste so much time to get it. In *Mississippi* (1935), a Negro coachman, made to look ludicrous in top hat and frock-coat two sizes too large for him, became the butt of a classic W.C. Fields joke: "Get along, you Senegambian!" Al Jolson, in and out of blackface in *Wonder Bar* (1934), visited a black heaven where a sepia Saint Peter and some ebony angels transformed God's paradise into an elaborate Pullman-porter playground. In *Go into Your Dance* (1935), Jolson, again in and out of black drag, was waited on by a knuckle-headed valet called Snowflake. Jolson often rubbed the servant's head—playing on an old Southern superstition: touch a nigger's head for luck! The actor who portrayed Snowflake in this film was also billed as such when he portrayed grotesque mugging domestics in *Twentieth Century, Lady by Choice* (1934), and *The Biscuit Eater* (1940).

To catalogue other movies in the early and middle 1930s in which the Snowflake type of black servant appeared without any significance would result in a plethora of titles. The change and the individualization of the servant came about gradually. In the films of the decade, one can trace a haphazard progression of the black character from field jester to house servant to domesticated servant to humanized servant to posthumanized eccentric. Stepin Fetchit was the actor whose roles marked the first transition from field clown to house handyman. He was as well the movies' first distinctive black personality.

High-Steppin' Sir Stepin

One newspaper carried the following item:

[He] has been missing appointments for 32 years ... is the world's champion job-loser. Because of his intolerable memory, he has been thrown out of all the best American race meetings, lost several distinguished positions as a shoe-black and forfeited one of the biggest starring contracts Hollywood had to offer—they could never find him.

Columnist Sidney Skolsky commented:

Fox has re-signed Stepin Fetchit. The colored performer who had such a promising movie career will be given another chance. They hesitated about signing Fetchit again. According to Helen Gwynn, they first called him in and told him that they were going to let him make a short.

He was told that if he behaved during the making of the short he would be given features. He was reminded that he was Hollywood's bad boy.

"You don't have to worry about me any more," said Fetchit. "You're not taking any chances at all. I've been reading history, and I've noticed that they all became big guys after they were 32. Napoleon, Washington, and Abe Lincoln. You don't have to worry about me any more. I'm 32 today."

In the year 1934—at the age of thirty-two—Stepin Fetchit was already a legend and one of movieland's few authentic oddities. Only a few years earlier, no one could have predicted that this actor who gave the appearance of being a lanky, slow-witted, simple-minded, obtuse, synthetic, confused humbug would take an entire nation and an era by storm. But Stepin Fetchit went far beyond anyone's predictions or expectations, and in his own inspired way he did so brilliantly. In the early 1930s he was the best known and most successful black actor working in Hollywood. At a time when contracts for black players were unheard of, Fetchit was signed, then dropped, then spectacularly re-signed by Fox Pictures. From 1929 to 1935, he appeared in some twenty-six films. Often working in as many as four movies at a time, Fetchit was the first Negro to receive featured billing, and special scenes were often written into pictures for him. He popularized the dim-witted, tongue-tied stammer and the phenomenal slow-lazyman shuffle. So successful was he with his slow gait that for years audiences thought Stepin Fetchit actually could not run. Negro bootblacks and bus boys were said to have imitated his notorious walk on the streets.

Fox Pictures, in promoting their first black star, did much to exploit his private life. What with Fetchit's own startling capacity for generating news, stories circulated of his flamboyant high style of life: his six houses, his sixteen Chinese servants, his two-thousand-dollar cashmere suits imported from India, his lavish parties, his twelve cars. (One was a champagne-pink Cadillac with his name emblazoned on the side in neon lights.) Whenever High-Steppin' Step came to town, so the stories went, two chauffeured limousines followed. The off-screen flamboyance and super-nigger highjinks whetted the public's appetite and at the same time often overshadowed the actual screen performances of a rather gifted personality.

Fetchit came to Hollywood in the late 1920s. Named after four Presidents, he was born Lincoln Theodore Monroe Andrew Perry in Key West, Florida, in 1902. He had first hoped (or so the press releases indicated) to enter the ministry, but before long he turned to vaudeville. With comic Ed Lee, he had an act called "Step and Fetch It." When a Fox talent scout spotted him, he was tested successfully for films, and his career began.

From the outset, Fetchit displayed an instinctive awareness of public tastes. No doubt he noted the popularity of toms, but he must have believed that toms were not much fun. Coons, however—those lazy, no-account, good-for-nothing, forever-in-hot-water, natural-born comedians—were enjoyed by mainstream audiences. Consequently, Stepin Fetchit developed into the arch-coon, and as such he had no equal, introducing to audiences of the 1930s all the antics and tomfoolery every later black comedian was to draw from. His very name fitted his image, for it conjured up a portrait of the plantation darky who must *step in* (the Big House), *fetch it*, and then go his way. His appearance, too, added to the caricature. He was tall and skinny and always had his head shaved completely bald. He invariably wore clothes that were too large for him and that looked as if they had been passed down from his white master. His grin was always very wide, his teeth very white, his eyes very widened, his walk very slow, his dialect very broken. But Fetchit was able to tie together all the disparate elements to create a stylized character. As if aware of his own effect, he gave performances that were often a series of extravagant poses. When he sang and danced in films, it was hard for audiences not to respond to the precise control of his body. "Mr. Fetchit's feet are like chained lightning as he performs," wrote one critic. Even when his characters were flamboyantly exaggerated, the master Fetchit was economic and in command of his movements. Never was there a false footstep. Never was there excessive excessiveness.

In his early films, as Highpockets in *In Old Kentucky* (1927), as Christopher C. Lee in *The Ghost Talks* (1929), as Joe in the 1929 version of *Show Boat* (1929), and as the call-boy Swifty in *Fox Movietone Follies* (1929), he was the embodiment of the nitwit colored man. Stepin Fetchit was always forgetful. Stepin Fetchit could

LEFT: The 1930s' archetypal coon, Stepin Fetchit.

BELOW: Abused and demeaned in picture after picture, Fetchit here takes orders from Will Rogers, an actor he was closely associated with in the 1930s.

never pronounce a word with more than one syllable. Stepin Fetchit seldom seemed to have his senses about him. In *Stand Up and Cheer* (1934), he was tricked into thinking a "talking" penguin was actually a shrunken Jimmy Durante. In *The World Moves On* (1934), he found himself a recruit in the French army! Whining and scratching his head in disbelief, he wondered how he of all people could be mistaken for a Frenchman! In *David Harum* (1934) Stepin nonchalantly soaked his aching feet in a tubful of hot water. When his wife berated him for using the hot water she was boiling to wash her dishes in, Fetchit calmly informed her that she had nothing to worry about. He had killed two birds with one stone, he said, as he lifted from the tub the family's dishes, which had been soaking right along with his feet. For movie audiences it was a classic comic moment.

Perhaps the most typical of the Fetchit features were *David Harum* and the other three in which he costarred with Will Rogers: *The County Chairman* (1935) and two movies directed by John Ford, *Judge Priest* (1934) and *Steamboat 'Round the Bend* (1935). In these four films, Fetchit was cast as the triflin', inarticulate, backward handyman who was there to do odd jobs for master Will Rogers. Throughout these films the black actor cowered, shuffled, or stammered, rendering himself almost unintelligible. Usually, he was demeaned and racially degraded. In *David Harum* he was traded to Will Rogers along with a horse in a shady horse deal. Afterwards, Rogers traded the same horse and Fetchit to another man. Later Fetchit and the bum horse were traded back again. Clearly, Stepin Fetchit's character was considered less than human. As Jeff in *Judge Priest*, the actor often found himself pushed, shoved, and yelled at by Will Rogers to the sheer joy of movie patrons. "Hey, boy, wake up there!" Rogers commanded him. In the film's finale, Fetchit led a notorious street parade, dressed in a mile-high top hat and an enormous fur coat, to the tune of "Dixie." Here, though, the actor triumphed over the role. Traditionally, movie audiences responded to spectacles and extravaganzas, and as Stepin Fetchit's character marched down the street, stepping high and caring less, he became a one-man carnival, an aesthetic happening for humdrum 1930s audiences. "That cloudy streak of greased lightning, Stepin Fetchit, is riotous as the judge's man of all or no work, and he is always threatening to drop the auditors into the Music Hall's plush aisles," wrote *The New York Times* when *Judge Priest* opened at Radio City.

Fetchit's antics eventually destroyed him, but in the early years they made him a star. Fetchit himself took pains to ensure his characters' "respectability." He shrewdly perceived that his coons, although extravagant and outlandish, must never be a threat to the white master, and, most important, they must be servants who could be reformed. Thus he created and popularized what he himself termed the "lazy man with a soul." He has been quoted as saying that he was the first to portray Negro characters who were acceptable to polite Jim Crow society. By the time Fetchit appeared in *Carolina* (1934) and *Steamboat 'Round the Bend* (1935), his characters had become integral parts of the household, involved in the affairs and troubles of the ruling families. They were still used for crude comic relief but at heart they were harmless creatures who, during crucial moments, would "come through." What Fetchit's "lazy man with a soul" ultimately did was to place the black character in the mainstream of filmic action and to remove him from the false idealization of the all-Negro movie. Between Fetchit's master and himself there was a spirit of good will and much mutual affection. These traits figured prominently in later Depression movies and were at the core of the developing master–servant syndrome.

Fetchit's heyday in films came to an end in the late 1930s. The self-demeaning tomfoolery he went through in film after film, as well as the superstitious chicken thieves or clownish show-offs or menial good-for-nothings he invariably portrayed, alienated him from black audiences. Whites had already viewed him as a representative of the American Negro. But black audiences knew better, and civil rights organizations were quick to criticize him. In films such as *Helldorado* (1935), *One More Spring* (1935), *36 Hours to Kill* (1936), *Dimples* (1936), *On the Avenue* (1937), and *Zenobia* (1939), even Fetchit began showing signs of disillusionment with his coon characters, and the quality of his work gradually declined.

Generally, though, there was a complex contradictory element to all Fetchit's appearances that was usually glossed over or ignored. Evidently, at least on a subconscious level, no one knew better than Fetchit the injustices and cruelties of the "benevolent" white masters in his films. Fetchit's great gift was in rendering his coons as such thoroughly illiterate figures that they did not have to respond when demeaned because they were always unaware of what was being done. When he was kicked in one film, Fetchit merely winked to his audience. When he was shoved in another, he merely moaned "Yessir" and went on his way. By removing his characters' intellects—indeed their psyches—from the real world, Stepin Fetchit's dimwits never had to acknowledge the inhumanity that surrounded them. They were inhabitants of detached, ironic, artistically controlled worlds. The ambiguity in Fetchit's work was so strong that audiences often asked, "Can he be serious?" That was something never asked of later black comics, and it was this aspect of Fetchit's work that distinguished him and made him more than just a stereotype figure. There was about him a sad, much-maligned, whining quality. Though he was a great comic figure, he seemed a bruised creature, and always his withdrawal within self—his retreat into a self-protective shell—indicated an overriding, often excruciating nihilism. This nihilistic aspect might explain in part his popularity in a disillusioned age. Yet it was not enough to save him, and when he became a target for the civil rights advocates, his career came to an abrupt end.

What no doubt helped to finish him was his own immaturity. With his penchant for high living, he reportedly went bankrupt, having run up debts of four million dollars with but $144 in the bank. Fetchit left Hollywood at the end of the 1930s and fell into obscurity. During the lean obscure years, he worked in a number of underground independently produced all-black features. Although removed from the Hollywood system that had always typed him, he continued playing the same coon character. In 1952, Fetchit appeared with James Stewart in a major studio film, *Bend of the River*. His comeback was casually dismissed. "We are sorry to note that Stepin Fetchit is back to play a clownish stereotype," wrote Bosley Crowther in *The New York Times*. Afterward, Fetchit made an appearance in John Ford's *The Sun Shines Bright* (1954). He had worked under Ford not only in his important films *Judge Priest* and *Steamboat 'Round the Bend* but in *Salute* (1929) and *The World Moves On* as well. This fifth feature with Ford, however, failed to revive Fetchit's career. He was not to be heard from again until 1968 when he denounced the television documentary "Black History: Lost, Stolen, or Strayed?" for "taking me, a Negro hero, and converting me into a villain." "It was Step," he said, "who elevated the Negro to the dignity of a Hollywood star. I made the Negro a first-class citizen all over the world ... somebody it was all right to associate with. I opened all the theaters."

To many, Stepin Fetchit may have sounded as if he were a man suffering from delusions. But his place in black film history remains significant, for indeed he did open studio doors to blacks in Hollywood. Today because his films are seldom shown and often neglected—to the point where his scenes are even cut when shown on television—the credit due him is generally denied. In his later years, he turned up in the entourage of Muhammad Ali and also appeared in the films *Amazing Grace* (1974, in which he gave a pathetic and embarrassing performance) and *Won Ton Ton, The Dog Who Saved Hollywood* (1976). Later audiences who saw a stale Fetchit had no idea what he was like when his routines were fresh. Fetchit died in 1985. His early characters remain the first of the white master's darling pets. After he arrived on the scene, a servant is a servant is a servant is a servant was no longer the case. When Fetchit ripped the door from the hinges, a slew of domesticated servants came romping through, most significantly in the films of two blond leading ladies.

Waiting on West and Serving Shirley

Mae West and Shirley Temple were worlds apart, but their servants were not. For both actresses, blacks became confidantes and playmates, and like the Stepin Fetchit of *Judge Priest* and *Steamboat 'Round the Bend*, they were also important plot fixtures.

Depression audiences viewing such prime Mae West features as *I'm No Angel* (1933), *She Done Him Wrong* (1933), and *Belle of the Nineties* (1934) could not help noticing the black maids who clustered about the platinum-blond heroine. The domestics were always overweight, middle-aged, and made up as jolly aunt jemimas. They wore patch-work dresses and colorful kerchiefs tied about their heads, and they had the usual names: Pearl, Beulah, and Jasmine. Their naive blackness generally was used as a contrast to Mae West's sophisticated whiteness. When set against white carpeting, white furniture, white decor—not to mention the white Miss West—the stout black figures hustling and bustling about served to heighten the hot white sexuality of their bawdy mistress.

Seldom did the black maids have lives of their own. Instead they were comments on their mistress. Hardly any moviegoer of the 1930s has forgotten how in *I'm No Angel* Mae West, after having bounced from her apartment a socialite who has snubbed her, quickly recovered her cool by giving the most famous instructions any movie maid ever received. "Beulah," she commanded, "peel me a grape!" Beulah (portrayed by Gertrude Howard) scurried into the room. Once again Mae West was in complete control of a situation. In the same film, Mae West, when trying on a new gown or testing her latest quip, gathered her chubby, affable servant gals around her to see their reactions. Often giggling and gaping or even literally kneeling before her as they checked a hemline, the Negro maids appeared to be paying homage to the supreme power of their white mistress. As she rattled off her sophisticated banter, the maids became her foils. "I wouldn't want no policeman to catch me without a petticoat," said maid Pearl in *She Done Him Wrong*. "How about a fireman?" cracked West.

Most important, Mae West's black maids were taken into her confidence and were pictured as knowing her better than any of her men. In *She Done Him Wrong*, maid Pearl (played by Louise Beavers) realized it was Cary Grant who had caught her mistress's eye. It was she who informed Miss West that Grant (portraying a Salvation Army officer) would be evicted from his mission settlement. The possible eviction proved crucial to the plot—and Mae West's romantic inclinations. Consequently, servant Pearl saved the day and proved herself the most dependable of loyal servants. In *I'm No Angel*, Gertrude Howard as Beulah performed the same function by testifying in her mistress's behalf during a hilarious courtroom sequence. In *Belle of the Nineties*, it was Libby Taylor as Jasmine who, upon learning her mistress had a date with a gentleman of dubious character, felt she knew her well enough to say, "Well, I'm surprised at you goin'," to which Miss West replied, "I'm surprised *you'd* think I was."

The implications throughout the films were that black women could not possibly be rivals to Mae West's femininity and that only black women were fit to wait on trollops. Because both blacks and whores were at the bottom of the social scale, Mae West could rely on her colored maids and enjoy a livelier camaraderie with them than she might with whites. Some of this camaraderie must have existed off-screen, too, for Libby Taylor, who portrayed Miss West's servant, had actually been her domestic. When she left New York to go to Hollywood, maid Taylor went with her.

What the blacks in the Mae West films represented was the second step in servant evolution—the domestic servant as trusted good friend. In some of the Shirley Temple features, audiences witnessed the first signs of the humanization of the black domestic.

Shirley Temple herself occupied a unique position in relation to Negroes in films. Of all leading ladies to be waited on by colored help, none was ever more dutifully attended to than little Miss Curlytop. Blacks appeared so often in her important films that there was an inside industry joke that a Temple picture was incomplete without at least one darky. In *Stand Up and Cheer* (1934), the elaborate musical that made Shirley Temple a star, a blues singer—actually a white performer, Tess Gardella, billed as "Aunt Jemima"—led a spiritual revival session. Stepin Fetchit was featured in this film as well as in *Dimples* (1936). In *Little Miss Marker* (1934) and *The Littlest Rebel* (1935), long, lean Willie Best was but one in a bevy of black actors. In *The Little Colonel* (1935), Hattie McDaniel, usually a tough and no-nonsense maid, was the picture of modesty as she portrayed Shirley's mammy. Later she was just as uncharacteristically subdued when she portrayed the faithful family maid to an adolescent Shirley in *Since You Went Away* (1944).

As a genuine Depression heroine who was as much a victim of hard times as anyone else, Shirley Temple sometimes associated with the low-lifers in her movies. But among Shirley and these low-lifers, particularly these black low-lifers—the livery keepers, the faithful old butlers, the big bossy maids, the doormen, the cooks—there was always a sense of community and an abiding feeling of order, as if everyone knew his place, accepted it, and therefore managed to make life bearable. With most adults, she was overbearing, outspoken, and forever in charge of the situation. Her common sense outranked theirs. But in her dealings with her black servants, there was occasionally some condescension or manipulation. Thus in *The Little Colonel*, audiences saw Shirley give commands to her crusty old grandfather, Lionel Barrymore, or offer advice to her distraught mother, or bring comfort to her desperately ill father. But with the hired help, Bill Robinson and Hattie McDaniel, Shirley Temple relaxed. She learned to pick up her heels and have some good clean fun. Robinson became the master in their relationship when he taught her the staircase dance routines.

Throughout her films, Shirley and her black servants were obvious buddies. The servants' vitality, spontaneity, and childlike qualities equaled her own. From them she learned to maintain good spirits in the face of adversity. As they danced and sang and laughed together, Shirley and her subservients gave Depression audiences their greatest gift; the impression that if everyone were kind to one another, the bad times would soon be over. Finally, to her, the black servants represented fellow children with whom she could sympathize more readily than with real (white) grownups or even with real children. When Shirley encountered her peers, especially the pickaninnies in *The Little Colonel* and *The Littlest Rebel*, she could be a real tyrant!

Mr. Bojangles: The Cool-Eyed Tom

Of all the black servants in the Shirley Temple films none was more closely associated with her than Bill "Bojangles" Robinson, who costarred with her in no less than four features. Theirs was the perfect interracial love match. For surely nothing would come of it. Indeed audiences so readily accepted them as a pair that in their biggest hit together, *The Littlest Rebel*, Robinson played her guardian, certainly the first time in the history of motion pictures that a black servant was made responsible for a white life. As Shirley's "Uncle Billy," Robinson reaped many condescending smiles and quaint compliments from nice little old ladies who were given to such comments as, "My, isn't he a sweet colored man." "Uncle Billy" was the perfect—perhaps the quintessential—tom role. But by then, 1935, that type of characterization was to be expected from Bill "Bojangles" Robinson.

Robinson had come to films only a few years earlier after a varied and legendary career as a tap dancer. The grandson of a slave, he was said to have never had a dancing lesson in his life, to have run away from his home in Richmond, Virginia, at the age of eight, and to have soon earned his living by dancing for pennies in saloons and on streets. He formally entered show business with a vaudeville act and in 1928 proved a smashing success in the *Blackbirds* revue. The hit *Brown Buddies* followed, and then spectacular appearances at the Palace Theatre in New York. Robinson coined the word "copasetic" which seemed to mean everything was just fine and dandy or better than okay. He originated the staircase tap dance. And Fred Astaire called him the greatest dancer of all time. Robinson's first film appearance was in *Dixiana* (1930) with Bebe Daniels and the comedians Wheeler and Woolsey. When he tapped away, his act was greeted by rounds of applause in theaters throughout the country. But it was when he returned to Hollywood in the mid-1930s that his movie performances climaxed his spectacular career.

Now, honey, all you gotta do is listen with your feet, he seemed to be telling Shirley Temple in their first feature, *The Little Colonel*, and as he tapped up the stairs with her, a star tom was born. In this film, Robinson proved himself a well-behaved, mannerly Negro attendant. When the old Southern colonel, Lionel Barrymore, fumed and fussed at him, good old Bill stood by patiently. He knew de ole massa didn't mean no harm. His respect won him audience approval, and he was rewarded for his "gentlemanliness" with more film work. From *The Little Colonel*, he went to *Hooray for Love* (1935), in which he not only sang "Got a Snap to My Finger" but was formally crowned the Mayor of Harlem. Later there were appearances as a genial servant to Will Rogers in *In Old Kentucky* (1935), a dancing sequence in *The Big Broadcast of 1936*, and finally what remains the definitive Robinson tom performance in David Butler's *The Littlest Rebel*.

ABOVE: Shirley Temple seeks aid from Bill "Bojangles" Robinson and the black community in *The Littlest Rebel* (1935).

RIGHT: The screen's first interracial couple: Temple and Robinson.

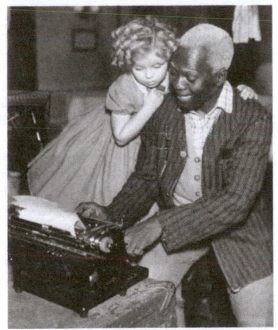

The Littlest Rebel was Shirley Temple's big Old South vehicle. As it began, she was the happiest of pint-sized Southern belles. An elaborate birthday party was being given for her, and Shirley was surrounded by her fair-haired mother, her tall, stalwart father, her tot friends, and the household slaves, of whom Uncle Billy was her favorite. Her chief delight was having Uncle Billy dance for her. When called upon, the good-natured servant always complied, and at this birthday party the highlight of the day's events was Uncle Billy's performance. But in the middle of the celebration, the ideal way of the Old South was interrupted by the war call. The party scattered. Later, Yankees invaded the plantation. Shirley made up in bootblack, pretending to be a harmless pickaninny. When the ruse failed, she turned to Uncle Billy. Now he must protect her from the Yankees. And he did just that. When Shirley's mother took ill and died and her father was captured by Union troops and hauled off to a Northern prison camp, Uncle Billy became her guardian-companion. Here his dancing ability again proved useful. Determined to finance a trip North so Shirley could help her father, but low on cash, he decided to tap up the deficit. Near a railroad station, he and Shirley performed energetically for all who passed by while another servant, portrayed by sleepy Willie Best, passed the cap to "help the cause." Thus the pair earned their fare to Washington. Together they visited President Lincoln and pleaded for the release of the girl's father. Lincoln pardoned him, and Uncle Billy and little Shirley lived happily ever after.

The actual performance by Bill Robinson in this feature as well as in the others was generally superficial and terribly unvaried. Indeed he often recited his lines as if reading from a blackboard. When he danced, however, audiences could not have cared less what he had to say. Robinson's greatest gift as a dancer in the movies was that his sense of rhythm, his physical dexterity, and his easy-going naturalness all combined to convey an optimistic—a copasetic—air. As he tapped across the room his sheer joy made audiences think that life after all was what you made of it. The real significance of a Bill Robinson performance was therefore never as much in what he had to say as in what he came to represent. His work in *The Littlest Rebel* was successful because he provided a reassuring framework for the film. Shirley Temple fans, forever anxious because of the plights and perils of their favorite heroine, could rest at ease as soon as Bojangles' name flashed in the credits. For it was obvious that if all the others in the movie lost their heads, Bill would be sure to keep his. He patiently listened to Shirley's chatter, understood her problems, sympathized with them, and ultimately made a decisive move to aid her— something no one else in the movie was capable of doing. "Uncle Billy can do anything. He can sing. He can dance. He can climb trees," said little Miss Curlytop. Audiences agreed. *The New York Times* wrote of Robinson: "As Uncle Billy, the faithful family butler, Bill Robinson is excellent and some of the best moments . . . are those in which he breaks into song and dances with Mistress Temple."

Tom and coon at odds with one another: Bill Robinson and Willie Best in *The Littlest Rebel*.

The Robinson figure was obviously the familiar contented slave, distinguished, however, because he was congenial, confident, and very, very *cool*. Unlike Stepin Fetchit, he was articulate too, and, more important, consistently reliable. His reliability and his detached urbane cool perhaps explain why there were seldom complaints about Bill Robinson's performances as there were against Fetchit's or even those of Willie Best.

Interestingly, Best made one of his typically somnambulistic appearances in *The Littlest Rebel*. Known for his outrageous coon portrayals, he served as a contrasting figure to point up the trustworthiness of Robinson. During the approach of Union soldiers fighting to free all the slaves, Best trembled. Robinson, still at ease, asked why he was so frightened, and Best replied that his mind told him not to worry but "my body don't believe it." In this scene, Best was the typical terrified darky, *scared of his own shadow*, whereas Bill Robinson came across even more than usual as the sensible and responsible Good Negro because of the contrast. Ironically, though, despite Robinson's earnest sobriety, it has to be admitted that of the two, Willie Best now certainly seems the funnier.

Bill Robinson's characters were all part of the humanized servant tradition. Humanization was nothing more than a softening or refinement of black characters. Perhaps it would be more appropriate to say that certain black actors, by individualizing their servants through their own unique and winning personalities, had proven that these black faces were not just escapist creations on the screen but realistic human ones, too. The humanized servants ushered in black dignity, and generally they escaped the self-demeaning antics that weighed other black servants down. Robinson was the most prominent of the male humanized figures.

Until the late 1930s, Bill Robinson's career was flourishing. Then the cracks in his screen popularity began to appear. Although he was to be loved by fans throughout his career, his courteous, humanized tom spirits gave way to more ribald, iconoclastic presences. After *The Littlest Rebel*, Robinson appeared in a serious role in *One Mile from Heaven* (1937), then as Aloysius in *Rebecca of Sunnybrook Farm* (1938—again with Shirley Temple), then later in 1938 in *Road Demon*, *Up the River*, and *Just Around the Corner*. In the last, as Corporal Jones, the doorman at Shirley Temple's hotel, he danced and sang "This Is a Happy Little Ditty." But the role was far from impressive and gone was much of his spontaneous effervescence. As his movie career ebbed, he wisely returned to the theater, making a successful comeback in 1939 in Mike Todd's *Hot Mikado*. After that success, he returned to Hollywood in 1943 to star in *Stormy Weather*. The movie had great entertainment segments, but, sadly, the cool *savoir-faire* of the old master Bojangles proved not half as interesting as the perfect beauty of the up-and-coming Lena Horne. Robinson died in 1949.

Clarence Muse: The Inhibited, Humanized Tom Standing in a Corner by Himself

An actor whose presence also distinguished his characters but who was virtually ignored during the 1930s was Clarence Muse. He was a short, stocky man with a large resonant voice, more inhibited than any other black performer of the period. Perhaps unable to produce the high-style flamboyance his fellow players so exuberantly displayed, he was instead very skillful at presenting mild-mannered docile manservants.

Muse's educational and theatrical background may in part explain why he was often so inhibited and restrained an actor. Born in Baltimore in 1889, he was a graduate of the Dickinson School of Law in Pennsylvania. He had worked for many years in the South with black acting troupes, and in New York he first appeared with the Lincoln Players and later the Lafayette Players. His training was generally in a more serious vein than that of most black performers, and he was not accustomed to working only for laughs.

When he first arrived in Hollywood, he was handled with a bit of care. In *Hearts in Dixie* he portrayed the old man, Uncle Napus. Here his tom character served as a dignified contrast to the broad foolery of Stepin Fetchit. Ironically, in *A Royal Romance* (1930), Muse found himself going through some of the same foolery. As the razor-totin' right-hand coon friend of a white detective, he helped look for spooks in an old deserted house. His befuddled antics were used for routine comic relief.

By 1931, Muse was back in top tom form when he appeared in *Huckleberry Finn* as the archetypal tom, the kindly Nigger Jim who sets out on the raft with Huck. Although he did not figure prominently in the film, Muse's Jim was still the congenial confidant and amiable alter ego of the adolescent Huck. What was most intriguing was that Muse seemed miscast because his slave was too intelligent. His dialect was obviously faked and forced, and during excruciatingly harsh close-ups used solely for laughs, audiences must have felt pained to see such a dignified and decent presence demeaned so. No other black performer of the period ever had quite such an effect, perhaps because most were able to forget themselves and become lost in the part. Muse always seemed to be standing at a great distance looking on with his large questioning eyes and sadly shaking his head.

Frank Capra's *Broadway Bill* (1934) was one of Muse's most important features. Muse had previously worked for Capra in *Rain or Shine* (1930) and *Dirigible* (1931), and the director, who affectionately called Muse his "pet actor," handled him sensitively. Cast opposite white actor Warner Baxter, Muse again played the amiable alter ego. The film is about a race horse, Broadway Bill, that Baxter and Muse hope to enter in the Kentucky Derby. Both are short on cash, and when Baxter discovers Muse's savings in the latter's boots, he uses the money of his black friend—who is called Whitey—for the racing enterprise. Throughout the film the two men are true compatriots. They sleep under the same roof. They share whatever food they can get. Still Muse's role called for much tommery and even some racking instances of Jim Crowism. In one scene, the film's producers upheld their self-imposed color bar by having Muse eat his food standing while Baxter remained seated. It would have been unheard of to have a black and white sit at the same table. Yet again Muse managed to strike at consciences through the depth of his own personality. Even the manner in which he walked—with head lifted, body erect, eyes straight ahead—indicated a self-respect and black self-awareness that other actors of the period lacked.

By 1935, Muse had appeared in an array of films including *Last Parade* (1931), *Secret Witness* (1931), *Woman from Monte Carlo* (1932), *Cabin in the Cotton* (1932), *Winner Take All* (1933), *Washington Merry-Go-Round* (1933), *From Hell to Heaven* (1933), and *The Count of Monte Cristo* (1934). Midway in the decade, he devastatingly went against the grain of the toms he proved so good at portraying when he appeared as a resurrected old mythic type, the black brute, in King Vidor's *So Red the Rose*. The film was a perfect example of the Old South (or Old South-oriented) pictures that were popular in the 1930s and very early 1940s. Others were *Carolina, In Old Kentucky, Steamboat 'Round the Bend, The Littlest Rebel, Jezebel* (1938), *Virginia* (1941), *The Vanishing Virginian* (1941), and, of course, *Gone with the Wind*. Romanticized and quasi-historical, *So Red the Rose* starred Margaret Sullavan as a Southern belle who is left stranded in the Big House with her dying father. Almost all the men are off fighting in the Civil War. When a rebellion erupts among her faithful slaves, the impetuous, headstrong, and ever-so-valiant Sullavan marches to the slave quarters to quench the rebellious fires. But who should be playing Cato, the renegade, rebel-rousing leader of the incendiaries but Clarence Muse! Muse played his upstart with an insolent conviction and anger that was perhaps *too* good. During the shooting of the film, the actor evidently was carried away by the rough-tough character he portrayed. In a climactic sequence when his Cato was to be slapped by the film's heroine, the actor refused to do the scene. Things were resolved by having actress Sullavan strike another black actor instead. Today it is obvious that Muse's performance lacked control, but it does reveal what can happen to a tom performer who is finally let loose.

Afterward Muse returned to tomming in *Show Boat* (1936), *Follow Your Heart* (1936), *Spirit of Youth* (1937), and *Way Down South* (1939). In this last film, Muse expanded his accomplishments. With writer Langston Hughes, he composed spirituals to be sung by the Hall Johnson Choir, as well as original music for Bobby Breen. More important, Muse co-authored the screenplay of the picture with Langston Hughes. Essentially an Old South melodrama, *Way Down South* told the story of an orphaned white Southern lad (Bobby Breen) and his devotion to the

Clarence Muse, the dignified, humanized torn.

slaves his deceased father had treated so humanely. When a Simon Legreeish character mistreats the slaves, young Bobby undertakes to save them, particularly his favorite, dear old Uncle Caton. This role was played by none other than Muse, who realized in 1935 that perhaps the most effective way for a black actor to come up with a solid role was to write that role for himself. In 1940, he co-wrote the script for *Broken Strings*, an independently produced film in which he starred as a concert violinist. Here the hint of dignity was brought to the forefront and made an integral part of the character. The role remains Muse's finest. In 1940, Muse played a coon minister in *Maryland*. This picture was a bad one not only for him but also for his black co-stars, Hattie McDaniel and Ben Carter. All three were abominable and fraudulently cute and homey. Thereafter, Clarence Muse was stuck with the tom character in films such as *Zanzibar* (1940), *Tales of Manhattan, Shadow of a Doubt* (1943), *Heaven Can Wait* (1943), *Watch on the Rhine* (1943), *Two Smart People* (1946), *Joe Palooka in the Knockout* (1947), and An *Act of Murder* (1948). In 1950, Muse returned to work under Frank Capra's direction in *Riding High* with Bing Crosby. The movie was a remake of *Broadway Bill*, and Muse re-created his role of the faithful servant. Nine years later he appeared in *Porgy and Bess*. Afterward Muse went into semiretirement, but he returned to films in 1972 in the role of Cudjo in *Buck and the Preacher* and in 1976 in a bit (as a shoeshine man) in *Car Wash*. Muse's early roles were neither great nor heroic, and taken out of their historical context they might seem far from impressive. They lacked the flashiness most black performances of the day were noted for. But they appeared at a time when being black and human in the movies was neither easy nor expected. Clarence Muse died in 1979.

Imitation of Life: Mother Knows Best

The humanization of the Negro servant was carried to new and highly publicized heights with the appearance of the first important "black film" of the 1930s, *Imitation of Life*. It arrived in 1934, at a time when a new social consciousness had infiltrated the motion picture industry. Already Roosevelt's election, the New Deal, the growing liberalism of the country, and the Depression itself had brought to American films a new world view and a new social order whereby many of the old racial proprieties were starting to be discarded. *Imitation of Life* was an outgrowth of this new conscious liberal spirit. It prided itself on its portrait of the modern black woman, still a servant but now imbued with dignity and a character that were an integral part of the American way of life.

Based on Fannie Hurst's best-selling novel, Universal's *Imitation of Life* was directed by John Stahl and starred the black actresses Louise Beavers and Fredi Washington as well as Claudette Colbert, Rochelle Hudson, Ned Sparks, and

Warren William. The film traced the lives of two widows, one white, the other black, who meet by chance and decide to throw their lots together. Both women are left with daughters to raise. The black widow, Aunt Delilah, will care for the house and Miss Bea's child, Jessie, while the white Miss Bea will work at a career and be the breadwinner. The early days are hard. The two suffer from the Depression realities of hunger and poverty. But fortune comes their way in the form of a pancake recipe. Passed down to Aunt Delilah for generations as a family secret, the pancake flour has such a wonderful flavor that Miss Bea decides to market it. In an act of magnanimity, she offers Aunt Delilah a 20 percent interest in the concern.

"You'll have your own car. Your own house," Miss Bea tells her. "My own house? You gonna send me away, Miss Bea? I can't live with you? Oh, honey chile, please don't send me away." When asked if she doesn't want her own house, Delilah replies, "No'm. How I gonna take care of you and Miss Jessie if I ain't here." She adds, "I'se your cook. And I want to stay your cook." Of the pancake recipe, Delilah says, "I gives it to you, honey. I makes you a present of it." Her submissiveness merely justifies Bea's exploitation. (The 1959 remake of *Imitation of Life* dropped the pancake recipe.)

And so the two women remain lifelong friends and successful business partners. Aunt Delilah's mix, as marketed by Miss Bea, is a phenomenal success, reaping prosperity for both. But ultimately the prosperity is coupled with heartache, then despair, brought on by the widows' respective daughters. Miss Bea's Jessie becomes her rival in a love affair. At an early age, Aunt Delilah's light-skinned daughter, Peola, becomes annoyed whenever her efforts to mingle with whites as a white are frustrated by the appearance of her very dark mother. Ultimately, she rejects her mother, leaves home, and attempts to cross the color line. Aunt Delilah's heart is broken.

The story is resolved with the death of the good Aunt Delilah, who is laid to rest with the one thing she wanted most: the biggest funeral the colored community ever did see. As directed by Stahl, it was super-deluxe Hollywood at its most extravagant, complete with white horses, a white hearse, and a full-sized band. The highlight of this orgiastically tearful funeral was the returning repentant daughter, Peola.

Because of its racial theme and some inspired casting, *Imitation of Life* turned itself into the slickest and possibly the best made tear-jerker of its time. On the surface, the film was a simple tale of motherly love and motherly woes. In the relationship between Beavers and Colbert, audiences were assured that differences between white and black, like differences between the rich and poor, could easily be done away with if everybody worked together. Beneath the surface, though, *Imitation of Life* was a conscious apotheosis of the tom spirit and an unconsciously bitter comment on race relations in America.

Louise Beavers' Delilah was a combination of tom and aunt jemima magnified and glorified in full-blown Hollywood fashion. But she introduced to the 1930s audience the idea of black Christian stoicism. She tells daughter Peola, "Open up

ABOVE: Service with a smile! Louise Beavers as the jolly, good-hearted, submissive cook in *Imitation of Life* (1934).

RIGHT: Beavers as the stoic Aunt Delilah and Fredi Washington as her wayward daughter Peola "passing" for white in *Imitation of Life.*

and say, 'Lord, I bows my head.' He made you black, honey. Don't be telling him his business. Accept it, honey. Do that for your mammy, your mother dear." In its historical perspective, this Christian stoicism—particularly because Beavers was able to make movie patrons believe that she herself believed it—"elevated" the Negro character in films by endowing him with Christian goodness far exceeding that of any other character. This same doctrine of Christian stoicism as first displayed by Beavers was later to inform the work of Ethel Waters and at times Sidney Poitier. Indeed, Beavers' bow-your-head sentiments with Peola were later skillfully re-created in 1949 by Ethel Waters in *Pinky*, but in a more realistic manner. Of course, the irony of this stoicism was that it made the Negro character more self-effacing than ever and even more resolutely resigned to accepting his or her fate of inferiority.

Imitation of Life's great contradiction, its single subversive element, was the character Peola. For the most part, her story was submerged. Originally, Peola had been conceived as a tragic mulatto type, the beautiful girl doomed because she has a "drop of Negra blood." But as played by Fredi Washington, Peola became a character in search of a movie. With eyes light and liquid and almost haunted, Fredi Washington made Peola a password for non-passive resistance. She seemed to be crying out that she simply wanted the same things in life other people enjoyed. She was the film's most complex character, its most heartfelt. To obtain the equality she wants, Peola has to rebel against the system. Peola was the New Negro demanding a real New Deal. But as *The New York Times* pointed out in its review of the film: "The photoplay was content to suggest that the sensitive daughter of the Negro woman is bound to be unhappy if she happens to able to pass for white." The explanation for Peola's rebellion is that she wants to be white, not that she wants white opportunities. Her weeping by her mother's casket was Hollywood's slick way of finally humiliating her, its way of finally making the character who had run away with herself conform to the remorseful mulatto type.

Regardless of its shortcomings, *Imitation of Life* was a solid box-office success. So responsive were audiences to its story that the film was revived in the 1940s and then remade in the 1950s. Louise Beavers and Fredi Washington became respected black actresses, although neither was to receive the recognition due her.

Iridescent Fredi: Black Girl in Search of a Black Role

For black Americans, Fredi Washington was for a time the great black hope. They saw in her a sophisticated and talented black actress with the range and the beauty to win leading roles. But in the end, she fell a victim to the times and her own peculiar looks.

Born in Savannah, Georgia, in 1903, Fredi Washington began her career as an entertainer in nightclubs and cafés. In Harlem society in the 1920s and 1930s, she and her sister, Isabelle, were legendary beauties, hotly pursued and discussed. After a brief career on the stage, Isabelle married Adam Clayton Powell. For Fredi, there was moderate success in a touring company of *Shuffle Along* and later on the stage in *Singin' the Blues* and *Porgy*. It was always a problem casting her, for, like Peola, Fredi Washington was a black girl who looked white. Her features were sharply defined, her hair long, dark, and straight, and her eyes a vibrant green. Press releases described her as looking French or Italian. Columnists were quick to relate the problems she had because of her white looks.

When she was cast opposite Paul Robeson in the play *Black Boy*, Fredi Washington portrayed a black girl passing for white. Therein her type was discovered. But in the film capital, it took some time before directors could decide on how best to use her. In *The Emperor Jones* (1933), opposite Paul Robeson, she played a light-skinned Harlem slut, but she proved too sophisticated and intelligent in the role. She also had been heavily darkened with make-up to look more Negroid. Washington said the producers didn't want it to look as if Robeson was playing a romantic role with a white actress. In the relaxed musical shorts she did with Duke Ellington and Cab Calloway in the 1930s, she seemed more at home. But it was as Peola in *Imitation of Life* that she emerged as the archetypal tragic mulatto for the Depression era. Her other films were *Drums of the Jungle* (1935) and *One Mile from Heaven*. In the former, she portrayed a villainous half-breed island girl. In *One Mile from Heaven*, she appeared opposite Bill Robinson as the radiant beauty who discovers a white foundling and wants to raise the child as her own.

Fredi Washington's characters were never happy ones, but for a while it looked as if her provocative and promising performances would make her a star. The newspaper *Afro-American* even asked in a feature article: "... who would her leading man be if Hollywood really let her go romantic?" Of course, there was to be no black leading lady. The movies were not ready for idealized tragic black heroines. Audiences preferred mammies and jemimas who could be laughed at or enjoyed or pitied but who would not strike at their consciences. Fredi Washington discovered that the spectacular looks that had opened the door for an important film role ultimately closed that door in her face.

In 1939 Fredi Washington returned to her stage career, making an impressive appearance in *Mamba's Daughters* as Ethel Waters' rebellious child. In the late 1940s, rumors spread that she would play the postwar mulatto heroine, Pinky, a perfect role for her. But by then she was too old for the part, and her name meant nothing at the box office. Fredi Washington died in 1994.

The melancholy and iridescent Fredi Washington.

Louise Beavers: The Black Guardian Angel

Louise Beavers, however, prevailed. Because of her humanized domesticity, she was for a time the most important black actress working in films. Even before she appeared in *Imitation of Life*, she had played an assortment of maid roles in Hollywood pictures, and she had been carefully groomed by herself and the studios to fit into the mammy-aunt jemima category. Before her there had been no distinctive mammy figure. And the studios realized Beavers was a perfect foil and background flavor for such Depression heroines as Jean Harlow, Mae West, and Claudette Colbert—women forced by the times to be on their own, yet needing someone in their corner to cheer them up when things looked too rough, to advise them when personal problems overwhelmed them.

Louise Beavers was a big-boned, robust woman with skin that was described as smooth as chocolate velvet, and eyes bright, large, and wondrously naive. In the late 1920s, when she was spotted by a studio agent in an amateur show, she was considered for a mammy role in Universal's *Uncle Tom's Cabin* because of her size and color. She was eventually assigned the role of a cook, however, because of her youthful appearance. She was heavy and hearty but not heavy and hearty enough. Thereafter she went on force-feed diets, compelling herself to eat beyond her normal appetite. Generally, she weighed close to two hundred pounds, but it was a steady battle for her to stay overweight. During filming, due to pressures, she often lost weight and then had to be padded to look more like a full-bosomed domestic who was capable of carrying the world on her shoulders. Another problem was her accent. Born in Cincinnati, she came to Los Angeles in 1913 and studied at Pasadena High. Consequently, her voice had no trace of a dialect or Southern patois. When the talkies came in, she schooled herself in the slow-and-easy backwoods accent compulsory for every black servant.

Another problem for Louise Beavers, certainly the least important but surely the most ironic, was that although she invariably was cast as a cook, she detested kitchen work and abhorred pancakes. During filming, professional white cooks had to prepare the food. Then Beavers was situated at the stove, smile intact and pancake flipper in her hand; thus the image of the jolly black cook was completely manufactured and presented for mass consumption. Once the contours of her screen personality were physically established, Beavers supplied the good-natured affability to round out the characters. She was always happy, always kind, always intricately involved in the private lives of her employers, so much so that she usually completely lacked a private life of her own.

Her early screen performances were in the 1931 films *Annabelle's Affairs*, *Girls Around Town*, and *Sundown Trail*. In 1932 she made some ten films, including George Cukor's *What Price Hollywood?* and *Divorce in the Family*. The following year she came into her own as the cheerful, hopelessly naive servant Pearl in Mae

West's *She Done Him Wrong* and again as a similar cheerful, naive servant Loretta in Jean Harlow's *Bombshell*. By 1933, during which year she appeared in seven other films, Louise Beavers was a standard fixture on the movie screen. Then came *Imitation of Life*.

Stories still circulate of the humiliation Louise Beavers endured once she had successfully tested for the role of Delilah. It was said that as the cast gathered to rehearse, when one of the little girls who played Peola at a young age, learned that Miss Beavers was to portray her mother, the child screamed that she did not want her. "She's black!" Later when Beavers requested that the word "nigger" be removed from the script, she won her case with the help of the NAACP. But when she was called afterward into the front office and made to pronounce "Negro" repeatedly as a means of punishment, she may have wondered if she had really won after all. Nevertheless, *Imitation of Life* was her great triumph. She was consistently singled out by the critics, and when the Academy failed to nominate her for an Oscar, columnist Jimmy Fiddler complained:

> I also lament the fact that the motion picture industry has not set aside racial prejudice in naming actresses. I don't see how it is possible to overlook the magnificent portrayal of the Negro actress, Louise Beavers, who played the mother in *Imitation of Life*. If the industry chooses to ignore Miss Beavers' performance, please let this reporter, born and bred in the South, tender a special award of praise to Louise Beavers for the finest performance of 1934.

Not long after her triumph, Louise Beavers appeared in another submissive and sympathetic role. Previously, she had made a mark by taking the black woman off the plantation. In *Rainbow on the River* she found herself right back there. In this Reconstruction days tale, she was cast as a former slave, Toinette, who raises and comes to love dearly a white child orphaned after the Civil War. When it is discovered that the boy has Yankee kinfolk, Toinette's heart is broken. But her Christian stoicism will not allow her to hold on to the child selfishly. As before, the performance went beyond the tom-mammy-jemima type because Louise Beavers played it with simplicity and sincerity. The most shameless thing, however (and something for which she might never be forgiven), was her intimation that during the Civil War she never wanted freedom anyway. Her masters had been so kind to her. To her credit or her chagrin, Louise Beavers played the scene beautifully and, worst of all, convincingly.

During the latter part of the decade, she made more than her share of mediocre films, and often she was required to do nothing more than giggle happily or smile knowingly. *Make Way for Tomorrow* (1937), *Wings over Honolulu* (1937), *Love in a Bungalow* (1937), *The Last Gangster* (1937), *Scandal Street* (1938), *Life Goes On*

The screen's favorite domestic or its biggest phony? Check Louise Beavers' sly smile and take one look at those beautifully polished nails. Those hands never touched a dish in their life.

(1938), *Peck's Bad Boy with the Circus* (1938), and *The Lady's from Kentucky* (1938) were some of the movies she made toward the end of the decade.

One of Louise Beavers' better roles was in David O. Selznick's *Made for Each Other* (1939). Selznick believed in American hearth and home, and to him this meant nothing less than two cars in the garage, a chicken in the oven, and a black cook in the kitchen. His *Gone with the Wind* and later his *Since You Went Away* featured Beavers' rival, Hattie McDaniel. His *Duel in the Sun* (1947) had Butterfly McQueen. But for *Made for Each Other* he selected Louise Beavers to portray dewy-eyed, devoted Lily, the servant to the Depression victims Carole Lombard and James Stewart. When Lily realizes Lombard does not have enough money to maintain her services, she saves her white mistress the embarrassment of having to let her go by saying, "Ah, never you mind, honey. I's a luxury." Before she leaves, she not only elevates Lombard's down-and-out spirits but offers the white woman some classic words of advice. "Lily's a whole lot older than you, honey, and she's learned one thing. Never let the seeds stop you from enjoying the watermelon.... Spit out those seeds before they stop you from enjoying the melon." Here, with even the tritest of lines, Louise Beavers remained the essence of Christian unselfishness. When seen today, her eyes do not convey any kind of grand sought-after truth. But they do evoke heartfelt kindness to the point where Louise Beavers is, as press releases liked to say, "a black angel."

In the 1940s, Beavers added her touch to *Shadow of the Thin Man* (1941), *Reap the Wild Wind* (1942), *DuBarry Was a Lady* (1943), and *Jack London* (1943). When it looked as if her career was just about finished, she appeared in *Mr. Blandings Builds His Dream House* (1948). Here she portrayed the family maid who supplies her employer, Cary Grant, with a winning slogan for baked ham. "Not ham! WHAM! If you ain't eating WHAM, you ain't eatin' ham!" she exclaims with a laugh. "Darling, give Gussie a ten-dollar raise," responds Grant. Thus the young advertising executive about to lose his job because he couldn't come up with the right slogan for a ham account has been saved from ruin! For Louise Beavers it was a small but important role. Again she was the black nourishing the white family.

When the "enlightened" post-World War II spirit virtually obliterated the servant figures, Louise Beavers made a slight image change to play Jackie Robinson's mother in *The Jackie Robinson Story* (1950). Moon-faced, still mellow, and marvelously meek, she was a touching presence. Her last important appearance was as the maid Beulah on the television series. Hattie McDaniel played the part on radio. After her death, Ethel Waters took over. Then Beavers. It remains one of the great perversities of the motion-picture industry that the three greatest mammies of the movies should ultimately portray the same jolly, docile cook. Afterward Beavers appeared as the maid in Mae West's nightclub act in Las Vegas. Before her death in the early 1960s, she made her final film appearances in

Teenage Rebel (1956), *Tammy and the Bachelor* (1957), *The Goddess* (1958), *All the Fine Young Cannibals* (1960), and *The Facts of Life* (1961).

The Green Pastures

"Gangway! Gangway! For de Lawd God Jehovah!" cried the black archangel Gabriel, and the screen was bombarded with the liveliest collection of agreeable toms, uncle remuses, aunt jemimas, and corn-patch pickaninnies ever assembled in one motion picture. It was *The Green Pastures*, the second of the important black films of the decade. In 1936, the year of its release, it brought the humanized servant tradition to an early apex.

The Green Pastures was an adaptation of Marc Connelly's enormously successful Broadway play. Directed by Connelly and William Keighley and released by Warner Brothers, it was the first major studio all-black spectacle since 1929. Because of the financial disappointment of the early all-black features, the major studios had steered clear of them. But a number of factors indicated the time might be ripe for another try. The box-office success of *Imitation of Life* had proved that blacks in important character roles could woo and affect audiences. At the same time the increase in ghetto theaters and the success of a number of independently produced all-Negro features had revealed that there was a growing Negro audience eager for any product even remotely touching on their own experiences. Finally, the long run of *The Green Pastures* on Broadway indicated that this was a property with meaning to many audiences. Warner Brothers decided to take a chance on it.

The Green Pastures was a very *likable* motion picture. Its simple theology, its naive philosophizing, and its "acceptable" portrait of black America as quaint and charming made it a gratifying experience. The story it told was simple. At a Sunday school class in Louisiana, a kindly Negro teacher, the good Mr. Deshee, visualizes the wonders of the Good Book so that his young pupils might better understand their meaning. Thus the biblical characters of old are transformed into contemporary Louisiana Negroes—in attire, in vernacular, and in customs. Adam and Eve are presented as a muscular bronze man and his vain coquettish mate. Cain the Sixth is a rough-and-ready no-account, and his high-yaller gal, Zeba, a high-strung strumpet. Moses becomes a clever conjurer. And Noah is a gregarious tom, complete with top hat and raincoat.

In heaven the angels, seraphim, and cherubim are also contemporary Negroes, strutting about with straw hats or uttering quaint Negro colloquialisms. "Being de Lawd ain't no bed of roses," moans the heavenly host. "Now you heared me. You want me to fly up there and slap you down?" belts out a mammy angel to her little no-account cherub son who rides a friendly cloud. In this heaven, de Lawd proudly passes out his most prized possessions: ten-cent seegars for everybody! Thus the heaven of *The Green Pastures* ultimately becomes a perpetual Negro holiday, one everlasting weekend fish fry. Harmony and good spirits reign supreme as the Hall Johnson Choir's resonant rendition of spirituals reminds everyone that there is no heaven like a black one.

A lively amalgam of sugar and subservience, *The Green Pastures* opened at Radio City Music Hall to unanimous praise from the white press and much of the black. *The New York World Telegram* called it "a beautiful film—the screen version of the tender, gently pathetic, curiously touching Negro miracle play." *The New York Times* commented:

> That disturbance in and around the Music Hall yesterday was the noise of shuffling queues in Sixth Avenue and the sound of motion picture critics dancing in the street. The occasion was the coming at last to the screen of Marc Connelly's naive, ludicrous, sublime and heartbreaking masterpiece of American folk drama.... It still has the rough beauty of homespun, the irresistible compulsion of simple faith.

In the *Afro-American*, however, one perceptive black reviewer wrote that the movie's characterization of the religion of the Negro was *only* caricature and that there was nothing in it except childlike faith. "Let *The Green Pastures* go for what it is: an interesting and entertaining spectacle with a cast of underpaid colored actors portraying Connelly's conception of ... unlearned earlier-day beliefs of heaven and the Bible. Any other viewpoint is outrageous."

Contemporary audiences tend to share the dissenter's viewpoint. It is now evident that *The Green Pastures* rested on a cruel assumption: that nothing could be more ludicrous than transporting the lowly language and folkways of the early-twentieth-century Negro back to the high stately world before the Flood. The movie played hard at exploiting the incongruity of angels with dirty faces. And in this juxtaposition of low with high, there were implied Negro ignorance and inferiority. All this went under the guise of a "Negro miracle play." Nothing could have been more absurd. For Negroes of the period never pictured historical or biblical events in terms of their own experience. Indeed, the problem was that they always dreamt of a white heaven and a white heavenly host.

But in 1936 few movie patrons linked sociology with films. Consequently, audiences found *The Green Pastures* a great cinematic treat. What transcended the shortcomings of the script, too, was the brilliance of the performances. Few film casts have ever equaled the sheer dynamics and unabashed delight that these actors showed. Among this crew of celestial lights, there was not one disagreeable or even remotely unpleasant type of performer. All put on a magnificent show of talent and spontaneous humor. Edna Mae Harris attacked the role of Zeba with great sly, vixenish relish, the kind audiences saw only when an actress was giving her once-in-a-lifetime performance—and knew it. The same was true of Frank Wilson's fine, ironic Moses. Oscar Polk portrayed the long, lean Gabriel with a surprisingly appropriate nonchalance and understatement. In this film, as in most of his others, Polk seems emasculated, but here it adds to the diversity of this black heaven. Eddie Anderson was a charming Noah. Also included in the cast were Clinton Rosemond, George Reed, Myrtle Anderson, and Ernest Whitman. Reed portrayed the kindly Mr. Deshee. Whitman appeared as a cantankerous loud-mouthing pharoah. He was a coon in ancient Egypt. Both Reed and Whitman were skilled performers and worked in a number of Hollywood films afterward. Whitman's later pictures included *White Hunter* (1936), *Daughter of Shanghai* (1937), *Congo Maisie* (1940), *Maryland* (1940), *Return of Frank James* (1940), *Drums of the Congo* (1942), *Cabin in the Sky*, and *Stormy Weather*. Whitman and Reed, however, were more fortunate than many of the other actors in *The Green Pastures*. After the movie was completed, a number of the performers returned to jobs as porters, cooks, and maids. Their holiday in Hollywood had come to an abrupt end.

Rex Ingram: First of the Freed Black Men

Of all the actors in *The Green Pastures*, Rex Ingram won the greatest recognition. As De Lawd, Ingram soared above all the sequences, all the characters, all the pageantry. He was a physically impressive actor. Tall, solid, yet athletically trim, with piercing eyes, skin that gleamed, and silver hair that gave him an ageless quality, he was the quintessence of Hollywood handsome. He was also an intelligent performer, the first black man to earn a Phi Beta Kappa key at Northwestern University and a graduate of that university's medical school in 1919. His early work included bit parts in silent movies and appearances on the stage in *Stevedore*, *Porgy*, and *Once in a Lifetime*. Among his first talking films were bits in *Trader Horn* (1931), *Sign of the Cross* (1932), *King Kong* (1933), and *The Emperor Jones*. *The Green Pastures* was a big opportunity, and with his stentorian voice that could in one moment be raised triumphantly in anger and in the next lowered in sympathy or remorse, Ingram made the most of that opportunity and proved a most befitting Lawd. His heavenly host was, as the script dictated, a backwoods preacher, but one ironically detached enough from himself so that he could play the role with moderation. He also portrayed Adam and Hedzrel.

Other important roles followed for Rex Ingram in *The Adventures of Huckleberry Finn* (1939), *The Thief of Bagdad* (1940), *Talk of the Town* (1942), *Cabin in the Sky* (1943), *Sahara* (1943), *Fired Wife* (1943), *A Thousand and One Nights* (1948), and *Moonrise* (1948). In all his movies, Ingram escaped the rigid typing most black actors had to endure. True, he was cast as a servant, but in none of his films was he required to tom or coon. In *The Green Pastures* he was an Uncle Remus of sorts, full of comic homespun wisdom. But generally, like Paul Robeson, Rex Ingram played men who seemed essentially free, slightly heroic, and removed from typical American life. In *The Adventures of Huckleberry Finn*, Ingram's character withdrew from conventional society by taking to the raft with the adolescent Huck. Rex Ingram's Nigger Jim was never servile like that of Clarence Muse in the earlier version or Archie Moore in the 1960 one. Instead, his Jim was a heroic guide leading Huck to manhood. And with his large chest and thick biceps Ingram seemed so powerful that audiences knew there were no chains strong enough to hold him down. *The Thief of Bagdad* and its remake, *A Thousand and One Nights*, cast him in the fantasy world of the Arabian Nights. As a towering genie finally released by Sabu from a bottle in which he had been trapped for centuries, Ingram screamed, "Free! I'm free at last!" And his call of freedom rang out far beyond the motion-picture screen.

Rex Ingram was frequently compared to Paul Robeson. Both men presented immensely dignified and self-contained black male characters. Yet there were differences. Although Ingram was not as good an actor as Robeson, nor as heroic a presence, he was able to express the one thing Robeson lacked: a gentleness, an overriding interest and sympathy in all of mankind. No matter how much producers tried to make Robeson a symbol of black humanity, he always came across as a man more interested in himself than anyone else. (It was precisely for this reason that he fared so well as the crafty, determined-to-survive-and-triumph egomaniac Emperor Jones.) Ingram's gentleness, coupled with his physical strength, made him more than appropriate as De Lawd and much later in his career as the Sudanese soldier who sacrificed his life for the troops in *Sahara*. These same qualities added depth to his performance in *Moonrise*, too, when he portrayed a kindly old Negro outcast who befriended a rebellious white boy. And, of course, the strength, the dignity, the gentleness, and the good spirits of his characters were what made them stand at the heart of the humanized tradition.

After 1948, Rex Ingram's career rapidly ran downhill. When he pleaded guilty to having transported a fifteen-year-old white Kansas girl to New York for immoral purposes, an abrupt end came to the grand performances. He still worked in movies—although not as consistently—but the spark was gone from his work. Eventually it appeared as if he had stopped acting altogether and that he was merely relying on the force of his voice and his physical presence to get him through his roles, so much so that by the time he did *Anna Lucasta* in 1958, he seemed nothing more than the perfect wreck the script called for. Before his death in 1968, Ingram appeared in *God's Little Acre* (1958), *Elmer Gantry* (1960), *Your Cheating Heart* (1964), and (in the bit role of the professor) *Hurry Sundown* (1967).

Stepin's Step-Chillun

In contrast to Rex Ingram's vigorous and humanized free black male characters were the highjinks of a lively set of coon figures who picked up Fetchit's mantle and by borrowing, stealing, or elaborating on his techniques were able to find employment at a time when he was on his way out. Although they had none of the master's ambivalent nihilism, they attained great popularity. The most prominent of Stepin's step-chillun were Willie Best, Mantan Moreland, and Louis Armstrong.

The first of the imitators and certainly the closest in style, technique, and physical appearance to the master was Willie Best. Best was born in Mississippi and came to Hollywood in the late 1920s. In films such as *Up Pops the Devil* (1931), *The Monster Walks* (1931), *Kentucky Kernals* (1934), *West of the Pecos* (1934), and *Murder on a Honeymoon* (1935), he was known as Sleep 'n' Eat, a name that, like Fetchit's, conjured up a darky image: the coon is content as long as he has enough to eat and a place to sleep. Also like Fetchit, Best was tall and thin, and he specialized in dense, dim-witted characters who walked about half awake, half asleep. He was usually treated shamelessly or acted shamelessly of his own accord. "Why is a shoe called a shoe?" he asks in *The Littlest Rebel*. "I spent all yesterday wondering why a horse is called a horse." In a typical Best film such as *The Ghost Breakers* (1940), he was the butt of crude racial jokes. During an electrical black-out in this film, Best trembles in fear of ghosts, but is soon reprimanded by his employer, Bob Hope, who tells the film's heroine, Paulette Goddard, "He always sees the darkest side of everything. He was born during an eclipse." Later Hope says to Best, "You look like a black-out in a black-out. If this keeps up, I'm going to have to paint you white."

Best's characters seemed even more self-demeaning than Fetchit's, for he lacked the latter's great style. Yet he endowed his characters with more warmth and humanity. They were not aesthetically perfect automatons, and although they were without complexities or ambiguities, they seemed more intensely alive. Best had the familiar dialect, but audiences could understand him. Moreover, he made his characters fit in to the whole conception of the film rather than rendering them as isolated happenings. Finally, Best was easier for the studios to manipulate. Consequently, when Fetchit's various scrapes with the law alienated him from audiences and when he had begun repeating himself in a deadly mechanized manner, Best inherited his coon crown and was steadily employed. In the 1930s alone, he worked in some twenty-five motion pictures, including *Two in Revolt* (1936)—in which he was billed as Willie Best for the first *time—Murder on a Bridle Path* (1936), *General Spanky* (1936), *Breezing Home* (1937), *Racing Lady* (1937), *Super Sleuth* (1937), *Merrily We Live* (1938), *Vivacious Lady* (1938), and *Nancy Drew, Trouble Shooter* (1939). In the 1940s he appeared in thirty-five movies, including *The Smiling Ghost* (1941), *Whispering Ghosts* (1942), *A-Haunting We*

Will Go (1942), *Cabin in the Sky* (1943) and *Thank Your Lucky Stars* (1943). In the 1950s, he appeared on the television series "My Little Margie" and "The Stu Erwin Show." He died in 1962.

Mantan Moreland was the second of the prominent Fetchit step-chillun. A round-faced, wide-eyed, cherubic coon, he did not come into his own until the late 1930s. But he endured throughout the beginning years of the 1940s, and as late as the early 1970s he was still making cameo appearances in films. In the 1930s Moreland was one of the few pure coons to attain popularity at a time when the humanized toms had taken over.

Mantan Moreland was born in Monroe, Louisiana, in 1902. By the time he was twelve he had run away from home and begun an informal career as a dancer. Later he met and toured in a comedy act with Tim Moore, a former prize fighter who later won fame as Kingfish on the television series "Amos 'n' Andy." After playing the black café-nightclub circuit for a number of years, Mantan Moreland finally caught the moviegoing public's fancy in 1938 with appearances in *Next Time I Marry, Frontier Scout*, and *Irish Luck*. Always cast as the faithful right-hand man, he added a perverse twist to the tradition. Generally, Mantan was always there *until* his white friend needed him. Then he took off for the hills. He was a fantastic cowardly lion with an uncanny command of stagecraft. In those films in which he was terr'fied of de ghosts, Moreland displayed an arsenal of gestures and grimaces that actors had traditionally used to steal scenes and develop characters. He was notorious for his perfectly timed double-takes. No other actor could widen his eyes like Moreland. Nor could any other manage his trick of appearing to run without actually moving at all. He always looked as if he were about to trip over his own feet as he tried to make a hasty departure. When he appeared in the Charlie Chan mysteries as the dubiously reliable chauffeur, Birmingham Brown, Moreland captivated audiences with his rapid, high-pitched, squeaky-voiced banter. Previously, Fetchit had appeared as Chan's servant in *Charlie Chan in Egypt* (1935) and even Willie Best had a stint in the Chan thriller *The Red Dragon* (1942). But neither lit up the screen with their terror as did Moreland. To such Chan features as *The Chinese Cat* (1944), *The Scarlet Clue* (1945), *The Jade Mask* (1945), *Shadow over Chinatown* (1946), *The Chinese Ring* (1947), and a host of others, Moreland brought demented energy to his chauffeur.

In the 1940s, Moreland was admittedly already an anachronism. Still, he was kept busy with the Chan series and such features as *Cabin in the Sky, Sarong Girl* (1943), *Revenge of the Zombies* (1943), *Melody Parade* (1943), *South of Dixie* (1944). Doubtless a reason for his durability was his great charm and his small stature. Because he was invariably shorter than the leading men of his films, audiences could accept his cowardice, his befuddled fumblings and mishaps. Sometimes his size elevated him from mere coon to a symbol of the universal little man. An independently produced all-black film, *One Dark Night* (1939), made excellent use

RIGHT: Ready for action but not for work, Willie Best gets a dressing down by Arthur Treacher in *Thank You, Jeeves* (1936).

BELOW: Mantan Moreland: the man with the fastest eyes in the West!

of Moreland as a perpetually jobless black father. When one of his far-out schemes finally works out, the comic-pathetic little man assumes his role as the big man of the house and heroically saves his daughter from the clutches of a villain. Here Mantan Moreland broke away from his formula roles to create a sensitive character. The actor considered this role his best. Much later in his career, Moreland ventured out into new types of drama. In 1957 he appeared off-Broadway in an all-black version of *Waiting for Godot*. As the tragic-comic Estragon, he received favorable reviews. Finally, when he returned to films in minor roles in *The Comic* (1969) and *Watermelon Man* (1970), Moreland finally escaped the humiliating antics that made him such a popular servant in the 1930s and 1940s, and at long last his characters were funny because of their human idiosyncrasies rather than their stereotyped racial shortcomings. Mantan Moreland died in 1973.

Louis Armstrong was the third of the important Fetchit imitators. His career on screen spanned four decades and two syndromes. Not only was he a reliable-servant figure in the 1930s, but in the 1940s and 1950s he was also the perfect entertainer. Armstrong first worked in films with his band in *Ex-Flame* (1931). He made his acting debut in Bing Crosby's *Pennies from Heaven* (1936), portraying the leader of a band appearing at Crosby's Haunted House Café. He sang a number that derived from the old racial stereotype of Negro fear and superstition titled "Skeleton in the Closet." Armstrong mugged and grinned his way through the song in the antics for which he later became famous. He was the perfect foil for Crosby. In *Artists and Models* (1937) Armstrong performed in a musical segment with Martha Raye (who was in blackface). In 1938 he appeared with Bing Crosby in *Doctor Rhythm* but his scenes were omitted from the released version. In *Going Places* (1939) his high-flung mugging madness just about stole the show. *The New York Times'* critic wrote of "a trumpet-tooting groom known to the jitterbugs as Louis (Satchel-Mouth) Armstrong. Satchel-Mo caught the Strand's [theater] audience going and coming. . . . Satchel-Mo' blows a mean horn; better still he's a solid man for comedy."

When Armstrong made later appearances in such films as *Cabin in the Sky, Jam Session* (1944), *Atlantic City* (1945), *Pillow to Post* (1945), *Young Man with a Horn* (1950), *Glory Alley* (1952), *High Society* (1956), and *Paris Blues* (1961), his work was neatly covered with a new veneer. Armstrong learned early that a layer of gregarious charm could make even cooning appeal to everyone, and, everyone loved seeing him sail away with his high-styled exhibitionism. When he attempted more serious roles after World War II, his charm proved vaporous. In the end, the thing that distinguished his film work was his music. When Satchmo played his horn—as when Bojangles danced—no one cared what he represented in the movie. He was a musician par excellence. His last film appearance was in *Hello, Dolly* (1969).

Louis Armstrong gives Bing Crosby a lesson in "natchel rhythm" in one of their early movies together.

All in all, the step-chillun were throwbacks to the earlier part of the 1930s. They represented a delayed crystallization of the prehumanized servant just as the congenial, uncomplicated creatures of *The Green Pastures* represented the ultimate distillation of the humanized servant tradition. The next and final stage in the evolution of the Negro servant in films was the posthumanized period. In the earlier period the acceptable, humanized black domestic was often forced to have a superhuman humaneness, a superhuman tolerance merely to point up his fitness for racial justice and to win audience sympathy. Thus Bill Robinson stood by stoically while the master bawled him out. Thus Louise Beavers sacrificed her own life and chances for fulfillment in order to serve better her white mistress. Here the Good Negro Servant's goodness was used to assert his equality. He *proved* his worth. But in the posthumanized servant tradition, no character ever gave a second thought to proving anything to anybody. This new set of eccentrics, led by Eddie "Rochester" Anderson, Hattie McDaniel, and Butterfly McQueen, lived in their own screwball worlds, did exactly as they pleased, and took little time to weigh the pros and cons of racial protocol. Seldom were they called upon to perform demeaning antics, and on those rare occasions when they were, they triumphed over the antics. Ultimately, this group brought an end to the servant syndrome as we think of it today.

Rochester: The Gentleman's Gentleman

There are two stories about how Eddie "Rochester" Anderson began his career. The first is that he sold newspapers as a child in Oakland, California, and while competing with other leather-lunged newspaper carriers, each outshouting the news of the other, the boy strained his vocal cords, eventually "ruining" his voice but in turn acquiring the inimitable gravelly quality.

The second story says that in 1937 comedian Jack Benny, on a trip West with his radio troupe, spotted a lively colored porter in a railroad car. The porter, Benny thought, was a natural-born philosopher-comedian, and soon afterward his radio-show writers decided to put such a character on the show. A search for candidates was begun. When a stocky, balloon-faced comic with a cement mixer of a voice appeared, they decided he was perfect for the role and thereafter christened him Rochester.

Both stories could be the fabrications of a press agent. But it is certain that Eddie Anderson's most distinct attribute was his gravelly voice and that he had his greatest success once he teamed with Jack Benny. In the late 1930s and into the 1940s, Anderson's alacrity and coherent tomfoolery as the agreeable valet Rochester made him the most popular black comedian in the movies.

The gentleman's gentleman: Eddie "Rochester" Anderson.

Eddie Anderson started working in films in the early 1930s, but it was a long time before he clicked. He had comic and chaotic moments in *What Price Hollywood?* and *Rainbow on the River* but nothing earthshaking. As Noah in *The Green Pastures*, he had a rare opportunity to play a character both comic and pathetic, a role he handled well. In 1937 he appeared in *Three Men on a Horse, Melody for Two, Bill Cracks Down, On Such a Night, White Bondage,* and *One Mile from Heaven.* In some of the pre-Benny features he was surprisingly subdued. In William Wyler's Old South epic *Jezebel* (1938) he played Bette Davis's loyal servant, stoically leading her through a disease-infested swamp so that she could be reunited with Henry Fonda. Although he performed well, the role consisted of little more than "yessims." In W. C. Fields's *You Can't Cheat an Honest Man* (1939), Anderson was more at home as a clever but minor circus roustabout named Cheerful. The role now proves arch Anderson. When he warns Fields that detectives are about to close in after one of bumble-nose's master plots has backfired, Anderson is ignored. Consequently, when the police do close in and arrest Fields, Anderson, shaking his head as the bossman is taken off, has the last laugh. The privilege of enjoying a joke at the boss's expense soon became an Anderson trademark. *Man About Town* (1939) established this trait beyond a doubt.

Man About Town was vintage late-1930s Paramount fluff. Directed by Mark Sandrich, it starred Jack Benny, Dorothy Lamour, and Phil Harris and featured Anderson as Rochester, the character he had by then already popularized on the radio. The plot was straightforward but contained enough mishaps to keep audiences confused and happy. Benny woos two wealthy socialites, unaware that their hot-tempered husbands are out to do away with him. Throughout the film, Rochester warns him of the consequences of "foolin' round." Benny pays no heed. But at the film's conclusion, it is Rochester who untangles all the entanglements and saves the boss's neck. In this film, he brought new dimensions to the servant figure. Fetchit had taken him indoors. Robinson had domesticated him. Now Rochester gave him full run of the house. When he first appears, he is found in typical coon position. He sleeps comfortably in the boss's chair, unaware that Benny has entered the apartment. Soon he is on his feet, the clever, manipulative servant who under the guise of working for the boss accomplishes much for himself. Later one merely has to see him with his feet propped casually on top of the table as he uses the boss's telephone, smokes the boss's cigars, and takes over the boss's apartment to realize that here was a servant who considered himself more a weekend guest than a subservient domestic.

In his second Benny feature, *Buck Benny Rides Again* (1940), Rochester again played a free uninhibited spirit. In his first scene, he has an important date with his girl friend and uses every excuse to get out of Benny's apartment. Finally, he says that the stork has presented his aunt with twins this very afternoon, and he must visit her. "If I remember correctly," says Benny, "the stork visited your aunt two months ago." "He sure gets around," replies Rochester. Finally the servant outwits the boss. Benny is going to a party and plans to wear his full-dress suit. Rochester tells him the suit is inappropriate and advises him to wear something else. Benny complies, wears another set of clothing, and then takes off. In the next cut, whom do audiences see driving up to his girl friend's apartment in the boss's car wearing the boss's top hat and the boss's dress suit but crafty old Rochester!

Some critics thought that in the first two films and the later Benny–Rochester features, *Love Thy Neighbor* (1940) and *The Meanest Man in the World* (1943), there was a father–son relationship between the two. Obviously, this was but one way of simplifying their camaraderie to fit into the great-white-father-poor-black-slave-son category. But for such a relationship to exist, one man must control or overshadow the other. That was never the case with the Benny–Rochester films. Rather one sensed that Rochester was far too independent to be completely subservient to anyone. In fact, judging by the number of times Benny was extricated from tight situations by the wit and resourcefulness of his valet, the master–servant relationship was close to being reversed. As an indication of his equal footing with his employer, Rochester addressed Benny as "Boss" or "Boss, Sir" rather than the traditional lone "Sir." Today such a privilege may seem grossly patronizing, but in the 1930s it was a step forward.

Ultimately, Rochester fused the tom and coon types into a gregarious eccentric presence. In a feature such as *Topper Returns* (1941), in which he portrays a chauffeur-turned-detective, he is the typical coon-in-the-haunted-house, terrified when he sees cigarettes floating in the air and scared out of his wits when he falls through a trick chair into a lake. Although he performed such antics, Rochester also rose above the old tradition because at heart his humor—along with the warmth and affection he engendered in his audience—was based more on his wisecracks and his shrewdness than on his color. When in film after film he warned Benny of dire consequences, audiences laughed not because of any racial jokes but because Rochester was a very bright little fellow who was bound to be proved right in the end.

Rochester's name was wedded to Benny's throughout his career. Indeed, it has always been said that Jack Benny owned the rights to the name "Rochester" and that he could have replaced Anderson and given the name to another actor any time he wanted. But Anderson-Rochester was such a distinct personality and such an instant radio success that this fate never befell him. In fact, many of the Benny–Rochester movies seemed more the valet's than the master's. "If Hollywood's other comedians are on their toes," wrote *The New York Times* in 1939, "the West Coast's domestic employment agencies may expect to be swamped any day now with requests for valets, preferably saddle-colored and answering to the name Rochester. For in Paramount's *Man About Town*, a sly little gentleman's gentleman—or comedian's comedian—called Rochester has restored Jack Benny to the comic map and cleared a sizable place there for himself." When Rochester and Benny appeared in *Love Thy Neighbor* the same newspaper commented: "Rochester is still putting Mr. Benny very much behind the eight ball and stealing as much of the show as he can get his hands upon. But enough, unfortunately, is not stolen. . . ."

In some of his movies, Rochester was granted a privilege usually denied black actors, namely some cinematic love life. Black actors in movies were generally denied black women, which was one way of making them sexless—therefore harmless—creatures. But Rochester's love life rounded out his creations. Theresa Harris, a beautiful brown-skinned actress who was to lose a chance at leading roles because of her darkness, first appeared with Rochester in *Jezebel*. The two had no romantic scenes together. Harris portrayed Bette Davis's scatterbrained maid, one of Hollywood's most excruciatingly demeaned characters. But later things went better for her when she appeared as Rochester's girl friend Josephine in the Benny features *Love Thy Neighbor* and *Buck Benny Rides Again* and also in *What's Buzzin' Cousin?* (1943). Harris also played unbilled roles in a lineup of films such as *Thunderbolt* (1929), *The Lady Escapes* (1937), *Big Town Girl* (1937), *The Women* (1939), *Cat People* (1942), *The Phantom Lady* (1944), and others. But on some occasions she found herself playing plum roles that broke some conventions of the time. In the pre-Code film *Baby Face*, she played Chico, the close friend of Barbara Stanwyck. Here the women were friends as was the case with Hattie McDaniel and Louise Beavers whose characters were also on friendly terms with their employers. But in some scenes, Harris was stylishly dressed and glamorized—and she had an undeniable sexuality. The same was true in *Professional Sweetheart* (1933) in which she was cast as the maid of Ginger Rogers. At a key point in the film, her maid character gets out of her uniform and into a slinky, glamorous gown. Seen surrounded by elegantly dressed, admiring white males, her character is a chic feminine ideal. Her talents as a singer are also revealed, and in the storyline, the character emerges as a radio star. In *Hold Your Man* (1933) with Jean Harlow and Clark Gable, she had a striking yet uncredited role. Also appearing in the 1937 race movie *Bargain with Bullets*, she was candid with the Negro press about the lack of opportunities for her in most Hollywood films. Nonetheless, her hip, smart, rather daring characters were modern and forward-looking. Houston-born Harris later worked in television and died in 1985.

The most obvious testament to Rochester's uniqueness as a personality and his ability to carry a picture alone came in the 1940s with *Cabin in the Sky*. The critics unanimously commended him for his performance. Under the sensitive direction of Vincente Minnelli, Anderson hit at an area his predecessors never approached: he touched his audience. As the forever scheming-dreaming Little Joe Jackson, he was at first engaging as he shot craps or wooed the sultry Lena Horne. But when his plots failed and particularly when his good wife, Petunia, was about to leave him for good, audiences did not feel embarrassed by wanting to comfort him. They were drawn to Rochester's charming, funny, and sad diminutive hero. Had he been given an opportunity to explore his wondrous admixture of the comic and the pathetic in other roles, there is no telling how great his contributions to American screen comedy might have been.

In the 1940s Anderson remained a great favorite, appearing in a long line of important productions such as *Kiss the Boys Good-Bye* (1941), *Birth of the Blues* (1941), *Tales of Manhattan, Star-Spangled Rhythm* (1942), *Broadway Rhythm* (1944), *Brewster's Millions* (1945), *The Sailor Takes a Wife* (1945), and *The Show-Off* (1946). In *I Love a Bandleader* (1945), he was touted as the highest paid black actor in Hollywood. His last film was *It's a Mad, Mad, Mad, Mad World* (1963). In the 1950s and 1960s, he appeared on television's "The Jack Benny Show." Anderson died in 1977.

Hi-Hat Hattie

Rochester's female counterpart was Hattie McDaniel, a massive, high-strung mammy figure. Often criticized because of her stereotype characters, she answered her critics just as tartly as she might have answered an employer in one of her movies, "Why should I complain about making seven thousand dollars a week playing a maid? If I didn't, I'd be making seven dollars a week actually being one!" McDaniel's statement gives a true picture of the options available to black performers of the 1930s. She played the fussy, boisterous, big-bosomed maid time and time again, using the stereotyped figure to display her remarkable talent and affinity for pure broad comedy. With her fiercely and distinctively American aggressiveness and her stupendous sonic boom of a voice, Hattie created rich, dazzling characterizations. Audiences of the 1930s responded to her excessive showmanship, her effrontery, and her audacity. She emerged as the one servant of the era to speak her mind fully, and the world of her eccentric characters was a helter-skelter, topsy-turvy one in which the servant became the social equal, the mammy became the literal mother figure, the put-on was carried to the forefront of the action, and the style of the servant overpowered the content of the script.

Hattie McDaniel came to Hollywood in the late 1920s. Born in Wichita, Kansas, in 1898, the thirteenth child of a Baptist minister, Hattie mastered her gospels and religious, self-righteous sauciness at an early age. Afterward she struggled upward from roles in road companies—billed as everything from the "colored Sophie Tucker" to the "female Bert Williams"—to appearances on radio and then finally parts in the movies. Once ensconced in the film capital, she was typed as a mammy. A powerfully built woman, she weighed close to three hundred pounds, was very dark, and had typically Negro features. With her enormous mouth, wonderfully expressive eyes, "pearly white teeth," and mammoth rounded face, Hattie McDaniel was one of the screen's greatest presences, a pre-Fellini-esque figure of the absurd and a marvel of energetic verve and enthusiasm.

One detects in Josef von Sternberg's *Blonde Venus* (1932) an attempt at first to pass her off as a humorless, less jolly version of Louise Beavers. The film stars Marlene Dietrich as a Depression heroine driven to shame by her poverty. Fleeing her husband who fights for custody of their young son and carrying the boy with her, Dietrich hides out in a small Southern town where she is befriended by a congenial local mammy. Not only does mammy McDaniel supply provisions and moral support, but she also serves as a lookout, quick to warn Dietrich before the detectives close in. The down-and-out heroine has come to rely on the servant as her last friend, and once again the prehumanized black domestic is the true and trusted companion out to aid the white world, not harm it. Hattie McDaniel seemed slightly miscast in even this minor role. For one thing, her distinctive booming voice did not seem right for a character the script says is submissive. Even nicely toned down by von Sternberg, Hattie's voice sounded as if it were meant to give commands, not take them.

Judge Priest (1934) cast McDaniel as a cheerful aunt jemima with Will Rogers and Stepin Fetchit. In her scenes with Fetchit, audiences could see evolving the great McDaniel rebellious spirit. Fetchit portrayed the arch no-account, Hattie the industrious domestic, fiercely interested in her work and unable to abide any niggerish foolery. "Cut that monkeyshine," she cries out when Fetchit dares to lounge and play his harmonica in the kitchen of the house. "Come on in here when I holler at you," she belts out to him at another point. Here she was the quick-tempered, outspoken black woman, not about to take any nonsense. Some of that same spirit was evident in her 1934 films, *Operator 13*, *Lost in the Stratosphere*, *Little Men*; and in her 1935 *Music Is Magic*, *Another Face*, and *The Little Colonel*. Then came the first of the classic roles in George Stevens' *Alice Adams* (1935).

In the careers of most important actors, there is a moment—in some play or movie or scene—in which they realize their own uniqueness and in which an observant director encourages them to reveal, or even revel in, that quality. The actor finally gives a super-deluxe, grand-slam, all-or-nothing performance. Great careers are made on such moments, and director George Stevens gave McDaniel hers. *Alice Adams* is about a small-town social climber, played by Katharine Hepburn, a poor girl actually brighter and more sophisticated than those higher up on the social ladder. She wants desperately to fit in. When she meets a handsome rich boy (Fred MacMurray), she leads him into believing that she too comes from a wealthy background. Her mother invites him to dinner. To impress their guest and ensure the evening's success, the Adamses hire a Negro cook to prepare and serve the meal. Well aware of the low status of the Adams family, she feels she is lowering herself by serving the dinner.

Hattie McDaniel plays her in a formidable and unorthodox fashion. From her entrance, she says things—amid some rambunctious gum chewing—that no other maid in the movies would ever have dared. When the mistress of the house tells her to serve the dinner soup, McDaniel counters, "But don't you think it's getting pretty hot for soup?" The weather does prove too hot for soup, and later when she is asked airily by Alice to "Please take this dreadful soup away," McDaniel merely stops dead in her tracks and stares at the girl imperially, indeed contemptuously, as if to say, "I done tol' you so!" Used by director Stevens not only for comic relief but to point up the pretenses of the Adamses, McDaniel's maid repeatedly makes fun of the family's foolish attempts to put on airs. She makes her dining-room entrances and exits lethargically, as if she could not care less. Why should she hurry for these no-'count white folks? She carries her tray in the most off-hand fashion. When Alice speaks French to impress her guest, McDaniel is there to undercut the girl's airs with a monosyllabic grunt.

After *Alice Adams*'s opening, one newspaper critic wrote: "The recital would be incomplete if it neglected to applaud Hattie McDaniel for her hilarious bit as hired maid during the classic dinner scene." Thus was fixed, in this film, the nature of Hattie McDaniel's relations with her white masters. Through her uproarious conduct, she puts them in *their* place without overtly offending them. Nor does she, as some might wish, pick up a gun to blow out their brains. Instead she struts about looking down on them, all the while pretending to be the model servant. But even the 1930s audiences knew Hattie McDaniel was putting them on.

In 1936, Hattie McDaniel appeared in eleven films: *Gentle Julia, The First Baby, Show Boat, Hearts Divided, High Tension, Star for the Night, Postal Inspector, The Bride Walks Out, Valiant Is the Word for Carrie, Reunion,* and *Can This Be Dixie?* Of these, *Show Boat* remains one of her better pictures. When she is first seen, it is evident that the toughness and assurance she carried with her in *Alice Adams* is still firmly intact. "Outta my way," an arrogant white dock worker tells her. "Who wants to get in your way!" she answers back. Later when he tries prying information from her on the doings of the showboat's leading lady, Julie, McDaniel answers with a sly, mischievous smile, "Ask me no questions, and I'll tell you no lies." Here Hattie McDaniel was talking back to Whitey, and there was nothing subtle about it.

In 1937 McDaniel appeared in seven films. Her most interesting role was as the maid in *Saratoga*, which starred Clark Gable and Jean Harlow. There was such a fine rapport between Gable and McDaniel that audiences lost sight of their master–servant roles. Never was McDaniel seen kowtowing. On those rare occasions when she attempted a "yes sir" or "no sir" with appropriate submissiveness, she came across as hopelessly fraudulent. *Saratoga* incorporated special scenes, too, to play on McDaniel's rich humor and infectious charm. In one scene, she joined in with other members of the starving proletariat to sing a let's-be-jolly-despite-the-Depression melody. Here she asserted herself as a social equal. Most important, in this film Hattie McDaniel's mammy emerged as a mother figure to Jean Harlow. McDaniel and Harlow had previously worked together in *China Seas* (1935). In that film Harlow's highflung legendary temperament had found its match. McDaniel had not screamed back at Harlow; she just did what she pleased in the film, disregarding her mistress. She knew better than any other actor in the movies—except for Gable, perhaps—just how to handle the irascible blonde beauty. In *Saratoga* she portrayed Harlow's fastidious maid. McDaniel was quick to note her mistress's quirks and kinks. She was adviser, protectress, and a source of nourishment. "You got a pencil smudge on your chin, honey," she tells Harlow just before Gable enters to pay a call. "Don't you want to fix up?" Harlow, as a true rebellious daughter, pretends to ignore her mammy maid's advice. But later she does clean off the smudge. When Harlow needs motherly comfort, particularly after a battle with Gable, Hattie is there to dry her tears. "Oh, Miss Carol. Why, honey, baby," she croons, taking her to her shoulder. But, like a dutiful mother, McDaniel refuses to take any nonsense. When a letter arrives from Gable for Harlow, she asks Harlow if she wants it read. Harlow screams no, but Hattie realizes the letter's import and reads it aloud anyway, oblivious to the blonde's outbursts.

One year and seven movies later when she appeared with Barbara Stanwyck in *The Mad Miss Manton* (1938), the mother-surrogate, social-equal aspects of McDaniel's personality were already familiar to audiences and roles were being tailor-made for her. Stanwyck portrayed a flighty society girl forever involved in pranks with a group of young socialite friends. McDaniel, as her maid, Hilda, has to pick up behind the society girls, but from the moment of her entrance, the audience knows that Hilda is not about to take anything from anybody. A solid mass of cantankerous confidence and vitality, she hurls verbal barbs with the speed and accuracy of an ace pitcher. At one point, she nonchalantly informs one of Stanwyck's young society friends that there is a telephone call for her. "Sounds like my date," says the giggling girl as she runs to answer the phone. "Sounds more like a pipsqueak to me!" counters McDaniel offhandedly.

Later, as Stanwyck begs Hattie not to be so rough on one of her society friends because "She's our guest, Hilda," McDaniel haughtily replies, "Umh! I didn't ask her up!" Obviously, if Stanwyck says "our guest," the apartment is as much the maid's as the mistress's. Just talking back was a triumph of sorts, and Hattie McDaniel was doing what every black maid in America must have wanted to do at one time or another. Throughout *The Mad Miss Manton*, as she orders Stanwyck and her friends about, criticizing their beaux, dissecting their schoolgirl chatter, and reprimanding them for their bad manners, Hattie McDaniel stands as an iconoclastic arbiter of taste. She also expresses a strong maternal concern for Stanwyck. Hattie demands approval of Stanwyck's boy friends, and she does not hesitate to listen in on phone conversations. Finally, as the true protective mother figure, she saves the heroine's life, mainly through her maternal interference.

McDaniel's flamboyant bossiness often can be read as a cover-up for deep hostility. Indeed, she seemed to time her lines to give her black audience that impression. In *The Mad Miss Manton*, as in all her best movies, Hattie McDaniel refused to accept typical domesticity, to yield to the meek brand of Christianity that characterized Louise Beavers. Only one year and one film separates the Hilda of *The Mad Miss Manton* from the Mammy of *Gone with the Wind*. In that film, McDaniel fused the elements of all her earlier screen performances to give what certainly was her finest characterization.

Gone with the Wind: Romanticizing Black Realities and the End of a Tradition

David O. Selznick's *Gone with the Wind* was the third and final feature of the 1930s spotlighting blacks. Based on Margaret Mitchell's novel, the story took more than two years to film and cost almost four million dollars. At heart, the film was nothing more than an elaborate romance, centering on the rebellious spirits of Scarlett O'Hara and her iconoclastic lover, Rhett Butler. The two were removed from politics and sociology, but in their own ways both saw through the sham and shame of their Old South world. Strangely enough, amid all the romantic unreality of this spectacular film, the black–white relationships were probably closer to the real ones of ante-bellum America than any ever before presented in the movies.

The problem with Civil War spectacles has never been that they presented Negroes as slaves—for how else could they be depicted?—but that the films have humiliated and debased them far beyond the callings of the script. *Gone with the Wind* was often criticized because the slaves were not shown taking up rifles against their former masters. *Gone with the Wind* omitted much that was significant about the lives of its slaves. Yet one can see the black actors struggling to transform their slaves into complex human beings.

Hattie McDaniel portrayed the O'Hara family's faithful Mammy. Boasting that she diapered three generations of O'Hara women, Mammy is proud of the mutual affection between master and servant. During the war years it is she who keeps Tara, the family plantation, going. Like earlier film slaves, Hattie McDaniel's character is motivated almost solely out of concern for the master family, but her Mammy also feels confident enough to express anger toward her masters. She berates and hounds anyone who goes against *her* conception of right and wrong, whether it be Mrs. O'Hara or Scarlett and Rhett. Not once does she bite her tongue.

But most significantly, Scarlett and Mammy maintain a complex mother–daughter relationship, much like those which actually existed in the old South, the kind of relationship that was either glossed over or treated condescendingly in other films. In *Gone with the Wind*, McDaniel's Mammy becomes an all-seeing, all-hearing, all-knowing commentator and observer. She remarks. She annotates.

ABOVE: Hattie McDaniel, the most outspoken servant figure in the 1930s, matches wits with Vivien Leigh in *Gone with the Wind* (1939). At the same time, Hattie lets her mistress know she's not about to take any nonsense.

BELOW: Life couldn't be better! So Hattie McDaniel and Ben Carter seem to think in *Maryland* (1940).

She makes asides. She always opinionizes. Shortly after the movie opens, Mammy is seen helping Scarlett into a corset, at the same time commanding her young mistress to eat before departing for a barbecue. It has already been revealed that Scarlett is upset because Ashley Wilkes, the man she loves, will marry someone else. Scarlett pines and moans, but only Mammy is aware of her feelings. When Scarlett refuses to eat the meal, Mammy does not hesitate to threaten her: "I ain't notice Mr. Ashley askin' for to marry you," she says, slyly smiling to let Scarlett know that she knows all about the infatuation. Her eyes widening in disbelief at being discovered, Scarlett, like the obedient, terrified daughter, eats! In her compliance, she becomes just as much a testament to Mammy's power as the giggling maids were to Mae West's.

It is Mammy who knows—and keeps secret—Scarlett's every plot. It is she who criticizes or advises, counsels or warns, protects or defends, but always understands. When Scarlett, just widowed, privately models a flashy new hat, it is Mammy who spies the action and promptly reprimands her. When Scarlett decides to return to Atlanta to request a loan from Rhett Butler, Mammy insists upon accompanying her. "No proper young lady is going there alone!" she snaps. She even makes a dress for Scarlett from the green drapes that once adorned Tara. As Scarlett walks the streets of Reconstruction Atlanta, Mammy literally clears the way, pushing aside the renegade blacks who line the sidewalks. Later, when Butler comes to pay a call after Scarlett is widowed a second time, Mammy, aware that Scarlett is not grieving at all (instead she's been hitting the bottle), informs Scarlett in the haughtiest manner, "I done tol' him you was prostrate with grief?" Delivered by McDaniel, it was the most perfectly timed, the funniest, indeed the most satiric line in the film.

Certainly *Gone with the Wind*'s script had much to do with presenting such an inspired Mammy. It has always been said that once Selznick had tested McDaniel for the role, he decided that only she could play Mammy and made script changes to meet with the special brand of McDaniel humor. Yet through the force of her own personality, McDaniel's character became free of the greatest burden that slavery—on screen and off—inflicted on blacks: a sense of innate inferiority. Her Mammy has a self-righteous grandeur that glows. Even audiences unaware of what a fine performer McDaniel was, sensed by her mammoth presence and her strong, hearty voice that here was an actress larger than her lines, bigger than her role. "Best of all," wrote *The New York Times*, "perhaps next to Miss Leigh, is Hattie McDaniel's Mammy." For her performance, Hattie McDaniel became the first Negro to win an Academy Award as Best Supporting Actress.

No two black actresses of the 1930s differed so widely as did Hattie McDaniel and Butterfly McQueen. Yet in an equally exciting and perhaps even subtler way, McQueen built up the comedy interludes of the character Prissy in *Gone with the Wind*, capping them with her own masterful bit of madness. McDaniel was tough and resilient and could take a small incident and magnify it into a mountain.

Butterfly, however, could take a big scene and condense it into the tiniest of lyrical poems. Her performance was marked by fragility, hysteria, and absurdity.

McQueen's Prissy is a servant girl for the O'Hara family. When the townspeople are deserting Atlanta in fear of Sherman's oncoming siege, Scarlett agrees to stay on to help Melanie through a difficult pregnancy *only* after Prissy has assured her that she can help with the delivery of the baby. "I'se knows all 'bout birthin' babies," Prissy declares, smiling with head lowered. But the day of the actual arrival, Prissy is nowhere in sight. When finally found by a panic-stricken Scarlett and told to take over, the girl stares into Scarlett's eyes, first in astonishment, then in absolute fright. "Lordy, Miss Scarlett," she cries in her high, tense, fluttery voice, "I don't know nothin' 'bout birthin' babies!" As Melanie moans and is near agony, Prissy nervously suggests to Scarlett, "My Ma says if you put a knife under the bed it cuts the pain in two." Throughout, McQueen delivered her lines with a sobriety that made them seem twice as funny.

Later, when Scarlett is about to flee Atlanta, Prissy gathers essentials. Packing chinaware amid thunderous cannon roars, she drops the dishes, screams in terror, and runs from corner to corner of the room. Finally, as the wagon, driven by Rhett Butler, departs from the city with Prissy, Melanie, and the newborn baby in the back, McQueen pops her head up every other frame or so, glimpses the flames of the city, and screams hysterically.

Some observers saw Butterfly as the stock darky figure. But there was much more to her performance. Had she been a mere pickaninny, she might have engendered hostility or embarrassed audiences. Instead she seemed to provide an outlet for the repressed fears of the audience. That perhaps explains why everyone laughed hysterically at her hysterics. For during the crisis sequences, the film built beautifully, and there was a need for release. Mere comic relief of the old type would have been vulgar. But because of her artistic mayhem, her controlled fright, and her heightened awareness and articulation of the emotions of the audiences, Butterfly McQueen seemed to flow wonderfully with the rest of the film. She had a pleasant waiflike quality, too, not in the patronizing style of *The Green Pastures*, in which the grown-up people behaved like rambunctious idiot children, but in a special, purely personal way. Tiny and delicate, Butterfly McQueen seemed to ask for protection and was a unique combination of the comic and the pathetic.

Usually little is said of the male servants in *Gone with the Wind*, particularly Oscar Polk, who played the emasculated Pork. His important scene occurs during the second half of the film when Scarlett presents him with a watch once owned by her father. Pork wants it desperately, but as a man who has had his brain, his soul, his individuality sapped from him during long years of servitude he cannot accept it at first. Here Oscar Polk expressed accurately that aspect of slavery that Hattie McDaniel soared above, the sense of inferiority. His was written on him in his stumped, bent-over posture and in his hesitant manner of speaking. He is a man

Butterfly McQueen as Prissy, the girl who knows all 'bout birthin' babies, with Clark Gable and Vivien Leigh in *Gone with the Wind*.

fighting to hold himself together. Polk's Pork was a valid comment on the slave system. But unfortunately in presenting something so real, the film made the character the focus of humor rather than pity.

Everett Brown appeared as the noble Big Sam, the former slave who rescues Scarlett from her attackers in Shantytown, and he did well in a minor role. *Gone with the Wind*'s most rigidly typed black character, and perhaps the one unredeemable black stereotype in the entire picture, was Uncle Peter, the clownish backwoods dolt who works for Aunt Pittypat. Surprisingly, the part was played by Eddie Anderson, and the only thing that saved him was that he was so buried under layers of make-up that audiences failed to realize their favorite was being used for the crudest comic relief.

Because they had carried the servant tradition to its highest point, the black characters of *Gone with the Wind* brought that tradition to a fitting close. In the 1940s, although the servants still appeared in films, the enthusiasm and creativity that distinguished figures such as Hattie McDaniel and Butterfly McQueen were gone. In the next decade, McDaniel appeared in some twenty-one features. Her presence still provided rich ribald humor, but her impact was not as great. In *Gone with the Wind*, her Mammy had brought to light a fact that white audiences had long ignored or suppressed: here was a black maid who not only was capable of running the Big House but proclaimed in her own contorted way her brand of black power. McDaniel scared her audience. Indeed, in the South there were complaints that she had been too familiar with her white employers. (There were similar Southern complaints against Rochester in the Benny movies.) In the 1940 film *Maryland* Hattie McDaniel was made too jolly and sweet. In films such as *Janie* (1944), *Since You Went Away* (1944), and *Margie* (1946), she was made too doggedly faithful. And perhaps worst of all, in *Song of the South* (1946), as she was seen merrily baking pies and singing cheerful darky songs, Hattie McDaniel displayed a newfound Christian domesticity that was the exact antithesis of her haughty grandeur in the late 1930s. Before her death in the early 1950s, McDaniel left the movies to play the wild and witty maid Beulah on radio.

Butterfly McQueen's screen personality was not as drastically altered as McDaniel's, but she, too, was stripped of some of her individuality in the next era. Her later films included *The Women* (1939), *Affectionately Yours* (1941), *I Dood It* (1943), *Cabin in the Sky*, *Since You Went Away* (her role was left on the cutting-room floor), *Mildred Pierce* (1945), and *Duel in the Sun* (1947). Her talents were often misused or misunderstood by directors and writers. In *Affectionately Yours*, she had to deliver what might be the most demeaning line ever uttered by a black in the movies. "Who dat say who dat when you say dat," she crooned. "I never thought I would have to say a line like that," the actress later said, obviously embarrassed. "I had imagined that since I was an intelligent woman, I could play any kind of role." Perhaps the final irony of that line and the best tribute to Butterfly

McQueen's comic talent was that her performance in *Affectionately Yours* was thoroughly disarming and considered by some critics the best in the movie. "[The] only glints of brightness ... are contributed by a hair-spring brownie called Butterfly McQueen, as a maid. Her frequent dissolves into tears upon the slightest provocation are ludicrous," wrote *The New York Times*.

McQueen's real problem, however, was that she had to be handled as a surreal creature rather than as the stock comic servant. Her comedic gifts were too special and delicate, too unique a blending of the comic and the pathetic, to be effective in ordinary dumb niggery roles. With her large expressive eyes, her bewildered and perplexed stare, and her quivering tremor of a voice, she seemed almost otherworldly. Surely, producer David O. Selznick and director King Vidor understood the peculiar nature of the McQueen personality. In their film *Duel in the Sun*, she was wisely cast as the mysterious Vashti, a mystifying character wandering in and out of the picture.

Butterfly McQueen's career took a disastrous turn in the late 1940s. There was little or no work. In the 1950s, when servants in the movies had all but vanished, she found herself in New York City struggling to survive as a sales clerk at Macy's, a waitress, a factory worker, a dishwasher, and as a companion to a Long Island white woman. In the early 1960s, when blacks were used in television commercials, many had hoped to see McQueen and other old servant figures pop up on the home screens. But network advertisers feared presenting a black as a maid in this new era of boycotts, protests, and militancy. (To cast McQueen as anything other than a maid also seemed out of the question.) Butterfly McQueen's story does have a somewhat happy ending. In the very late 1960s, she was rediscovered by a whole new generation when she appeared in the off-Broadway play *Curley McDimple*. *Gone with the Wind* was reissued. And she was a name again. She still was not overrun with offers, but at least she was out of the kitchen and back before the lights.

Before leaving the 1930s, a final word should be said about the one black actor who stood apart from the rest of the servant figures, who seemed to tower above the era itself. He still has a special place in the history of American entertainment and politics.

Paul Robeson: The Black Colossus

By the Depression era, Paul Robeson was already an authentic legendary figure in twentieth-century America. The son of a former slave, he had a rare intellect and athletic ability that enabled him to reach out for all the best white America could offer. Born in Princeton, New Jersey, in 1898, by the time of high school he was an academic *cause célèbre*. An honor student, he won a scholarship to Rutgers

University at a time when they were virtually unheard-of for black students. At Rutgers he distinguished himself as an athlete of astounding skill, a four-letter man and a terror on the football field. When he was named to the All-American football team in 1918, he was called "the greatest defensive end who had ever trod the gridiron." Robeson's academic record was equally impressive. He was elected to Phi Beta Kappa in his junior year, graduated with honors the next, then went on to Columbia University's law school. Always proud and quick-tempered, he attained new triumphs as an actor and concert singer. Eugene O'Neill's plays *The Emperor Jones* and *All God's Chillun Got Wings* took on new dimensions with Robeson as their star. The plays *Stevedore*, *Taboo*, and *Black Boy* are recalled today simply because he appeared in them. Later his *Othello* had the longest run of any Shakespeare play to appear on Broadway. Robeson seemed to have achieved all that a man can hope for, but ultimately his life mingled irony with heartache, idealism with disillusionment, a love for his people with an eventual rejection by them. He became a victim.

It is one of the less pleasant aspects of the American way that when a black artist is successful and silent, he remains a national favorite. But when a black artist becomes important enough to want better roles (usually those with more dignity and less racism inherent in them) or when the artist makes some comment against the social-political climate of the country, he becomes a doomed man. When Robeson became associated with the Communist Party in the mid-1930s, when he spoke out against American discrimination and segregation, when he began making trips to the Soviet Union, he was singled out and finally silenced. Eventually the concert halls were closed to him. Negroes on the streets whispered his name in fear or shame. Reportedly, the State Department refused to let him leave the country. At another time, they did not want to let him back in. And Paul Robeson became the first of the controversial black political prisoners, the first of our great black artists to have his art denied him because of his political beliefs.

Because Robeson was denied a platform on which to display his art, the legend about him was to grow. Was he really the greatest baritone of all time? Was he actually America's greatest actor? Was he really so incredibly handsome? Was he actually too much of an assertive black male in his plays and films for white America to permit him to continue? Was his smile the key to understanding his enigmatic personality? The questions about Robeson had really begun as early as the 1920s, and they continued with rapacious fervor throughout subsequent decades. If there ever have been any answers, they were found in his movies, and audiences of the 1930s, like those today, went to see his pictures to learn more about the myth and the man, the mask and the mystique.

Most of the important Paul Robeson features were made abroad. He was the only black star of the 1930s to work in foreign pictures, where he could escape typing—or so he thought. But like his Hollywood features the foreign films seldom met with his approval. Always Robeson went into a motion picture with the hope that it would elevate the state of his people. But after completing a role Robeson would discover that if anything his talents had been exploited and used to demean the black man's struggle for equality and full independence. His first foreign film, the silent *Borderline* (1928), starred him opposite his wife Eslanda and the poet Hilda Doolittle and had little to offend anyone. But his second, *Sanders of the River* (1935), an African drama that he agreed to star in for British producer Zoltan Korda out of a "passionate concern with African culture," was transformed into a glorification of British colonial rule. Scenes in which he did not appear had been rewritten without the actor's knowledge, and at a special preview an irate Robeson stormed out of the movie house in protest.

In most of his other European motion pictures—Song *of Freedom* (1938), *Dark Sands* (1938), *King Solomon's Mines* (1937), and *The Proud Valley* (1941)—Robeson was cast as an "undercover servant," exploited in much the same way Sidney Poitier was to be some twenty-five years later. He was always at the service of some white friend in the films—but the friend was little more than the old white massa figure. Robeson's films were the first to use this technique. In *Sanders of the River* he was Bosambo, the trusty right-hand man of Sanders, the white "man of iron" who rules the dark, backward tribes of Africa. Robeson provided not only physical strength for his master but some comic and romantic interludes for the mass audience. In *King Solomon's Mines*, Robeson was Umbopa, the Mashona chief who aids the white Sir Cedric Hardwicke in his search for the legendary mines. In *Proud Valley*, the film Robeson felt proudest of, he was again the black servant, a strong, heroic coal miner who sacrifices his life so that his white brothers may live. The servant proceedings were slightly altered in *Song of Freedom*; here Robeson portrayed a successful concert singer in England who suddenly discovers he is a descendant of a West African queen whose tribe is now in need of a leader. As the archetypal modern black man, Robeson was also depicted as still having the jungle blood running through his veins. That he can never escape. The classic aspect of *Song of Freedom* was its fascinating but unconscious homage to colonial rule. As an industrious British black man, Robeson was the epitome of black middle-class sobriety. He has been trained by whites and adheres to their value system. His wife is a fair-skinned, straight-haired, proper mulatto. And he has a dark-skinned coon servant. When he journeys to deep dark Africa, he takes his British manners and mores and civilizes the savage natives. Great Britain could not have asked for a more loyal subject.

In a way, these films were dishonest. Audiences may have deplored the master–servant antics of even so enlightened a pair as Benny and Rochester, but at least with them patrons knew where they stood. There was no attempt to trick the audience into believing they were viewing something modern and significant. In contrast, the Robeson films were meant to reflect the liberal and even radical attitudes of the day. Yet they now seem dated and false.

Paul Robeson and Nina Mae McKinney in *Sanders of the River.*

What was impressive about the Robeson films, however, was Robeson himself. In all his movies, audiences were aware of his great bulk and presence. His eyes gleamed. His smile was brilliant and infectious, often revealing the complete joy of the actor as he sang, sometimes masking an ambivalent, ironic side of his personality. But always Paul Robeson used his smile to draw his audience to him. Physically, Robeson was such a towering figure, a colossus actually, that he immediately suggested strength. One could never imagine him portraying a weakling. He was made for heroic parts in the classical sense. He seemed a man of instinct and intuition, and seldom played characters of intellect. Robeson was all heart or all guts or all bombast or all passion or all fury, elemental and pure. His lack of intellectual control added to the excitement and theatricality of each performance.

Robeson's greatest contribution to black film history—and the aspect of his work that most disturbed American white moviegoers—was his proud, defiant portrait of the black man. In his best known film, *The Emperor Jones* (1933), Robeson portrays O'Neill's black man who refuses to kowtow to anyone—Brutus Jones, an arrogant, strong-willed braggart, who rises from Pullman porter to autocrat. In one particularly interesting scene on a railroad car, Robeson goes through the stock "yes sirs" and "no sirs" to his white employers, but is so full of energy and self-mockery that his behavior is not self-demeaning. Later when he attempts to blackmail his employer (and afterward when he mocks the employer for the benefit of his black woman), he is a black man consciously asserting himself, consciously cutting The Man down to size.

The Emperor Jones made Paul Robeson a symbol of black confidence and self-fulfillment. When he argues with a friend in a crap game, he kills him, then is sent to a chain gang. When a sadistic guard there whips Jones, he kills the guard, escapes, and sets off for Jamaica. There he works for a white trader, maneuvers (and eventually forces) his way into a partnership, and then usurps the throne of the island's black king. For the next two and a half years, he struts through his palace in his high patent leather boots. He gazes at himself in his corridor of mirrors. "King Brutus!" he proclaims. "Somehow that don't make enough noise." He pauses. "The Emperor Jones!" And thus a ruler is born.

Surely, as Robeson was seen standing by his throne with a crown on his head and a scepter in his hand, as he ordered his old white partner about, black audiences must have felt immensely proud and fond of that badd nigger up there on the screen, telling them white folks to get outta his way to give him room to breathe. Despite the fact that at the end, in punishment for his iniquities (and we might assume his self-assertion), Robeson's Brutus is hunted in the jungle and killed, and despite the fact that in the jungle sequences Robeson, with his chest bare and a terrified expression on his face, was often a black brute figure, black audiences still saw a black male completely unlike the servile characters of most American movies.

The Emperor Jones gave Robeson his finest screen role. One of his few American projects, it was independently produced by John Krimsky and Gifford Cochran and directed by Dudley Murphy. Yet it was thought tainted (by Robeson himself on occasion) because it presented the Negro as a murderer and a rogue.

Robeson did not fare as well in his three other American pictures. His first, *Body and Soul* (1925), was a silent independently produced by Oscar Micheaux. The plot was badly jumbled, and Robeson without his voice was merely beautiful and mysterious. *Show Boat* was a film Robeson might not have cared for, but, curiously, today he seems more relaxed and less stagey in this movie than in any other. The picture itself had an interracial theme, which was handled melodramatically but nonetheless well. Among the traveling troupe of entertainers who perform on the showboat there is a somber, good-hearted beauty named Julie. She becomes a victim of racism when it is discovered that she has "Negro blood." When word reaches the showboat company, Julie's white husband swiftly cuts her hand with a knife and sucks her blood. Miscegenation is a crime in the South. The husband performs this ritual because "One drop of Negro blood makes you a Negro in these parts." Afterward Julie and her now-mulatto husband slowly depart from the showboat hand in hand. Later the tragic Julie becomes an alcoholic. The white blues singer Helen Morgan played Julie in the film. Robeson and Hattie McDaniel portrayed the comic servants, Joe and Queenie. Both performers went through stereotype routines, but Robeson never fully demeaned himself, and when he sang "Ole Man River" and "Ah Still Suits Me" (with Hattie McDaniel), he lifted the entire movie onto his massive shoulders and carried it to moments of eloquence and greatness.

In *Tales of Manhattan* (1942), which also featured Ethel Waters and Eddie Anderson, Paul Robeson played his last American film role. Unfortunately, the movie was a personal disaster. Robeson portrays a backwoods Southern coon who discovers a satchel of money that has been dropped into his cotton field from an airplane. Immediately, he and Waters thank de almighty Gawd in de hebben above. Throughout the film the blacks sing in the fields, dance in the churches, clap their hands in joy, and stand tremblin' 'fore de power and de glory above. Again superstition had been substituted for the genuine intensity of the black religious experience, and the Negro sequence of this all-star film alienated black audiences and aroused great controversy. Surprisingly, N A A C P Secretary Walter White defended the film. But other civil rights groups picketed it, and publications such as *PM* and *The Daily Worker* criticized it vehemently. Star Robeson joined in the protests. "I wouldn't blame any Negro for picketing this film," he announced after having seen a completed version. Thereafter he picketed the film *and* Hollywood. He narrated the movie *Native Land* (1942), but he never accepted another motion-picture role. During the last years of his life, Robeson lived in virtual seclusion at the home of his sister in Philadelphia. He died in 1976.

Paul Robeson was the last major personality in the 1930s gallery of black artists. All the actors distinguished themselves not so much through characters as through their interpretations. Ultimately, they just about exhausted themselves. They used up their supply of ingenuity. Indeed, their servant characters had become so rich, so dazzling, so individualized—in short, so real, significant, and perhaps even threatening—that the servant syndrome could be developed no further. The great black character actors had invigorated the era with their idiosyncrasies and style. In later eras, although the black actor was to be given bigger and better roles and more prominence in films, the actors themselves were rarely able to take their audiences to such idiosyncratic wacky heights. But the servants ended by serving themselves better than the masters, and they provided American movies of the Depression with some of their most imaginative and absurd moments.

Because he was one of the few black actors to triumph in an independently produced black film, Paul Robeson now serves as a lead-in for the next great phase of blacks in films—the period of the black moviemakers, when independent directors and producers made movies to tell the world what being black was really about.

4 THE INTERLUDE: BLACK-MARKET CINEMA

In Chicago—as early as 1912—a black man named William Foster produces a series of all-black comedies ... The scholarly secretary of Booker T. Washington sets out to make a Negro-accomplishment movie, ends up by turning out a prodigious flop, yet fathers a movement.... In Nebraska, Kansas City, Chicago, New York, and other cities and states independent filmmakers set up shop to supply ghetto theaters with relevant all-black movies.... Stepin, Mantan, Nina, and a score of other old-timers and newcomers find employment in movies made outside of Hollywood... And an oversized, charismatic man named Oscar Micheaux becomes America's first legendary black filmmaker.

After *The Birth of a Nation* was released in 1915, there came the great public furor against its racism. At the time, a standard reply to protests about how Negroes were depicted in American films was that blacks should develop their own crop of filmmakers. To some extent that standard reply prevails today. The truth is that black Americans have made their own films for many years. While the mainstream of Hollywood filmmakers demeaned and ridiculed the American Negro, an underground movement gave rise to a group of independent black filmmakers who flourished in the late 1920s and the 1930s. They tried to present realistic portraits of black Americans, but more often than not were trapped by the same stereotype conceptions as their white competitors. And always they were plagued by financial, technical, and distributing problems. Yet some came up with remarkable achievements that survive today. A host of black writers, directors, producers, and technicians gained valuable experience from working on these films. In fact, had it not been for such underground features—sometimes called *race movies—many* blacks would never have worked in films.

The films also offered employment for a great number of actors. Paul Robeson, as we have seen, started his movie career in a film directed by Oscar Micheaux. The only surviving recorded performance of the legendary black stage actor Charles Gilpin was in an independently produced black film. During the late 1930s and early 1940s these films offered exposure and experience to Lena Horne, Eddie Anderson, Spencer Williams (who later starred as Andy on the television series "Amos 'n' Andy"), Nina Mae McKinney, Mantan Moreland, Louise Beavers, Herbert Jeffery (also known as Herb Jeffries), comics Moms Mabley and Pigmeat Markham, and even Stepin Fetchit. All in all the underground black film movement provided film history with an exciting interlude, perhaps now of greater interest for sociological rather than artistic reasons.

In this period of the independents, producers explored and experimented with black themes. Films were made exclusively to please black audiences, and on occasion revealed black fantasies. The era had begun inauspiciously with the appearance of a black man named William Foster. Born in 1884—and a veteran in the tough world of show business, having worked as a press agent for black shows starring the comedy team of (Bert) Williams and (George) Walker—Foster, while living in Chicago, scrambled together enough money to produce his first short black-cast film *The Railroad Porter* around 1912, followed by *The Fall* Guy and *The Barber.* Later at Pathé Studios in Los Angeles, he did a series of shorts starring the legendary black team of Buck and Bubbles. His early films may have been crude but they marked a beginning.

In 1913, Biograph Pictures in New York undertook an ambitious project, a film starring Bert Williams, the legendary black Broadway star and the groundbreaking comedian of the Ziegfeld Follies. Here Williams appeared with a black cast, including actress Odessa Warren Grey as his love interest. Also in the film was a Cakewalk sequence, a stunning record of the historic dance craze that had swept through Black America. Throughout, Williams wore his customary blackface makeup which is puzzling because the other black actors are not in blackface. But blackface was part of Williams's stage identity; apparently, he was unwilling to part with it. Or perhaps the filmmakers did not want to part with it either. Three unidentified directors worked on the film: one, black; two white. Believed to have been conceived as a 35 to 40 minute feature, the movie, however, did not see the light of day. For some reason, it was neither completed nor released. Almost a century later, the unedited 35 millimeter reels, which included footage of the performers with the directors, was rediscovered by a curator at New York's Museum of Modern Art. They had lain in storage at the Museum for decades. "The reels were part of a collection of 900 unprinted negatives that came from the defunct Biography company," reported Felicia R. Lee in the September 20, 2014, issue of *The New York Times*. "Its journey to the public began in 1976, when a curator copying the footage noted Bert Williams' appearance." Afterward the restoration of the film and research on its background began. The film has been titled *Lime Kiln Club Field Day*.

This was not, however, Bert Williams's only movie appearance. In 1914, he starred in *Darktown Jubilee*, also lost. But by 1916, the popular Williams appeared in the Biograph shorts *Natural Born Gambler* and *Fish*, which *do* survive! With Williams's movie roles, there soon emerged the idea of using such a star to reach a new kind of audience, an African American one.

Then there appeared a mild-mannered scholarly man named Emmett J. Scott. At one time the secretary of Booker T. Washington, Scott set his sights on making a major black film. After the release of *The Birth of a Nation* a number of American blacks hoped to produce a short film to cite the accomplishments of colored America as a counterattack to Griffith's alleged racist propaganda. The NAACP toyed with the idea but eventually decided to fight the Griffith feature through the courts and picket lines. As the NAACP shied away, the scholarly Scott strolled to the foreground. He enlisted the aid of the black bourgeoisie, which furnished him with the capital for *Lincoln's Dream*. Initially, Scott hoped to tack this Negro-achievement short onto *The Birth of a Nation* as a prologue. But later Scott's modest proposals stretched to larger proportions. Scriptwriter Elaine Sterne expanded the short project into a feature. The script was submitted to Universal but rejected. Finally, the movie was shot in Chicago and Florida, where the company was haunted by bad weather, poorly designed and constructed sets, an inexperienced cast and crew, and inadequate lighting facilities. When the production ran into dire financial difficulties, Scott had to seek support from white backers, who altered his film's theme and sentiments. After three long hard years, *Lincoln's Dream* was some twelve reels long, ran three hours, and was retitled *The Birth of a Race*. Publicity posters promoted it as "The Greatest and Most Daring of Photoplays . . . The Story of Sin . . . A Master Picture Conceived in the Spirit of Truth and Dedicated to All of the Races of the World." It opened at Chicago's Blackstone Theater in 1918 and was a disaster artistically and financially. Yet it served as an impetus for others.

The organization to pick up where Scott had left off, the first of the black company pioneers, was the Lincoln Motion Picture Company. Incorporated in 1916 (before Scott's film was even completed) and based in Nebraska, the organization was the brainchild of black actor Noble Johnson and his brother George. *The Realization of a Negro's Ambition* was one of the company's first products. The film extolled Negro achievements. Another release, *Trooper of Troop K*, was about the massacre of the Negro troops of the famous Tenth Cavalry and the historic rescue of Captain Lewis S. Morey by the "unknown and unhonored" Trooper K. Both films were distributed to ghetto theaters. George Johnson had shrewdly noted that because of segregation in the South and de facto segregation in the North, a number of all-black theaters were opening. A growing black audience was anxious for black merchandise. The Lincoln Motion Picture Corporation made movies for the black market until the early 1920s, turning out approximately ten films, each no longer than three reels.

Moon Over Harlem

All-Negro Cast Films

BIG TIMERS
Stepin Fetchit in a mix-up with a chamber maid.
44 minutes $10

THE BLOOD OF JESUS
Undoubtedly the most powerful All-Negro motion picture ever produced. A great religious epic.
60 minutes $15

BROKEN STRINGS
Clarence Muse appears as a famous violinist who overcomes adversity with his son's help.
70 minutes $15

BRONZE BUCKAROO
Herbert Jeffrey and the Four Tones. Another fine Western with an all-star cast.
60 minutes $15

DARK MANHATTAN
Ralph Cooper stars in this smashing underworld drama.
66 minutes $15

THE DEVIL'S DAUGHTER
Nina Mae McKinney, Hamtree Harrington. A burning drama of love and hate in the tropics.
70 minutes $15

DOUBLE DEAL
Monte Hawley, Jeni Legon, Florence (Sulumai) O'Brien. His best pal gives him a double deal.
70 minutes $15

THE EXILE
Stanley Murrell and an all-star cast.
70 minutes $15

GANG WAR
Ralph Cooper
See this machine gun thriller.
70 minutes $15

GO DOWN DEATH
Saturday sinners and Sunday saints clash in the battle of Good against Evil.
70 minutes $15

HARLEM BIG SHOT
A. B. Comethiere and Lorenzo Tucker, "the Negro Valentino."
70 minutes $15

HARLEM IS HEAVEN
Bill Robinson
A fun-fest of joy, with Eubie Blake's Orchestra.
70 minutes $15

GOD'S STEPCHILDREN
From the story "Naomi, Negress," of a baby that looks white.
70 minutes $15

IT HAPPENED IN HARLEM
The owner of the Paradise Cafe finds a new singing star at the drug store.
30 minutes $7.50

LYING LIPS
Edna Mae Harris and an all-star cast.
70 minutes $15

A page from the 1958 Ideal Pictures catalogue listing all-Negro films available for rental. Unfortunately, most of the movies made by the independents have been destroyed or remain undiscovered.

The Reol Motion Picture Corporation, headed by Robert Levy, emerged after World War I. *The Call of His People* was an early project. This film, made in Irvington-on-the-Hudson, New York (the estate of the Negro millionairess Leila Walker), was an adaptation of the novel *The Man Who Would Be White* by the black writer Aubrey Browser. Its theme—the Negro light enough to pass for white—later developed into a favorite among the independents. More often than not, these "passing" films seemed to be wish-fulfillment yearnings of their producers. But the theme revealed the preoccupation of black America at the time: how to come as close as possible to the great White American Norm. Other Reol films included *The Jazz Hound*, *The Burden of Race* (the best title of the lot), *Easy Money*, *The Spitfire*, *Secret Sorrow*, and *Sport of the Gods*, the last based on a work by black poet Paul Laurence Dunbar. Reol was one of the first companies to make film versions of black classics. The company also boasted of a circuit of three hundred theaters throughout sections of the South and in many of the Northern big-city ghettos. Finally, Reol titillated the black mass imagination by launching the first colored movie star! Edna Morton was billed as the "colored Mary Pickford" and was described as a "teasing brown" torrid dancer "with the grace and abandon of her race."

Whereas Reol had its "colored Mary Pickford," another black company soon boasted of its "black Sherlock Holmes." This was the title of the film with which the Chicago-based Ebony Film Corporation formally opened. The company specialized in a series of one-reel comedies, mostly parodies on popular white vehicles, as the Holmes title suggests.

According to film historian Thomas Cripps in an article in *Negro Digest*, a rash of film companies grew to supply the seven hundred or so ghetto movie houses that had sprouted up by the late 1920s. In the years to come, more than one hundred firms and corporations were founded to produce Negro films. Among them were the Foster Photoplay in Chicago; the Gate City Film Corporation in Kansas City; Constellation Films, formed in 1921 in New York; the Renaissance Company, which produced all-Negro newsreels and was headed by black actor Leigh Whipper in New York in 1922; and Dunbar Pictures and Roseland Pictures and Recording Laboratories, both based in New York in 1928 and 1929. From Jamaica, Long Island, Buddy Holman headed Paragon Pictures in 1932. The company released the films *The Dusky Village* and *Crimson Fog*.

During this period a number of whites moved in and began making all-black films for ghetto audiences. White backers organized the Famous Artists Company in 1927. Octavus Roy Cohen produced a series of all-colored shorts in the mid-1920s. Usually his films made fun of Negro lawyers and doctors by depicting them as familiar coons. Often Cohen required his black actors to go in blackface. Much later the Cohen viewpoint—depicting Negro professionals as just as idiotic as the servant figures of the Hollywood films—was to be popularized on radio's and

LEFT: Scene from Herald Pictures Incorporated's *Miracle in Harlem* (1947). The picture, a mystery melodrama, was considered a technical landmark in the history of ghetto cinema. BELOW: Three spade detectives in *Miracle in Harlem*.

television's "Amos 'n' Andy" series. The Cohen shorts no doubt represented the underground movement at its worst, but in some cases a few curiously valid products were made. Whites were behind the Colored Players of Philadelphia, yet this company produced two remarkable films: *Ten Nights in a Barroom* with Charles Gilpin in 1926 and *Scar of Shame* in 1929. The latter remains an effective piece of work. Slow-moving and melancholy, *Scar of Shame* tells the story of an ill-matched marriage between a black concert pianist and a poor lower-class black girl. Secretly ashamed of his wife, the young man keeps her hidden from his socially prominent middle-class mother. At the same time, the girl's derelict drunken father plans to kidnap her, in hopes of having her sing at the nightclub of one of his racketeer friends. During a confrontation between the girl (who is about to leave her husband when she learns he is embarrassed by her), the racketeer (who is about to take her off for his nightclub), and the husband (who pleads with her to stay with him), the husband accidentally shoots and disfigures the wife. He is sent to prison but later escapes. He begins life anew and falls in love with another woman, only—through circumstances beyond his control—to meet up with the wife again. She still loves him but knows she can never be his equal. Socially—despite the fact that both are black—they are of different worlds. Despondent, the wife commits suicide. Afterward the husband marries the new girl of his dreams—who is his social equal. Melodramatic but effective, *Scar of Shame* was an eloquent statement on the color caste system and the divisions that exist among black Americans. (The girl's father is very dark; so, too, is the racketeer. Almost all the other characters are fair-skinned. The girl is clearly a victim of her "dark" biological background.) This movie was possibly the finest product of the entire independent movement.

Despite the rapid growth of the new black audience, particularly between 1915 and 1923, a number of unfortunate events halted the burgeoning black industry. A flu epidemic in 1923 had a devastating effect, closing many ghetto theaters and amplifying the problem of distribution. When talkies came in, many companies lacked the capital to keep up production and to acquire the sound equipment the new era demanded. The release of the big studio productions *Hearts in Dixie* and *Hallelujah* spelled disaster for the small independents. Finally, the Depression finished off all but the sturdiest.

During the Depression, independent black films for black audiences were being made almost entirely by white moviemakers; thus, the underground movement then went into a bizarre second phase. The new films concentrated on major Hollywood genres: mystery, melodrama, boy-meets-girl love story, musical, western. White writers and directors, using pseudonyms, constructed the vehicles. In the late 1930s, producer Jed Buell filmed *Harlem on the Prairie*, touted as the first Negro western. Buell also filmed *Lucky Ghost*, which featured an eye-rolling coon hero, and a series of successful films with Mantan Moreland.

During this second phase, there were films that treated blacks sensitively, among which *The Emperor Jones* was probably the best of the lot. The Southland Pictures Corporation released Bud Pollard's *The Black King* in 1932. Filmed in Fort Lee, New Jersey, the movie centered on a back-to-Africa movement reminiscent of Marcus Garvey's endeavors. In 1937 National Pictures released *Spirit of Youth*, dramatizing the meteoric rise of a black boxer. Joe Louis played the central character, a figure closely related to the champ himself. As might be expected, Louis's acting was wooden. Also featured in *Spirit of Youth* were Clarence Muse, Mantan Moreland, and Clarence Brooks. Afterward, in 1940, Muse was able to write and star in *Broken Strings*, technically one of the better-made features of the period. Spencer Williams, too, with white backers, wrote, directed, and co-starred in *Go Down Death* in 1944. Williams also directed *The Blood of Jesus*. Both films were serious but unsuccessful attempts to analyze the black religious tradition.

Some of the more prominent white-backed film corporations were Astor Pictures, Herald Pictures Incorporated, and Million Dollar Pictures. Astor, headed by the white Southern-born Robert M. Savini, turned out comedies such as *Tall, Tan, and Terrific* in 1946 with Mantan Moreland and *Big Timers* in 1946 with Stepin Fetchit. It also released black musicals such as *Beware*, directed by Bud Pollard in 1946 (a forty-five-minute feature starring the jazz musician Louis Jordan) and *Ebony Parade* in 1947. Two energetic brothers, Jack and Dave Goldberg, organized Herald Pictures, Incorporated. The company released shorts starring the black blues singer Mamie Smith as well as such features as *Harlem Is Heaven* with Bill Robinson and *Miracle in Harlem* in 1947 with Stepin Fetchit. The latter, a combination mystery-gangster melodrama, was considered a technical landmark in the history of the race movie. Richard C. Kahn formed Hollywood Productions, which released the Western *The Bronze Buckaroo* in 1938. It remains interesting because of its "color design." The light-skinned performers Herbert Jeffrey and Artie Young played the leads and were actually white figures. As a singing cowboy, Jeffrey went through the expected Tex Ritter–Gene Autry heroics and exploits. Jeffrey, out to find the murderer of the heroine's father, was always immaculately dressed in tight riding clothes and fancy silver spurs and guns. At the movie's conclusion he captures the murderous culprit, and then he and his light-skinned, ever-so-polished middle-class heroine ride off into the sunset. Jeffrey's light skin classified him as a hero for ghetto audiences. Conversely, the supporting players, the comic, eye-rolling Dusty and the sinister villain, were played by the dark actors Lucius Brooks and Spencer Williams.

Million Dollar Pictures was organized by the handsome black actor Ralph Cooper and a group of white associates. The company turned out a healthy series of hits in the late 1930s and the early 1940s. One of the company's first big hits was a black gangster movie, *Dark Manhattan*, in 1937. *One Dark Night* featured Mantan Moreland in a serious role. In *Reform School* Louise Beavers undid her kerchief for one of the few times in her career. This film was so successful that Million Dollar Pictures later made a sequel to it. The company also released *Bargain with Bullets* and *Life Goes On.* Still noteworthy today is Million Dollar's *The Duke Is Tops* which starred Ralph Cooper opposite a pretty little "bronze colored gal" then making her movie debut. That gal was Lena Horne, who afterward returned periodically to star in other independent all-black productions.

From phase one to phase two, the black independents supplied ghetto theaters with an array of entertaining black products. Even when blacks could view films at white theaters, most still preferred the ghetto movie houses, where they could "give full rein to their feelings and impulses." The sociologist E. Franklin Frazier has said that it was in these ghetto theaters, some battered and broken down, others poorly heated or ventilated, that black audiences felt most comfortable because they were with their own people. In this respect, the black market cinema was a triumph of sorts. The films today might appear dated or naive, but they were a source of pride to black America. And the independent underground black film movement did provide American film history with at least one astounding presence.

Oscar Micheaux

The one filmmaker who survived the flu epidemic, the competition from the Hollywood studios, and even the financial pinch of the Depression was Oscar Micheaux. This fiendishly aggressive young entrepreneur started his Oscar Micheaux Corporation in 1918 with short features, then produced full-length films. In 1931, when most black independents were closing up shop, he released *The Exile*, one of the first all-talking motion pictures made by a black company. For almost 30 years, Micheaux wrote, directed, and produced from 30 to 40-some films. His last was promoted as the "Greatest Negro photoplay of all time."

Mystery and myths have long surrounded the corporation and the man Micheaux. His widow, Alice B. Russell, an actress who appeared in a number of his films, lived for years in virtual seclusion in New York City, refusing to comment on her husband's life or work. Through her silence, the aura enveloping her husband merely intensified. How he learned anything about films remains part of the mystery. But it is certain that Micheaux, born in Illinois in 1884, began his professional career as a novelist. Later his fervid enthusiasm for making movies carried him from South Dakota to Chicago and New York.

In a ten-year period Oscar Micheaux wrote approximately ten melodramatic novels, having formed his own company to publish them. *The Homesteader, The Wind from Nowhere, Masquerade,* and *The Case of Mrs. Wingate* were some. The novels might easily have sat unread had it not been for their author's ingenuity.

Micheaux well understood the mass imagination, and by catering to its wants and needs he was able to survive and become successful. His philosophy on literature later extended to his films: Learn from the masses; then teach them. And teach he did.

Once a novel was completed, Micheaux arranged aggressive promotional tours to launch it. During these tours, Micheaux assertively and energetically traveled by car through sections of the country, making sure to hit the black belts. Meeting with leaders of the black communities—doctors, lawyers, businessmen, and schoolteachers—as well as with black laborers, domestics, and farmers, he lectured in schools, in churches, even in homes, promoting himself and his work. Gradually he acquired a certain following and established a name for himself that quickly circulated through the black grapevine. He also sold his books to white farmers.

Indeed, so widespread had the Micheaux reputation become that soon after the formation of the Lincoln Motion Picture Company, Micheaux was approached by the Johnson brothers for the screen rights to his novel *The Homesteader*. He accepted an invitation to come West to confer on the project but traveled a roundabout route, stopping in Oklahoma and other states to promote his latest novel. During this trip, Micheaux, already fascinated by films and determined to make his own, decided to sell the rights to the novel *only* if he was able to direct the film version. When his bid was rejected, Micheaux headed east again, resolved more than ever to make movies. Taking a similar roundabout route back, he enlisted on the way the support of a group of Oklahoma farmers to whom he had previously sold his novels. Who gave what or how much is still unknown, but Oscar Micheaux rounded up enough capital to get his project off the ground. His first movie was *The Homesteader* in 1919. Soon afterwards a host of others appeared: *Within Our Gates, The Brute, Symbol of the Unconquered* in 1920; *Gunsaulus Mystery* and *Deceit* in 1922; *The Dungeon, The Virgin of the Seminole*, and *Son of Satan* in 1922; *Jasper Landry's Will* in 1923; *Birthright* and *Body and Soul* in 1924; *The Spider's Web* in 1926; *Millionaire* in 1927; *When Men Betray* and *Easy Street* in 1928; *Wages of Sin* in 1929; *Daughter of the Congo* in 1930; *The Exile* and *Darktown Revue* in 1931; *Veiled Aristocrats, Black Magic*, and *Ten Minutes to Live* in 1932; *The Girl from Chicago* and *Ten Minutes to Kill* in 1933; *Harlem after Midnight* in 1934; *Lem Hawkin's Confession* in 1935; *Temptation* and *Underworld* in 1936; *God's Step Children* in 1937; *Swing* in 1938; a *Birthright* remake and *Lying Lips* in 1939; *The Notorious Elinor Lee* in 1940; *Betrayal* in 1948.

Micheaux used the same techniques in promoting and financing his films that he had used with his books. But he had a new dash and flair, befitting a motion-picture director. A hefty six-footer, given to wearing long Russian coats and extravagant wide-brimmed hats, Micheaux is said to have toured the country, stepping out of cars and into meeting halls as if "he were God about to deliver a sermon." "Why, he was so impressive and so charming," said Lorenzo Tucker, one of the most important of Micheaux's leading men, "that he could talk the shirt off your back." Just this sort of charm enabled Micheaux to persuade Southern theater owners to show his films. On his tours, Micheaux approached white Southerners and told them of the new black audience. At first they shied away, but when he spoke of the cash register, theater managers listened. It was soon arranged to have Micheaux features shown at special matinee performances held for black audiences. His movies were also sometimes shown at midnight performances for white audiences eager for black camp. Aware of the mystique of black nightclubs, he inserted into his films cabaret scenes that would appeal to whites.

As for his actors, Micheaux generally gathered them from black acting companies such as the Lafayette Players in New York. But he came across some of his stars under bizarre circumstances. Legend has it that Micheaux would spot a figure or note a gesture or be struck by the way the light fell across a face and would immediately sign the person up. Lorenzo Tucker said he was first spotted by Micheaux in Philadelphia. Having gone there to audition for a show, he was sitting in the lobby of the Dunbar Hotel when crafty Micheaux, whom he did not know, approached him and asked if he was an actor. "You're one of them who *thinks* they are," Micheaux added. Afterward, Tucker went to see Micheaux in New York. He was given a part, and all in all worked in some fourteen Micheaux productions.

Micheaux cast his actors on the basis of type. He modeled his stars after white Hollywood personalities and publicized them as black versions. Handsome and smooth Lorenzo Tucker was first referred to as the "black Valentino." Later when talkies came in, he was the "colored William Powell." Sexy and insolent Bee Freeman, a vamp figure, was the "sepia Mae West." Slick Chester, a character actor who played gangster roles, was the "colored Cagney." Lovely Ethel Moses was sometimes touted as the "Negro Harlow." The leads in Micheaux pictures were usually played by light-colored Negro actors, and in later years Micheaux was to be severely criticized by more militant black audiences for selecting "light-brights."

Once Micheaux had completed a film, he carried stills from it to theater managers. "Here's my black Valentino. The girls love him," he would boast. "If I can get the right backing, I'll star him in my next film, too." In this way he was often able to solicit financing for his *next* picture. He also sent his stars on personal-appearance junkets to Northern ghetto theaters. By these vigorous promotion tactics he established himself as the most successful black moviemaker of the period.

Despite clever campaigns, Micheaux was repeatedly dogged by financial problems. The little money he gathered was still far from what was needed to see a film through production, and he was compelled to work on the tightest of budgets. A picture was usually completed within six weeks. When shooting in New York, he worked with a minimum crew, all union workers. Usually he hired his cameraman for one day at a time. Often a scene was made in a single take. Generally, camera

LEFT: Lorenzo Tucker, the "black Valentino."
BELOW: The "sepia Mae West," Bee Freeman, with Oscar Polk in Oscar Micheaux's gangster thriller, *Underworld* (1936).

ABOVE: The stalwart good colored fellow goes to savage Africa to rescue a pretty Negro girl in Micheaux's *Daughter of the Congo* (1930).

RIGHT: One of Micheaux's favorite leading ladies, the fair-skinned Ethel Moses, seems to be losing her scarf.

setups were basic: nothing fancy. Since he was forced to shoot scenes so rapidly, he seldom was able to do retakes. Consequently, audiences might see an actor flub his lines and then just pick up the pieces of his sentence and keep on going. Sometimes important sequences in his films centered around one set. In *God's Step Children*, several early scenes occurred in front of a staircase. Filming in the home of a friend, Micheaux discovered that the staircase area offered the best lighting angles, and thus worked his big scenes around it.

Filming on location at actual homes or offices was almost standard procedure for the Micheaux Company. It saved money and time. Micheaux might be visiting friends when he would nonchalantly pan the room, noting a particularly photogenic style of furniture or decor. He rarely had any difficulty charming his hostess into permitting him to film scenes for his next movie there.

Micheaux's silent films are far more fluid and less formulaic than his talkies, which were similar to Hollywood B movies with obvious technical problems. One sees him struggling with the sound medium. (The Hollywood studios also struggled to perfect their early talkies.) Lighting and editing were often poor, and the acting could be dreadful. Still, the standards of the Micheaux feature were often better than those of the other black independents. Intertwined in his films was the race theme. Just as Negro newspapers and magazines took major news stories and reported on them from a black perspective, Micheaux often—especially in the talkies—took the typical Hollywood script and gave it a racial slant. *Underworld* was a gangster film with black gangsters and a black gun moll. *Daughter of the Congo* was an African adventure story with a colored cavalry officer bent on rescuing a young rich Negro girl lost in the savage tropics. *The Deceit* and *The Dungeon* were conventional melodramas. *Temptation* was a sophisticated sex drama in the De Mille vein.

There were important exceptions, especially in some of his silents in which he focused on the race theme. In *Birthright*, a young black Harvard graduate returns to his home town in Tennessee bent upon founding a colored college "to uplift the race." Naturally, he encounters opposition; but, surprisingly, it comes not only from the white community but from blacks, too, who agree with white Southerners that education ruins a Negro. In its own silly and sly way, *Birthright* made a definite plea for black unity while seriously satirizing the old-style toms. On the other hand, Micheaux's 1937 melodrama *God's Step Children* zeroed in on the problem of the light-skinned black attempting to "pass" for white. The movie seems corny today, but better than others of its time it captured the racial philosophy of the black middle classes in the 1930s and 1940s.

What remains Oscar Micheaux's greatest contribution (and something revealed explicitly in *God's Step Children*) is often viewed by contemporary black audiences as his severest shortcoming. That his films reflected the interests and outlooks of the black bourgeoisie will no doubt always be held against him. His films never centered on the ghetto. They did not deal with racial misery and decay. But that didn't mean they did not acknowledge racial problems. Usually, though, the films concentrated on upright middle-class protagonists. At times, one may feel he's created a world that's part fantasy, part reflective of a segment of the black bourgeoisie. He seems determined to depict blacks as just as affluent, just as educated, just as "cultured" as white America. Though Micheaux's films—with their light bright leads and their darker "lower" classes—might embarrass later audiences, they represent an important part of black film and social history. Often he seems to adhere to W. E. B. Du Bois's "talented tenth" theory. His heroic leads are the educated go-getters who believe they must do something to "further the race, not hinder it." To appreciate Micheaux's films, one must understand that he was moving as far as possible away from Hollywood's jesters.

Eventually, Micheaux and the few other companies that hung on into the 1940s were killed off after World War II. Ironically, Micheaux's last movie, *The Betrayal*, opened in 1948 at a white theater in downtown New York. It drew major review attention, but the movie was received poorly and was a failure. Afterward there were no others. Micheaux died in 1951 in Charlotte, North Carolina, in relative obscurity. For years, many of his films vanished.

As Micheaux films resurfaced in later decades, new audiences were able to understand better the scope of his work and contributions with such films as *Veiled Aristocrats, Murder in Harlem* (also known as *Lem Hawkins' Confession*), and *Symbol of the Unconquered*. His *Body and Soul*, in which Micheaux focused on a shifty minister, marked the screen debut of Paul Robeson.

But most startling was his 1920 film *Within Our Gates*, which was lost for almost seventy years. Originally rejected by the Chicago Board of Censors, *Within Our Gates* sparked a controversy because of an explosive lynching sequence—and the fear that it might cause race riots. When the film finally opened in Chicago, it played to a packed house. But its national distribution was limited. Southern theaters refused to book it. Later it disappeared.

Then in 1990, a print was discovered at the Spanish Film Archives in Madrid (with Spanish subtitles). Afterwards it was shown publicly, notably in 1992 at a theater at New York's Lincoln Center. Now audiences had the rare opportunity to see a pioneering African American director examining—with passion and commitment—the "race theme" (using an interracial cast): here Micheaux looked at tensions between black and white in the South—and also turned his focus on such other "explosive" issues as rape, miscegenation, and urban crime. Significantly, he focuses on a young, educated African American woman who works for a better day for her people.

Another early pioneering black director whose films—such as *The Blood of Jesus, Go Down Death*, and *Juke Joint*—reached new audiences in later years was Spencer Williams.

Still, what killed off the efforts of even the sturdiest of the independents in the late 1940s were the Negro Problem Pictures that took up racial themes. The independents could not compete with these Hollywood-made features. Soon their products were no longer distinct. But the independent black filmmakers, whose body of work yet deserves close attention, kept the faith for as long as they could and for a long time before it was fashionable.

5 THE 1940s: THE ENTERTAINERS, THE NEW NEGROES, AND THE PROBLEM PEOPLE

Lena Horne stands, looking elegant and sophisticated, singing of love and loneliness.... A black G.I. lies in a hospital, yet to recover from a wartime racial incident that has left him paralyzed and amnesiac.... Hazel Scott, seated at a piano and spectacular in a form-fitting, low-cut gown, plays Gershwin in her inimitable style.... A light-skinned young Negro woman called Pinky returns south to a life of racial agony after having passed for white in the North.... Duke Ellington, Count Basie, Lionel Hampton, and Louis Armstrong perform their music to the delight of a war-fatigued nation.... A prosperous New England family confesses to their staid community—and themselves—that they are Negroes and have been "passing" for the last twenty years.... Ethel Waters and Rochester sing a lively duet and turn Cabin in the Sky *into a hit movie fantasy.... A proud Mississippi Negro maintains his dignity—and his manhood—as his Southern neighbors set out to lynch him.*

These were the black film people of the 1940s. The villains were forgotten. The jesters had had their day. And the servants, now that the great financial slump had ended, exchanged their mops and pails for zoot suits and sequined gowns. The new era began enthusiastically by presenting a lively set of Negro entertainers. Singers, dancers, musicians, acrobats, and clowns abounded, and the ring and roar of the cash register reflected their ability to entertain. For a time, it appeared as if the era would be exclusively theirs. But before its end the entertainers were to be virtually shoved aside as a puzzling set of people appeared and revealed that in America there was such a thing as a race problem.

For the film industry the 1930s had been consistently frivolous, spirited, and screwballish, but the next era was not so clearly defined. Its identity was split in two by a war abroad and then the emergence of one at home. Before the 1940s ended, the decade proved to be the most bizarre and certainly broke the most ground of all for blacks in American films.

The Entertainers

Although it flowered in the early 1940s, reached its apex with two important all-black musicals, and was to be used throughout the war years as the standard procedure for handling black personalities, the Negro Entertainment Syndrome was not really new. The servants dominated the important movies of the 1930s, but the entertainment aspect was never ignored. Indeed, in almost every American movie in which a black had appeared, filmmakers had been trying to maintain the myth that Negroes were naturally rhythmic and natural-born entertainers. With their cast of darkies singing and dancing, *Hearts in Dixie* and *Hallelujah* had obviously presented blacks not only as jesters but as uninhibited entertainers too. Even as Bessie Smith cried the blues in *St. Louis Blues*, she was at heart the entertainer.

Ethel Waters sang "Am I Blue" in her first film, *On with the Show* (1929), and in an early short of the 1930s, *Rufus Jones for President*, she held a tot named Sammy Davis, Jr., on her lap as she rocked him to sleep with a lullaby. Sometimes the entertainment aspect was implied in the servants' performances, even though there was no singing or dancing. The actor seemed to express himself in a musical or rhythmic way. At other times the entertainer aspect was more explicit. Hattie McDaniel sang an extemporaneous homecoming celebration number in *The Little Colonel*. In *Judge Priest* she sang "In My Old Kentucky Home" in one episode, and in another she performed a merry work song. "I got to take down the clothes and take 'em in the house . . . yes, lawd," she crooned, glorifying her servitude in song. In the same film, Stepin Fetchit led the "Dixie" street parade. Rochester sang and danced in *Man About Town*. Bill Robinson had at least one tap-dancing number in all his films.

Often clusters of blacks would perform exaggerated revival sessions, as in *Belle of the Nineties* and *Stand Up and Cheer*. On rare occasions individual black entertainers were able to move audiences with their song. Paul Robeson's mighty voice poured over from the screen to fill theaters as he sang, and even in his great, serious movies such as *The Emperor Jones* or *Song of Freedom* there was at least one musical selection by the handsome baritone. In *Gold Diggers of 1933*, the lovely Etta Moten became the Negro girl of every Depression man's dream as she crooned the sentimentally charged "Remember My Forgotten Man."

In the mid-1930s, as the swing era reached its zenith, blacks were employed even more as musical entertainers in Hollywood films. Duke Ellington—elegantly dressed in white—not only was featured with his band in Mae West's *Belle of the Nineties* but also starred in a number of musical shorts and *The Hit Parade of 1937*. Cab Calloway, who had appeared in talkie shorts, also performed "Reefer Man" (dressed in white) in the W. C. Fields feature *International House* (1933). Before the decade ended, Calloway was cast in *The Singing Kid* (1936) with Al Jolson and in *Manhattan Merry-Go-Round* (1937). Louis Armstrong was one more talented musical performer imported to the West Coast to be featured in films. Such shorts as *Rhapsody in Black and Blue* (1932), *Bundle of Blues* (1933), *Jitterbug Party* (c. 1933), *Symphony in Black* (1935), and *Hi-De-Ho* (1935) were only a few in a long array at the beginning of the swing era that featured one or another of these three musicians.

Gradually, as the Negro performers grew in popularity, there evolved a special platform for displaying the entertainer to his best advantage. Rather than include him in the regular plot of the movie and have to stop in the middle of the serving scene while a Negro sang his song, producers introduced specific musical interludes in which the entertainer could perform unhampered by a story line. Frequently a nightclub scene was introduced into the movie so that the performer would have a natural setting. The interludes were casually inserted in the films. The central characters might be planning a big event—such as a political rally (as in *Every Day's a Holiday*, 1938), a stage show (*Belle of the Nineties*, 1934), or the launching of a swanky new café (*Pennies from Heaven*, 1936)—and would need a spectacular show-stopping routine to attract attention. Luckily Louis Armstrong or Duke Ellington or Cab Calloway was never far away! The entertainer would provide a dazzling interlude and then fade from the scene, leaving the plot to continue without him.

It was not long before the entertainers became so successful in this format that there was hardly a *Big Broadcast* or a *Broadway Melody* or a *Hit Parade* in which there was not at least one number by a black personality. Even as late as the 1950s, remnants of the entertainer syndrome were present in films such as Fritz Lang's *The Blue Gardenia* (1953) and Jean Negulesco's *A Certain Smile* (1958), in which Nat "King" Cole and Johnny Mathis sang in nightclub interludes. But in the 1940s the tradition had its heyday.

The gregariousness and energy of the entertainers were used in the 1940s to ease the tensions of a war-depressed nation. It was during the war years, more than ever before, that the great gift of the movies, that of allowing people to escape to other worlds where blues, bad times, and heartaches could be forgotten, was most consciously employed. In part, they were used to boost the nation's morale and to promote patriotism. USO troupes were entertaining the boys overseas while at home the black entertainers stated through their song and dance that America was indeed a good and decent country full of joy and unity, a place well worth fighting for. Like the servants of the 1930s, the entertainers, too, set out to delight and please

Ethel Waters.

without at all changing anyone's life. Yet unlike the servants, whose familiarity with the stars of the 1930s films had irritated some patrons, the entertainers syndrome was clearly a safe device. Because musical numbers were not integrated into the script, the scenes featuring the blacks could be cut from the films without spoiling them should local (or Southern) theater owners feel their audiences would object to seeing a Negro. The whole procedure now seems ridiculous and archaic; it was but another way in which motion pictures catered to audience prejudices.

Two Negro personalities who prospered and perished because of this built-in cutting procedure were among the era's big favorites as well as two of its big rebels and the 1940s' most prominent and handsome black creations. One was always strategically seated at a piano, the other conspicuously draped around a column. One was Hazel Scott, the other Lena Horne. Each entertainer—a remarkable pianist and a sultry song stylist—brought to the movies her own concept of black pride and steadfastly adhered to it.

Hazel Scott: Miss Proper Middle-Class Lady

Hazel Scott remained important in later decades mainly because she was considered so important by her own generation. In the early 1940s she was an immensely popular performer, acclaimed for her successful nightclub appearances and noted for her fiery temperament. A proud and demanding performer, who never tried to conceal either her color or her anger, Hazel Scott was one of the first black artists to refuse to appear before segregated audiences. In the end, her militancy may have put a damper on her career and brought a halt to her meteoric rise in the 1940s. But for a brief spell she was an important personality in Hollywood films.

Hazel Scott, born in 1920 in Port of Spain, Trinidad, came to the movies in 1943 after a legendary childhood. She was the daughter of two creative parents. Her father, R. Thomas Scott, was a well-known Negro scholar; her mother, Alma Long Scott, a musician and a Trinidad aristocrat. When the Scotts migrated to Harlem in 1924, their young daughter was already a child prodigy. She read at three. It was found that she had perfect pitch at three and a half. She played the piano at four. She had mastered the classics—and was improvising—at five. Afterwards, she studied privately with a professor from the Juilliard School of Music. At the age of twenty Hazel Scott made her professional nightclub debut at a Greenwich Village club, Café Society Downtown. She was an overnight sensation and soon became the rage of New York City. Two years later, director Gregory Ratoff filmed sequences of her at the piano to be inserted in Columbia Pictures' *Something to Shout About* (1943). When the Columbia executives viewed the sequences, they were so impressed they wrote in a part for Scott and asked her to come to Hollywood.

Hazel Scott immediately distinguished herself from the blacks who had previously worked in the movies. She had developed into a shrewd and articulate

Hazel Scott.

young woman and a very self-assured one as well. She had no doubts about either her talents or her superiority. And she did not hesitate to make demands. Thus she refused to play a role in a film, well aware, as she informed *Ebony* in 1945, that black women were too often cast as whores or maids. Instead she always appeared in movies as herself, seated at the piano just as she would be in a nightclub.

The Scott specialty—the aspect of her musicianship which made her a star—was a unique and daring blending of the classics and swing music. *Time* magazine described her technique:

> Where others murder the classics, Hazel Scott merely commits arson.... She seems coolly determined to play legitimately, and, for a brief while, triumphs. But gradually it becomes apparent that evil forces are struggling within her for expression. Strange notes and rhythms creep in, the melody is tortured with hints of boogie-woogie, until finally, happily, Hazel Scott surrenders to her worst nature and beats the keyboard into a rack of bones. The reverse is also true: into "Tea for Two" may creep a few bars of Debussy's "Clair de Lune."

The Scott technique was on display in a number of 1940s products: *I Dood It* (1943), *The Heat's On* (1943), and *Broadway Rhythm* (1944). Perhaps her typical performance—the one her devotees called the "quintessential Scott"—was in Warner Brothers' *Rhapsody in Blue* (1945), a schmaltzy biography of George Gershwin directed by Irving Rapper. She made an unforgettable appearance at a Paris nightclub singing Gershwin's "The Man I Love." Stirring as this five-minute sequence was, it was cut from the film by Southern censors. But *Rhapsody in Blue* best revealed Hazel Scott's ability to invest her characters with "refinement" and "taste." She sits upright at the piano, back perfectly erect, and looking altogether magnificent. She is immaculately gowned and coifed. She lifts her chin in subdued condescension. Surely in 1945 it must have been marvelous for black audiences to see a black woman so supremely confident. Yet one of the perverse ironies of Hazel Scott's work was that later younger black audiences (of the late 1960s/early 1970s) found her too bourgeois (too *bourgsee*) and rather affected. For them, she looked as if she had to *prove* something, perhaps how good she was, for the sake of her race. (Still later generations, however, would view her simply as an assured high-flung diva.) Paradoxically, in a movie like Vincente Minnelli's *I Dood It*, she sometimes slipped, without even realizing it, into the kind of category she fought to escape. Here Scott—decked out in a luxurious white fur coat and a low-cut, form-fitting, dark sequined gown—rehearses on a stage with a group of Negro singers, all of whom are elegantly dressed. Among them is Vivian Dandridge, the older sister of Dorothy Dandridge. First, Scott performs a great rendition of "Taking a Chance on Love" on the piano. Then she joins Lena Horne, who performs a song called "Jericho." It's an energetic, spirited number that transforms the stage into a pop-style revival session. Scott glided through the sequence on the strength of her great style, yet she may have had some battle scars. American audiences congratulated themselves for appreciating this "cultured" black woman who knew the classics so well. But in retrospect those audiences were just like the blue-haired ladies in the 1950s who watched Harry Belafonte in his tight pants and open shirts and left the theater raving about the "anthropological research" that enriched his folk tunes. Either the ladies had not seen straight or they were not saying what they really did enjoy about a Belafonte performance. With Hazel Scott, "culture" was the cover-up explanation for what her presence actually sometimes represented. In the context of the white films in which she appeared, Scott may have appealed to some moviegoers as a new variation of the age-old "exotic black woman." Certainly critic James Agee realized it when he criticized Scott for exploiting her breasts and armpits. And it was something that audiences may read into her sequence in *I Dood It.* There sat Hazel Scott on display. Her style might be seen as a come-on. And even in her smile there was a lewd suggestiveness that remains intriguing. Scott was far sexier than most may have admitted. Scott, however, fought to maintain her dignity in her films. In the mid-1940s, her movie career came to a halt when she clashed with Columbia Pictures studio head Harry Cohn over costumes which she felt stereotyped blacks. She said that Cohn told her she'd never work again in Hollywood. "I was already signed for *Rhapsody in Blue.* So I made that," said Scott. "And then he was as good as his word. I never made another Hollywood film." She appeared in only one other feature, the 1961 French film *The Night Affair.* Yet she became a permanent footnote in black political history when in 1945, she became the second wife of the foremost black politician of her time, Adam Clayton Powell, Jr. The marriage ended in 1961. She died in 1981.

Lena Horne: Black Beauty in Residence

Hazel Scott's greatest rival during the period was Lena Horne. Actually, it would be better to say that the nearest thing Lena Horne had to a rival was Hazel Scott. For Lena Horne was unquestionably the 1940s' biggest Negro attraction.

By now one of the entertainment world's legendary figures, Lena Horne was born in 1917 in a small Brooklyn hospital. Stories are still told of how the nurses excitedly carried the newborn infant through the corridors and the wards, raving about her unusual "copper color." That was but the first in a long line of such exhibits throughout Lena Horne's career, and, as she herself admitted, most of her successes came from exhibiting that extraordinary copper skin tone.

Lena Horne was already en route to stardom by the time she migrated to Hollywood in the early 1940s. She had appeared at the Cotton Club at age sixteen, had successfully performed in Lew Leslie's *Blackbirds of 1939,* and had worked her way up to appearances at the smart New York night spot Café Society Downtown.

Lena Horne.

Everywhere she was touted as the *café au lait* Hedy Lamarr. In Hollywood, everyone waited eagerly to see what roles she would be assigned in films. NAACP Secretary Walter White took a personal interest in her career. He was convinced that Lena Horne could alter the trend of Negroes in American movies.

Lena Horne's first Hollywood film was *Panama Hattie* (1942) starring Red Skelton and Ann Sothern. In two musical episodes directed by Vincente Minnelli, Lena Horne came on, sang her songs, danced with the Berry Brothers in one number, then exited. Brief as the appearances were, her presence had impact. Shortly thereafter MGM received a number of letters from whites asking who their new *Latin American* discovery was. MGM was also accused by some irate Negroes of attempting to pass her off as white. Lena Horne's next film, *Thousands Cheer* (1943), was what she called her first big, all-star musical. "They didn't make me into a maid," she has said, "but they didn't make me into anything else either. I became a butterfly pinned to a column singing away in Movieland." Her films were constructed so that Horne's scenes could easily be cut when the movies were shown in the South.

Henceforth, like Hazel Scott, Lena Horne came on as herself. She was always elegantly and sensuously dressed. She did her bit, then vanished. In her "Love" musical number in *Ziegfeld Follies*, she was something of a sensual exotic—dressed suggestively in a tight, colorful costume—while performing in a sexy, heated club with other black cast members. When Lena Horne finally played her two big starring roles, the sex-object syndrome (actually nothing more than the tragic mulatto without the tragedy) was carried a step further by casting her as exotic sirens. But to everyone's surprise—and perhaps to the credit of Lena Horne—she always proved herself too much the lady to be believable as the slut. Indeed her Georgia Brown in *Cabin in the Sky* was more a tease than anything else, and her startling freshness and untainted wholesome beauty in this film and in *Stormy Weather* made her an object of contemplation rather than one of possession.

I Dood It, Swing Fever (1943), *Broadway Rhythm* of 1944, *Two Girls and a Sailor* (1944), *Ziegfeld Follies* (1944), *Till the Clouds Roll By* (1946), *Words and Music* (1948), and *Duchess of Idaho* (1950) were other Horne pictures. In all these films, Lena Horne looked lovely as ever, but she never seemed to be enjoying herself. She sometimes came across as aloof and remote. Yet curiously, it was this very aloofness and artistic detachment that added to her allure and mystery.

Toward the end of the 1940s, Lena Horne had trouble with her studio. In her autobiography, *Lena*, the actress reported that relations with MGM were never very friendly once she became involved with the white musician Lennie Hayton, whom she later married. Then, too, Horne became more selective about the roles she wanted to play. For a time, MGM made it difficult for her to get nightclub assignments. When the studio remade *Show Boat* in 1951, Lena Horne yearned for the role of Julie, the mulatto. But the part went to Ava Gardner. Later in 1953 when MGM cast *Bright Road*, their first "serious" black-cast film of the 1950s, Horne was bypassed for the lead, which went to Dorothy Dandridge. Later she lost *Carmen Jones* to the same actress. In the early 1950s, too, she was listed in Red Channels, and consequently was blacklisted from television and some radio appearances. Because of her friendship with Paul Robeson and her interest in the Council for African Affairs, she was resented by many conservatives in the entertainment industry. For a while it looked as if the legendary beauty's star was on the descent. But Lena Horne worked her way back into the mainstream, returning to the studio that had once shunned her for another musical stint in *Meet Me in Las Vegas* (1956), then triumphing on Broadway in *Jamaica*. In the 1960s, she came back strong with concert and stage performances, then finally a movie role—as Richard Widmark's mistress in *Death of a Gunfighter* (1969). In the film she was a unique admixture of middle-class haughtiness and downhome, nitty-gritty daredevilment. Horne died in 2010. Today, however, Lena Horne is still thought of as *the* black leading lady of the war era. As such, she starred in the period's two big all-black spectacles: *Cabin in the Sky* and *Stormy Weather*, both released in 1943, both taking the entertainer syndrome to its apex.

Cabin in the Sky

MGM's *Cabin in the Sky* was based on a successful Broadway show that had starred Ethel Waters, Dooley Wilson, and the Katherine Dunham dance troupe. It had sat on MGM's shelves, since all-Negro productions were still financial risks. But once the studio finally gave the go-ahead signal to producer Arthur Freed, they went all the way, and their all-Negro musical—the first in nearly fourteen years—was launched with tremendous fanfare.

Ethel Waters was signed to repeat her role as the good wife, Petunia. Eddie Anderson was cast in the lead male role. And the studio's black-beauty-in-residence, Lena Horne, was set to portray the temptress Georgia Brown. Vincente Minnelli was assigned to direct. To it he brought his sensitive, sometimes airless style, one nonetheless appropriate for the story. A handsome sepia-tone surface was employed effectively, and the film had the studio-made period glow MGM prided itself on.

A light and ingratiating fantasy, *Cabin in the Sky* told the story of Little Joe Jackson, a harmless *little colored* man who enjoys shooting craps and raising a bit of cain. He is married to a decent God-fearing woman, Petunia, who worries plenty about him. But neither Joe nor Petunia knows of the battle between the general of heaven and Lucifer, Jr., of hell for the rights to Jackson's soul. To win his victim, Lucifer, Jr., throws everything—including a winning sweepstakes ticket and the temptress Georgia Brown—Little Joe's way. But, in the end, Petunia's prayers save him, and together the two are able to walk to their cabin in the sky.

The plot, characterizations, and naive sentiments of *Cabin in the Sky* now seem passé. No doubt the film's world was remote even in 1943. But what gave it charm was the wit and innocence the director and actors poured into it. As for the actors, it was not as important what they did as who was doing it. The film was advertised as an all-star production. For once not even the MGM publicity department could be accused of luring an audience under false pretenses. Just about everybody was in it.

Rex Ingram, in multiple roles, stood out as an immaculately gleaming Lucifer, Jr. Oscar Polk played Deacon and Fleetfoot. Butterfly McQueen was Lily, the pious I-told-you-so. Ruby Dandridge, the mother of Dorothy and a popular actress in her own right, appeared as a chatty churchgoer. John "Bubbles" Sublett of the Buck and Bubbles team did a virtuoso stick-and-staircase dance sequence—while Duke Ellington played a rousing rendition of "Shine." Newcomer Kenneth Spencer, then just fresh from a serious role in *Bataan* (1943), was so impressive as heaven's general that he was touted as a new Robeson. Included also were Willie Best, Mantan Moreland, and Louis Armstrong, all at their incredible coon best. Rochester and Horne stopped the show with their "That Ole Debbil Consequence." And Ethel Waters, who had temper tantrums throughout the filming, was beautifully restrained. When she sang "Happiness Is a Thing Called Joe," the fantasy world of *Cabin in the Sky* vanished and the reality of a strong, heartfelt experience entered. "The main thing," wrote one reviewer, "is that Ethel Waters is on hand, for there are songs to be sung . . . and in that respect, she is incomparable."

Impressive as the cast was, *Time* magazine commented perceptively: "Like many star-filled pictures, this one never really shows off its crowded heavens. The Negroes are apparently regarded less as artists (despite their very high potential of artistry) than as picturesque, Sambo-style entertainers." As good as the performers are, they still seem locked in and artistically restrained by very old concepts.

In subject matter, *Cabin in the Sky* resembled earlier black films. Again Negroes were removed from the daily routine of real American life and placed in a remote idealized world. As in the past, the exotic features of black existence were played up. There was the familiar theme of the Good Colored Boy who leaves at home the Christian Good Woman to take up with the Bad Black Girl. The basic poverty in which the characters live was glossed over. So was the fact that Little Joe can neither read nor write.

Apparent as the distortions of *Cabin in the Sky* were, the picture received favorable notices. The *New York Post* commented: "It's a spirited and charming fable which Vincente Minnelli has directed with great gusto and delicious abandon." *The New York Times* said: "*Cabin in the Sky* is a beautiful entertainment . . . sparkling and completely satisfying . . . by turn an inspiring expression of a simple people's faith in the hereafter and a spicy slice of their zest for earthly pleasures." Apparently by 1943 this false image of American Negroes had been so thoroughly ingrained in the psyches of moviegoers that, had the movie been made straight, it would have been considered an unbelievable portrait of Negroes.

ABOVE: *Cabin in the Sky* (1943) and the eternal triangle in black musicals: Lena as the bad black girl; Eddie Anderson as the good colored guy; Ethel Waters as the long-suffering Christian woman. LEFT: Lena Horne and Fats Waller in *Stormy Weather* (1943).

Stormy Weather

Those Negro entertainers who did not appear in *Cabin in the Sky* had a second chance for glory in the all-black production of *Stormy Weather* (1943). Directed by Andrew Stone and released by Twentieth Century–Fox, the film was a thinly veiled dramatization of the life of Bill Robinson, who starred in it with Lena Horne. The cast also included the jazz musician Fats Waller, the comic Flournoy Miller, the Cotton Club singer Ada Brown, the anthropologically oriented Katherine Dunham dancers, the phenomenal hi-de-ho man, Cab Calloway, and two of the movies' truly extraordinary dancers, The Nicholas Brothers.

Stormy Weather was not the undiluted fantasy its predecessor had been, but it was not without its aura of unreality. The musical was a cavalcade, a revue of Negro entertainment from 1918 to 1943, seen through the eyes of its star, Robinson, and told in a series of entertainment sketches with Horne singing, Cab clowning, and Bojangles tapping. In between the musical shenanigans was the usual backstage drama in which two entertainers—Robinson and Horne—fall in love, break up, and then fall back in love again in an extravagant grand finale. The plot did not amount to much and was shamelessly illogical, but fortunately there were some good songs and some wonderfully diverting performances. Fats Waller and Ada Brown provided spicy renditions of "Ain't Misbehavin'" and "That Ain't Right." Dooley Wilson did not have a chance really to sing, but he proved thoroughly ingratiating as the quick-witted, smooth-talking Gabriel. Cab Calloway, splendidly arrayed in a zoot suit ten times too large for him and with hair falling onto his face, displayed appropriate razzmatazz. Bill Robinson, although far from being the great dancer he had been in his prime, hoofed with agility and precision in his riverboat sequence. Most spectacularly, the Nicholas Brothers, noted for their somersaults, flips, and twirls, actually spiraled beyond and around the movie, framing the film with their fierce energy. Their great style more than compensated for the movie's lack of substance. Finally, Lena Horne, so tightly controlled in her acting that she appeared to be the biggest black bourgeois phony the movies had ever seen, managed somehow to be perfect as Selina. In her important scene, when she sang the title song, "Stormy Weather," Lena Horne's beauty and melancholy brought depth to the lyrics. The song was a hit, went on to establish her reputation in Europe, and was ever afterwards associated with her.

Stormy Weather may not have been the best movie of the year, but audiences of 1943 would have wanted it to be no different. The film represented wartime escapist entertainment at its peak. Curiously, in its own naive way, it attempted also to break away from stereotyped situations and characterizations. Proudly announcing how the movie had avoided the use of the standard crapshooters and no-accounts, producer William Le Baron explained how one line of dialogue was eventually cut. When a character was asked where he got his new suit, his reply had been, "I won it in a crap game." This touch might now seem hopelessly naive, especially because

Stormy Weather was really no major departure from past movie depictions of African Americans as gentle folks. Still, by the very nature of its all-black cast, *Stormy Weather—and Cabin in the Sky*, too—was an exception to the rules of 1940s moviemaking. Each showcased the entertainer syndrome at its very best. In the South, where all-Negro films were usually shunned, these two reached the all-black movie houses, and black audiences greeted them enthusiastically. They were also shown at army camps (where Lena Horne was a great favorite) and abroad. Ironically, although neither was what Hollywood called a box-office success, each found an audience.

Bits and Pieces of Black Action

The entertainment syndrome endured a bit past the mid-1940s. Ultimately it wore itself thin and died. But before its demise, the syndrome had some sparkling and unforgettable moments when black faces appeared, parading their wares, showcasing their talents, and invigorating wartime films with some exciting black action.

The Nicholas Brothers, Harold and Fayard, captivated audiences with their stylized acrobatics and proved themselves the greatest dance team ever to work in American movies. They appeared in *Pie Pie Blackbird* (1933), *The Big Broadcast of 1936, Down Argentine Way* (1940), *Sun Valley Serenade* (1941) with Dorothy Dandridge, *The Great American Broadcast* (1941), *Orchestra Wives* (1942), *Carolina Blues* (1944), and Vincente Minnelli's *The Pirate* (1948). As they flipped and leap-frogged, even a casual observer could see that all dancers, including Fred Astaire, had picked up steps, routines, and distinctive rhythmic quirks from this unusual team.

Another distinctive black dance team that was to prove successful and influential was the Katherine Dunham company. The attractive founder and leader was an anthropologist and lecturer with a Ph.D. During her student days, Dunham had lived among isolated maroon people in Jamaica. She carefully analyzed their rituals and primitive dance rhythms, and later incorporated their movements into her choreography for dances done to swing music. The company was spotlighted in *Star-Spangled Rhythm* (1942)—in which Dunham and Rochester danced an extravagant tribal jitterbug. Dunham was the choreographer on several other Hollywood films, and in *Casbah* (1948) she played a dramatic role. After a brief hiatus from moviemaking, she returned in the 1950s to portray Silvana Mangano's dancing teacher in Robert Rossen's *Mambo* (1955). In the same era, her pupils Eartha Kitt and Marlon Brando made names on their own.

Still another interesting and offbeat performing group was the Hall Johnson Choir. Considered by many the greatest choral company in the country, this group had first sung its stoic spirituals in *The Green Pastures, Lost Horizon* (1937), and *Way Down South* (1939). In the 1940s they worked in *Swanee River* (1940), *Lady for a Night* (1941), and *Tales of Manhattan*.

The entertainment era's greatest dancers: the Nicholas Brothers.

Other 1940s products featured individual Negro performers. Duke Ellington appeared in *Reville with Beverly* (1943). *The Hit Parade of 1943* showcased Dorothy Dandridge with Count Basie's band, while *Pillow to Post* (1945) featured a lively duet between Dandridge and Louis Armstrong. Cab Calloway worked in *Sensations of 1945*. The same year Warner Brothers released a startling all-black jazz documentary *Jammin' the Blues*. Directed by Gjon Mili, this moody, well-textured short featured Marie Bryant (singing "On the Sunny Side of the Street" in a way in which it has never been sung since), Lester Young, and a host of other prominent jazz artists. Ben Carter, one of the most rigidly stereotyped and at times most embarrassing black actors to work in American movies, played the crusty old John-Henry in the Judy Garland musical *The Harvey Girls* (1946). Otto Preminger's *Centennial Summer* (1946) featured Broadway star Avon Long in an 1876 saloon number. Pearl Bailey made her motion-picture debut singing "Tired" in *Variety Girl* (1947). Later she appeared in *Isn't It Romantic* (1948). And *New Orleans* (1947) not only featured Louis Armstrong but also Billie Holiday who previously appeared in the short *Symphony in Black* (1935). Here, however, she played a maid. Yet when she sang, Billie Holiday was a lush, romantic ideal.

An independently produced, all-black, three-reel musical, *Ebony Parade* (1947), starred Count Basie, Cab Calloway, June Richmond, the Mills Brothers, and Dorothy Dandridge, then a newcomer. The picture was promoted by the black press, but it ended as a great disappointment. And the black community's hopes of cashing in on the entertainment vogue sweeping the country went down the drain. But there were consolations as more and more African Americans appeared in major industry productions.

All in all the entertainers were having a grand old time, but the quality of their work and their films seriously declined. Their overexposure and exploitation became obvious at the end of World War II. There were literally scores of other films with Negro dancers and singers, far too many, far too random, to permit specific discussion. It is hard, too, to pin down the exact time when the entertainment syndrome had had its day and had lost its appeal to the mass audience. But in many respects, a picture which spelled the ultimate end to the syndrome was Walt Disney's *Song of the South* in 1946. It provided a sad last look at the servant syndrome, too.

Song of the South

Stylistically, *Song of the South* was a great novelty. It was a live-action spectacle with clever animated sequences interspersed throughout. But its theme, that of the pastoral Old South, was familiar terrain. It took place on an Atlanta plantation where contented servants toiled joyously in magnificently photographed Technicolor work fields. Hattie McDaniel was the family mammy. James Baskette portrayed dear old Uncle Remus, a character glowing with sunshine and joy. In his spare time, Uncle Remus sings as animated bluebirds and butterflies whiz past. And his greatest delight is telling wondrous stories to the dear little white massa. Everything's just zip-a-dee-doo-dah.

Had the film been made in 1929, audiences might have excused it as merely naive and innocent. But in 1946 *Song of the South* was a corruptive piece of Old South propaganda put together to make money. Even the actors seemed weighed down, entrapped in the mud of the money minds who wanted none of the diversions or perversities that had distinguished the servants of the 1930s and the entertainers of the early 1940s. Instead they sought only a plasticized sense of order.

James Baskette, in the role Rex Ingram had turned down, presented Uncle Remus as the paragon of contentment and domesticity. His storytelling was skillful and slick. Yet the one virtue of the Joel Chandler Harris tales, on which the movie was based, was that, although they distorted the black plantation experience, at least they revealed the moral insights of Uncle Remus. His gift had been to transliterate the social framework of his own community into animal adventures. In the movie the animated Br'er Rabbit and Br'er Fox were a delight, an example of clever animation. But their escapades were a showcase for the Disney speciality rather than any comment on the old Negro character's philosophical outlook.

James Baskette was awarded a *special* Oscar for his performance, and *Song of the South* did yield its producers a profit. But the movie was criticized. The Manhattan Council of the National Negro Congress called on the people of Harlem to "run the picture out of the area," then out of New York State. The NAACP joined the criticism, insisting that the movie gave "an impression of an idyllic master-slave relationship which is a distortion of the fact."

Song of the South glaringly signaled the demise of the Negro as fanciful entertainer or comic servant. The towering eccentric billboard figures had at last been cut down to cheap comic book size. Neither the songs nor the servants had worked. Afterwards, Hollywood ignored them both.

The New Negroes: An Interim

Between the entertainers and the problem people, there was an interim period in American motion pictures, during which the New Negroes came into being. The New Negroes were an outgrowth of the social spirit of the day, and the following article from *The New York Times*, February 1943, indicates just how and why they came about.

Two major studios, Metro-Goldwyn-Mayer and Twentieth Century–Fox, in producing pictures with all-Negro casts, are following the desires of Washington in making such films at this time. Decisions to produce the pictures, it is stated, followed official expression that the Administration felt that its program for increased employment of Negro citizens in certain heretofore restricted fields of industry would be helped by a general distribution of important pictures in which Negroes played a major part.

The *Times* article underlined the new attitude that began to emerge during America's troubled war years. The nation had but recently recovered from a Depression that had unearthed social ills and injustices. Now the United States was threatened by the rise of fascism in Europe. Simultaneously, the nation was reminded by vocal civil rights groups of the bigotry and racial discrimination still operating in America's industries and even in its armed forces. At this time many Americans underwent their first pangs of guilt. Many people experienced a "liberal" urge to right old wrongs. Often the old wrongs were corrected in a patronizing or condescending manner, but significant social changes did come about. Pressured by A. Philip Randolph's proposed March on Washington in 1941, President Roosevelt issued Executive Order 8802, which forbade racial and religious discrimination in war industries. Under heavy criticism, the War Department had formed the first Army Air Corps squad for Negro cadets. Later the government pushed for integration in all areas. Soon the motion-picture industry, in tune with this new spirit, offered more movie roles to blacks. The new opportunities benefited the entertainers while paving the way for the emergence of sympathetic Negro character roles in feature films. Generally, these New Negro characters were used for social statements, and they often paid homage to the democratic way of life. In fact, however, the New Negroes were not entirely "new."

Sympathetic Negro characters had appeared in American movies before the 1940s, but there had been very few. The talkie era's first such character was the black Dr. Marchand in John Ford's *Arrowsmith* (1931). Played by Clarence Brooks, Marchand stood straight and confident as he introduced himself as a graduate of Howard University's Medical School. Surely this was the movies' first *professional* black character. Marchand became a hero when he helped star Ronald Colman fight the plague sweeping through the West Indies. He offered the white man the chance to experiment with a new serum on the island's black natives. "And if you succeed," said Marchand, "it will be a privilege for my people to have served the world." Few viewers forgot Brooks's characterization or his extraordinary self-containment.

One year later another sympathetic Negro made a brief appearance in Mervyn LeRoy's attack on penal institutions, *I Am a Fugitive from a Chain Gang* (1932). When hero Paul Muni escaped from the inhumane chain gang, he was aided by a massive Negro prisoner. Later director LeRoy employed another sympathetic black man in *They Won't Forget* (1937). In this film a Negro janitor, Tump Redwine

(Clinton Rosemond), discovers the body of a murdered white girl and is forced to undergo a brutal interrogation by the small town's racist police force. LeRoy used the janitor not only to point up racial injustices committed daily by ordinary folks but, because of the janitor's innocence, as a symbol of all the oppressed, exploited peoples of the world. In addition to *Arrowsmith* and the LeRoy features, the films of Paul Robeson throughout the 1930s had centered on "noble" black characters. But there were not enough of these sympathetic Negroes to constitute a trend. Nor were they representative of standard policy for the handling of black characters. In the early and middle 1940s, there were, in retrospect, not many more sympathetic black roles. But there were enough. And audiences noticed the intelligent, socially significant New Negroes who appeared in a number of important dramas.

The lanky and emaciated actor Leigh Whipper was cast in a trio of sympathetic New Negro roles. Lewis Milestone's *Of Mice and Men* (1940) found him as Crooks, the crippled, battered old man who aids the film's derelict heroes, George and Lennie. In William Wellman's *Ox-Bow Incident* (1943), Whipper portrayed the somber Negro preacher Sparks. The film dealt with three men wrongly accused of a crime and lynched for it by an unruly mob. Throughout the movie Whipper's weary, weathered Sparks stands up to the angry mob, pleading for mercy. In a curiously moving sequence just after the hanging, he falls on his knees singing, "You got to walk that lonesome valley. . . ." Later Whipper worked in scores of vintage 1940s movies, often portraying relatively dignified servants or farmhands. With the exception of his work as Haile Selassie in Michael Curtiz's *Mission to Moscow* (1943), none, however, was to be as successful or important as these first two early performances.

Another black actor to give an impressive performance in a serious role was newcomer Ernest Anderson. Featured with Bette Davis, George Brent, Olivia de Havilland, and Hattie McDaniel in John Huston's *In This Our Life* (1942), Anderson portrayed an intelligent young law student arrested on hit-and-run charges. He maintains his dignity despite much badgering, until the real driver—Bette Davis—admits her guilt. Anderson's performance and the film's racial theme proved the only commendable things in an otherwise dull and ordinary motion picture. "This last . . . is the one exceptional component of the film—this brief but frank allusion to racial discrimination," wrote critic Bosley Crowther. "And it is presented in a realistic manner uncommon to Hollywood by the depiction of the Negro as an educated and comprehending character. . . . Ernest Anderson is remarkably good as the Negro boy."

Note that the reviewer referred to him as a *boy*, not a *young man*. Good as Anderson was, his career was often a series of unbilled roles (or bits) in such movies as *Yankee Doodle Dandy* (1942), *The Palm Beach Story* (1942), *The Hoodlum Saint* (1946), and others in the late 1940s and 1950s. Always he carried his composure with him. His other important role came in the searing 1951 race drama *The Well*. Here he and Maidie Norman (another composed performer) portrayed the distraught parents of a missing five-year-old girl. Unknown to the parents and the townspeople in their racially mixed community, the child has fallen into a well. When rumors spread that the little black girl was last seen with a mysterious white stranger, the situation turns explosive as long festering racial divisions rise to the surface. When the girl is discovered and rescued alive from the well, the community has learned something about itself and its unacknowledged racial tensions. A low-budget film directed by Leo Popkin and Russell Rouse, *The Well* had a potent raw energy. Afterward, Ernest Anderson returned to small and again often uncredited roles in such films as *The Band Wagon* (1953), as the porter in *North by Northwest* (1959), and as the ice cream vendor in *What Ever Happened to Baby Jane?* Maidie Norman also appeared in the latter film as the sensitive housekeeper who tries to defend Joan Crawford's invalid character but who comes to a terrible end at the hands of the character played by Bette Davis. Ernest Anderson worked in television until 1978.

While *In This Our Life* presented the intelligent New Negro in civilian life, the 1943 films, *Bataan*, *Crash Dive*, and *Sahara* spotlighted the New Negro in the military. By 1941, Benjamin O. Davis had already been appointed brigadier general, becoming the first Negro general in the history of the United States armed forces. Consequently, by 1943 the film industry had no qualms about playing up black military heroism. *Bataan* featured Kenneth Spencer as a black demolitions expert. Not only does Spencer's Wesley Eeps lead the company's prayer services for their dead captain, but he later saves a white soldier from walking into enemy gunfire. Finally he dies heroically with the other men—all white—in his patrol. Similarly, the war film *Crash Dive* featured Ben Carter as Oliver Cromwell Jones, a character modeled on Dorie Miller, the Negro messman on the USS *Arizona* who manned a machine gun during the Pearl Harbor attack and downed four enemy planes. In the British import *Sahara* Rex Ingram was a magnificent Sudanese soldier, engendering audience affection as he heroically killed a Nazi and then sacrificed his own life in the name of the free world! And the government filmed *The Negro Soldier* (1944) and *The Negro Sailor* (1945), both hymns of praise for the wonderful work the nation's "colored boys" were contributing to the war effort.

Related to the military films but with far broader implications was Alfred Hitchcock's *Lifeboat* (1944). The film was about a group of Americans holed up in a battered lifeboat after their passenger freighter is torpedoed by the Germans. All the passengers symbolize specific elements in a full democratic society. A black steward, pensive and inarticulate, represents America's vast second-class citizenry. "Hey, Charcoal," the steward is greeted by Tallulah Bankhead. But when it is revealed that "Charcoal" has saved the life of a drowning white woman and her child, he becomes "Joe" and takes on heroic dimensions. The role was played with somber dignity and intelligence by Canada Lee, the Broadway actor previously acclaimed for his work in the Orson Welles production of *Native Son*.

From the Hitchcock picture, Canada Lee moved on to other sympathetic New Negro appearances. Robert Rossen's *Body and Soul* (1947) cast him again in the heroic mold when he portrayed a boxing champion, first defeated by a white man (John Garfield), then signed on as his former opponent's trainer, and ultimately revealed (like the faithful tom servants of old) as the new champ's only friend. *The New York Times* in reviewing the film said:

> It is Canada Lee who brings to focus the horrible pathos of the cruelly exploited prize-fighter. As a Negro ex-champion who is meanly shoved aside, until one night he finally dies slugging in a deserted ring, he shows through great dignity and reticence the full measure of his inarticulate scorn for the greed of shrewder men who have enslaved him, sapped his strength, and then tossed him out to die. The inclusion of this portrait is one of the finer things in the film.

Later in his career, Canada Lee appeared in *Lost Boundaries* (1949) and most memorably in *Cry, the Beloved Country* (1952). He remains one of those strange cinematic character presences who brought quiet strength and sensitivity to all their roles.

Possibly the most popular of the New Negroes was a shy little colored man who sat at a piano and sang "As Time Goes By" in Michael Curtiz's *Casablanca* (1942). The song became a national anthem for lovers and loners; the movie a box-office favorite, and the character Sam a byword for the friendly, congenial type of Negro everyone still cherished. Slick and smooth as actor Dooley Wilson was, his Sam was little more than an updated combination of faithful servant and entertainer. "Play it, Sam," Humphrey Bogart says, and Wilson goes into action. But the easygoing camaraderie between him and the film's star was without the normal racial barriers. It struck very close at what can only be termed the movies' *huckfinn fixation.*

The essential scenario for the exploration of the huckfinn fixation is quite simple: A good white man opposes the corruption and pretenses of the dominant white culture. In rejecting society, he (like Huck Finn) takes up with an outcast. The other man (like Nigger Jim) is a trusty black who never competes with the white man and who serves as a reliable ego padder. Traditionally, darkness and mystery have been attached to the American Negro, and it appears as if the white hero grows in stature from his association with the dusty black. Blacks seem to possess the soul the white man searches for. The huckfinn fixation, although treated superficially, had already run through the two film versions of the Twain classic in 1931 and 1939 (as it was to appear later—superficially again—in the 1960 version). It had popped up even in a typical 1930s product such as *Judge Priest*. Obviously, star Will Rogers could relax with servant Stepin Fetchit because the latter was not caught up in any phony social etiquette.

In *Casablanca* Bogart was the cynical, soured rebel, and it was appropriate that in rebelling against society's trumped-up phoniness, he should enjoy the friendship of a black man, someone equally undermined by the system. As the black man plays "As Time Goes By," Bogey is consumed by a sentimental longing for the past when the world seemed good and pure.

The huckfinn fixation perhaps represents the white liberal American's dream of lost innocence and freedom. To fit into society, one loses the "spirituality" the Negro is believed to thrive on. Regardless of its real meaning, the fixation made its way into other 1940s films. The screen adaptation of black novelist Frank Yerby's *Foxes of Harrow* (1947) starred Rex Harrison as a reckless, daredevil plantation owner who was most comfortable with his gambling cronies or his black slave, Achille (portrayed by former football star Kenny Washington). So close is Harrison to Achille that he wants the black man's son to become the personal manservant to his child. In a curiously bitter scene, Achille's wife, an African princess, drowns herself rather than live to see her child enslaved. In *Moonrise* (1948), Dane Clark as a young, restless community outcast, Danny, meets in the woods an old colored man, Mose (Rex Ingram). The two hunt, fish, hike, and live together until Mose discovers that Danny has killed a rich banker's son. He advises the white boy to go back and fight his outcast role. With such advice, Mose attempts giving the boy his manhood.

The huckfinn fixation, closely aligned to the master–servant syndrome yet with far deeper connotations, was represented in the 1950s with its great moments with Ethel Waters and Julie Harris in *The Member of the Wedding* (1952), with Sidney Poitier and John Cassavetes in *Edge of the City* (1957), with Poitier and Rock Hudson in *Something of Value* (1957), and with Frank Sinatra and Sammy Davis, Jr., in occasional scenes from their clan pictures. In the 1960s, the tradition was upheld by Poitier and Rod Steiger in *In the Heat of the Night* (1967) and by Arlo Guthrie and his black college friend in *Alice's Restaurant* (1969). Though the fixation was to attain its full complexity in these later films and was eventually to be incorporated into standard television social dramas (such as the "Mod Squad" series), it was first innocently played with in 1942 in *Casablanca*.

Curiously, the most eloquent of the New Negro sentiment appeared not in an American movie but in Roberto Rossellini's Italian film *Paisan* (1948). In one episode of the film a black G.I. and an Italian shoeshine boy meet on the streets of Naples during World War II. The lonely G.I. takes to the child, but the boy hopes merely to steal the soldier's shoes once he sleeps. As the two talk, the weary G.I. reminisces, boasting of life back home. But when he looks into little Francisco's eyes, the black man is shamed and admits his home is no more than a dirty shack in Mississippi. As he speaks, the similarities between bombed-out Italy and the poverty-stricken South become apparent, and both the shoeshine boy and the G.I. are revealed as victims of a war and a system. "Don't go to sleep," the child warns his new friend, "for I will have to steal your combat shoes." In spite of the warning, the

G.I. sleeps, and Francisco takes the shoes. The next day the soldier finds the child at his home place. But the black man is saddened by the horrible hopeless squalor and the boy's crippled grandfather. "Those are not my shoes," he says and drives off.

Paisan was followed by *The Quiet One* (1948), which had a commentary written by James Agee. It was a sensitive study of a lonely Negro boy, withdrawn and cynical, who is brought back through compassion and understanding. In a glowing review of the film, *The New York Times* wrote:

> Out of the tortured experiences of a 10-year-old Harlem Negro boy, cruelly rejected by his loved ones, . . . a new group of local filmmakers has fashioned a genuine masterpiece. His [director Sidney Meyers] handling of Donald Thompson, the Harlem youngster who plays the principal role, is a brilliant piece of directing, for he has got from this normal lad such attitudes and expressions as haunt the memory. In the shadows that drift across his countenance and in the very manner of his walk are mirrored the confusion and rebellion, the hope and relief of a tortured child.

Donald Thompson's fine performance remains one of the first intelligent treatments of the black child in American movies, a far cry from the pickaninny absurdities of Farina. A few years later another sensitive depiction of a black child was revealed in the work of young Philip Hepburn in *Bright Road* (1953), and in 1972 Kevin and Eric Hooks were to give effectively moving portrayals in *Sounder*. Today *Paisan* and *The Quiet One* stand out as perhaps the definitive statements on the New Negro. Others appeared in movies such as *The Lost Weekend* (1945), *Till the End of Time* (1946), and *Any Number Can Play* (1949), but the Agee and Rossellini vehicles sensitively characterized their black heroes without stress or strain.

The interim provided by the New Negroes was neither golden nor necessarily illuminating. Yet it was not without significance. For the New Negro characters demonstrated that blacks could be handled sympathetically without relying on the old types. Black characters could be made amusing or interesting without set "nigger" traits. Finally, it was apparent that this new kind of handling could contribute to the quality of serious and successful motion pictures. The New Negroes served as warm-up exercises, paving the way for the Negro as Leading Character, for the Negro Problem as Motion Picture Theme. After World War II, however, the New Negroes were not strong enough to meet the new audience demands.

The Problem People

The postwar movie audience of the late 1940s was prosperous but not very relaxed. World War II had further complicated American lives, bringing into sharp relief basic political and social issues. For audiences that still had the terrorism of Hitler and Mussolini fresh on their minds, the old-time war call for solidarity was not muffled or toned down but heightened. Indeed, the 1930s concept of "equitable treatment for all" was finally extended so that the *all* included America's black people, too.

In films, the postwar audience demanded recognizable problems and issues, particularly on racial matters. The random self-indulgence and idealization of the old all-black spectacles now seemed remote. They were too diverting, too entertaining, too reflective of a corruptly innocent time when Hollywood had no conscience. American moviegoers now wanted to be pounded over their heads with facts, with guts, with realism. And they were willing to accept controversy. Thus the tone of American movies underwent its first stage of radical change.

In 1947, while answering the demand for facts and guts, Hollywood simultaneously satisfied the masochistic cravings of the postwar audience with the release of *Crossfire* and *Gentleman's Agreement*. Each focused on a subject that had once been taboo: racial discrimination. Both condemned anti-Semitism in America. Audiences and critics responded to the films favorably and indicated they were ready for more. The movies could go a step farther. And so finally by 1949, the audience expectations and demands, their quirks, their insecurities, and their guilt feelings created more surely than anything else a cycle of penetrating motion pictures that investigated the race problem in America. The Negroes of the films had their color stamped indelibly upon them, and they suffered, struggled, bled, yet endured. But as Hollywood had it, they always won their battles.

Home of the Brave and the Postwar Good Sensitive Negro

Home of the Brave (1949) launched the cycle of problem pictures. Independently produced by a thirty-five-year-old fledgling moviemaker, Stanley Kramer, directed by Mark Robson, and written by Carl Foreman, the picture went against all the accepted theories of Hollywood moviemaking. It was made on a low budget. It featured Frank Lovejoy, Steve Brodie, Lloyd Bridges, Jeff Corey, and newcomer James Edwards, none big-name stars. The subject matter was offbeat. As a successful Broadway play, Arthur Laurents' *Home of the Brave* had had an anti-Semitic theme. Its hero was a young Jewish soldier. Producer Kramer shrewdly substituted a Negro character for the Jewish protagonist. At the time a few major studios had already announced plans for "Negro tolerance" projects, but their properties were far from completion. Well aware that the first Negro tolerance picture released would garner the most publicity and reap the largest profits, Kramer swore his crew and cast to secrecy. His movie was filmed under the title *High Noon* (later used for another Kramer hit). When it opened, it took the entire film industry and the country by surprise.

Home of the Brave described, in a series of flashbacks, the emotional breakdown of a young Negro private, Peter Moss. As he undergoes examination by a sympathetic medical captain, Moss unravels his tale, revealing a number of racial incidents he endured while on a special five-man mission to a Japanese-held island. Repeatedly excluded and harassed, Moss had cracked up under the pressure. In the psychiatric sessions, it is revealed, however, that it was not the island experience alone that led to the soldier's disintegration. It is the American way of racism that has always forced the Mosses of the world "outside the human race."

"I told you I heard something in the middle of the night once," Moss tells the psychiatrist. "Some drunk across the hall from my aunt's yelling: 'Throw out the dirty niggers!' That was us. But I just turned over and went back to sleep. I was used to it by then. Sure I was ten. That's old for a pickaninny." Later he adds, "I learned that if you're colored, you stink. You're not like other people. You're—you're alone. You're something strange, different . . . Well, you make us different, you rats."

Home of the Brave concluded on a conciliatory note. As Moss is about to leave the military hospital after his recovery, the easygoing white soldier Mingo approaches him. The war now over, Mingo offers to be a partner in a bar that Moss hopes to open. Genuinely touched, the Negro accepts, free of the past and equipped with a new philosophy. "I am different," he says. "Everybody's different. But so what! Because underneath we're all guys."

Today *Home of the Brave*'s optimistic ending may strike many as "rigged" and false. The ending lessens the impact of much that preceded it. Mingo's gesture is "noble" enough, yet it is believable only in the movies. There is even a tinge of white patronage because it is the white man offering his hand to the black man. No doubt *Home of the Brave* affected audiences in 1949 in the same way. But there was something decent about its optimism. No matter how much one rejects it intellectually (and the times would bear out this rejection), the bright ending had the type of fairy-tale idealism movie patrons thrived on. Audiences wanted to believe racial problems could be abolished if black and white simply took one another's hands, and here the movies reaffirmed that naive wish. Thus it was no great surprise that patrons left the picture content that everything would work out. Even for black audiences, comparing the film's dialogue to Louise Beavers' "Oh, honey chile, please don't send me away," Moss's words must have sounded like a black declaration of independence. In the end, *Home of the Brave* justified itself by meeting the requirements of its age.

The film was a solid commercial and critical success and was hailed as a Hollywood breakthrough in the presentation of racial discrimination as a central theme. *Time* magazine wrote: "[It] . . . has novelty, emotional wallop, and excitement that comes from wrestling with a real problem, rather than fencing with a cooked-up plot.... Even when it fumbles the statement of its message, the movie retains a sort of rough-and-ready strength." Surprisingly, even Southern movie critics liked the picture. *The Dallas Morning News* called it "brilliant," commenting that it "abashes the white man for both his habit of Negro prejudice and worse, his unconscious tactlessness." "Let no smug section of the nation think [the Negro Problem] is exclusively the South's baby," warned *The Memphis Commercial Appeal* in its review. "It belongs to us all." The movie played to full houses in major Southern cities such as Memphis, New Orleans, Chattanooga, Fort Worth, and Dallas.

Those connected with the film reaped the benefits. Producer Stanley Kramer became the high priest of the message-problem pictures of the 1950s and 1960s, spearheading with such films as *The Defiant Ones* (1958), *Pressure Point* (1962), and *Guess Who's Coming to Dinner* (1967). Mark Robson directed a series of successful melodramas. Carl Foreman emerged as a top scenarist. Black actor James Edwards went on to other starring roles. It looked as if he would become *the* black leading man in American movies of the 1950s. Unfortunately, Edwards' career was cut short just as it was beginning to flourish. James Edwards now remains one of those misplaced personages of the movies. He was a fine actor, but he was ahead of his time.

Born in Muncie, Indiana, Edwards studied speech and drama at Indiana and Northwestern universities, and served as a first lieutenant during World War II. He appeared in several Broadway productions before winning recognition as the hero of *Deep Are the Roots*, a long-running drama about a Southern household during the war years. He migrated to Hollywood and landed a role as a butler in *Manhandled* in 1944. There followed much later an important supporting role as the sensitive black prize fighter in Robert Wise's *The Set-Up* (1949). After *Home of the Brave*, he was cast in *The Steel Helmet* (1950) as a patriotic black American soldier, quick to defend America rationally and to put down the "Commies." In *Lights Out* (1952) he appeared as a blind soldier befriending a bigoted blind white military man. When the white soldier learns his friend is a black man, he is guilt-ridden and frustrated. All the stupid, foolish years in which he has accepted and promoted racial discrimination are suddenly brought into focus. At the end of the film, the white man has learned the meaning of tolerance and humanity from his black friend.

In these early films, Edwards presented a heightened portrait of the postwar American Negro. He is sensitive. He is intelligent. He is articulate. He is innately good. At times, he seems little more than a dressed-up tom. But as a prerogative reserved only for the postwar freed black man, he is capable of choosing to fight his white opponents (although often he chooses not to). Most important, though, Edwards' postwar Negro was the screen's first black hero (with the possible exception of Robeson) governed by a code of fundamental decency, courage, and compassion. Throughout his films, he stands tall and detached. He can easily pounce on his white friend, but his code of decency prohibits this move. Instead he waits patiently, ready to aid the white man when the time comes. Always he lies in wait for acceptance. The code first displayed by Edwards as well as his reasoned goodness and his middle-class qualities were later lifted almost intact to establish the Sidney Poitier star personality in the 1950s.

Impressive as Edwards' early performances were, he did not develop into a star. In the ambivalent late 1940s and the apathetic early 1950s, racial tolerance as a theme was fashionable but Negro actors were not. A nervousness and sexual ambiguity alienated him from white movie audiences. Sexy black men were never very popular in American motion pictures. In his features, Edwards was rendered sexless because he seldom had a love interest. Yet his sexuality was still evident—even in the way he walked. He smiled, not in the boyish or romantic way of a Sidney Poitier, but in a tentative and lewdly suggestive manner. Always his eyes looked straight ahead, burning with passion and resentment. His nerves seemed to be as taut and tense as his muscles. He was attractive and aggressive, and there was a distinctive nervous charge in his voice. He seemed dangerous. The very first of the Good Sensitive Postwar Negroes scared his public, and for that reason he was denied movie stardom.

Edwards' career underwent its great decline in the mid-1950s. Like Paul Robeson, he had refused to testify before the House Un-American Activities Committee, and his career suffered because of it. In 1952, he lost an important role in *Red Ball Express* to the up-and-coming—and safe—Sidney Poitier. His subsequent appearances in *The Member of the Wedding*, *The Caine Mutiny* (1954), *Innocents in Paris* (1955), *The Phenix City Story* (1955), *The Killing* (1956), *Battle Hymn* (1957), *Men in War* (1957), *African Manhunt* (1957), *Fraulein* (1958), *Tarzan's Fight for Life* (1958), *Pork Chop Hill* (1959), *The Manchurian Candidate* (1962), and *The Sandpiper* (1965) were decent supporting roles but seldom significant ones. His last appearance before his death in 1970 in *Patton* was entirely forgettable.

Lost Boundaries' Tragic Mulattoes

Louis de Rochemont's *Lost Boundaries* (1949) was the second of the problem pictures. Alfred L. Werker directed the film, which was based on a *Reader's Digest* true account of a New England Negro family that had lived as whites for twenty years. Producer de Rochemont took his crew and his cast of unknowns to Portsmouth, New Hampshire, where he shot on location, using community residents in small roles and bringing his film in on a shoestring budget of $600,000. Thus *Lost Boundaries* was made to seem starkly realistic with almost a documentary flavor.

The film struck at the deep-rooted prejudice of the American small town. When Scott Carter, a handsome light-skinned Negro doctor, is unable to find employment at Negro hospitals (where he is rejected because he looks too white) or white hospitals (where he is rejected because he admits to being a Negro), he moves with his fair-skinned wife to a staid New England community. There they merely stop telling people what they are. The Carters win the friendship and respect of their neighbors, quietly rear a son and daughter, and participate actively in community affairs. The years pass without incident. But ultimately Carter's great patriotism proves to be his undoing. He enlists in the Navy as a commissioned officer and is warmly accepted until a naval investigation uncovers his Negro heritage. "Failure to meet physical qualifications," is the Navy's explanation for his rejection. Suddenly, the past years are brought into the present. The Carters are compelled to "confess." "Why didn't you tell me I was Negro!" cries son Howie upon hearing the news. Thereafter he leaves home to search for his "cultural roots" on the streets of Harlem. Daughter Shelly remains confused. As for the good, principled people of the community, once they learn the awful truth they turn against their former friends. Not until a special sermon on tolerance is delivered by the town's white minister do the townspeople, shamefaced and guilt-ridden, extend their hands again to their friends.

Dramatically, *Lost Boundaries* was without the didacticism of *Home of the Brave*, and its events flowed more naturally. Its sequence of the troubled Howie wandering through a circus-style Harlem was melodramatic and overdone, but its quiet moments more than compensated. "They've been saying your folks are colored," says Shelly's boy friend, pleading as he speaks that she will tell him the rumors are untrue. "Are they saying *bad* things about us?" she asks in one of the finest moments of the film.

Lost Boundaries received glowing reviews. *Time* called it "not only a first-class social document, but also a profoundly moving film." Bosley Crowther commented in *The New York Times:* "One of the many bitter aspects of racism in our land—the in-between isolation of the Negro who tries to 'pass' as white—is exposed with extraordinary courage, understanding and dramatic power in the new film titled 'Lost Boundaries.' . . . Viewed as emotional entertainment, as social enlightenment or both, it is one of the most effective pictures that we are likely to have this year." In the South, reactions were diverse and divided. Although banned in Atlanta ("Contrary to the public good," said its movie censor), the picture met with success in Norfolk, Miami, Richmond, Houston, Louisville, Raleigh, San Antonio, and some twenty-five smaller Southern towns.

Despite its success, *Lost Boundaries* was weakened by its compromises. In 1949, the Carter family appeared to be a new "relevant" fixture on the screen. But actually its characters were the old-time tragic mulattoes. By dealing with such characters and such a remote problem as "passing," the movie, like most Hollywood productions, had created a dream situation, an isolated fantasy world no more real than those of the all-black musicals. And the film further compromised itself by

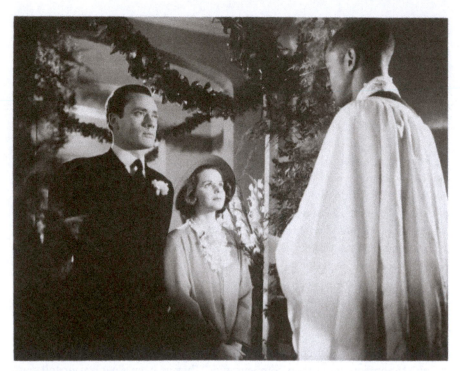

Mel Ferrer and Beatrice Pearson as the tragic, tragic mulattoes who marry and then leave the black community to pass for white in *Lost Boundaries* (1949).

James Edwards, Lloyd Bridges, and Frank Lovejoy in *Home of the Brave* (1949).

casting white actors in the leading roles of the suffering blacks. Here it fell in line with a long list of productions which cast whites in important Negro roles to insure audience identification and box-office success. The film versions of *Show Boat* in 1929 and 1936 had featured white actresses as the doomed mulatto Julie. (The 1951 version was to repeat the casting procedure; so, too, did the 1959 version of *Imitation of Life*, in which a Jewish actress portrayed the rebellious black daughter.) Likewise all the films about *Cleopatra* from Theda Bara's to Claudette Colbert's to Vivien Leigh's, right up to Elizabeth Taylor's in 1963, used lily-white actresses to portray the "dark queen of the Nile." *Lost Boundaries* was cast with whites for the same reasons its predecessors were. The idea underlying the deluxe gloss was how awful it is that these good white people should have their lives ruined simply because of Negro blood. White audiences could readily extend their sympathy to these fair-skinned blacks because, as played by Mel Ferrer and Beatrice Pearson, they were literally no different from themselves. The audience could not fail to spot the intolerance heaped upon them.

Lost Boundaries' final compromise was that while it quickly pointed up the hypocrisy of the white townspeople, it failed to hit at them with a wallop. The whites' viciousness was understated at a time when it should have been emphatic. The light-skinned Negroes appeared to have wronged the town by keeping such a secret, and the guilt was placed on their shoulders, making the blacks the tragic characters. Curiously, this and the other compromises of *Lost Boundaries* were repeated in the next problem picture.

Pinky's Tragic Mulatto and Its Strong Black Woman

In 1949 Twentieth Century–Fox contributed *Pinky* to the cycle of problem pictures. Produced by Darryl F. Zanuck and directed by Elia Kazan, it starred Jeanne Crain, Ethel Waters, and Ethel Barrymore with William Lundigan, Frederick O'Neal, and Nina Mae McKinney in supporting roles. The feature was a slickly put together product. Its clearly defined black and white photography, its carefully composed scenes and its theatrical sets aided director Kazan in fashioning an insulated unreal world. The movie shifted the emphasis to an area more closely associated with racial hostilities: the Deep South. It explored other new turf, too. Not only was *Pinky* the first feature to deal with an interracial romance, but in the grandiose performance of Ethel Waters it presented the archetypal strong-black-woman character.

The film's plot is straightforward. A fair-skinned Negro nurse, Pinky, revisits the South after having passed for white in the North. She is depressed by the life she returns to—the squalor of her home, the daily threats and insults. She is attacked by a knife-carrying black woman. Later she is arrested by the police, who have come to her defense only to turn against her once they learn she is not white. She is followed and chased by two drunken thugs. "She's the whitest dinge I ever seen," one says, laughing. Pinky plans to return north to her white fiancé and her life as a white woman in a free society. But her hard-working grandmother saddles her with an obligation to care for an old aristocratic white woman, Miss Em. The woman is now impoverished and near death, but her pride and arrogance epitomize to Pinky the South's racist code. The twist of the story is that while caring for this crusty old woman (Ethel Barrymore), the mulatto attains maturity and stature. "Nobody deserves respect as long as she pretends she's something she isn't," the woman tells her. And Pinky realizes that if she returns north and passes for white—something she isn't—she can never have self-respect. When Miss Em dies, leaving her decaying mansion to Pinky, the girl fights to keep the property. She painfully comes to understand responsibility and justice. "Tom, you can change your name," Pinky tells her white fiancé after winning her property suit. "I wonder if you can change what you are.... I'm a Negro. I can't forget it. I can't deny it.... You can't love without pride." She ends her romance, opting to remain in the South and work with her people. In the movie's final and memorable shot, Pinky stands before Miss Em's mansion, which is now converted into a black nursing clinic. She is content because she has pride in her race. Yet Pinky is aware that she has sacrificed personal happiness. And so, as is true of all tragic mulattoes, Pinky ends as a wiser woman but one not completely fulfilled.

As a motion picture *Pinky* also ended not completely fulfilled. The reviews were conflicting. *Newsweek* glowed: "Elia Kazan ... here does an admirable job of blending a courageous approach to racism and the strictly emotional factors of Pinky's personal history." But *The Daily Worker*, noting that Pinky "finds herself" through the aid of Miss Em, called the film a deception which insisted that "the solution to its [Negro] problems will come from the white ruling class and that they will be rewarded individually by the measure of simple goodness, not by organization or political struggle."

The Daily Worker pointed up but one of the compromises that diluted *Pinky's* power. There were others. In *Quality*, the novel by Cid Ricketts Sumner on which it was based, Pinky won her courtroom case, but the Ku Klux Klan burned down Miss Em's house in retaliation. That ending was far more honest than the optimistic everything's-gonna-work-out-fine tone at the film's end, when a group of cute ebony nurses are seen laughing in the converted hospital.

But the film's greatest compromise was casting white actress Jeanne Crain in the lead role. More than any other film in which a white has played a black role, *Pinky* typified the movie industry's methods of grasping audience identification. In a number of scenes, Ethel Waters as Granny, the typical Negro domestic, is shown washing, ironing, or performing other menial chores. No one expected any more from her, and audiences were neither surprised nor outraged by her behavior. But when Jeanne Crain's Pinky was forced to take in washing to earn money for her lawyer's fees—as she stood over a scrubbing board with the carefully placed studio sweat rolling off her perfect porcelain-white face—white audiences were automatically, shocked and manipulated so that they sympathized with this lovely white girl compelled to work like a "nigger." To Kazan's credit, that scene came across as intended, and by the time Jeanne Crain entered the courtroom, movie patrons of 1949 felt she had been through enough to earn winning the case. Likewise the insults and threats she underwent seemed twice as menacing because they were committed against a white actress. And by the same token, her "interracial" romance with actor William Lundigan upset no one because, in actuality, it was no such thing at all. (Still the pair were not permitted to marry.) Jeanne Crain as Pinky made a far more successful movie but a far less honest one, too.

Compromises aside, where *Pinky* shone through with brilliance was in Ethel Waters' moving portrayal of Granny. She is an old laundress, known to the townspeople as Aunt Dicey, who cannot even read. But she burns with humanity. In the Philip Dunne–Dudley Nichols screenplay the character was a combination tom and mammy, a further elaboration on Aunt Delilah of *Imitation of Life*. But Ethel Waters' great gift as an actress was that regardless of the script or character or the contrivance of the movie itself, she exhibited ambiguities and contradictions that seemed to come from her own personal experience. Unlike previous screen mammies, she was never emotionally one-sided, neither all Christian resignation (like Louise Beavers) nor all rage and indignation (like Hattie McDaniel). In *Pinky*, her great humanity bursts through as she is viewed washing the filth from the clothes of the town's whites in order to send money north to her granddaughter. Her humanity is further revealed as the single member of the town whose sympathy extends to the rich cranky white lady up in the Big House.

As she appears in the courtroom wearing an absurd black hat or as she sits on her rocker on the broken-down porch describing her feelings for the dead woman and expressing her gratitude for the clothes and shoes Miss Em has left her, Ethel Waters' character is not the old tom trying to ingratiate in order to save his position. Rather she is a strong woman concerned with all humanity and dedicated to her own sense of truth and loyalty. Yet her character is complex enough to reveal another side of her personality: she can explode and revel in righteous anger. When she learns that her granddaughter has passed for white, she commands that the girl immediately fall to her knees and repent. "That's a sin before God, and you know it.... Denying yourself like Peter denied Jesus. Get down. Ask the Lord to forgive you." Later she adds, "I worked hard to give you an education. If they done educated the heart out of you, then all I did was wrong. Now go up there to Miss Em or I'm going to whip the living daylights out of you!" To her credit as a remarkable actress, Ethel Waters played the scene as no other black actress could have done without ever seeming ludicrous, her voice so large and her strength so apparent that no one dared laugh at the lines. And thus she lifted her character from the pages of the script and

RIGHT: Black shoulders were made to cry on. So Jeanne Crain learns from Ethel Waters in *Pinky* (1949).

BELOW: *Intruder in the Dust* (1949) starred Juano Hernandez as the defiant, aristocratic Lucas Beauchamp. Hernandez's performance remains one of the strongest black male portraits in film history. At right, David Brian.

transformed Granny into a heroic figure. In *Pinky* she made the archetypal strong black woman a figure that transcended the stereotype of her role. So forceful was her presentation that she won an Academy Award nomination for best supporting actress of 1949. Her performance spelled the death of the one-sided mammy figure.

Intruder in the Dust and the Defiantly Proud Black Man

MGM brought a close to the 1940s' cycle of problem pictures in 1949 with Clarence Brown's adaptation of William Faulkner's *Intruder in the Dust*. Considered by many the finest of the quartet of problem dramas, the movie remains one of the more faithful and intelligent of the Faulkner screen adaptations. It also introduced actor Juano Hernandez, whose performance and extraordinary presence still rank above that of almost any other black actor to appear in an American movie.

Like the first two problem pictures, *Intruder in the Dust* strove for realistic effects. Director Brown made his film without the big-studio machinery to which he was accustomed, taking his cast and crew from Hollywood to Oxford, Mississippi, to shoot most of his movie. More than five hundred townspeople of Oxford, including some hundred and twenty blacks, gladly worked as extras. Brown's great pains paid off, for his film captured not only the character of one massively impressive black man but the character—savage and venomous—inherent in one "typical" small American town.

Intruder in the Dust was many things—a melodrama, a detective story, a murder mystery, a condemnation of mob rule. But mainly it was a subtle study of a fearless and proud black man, Lucas Beauchamp. When he is accused of killing a white man, the tensions of his Southern townspeople mount. "He won't need a lawyer. He won't even need an undertaker," an angry mob shouts. But Lucas Beauchamp is on trial for more than murder. For Beauchamp, confident, aristocratic, and "insufferable," is a black man who—through his independence—has dared to act like a white, and the townsmen want him cut down to size. Beauchamp turns to a teenage white boy, Chick. The summer before, during a hunting trip, Chick was saved from drowning by the black man, who literally lifted him from the sea, taking the boy to his home, offering him food and shelter. Because of the rigid racial-social codes of the South, the boy feels compelled to repay Lucas for the rescue. But the man refuses payment for an act of human compassion. Afterward the boy feels guilty. He owes something to a nigger. Now Lucas enlists Chick's aid, acting on an old Negro saying: If you want anything "out of the ordinary" accomplished, set women and children to working on it. Ultimately it is through Chick (the child) and an old spinster schoolteacher (the woman) that the out of the ordinary is accomplished, and Beauchamp is found innocent of the crime.

But most startling is the fact that not once does the black man bend. Not once does he stoop to prove he is as good as a white man. That's something only a man who does think he is inferior would do. And Lucas Beauchamp has no doubts about his equality. When it is revealed that Beauchamp has known the identity of the real murderer but kept it secret throughout his prison ordeal, he is asked by the white lawyer, "Why didn't you tell the truth when you were in jail?" "Would you have believed me?" Beauchamp replies bitterly. And the lawyer (as well as the townspeople) realizes, "He wasn't in trouble. *We* were in trouble."

Tough-minded and complex, *Intruder in the Dust* unearthed, among a number of things, a somber piece of Americana: a black man on trial has little chance for justice in our country, said the film, more than twenty years before such statements were fashionable. For the most part, the movie received excellent notices. Yet because it appeared at the end of the problem picture cycle it was overlooked and did not fare as well commercially as its predecessors. But *Intruder in the Dust* did bring well-deserved attention to its star, Juano Hernandez. Because of it he remains one of the great black male movie symbols. He might also qualify as another of our great black victims.

Hernandez came to the screen after a varied and sometimes hazardous career as a circus performer, vaudeville trouper, and radio actor. Born in 1901, he was the son of a Puerto Rican seaman. Self-educated and always self-assured, he spent a childhood in Brazil singing and performing acrobatics on the streets to raise pennies for food. Later he worked in a Cuban circus as a tumbler, strong man, acrobat, singer, and boxer. In America, he appeared in vaudeville. He worked in the chorus of the 1927 stage production of *Show Boat*, had engagements at the Cotton Club, and then scored in *Blackbirds*. But his biggest success came on radio, where for many years he was the only Negro actor consistently used for all kinds of roles. He portrayed everything from Mandrake the Magician to Benito Mussolini, Haile Selassie, and Chiang Kai-shek on the "Cavalcade of America" show.

Intruder in the Dust was Juano Hernandez's first major film. He proved to be its greatest asset and virtue. His physical presence, like Robeson's, was towering. With massive shoulders, large hypnotic eyes, and jawbones that looked as if they were chiseled from granite, he loomed larger than the film. In an early scene, director Brown shrewdly photographed him from his feet upward—from his massive boots to his iron-jawed face—so that the audience sensed the growing stature of the man. Hernandez played his character with skill and insolence. He strode through the film with a haughty arrogance that made him seem like a wise, many-faceted version of Hattie McDaniel. "The stance and magnificent integrity," wrote *The New York Times*, "that Mr. Hernandez displays in his carriage, his manner and expression, with never a flinch in his great self-command, is the bulwark of all the deep compassion and ironic comment in the film." Not surprisingly, when the Oscars and The New York Film Critics' Awards were passed out, Juano Hernandez was overlooked. But he did receive two foreign acting awards for his portrayal.

In Hollywood, Hernandez found steady employment, and his career showed great promise. The western *Stars in My Crown* (1950) featured him once more as a Negro falsely accused of murder. "And Juano Hernandez," wrote *Newsweek*, "again puts quiet dignity into his rendition of a colored man nearly hanged by some of his white neighbors." *Young Man with a Horn* (1950) co-starred him opposite Kirk Douglas as a sympathetic jazz musician. *The Breaking Point* (1950), a dramatization of Hemingway's *To Have and Have Not*, starred him as the tough and stanchly honest fishing-boat partner of the wayward John Garfield. When Garfield becomes involved with gangsters, the mighty Hernandez tells him he must go straight. "Juano Hernandez," wrote Bosley Crowther, "is quietly magnificent as Harry Morgan's helper and friend. As a matter of fact, the suggestion of comradeship and trust that is achieved through the character played by Mr. Hernandez, and the pathos created by his death, is not only a fine evidence of racial feeling, but it is one of the most moving factors in the film." The film's director, Michael Curtiz, added: "Hernandez is the 'new Negro' in our movies. Now we have a dignified, intelligent, *big* man." In 1955 he appeared in *Trial*, an explosive courtroom drama in which he portrayed a judge determined to give a Mexican boy a fair trial, and *Kiss Me Deadly*.

In all these early appearances, Juano Hernandez presented a compelling, invigorating figure. He was the single black actor in the movies who appeared not to fight the dominant culture, not to be buried under by it, not to have been scarred by it. Whereas James Edwards (and later Sidney Poitier) presented sensitive, easily bruised, slightly confused young men, Hernandez was always the confident, archly independent strong black man. Hernandez in films was usually the separatist, usually the withdrawn, proud individualist. He was perhaps the movies' Stokely Carmichael figure, arriving on the scene at a most unexpected time, proclaiming his own brand of black power, completely scornful of the petty rules of the white world.

Sadly, Hernandez seems to have lost out precisely because of his black assurance. An early Stokely Carmichael was not what audiences of the 1950s wanted to see in the movies. His career, as perhaps is now to be expected for a serious black actor, took a downward turn in the mid-1950s. In subsequent films, his roles were slight and vaporous, and audiences watched him floundering to invest his characters with significance. As the religiously fanatic father in *St. Louis Blues* (1958), he was much too good and involved for this B movie. Because of the mediocrity of most the other actors, Hernandez's talents seemed out of place. In *Something of Value* (1957), Sidney Poitier was the star, and Hernandez was reduced to the role of an African chieftain. When he appeared in a supporting role in *The Pawnbroker* (1965), critic Pauline Kael wrote: "The great old Juano Hernandez, as the man who wants to talk, gives the single most moving performance I saw in 1965." As a man whose spirit has visibly been crushed, a misplaced person seemingly coming from nowhere and then going back, mumbling and fumbling and pathetic and lost, Hernandez was nothing short of brilliant. But the performance failed to resurrect his career. In *The Reivers* (1969), as the black patriarch, Uncle Possum, his dignity was ever present, but the physical man had begun to decay. By the time of Sidney Poitier's *They Call Me MISTER Tibbs* (1970), Juano Hernandez, as a toothless morally decayed janitor, had become a joke to a new generation unaware that without his earlier work there perhaps would not have been a Poitier.

Juano Hernandez and the cycle of problem pictures appropriately ended the schizophrenic 1940s. As well as anything else happening in the arts—on the stage or in fiction or poetry or even politics—these movies indicated that America's racial problems could no longer be kept in the background. In many respects, the problem pictures set the tone and pace for the new films of the 1950s and early 1960s, and although the problem pictures themselves were compromised and in some ways as confused as their age, they signaled a coming of age of the racial theme in American motion pictures; ground for intelligent statements on the black experience in the movies had at long last been broken. Today they appear as the calm before the racial storm. But after them, never would the black character be so obviously exploited and demeaned as in the previous eras.

6 THE 1950s: BLACK STARS

Ethel Waters is stoic and reassuring as she sings "His Eye Is on the Sparrow," and suddenly, becomes—for a new generation—its great earth-mother figure. . . . Dorothy Dandridge, first as Carmen, then as Margot, later as Bess, acts her heart out, wins her Oscar nomination, and emerges on screen and off as the living embodiment of the tragic mulatto. . . . Sidney Poitier enters the era shyly as a young unknown in No Way Out, *only to close the decade as one of the most important leading men—black or white—in the movies. . . . Writer Richard Wright, baseball player Jackie Robinson, boxer Jersey Joe Walcott, tennis champ Althea Gibson, football player Woody Strode, trumpeter Louis Armstrong, crooner Nat "King" Cole, songstress Eartha Kitt, comedienne Pearl Bailey, jazz stylist Ella Fitzgerald, and calypso artist Harry Belafonte invade the movies and go "dramatic." . . . And problem pictures continue, alternately engaging and alienating their audiences.*

It was the 1950s, an era to be remembered as apathetic and sleepy-eyed, vulgar and hypocritical, grandiose, spectacular, and tasteless. Yet the Eisenhower age was one of change and turbulence, a decade that encompassed an array of incongruities: McCarthy in the Senate, troops in Korea, a Nobel Peace Prize for Ralph Bunche in Sweden, the National Guard in Cicero and Chicago, the Supreme Court Decision of 1954, Marian Anderson at the Met, Emmett Till lynched in Mississippi, bus boycotts (later bombings) in Montgomery, the rise of Martin Luther King, sit-ins in Oklahoma, federal troops in Arkansas.

The 1950s' social-political whirl penetrated the motion-picture industry, which like the rest of the country, had to undergo change. Already the industry had lost some of its best talents because of blacklisting. Slowly, too, the look of the American feature film was altered, no longer stamped with the big-studio gloss but marked now by the individual signature of the independent director or producer. Television sets had come into homes across the nation and when box-office attendance, after its great boom in the war years, tapered off drastically the film industry offered the giant wide screens—Cinerama, CinemaScope, VistaVision, 3-D—as a desperate means of holding the audience. Likewise the industry picked up bold themes in part to lure the television audience away from home and in part as a realistic reflection of the growing chaos in the streets of America and in the psyches of its citizens. Gone almost entirely was the magical, romantic, bigger-than-life daydream quality of the old movies as independent filmmakers brought to the public not only more problem pictures but "message" pictures, "serious" pictures, "thoughtful" pictures, "studious" pictures, and "controversial" pictures, all interchangeable but carrying different labels.

For black actors this era of silent change was important. The great gains of the late 1940s were continued in the 1950s with the emergence of distinct black personalities who, through their own idiosyncrasies, invigorated the Negro Lead Character and the Negro Theme. Almost immediately three diverse black personalities stood out prominently, and they were to remain so throughout the decade, making the greatest breakthrough for the black actor in American motion pictures. Sidney Poitier, Dorothy Dandridge, and Ethel Waters transformed the history of blacks in films from a study of pictures or parts or personalities to one of star dimensions.

As already seen, in the early days of moviemaking black actors were rigidly consigned to mythic types. Through the push and power of their personalities, some actors had created great pop figures. Everything in Hollywood was a game, they knew, and they did not expect to be taken very seriously. Movie audiences loved and laughed at these great comic strip characters. They left theaters having enjoyed themselves but with little reason to think twice about what they had seen. No one ever cared what Bill Robinson was really thinking as he danced up the staircases with Shirley Temple. Nor did anyone give a second thought to how Hattie McDaniel must have felt as she ripped the bandana from her head after a particularly humiliating scene.

Occasionally, with black actors such as Stepin Fetchit or Lena Horne or Paul Robeson, because their off-screen exploits paralleled their on-screen images and because they were publicized by their studios, audiences felt they had some insight into the person on celluloid. But still unlike the important white stars—such as Garbo and Gable—the old black actors were not monolithic figures. They did not symbolize disparate elements of their audience's personalities. They were not able to affect lives dramatically or touch on the mass imagination. Indeed, the moviegoing public was not yet prepared to be swept off its feet by the intrigues of a colored personality.

But in the 1950s Poitier, Dandridge, and Waters reached out and affected the imagination of the mass audience. Patrons believed in them. Often because of their private lives or because of a strongly rooted image, the trio overpowered the films in which they appeared. Moreover, in this strange psychoanalytic age when audiences started dissecting not only their own inner selves but those of their movies and movie stars as well, when patrons went to see black performers not for mere entertainment but for a comment on the black experience, these three performers became popular because of what they represented to moviegoers. Like all great stars, they were aesthetic beings in themselves. To contemplate Waters' humanity or Dandridge's beauty or Poitier's code of decency was worth the price of admission, and the three made a slight dent at the place Hollywood has traditionally cherished most: the box office.

Ethel Waters: Earth Mother for an Alienated Age

Ethel Waters was the first of the three to win mass audience approval. She had been around for a long time, and her life and career were a tale of disorder and much early sorrow. Growing up in Chester, Pennsylvania, she had stolen food to eat, run errands for whores, been a lookout for pimps and underworld figures. At thirteen she was married. At fourteen she was separated. At fifteen she was a chambermaid and laundress at a Philadelphia hotel where she earned $4.75 a week. Then almost miraculously she rose from poverty to international acclaim, first in the cellars and cafés where she was billed as "Sweet Mama Stringbean" and later on the stage in such successful productions as *Africana*, *Blackbirds of 1930*, *Rhapsody in Black*, *As Thousands Cheer*, *At Home Abroad*, *Mamba's Daughters*, and *Cabin in the* Sky.

Ethel Waters later reached a whole new audience with her impressive film work. But suddenly her spiraling career fell flat in the mid-1940s. Overwork, exhaustion, exploitation, and personal unhappiness had made her "difficult" and chronically suspicious of everyone. Her outbursts on the set of *Cabin in the Sky* remain a part of Hollywood legend. Subsequently there was a six-year period of unemployment in the film capital, and by 1948, when Darryl Zanuck asked her to test for Granny in *Pinky*, Ethel Waters was almost at the point of begging for a role. Her Granny was an old typed vehicle but she got mileage out of it, and her career swung back into full gear. Today, because of her appearances in such films as *Cairo* (1942), *Tales of Manhattan*, *Cabin in the Sky*, *Stage Door Canteen* (1943), and *Pinky*, many still think of Ethel Waters as an exclusively 1940s figure. It was during this period that, singlehanded, she brought a new style and substance to the time-worn mammy. But as significant a figure as she was in the 1940s, it was in the Eisenhower era, in the film version of Carson McCullers' play *The Member of the Wedding*, that she scored her greatest screen triumph and an overwhelming personal victory.

The Member of the Wedding was more than simply a movie. It was in two very important respects a motion-picture event. Foremost, it marked the first time a black actress was used to carry a major-studio white production. Secondly, the movie was another comeback for Ethel Waters. Her autobiography *His Eye Is on the Sparrow* had recently been published and was a best seller. In it, she told all the lurid details of her life—the fights, the lovers, the marriages, the career troubles. Curiously, instead of alienating her audience, the turbulent events in the autobiography convinced patrons that Ethel Waters, who had always portrayed long-suffering women, was indeed the characters she played. Moreover, audiences knew Ethel Waters had truly suffered. Now patrons rooted for her to succeed—to triumph. When *The Member of the Wedding* finally opened, audiences got just that.

The Stanley Kramer–Fred Zinnemann feature was a serious, oddly structured film for 1952 American moviegoers. It starred the original Broadway cast. It had little plot, and focused instead on the interactions of three outcasts: Frankie Adams (played by Julie Harris), a twelve-year-old motherless girl entering adolescence and wanting desperately to belong; John-Henry (Brandon de Wilde), Frankie's six-year-old sickly cousin-playmate; and the weathered and beaten family cook, Berenice. In the course of the film, Berenice is revealed as the guiding spirit in the children's solitary lives. She is cook, housekeeper, protectress, reprimander, adviser, and confidante. "Come on. Let us play a three-hand game of bridge," says Berenice as she and the children sit in the kitchen. "Play the King, John-Henry," she tells the boy when he is about to cheat at their bridge game. "You know you got to play the rules of the game." In these quiet or sometimes turbulent moments among the three, author Carson McCullers' great lyricism was apparent as much as her theme of human loneliness and alienation. "We go round trying one thing. Then another. Yet we're still caught," Berenice tells young Frankie. At another time, in her most moving monologue, she explains to the two children the fragmented blind alleys of her life. "He was the first man I ever loved. Therefore I had to go and copy myself forever after and what I did was to marry off little pieces of Ludi whenever I run across them. It was my misfortune that they all turned out to be the wrong pieces." She comforts the two and helps them grow from her experiences. She sings to them "His Eye Is on the Sparrow." The film is resolved with Frankie grown and over that aching period of adolescence. Berenice stands alone in the kitchen of the house. She is leaving to work elsewhere, and we understand that her talents as an earth mother, to nourish and comprehend, are needed in a new household.

The Member of the Wedding was a critical success, but reports of its strange plotlessness and unconventional characters scared off many viewers. Others found them baffling. But Ethel Waters, the actress and the human being, was praised by everyone, even by those who did not like the film. Berenice was a perfect role for her, and there were obvious parallels between the seamy, confused tragic life of the movie's heroine and the legends about the entertainer. In the film version of *The Member of the Wedding*, the role was so well written and the character so well etched that Waters at long last had the material for a bravura performance. In her

Even in the 1950s, black shoulders were still made to cry on. In *The Member of the Wedding* (1952) Julie Harris goes to Ethel Waters for comfort.

hands, every line, even a seemingly unadorned statement, was delivered with a warmth and irony that went beyond the script. "Can't bid," she said during the card game. "Never have a hand these days." "All my life I been wanting things I ain't been getting," she uttered plaintively. Ultimately, because *The Member of the Wedding*, with its skinny tomboy heroine and its pint-sized bespectacled leading man, was so unlike the typical Saturday evening movie fare, audiences tended to accept Ethel Waters and her life rather than the lives portrayed in the film. She emerged now as more than just a representative of the long-suffering, strong black woman. She was a great "serious" popular myth come true. For black audiences, Ethel Waters was the personification of the black spirit they believed had prevailed during the hard times of slavery, and they felt she brought dignity and wisdom to the race. For the mass white audience, Ethel Waters spoke to an inner spirit of a paranoid and emotionally paralyzed generation that longed for some sign of heroism. Movie stardom itself has often been based on a thin line between actress and myth, and with this performance Ethel Waters became a genuine movie star. Her personality, rather than her character or her movie, had grasped the public imagination, and thus the history of the Negro in American films gained a new perspective.

But if Ethel Waters altered black film history, she was perhaps the last to know about it. For in spite of her impressive performance, she curiously became in the mid-1950s a victim of audience indifference. From *The Member of the Wedding* she went on to important Broadway appearances. There was also the successful television series "Beulah." Then new troubles arose: income-tax evasion and other debts. Finally, her debts and problems mounted so high that she was forced to make an excruciatingly painful appearance on the television quiz show "Break the $250,000 Bank." The great actress stood before millions in their homes trying to win money to pay her taxes. Surprisingly, audiences took her plight in stride. There was neither outrage nor great sadness. In a frightening way, Ethel Waters' public sorrow and humiliation were considered fitting for the tough endurable mythic figure who had always shown America that she could prevail, even under the most trying situations. When her next film, *The Sound and the Fury* (1959), was released, Twentieth Century–Fox's publicity department announced that "everybody's favorite," indeed "America's favorite," Ethel Waters, was back. As Dilsey, the "indomitable skeleton," the part Faulkner himself might have written for her, Waters again acted the strong black woman in grand style. The movie at first looked promising, with a cast that included Yul Brynner, Joanne Woodward, and Margaret Leighton. But the actors floundered in one mess of a script, and Waters fought to stay afloat. It was her last film of the decade.

The 1950s ended with Ethel Waters having appeared in but two motion pictures. But for this anemic, insecure age, one scared of its own shadow and terrified of taking risks, she was an echo of the past. Ethel Waters seemed to be some noble part of our heritage that was quickly becoming extinct. In a period of mass uniformity, she was the individualist foolish enough to assert herself yet strong enough to pay for the consequences. In the end, her image—the myth she lived out—loomed larger than life over the decade. Through the 1950s into the early 1970s, Waters made occasional television appearances on such programs as "Route 66," "The Great Adventure," and "Owen Marshall," again playing the strong matriarchal heroine. In her later years, she appeared with Billy Graham's Crusades. In 1977, Waters died at age 80.

Dorothy Dandridge: Apotheosis of the Mulatto

Dorothy Dandridge was the second of the black stars. Before the apathetic Eisenhower age ended, she had infused it with her great intensity and risen as its most successful black leading lady. For a period that prided itself on appearances, hers was a startling presence. She was a great beauty. Her eyes were dark and vibrant, her hair long and silky, her features sharply defined. And she had the rich golden skin tone that had always fascinated movie audiences, black and white. Moreover, she was a distinctive personality, schizophrenic, maddening, euphoric, and self-destructive. Before her Nina Mae McKinney had displayed uncontrolled raunchiness. Fredi Washington had symbolized intellectualized despair, and Lena Horne had acquired a large following through her reserve and middle-class aloofness. On occasion, Dorothy Dandridge exhibited all the characteristics of her screen predecessors, but most important to her appeal was her fragility and her desperate determination to survive. In a way never before demonstrated by a black personality, she used her own incongruities and self-contradictions to capture and extend the mass imagination. Her life and career were vigorously reported on by the white and black press. At times she seemed to bask in her own publicity, and it was obvious that she took pains to create an image, to package it, and then to market it for mass consumption.

The irony that overshadowed Dorothy Dandridge's career was that although the image she marketed appeared to be contemporary and daring, at heart it was based on an old and classic type, the tragic mulatto. In her important films Dorothy Dandridge portrayed doomed, unfulfilled women. Nervous and vulnerable, they always battled with the duality of their personalities. As such, they answered the demands of their times. Dorothy Dandridge's characters brought to a dispirited nuclear age a razor-sharp sense of desperation that cut through the bleak monotony of the day. Eventually—and here lay the final irony—she may have been forced to live out a screen image that destroyed her.

Dorothy Dandridge: the 1950s' tragic mulatto.

Dorothy Dandridge came to films after a lengthy and arduous career as a stage entertainer. The daughter of a Cleveland minister and a comedienne-actress named Ruby, she performed as a child with her older sister Vivian in a vaudeville act billed as "The Wonder Kids." At fifteen she and Vivian along with another black girl appeared as the Dandridge Sisters, touring the country with the Jimmy Lunceford band. At sixteen, Dorothy Dandridge performed at the Cotton Club, where she met Harold Nicholas of the dancing Nicholas Brothers. She married him and bore him a daughter. Later the pair divorced. Throughout the 1940s, she worked in nightclubs as well as in a string of films such as *Lady from Louisiana* (1941), *Bahama Passage* (1942), *Drums of the Congo* (1942), *Ebony Parade*, and *The Hit Parade of 1943*.

In the early 1950s, a trio of low-budget movies in which she played "good girl" roles served as springboards for Dorothy Dandridge's rise. The first, *Tarzan's Peril* (1951), was typical jungle fare with one twist. In a crucial episode, Dandridge, as a kidnaped African princess, was tied to the stakes by a warlike tribal leader. As she lay with legs sprawled apart, heaving and turning to break loose, it was apparent that never before had the black woman been so erotically and obviously used as a sex object. From the way Lex Barker's Tarzan eyed the sumptuous Dandridge, it was obvious, too, that for once Tarzan's mind was not on Jane or Boy or Cheetah!

In Columbia's *The Harlem Globetrotters* (1951), Dandridge was cast as a sympathetic young wife trying to keep a decent husband from going bad. She had little more to do than look lovely. MGM's 1953 all-black *Bright Road*, followed, giving Dorothy Dandridge her first starring role. As a grade-school teacher working to reach an unhappy wayward student, she was cast opposite child actor Philip Hepburn and a shy newcomer named Harry Belafonte. Here she revealed a soft, radiant, melancholic quality. "Her work in MGM's *See How They Run* [the title was changed upon release] projects sultry Dorothy Dandridge into the enviable role of Hollywood's No. 1 female star," wrote *Ebony*. *Life* magazine also ran a special article on the film, spotlighting its leading lady. Thus by 1953, the momentum for Dandridge's career was well under way. Had she continued playing such nice-girl roles, her career might have been entirely lackluster. But Dorothy Dandridge learned early that there were better things ahead on the other side of virtue.

Carmen Jones was the celebrated movie that established her as the definitive tragic mulatto. It also contains the definitive Dandridge mulatto performance. The legend of how director Otto Preminger first decided to cast Dandridge for the lead in his film reads like a press agent's dream tale, but it appears to be true. Initially, Preminger had thought her too sleek and sophisticated for the role of a whore. But he underestimated the talent and determination of the actress. When it appeared as if she had lost the role altogether, Dorothy Dandridge completely redid her appearance and style. She taught herself a Southern dialect. She mastered wildly uninhibited body movements. She shrewdly exploited her own nervous tension. With her new image perfected, she tossed her hair about her head, made up her eyes darkly, dressed herself in a sheer low-cut blouse and a long, tight skirt, and then audaciously strutted into Preminger's office. Vivacious, sportive, alluring yet somehow haunted and vulnerable, Dorothy Dandridge was the living embodiment of the director's Carmen. The role was given to her.

Carmen Jones, released in 1954, was a lavish, highly publicized, and very successful all-black spectacle. If audiences truly yearned for relief from the tedium and routine of their lives, surely this was perfect pop entertainment. Based on Bizet's comic-strip opera Carmen, it cleverly transformed the opera's colorful Spanish cigarette girl into Carmen Jones, a sexy black factory worker in the South. Her foil is a Good Colored Boy, Joe, portrayed by Harry Belafonte. Carmen lures him into deserting the army, goes with him to a sleazy Chicago hotel where they evade the law, then deserts him for a prize fighter, and finally is strangled by him for her unfaithfulness.

The plot and the characters of Carmen Jones were pop creations, and the film relied on the stock situations: hair-pulling fights between black females, the inevitable barroom brawl, the exaggerated dialects, the animalistic passions and furies of the leads. Old-style kitsch, it was made impressive nonetheless by its director's exuberant style and its cast's great élan. Everyone seemed to be there to have a good time. Diahann Carroll had a small decorative role as one of Carmen's good-time girl friends. Olga James portrayed the submissive Cindy Lou. Brock Peters snarled gloriously as the villainous Sergeant Brown. Joe Adams as prize fighter Husky Miller was such an overtly sexual performer that audiences could understand why he never went far in films. White audiences still found sexually assertive black males hard to accept. Pearl Bailey was an open delight as she belted out a rousing "Beat Out That Rhythm on a Drum." Also in the glittering cabaret sequence, there were the great drummer Max Roach on the drums naturally; and the great dancers, (a young) Alvin Ailey and (with her ponytail intact) Carmen de Lavallade. But Dandridge's Carmen dominated the production. On the one hand, cool, calculating, and perfectly confident, on the other, reckless and insecure, she is animalistic and elemental. When pursued by Belafonte, she kicks, she screams, she claws, she bites, and at one point, she crawls on all fours. Belafonte must tie her hands and feet to prevent her from escaping. Here again Dorothy Dandridge was the jungle queen tied to the stakes. But her performance was curiously detached. Certainly, audiences knew that here was a woman who was acting. But the sheer theatricality, the relish she poured into her role, made audiences forget the incongruities of the plot and instead delight in Preminger's black fairy tale and this extravagant, high-strung bumblebee. "Looka here, baby," she seemed to say, "it ain't real, but I am!" Living in a social world controlled by men, her Carmen is constantly in opposition to the rules of that society. The film, however, ties her determination

Scenes from the 1950s' most lavish all-black musical, *Carmen Jones* (1954).
ABOVE: Joe Adams (left) and Harry Belafonte vie for the attentions of Dandridge.
BELOW: *Carmen Jones*'s three good-time gals are out for a night on the town: Pearl Bailey, Dandridge, and Diahann Carroll.

to make her own choices primarily to her sexuality. She chooses the men in her life the way men choose a woman. Yet always Carmen's freedom—her fundamental independence—is what concerns her most. In a key scene in a seedy hotel room, her lover played by Belafonte becomes possessive and tells her that he loves her and that gives him the right-----. But she cuts him off, saying it doesn't give him the right to own her; only one person does, she lets him know. "Me. Myself." She adds: "I might come back" as she walks out on him. For the Eisenhower era, it was a wholly startling sequence. It still is today. In the movies, African American women, more often than not, were not depicted in such a forceful, self-determining way. Of course, *Carmen Jones* punishes Dandridge's Carmen for her independence—when ultimately she is killed by her lover. But a statement has already been made on black female autonomy and self-empowerment.

"The range between the two parts [*Carmen Jones* and *Bright Road*] suggests that she is one of the outstanding dramatic actresses of the screen," wrote *Newsweek*. "Of all the divas of grand opera—from Emma Calvé of the 90s to Risë Stevens— who have decorated the title role of *Carmen* and have in turn been made famous by it, none was ever so decorative or will reach nationwide fame so quickly as the sultry young lady ... on *Life's* cover this week," wrote the editors of *Life* when Dorothy Dandridge became the first black ever to grace its cover.

Carmen Jones made Dandridge a star. Her performance earned her an Oscar nomination as best actress of the year. Although she lost the award to Grace Kelly, no black performer had ever before been nominated for a leading actor award. (Hattie McDaniel's award and Ethel Waters' nomination were for best supporting actress.) Afterward the first rushing whirl of publicity closed in on her. *Paris-Match* and *Ebony* ran cover stories on her. A score of other publications, from *Time* to *Confidential*, carried feature articles about her. Dorothy Dandridge was reported on, probed, studied, dissected, discussed, scrutinized, and surveyed. There were incredible rumors and stories about her that yet live on in Hollywood, tales about her retarded daughter, her "hidden" son, her white father, and, in keeping with the image gradually growing about her, of her white lovers. She was said to be involved with everyone in Hollywood from Tyrone Power to Otto Preminger to Peter Lawford to Michael Rennie to Abby Mann to Arthur Loew, Jr. What with the publicity and gossip, Dorothy Dandridge now seemed a star of the first magnitude.

But despite the great fanfare and recognition after her triumph in 1954, Dorothy Dandridge sadly discovered there was no place for her to go. Bigotry and bias still had their place in Hollywood. Very few film offers came her way. Those that did were little more than variations on Carmen. Always she was to be cast as exotic, self-destructive women.

Just such a character was Dandridge's Margot in Robert Rossen's *Island in the Sun* (1957). Here she was cast in the first of her interracial-love roles. Today some might think it totally unimportant that Dorothy Dandridge was the first black woman ever to be held in the arms of a white man in an American movie. Yet, because she was permitted to bring integrated love to the mass audience in an age about to erupt in chaos over the issue of integration, she remains a socially significant figure in this film. It was a testament to her importance as a star that Twentieth Century–Fox risked featuring her opposite white actor John Justin. But, significant as the move was, *Island in the Sun* was marred by compromises. Even its producer, Darryl F. Zanuck, has admitted not liking the finished film because of them. Because of its theme of miscegenation, *Island in the Sun* was controversial even during the shooting. Before its release, some theater owners (mostly Southern) threatened to boycott it. The South Carolina legislature even considered passing a bill to fine any movie house that showed the film $5000. That bill was never passed, but the threats had their effect. Cautious steps were taken to avoid too much controversy. In the movie, Dandridge and Justin held hands and danced together, but little else happened. "The one scene I objected to seriously was the one in the summerhouse where John confesses his love for me," Dandridge later said. "We had to fight to say the word *love.*" The studio also refused to let the two kiss. In the summerhouse scene, Dandridge's Margot seemed tense when asked about her background. Audiences associated that nervousness with the character rather than the actress. As patrons watched Dandridge and Justin dance together, surely they thought how lovely the pair looked and how happy they could have been if only the jittery beauty weren't *colored.* She had everything else going for her! Surprisingly as controversial as some thought the miscegenation theme to be, it attracted movie audiences. *Island in the Sun* was made for $2,250,000 and grossed $8 million.

That same audience reaction, however—pity for the poor racially "tainted" beauty on screen—seemed built into the subsequent Dandridge films *The Decks Ran Red* (1958), *Tamango* (1957), and *Malaga* (1960). The latter two were filmed abroad.

Like Paul Robeson, Dorothy Dandridge fled this country, hoping to find in Europe an opportunity to play diversified, untyped characters. But she too encountered only disillusionment and repeated compromises.

Tamango cast her as a mulatto slave loved by a white ship captain (Curt Jurgens). Two versions, one French, the other English, of all the love scenes were filmed. Then because of the interracial love theme no major American company would distribute the picture, and it failed. *The Decks Ran Red* fared a little better. In this tempestuous tale of a ship mutiny, Dandridge was surrounded by a trio of handsome white actors, James Mason, Stuart Whitman, and Broderick Crawford. As all three furtively undressed her with their eyes, it was apparent that had she not been black she would have ended up in the arms of one or the other before the picture's conclusion. In *Malaga*, Edmund Purdom and Trevor Howard were her leading men. As a woman torn between two loves, Dandridge was peculiarly remote and melancholy. So immersed was she in despondency that her performance at times

ABOVE: Dorothy Dandridge as the exotic slave in *Tamango* (1957) with Curt Jurgens cautiously eyeing her.
LEFT: *Porgy and Bess* (1959), the last of the era's extravagant all-black musicals, with Sammy Davis, Jr., Dandridge, and Sidney Poitier.

seemed separate from the rest of the movie. Here Dandridge was fully stripped of the fire and passion that dominated her Carmen. Instead she appeared at her most vulnerable. What weighed her down was not so much her character's dejection as her own. "No one knew what her nationality was to be in the picture," her manager, Earl Mills, later reported. "The problem as to whether Trevor Howard should kiss her on the screen was called ridiculous. This was Dorothy's most frustrating acting experience by far."

Curiously, the important aspect of her two European movies (as well as *Island in the Sun*) was that Dandridge was bringing her own personal disappointments and frustrations to her characters. Audiences responded to the sadness on screen as an outside force. Perhaps they told themselves that the reason Dorothy Dandridge—this exquisite black love goddess—was unfulfilled was because of that drop of Negro blood. It was wrecking her chances for fulfillment. And indeed, for Dorothy Dandridge, on screen and off, in the mass imagination, the tragic flaw was her color.

Dandridge's last important American film was *Porgy and Bess* in 1959. As Catfish Row's torrid Bess, she put her star qualities on brilliant display. Designer Irene Sharaff's long tight skirt and dark wide-brim hat made Dandridge a stunning creation. As she walked through the theatrical sets of the film, she was Dorothy Dandridge. Even star performers Pearl Bailey and Sammy Davis, Jr., failed to take the screen from her. Co-star Sidney Poitier was literally dwarfed. Again Dandridge portrayed the woman at odds with society, again the Bad Black Woman trying to go right, again the tragic heroine who ends up leaving the good Porgy to wander up No'th to Harlem with Sportin' Life. Dandridge gave a highly unusual interpretation of Bess, a less obviously sexual woman (she refuses to play Bess as a whore), a far more haunting one. The performance won her a Foreign Press Golden Globe Award nomination as best actress in a musical.

The rest of Dorothy Dandridge's career was a sad story. She appeared in but two more pictures. Producers and directors seemed unable to think of her in any terms but that of the exotic, doomed mulatto, and already by the late 1950s and early 1960s the mulatto figure was dated. There was talk of starring her in *Cleopatra*, but the plans fell through. Off-screen she was beset by a number of personal conflicts. In many respects, she epitomized the confused, unsatisfied movie star dominated by the publicity and life style that informed her screen image. She was openly seen with white actors. And the stories circulated that she was attracted to white men only. In the late 1950s her marriage to the silver-haired white restaurateur Jack Denison seemed to confirm suspicions that Dorothy Dandridge had fallen victim to acting out her screen life in private. But as both Dandridge's closest friend Geri Branton and also her sister Vivian were quick to say, she operated in a professional world that excluded black men. In 1962 her troubles were heightened when after her divorce from Denison she found herself bankrupt. There were no movie jobs, few club offers, and only occasional television appearances. Dorothy Dandridge found herself a has-been, an anachronism unwanted in a new Hollywood. Slowly, it was rumored, she drifted into alcohol, pills, and self-destructive love affairs. Then in 1965, at the age of forty-two, Dorothy Dandridge was found dead, the victim of an overdose of anti-depression pills.

Sidney Poitier: Hero for an Integrationist Age

Sidney Poitier was the 1950s' third black star. His career proved more substantial, professionally and personally, than those of his predecessors. Poitier came to the movies almost accidently. Born in Miami in 1927, of Bahamian parents, he was the youngest of eight children. He grew up in the Bahamas and also lived later in Miami before coming to New York in the 1940s. With no thought of a film career, he worked in New York at odd jobs as a dockhand, dishwasher, chicken plucker, and bus boy. One day while thumbing through New York's black newspaper *The New York Amsterdam News*, he stumbled on an ad for actors at the American Negro Theater. He auditioned—with disastrous results. But soon he became determined to be a successful actor. After minor stage roles and some road tours, Sidney Poitier came to films and just about took over.

Poitier's ascension to stardom in the mid-1950s was no accident. There were three important reasons why he succeeded and won an audience at a time when other black actors such as Hernandez and Edwards were losing out. Foremost was the fact that in this integrationist age Poitier was the model integrationist hero. In all his films he was educated and intelligent. He spoke proper English, dressed conservatively, and had the best of table manners. For the mass white audience, Sidney Poitier was a black man who had met their standards. His characters were tame; never did they act impulsively, nor were they threats to the system. They were amenable and pliant. And finally they were non-funky, almost sexless and sterile. In short, they were the perfect dream for white liberals anxious to have a colored man in for lunch or dinner.

Poitier was also acceptable for black audiences. He was the paragon of black middle-class values and virtues. American Negroes were still migrating north and were gradually increasing their political power. The rising middle classes and the power (limited as it might have seemed) of their money supported Poitier. Black America was still trying to meet white standards and ape white manners, and he became a hero for their cause. He was neither crude nor loud, and, most important, he did not carry any ghetto cultural baggage with him. No dialect. No shuffling. No African cultural past. And he was almost totally devoid of rhythm. In short, he was the complete antithesis of all the black buffoons who had appeared before in

American movies. This was one smart and refined young Negro, and middle-class America, both black and white, treasured him.

But the second reason for Poitier's ascension was that in many respects his characters were still the old type that America had always cherished. They were mild-mannered toms, throwbacks to the humanized Christian servants of the 1930s. When insulted or badgered, the Poitier character stood by and took it. He knew the white world meant him no real harm. He differed from the old servants only in that he was governed by a code of decency, duty, and moral intelligence. There were times in his films when he screamed out in rage at the injustices of a racist white society. But reason always dictated his actions, along with love for his fellow man. Most important, he did not use his goodness only as a means of saving a position. Past good Negroes in the movies, notably Bill Robinson, were usually concerned about pleasing the master in order not to be booted out of the Big House. But Poitier did not care about the Big House. Nor did his goodness issue from some blind spot of Christian faith (as with his screen "mother" Louise Beavers). He acted as he did because an overriding intelligence demanded that his characters be humane.

Finally, Poitier became a star because of his talent. He may have played the old tom dressed up with modern intelligence and reason, but he dignified the figure. Always on display was the actor's sensitivity and strength. One can trace in all the Poitier features of the 1950s the qualities that made him a national favorite. Interestingly, the evolution of the Poitier screen personality was swift. In his first film, *No Way Out* (1950), audiences saw all the qualities that would make Poitier characters so "laudable" for the rest of the decade.

Joseph Mankiewicz's *No Way Out* launched not only Poitier's career but the cycle of problem pictures in the 1950s. Literate and sophisticated, the movie spotlighted the race riots that had broken out after World War II, at the same time presenting a sensitive portrait of the educated Negro. The plot centers on a young Negro doctor, Luther Brooks, at a large metropolitan hospital. When two white hoodlums are wounded during an attempted robbery, Brooks tends the pair. One of the men dies. The other then accuses Brooks of murder. Thereafter the young doctor is embroiled in controversy, and he fights to prove his innocence. When the remaining white hoodlum organizes a group of racist friends to attack the ghetto area, the city verges on a major race riot. By a lucky stroke of Hollywood imagination, Brooks proves his innocence through an autopsy, and equilibrium returns to the city.

With its crisp and quick-witted dialogue, *No Way Out* to some degree captured the mood of postwar America and summed up its repressed racial hostilities. Likewise its Negro characters were walking exponents of the postwar black doctrines of racial integration and *overprove*. "You got 'em. All A's," the doctor's wife tells him. "No wonder you're tired. Even I'm a little tired. Cleaning up after parties.

ABOVE: In the tradition of the dying servant, the good Poitier character sacrifices himself for his white friend John Cassavetes in *Edge of the City* (1957).

BELOW: Later, Poitier performs a sacrifical act for his white friend Tony Curtis in *The Defiant Ones* (1958). Distorted as both pictures might now appear, they were crucial in the emergence of Sidney Poitier as a full-fledged star in the late 1950s.

Eating leftovers. One day off a week to be with my husband. To be a woman.... We've been a long time getting here. We're tired, but we're here, honey. We can be happy. We've got a right to be."

No Way Out garnered critical praise. *The New York Times* called it "a harsh, outspoken picture with implications that will keep you thinking about it long after leaving the theater." But strong, original, and honestly stated as the movie was, it failed to win a large audience. The public was already weary of the Negro-struggle film, perhaps because the struggles of previous cinematic Negroes such as the mulattoes Pinky and Carter had been so hokey and superficial. From its advertising campaign, *No Way Out* must have seemed only one more in the lot.

What distinguished the picture was Sidney Poitier. As Brooks, he had the archetypal modern integrationist tom role. He was a brilliant young doctor whose achievements—the all A's, the correct diagnosis—summed up the equal-by-being-superior philosophy. He was handsome. He stood straight, spoke well, and never trod on anybody's toes. He was a man who could be reasoned with. He and his wife represented the average middle-class black aspirants trying to make it. But he never made a move against the dominant white culture. Instead he nourished it. In one scene, after having been shot by the white hoodlum, Poitier struggles to save that man's life. In a purely Christian way, he forgives his opponent, saying: "Don't you think I'd like to put the rest of these bullets through his head? I can't . . . because I've got to live too. . . . He's sick. . . . He's crazy . . . but I can't kill a man just because he hates me." What red-blooded all-American white audiences in this Eisenhower age of normalcy could not have liked this self-sacrificing, all-giving black man? What integrationist-aspiring black audience would not be proud of this model of black respectability? Poitier was clearly a man for all races.

When one thinks of how much of Luther Brooks was to remain with actor Poitier, he is tempted to ask if scriptwriters Mankiewicz and Lesser Samuels should not be credited with creating the most important black actor in the history of American motion pictures. Obviously, what they did create was the character, the screen persona that Poitier was to popularize and capitalize on. In the early days, Poitier no more molded his image than did Stepin Fetchit; he lived out Hollywood's fantasies of the American black man.

The actor's second film was Zoltan Korda's 1952 adaptation of Alan Paton's South African drama, *Cry, the Beloved Country.* The feature starred Canada Lee as an old village priest journeying to Johannesburg in search of a son gone astray. In the city, where he is saddened by the poverty and filth and bewildered by the racism, he is aided in his search by a young priest played by Poitier. The movie made an ultimate plea for racial harmony and conciliation. Canada Lee had the finest role of his career. Poitier was a supporting player, but he brought good humor and a relaxed gregariousness to his priest. Moreover, the young Poitier was there to help a battered old man no one else in Johannesburg had the time for, and the humanity of his character (in keeping with his heroic code) merely added to the momentum of his career.

His next two films, *Red Ball Express* (1952) with Jeff Chandler and *Go, Man, Go* (1953) with the Harlem Globetrotters, cast Poitier in conventional bland supporting roles. *Red Ball Express*, a military adventure tale, did provide audiences with glimpses of one of Poitier's great prerogatives as a postwar freed black man, the emotional explosion. "Look, *boy*, where I come from you don't give orders. You take 'em," a racist soldier shouts when Poitier asks for a cup of coffee. But Poitier jumps upon him with passion and regains any lost dignity. Young black audiences loved him for it. Here at long last was a sane black man, free and strong enough to shout back to whitey.

Shouting back was very much a part of *The Blackboard Jungle* (1955). In this harrowing exposé of American high schools Poitier was costarred with Glenn Ford, Anne Francis, and Vic Morrow. He portrays Gregory Miller, an intelligent, complex student who fears that in the outside world there will be no place for a second-class citizen to take the lead. He hounds and torments white teacher Ford, who represents the oppressive system. He snarls, acts tough, and displays his virility more effectively than in any other film. "Come on! Go ahead! Hit me!" he yells to Ford. Here the disaffiliated young of the 1950s saw a man with a choice. He didn't have to take anything. Even before it was fashionable, he was bucking the corroding system. Yet at the same time, Poitier's Miller was an easily hurt, sensitive young man forced to live outside society. He was the classic loner of the 1950s, much like Marlon Brando and James Dean. And young audiences understood his loneliness, his confusion, and his entrapment because it was a comment on their own in the Eisenhower age. At *The Blackboard Jungle*'s conclusion, when he aids teacher Ford against a student with a switchblade, some of his earlier impact is diminished, but his code of decency is reaffirmed, and Poitier's Miller becomes a hero for young and old.

During the next four years Sidney Poitier worked in six motion pictures. In *Something of Value*, with Rock Hudson, *Band of Angels* (1957), with Clark Gable and Yvonne De Carlo, and *The Mark of the Hawk* (1958) with Eartha Kitt and Juano Hernandez, he was an unlikely amalgam of *The Blackboard Jungle*'s Gregory Miller and *No Way Out*'s Luther Brooks. Sullen, angry, quick-tempered, and headstrong, he rebelled in many of these films, occasionally playing a modernized version of the black brute. (In the movies, most black men politically militant or merely politically motivated are simplified by the scenarists into the unreasonable, animalistic brutes of old.) But always, as if to save Poitier's image and the scriptwriter's white supremacist neck, the features concluded with Poitier's goodness and humanity reasserted, and once more audiences discovered him to be on the side of the angels. In this four-year period, the archetypal Poitier roles—the two that remain among the finest in his gallery of characters—were as Tommy Tyler in *Edge of the City* (1957) and as Noah Cullen in *The Defiant Ones* (1958).

The David Susskind–Martin Ritt production *Edge of the City* was an adaptation by Robert Alan Aurthur of his own television drama "A Man Is Ten Feet Tall," in which Poitier had already appeared. The story is about two men, a white and a black. In a true gesture of integrationist harmony, railroad worker Tommy Tyler befriends a wayward and confused army deserter (John Cassavetes). The story has a twist because for once it was the black man extending his hand to the white. Poitier helps the white man find a job, and then as his greatest manifestation of friendship invites him home to meet his wife (Ruby Dee) and have dinner. A Christlike figure, he stands for conscience and humaneness. But he is destroyed by his kindness and loyalty. During an argument with a fellow white worker in which Poitier defends Cassavetes, a fight breaks out. Poitier is winning. But he begs his white opponent to quit. When he turns to walk away, the white man stabs him in the back. Poitier dies in Cassavetes' arms.

Poitier's role won him great favor with the critics. *The New York Herald Tribune* called his black man one of deceptive simplicity. "With his quick smile and exhilarating talk," wrote the reviewer, "he can cajole the boy out of deep gloom. With a joke he can stop an ugly fight before it begins. But underneath he is a man of serious faith and deep strength, and when it's time for him to listen sympathetically or to say something important, he is the finest kind of friend." After *Edge of the City*, no moviegoer in America had any doubts about Poitier's talents. Nor did any fail to see what he represented. He was fast becoming a national symbol of brotherly love.

Oddly, when viewed today, the incongruities and disparities ignored by the audience of 1957 are blatantly apparent. Poitier's character falls into the tradition of the dying slave content that he has well served the massa. His loyalty to the white Cassavetes destroys him just as much as the old slave's steadfastness kept him in shackles. In this case, writer Aurthur smooths over the black man's death by having the white Cassavetes hunt down the killer.

Curiously, *Edge of the City* also revealed Sidney Poitier as a colorless black. The dinner scene between Poitier, his wife, and their white friends is not an interracial summit meeting because there are no cultural gaps. Nor are there any cultural bridges to cross. All four are decent American citizens. Poitier also seems sexless in this movie. In previous features, scriptwriters were sure to keep Poitier's sexuality well hidden. He seldom had a serious movie romance. In those films in which he was married, it was generally to a sweet homebody type who seemed devoid of sexual passion. Mildred Joanne Smith played this part in *No Way Out*. In *Edge of the City* it was Ruby Dee. She now remains the model movie mate for Poitier. (They have appeared in five films together.) An intense and talented actress, Ruby Dee is known for deft performances as unfulfilled, timid, troubled women. Certainly in

Edge of the City, as she smiles sweetly at Poitier or proves how understanding and sensitive she is, audiences must have found the two a well-scrubbed sexless pair. One can understand why later militant patrons would view them both as sterile products of a decadent, materialistic Western culture. It should be noted that in one of their next films together, *A Raisin in the Sun* (1961), they effectively portrayed a couple with bedroom blues. Poitier's romantic apathy just about drives Dee up the wall in this film, and it is one reason why she wants to abort their expected child.

In the 1960s, Sidney Poitier's sexual neutralization became embarrassingly apparent, particularly when Hollywood provided romantic interest for him, albeit in a compromised manner. In *The Long Ships* (1964), when as a villainous Moor he kidnaps a beautiful white woman, he has been made to take a year's vow of celibacy. Therefore Poitier's sexual impulses remain safely suppressed. In *A Patch of Blue* (1965) he has a brief screen kiss with a blind white girl (Elizabeth Hartman). Everyone knows there is a romance developing between the two, but at the movie's end, rather than assert himself and bed the girl, he dutifully ships her off to a school for the blind. And in the notorious *Guess Who's Coming to Dinner* (1967) he wins the hand of a white girl in marriage, but they are a peculiarly unromantic couple who are seen kissing but once in the film, and the audience views this passionate event through a cabdriver's rear-view mirror. Later, in *They Call Me MISTER Tibbs*, Poitier was finally cast opposite a vibrant, overtly sexual black woman, Barbara McNair. But audiences were openly baffled at seeing this beauty made up (with hair neatly groomed and clothes nicely dull and "tasteful") to look like Ruby Dee! Poitier's sexuality was still a problem for Hollywood moviemakers, and the attempts to keep him cool were so obvious that he seemed ludicrous. In the 1950s, however, audiences accepted the neutrality and rather respected him for it.

The Defiant Ones was Sidney Poitier's most important film of the decade. In it he played Noah Cullen, a black convict handcuffed to a white (Tony Curtis) as the two escape the law. Neither man likes the other. But before the picture ends, something akin to love has developed. For, once they have been unchained, the good Poitier comes to the rescue of Curtis, not out of necessity but out of brotherly love. Again he sacrifices himself, this time not with his death but his freedom, all for the sake of his white friend. In this film, one of his biggest hits, Poitier alienated a certain segment of the audience. When he saved his honky brother, he was jeered at in ghetto theaters. Black audiences were consciously aware for the first time of the great tomism inherent in the Poitier character, indeed in the Poitier image. Yet to Poitier's credit, his power as an actor demanded that the role and the film be taken seriously. There are sequences of great sensitivity and power when Poitier's Noah discusses his life before prison. He received an Oscar nomination for best actor of the year.

Porgy and Bess was Poitier's last film of the 1950s. The movie portrayed blacks as the singing, dancing figures of old. Poitier accepted the role of Porgy only after much pressuring, and, although his performance was engaging, he seemed out of place. Here it was 1959. There was Martin Luther King. There were sit-ins, demonstrations, and boycotts. And what was America's black idol doing? There he stood singing, "I got plenty of nothin', and nothin's plenty for me."

In retrospect, it can be said that all the Poitier films of the 1950s were important and significant. Because they were all made to please a mass white audience at a time when the main topic of conversation was school desegregation, today their messages may seem rigged or naive. But they retain a certain raw-edged bite and vigor. Audiences still respond to the actor's sophistication and charm, to his range and distinctly heroic quality. In the 1960s, Hollywood belittled and dehumanized Poitier's great human spirit by making it vulgarly superhuman. He became SuperSidney the Superstar, and he was depicted as too faithful a servant, the famous Poitier code then a mask for bourgeois complacency and sterility. But in the 1950s his work shone brightly. For black and white Americans he was a marvelous reason for going to the movies. And whether an integrationist or a separatist age likes it or not, Sidney Poitier's movie characters in the 1950s singlehandedly made audiences believe things would work out, that they were worth working out. It was still just a beautiful dream, but often that's what great movies and careers are all about.

Black Odds and Ends

Although the major black films of the 1950s featured Dandridge or Poitier, the era could also boast of a few offbeat and intriguing black cinematic diversities. Film biographies of two black athletes and one black composer were ghetto favorites. And audiences also enjoyed watching some of the beautiful blunders made by nonactors—athletes, musicians, singers, comedians, and one highly respected novelist—in serious dramatic roles. Minor problem pictures appeared, and there were some new variations on the old tragic mulatto theme.

The dramatization of Richard Wright's *Native Son* (1951) was one of the era's earliest problem pictures and also one of its first casualties. For some ten years since its publication, *Native Son* had been black America's proudest literary achievement. The story of the rebellious and angry ghetto youth, Bigger Thomas, who finds his *raison d'être* in two violent crimes, deeply affected black people who could identify with his quest for identity. Wright's work had visual power and sweep, and the dialogue was tense and dramatic. The writer himself had long hoped to see his novel filmed. When no Hollywood company would finance the project, he went to foreign financiers. But *Native Son* proved a fiasco, ill conceived and technically poor. Wright had authored the screenplay, which faithfully followed the novel, but key scenes and character details were missing. Filmed in Argentina, the movie lacked the sense of place essential for its story. Audiences felt neither the oppressiveness of the system nor that of its setting, Chicago. The actors did not help matters. Jean Wallace was rather stiff as the white girl accidentally murdered by Bigger, while newcomer Gloria Madison was perhaps too fluid as the black girl, Bessie. *Native Son's* greatest liability was Richard Wright himself, who starred as the seventeen-year-old Bigger. At the time, Wright was fifty. Too old, too fat, too weary, too middle class, and too successful and sophisticated, Richard Wright was thoroughly implausible in the role of a tortured deprived youth. A disappointing remake of *Native Son* appeared in 1986 with Victor Love as Bigger.

Another nonactor who acted in the 1950s was Jackie Robinson. The Dodger's star baseball player portrayed himself in *The Jackie Robinson Story* (1950), an inexpensive and quickly produced movie tracing the ball player's slow, steady rise. The movie also had a slow, steady rise before its filming. When Robinson had testified against Paul Robeson before the House Un-American Activities Committee he endeared himself to red-troubled white America. No studio could have objected to filming a low-budget version of his life. Yet two studios turned the project down because the promoters of the picture refused to film the story with a white man teaching Robinson how to be a great ball player. Self-reliant Negro heroes were still unfashionable. *The Jackie Robinson Story* was finally filmed by Eagle-Lion Studios for about fifty thousand dollars. A throwback to the race-achievement pictures of the black independents, the movie was too busy making viewers appreciate the hero's "credits to the race" to let them relax and enjoy a good story. In the end, it lacked drama and direction, plodding along on its star's name. Still it is doubtful if anyone has forgotten Joel Fluellen's sensitive portrayal of Jackie's college-educated, Olympic-winning brother, who works as a street cleaner. Nor could anyone fail to be charmed by Ruby Dee's bright appearance as the dedicated wife. There was Louise Beavers, too, large and lonesome as the champ's hard-working ma. And, finally, there was Jackie Robinson as Jackie Robinson. "Mr. Robinson," wrote *The New York Times*, "doing that rare thing of playing himself in the picture's leading role, displays a calm assurance and composure that might be envied by many a Hollywood star." Although few patrons were as enthusiastic about Robinson's performance (many thought him wooden), almost everyone agreed that during the action shots on the diamond Jackie Robinson was nothing short of fantastic.

Boxer Joe Louis was the subject but not the star of *The Joe Louis Story* (1953), a chronicle that recaptured highlights of a two-decade career, opening in 1934 and ending with the bout with Marciano. The movie starred Coley Wallace as the champ. James Edwards (with head shaved clean) was cast as trainer Jack Blackburn, and Hilda Simms (the original Anna Lucasta of the stage) played Joe's wife.

Unfortunately, the picture failed to reach a large audience. But many a ghetto kid was to cherish it.

Jersey Joe Walcott, Althea Gibson, and Woody Strode were other athletes who went dramatic in the 1950s. Boxer Wolcott was appropriately cast as a fight trainer in *The Harder They Fall* (1956) with Humphrey Bogart. Tennis champ Gibson portrayed Constance Towers' maid in John Ford's Civil War epic *The Horse Soldiers* (1959). Controversy arose over Gibson's role; civil rights groups protested that it was a step backward and much too undignified for an Olympic champion to be cast as a servant. But the organization that should have complained was the Screen Actors Guild, for Althea Gibson was hardly anyone's idea of an actress.

Former Los Angeles Rams football player Woody Strode made the most successful transition from sports hero to movie personality. With his magnificent physique and spectacular style—quick eyes that flash and dart malevolently, gleaming white teeth fixed in a broad smile, and biceps and triceps that he was quick to flex—Strode became the movies most notable black muscleman, appearing in adventure stories and spectacles. *Androcles and the Lion* (1952) featured him as the lion in close-ups. On the television series "Mandrake the Magician," he appeared as the enormous Moroccan bodyguard of the comic-strip hero. Other Strode films of the 1950s included *The Gambler From Natchez* (1954), *The Ten Commandments* (1956), *Tarzan's Fight for Life* (1958), and *Pork Chop Hill.* With nothing to do but be blankly beautiful, Woody Strode always seemed but one more elegant period piece provided by an imaginative set designer.

Strode had his most serious (and best) role in John Ford's *Sergeant Rutledge* (1960). The film also marked an important step in the evolution of the racial consciousness of director Ford. Previously, Ford, in his depiction of blacks, had gone from one extreme to another. On one hand, his *Arrowsmith* had been startling and ahead of its time in its humane and sensitive depiction of the black Dr. Marchand. On the other hand, his films *Judge Priest* and *Steamboat 'Round the Bend* had followed the accepted notions of their time. Each had demeaned and exploited Stepin Fetchit. In 1949, after conflicts with Ethel Waters over her interpretation of the character Granny in *Pinky*, Ford had been taken off the picture by producer Darryl F. Zanuck. "It was a professional difference of opinion," Zanuck later said. "Ford's Negroes were like Aunt Jemima caricatures." Then in 1959 the director was criticized for his handling of Althea Gibson in *The Horse Soldiers.* But *Sergeant Rutledge* seemed an apology for all his past racial indiscretions, and he attempted to present the Negro as a dignified and noble figure. Unfortunately, the picture itself did not succeed in the way Ford might have wanted, and Woody Strode's performance was the only aspect of the movie fully appreciated by the critics. Here Strode portrayed a Negro soldier on trial for double murder and the rape of a white girl. "*Sergeant Rutledge* may not add up to Mr. Ford's finest hour," wrote *The New York Times'* reviewer, "but it certainly is Mr. Strode's." Throughout the film, as he is badgered and hounded, Strode maintains his integrity and his composure. At the film's conclusion his heroism is not only confirmed but his innocence is discovered too. Because of what most critics considered impressive work (seen today, Woody Strode comes across as very wooden), a whole new career appeared to be opening up for Woody Strode. But Ford's epic was an exception to the general run of movies Strode worked in. In subsequent films such as *Spartacus* (1960), *The Last Voyage* (1960), *The Sins of Rachel Cade* (1961), *Two Rode Together* (1961), *The Man Who Shot Liberty Valence* (1962), *The Professionals* (1967), and *Shalako* (1968), Woody Strode found himself again bare-chested with muscles bulging and teeth gleaming. Later he starred in *Black Jesus* (1971) and *Black Rodeo* (1972).

William Marshall was the 1950s' other physically overpowering black man. Although he was not an athlete, he looked like one; he stood six feet tall and weighed two hundred and twenty-five pounds. His appearance in *Lydia Bailey* in 1952 was memorable not so much because of his acting as due to his particular character. The movie was about Toussaint L'Ouverture's Haitian revolt at the end of the eighteenth century. Marshall was cast as a strong, and domineering islander. His costumes exposed and exploited his massive body. The studio sweat glistened on him. As he paraded his assortment of eight wives, it was apparent that here stood a man of prodigious strength and passionate desires. If audiences had any doubts about either the strength or the desires, they promptly forgot them when Marshall's character's name was revealed. He was called King Dick. Not too much irony or subtlety there. Clearly, William Marshall, like Woody Strode, was the 1950s version of the black buck. Marshall's other important role was as King Glycon in *Demetrius and the Gladiators* (1953). Later he appeared in *Something of Value* (1957), *The Boston Strangler* (1968), and a string of other films. With his deep Robesonesque voice and his powerful presence, he was always a pleasure to watch, even later as the star of the black-vampire film *Blacula* (1972).

The athletes-gone-dramatic were joined by the entertainers-gone-serious. In *The Strip* (1951) and *High Society* (1956), Louis Armstrong was bugle-blowing Louis. But in *Glory Alley* (1952), he portrayed Shadow Johnson, a good-humored bartender. Someone cracked that with this performance "de shadow done returned." Armstrong had a chance for some intensified tomming as he tried untangling the love problems of the film's stars, Ralph Meeker and Leslie Caron. But as could be expected, old Satchmo came off best in the musical interludes. *The New York Times* wrote: "Every now and then, Louis Armstrong sticks his broad, beaming face into the frame and sings or blasts a bit on his trumpet. That makes the only sense in the whole film." Armstrong was also the subject of the 1957 documentary *Satchmo the Great*. Edward R. Murrow and Fred Friendly produced the film, which followed Armstrong on a European tour and on a trip to Africa's Gold Coast.

Ella Fitzgerald, too, was better when she forgot her dramatics. In *Let No Man Write My Epitaph* (1959) she portrayed a washed-out drug-addicted blues singer. Somehow her bluesy life never seemed very blue, and Ella looked mighty healthy for such a sick chick. She was much more at home when she appeared as herself in *Pete Kelly's Blues* (1955) and *St. Louis Blues.*

Big-name singing stars who went dramatic with more flourish but just as little success were Nat "King" Cole and Eartha Kitt. For a time, it looked as if Cole would be promoted into a black leading man. When he sang background music in a number of 1950s films such as *The Blue Gardenia* (1953), *Small Town Girl* (1953), and *Istanbul* (1957), Cole epitomized black cool. But cast as a French Foreign Legionnaire in *China Gate* (1957) he played the part a little too hotly and lost his bearings.

Cole's big picture of the 1950s was the all-black *St. Louis Blues*, a highly fictionalized biography of the black jazz composer W. C. Handy. Here he was teamed with an array of talented black performers—Eartha Kitt, Cab Calloway, Pearl Bailey, Ruby Dee, Juano Hernandez, Mahalia Jackson, and Ella Fitzgerald. Modestly budgeted but heavily promoted by the black press, *St. Louis Blues* looked like a winner at first. Unfortunately, however, neither the film nor its cast came off very well. Mahalia Jackson used her powerful voice effectively and Pearl Bailey supplied some much-needed gusto, but they were not enough to save this routine, implausible melodrama. Worst of all, Cole proved the least interesting of all the cast. Thin and anemic and much too suave and courteous, Cole seemed out of place, and it was apparent that he lacked the strength and range to carry the picture. The following year he worked in *The Night of the Quarter Moon* (1959), but the studios lost all hope of transforming him into a leading man.

St. Louis Blues' other casualty was Eartha Kitt. On the stage, Eartha Kitt had been a marvel of wicked insouciance. Vain, naughty, obdurate, and teasing, she purred and pouted and won a vast following. Eartha Kitt epitomized the exotic black woman born to be pampered. The songstress had the polish and the playful wit and intelligence to make herself a highly prized sex object. For café society she represented the ultimate kept woman. Only a man with a large expense account could afford her. Only a man with a certain *savoir faire* could excite her. In films, however, Eartha Kitt proved much too distinctive and unusual to please the mass audience. In *New Faces of 1952*, she was an engaging novelty. Because patrons did not have to see a great deal of her, she was tolerated. But in her starring roles in *St. Louis Blues*, *The Mark of the Hawk*, and her most spectacular flop, the all-black *Anna Lucasta* (1958), she alienated her audience. She had been noted for her "cat" songs, but in these films she looked and sounded like a cat. A terribly affected and studied actress with too many self-conscious kinks and quirks and in need of a strong director to break down the defenses she had built up for herself, Eartha Kitt had an arch independence and what some saw as an underlying bitchiness that antagonized filmgoers. Easily intimidated audiences may have found her demonic and dangerous. In 1965, she returned to films after a lengthy absence for a rather solid performance in *Synanon*. But the picture failed, and Eartha Kitt went back to her nightclub appearances and her cat songs.

The two most successful entertainers-gone-dramatic were Pearl Bailey and Harry Belafonte. Yet neither was to live up quite to audience expectations. Both performed best before a live audience, where they could improvise or play on a mood or sustain a tone. Bailey's movie roles offered her greater flexibility than did those of Belafonte, and because her characters were such zany, uninhibited types she fared better.

In Pearl Bailey, moviegoers saw a brief return of the wisecracking, manipulative black woman Hattie McDaniel had popularized in the 1930s. As the good-time girl Frankie in *Carmen Jones*, as the audacious, clever maid Gussie in *That Certain Feeling* (1956), as the vivacious aunt in *St. Louis Blues*, and as the cynical Maria in *Porgy and Bess*, Pearl Bailey could be counted on to be sassy, sensible, and inventive. She was not taken in by sham, and never in her lifetime was anybody going to pull the wool over her eyes. Yet, independent and sure-footed as she was, Bailey was never pure cantankerous mammy. There was a streak of gentleness to her, and at times she was the cheerful aunt jemima who might rousingly speak her mind but who at heart meant no one any harm. Her distinguishing characteristic throughout her career was her astounding vivacity. Who could forget how she lifted *Porgy and Bess* from its idealized, insulated world? As the shrewd, perceptive Maria she presented audiences with a presence who could not abide idealization or falsification. If anything, her subdued performance helped uncover the shallowness and dishonesty of the stereotype figures that dominated the production. Pearl Bailey was genuine.

Pearl Bailey's most serious and offbeat role in the decade (a role in which the director Michael Anderson tried wedging her into the Ethel Waters nurturing strong-black-woman category) was as the boozed-out, Bessie Smith-type blues singer in *All the Fine Young Cannibals* (1960). She aids a young white musician (Robert Wagner) in his rise to jazz fame. The pair openly live together, but the script dishonestly tries to make their relationship platonic. Bailey was so blatantly miscast that audiences probably wished it were a platonic affair. She was too self-aware, too full of common sense and sheer curiosity to be credible as the self-pitying, self-destructive entertainer.

After *All the Fine Young Cannibals*, there was a long absence from the movies for Pearl Bailey. In between she made nightclub appearances and had great success on Broadway in *Hello, Dolly!* Later she was signed to star in her own television series, and then moviegoers saw her return to films for the role of Marge in *The Landlord* (1970). Pearl Bailey died at age 72 in 1990.

"From the top of his head right down to that white shirt, he's the most beautiful man I ever set eyes on," Diahann Carroll once said of Harry Belafonte. In the 1950s, those were the sentiments of American females, white and black. So handsome and slick a black dude was Belafonte that he seemed a born movie star, a natural new-style romantic hero. Hollywood capitalized on his looks and his sexuality, yet at the same time, in film after film, it appeared that the motion-picture industry feared them. Belafonte was usually cast in good-guy roles where his island-boy sensuality could be made safely antiseptic. And Belafonte himself lacked the gutsy style to break through the Mr. Clean roles and put forth the sexual raunchiness Hollywood secretly valued him for. Obviously, he fell into the black buck category. Even at that he could have been tolerable and at least a diversion from Poitier's noble tom characters. But if a black buck is not going to be daring or flashy or uninhibitedly sexy, then what good is he? That's just the question moviegoers asked themselves as they watched the even-tempered, mild-mannered Belafonte.

His first film, *Bright Road*, cast him as the understanding elementary school principal who pines for schoolteacher Dorothy Dandridge. But the film doesn't let him make his move, hardly a believable predicament for a handsome leading man. In *Carmen Jones*, Belafonte's Joe was obviously no match for the movie's spitfire heroine. His naiveté and antiseptic air were in keeping with the plot and the character, but Belafonte's own shortcomings as an actor were evident. Once audiences had looked over his face and body and after the camera had finished playing up to him, there was little else to engage the viewer. If anything, Harry Belafonte had proved that looks alone (without passion or humor) mean very little.

The political potboiler *Island in the Sun* (1957) provided the actor with his meatiest character. He played David Boyeur, a political upstart, an island boy turned radical, a man of strong political and possibly sexual drives. Not only does he take the election right out of the hands of the rich white candidate, but he woos and captivates an aristocratic white matron, Mavis. In the person of Belafonte, Boyeur is a decent, colored chap trying to do right. But politically and emotionally, he is too phlegmatic and sedate to be credible as a revolutionary. Nothing seems locked up within him. Even his voice lacks variety and strength. But worst, as Mavis's would-be lover, he seems—at first—to have a good come-on, but surely audiences wanted to accuse him of false advertising. All Mavis (and an expectant audience) got from this rebel-rouser was a lot of talk. Midway in the film, he also sings a work-song, which doesn't do much to strengthen the character either. It just slows things down. The two do drink out of the same coconut (but from different sides). It's Hollywood at its most compromised—a supposedly interracial romance without romance or physical contact. Although one could blame Boyeur's inhibition on the scriptwriters, Harry Belafonte as an actor failed to look either passionate or even remotely interested in white actress Joan Fontaine. Instead he seemed to stand by merely to pay homage to her as a white woman. As a result, no one cared much about the character. *Island in the Sun* did nothing to advance his film career.

In 1959 with *Odds Against Tomorrow* and *The World, the Flesh, and the Devil,* Harry Belafonte handled himself decently enough. But he still lacked conviction and humor. On the whole, his venture into motion pictures was a disappointment in the 1950s. Eleanor Roosevelt had said he could mesmerize audiences in concert halls, and on stage Belafonte did have a way of projecting oddly melancholy moods or strong gutsy rhythms. But in the movies he was strangely bland and innocuous. Surprisingly, just when everyone was about to write him off as an actor, he returned to the movies after an eleven-year absence. In *The Angel Levine* (1970) he gave a decent but uninspired performance. Then in *Buck and the Preacher*, Belafonte turned in a wonderfully developed and stylized performance as a Bible-totin', pistol-whippin', tooth-decaying, ornery backwoods preacher. No longer was he simply Mr. Beautiful Black America; now Belafonte had discovered in himself, at forty-four, a rough-and-ready, gutsy quality that delighted audiences. Later, Belafonte won the New York Film Critics Circle's Best Supporting Actor Award for his performance as a gangster in Robert Altman's *Kansas City* (1996). He also starred opposite John Travolta in the racial/political satire *White Man's Burden* (1995).

In the 1950s, the tragic mulatto seemed in for a massive resurrection, and a number of white actresses had opportunities to bemoan a mixed fate. The 1951 version of *Show Boat* featured Ava Gardner as the mulatto Julie. In *Band of Angels* Yvonne De Carlo portrayed a Kentucky-bred belle who is sold into slavery when it is learned her mother was a Negress! But because actress De Carlo is not black at all, the film's hero (Clark Gable) first buys her, then falls in love with her. If a movie mulatto is really white, her chances for happiness are usually better. In the World War II melodrama *Kings Go Forth* (1958) Natalie Wood portrayed a beautiful French girl pursued by infantrymen Tony Curtis and Frank Sinatra. When word leaks out that her father was an American Negro she is deserted by both men. She attempts suicide but recovers and in the end transforms her family's posh villa into a hostel for war orphans, those just as deprived of love as herself. Luckily, Natalie Wood is really white. Therefore Frank Sinatra can return (minus an arm lost in combat) to ask forgiveness—a broken man for a broken woman.

Natalie Wood was most blessed. Other heroines were not. Julie London had a horrendously rough time in *Night of the Quarter Moon* (1959). When she weds a wealthy San Francisco lad (John Drew Barrymore), Julie London informs him that she is a quadroon. No matter, he says. When the couple arrive in San Francisco, however, the young man's family does everything it can to dissolve the marriage. But Julie London's problems were nothing compared to those of the mulatto in *Raintree County* (1959). In this drama a Civil War Southern belle (Elizabeth Taylor) is driven to a frenzy because she *thinks* she is part Negro. First she is carted off to a mental institution; later she is found dead under the raintree. Of course, Taylor is revealed as being all white, but the movie shows how awful just the thought of black blood can be.

By far, the 1950s' greatest mulatto was the heroine Sarah Jane in Douglas Sirk's remake of *Imitation of Life* in 1959. Version two's Sarah Jane is no happier than the original's Peola. Nor is her mother Annie (Juanita Moore) any more content about her daughter's "affliction" than was Louise Beavers. Not only is Sarah Jane severely beaten by a white boy friend (stunned by the "discovery"), but she is so wretched that she drives herself to self-degradation by becoming a singer in a sleazy red-light district. The film concludes with her return to her dead mother, weeping over the casket and again causing a flood of tears in movie theaters. White actress Susan Kohner was a sinister but convincing Sarah Jane, and Juanita Moore, as Annie, gave a touching and now underrated performance that earned her an Academy Award nomination for best supporting actress. Unfortunately, Moore was later saddled with unchallenging roles in *Walk on the Wild Side* (1962), *The Singing Nun* (1966), *Rosie* (1967), *Uptight, Abby* (1974), and *Thomasine and Bushrod* (1974).

The remake of *Imitation of Life* was successful at the box office, revealing that audiences could still respond to the old corn. It also gave birth to a number of similar films in the early 1960s, most notably *I Passed for White* (1960). Here white actress Sonya Wilde portrays a fair-skinned Negro lass who migrates north, where, to no one's surprise, she passes for white. Everything seems fine as she settles down with a white husband. But then her child is born and in terror she screams to the nurse, "Is the baby black?" No, the baby is not black. But word is soon out that his mama is. And thus tragic consequences finally catch up with the doomed mulatto.

In a final look at the 1950s, *The Last Angry Man* (1959) should be mentioned. *The Last Angry Man* was mellow in subject matter or tone. An old-style sentimental problem picture about a kindly white doctor, it remains of interest chiefly because of Paul Muni's moving performance and the gallery of new black faces it introduced: Claudia McNeil, Cicely Tyson, Godfrey Cambridge, and Billy Dee Williams. Each was to go on to some critical or commercial success in subsequent decades.

The products and personalities of the Eisenhower age may now seem as ludicrous or irrelevant as those of earlier decades. But the era has to go on record as a self-consciously and self-righteously sincere period in which racial issues were confronted and dealt with in relatively honest terms, at least with as much integrity as the film industry was capable of giving. Films still ended happily, and if any black anger—such as that expressed in Poitier's emotional outbursts—popped up in movies, its impact was lessened by the picture's conclusion, when all difficulties and problems were resolved. Perhaps the tidying-up process was the major shortcoming of this decade's films. Movies such as *Edge of the City, Island in the Sun,* and *The Defiant Ones* failed to record black anger and anguish realistically.

They naively announced that integration would solve our problems. Other films such as *Carmen Jones*, *St. Louis Blues*, *Anna Lucasta*, and *Porgy and Bess* returned to idealized, fake black worlds.

By 1959 America was approaching a social upheaval, a new period in which racism would be revealed as a national sickness, in which the doctrine of integration would be uncovered as too simple an answer to so complex a situation, and in which the American black man would assert himself culturally to articulate the rage he had suppressed through the years. That great social and political change—and its impact on Hollywood films—would render obsolete much of the work of the black stars and personalities of the 1950s and would usher in a totally new type of black film and even a new type of black star.

7 THE 1960s: PROBLEM PEOPLE INTO MILITANTS

Sidney Poitier, Ruby Dee, Claudia McNeil, and Diana Sands star in A Raisin in the Sun *as a Chicago ghetto family cooped up in an inferno of a three-room apartment. . . . Shirley Knight is the Great White American Bitch and Al Freeman, Jr., is the Good Black Boy she leads to death in* Dutchman. *. . . De New South replaces de massa's ole plantation as Beah Richards, Robert Hooks, and Diahann Carroll whoop it up in* Hurry Sundown. *. . . An idealistic white girl arrives home in the affluent suburbs carrying Mr. Perfect Negro on her arm—who else but Sidney Poitier—as she announces* Guess Who's Coming to Dinner. *. . . Jim Brown makes his way through westerns, prison yarns, and adventure tales to become a box-office favorite and a challenger to the old way of black movie herodom . . . Raymond St. Jacques leads a conclave of black revolutionaries armed with guns and slogans in* Uptight. *. . . Ossie Davis and Dionne Warwick are the stoic slaves who take over the Big House in* Slaves. *. . . The Learning Tree spotlights a young black boy growing up in Kansas in the 1920s and dramatically confronting the violence and self-destructiveness that are a part of this period. . . .* Putney Swope *showcases a troupe of high-flung, far-out jive-ass niggers storming through an advertising agency and out to get whitey.*

Turbulent, guarded, and paranoid—that was the steaming 1960s when the streets and then the screens exploded with anger and insolence. The nature of the times catapulted the movies' problem people of old into militants of new. No longer were sad-eyed black people trying to prove their worth in order to fit into white worlds. No longer were submissive, patient Negroes pleading for acceptance. Instead, the headstrong militants appeared. Black hearts were still broken, and black lives were still ruined. But with the militants, black rage, black anger, and black power began their maddening stomp, overturning the old placid way and lifting eyebrows as they introduced to America the deep-seated bitterness so long ignored.

Politically, the 1960s may prove the most important decade in the twentieth century for black Americans. An era of great change, the beginning of a transition period of which we have yet to see the end, it started with sit-ins, boycotts, and marches and ended with riots, demonstrations, and a series of horrifying assassinations. In 1960, Negroes were quietly asking for their rights. By 1969, blacks were demanding them. The decade moved from the traditional goal of cultural and academic assimilation to one of almost absolute separatism and the evolution of a black cultural aesthetic.

The movies of the period reflected the great transition. They were a mixture of old and new. It was almost exclusively a period of so-called significant films rather than great personalities. Sidney Poitier was still the top black box-office draw in the country, but at times even his movies overpowered him as a performer. For the most part, his features dealt with familiar aspects of integration and succeeded critically and commercially. Yet they seemed out of place in this separatist age, and they found competition from a number of motion pictures removed from the mainstream of American moviemaking. These films, in which the evolving militants were first to appear, presented a world heretofore ignored on the American screen—ghettos, whores, hustlers, addicts, pimps, and pushers, a world of racist sickness, of oppression, of black despair and rage. These new movies studied poverty, interracial marriages, the state of being black and finding fulfillment in the narrow confines determined by a hostile white world. As the era progressed—and as social pressures mounted—the first steps in the evolution of a new black film began with the appearance of black scriptwriters, providing films with startling dialogue and realistic characters. Later the evolution was just about completed with the appearance of America's first major black movie director. Ultimately, the new black film advanced in two directions. One approach was serious, lyrical, and poetic. The other was farcical, high-spirited, and flashy.

Steps Forward

Take a Giant Step (1960), an amalgam of old and new, launched the new decade. Rock 'n' roll singer Johnny Nash starred as a black boy approaching manhood, full of unanswered questions and stifled by the white environment in which he must function. Ruby Dee made an offbeat appearance as a housekeeper who helps Johnny out with some of his questions about sex. Appearing as Johnny's middle-class mother was Beah Richards. Frederick O'Neal portrayed the singer's father. O'Neal had already appeared in a number of stage productions and had worked in *Pinky*, *Something of Value*, and *Anna Lucasta*. Later he became a figure in theatrical history when he was elected the first black president of Actors' Equity. *Take a Giant Step* had little in the way of performances or direction to distinguish it. Its chief virtue was that black playwright Louis Peterson had adapted the movie from his successful off-Broadway play. Black screenwriters were a rarity in Hollywood. One only regrets that Peterson's venture did not fare better.

The film adaptation of Lorraine Hansberry's *A Raisin in the Sun* (1961) proved more successful. Directed by Daniel Petrie and produced by David Susskind, the film was a disorganized integrationist drama. Still it contained enough unusual twists and insights to move audiences. Set in a tiny Southside Chicago apartment, *A Raisin in the Sun* examined the Younger family. For years, matriarch Lena Younger has dreamed of getting out of the flat she shares with her son Walter, his wife Ruth, their child Travis, and her daughter Beneatha. Her deliverance comes in the form of a ten-thousand-dollar insurance policy left to her by her husband. With the money, Lena Younger will buy a house in the integrated suburbs. As she makes her plans and dreams her dream, the personal problems of each member of the household clash with those of the others. Author Hansberry captured the tension of blacks enduring lives of violent desperation, and she hit with unerring exactness on a number of things never dealt with before in the movies. Her drama took the average filmgoer into the grime and grit of the ghetto. It exposed the matriarchal set-up in black homes and examined the emasculation of the black male by a hostile white society. Hansberry framed her work with the gentle humor and wisdom a race of people had developed out of their heartache and anguish. *A Raisin in the Sun*'s message may seem dated today, but even though the film celebrated integration and ultimately paid homage to the America of free enterprise and materialism, it mirrored a timeless sense of oppression and despair, and it contained performances that, if at times overblown, were often rich and effective.

As the restless, wayward son Walter, Sidney Poitier gave one of his most exciting performances, heightened because his character was so different from the established Poitier image. "I open and close car doors all day long. I drive a man around in his limousine and I say, 'Yes, sir,'" he cried. "Mama, that ain't no kind of a job . . . that ain't nothing at all." His Walter was a deeply troubled man with whom black audiences could identify.

Newcomer Diana Sands portrayed the uninhibited, intellectual sister Beneatha. Hers was a witty and winning characterization. As she screamed out in comic-pathetic rage that there was no God, she revealed herself as a magnetic, compelling actress. Diana Sands ushered in the contemporary, untyped intelligent black woman. She was neither mammy nor mulatto. After *A Raisin in the Sun* she made an appearance in an entirely forgettable film titled *An Affair of the Skin* (1963). But later she was very successful in such stage productions as *The Owl and the Pussycat*, *Blues for Mr. Charlie*, and *Phaedra*. She returned to films in the 1970s with a sensitive performance as the black girl made pregnant by the white boy in *The Landlord* (1970). Somber, slightly hoarse, near tears but not about to break down, Diana Sands managed, amid heavy dramatics, to impart a comic, lighthearted side

RIGHT: In 1951 Jackie Robinson temporarily left the baseball field for the movies, but he didn't forget to carry his glove along with him. Here he appears with Ruby Dee in *The Jackie Robinson Story*.

BELOW: The grime and grit of the ghetto as never seen before: *A Raisin in the Sun* (1961), with Sidney Poitier, Ruby Dee, Claudia McNeil, and Diana Sands.

to her character. Even in the sudsy, exploitative soap opera *Doctors' Wives* (1971), she gave a clever, adroit performance, proving that talent could transcend material. No doubt her most intriguing screen role was in the bizarre, uneven *Georgia, Georgia* in 1972. Sands also appeared in *Willie Dynamite* (1973) and *Honeybaby, Honeybaby* (1974). In 1973, shortly after she began work on what might have been her most successful film—the title role in Claudine—Sands was stricken with cancer and was replaced by Diahann Carroll. Diana Sands died at age 39 in 1973.

Generally, Claudia McNeil received glowing notices for her work in *A Raisin in the Sun*. *Time* magazine did cattily remark, however, that she often came across "like a mean old man in a wig." And it has to be admitted that the news magazine had its point. Seen today, McNeil seems grossly like the mammy of Hattie McDaniel vintage, but without the humor and spontaneity. She had the power but not the pathos required, and her work was most effective when she was hooting, yelling, and reprimanding.

Surprisingly, the one performance in *A Raisin in the Sun* that retains its full intensity is Ruby Dee's Ruth. As the wife who agonizes over cleaning someone else's home and then returns to find she has none of her own, Ruby Dee proved successful with a difficult character. She also showed that if given the chance she could do complex and delicately shaded work. Before *A Raisin in the Sun*, Ruby Dee had run through the perfect wife-girl-friend bit to the point where she was—as one newspaper called her—"the Negro June Allyson." In films such as *No Way Out; The Jackie Robinson Story; Go, Man, Go; Edge of the City; Virgin Island* (1960); and *Take a Giant Step*, she was either pleasantly understanding or sincerely forgiving. Although she occasionally rose above her material—her breakdown after Poitier's death in *Edge of the City* was extremely powerful—even in her good work, Ruby Dee never seemed a complete person. She appeared to be the typical woman born to be hurt. Everything about her suggested frustration and pain. Her voice trembled and broke. There were deep shadows under her eyes. She looked thin, anemic, weak, and terribly underfed and unloved. She always seemed to force a smile while standing by nervously and accepting whatever her men might throw her way. Often, because her performances were as inhibited and keyed up as her characters, she seemed limited in range as an actress, and audiences longed to see her break loose. But in *A Raisin in the Sun*, Ruby Dee forged her inhibitions, her anemia, and her repressed and taut ache to convey beautifully the most searing kind of black torment. The rest of the cast exploded with obvious rage, but Ruby Dee's tension, in contrast, was all the more immediate because it was so well controlled. *A Raisin in the Sun* must have been a liberating force for the actress; afterward she temporarily broke the mold of her frustrated heroines with appearances as a prostitute in *The Balcony* (1963) and as the pigtailed pickaninny in *Gone Are the Days* (1964). Neither film was successful, and soon Ruby Dee was back in the old mold in *The Incident* (1967), another of her better performances where she again *used* her inhibitions, and *Uptight* (1969). Later, in *Buck and the Preacher*, Ruby Dee, like Harry Belafonte, gave an admirable performance. As Sidney Poitier's long-suffering wife, a woman simply hoping to escape racist America and live her life without having to fight battles, she delivered a moving monologue. The role might be classified as a typical Ruby Dee understanding-endurable-sensitive-wife character, but that seemed a bit beside the point here. The important thing was that she played her role so well.

The integrationist theme of *A Raisin in the Sun* also informed Roger and Gene Corman's cheaply made *The Intruder* (1963). Centering on a mysterious white man who enters a small Southern town and sets off racial animosities resulting in bombings, burnings, and night rides of the Klan, the film had neither aesthetic nor great social significance. But *The Intruder* did go into something still very much on the nation's mind: school desegregation and the hysteria growing out of it. Moreover, the film revealed that the racial theme and pro-civil-rights issues were acceptable enough to infiltrate the American B movie.

Black Art Films

During the first half of the 1960s, a quartet of inexpensively but sensitively made motion pictures offered grimly realistic and cynical looks at black America. *Shadows* (1961), *The Cool World* (1963), *One Potato, Two Potato* (1964), and *Nothing But a Man* (1964), all apparently not made only for commercial reasons, presented "art-house style" depictions of America's racial problems. Audiences viewed black protagonists demanding a chance to fulfill themselves on their own terms without having to live up to white standards. Behind their placid exteriors, there shone the evolving great militant spirit.

John Cassavetes' *Shadows* picked up the old tragic mulatto theme and turned it inside out. Here a black girl who looks white falls in love with a white man. She neglects to tell him she is black not because of any shame. She simply believes it unimportant. By the picture's end (and after the white man has rejected her upon discovering her racial heritage), the girl has learned that in America such problems are never unimportant. Filmed in *cinema vérité* style, *Shadows* unearthed squarely and honestly the hazards of an interracial romance.

By 1963, most movie patrons were accustomed to reading about the Freedom Riders in the South and the various protest activities of Martin Luther King. Civil rights involvement was becoming respectable, and the great white liberal movement was in full swing. But not even the liberals—and surely not the majority of the moviegoing public—were acquainted with the world Shirley Clarke's camera probed in *The Cool World*. Here the camera focused on previously unexplored turf—Harlem. Based on Warren Miller's novel, the film showed the plight of a fifteen-year-old ghetto victim, Duke, and his gang, the Pythons. Duke searches for a gun, the great power symbol that will assure him of his leadership and help him defeat the rival gang, the Wolves. In between the search for the gun, director Clarke presents a disciplined and realistic portrait of Harlem as Divine Hell. The Pythons trade comic books for marijuana, share their gangland whore, drink booze, snatch purses, storm the city streets in anger, in boredom, in utter hopelessness. At the same time, Clarke turns her camera to other faces of the city: Strollers along Fifth Avenue, unaware of the tension on the sidewalks of 125th Street and Lenox Avenue. Duke was played by the talented Hampton Clanton who later (billed as Rony Clanton) starred in *The Education of Sonny Carson.*

An honest and difficult film, *The Cool World* was produced by Frederick Wiseman (now known for his brilliant documentaries on hospitals and high schools) and features a number of impressive performers, some of whom, like Gloria Foster and Clarence Williams III, would be heard from again before the decade ended. Shirley Clarke was co-author of the script along with Carl Lee (the son of actor Canada Lee), who also played Priest. Here again a perceptive black writer was able to bring new insights to a filmic exploration of the black experience. Four years after *The Cool World,* Shirley Clarke returned to a treatment of a black subject with *Portrait of Jason* (1967), a devastating documentary study of a black male prostitute.

Sam Weston and Larry Peerce's *One Potato, Two Potato* was the screen's first study of an interracial marriage. (Other features had dealt with interracial romances; there is a difference.) The film centered on a custody battle between a divorced white couple for their young daughter. Previously, when the woman had been deserted by her husband, she had met and fallen in love with a black man. Against opposition mainly from his family, the two married, taking her child by the previous marriage to live with them. Despite social pressures, their marriage is working, and the black husband's parents have developed a deep feeling for their daughter-in-law and her little girl. But when the former husband learns of his daughter's whereabouts, he initiates a court battle to take the child away. He wins his suit, and the film concludes with his driving off with the confused child.

Skillfully photographed in Painesville, Ohio, *One Potato, Two Potato* was a somber film, its approach restrained and decent, its direction adroit. Its modest success (along with the critical interest in *Shadows*) surely led the way for such major-studio studies of the interracial marriage-romance in *A Patch of Blue* and *Guess Who's Coming to Dinner.* All its performances were well handled. Barbara Barrie deserved her Cannes Film Festival Award as best actress for her portrayal of the wife. Robert Earl Jones (the father of James) and Vinnie Carroll played the hostile black parents ultimately unable not to love the little girl. But *One Potato, Two Potato*'s chief virtue was Bernie Hamilton's charming portrayal of the Negro husband. For a number of years, Hamilton had been working on and off in films, appearing in *The Jackie Robinson Story, Let No Man Write My Epitaph* (1960), *The Young One* (1961), and *The Devil at Four O'Clock* (1961). But never before had he a role he could do anything with. Here in *One Potato, Two Potato* he presented a portrait of a decent and intelligent black man without glamorizing or idealizing the character. Later he appeared in *Synanon* and *The Swimmer* (1968).

That same quality of screen honesty shone through Ivan Dixon's fine performance in *Nothing But a Man*. The film itself was as neatly restrained as the actor. It dealt with a black railroad laborer, Duff Anderson, living in the Deep South. When he marries an attractive schoolteacher (Abbey Lincoln), the film records the pressures in his home and outside it which nearly crush the pair. Duff's independence from his white bosses marks him as a target for their racism. Fired from one job after another, taunted and hounded, he eventually takes out his frustrations on his wife. He leaves her and sets out on a black odyssey that carries him to Birmingham, where he visits his self-destructive alcoholic father. There he sees a man dying with nothing, denied even his manhood. Deeply affected, Duff returns to his wife, taking his own illegitimate son with him, and attempts to re-establish the relationship.

Shot in distinct black and white, quiet in tone, notable for its subtlety, *Nothing But a Man* told its deep, dark tale simply. The film owes much of its power to its performers. Julius Harris portrayed the alcoholic father. Although director Michael Roemer never points a finger at racist white America for Harris's condition, and although Harris never cries out in self-pity as a victimized black man, the implications are there nonetheless. As the understanding wife, jazz vocalist Abbey Lincoln (in her acting debut) provides appropriate strength and passion. It is one of the warmest black female characterizations of the decade. The other impressive female performance in *Nothing But a Man* is that of Gloria Foster. She had already revealed herself in *The Cool World* as an introspective actress of great power. Here cast as the stoic mistress of Julius Harris, Foster is a marvel of intensified pain. Fine as that performance is, she has made few film appearances since then. With her marriage to Clarence Williams III, of television's "Mod Squad" series, she moved to California from New York, where she had had great success in off-Broadway productions. In California she made many television guest shots; with astounding skill, she managed even on the tritest of shows to be convincing and to present herself as a totally contemporary black woman. Her style is the most naturalistic of any black actress in American pictures. Foster's subsequent films included *The Comedians* (1967), *The Angel Levine*, and *Man and Boy* (1972).

Moving as the other actors were, *Nothing But a Man* marked a personal triumph for actor Ivan Dixon. A black performer of great skill, Dixon had previously appeared in scattered empty roles in films such as *Something of Value* and *Porgy and Bess* and in a few television programs. As the African beau of Diana Sands in *A Raisin in the Sun*, he had a fleeting opportunity to show his mettle, but it did little

ABOVE: The interracial marriage comes to the screen—Barbara Barrie and Bernie Hamilton in *One Potato, Two Potato.*

BELOW: Brock Peters, who emerged in the 1960s as the era's most prominent black brute figure.

to advance his career. Today *Nothing But a Man* remains his finest work. His Duff was a fitting precursor to the militant spirits about to burst on the scene. His character's quarrel was not only with his white oppressors but with those blacks who permit oppression. Dixon affected his audience without relying on histrionics. Both he and Bernie Hamilton ushered in a new style of black sexuality in the 1960s. Through the way they walked, through the way they eyed and held women, these two actors let audiences know they were sensitive, tortured men as well as sensual ones. Unfortunately, neither actor was to work steadily in movies. Dixon later appeared in a thankless role in *Patch of Blue.* In 1972, he directed Robert Hooks in *Trouble Man.*

A Step Backward: Ossie Davis and *Gone Are the Days*

Whereas the art-house films attempted to present untyped black characters, the 1964 film adaptation of Ossie Davis's play *Purlie Victorious* carried audiences back to the old stereotype figures. Retitled *Gone Are the Days*, the movie centered on a fast-talking, slickster minister, Purlie, whose ambition is to convert a battered barn (the property of a staunch Southern aristocrat) into an integrated church. He enlists as many as he can in his community—the local mammy and the local tom and the local pickaninny and the local white liberal—to aid him in his plan. In the end, Purlie gets his church. As a film *Gone Are the Days* was often humorless. Had Ossie Davis not been associated with it, the picture would hardly be worth mentioning.

By 1964, Ossie Davis had already acquired a following that included white liberals and members of the black bourgeoisie. Through sheer push and panache, he had promoted himself into the leading-man category, replacing Poitier on stage in *A Raisin in the Sun* and then winning decent reviews for his work in *Purlie Victorious.* In motion pictures, Davis met with moderate success. He gave serious though hardly commanding performances in such features as *No Way Out, The Cardinal* (1963), *Shock Treatment* (1964), and most notoriously in *Slaves* (1969). He did have some fine moments in *The Hill* (1965) and *The Scalphunters* (1968).

It was evident that Davis was essentially a character actor and not a leading man like Poitier. But there was a place for Davis in the film world. He was usually cast as a stoic, relatively dignified tomlike character. He was an educated Negro priest in one film, a Latin scholar of sorts in another. Like Poitier, he was a model integrationist hero: intelligent, reasonable, reliable, and well-mannered. But Davis's characters were not very compelling. Sometimes their distinguishing characteristic was that they appeared to be masochists. If any reactionary white audience wanted to see a black man get his due, an Ossie Davis film was the thing to see. In Otto

Preminger's *The Cardinal*, Davis portrayed a Southern priest journeying to Rome to cry out against discrimination in the Catholic church. Practically everyone in the theater knew the journey would be of no avail. Almost anyone could have predicted that retaliation would be taken against this outspoken black man. Consequently, when the gentle and well-bred Davis was brutally attacked by the Ku Klux Klan, no audience member was terribly surprised—or upset. Admirable or heroic as Davis's character was, he had been asking for trouble. For moviegoers, it looked like a set-up. The same was true of his kind-hearted tom character in *Slaves*. Here again Ossie Davis was brutally beaten, and once more through his stoicism, he seemed to encourage his own abuse and mistreatment. Regardless, in all his early films, Ossie Davis at times proved interesting. Much later when Davis appeared in such films as *Do the Right Thing* (1989), *Jungle Fever* (1991), and *Get on the Bus* (1996), he became surprisingly commanding. With age, Davis learned how to hold the screen. He would be wonderful to watch. But early in his career, he was far from overwhelming.

As an actor, so, too, as a writer in the early 1960s. Ossie Davis's *Gone Are the Days* proved mildly diverting in bits and pieces, namely, in the idea behind the work. But as a whole the movie was far from the great farce its author envisioned. Davis believed American audiences, black and white, were sophisticated enough in the early 1960s to enjoy the old stereotypes and laugh at their exaggerations. He intentionally played with types, clichés, and platitudes. Unfortunately, the actors were not at their best. Godfrey Cambridge's tom was static and emotionally anemic. Beah Richards's mammy was intolerable. Davis himself was a crackerjack talker, dazzling with his razzmatazz but ultimately too one-dimensional. Ruby Dee turned up surprisingly as an uninhibited pickaninny named Lutiebelle, and, surprisingly too, she was the only funny character in the picture. *Gone Are the Days* was a prodigious disappointment. Under the direction of Nicholas Webster, Ossie Davis's parody of stereotypes had not worked, and Davis may have pined over this—but not for long. Later his idea that audiences were removed enough from the stereotypes to respond to them if they were exuberantly presented was proven true with the enormous success of the Broadway musical *Purlie* (based on *Purlie Victorious*) and the Davis-directed movie *Cotton Comes to Harlem* (1970). If anything, *Gone Are the Days* was the first step in the evolution of the new-style all-black movie.

Along the Road, in Harlem, and on the Subway

The far-fetched efforts of Ossie Davis were followed by the serious approaches of the so-called little pictures *Black Like Me* (1964), *The Pawnbroker* (1965), and

Dutchman (1967). *Black Like Me,* based on John Howard Griffin's bestselling book, reversed Hollywood's great theme of passing the color line. Playing the author, who actually performed this social experiment, James Whitmore, as a white man, undergoes a special chemical treatment to darken his skin. Then he hitchhikes across the South passing as a Negro. During his travels in a black man's America, the white man witnesses the cruelty and hatred that infest the land. He is shoved on buses, chased by white hoodlums, abused by employers, refused employment, questioned about his sex life, and repeatedly subjected to humiliation.

Critics of *Black Like Me* still view it as merely another example of the white man slumming at a black man's expense. Others have seen it as a continuation of the tragic mulatto theme and nothing more. (Indeed, the film's thesis was that here was a white man being treated so shamelessly simply because his skin was darkened.) But the more relevant fact was that, crude and shoddy as this B movie was, it was an earnest attempt to confront and expose racism in America.

The production's earnestness was greatly aided by the engaging work of a line-up of new black faces. Al Freeman, Jr., appeared briefly as a quick-tempered 1950s-style sit-inner. As Mr. Educated Negro, Roscoe Lee Browne provided an appropriate insolent and neurotic flair that went a little deeper than his written role. He was a stage actor with only one previous screen credit—in Shirley Clarke's *The Connection* (1960). Some of his mannered theatrics did not work to full effect. But he introduced in this film a new type of black character of which he would be the chief exponent and which would be more fully developed in his subsequent films *Uptight* and *The Liberation of L. B. Jones.* His characters were cynical, lost, sterile toms, products of a decadent black bourgeoisie. Perhaps his were the most realistic toms ever presented in American films. Having sold out, they have profited economically, but they have lost their self-respect and always seem to be verging on emotional breakdowns. Browne's most likable role, an exception to his lost tom characters, was as the dapper, cane-carrying dandy in *The Comedians* (1967). *Black Like Me* also introduced a slender and surprisingly pleasant Raymond St. Jacques, as a middle-class black businessman, and the delightful Thelma Oliver, as a black girl who talks too much although she tries her best not to. Both also appeared in *The Pawnbroker.*

Sidney Lumet's *The Pawnbroker* did not have a black theme, but the picture was set in Harlem, and it prominently featured a number of black actors. Like the film's disillusioned Jewish hero, the blacks were inhabitants (sometimes victims; other times, predators) of a world that daily assaults and dehumanizes them. Thelma Oliver was moving and resonant as the broken-spirited black girl ready to sell everything, including herself, to save her lover. Oliver's black whore was a beautifully defined and individualized figure, a creature as comic as she was sad. In a minor role, Raymond St. Jacques proved adequate—no more, no less. On the other hand, Juano Hernandez was excellent in his role.

Although he was not the most impressive black actor in the picture, Brock Peters nonetheless merited close attention. He was cast as a sinister hood terrorizing the Jewish pawnbroker. For Peters, the role as the tough was nothing new. His previous performances as Sergeant Brown in *Carmen Jones* and as Crown in *Porgy and Bess* had been personifications of the classic black brute. Brock Peters was pitch black (that was enough to frighten any white audience) and without the healthy good looks of a Poitier or a Belafonte. He perfected a vicious snarl and as he malevolently eyed the other characters in his films he suggested uncontrolled violence. Finally, when he pounced upon his opponents, he was the incarnation of unbridled brutality. Even when cast later as the homosexual West Indian Johnny in the British film *The L-Shaped Room* (1963) or as the emasculated farmhand on trial for rape in *To Kill a Mockingbird* (1962), his characterizations had raw edge and bitter power. In *The Pawnbroker*, Peters was in top brute form. Belligerent, hostile, and downright nasty, he played his part well, but it was apparent that he was playing a type and doing little more. He continued in this tradition with his black supremacist work in *The Incident* (1967) and later in *The McMasters* (1970).

When adapted for the screen, LeRoi Jones's one-act play *Dutchman* was expanded to fifty-five minutes. Directed by Anthony Harvey in England, *Dutchman* was a grim little parable, beginning with a subway ride and ending with a nightmarish dance of death. On a New York subway train, a psychotic white woman, Lula, meets a respectable middle-class black man, Clay. By the time the ride has ended, Lula has stabbed Clay to death before a trainload of passive passengers and is well on her way to doing in a second black victim. By its conclusion, too, *Dutchman*, better than any other piece of dramatic writing of the decade, articulated the options left open to a black man in white America: either he can survive by joining the ranks of the black bourgeoisie (those apers of white manners who are doomed to lives without their manhood) or he can lash out at the dominant culture and run the risk of being chopped down. Jones's thesis was not particularly pleasant. Nor was the film. But they worked dazzlingly.

Dutchman owed most of its power to its high-charged theatrical dialogue and the acid performances of Al Freeman, Jr., and Shirley Knight. Today this is still Freeman's best screen performance, and his character is typical of the sort he played during the 1960s. His Clay is a number of things. For the first three-fourths of the picture he is the educated tom, a "civilized" Negro who quietly turns the other cheek. In the last quarter, Freeman violently explodes, asserting himself as he protests the injustices and atrocities black Americans live with daily. Clearly, Freeman's Clay is a middle-class creation. But he is a radicalized one. Not content to be intellectually stagnant, he is transformed into a forceful militant. In *Dutchman* and his other films *Black Like Me, The Troublemaker* (1964), *The Detective* (1968), *Finian's Rainbow* (1968), and *The Lost Man* (1969), Al Freeman, despite the fact that he played supporting roles, emerged as the movies' best black spokesman on militancy and intellectualized hostility. Never were his characters portrayed as the typical black brutes (as most movie militants were to be depicted). Each of his performances was so well thought out and so expertly tempered that his emotional outbursts were never just uncontrolled hatred. Instead they were explanations of why black America had so much pent-up anger. For this reason, Freeman's work still outshines that of many name actors of the period.

Way Down in de New Ole South with Tom-Tom, Miss Bronze Barbie Doll, and Ms. Militant Mammy

Otto Preminger's *Hurry Sundown* (1967) was the first major, big-budget, star-studded motion picture to center on the militant spirit of the mid-1960s and the black revolt. Preminger based his film on K. B. Gilden's sprawling, best-selling novel about the post-World War II New South. He shot his movie in Baton Rouge, Louisiana (where crew and cast were often threatened by the Ku Klux Klan), and he lined up an impressive roster of actors: Michael Caine, Jane Fonda, John Philip Law, Faye Dunaway, Burgess Meredith, and the black actors Robert Hooks, Diahann Carroll, Rex Ingram, and Beah Richards.

Hurry Sundown was, in many respects, a summation of almost every Southern white and black cliché the movies had ever relied on. The Southern Belle, the Simon-Legree massa, the white idiot child, the faithful mammy, the white Liberal, the New Educated Black Woman (a la Pinky), the New Good Sensitive Negro, the Corrupt Old White Bigot, the Po' White Trash—all had their place in this drama. The plot was complicated and circuitous. A corrupt simon-legreeish Michael Caine wants to make an important land deal, selling property belonging to his wife (Jane Fonda). But he also needs that of his wife's cousin Rad (po' white trash portrayed by John Philip Law) and his wife's mammy (Beah Richards) to complete the transaction. Through much wheeling and dealing, with many heated passions and bed scenes in between, Caine is able to persuade Fonda to take her mammy's land. "That old woman was my mammy," she protests at first, "and she loved me. There was a time when she was the only one in this whole world I knew loved me. And I *cain't* go against her!" But, of course, she does. Still, before Caine knows it, the po' white trash cousin Rad (who's a war veteran) has joined with the mammy's uppity militant son Reeve (also a war veteran, portrayed by Hooks) to keep their property and to work it together. Theirs represents the new postwar spirit, that of integration, and Preminger implies that this spirit will defeat their common enemy, the white supremacist.

The film builds to two heady climaxes. The first is in a courtroom session at which a white bigoted judge (Burgess Meredith) presides. Before the session ends, Diahann Carroll has chased Fonda into a white ladies' room, has berated her for sticking by a man who means her no good, and has brought about such a drastic transformation that Fonda marches back into the courtroom and demands that the proceedings be stopped. She drops her case. Black Reeve and white Rad are victorious. Or so they think. For during the second climax, greedy Caine has dynamited Rad's farm. But the movie's liberalized conclusion announces that the postwar integrationist spirit will not be destroyed so easily. Black Reeve and his black church-and-farm friends march with white Rad to help him rebuild his farm. Throughout a black chorus sings dat dey don't mind de sufferin' cause de sundown's a comin'. And thus we see the dawn of a new South.

Preposterous as *Hurry Sundown* may sound, it remains a key pop work of the 1960s, and it contains some intense, if at times outlandish, performances by its black players. Screen newcomer Robert Hooks portrays Reeve, the World War II veteran returning home to fight another battle. He accepts insults and humiliations until he can take no more, then joins forces with his white friend. Hooks's character was to symbolize a new type of militancy in tune with the outspokenness of a Stokely Carmichael. But in actuality he is little more than the postwar Negro figure of the 1940s, a sort of pepped-up James Edwards. He is a tom's tom, pliable and decent, and the character is made redeemable only because of the actor's personal charm and healthy good looks. If *Hurry Sundown* did nothing else, however, it revealed that with the right roles Robert Hooks could have developed into a black matinee idol.

Diahann Carroll plays the part of the pretty schoolteacher Vivian. It is a role she was perfect for, but perhaps for all the wrong reasons. It seemed as if Diahann Carroll had been grooming herself throughout her career for this role as the post-integrated black woman. In her first films, *Carmen Jones* and *Porgy and Bess*, Carroll was cast as a pleasing, unadorned plain Jane. She was pretty and pert but hardly glamorous. She was slightly sensual but far from seductive. All in all Diahann Carroll came across as the nice, innocent girl next door. But in the 1960s, this engaging naiveté was lost; Diahann Carroll's film style underwent a drastic change. (The image she presented in nightclub and television appearances and on Broadway in *No Strings* underwent the same change.) It was in *Paris Blues* in 1961 that she first emerged as a plasticized, middle-class Negro lady type. ("I'm acceptable," she later explained in the March 14, 1970, issue of *TV Guide*. "I'm a black woman with a white image. I'm as close as they can get to having the best of both worlds. The audience can accept me.... I don't scare them." Truer words were never spoken.) Here she portrayed a young American woman off to learn about life and love in France. Her best friend is a white woman, played by Joanne Woodward, and it is obvious that culturally and philosophically the two are of the same world, except perhaps that Woodward exhibits a bit more spunk and spontaneity.

Black leading ladies had always been cast close to the white ideal, but always, of course, even in the cases of Lena Horne and Dorothy Dandridge, there was some trace of the ethnic experience, something "cullid" about them that black audiences could identify with. In *Paris Blues*, however, Diahann Carroll came closer in speech, dress, mannerism, looks, and life-style to the great white ideal than any black actress before her. But more disturbing (or perhaps enlightening) was that she revealed how sterile and shallow such an ideal was. On the screen, not one hair was out of place. Not one word was mispronounced. There was not one false blink of the eyes. So perfectly planned and calculated was she that Diahann Carroll seemed more an automaton—some exquisite bronze Barbie Doll—than a leading lady. For politically sensitive black audiences, Diahann Carroll represented one more dehydrated and lifeless accruement of a decadent capitalist society. And curiously the elegant sterility may explain her magnetism.

In *Hurry Sundown*, that magnetic sterility and decadence were out of place, but with it Carroll gave her definitive bronze Barbie Doll performance. Here she portrayed an outspoken, educated black woman just returned from the North. Her character was to be horrified and indignant over segregation yet bright and resourceful enough to work her way around difficult situations. Curiously, Carroll seemed more bored by the racism in the picture—or amused—than irritated. She is obviously a woman accustomed to getting what she wants, one who really doesn't have any great feelings of discrimination. She knows oppression only on a superficial level. The scene in which she follows Jane Fonda into the white ladies' room and slaps her face seems somewhat ludicrous. In the first place, Carroll looks as white as Fonda—and acts it, too. So why the fuss over her entering the white ladies' room? Secondly, Carroll's pleas for her rights are almost laughable because she seems too far removed from the harsh black experience to fully understand it. Perhaps for this reason, though, her work has a certain daffy effectiveness. She herself clearly symbolizes the post-integrated black woman. Her color will never make her feel shame, and she is to be respected for that. But she has entered a free society at the expense of her own individuality. She has adopted so many white values that she has lost her own soul.

This type of black woman—and some of the decadence she acquires by fully accepting the values of the dominant culture—could have been fascinating if properly handled. Later, William Wyler toyed with it in *The Liberation of L. B. Jones*. But he unwisely cast his picture with a black whore type (Lola Falana) rather than a black decadent middle-class lady figure. This type of character is one that the movies, even black fiction and poetry, have yet to deal with. But if ever it was to be dealt with, Diahann Carroll would have been the actress to represent it best in American movies. Regardless, she came close after *Hurry Sundown* in parts of *The Split* (1968). Later, she had her most notable success as the Doris Day-like character on the television series "Julia."

Beah Richards, as Mammy Rose, came off better than any other black actor in *Hurry Sundown*, presenting to audiences a middle-class mammy in revolt. Previously Richards had appeared in movies such as *Take a Giant Step*, *The Miracle Worker* (1962), and *Gone Are the Days*. Later she appeared as the mother in *Guess Who's Coming to Dinner*. In all these films—and even in *In the Heat of the Night* (1967) in which she was uncharacteristically cast as a whore—Beah Richards was always the paragon of black respectability—at least at first glance. One always imagined her wearing white gloves and having a bridge party to attend. But unlike the middle-class Diahann Carroll, Richards had a humorous side, and emerged as the prim little black lady whom audiences secretly loved to hate. There had never been anyone quite like her before. She was so soft-spoken and genteel (notably later in *Guess Who's Coming to Dinner*) that audiences knew she had to be acting. Beah Richards just did not look like the typical middle-class black woman. For one thing, she was very dark and had "Negroid" features. Almost always middle-class black characters, on screen as off, were thought of as being light-skinned—as close in complexion to whites as they were in their life-styles. For another thing, she looked hard and "evil," as if she would bite back in a minute if anyone dared step on her toes. She struck moviegoers as the kind of woman who had been exposed to a harsher black experience, be it urban or rural. There was something definitely "cullid" about her, and audiences just wanted her to drop the middle-class sweetness and phoniness and scream out in anger. In *Hurry Sundown*, Beah Richards was once again cast as the sweet, lovable, pious, well-spoken, pliant black woman. But this time, audiences saw the obviously fake middle-class black lady break loose.

Made up to look at least two-hundred and fifty years old, with a head of hair that looks like a cotton patch, Richards's character, Mammy Rose, was at first the essence of the Louise Beavers type of submissive, cheerful domestic. "Sometimes, Rose," says white actress Fonda, "I think you just about invented love." The proper, intelligent, polite Mammy Rose smiles. But within a few minutes when she is asked to give up her property, she collapses with a heart attack. Then, like a pepped-up, enraged version of Ethel Waters, she cries out to her son, "I was wrong. . . . I was a white folks' nigger. I was. . . . You got to fight. . . . Swear to it. . . . You'll know at the end you won't have this agony. This taste of bitterness and gall. In these last minutes, you know what I feel most of all. Anger. And hateful. Not so much of them but for what they done to me. . . . And myself for helping them to do it. . . . I truly grieve for the sorry thing that has been my life." In the context of the film, the scene is comic. No one acquires that much insight in five minutes. But at the movies anything can happen. And, most important, because actress Richards was finally saying the lines it looked as if she should have been crying out throughout this picture (and perhaps her previous ones), the sentiments appeared real. The middle-class mammy had dropped the airs and become real. The audience forgot the rest of the film and picked out those parts it held closest. And Beah Richards came off as a heroine of sorts.

Beah Richards's success in *Hurry Sundown* epitomized the things that went into making this particular movie a success with black audiences. Like Richards's character, the film dealt with issues, questions, even taboos that were on everyone's mind. And in dealing with these the film spelled everything out without attempting ambiguity or nuance. "If we want to make it better," said Robert Hooks's Reeve, "we gotta make it better. Nobody's going to do it for us." Coming from Hooks's tom, the words were ridiculous. But they summed up the mood and the attitude (simplified, of course) of militants in the 1960s. Consequently, the audience forgot about the character saying the lines and instead responded to the lines themselves. "On your feet," said a white judge when he found Diahann Carroll sitting in his office. "What has come over you people? Have you no sense of decorum? Isn't there a trace of respect left in any of you?" Later the same judge asks during a courtroom procedure, "Are you aware of how extraordinary it is for a white man to come into my court to represent a black boy?" "Well," replies the white lawyer, "no more than it was for my daddy to present me a negra half-brother!" "Don't rattle your skeletons in my face!" the judge commands.

But *Hurry Sundown* rattled everyone's skeletons in everyone else's face. It presented archetypal scenes and characters that audiences associated with the South, with bigots, with liberals, and with touchy racial situations. Although it was cluttered with clichés and misrepresentations, *Hurry Sundown* was directed as one big glorious comic strip with pop scene after pop scene, and thus it succeeded on a primal level as a popularization of current events. Eventually, because of its inadvertent satire and parody, the movie pointed a new direction for the handling of the Negro problem. It led the way to the pure satire and madness and the intentional use of stereotypes and clichés found in *Putney Swope* and *Cotton Comes to Harlem*.

A Man Called Adam and Sammy Davis, Jr.'s, Bid for Movie Stardom

At the same time Preminger's rambunctiously absurd effort appeared, movie viewers were also presented with a psychodrama, *A Man Called Adam* (1966). The film starred Sammy Davis, Jr., with Cicely Tyson, Peter Lawford, and Ossie Davis. Except for Tyson's sensitive and intelligent work as the ingenue, the acting and direction were pedestrian at best. In fact, the only saving grace of this drama about a disturbed and difficult jazz musician wallowing in self-pity was that it unintentionally revealed the confused anger then felt in American inner cities.

The feature seemed to have a certain oppressiveness. A few minutes into the film, some moviegoers were probably ready to get home. Yet the idea of a jazz film itself certainly appealed to black audiences. So, too, did the idea of a new black heel of an antihero. (This idea was successfully picked up in 1971 in *Sweet Sweetback's Baadasssss Song*.) The sounds for Davis's trumpet were actually performed by Nat Adderly. And it was fascinating to see the great Louis Armstrong cast as the old musician Sweet Daddy. Still not an actor, Armstrong nonetheless endowed the film with pathos and feeling. But the movie's great failing was what the producers had thought was its great asset: Sammy Davis, Jr. He makes a valiant effort and has a great intensity but he can't get a hold on the character.

Throughout the late 1950s and early 1960s Sammy Davis, Jr., had had a spectacularly lackluster film career. He always received featured billing in movies. Because he had been an entertainer nearly all his life, beginning as a tot with his father in the Will Mastin Trio, the black press often sentimentally gave him good coverage. Other times, though, the black press was critical of him. Audiences had been conditioned to think of him as a show-business legend. Yet his actual film performances were far from outstanding. His first film of the 1950s, *The Benny Goodman Story*, was hardly memorable. In his next feature, *Anna Lucasta*, he and Eartha Kitt were billed as "the entertainment world's most electrifying pair." Yet there was little electricity to the coupling. As the hard-as-nails sailor boy friend Davis was miscast and totally unconvincing, clearly lacking the physical presence and personality for a lead role. Afterwards there came his most publicized appearance, as the flashy, jive-ass Sportin' Life in *Porgy and Bess*. Here he seemed more at home, but the Gershwin music was more interesting than the character. At times, too, Davis came across like a shrimp trying to act like a big fish. The secret to playing Sportin' Life was to be slick and devilishly sexy but to do it with the greatest of ease. Sammy Davis, Jr., seemed to be trying too hard. Black moviegoers had very mixed feelings about him throughout the era.

In the features that dominated his career, the rat-pack movies in which he costarred with Frank Sinatra, Dean Martin, and Peter Lawford, he alienated black movie patrons because he was too much the tagalong figure. On the surface the rat-pack pictures were egalitarian affairs, but underneath there was something hypocritical about their treatment of Davis. In *Ocean's Eleven* (1960), Davis portrayed the agreeable sidekick. In an era in which Negroes were popping up in offices throughout America, he became the "showcase Negro" for the white stars. To maintain that privileged position, he sometimes endured awkward moments. Though he often cut a very elegant figure in *Robin and the 7 Hoods* (1964)— wearing tailored suits, ties, and hats, at times, he playfully used dialect, which for blacks in the 1960s seemed passé. In a scene in which he searched for a missing telephone, he even played it like a befuddled Willie Best. For later generations, the conclusion—with Davis, Martin, and Sinatra all dressed as Santa Clauses—is fairly tame. But for mainstream 1960s audiences, the racial joke of a *ludicrous* black Santa was at Davis's expense. In that same film it was apparent that Sinatra ordered him about as he never did the white actors.

In *Sergeants 3* (1962), in which he was actually cast as a diligently faithful servant, the movie tried prettifying the situation by making him a hero. But Davis seemed too eager to please his white co-stars, and consequently failed to satisfy black audiences.

With *A Man Called Adam* Sammy Davis, Jr., may have wanted to redeem himself. But he was dramatically unprepared for the role, and he failed terribly in the scenes in which he whined or broke down. Later he returned to his comic sentimental figures when he co-starred with Peter Lawford in *Salt and Pepper* (1968) and its sequel *One More Time* (1970). As he portrayed Lawford's loyal man-Friday, Sammy Davis, Jr., was—at the time—a regrettably embarrassing figure with little spunk. For later generations, Davis would be interesting to watch—just to see such a famous talent. But his movies failed to provide him with roles in which that talent could be as brilliantly displayed as it was in theaters and nightclubs.

Super Sidney of the 1960s

Sammy Davis, Jr., did not make it as a leading man, but audiences did not seem to mind. They simply stuck by their old reliable leading man now transformed into a superhero, Sidney Poitier. By 1967, the year Poitier's biggest hit of the decade, *Guess Who's Coming to Dinner*, was released, the actor had already ascended to the ranks of superstardom. It was evident that he had no rivals. His screen personality was still that of the intelligent, kindhearted black man, and his code had remained intact throughout a series of alternatively entertaining and dull motion pictures. *Paris Blues* had supplied the heretofore sexless leading man with some romance in the form of Diahann Carroll, but the pair's moments on screen were torpid. *All the Young Men* (1960) and *Pressure Point* had proven disappointing, and not even the drawing power of the Poitier name could save them. Likewise *The Long Ships* had failed to make him a romanticized villain.

But just then when the career of an ordinary screen presence might have disintegrated, there had appeared the wildly successful *Lilies of the Field* (1963). Under Ralph Nelson's direction Poitier starred as the easygoing Homer Smith, an ex-G.I. who stumbles across a group of refugee nuns in the Arizona desert. They hope to build a chapel, and they see him as their savior. Before Homer knows it, he has begun work on the chapel, and is devoting all his time to it, and has even taken a part-time job to earn money to buy additional materials. Charming but light, *Lilies of the Field* offered Sidney Poitier an opportunity to flex his muscles and be the ingratiating and dependable character he was so good at portraying. It earned him an Academy Award, thus making him the first black man to win one. His career soared to undreamed-of heights afterward.

Paradoxically, while *Lilies of the Field* won Poitier an even larger following, it revealed more of the cracks in the great idol's armor. In the 1944 production of *Since You Went Away*, Hattie McDaniel had portrayed a long-time loyal servant to Claudette Colbert's family. When they saw her taking a part-time evening factory job to help the war-stricken family through their financial difficulties, black audiences laughed at Hattie McDaniel. Even in 1944, her character's obvious tom quality seemed ludicrous. Twenty years later, when Poitier took a similar part-time job for similar reasons—to help the white nuns—it seemed to black audiences, if not to white, that he was now leading the black character back in his place as a faithful servant. Worst of all, his character was not a pop figure who could be laughed at, but something deadly serious.

After his Oscar, Poitier was made even "nicer" by Hollywood scenarists, and it appeared as if he were going along with the program. In *The Slender Thread* (1965), with Anne Bancroft, he became the black savior of the crazed white woman who had taken an overdose of pills; in *A Patch of Blue* the seeing-eye dog for a poor blind white girl; in *Duel at Diablo* (1966) a conventional cowboy; in *To Sir, with Love* (1967) a schoolteacher oddly representative of the system that the old Poitier of *The Blackboard Jungle* had rebelled against. Most of the Poitier features of the 1960s were solid entertainment vehicles. They pleased audiences but failed to satisfy them completely because the social significance and political implications of the 1950s Poitier features were lacking, and a surprisingly mannered ideal black man, so far above the masses who loved him, was emerging. *Guess Who's Coming to Dinner* paid homage to that new superblackman, and, while it was enormously successful, it was the one that jolted Sidney Poitier as he sat on his throne.

Directed by Stanley Kramer, *Guess Who's Coming to Dinner* was really an innocuous film. Poitier starred with Katharine Hepburn, Spencer Tracy, Katharine Houghton, Beah Richards, and Roy Glenn, Jr., in a story that tackled the touchy subject of interracial marriage. A white girl comes home to mother and dad in the suburbs with a tall handsome black man whom she wants to marry. Everybody goes into a dither, but of course, in the end, after a major summit meeting of both the bride's and the groom's parents, everything is worked out.

Guess Who's Coming to Dinner was pure 1949 claptrap done up in 1940s high-gloss MGM style. By concentrating on nice decent people entangled in personal heartaches, director Kramer diverted the audience from real issues. There stood Poitier, charming, good-looking, mannerly, and brilliant. Who could refuse him for a son-in-law? That was part of Kramer's point, of course. But it was far too simplistic. There also was no big romantic scene between Poitier and the young woman he wants to marry. The two were seen kissing from the rear-view mirror of a taxi cab. That was it. The film seems to show as subtext the fear of black male sexuality. Large mainstream audiences, taken in by the picture's clever advertising campaign and its star packaging, turned the picture into a tremendous commercial success. It was received well critically, too, and Beah Richards received an Oscar nomination as Best Supporting Actress for her rather idiosyncratic performance. Richards was a great actress but her role as written was pallid. Still, she can be oddly fascinating to watch. The movie proved one of the last of the explicitly integrationist message pictures. And the newspaper and magazine articles by black and white attacking Poitier and Kramer flowed after its release. The now feature article by black writer Clifford Mason that denounced Poitier characters as too limited and unrealistic to continue having much impact, was run in *The New York Times* under the title: "Why Does White America Love Sidney Poitier So?" "Civil Rights is one thing," maid Isabelle Sanford had said in *Guess Who's Coming to Dinner*, "but this here is another." That no doubt will remain the final comment on the film and Poitier's role in it.

Sidney Poitier's next films were *In the Heat of the Night* and *For Love of Ivy* (1968). The former told the story of a Negro police officer (from the North) Virgil Tibbs investigating a Southern murder case. During the process of solving the crime, he comes face to face with racism. But, true to the new super dynamics of Sir Sidney, he not only uncovers the murderer's identity but also wins the admiration and friendship of a bigoted police chief, played by Rod Steiger. The Best Actor Oscar went to Steiger that year.

Yet, ironically, Poitier gave one of his strongest, most measured performances. He had two scenes that brought out cheers from black viewers. At one point, the bigoted police chief refers to Poitier's character as boy; he also uses the n-word. When he asks Poitier what they call him up North, Poitier answers with a *slow burn* that explodes with real anger: "They call me MISTER TIBBS!" In another scene, an aristocratic white Southern racist slaps Poitier. Without missing a beat, Poitier slaps him back! These were great moments for Poitier in the film. Black audiences loved those sequences with a defiant Poitier. Yet still the film had Poitier basically helping whites. Why should he really (no matter what the script wants us to think) stick around in the South to help them? Still, this basically well-put-together film walked off with the Best Picture Oscar for 1967.

For Love of Ivy was a Doris Day–Rock Hudson style romantic comedy done with black actors. A faithful servant (Abbey Lincoln) announces she will leave the family that has employed her for years. The family does everything to persuade her to stay, even offering her a trip to Africa! Finally, the family's hip teenage son decides Ivy needs a lover. He tricks local stud Poitier into romancing the maid. The two fall in love and have a big sexless sex scene, and everything turns out just right. Despite the corn, *For Love of Ivy* distinguished itself because it offered the first love scene between blacks in a popular movie. Otherwise, it seemed hopelessly out of

The picture that made a mint but was the last of the old-style integrationist dramas: *Guess Who's Coming to Dinner* (1967) with Katharine Hepburn, Katharine Houghton, and Poitier.

time and tune, and leading man Poitier seemed almost obsolete. A sign of the fickleness of movie audience tastes is that this film looks much better today. Abbey Lincoln's charm has not diminished, and the romantic ease and agility of the film now are apparently coming back into vogue.

What remains the most intriguing aspect of the 1960s, particularly the mid-to-late 1960s, is the rapidity with which attitudes, outlooks, and opinions changed. In dealing with racial situations, moviemakers had been accustomed to moving in cautious steps, in tune with the cadence of the mass audience. During the Johnson era, however, Hollywood appeared to lose track of the speed with which the mind of the mass audience was moving. By 1966 Martin Luther King's philosophy of nonviolence was just about dead, although only a few years earlier he had been the unchallenged spokesman for black America. Yet the film industry was still coasting along on the King attitudes. Malcolm X had been assassinated. Stokely Carmichael had arrived. H. Rap Brown had said violence was as natural in America as apple pie. Watts, Detroit, Harlem, South Philadelphia, Cleveland, and Washington, D.C., had exploded with riots. The President's National Advisory Commission had reported that America was "moving toward two societies, one black, one white, separate and unequal." And yet the industry continued with its brotherly-love everything's-going-to-be-dandy escapist movies, assuming that audiences would still believe in them. But the new audience was exposed to much more. Television familiarized people with incredible scenes of blood and brutality in their own living rooms. Added to the physical brutality was a new interest and awareness of the black experience. It was becoming "chic" and "hip" to understand the black man's style, even to speak in his jazzed-up dialect. By the end of the 1960s, the motion-picture industry caught up, jumping on the bandwagon before it even knew what was really happening. As a consequence, there appeared two new phenomena. One was the final evolution of a new kind of black film. The other, which actually came first, was the extraordinary rise of an actor named Jim Brown.

Jim Brown: Black Buck Hero for a Separatist Age

He came to the movies in the mid-1960s after a phenomenal college and professional career as an all-star football player. When he decided to switch careers, the news certainly must have seemed a joke to movie executives, to football commissioners, indeed even to film audiences. But Jim Brown had the last laugh on virtually everyone. He arrived in motion pictures at a time when the mass black audience was in desperate need of him. Even though he was to be nothing more than the black buck of old, he answered—because of his unique charisma and astounding physical presence—the need for a viable black-power sex figure.

Before Jim Brown, the black leading man had been physically self-sufficient, but never overpowering. Robeson and on occasion Rex Ingram came close to it, but generally their films were realistic ones, not pop pictures, and therefore they could not overstep reasonable bounds of strength. Jim Brown suggested violence and power, a dash and daring never before exhibited by a black male. On a physical basis alone, he was impressive. He stood six feet, two inches, weighed well over two hundred pounds, and had a forty-five inch chest. Brown had been acclaimed as the most powerful and elusive running back in the history of professional football. Off the field he made headlines when he was arrested for allegedly throwing a girl off a balcony and a full-grown man over a car. All of these added to the Brown mystique. He was big. He was black. He was outspoken. He was baaaddddd. In films, Jim Brown simply played the big, black, baaadddd nigger parts it seemed he was born to play. The fact that he lacked enough talent to play them did not much matter.

In his first features, the western *Rio Conchos* (1964) and the graphic war drama *The Dirty Dozen* (1967), he was wisely cast as men forced to operate in worlds where they were motivated by their physical strength rather than their sensitivities. Brown had ample opportunities to show his stuff, notably in *The Dirty Dozen*, with astounding vigor and occasionally with what seemed like overzealous sadism.

The first films established Brown as a rugged, insensitive yet surprisingly sincere and dependable adventurer. He made his way through a series of similar rough-and-ready exploits in subsequent films: *Dark of the Sun* (1968), *The Split, Kenner* (1968), *100 Rifles* (1968), *Ice Station Zebra* (1968), *Riot* (1969), *The Grasshopper* (1970), *Tick . . . Tick . . . Tick* (1970), and *El Condor* (1970). Jim Brown was always a bold man, decisive, anxious for action, and completely confident of his own power. Males relished the situations in which he was cast and his skill in getting out of them while keeping his cool. Young black children in the ghetto liked him because he was a black man who could shove back to whitey the violence whitey had originally dealt out. And women responded to him because his intense sexuality was closely related to his power. Directors were quick to show him with his chest bare, with his thick legs exposed. The blackness of his skin and his sheer physicality took audiences back to the myth of the black man as a pure creature of astounding sexual prowess.

Another reason for Brown's success with females (notably white ones) was his apparent lack of sensitivity. When he took Raquel Welch to bed in *100 Rifles*, it was evident that his character lacked the tenderness and humanity which in the past had always redeemed the most violent of movie heroes in the eyes of female fans. Consequently, the main thing women could respond to in Jim Brown was his beautiful physical being. Surprisingly, there were not many black women among

Tough, arrogant, and a master of machismo, actor Jim Brown emerged in the late 1960s as the perfect black hero for a separatist age.

his fans. His lack of feeling and passion made him seem just as sterile as certain white adventure heroes. On the other hand, Brown's characterizations may have won him a certain homosexual following. One scene in his prison drama, *Riot*, seems to have been inserted not only to shock the sensibilities of the mass audience but also to titillate some of the homosexual patrons. In the film Brown is approached by a white prisoner who begs to spend the night with him. As Brown's character remains aloof and implausibly untouched, the homosexual's passion merely grows. Brown's low-keyed, understated sadism obviously turns him on.

The most interesting aspect of Jim Brown's characters in the 1960s was that their strength was always used to work with the dominant white culture rather than against it. Whites applauded him and gave him their stamp of approval because he aided them. Thus in *The Dirty Dozen* his violence was directed against enemy troops. In *Riot*, it is directed against the corrupt white warden and in aid of mistreated prisoners, white and black. In *Dark of the Sun*, his strength united with that of white mercenaries trying to rid an African nation of revolutionary simbas. Jim Brown's brute force, if not properly guided, would be blind and indiscriminate and too much of a threat to white males in the audience; thus he could never be cast as a politically militant black man.

Regardless, Jim Brown proved himself an exciting new presence in American motion pictures. He starred in almost nothing but B movies. Yet they succeeded because of him, seeming to subordinate themselves to his presence. Curiously, although patrons did not go to see Jim Brown movies for their social significance, the Brown vehicles carried some political weight simply because there was a black man up there on the screen, raising cain, strutting like a glorious prima donna, and sure to let everyone know that he could not care less whether he was liked or not. And he seemed to be avenging all those earlier black males who had to bow and kowtow. Jim Brown was a hero for a distinctly separatist age, and he proved in the separatist late 1960s that he was the right actor at the right time in the right place. His following dwindled somewhat when audiences saw through the transparency of his buck heroes, but Jim Brown's one-dimensional comic book adventurers were precursors of the independent, arrogantly aggressive buck heroes that dominated black movies in the early 1970s. Brown himself remained an important star in the next era. In tune with the changing times, his screen persona was mildly politicized in a film like the 1974 *Three the Hard Way*: along with Fred Williamson and Jim Kelly, he's in pursuit of a white supremacist with a black genocide scheme.

The New-Style Black Film

The 1960s' most curious phenomenon, the new-style black film, made its way onto American screens with the 1969 appearance of the movies *Uptight*, *Slaves*, *The*

Learning Tree, *The Lost Man*, and *Putney Swope*. Each conformed to a broader type of film then rising in popularity, the let's-hate-ugly-corrupt-America motion picture. All were indictments of the system. Each focused on some aspect of the new black militancy, often applauding separatism. Significantly, too, most of these films had blacks working behind the cameras as well as in front.

Jules Dassin's *Uptight* was the first American movie to spotlight black revolutionaries and the separatist movement. Set in the Hough ghetto area of Cleveland shortly after the assassination of Martin Luther King, the film takes up the theme of nonviolence. Nonviolence died with King in Memphis, declare the dashiki-clad revolutionary protagonists as they arm themselves with guns and slogans. When one of the group's leaders is turned into the police by a fellow member of the organization, the militants track down and assassinate the informant. Little else happens in the film.

Most considered *Uptight* a major disappointment. Audiences had waited anxiously for a film that would dramatize the chaos of the streets. On the surface, with its trappings—the ghetto, the beards, the beads, the afros, the armaments— the film looked contemporary, but underneath it was compromised and dishonest, revealing its white director's inability to see a black story from a black point of view. Preachy and didactic, Dassin's movie was based on John Ford's 1935 film *The Informer*. Dassin and his black screenwriters, Ruby Dee and Julian Mayfield, had substituted black revolutionaries for the Irish rebels of the Ford drama. But by this substitution, the trio exposed their failure to grasp the complexities that distinguish the new black movement from any other in the history of Western man. Moreover, their characters lacked commitment and passion, and as they stormed about the streets of Cleveland they emerged as little more than one-dimensional, pent-up black brutes. In fact, if *Uptight* made any statement at all, it was that blacks were effectual only at wiping out one of their own. Never did audiences see a heated black–white confrontation.

But the most disturbing aspect of *Uptight* was its actors. Individual militant performances could have invigorated the platitudes, the didacticism, and the brute stereotypes. But unfortunately Dassin cast his picture with dull American actors. As the black whore, Ruby Dee still touched audiences with her vaguely pathetic smile, but she seemed all wrong for the part. Writer Julian Mayfield should have stuck to the books; portraying the alcoholic informer Tank Williams, he was little more than a walking vacuum.

Uptight's greatest liability was Raymond St. Jacques. Before his appearance in the Dassin feature, St. Jacques had been building up a following. Audiences, ignoring his uncharacteristically agreeable portrayals in *Black Like Me* and *The Green Berets* (1968), had been attracted to the shrewd and insolent air he exhibited in minor roles in such 1965 films as *Mr. Moses*, *The Pawnbroker*, and *Mr. Buddwing*. The crowning point of his career had come with his performance as the sadistic captain of the Haitian police in *The Comedians* (1967). Here he had used his deep, resonant voice splendidly, and his menacing *sang-froid* had conveyed appropriate hostility and aggression; as he strutted about in his dark glasses or shoved Lillian Gish onto the pavement, Raymond St. Jacques was the incarnation of militant anger. Thereafter he was touted as the new revolutionary hero. But the touting proved premature.

When next cast as the hard-as-nails, no-nonsense convict in the adaptation of Chester Himes's *If He Hollers, Let Him Go* (1968), Raymond St. Jacques had his first starring role, but he was not strong or interesting enough to carry the picture throughout. Some of his defects were quite apparent, too. His voice was still resonant but unvaried. At times his delivery was dry as a biscuit and his monosyllabic grunts and groans made him sound as if he were suffering from cinematic constipation; one hoped he would find the bathroom before the movie ended. In *Uptight*, in a role for which he was physically perfect because he resembled so much the real revolutionary H. Rap Brown, the underlying lack of charisma in St. Jacques's personality was used by director Dassin not only to undercut but to deglamorize the black militant spirit by presenting so unpassionate and uninspiring a leader. At best, his work could be called competent, but it was not enough to charge the movie with the vitality it needed. Later, in *Cotton Comes to Harlem, Come Back Charleston Blue* (1972), *Cool Breeze* (1972), and *The Final Comedown* (1972) he was more successful in roles that demanded less. His last appearance before his death was in *Glory* (1989).

Radicalized plantation slaves were the protagonists of Herbert Biberman's *Slaves*. Through this undercover remake of *Uncle Tom's Cabin*, director Biberman hoped to draw an analogy between the brutal America of the past and the violent America of the 1960s. But the analogy was uncalled for because it was already so vividly self-evident, and surely if anything was superfluous in 1969, it was a replay of Stowe's saintly (and actually more complex than most filmmakers were willing to admit) hero. As it turned out, *Slaves* relied on stock characters and episodes: the inhuman slave auction; the sadistic white master; the beautiful mulatto mistress in the Big House; the kindly, loyal black manservant. In 1977, the television miniseries "Roots" would explore the same type of situations and characters but with great conviction, a deeper comprehension of the slave system, and remarkable performances. Decades later Quentin Tarantino's *Django Unchained* would turn the old movie-style images on their heads to present a violent, bloody portrait of slavery, and Steve McQueen's *12 Years A Slave* in 2013 would rewrite movie history to present a nuanced, powerful portrait of slave lives. In *Slaves*, the script does little to distinguish the masochistic tom character. But Ossie Davis gives it a valiant try. Newcomer Barbara Ann Teer provided the picture with its genuine moments of anguish and pain. As the slave wife about to see her man sold to another plantation, her cry, "It just ain't fair, it just ain't fair," was urgent and real but still not enough to elevate a film already weighed down by an inadequate script and a melodramatic, heavy-handed piece of direction. Finally, as the master's black mistress, singer Dionne Warwick was, to put it kindly—sweetly preposterous. But like Jackie Robinson when he had made his film debut, she was great in the action shots as she roamed discontentedly through the plantation, singing, singing, singing 'bout slavery.

Black novelist John O. Killens was employed as one of *Slaves*'s scriptwriters. Killens had turned in professional work with his screenplay for *Odds Against Tomorrow*, but here he seemed overwhelmed by a white director's demands. In one interesting scene the corrupt slave master (Stephen Boyd) relates the rich history and accomplishments of African tribes to his white friends. Because the achievements are indeed real, the scene has a startling impact. Surely, Killens had something to do with writing it. But ultimately the achievements are turned against them and are used by the film as one further assertion of white power. For, rich and productive as the African tribes were, the almighty white man, as usual, conquered them.

Uptight and *Slaves* were moderately successful. False and hollow as they were, the films offered black audiences recognizable images. Here at least were products that acknowledged the violence and cruelty of the white American way of life. Black audiences accepted them but with the hope that something better might come along.

Gordon Parks's *The Learning Tree* was something better, although it was not to meet with as much success as its predecessors. In 1963 Parks, a distinguished black photographer for *Life* magazine, had added another entry to an impressive list of credits when his autobiographical novel *The Learning Tree* was published and widely praised. When Warner Brothers signed him to adapt his book for the screen, Parks became the first black man to direct a major American movie. With a cast that included young Kyle Johnson, Alex Clarke, Mira Waters, Estelle Evans, Dana Elcar, and the fine character actor Joel Fluellen, Parks shot his movie in his home town, Fort Scott, Kansas.

The Learning Tree was a nostalgic evocation of a period and a place seemingly remote in 1969. It records the events in Parks's childhood in Kansas during the 1920s. At first glance it is an innocent time when the picture's hero, Newt, can do cartwheels in a field of flowers or steal apples from a vineyard with his buddies. But it is also an age polluted by violence and racism. A creek where Newt swims suddenly turns red from the blood of a black man senselessly shot by a bigoted white sheriff. In an old country barn a white man is mercilessly beaten to death by a black. In the town courtroom, that same black man flees an angry group of townspeople and blows out his brains before they have a chance to do it for him. On second glance, Newt's age is not so remote from the late 1960s after all. "Some of the people," the hero's mother tells him, "are good and some of them are bad—

just like the fruit on a tree . . . think of it like that till the day you die—let it be your learnin' tree."

Simply and sensitively, Gordon Parks's film presents a boy who is black but not tortured by his blackness. He is like other boys, no matter what the color or place or time. Yet he is not colorless. Nor indistinct. He knows what it is to be told to leave a restaurant, to be advised that college is not for colored boys. He knows violence and cruelty. But unlike other black characters in the late 1960s (most notably the brute protagonists of *Uptight* and *Slaves*), he does not suffer consciously. Nor does he cheaply parade his discontent. Parks's hero, played beautifully by Kyle Johnson, observes the world. Bruised by it, he learns from it nonetheless.

As good as it was, *The Learning Tree* did rely on a number of clichés. But to director Parks' credit, he presented them with such feeling as to render them new, and he resensitized his audiences so that they experienced again the pain of being told to leave a restaurant because of their color. In the end he restored the clichés' original meanings, and his film remains a lyrical and eloquent statement on the black experience in America.

The Sidney Poitier vehicle *The Lost Man* seemed in many respects a successor to *Uptight*. Based also on an old movie (*Odd Man Out*, 1947) about the Irish Revolution, its transatlantic substitution of blacks for Irish rebels failed to be dramatically convincing or coherent. Black militants prepare to overtake a city (Philadelphia) through an "infallible" payroll robbery. Amid decaying brownstones and deserted, littered lots, Poitier stands lean and pure as ever. Outfitted with dark glasses as he raps with the brothers, he is not the out-and-out tom of old, but he is not the radicalized brute the movie wants him to be either. Flat and pretentious, *The Lost Man* failed at the box office, and the trumped-up romance between the black hero and the white society girl almost set ghetto theaters aflame with indignation. In this separatist age, such white–black alliances were clearly out of place.

A film that seemed out of whack with the times but spotlighted a new black talent was Mark Rydell's breezy adaptation of William Faulkner's *The Reivers* (1969) with Steve McQueen and black actor Rupert Crosse. McQueen played the likable roguish hero while Crosse gave a comic and well-shaded performance as a black slickster/sidekick. With only a few previous screen credits such as a role in Cassevetes's *Shadows* and another in *Waterhole #3* (1967), Crosse proved effective enough to win an Academy Award nomination as Best Supporting Actor. It was the first time a black actor had ever been nominated in that category. In the years to come, a number of black performers (Howard Rollins, Jr., Alfre Woodard, and Margaret Avery) were finally, like Crosse, to receive this type of industry recognition for their work, winning those all-powerful Oscar nominations, which was no small feat. Afterward Crosse appeared mostly on television. He died, however, at age 46 in 1973.

ABOVE: An undercover remake of *Uncle Tom's Cabin* passed as a "new style black film": *Slaves* (1969), with Stephen Boyd as the wicked massa, Ossie Davis as the stoic, masochistic slave, and Dionne Warwick as that mysterious black gal livin' up there in de massa's Big House.

BELOW: The trials and tribulations of a decadent middle-class black couple (Lola Falana and Roscoe Lee Browne) were sensationalized and distorted in *The Liberation of L. B. Jones* (1970).

Robert Downey's *Putney Swope* closed the decade and was the first of the new black films to take a farcical look at black America. The film was part parody, part put-down, part satire—of stereotypes, power manipulations on Madison Avenue, capitalism, and the various hang-ups infesting the American way of life. Downey achieved his end by reversing the racial scales.

Putney Swope's plot is simple. A black token figure in an advertising agency is accidentally elected chairman of the board. "I'm not going to rock the boat," Putney announces upon his election. "I am going to sink it!" Thereafter in one superbly edited sequence the board of directors is no longer the line of pole-faced white cadavers, corrupt and hungry for money and power. It has been replaced by a new vital black staff equipped with dashikis and afros, later with guns and munitions. The agency changes its name to Truth and Soul, Inc., and it sets out to shake up the sensibilities of just about everyone.

By the time the film ends Putney and company have sunk the boat and at the same time revealed blacks to be just as corrupt and power-hungry as whites. Their black Establishment (best symbolized by Mrs. Swope berating and hounding her scrawny white maid) proves no better than its white predecessor. White has been turned black and black turned white, and everybody is made ugly.

In reviewing *Putney Swope*, Arthur Knight of *Saturday Review* said the film "just goes to show what might happen should blacks ever get control of the power structure in this country." In actuality, *Putney Swope* was merely what Mr. Knight, Mr. Downey, and others thought would happen in America should black citizens attain economic or political control. To substantiate his view, director Downey relied on the misconceptions and myths about blacks that had pervaded and polluted white America for so long. The blacks of *Putney Swope* were depicted as supercharged athletes, as high-powered sexual beings, as loud-mouth do-nothings. Instead of picking at any genuine black follies to prove his point, the director chose to satirize the lies, myths, clichés, exaggerations. For some, *Putney Swope* is an entertaining film. But for others, it is a work admirably filmed in segments but horribly distorted with black brutes and bucks and exotic whores that hark back to the days of D. W. Griffith.

Putney Swope and the other new black films of the late 1960s may today seem like historical pieces and not very powerful stuff. But they do reveal the manner in which films were being used almost explicitly to make political statements. The new motion picture makers—for whatever reasons—wanted their products to take a stand on current social, political, and even economic issues. Statement-making continued and ultimately the new black films of this period proved to be merely the genesis of a new style and a new attitude on what movies should be all about. It was in the next decade, however, that the new black film further evolved.

Billy Dee Williams and Diana Ross, the era's king and queen of black pop, in *Lady Sings the Blues* (1972). The film was a simplified dramatization of Billie Holiday's very complex life but succeeded nonetheless as an entertaining, escapist movie romance.

8 THE 1970s: BUCKS AND A BLACK MOVIE BOOM

A trio of unlikely protagonists—Sweetback, Shaft, and Super Fly—storm across the screen, stomping down whitey, then waltzing off into the urban sunset, while becoming heroes for a new generation of young black moviegoers. . . . Diana Ross and Billy Dee Williams emerge as the dream queen and king of black romantic pop in Lady Sings the Blues *and* Mahogany. . . . *Cicely Tyson and Paul Winfield win critical acclaim for their powerful dramatic performances in* Sounder. . . . *Jim Brown and Fred Williamson, in a maddening bid for stardom, lead a host of athletes coming to the silver screen. . . . Sidney Poitier, Ossie Davis, and Michael Schultz are among the era's new film directors. . . .* Claudine *and* Sparkle *are movie rarities: dramas focusing on the tensions and turmoils of black women. . . . And, surprise of all surprises, a comedian from Peoria, Illinois, none other than Richard Pryor, becomes a leading man in the movies and is en route to full-fledged stardom.*

It was the 1970s, that slick, trendy, and contradictory era that opened with politics and social issues very much on the minds of most Americans. Student campus takeovers continued. So, too, did protests against the war in Vietnam. What with the Black Nationalist movement, the youth movement, and the rising tide of feminism, the 1970s looked as if it, like the 1960s, would be propelled along by political activism. But within a few years, the national mood had dramatically changed. Following Watergate and Richard Nixon's resignation from the presidency, the nation's citizens grew increasingly cynical and disillusioned about their government. During the years of Gerald Ford and Jimmy Carter, Americans seemed to focus less on social concerns and problems and more on personal goals and ambitions. The various trends and national fixations of the mid- and late 1970s—whether it be the jogging enthusiasts, the health food advocates, the disco devotees, or the openly (and joyously) self-analytical—all were signs and symbols, so the social historians believed, of a nation whose citizens had become obsessed with themselves. A period that had been known for its political fervor was now labeled a self-indulgent "me" decade instead.

The movies, of course, reflected the shifting outlooks and attitudes. No other period in black movie history, however, has been quite so energetic or important as the frenetic 1970s. More black actors and actresses worked in films than ever before. Black writers such as Richard Wesley, Bill Gunn, and Lonne Elder III wrote scripts for important productions. Such black directors as Gordon Parks, Sr., *and* Gordon Parks, Jr., as well as Sidney Poitier, Michael Schultz, Stan Lathan, Hugh Robertson, and Ossie Davis all made major studio films. For the first time in film history, the studios produced black-oriented films pitched directly at pleasing blacks. Audiences saw black movie characters speaking in a new idiom and rhythm. Movies sought to give some semblance of a black community with a set of attitudes, aspirations, and grievances all its own.

But while images of the 1970s were far different from those of previous decades, often enough the old stereotypes resurfaced, simply dressed in new garb to look modern, hip, provocative, and politically "relevant." The early years of the era might best be described as *the age of the buck*, a period when a band of aggressive, pistol-packing, sexually-charged urban cowboys set off on a heady rampage, out to topple the system and to right past wrongs. Other familiar faces also appeared: the beautiful doomed light-skinned black woman (yes, the long adored tragic mulatto) and some fast-talking coons. Then, too, while the 1970s opened with films with some political heat, the age closed with movies that were increasingly more escapist. By the era's end, there was even the return of a large-scale all-black musical.

Preludes

At the start of the era, black audiences, like those of the 1960s, sat in wait, picking through this picture or that, in search of a film or character that would directly address America's racial issues and conflicts. A film like William Wyler's 1970 *The Liberation of L. B. Jones*, which examined nasty race relations in a small Southern town and touched on the ties between sex and racism, generated some interest. Black audiences tended to ignore the film's nominal stars (Roscoe Lee Browne as a bourgeois tom, Lola Falana as his "slutty" wife) in favor of the militant character played by Yaphet Kotto, who, at the film's climax, threw a tough old Southern racist into a hay cropper. Here was a black man clearly taking matters in hand—and refusing to back away from violence as retribution. Audiences also responded to James Earl Jones as the defiant and outspoken boxer Jack Jefferson (based on the first black heavyweight champion, Jack Johnson) in Martin Rites *The Great White Hope*. Jones's performance was stagy and overblown but powerful enough nonetheless to win him an Academy Award nomination as Best Actor. Jones later appeared, with varying degrees of success (he remains a rather overrated screen actor), in *The Man* (1972), *Swashbuckler* (1976), *A Piece of the Action* (1977), *Conan the Barbarian* (1982), *Matewan* (1987), and *Gardens of Stone* (1987). But for a brief spell in the early 1970s, it looked as if he might become an important leading man in American movies.

Hal Ashby's *The Landlord* also featured black characters that the audience could identify with. This underrated satiric comedy-drama featured Diana Sands as a woman who has an affair with the young white landlord (Beau Bridges) of her Brooklyn tenement. When her husband (Louis Gossett, Jr.) learns she has become pregnant by the young white man, he grabs an axe and threatens Bridges. The husband's anger, doubtless intensified through years of pain, and powerfully defined by Gossett, is so real and focused that here audiences saw a black man entrapped in a tight, oppressive system that daily eats away at dreams and wrecks lives.

In a very moving sequence, Sands's character—saddened, guilt-ridden, and heartbroken by the callousness of the white man—lies solemnly in a hospital bed. She wants Bridges to put their son up for adoption—but as a white. "Why?" he asks. "Cause I want him to grow up casual," she answers, "like his daddy." Here Sands gives what may be her best performance.

Other solid performances came from Mel Stewart, Robert Klein, Marki Bey, Marlene Clark, Lee Grant, and Pearl Bailey. Much of *The Landlord*'s strange, moody, dreamy tone and its perceptive, deeply-felt depiction of ghetto life, can be attributed to black writer Bill Gunn's sensitive screenplay. The film was based on a novel by black writer Kristin Hunter.

The picture that launched much of the energetic, optimistic spirit of the 1970s was Ossie Davis's *Cotton Comes to Harlem*. Based on a novel by black writer Chester Himes, the film's heroes were two gritty black detectives, Grave Digger Jones (Godfrey Cambridge) and Coffin Ed Johnson (Raymond St. Jacques). Its plot was standard cops-and-robbers stuff, its portrait of Harlem still that of a picturesque merry-go-round, populated by a crew of congenial coons, toms, and painted ladies. It not only played up to black fantasies (on a black world order) but also to white fantasies of a black world full of harmless stereotypes.

Its shortcomings aside, Davis's high-spirited, boisterous romp—reminiscent of the best race movies—managed to revive the old ethnic humor. Unlike a white director who might have treated the material with condescension, Davis delighted in the spark and vigor of his cast, which included Calvin Lockhart, Judy Pace, Emily Yancy, Frederick O'Neal, Helen Martin, Cleavon Little, Theodore Wilson, and most notably, that grand old master of the "chitlin circuit," Redd Foxx.

Cotton Comes to Harlem seemed to be telling black audiences that it was now all right to laugh at the old dum-dum characters which would have infuriated audiences of the 1960s. Now the old ethnic humor seemed blessed with a double consciousness: rather than cooning or tomming it up to please whites (as Fetchit had had to do), the black comic characters joked or laughed or acted the fool with one another. Or sometimes they used humor combatively to outwit the white characters. (Of course, Eddie Anderson and Hattie McDaniel had always done this, on the sly.)

With *Cotton Comes to Harlem*, a black director had now also turned out an unabashed moneymaker. The film was an unprecedented success. It had a record opening in Chicago, and *Variety* predicted that "even Southern exhibitors will want a piece of the action." Davis continued directing films: adaptations of Wole Soyinka's *Kongi's Harvest* (1971) and also black female playwright J. E. Franklin's *Black Girl* (1972). The latter looked at three generations of black women and featured a lineup of vivid actresses: Claudia McNeil, Louise Stubbs, Ruby Dee, Leslie Uggams, Loretta Greene, Gloria Edwards, and young Peggy Pettitt. Later Davis directed *Gordon's War* (1973, starring Paul Winfield as a Vietnam veteran who sets out to clean up the drug-infested streets of Harlem) and *Countdown at Kusini* (1976).

Melvin Van Peebles: The Black Movie Director as Folk Hero

The film, however, that clearly introduced the new-style defiant buck hero and galvanized the new audience was Melvin Van Peebles's *Sweet Sweetback's Baadasssss Song*. The picture was the third of a director who had already led a rough-and-tumble life. Born in Chicago in 1932, Van Peebles had graduated from Ohio Wesleyan University, later lived in San Francisco, then moved to France where he wrote five novels and tried his hand at filmmaking. His first feature, the European-made *Story of a Three-Day Pass* (1967, based on his novel), about an interracial love affair, received a mixed but encouraging reception from American critics. His second film, the 1970 *Watermelon Man*, was no great success either; its distinction was that it now ranks as the classic tragic mulatto movie of the early separatist 1970s. Godfrey Cambridge stolidly portrayed (in whiteface) a white insurance man transformed overnight into—heaven help us—a Negro! Thereafter his wife deserts him, and he suffers an identity crisis. That old black blood—which always brews trouble—has made his life wretched and intolerable. *Watermelon Man* dramatized a great white fantasy-nightmare (and perhaps marginally a great black fantasy about whites)—that of mysteriously losing lily-whiteness and turning coal-black. Yet as a motion picture that supposedly addressed itself to the black experience, it seemed remote. But with *Sweet Sweetback's Baadasssss Song*, director

Van Peebles, who also wrote the script, discovered not only his audience but his style and subject too.

The film centers on a cool-as-a-cucumber black stud, Sweetback. When he sees two white policemen cudgel an innocent black youth, he lays waste to them, smashing in their heads with their own handcuffs. Then he flees. After a series of chase sequences and hot sexual adventures (he is the most extravagantly sexual hero audiences ever saw), he manages to escape the law. The film ended with the message: A BAADASSSSS NIGGER IS COMING BACK TO COLLECT SOME DUES. The fact that a black man met violence with violence and triumphed over the corrupt white establishment appealed not only to the mass black audience (particularly, the black young, who flocked to it) but to some young white audiences as well. Then, too, after decades of comic asexual black male characters and an era like the 1950s when Poitier and Belafonte, while considered sexually attractive, were rarely permitted to be sexually aggressive in their films, audiences were ready for a sexual black movie hero.

Sweetback was a blazing commercial success, and it gave birth to a series of imitations. Widely reported on by the press, the film also set off a wave of controversy because of its violence and raw sexuality. White critics tended to hate the film flat out. "Whites would have to be masochists to accept the unrelenting portrait of their fellows," wrote Archer Winsten in *The New York Post*. In *The New York Times*, Vincent Canby called it "almost psychotic" and "an absolutely mindless and dirty political exploitation film." Within the black community, the film was also debated.

"There is a certain grim white humor," wrote Lerone Bennett in *Ebony*, "in the fact that the black marches and demonstrations of the 1960s reached artistic fulfillment in the 1970s with Flip Wilson's Geraldine and Melvin Van Peebles's Sweetback, two provocative and ultimately insidious reincarnations of all the Sapphires and Studs of yesteryear." Bennett's article attacked the film as trivial and tasteless and labeled it a negative classic "because it is an obligatory step for anyone who wants to go further and make the first revolutionary black film."

During this period of obvious social flux and of the evolution of a black cultural aesthetic, which insisted that black art give the black community some political and social direction, *Sweetback* seemed—for older members of the black intellectual community—to offer not direction but a daydream of triumph. At heart, its hero, of course, was the familiar brutal black buck. In some respects, the picture may be viewed as having fed white hysteria and paranoia. Yet as a bold declaration of war that refuses to make concessions to please a white audience, the film enjoys jerking white audiences around and unleashing age-old fears.

But the film also succeeded partly because it played on a certain social/political philosophy prevalent in some sectors of the black community in the late 1960s and early 1970s. During that time, in rejecting the black bourgeoisie, which had seemingly often aided and abetted White America through attempts at cultural

Three of the early 1970s most popular heroes: Melvin Van Peebles, the director, producer, and star of *Sweet Sweetback's Baadasssss Song* (1971); Ron O'Neal as the moody character Priest in *Super Fly* (1972); and Richard Roundtree, gun in hand and ready for action, in *Shaft* (1971).

assimilation, the new militant separatist black classes sometimes came to identify blackness with the trappings of the ghetto: the tenements as well as the talk, the mannerisms, and the sophistication of the streets—all of which appeared to mark a life lived close to one's black roots. Ghetto residents seemed to have a greater ethnic identity. Eventually, poverty and ghetto life (sometimes the very degrading constraints imposed on Black America by White America) were frequently idealized and glamorized. (This was frequently done by the educated, politically committed children of the black bourgeoisie.) With the glamorization of the ghetto, however, came also the elevation of the pimp/outlaw/rebel as folk hero. Van Peebles played up to this new sensibility, and his film was the first to glorify the pimp. It failed, however, to explain the social conditions that made the pimp such an important figure. At the same time, the movie debased the black woman, depicting her as little more than a whore. His film remains, however, a striking social document on the nature and certain attitudes of the new era. Just as importantly, in its own way, *Sweetback* revealed through music and movement a communal spirit—call it tribal if you will—existent in Black America alone. Throughout Sweetback was aided by members of the community wherever he went, and surely, at the conclusion, the community had contributed to the individual's triumph as much as the man himself.

Afterwards Van Peebles emerged as something of a folk hero for the black community, partly because of the daring way he had produced his movie outside the Hollywood system. Working under the pretense of making a porno, Van Peebles used a nonunion crew (blacks and whites) and shot the picture in nineteen days, all on a budget of $500,000. At one point, Bill Cosby loaned him $50,000. After most distributors refused to touch the film, Cinemation picked it up. Within a few months, *Sweetback* grossed $10 million. In interviews Van Peebles used the tone appropriate for the times. "Of all the ways we've been exploited by the Man, the most damaging is the way he destroyed our self-image," he told *Time* in its August 16, 1971, issue. "The message of *Sweetback* is that if you can get it together and stand up to the Man, you can win." Later Van Peebles wrote the Broadway shows *Ain't Supposed to Die a Natural Death* and *Don't Play Us Cheap*.

For a time, he was one of the most visible black personalities in the public eye. His 1973 screen version of *Don't Play Us Cheap*, however, proved disappointing and was poorly distributed. In 1976 he wrote "Just an Old Sweet Song" for television. But no other features followed in the 1970s.

In the early 1980s, he directed theater productions and also wrote and appeared in the television drama "Sophisticated Gents." In the mid-1980s, he became the only black trader on the American Stock Exchange. Was there ever a greater irony for a one-time maverick black film director? Later he appeared briefly in *Jaws The Revenge* (1987) and directed (1989) *Identity Crisis* both featuring his son, actor Mario Van Peebles.

In the 1970s, though, Melvin Van Peebles changed the direction of black movies. Now audiences had been introduced to the new style black film (based on dissent and anger) in which the black male's sexuality, for too long suppressed, had come to the forefront. Now the bucks took center stage.

Shaft: He's a Badd Mother—Shut Your Mouth

Shaft also appeared in 1971. This little picture, which its studio, MGM, thought might make a little money, instead made a mint—some $12 million within a year in North America alone—and single-handedly saved MGM from financial ruin.

Directed by Gordon Parks, Sr., *Shaft* starred newcomer Richard Roundtree as a tough, renegade black detective, John Shaft, who lives in a swanky book-lined Village apartment, is confident enough to down any cat who crosses his path, and is a whiz with the ladies. "Hotter than Bond. Cooler than Bullitt," read the advertisements. Based on a novel by white writer Ernest Tidyman, *Shaft* essentially was a standard white detective tale enlivened by a black sensibility. As Roundtree's John Shaft—mellow but assertive and unintimidated by whites—bopped through those hot mean streets dressed in his cool leather, he looked to black audiences like a brother they had all seen many times before but *never* on screen. Isaac Hayes's pulsating background music also added to the film's texture. When the lyrics to the title song announced that Shaft was a "baad mother" and then a chorus cut in quickly saying, "shut your mouth," well, it was hard to be completely critical of the film. Hayes's "Theme from *Shaft*" won the 1971 Academy Award as Best Song, marking the first time a black man had ever won the Oscar in this category. Two innocuous and jumbled sequels appeared: *Shaft's Big Score* (1972, directed by Parks) and *Shaft in Africa* (1973).

Gordon Parks later directed *The Super Cops* (1974). But *Lead-belly*, his 1976 romanticized biography of folk singer Huddie Ledbetter, was poorly handled by its studio Paramount and died at the box office. Parks made no other feature films. His career, like Van Peebles', pointed up the basic fact that while black directors were to work on major films in the 1970s, those very directors also found it hard to sustain their careers. The same would prove true of many of the era's black performers including Richard Roundtree who starred in *Shaft* sequels as well as *Charley One-Eye* (1973), *Earthquake* (1974), *Man Friday* (1976), *One Down, Two to Go* (1983), as well as *City Heat* (1984) with Clint Eastwood. He also made a nostalgic cameo appearance, along with director Parks, in the remake of *Shaft* in 2000.

Super Fly: Mixed Messages

A year after *Shaft*, *Super Fly* (1972), independently produced by Sig Shore and directed by Gordon Parks, Jr., appeared. Within two months, it made $11 million and for a spell, outgrossed every other movie on the market. Within the African American community, however, many were outraged by the glorification of its hero, a Harlem cocaine dealer named Priest (Ron O'Neal). It has to be admitted that hero Priest, dressed like an urban prima ballerina in long, sweeping coats and large wide-brimmed hats, is a romanticized version of the Harlem pimp.

Super Fly looks authentic: the Harlem settings, the streets and alleyways, the bars, and the tenements all paint an overriding bleak vision of urban decay, new terrain for commercial cinema. It's a war zone where corrupt drug kingpins and pushers battle for control. Priest has risen to power by standing outside the law. The law itself, so the picture reveals, is perverted and corrupt. The film ends with Priest defeating his white opponents (including the drug boss) and leaving the cocaine business with a hefty bankroll to boot.

At heart, *Super Fly* sends out mixed messages. At one point when a disgruntled Priest announces he wants to get out of the drug trade, his friend Eddie (Carl Lee) dismisses such thoughts. After all, so Eddie reasons, Priest has everything America is taught to value: the fabulous apartment, the stereo, the car, the fine *vines* (clothes), even the women who are considered part of such a package. Fundamentally, the film tells audiences that the American dream of success has become polluted and perverted into a nightmare of cold, hard materialism. Priest, however, is no political rebel with an agenda of political alternatives. This grand-style individualist just wants out. Yet he plans to take with him his material acquisitions and comforts (represented by the cache of money he holds onto at the end of the film).

Audiences, however, chose to overlook the contradictions, enthusiastically accepting the wish-fulfillment ending. No one wanted to see a black hero defeated. Thus the main point again was that here was a black man living on his own terms. Like Shaft and Sweetback, Priest was also, you might say, *sexually audacious*.

Curiously enough, the big sex scene in *Super Fly* (it's a bathtub sequence with lots of suds covering some vital areas) like the sex scenes in other black films—*Melinda* (1972), *Slaughter* (1972), and *Shaft*—frequently was more graphic and lingering than any such scene in white movies of the time and looked as if it had been inserted simply to play on the legend of blacks' high-powered sexuality. While the movies assiduously sought to avoid the stereotype of the asexual tom, they fell, interestingly enough, into the trap of presenting the wildly sexual man. Rarely was there a mature male view of sex as depicted in a movie like *Nothing But a Man*. Then, too, the women are rarely defined in any way other than as the hero's love interest.

Technically, *Super Fly* was adequate. Some of its drive could be attributed to Curtis Mayfield's sensual score. There was also actor Ron O'Neal's performance—or perhaps his perceptive lack of one. O'Neal presented an arrogant, enigmatic hustler who was careful not to reveal too much. In 1973 a fairly terrible sequel, *Super Fly T.N.T.* appeared, starring and directed by O'Neal with a script by Alex Haley. In 1990, there was a sorry attempt to revive Super Fly in *The Return of Super Fly.*

Ron O'Neal later appeared in such films as *The Master Gunfighter* (1975), *Brothers* (1977), and *Red Dawn* (1984). Director Gordon Parks, Jr., also directed *Thomasine and Bushrod* (1974, with Max Julien and Vonetta McGee), *Three the Hard Way* (1974), and *Aaron Loves Angela* (a 1975 modern Romeo and Juliet story, starring Kevin Hooks and Irene Cara). In 1979 Parks, at the age of forty-five, was killed in a plane crash in Kenya.

Buckmania

The success of *Sweet Sweetback's Baadasssss Song*, *Shaft*, and *Super Fly* snapped the industry moguls to attention. Soon black films began turning up with startling regularity. Sometimes it even looked as if the same movies were being remade time and again. First there was *The Legend of Nigger Charley* (1972), then *The Soul of Nigger Charley* (1973). There were *Black Caesar* (1973), *Black Samson* (1974), *Black Jesus* (1971), and *Sweet Jesus, Preacher Man* (1973). There were *Slaughter* and *Slaughter's Big Rip Off* (1973, an appropriate title if there ever was one), also *Blacula* and *Scream, Blacula, Scream* (1973). There were also *The Bus Is Coming* (1971), *Top of the Heap* (1972), *The Final Comedown* (1972), *Hit Man* (1972), *Cool Breeze* (1972), *Detroit 9000* (1973), *The Black Godfather* (1974), and *The Mack* (1973).

"Talented black actors, directors and writers were suddenly plucked out of studio back rooms, modeling agencies and ghetto theaters, and turned loose on new black projects," wrote *Newsweek* in its October 23, 1972, cover story on the new black movie boom. "But an astonishing number of black films have been paying off at a rate to put their white counterparts in the shade—and . . . have . . . produced the first gold mine in years for a struggling industry." The black audience's support of the new black films may well have saved the commercial film industry at a time when general ticket sales were in a slump.

For the most part, the films were heady male action fantasies, with tenacious buck protagonists performing deeds of derring-do, while self-righteously giving lip service to the idea of political commitment. The films would have us believe the heroes were out to clean up the ghetto of its ills. Actually, the best way to have cleaned up the ghetto might have been to have first rounded up the producers of some of these vehicles.

What became most disturbing was that while these movies appeared to be black (in concept, in outlook, in feel) and while they were feverishly promoted and advertised as such, they actually were no such thing. Many of the new black-oriented films were written, directed, and produced by whites. (The same, of course, had been true of the latter part of the race movie movement.) Worse, many of the new movies were often shot on shoestring budgets, were badly directed, and were technically poor. The film industry hoped simply to make money by indeed exploiting an audience need. Eventually, there was the rise of what came to be known as the "blaxploitation film": a movie that played on the needs of black audiences for heroic figures without answering those needs in realistic terms.

Within the black community, protests were voiced. "We must insist that our children are not constantly exposed to a steady diet of so-called black movies that glorify black males as pimps, dope pushers, gangsters and super males," announced Junius Griffin, the head of the Hollywood branch of the NAACP.

One can readily understand why black audiences responded to the theme of these movies, which touched on the fundamental dissatisfaction of dispossessed people. One can also understand the appeal of the new characters, who were menacing figures far different from the passive "conciliatory" black types of the past. The films touched also on another need: that of entertainment. But the worlds those films frequently presented, despite the posturing and the attitudinizing, were often just as false as those of previous all-black Hollywood movies. And often the rough-tough-cream-puff militant-stud-buck heroes were no more authentic than the servants of the 1930s or the entertainers of the 1940s.

Yet something else cannot be overlooked. No matter what their distortions and dishonesties, many films from this period today retain a certain edge. Their collective subtext attracts or sometimes repels us. Often political and social messages crept through, providing insights and comments on the quality of life in America. They touched on a mass hope for an overturn of a corrupt racist system. The violence, the sense of betrayal and the relentless double-crossing maneuvers that are so much a part of these films are no doubt as much an outgrowth of the violence in Vietnam and the later corruption of Watergate as they are of the rage and despair of racial inequities in America. Ultimately, the success of the black-oriented films helped change the look and feel of the American feature in ways some might not have expected. Surely, the social realism of urban buck dramas—the idea of an ethnic hero with a distinct ethnic style—had an influence on such movies as Martin Scorsese's *Mean Streets* (1973) and *Taxi Driver* (1976), Sidney Lumet's *Dog Day Afternoon* (1975), and even the underclass struggle of Stallone's *Rocky*.

The Jock as Movie Star

Amid the black boom of the early and mid-1970s, there was a new phenomenon: the rise of the black athlete—the jock—as movie star. All types of athletic stars now appeared in films: former Olympic champ Rafer Johnson in *Soul Soldier* (1972);

football player O. J. Simpson in *The Klansman* (1974), *The Towering Inferno* (1974), in which he had the distinction of rescuing a cat, and in *Capricorn One* (1978); Muhammad Ali in *The Greatest* (1977), a weak look at the champ's life; football player Bernie Casey (possibly the best of the athletes-turned-actors) in *Hit Man; Maurie* (1974), *Cornbread, Earl and Me* (1975), *Brothers,* and later *Sharky's Machine* (1981), and *Never Say Never Again* (1983). The unbelievably stiff martial arts champ Jim Kelly also karate-chopped his way through *Enter the Dragon* (1973), *Black Belt Jones* (1974), *Golden Needles* (1974), and *Hot Potato* (1976). And boxer Ken Norton appeared as a part noble tom/part sexy buck in those sadomasochistic Old South wonders *Mandingo* (1975) and *Drum* (1976).

But why were there so many athletes on screen in the 1970s? Actually, in the past athletes Joe Louis, Jackie Robinson, Kenny Washington, Woody Strode, Althea Gibson, and others had all appeared in movies. When brought to the screen, the black athlete has always been a safe commodity because, without ever having made a picture, he or she is already a box-office name. (An audience may pay simply to see him make a fool of himself.)

Then, too, in American culture, the black athlete, powerful and seemingly of superhuman strength, has always been a double-sided social/political figure, both celebrated and feared because of his remarkable skills. The film industry, aware of this ambivalent attitude, has shrewdly learned how to manipulate the myth of the athlete and to alter his legend to fit the mood and tone of the times. The basic use of the black athlete has almost always been the same: if the "name" athlete, with strength and force enough to oppose the culture successfully, chooses instead to support it, his endorsement serves as a cue to all us mortal weaklings with thoughts of rebellion to *cool it.* Consequently, on screen athletes have traditionally been packaged to proclaim the pleasures of a great capitalistic society. Usually, the athlete is used to reinforce our daffy notions that heroics are measured in physical actions. Seldom has the athlete as movie hero been a thinker, questioning his role in society. And almost always, when examining their movies, one sees that the politics of the black athletes are far more populist than revolutionary.

The two busiest athlete-actors were Jim Brown and Fred Williamson. Brown appeared mostly in formula action pictures: *Slaughter, Black Gunn* (1972), and *I Escaped from Devil's Island* (1973), all of which made him look like the king of the bucks. Occasionally, he was used more effectively than even he might have wanted to be. In 1970 *The Grasshopper* cast Brown as a former football star, who works as a "greeter" at a Las Vegas hotel. He marries a beautiful young white woman (Jacqueline Bisset), who is sadly adrift. (The idea may have been that a white woman would have to be adrift to marry a black man like Brown.) Often Brown looked as if he were playing himself, but for a change, he did a halfway credible job of it. He communicated rather dexterously the subtle forms of self-disgust that tear at a man who is merely a token of his past glory. He's an athlete out of place in the real world.

By the late 1970s when he was no longer a box-office power, Brown was cast in James Toback's atmospheric *Fingers* (1978) as a kind of sepia Nietzschean Superman. Ironically, he was also reduced to his most blatant form of buckdom. In this feverish drama that focuses on Harvey Keitel as a concert pianist who collects "debts" for his gangster father, Brown played Dreems, a man who is powerfully built, physically unconquerable, and sexually all-consuming. In a scary sequence, Brown parades two of his young white women (his love slaves) before Keitel. To give a warning of what could happen should he ever be crossed, Brown's Dreems suddenly turns violent: he grabs the two women and smashes one's head against the other's. It is a jolting and unforgettable sequence. Here Brown is brilliantly showcased *and* exploited. Under Toback's direction, Jim Brown had never been more menacing. Yet he was all buck (perhaps the scariest the movies had ever seen): the white man's notion of the all-powerful brutal black man, superhuman but not quite human either. Toback used Brown's character to play on white paranoia and fascination with black male strength and sexuality.

Former football player Fred Williamson proved more relaxed in a long lineup of features: *Tell Me That You Love Me, Junie Moon* (1970), *M*A*S*H* (1970), *The Legend of Nigger Charley*, *The Soul of Nigger Charley*, *Black Caesar* and its sequel *Hell up in Harlem* (1973), *That Man Bolt* (1973), *Hammer* (1972), *Boss Nigger* (1975), and *Bucktown* (1975). In a film like *Black Eye* (1974), he played his detective hero in such an unassuming, laconic manner that it was apparent that inside Fred Williamson there was a halfway decent actor struggling to get out. And in such he-man films as *Three the Hard Way* and *Take the Hard Ride* (1975), he was also a pleasant, breezy contrast to his co-stars: the stolid and wooden Jim Brown and, yes, the stolid and wooden Jim Kelly.

Eventually, forming his own production company Po' Boy Productions, Williamson began directing (sometimes producing and writing) and starring in his own vehicles. *Death Journey* (1976), *Mr. Mean* (1978), *The Big Score* (1983), *The Last Fight* (1983), and *One Down, Two to Go*. His films, however, were frequently poorly made. And he failed to stretch whatever acting talents he had. Audiences eventually lost interest in him.

The buck era remained in full steam from around 1972 to 1975. Afterwards most of the athletes vanished from the screen. Years later, black filmmaker Keenen Ivory Wayans satirized the era in his film, *I'm Gonna Git You Sucka* (1988).

Lady Sings the Blues: Black Stars, Black Romance

Early in the era, black audiences searched for a different type of picture, one less action-oriented and more focused on relationships. One of the first films to veer in such a direction was *Lady Sings the Blues* (1972). Based on Billie Holiday's autobiography and starring Diana Ross, this Motown/Paramount production simplified a complex life, often resorting to the clichés found in many 1940s movies, stories of showbiz folk rising from rags to riches, then bringing about their own sorry downfall. In depicting the bigoted racial climate of Holiday's time, the movie frequently turned melodramatic with an overheated lynching episode and another overcharged confrontation with the Ku Klux Klan. The film also completely glossed over Holiday's love life, carefully editing out the various husbands and lovers, substituting instead a dream prince charming in the form of Billy Dee Williams as Louis McKay.

Yet criticism aside, the movie was vastly entertaining and emerged as the screen's first full-fledged black romantic melodrama. It did indeed treat its central character with respect. One of the film's most memorable sequences occurred at a nightclub where Ross and Williams—just getting to know one another—flirt and play the traditional male/female game of cat and mouse. When he asks her to dance, saying he's really in the mood for dancing, she responds by telling him, "Well, go on and dance then. Ain't nobody stopping you." Of course, the two do dance as she admits, "Mr. McKay, I have a confession to make. This place is fantastic—and so are you." For an audience that had seen Priest in *Super Fly* relating primarily to his woman in a sexy bathtub scene or that had watched Sweetback bed a woman as if he were blessing her with a divine gift, it was a new sensation to watch a black man actually court and cajole a black woman. Rarely before had movies given audiences the idea that black characters could be romantic. *Lady Sings the Blues*, if it accomplished nothing else, presented audiences with some of the most romantic scenes thus far in the history of blacks in films. The film also was enlivened by the performance of Richard Pryor as the Piano Man, who was so hepped-up and high-spirited that he looked as if he might get out of control and inject the film with another level of reality.

In the past, Oscar Micheaux had believed in his colored star system: he had hoped to reach the mass audience with lavish entertainments and dazzling, charismatic personalities. Had he seen *Lady Sings the Blues*, he might well have been entranced (and vindicated). He had been right: the mass black audience was waiting for just such a project.

For her performance, Diana Ross won an Oscar nomination as Best Actress. No one had thought this skinny, girlish Detroit-born goddess (all shiny razzle-dazzle extrovert) capable of playing Billie (the essence of still, moody quiet fire). Frankly, one never forgets one is watching Diana Ross. But hers is a splendidly developed star performance in the classic sense.

For Williams, the film marked a turning point in a career that, until then, had not taken off. After such films as *The Last Angry Man* and *The Final Comedown* (1972), he had now finally emerged as a romantic hero. Hollywood handsome and decked out in dapper suits, he touched on a type of black male elegance—similar to Duke Ellington's—that had flourished in the 1920s. Women liked him also because of the sensitivity he showed toward Ross. Yet genuine matinee idol that he was, afterward Hollywood rarely cast him in larger-than-life romantic roles.

Sounder

No black film of this early period was as highly praised as *Sounder* (1972). Sensitively directed by Martin Ritt, the film centered on a family of sharecroppers in the South during the Depression. The father (Paul Winfield), struggling to keep food on his family's table, steals meat and thereafter is sentenced to a year of hard labor. While imprisoned, he fights not only to hold his family together but to hold himself together as well. The film followed the efforts of the mother (Cicely Tyson) to care for her three children and to keep their land going during the father's absence. It also focused on the oldest child, wonderfully played by Kevin Hooks, about to come of age.

"*Sounder* is an outstanding film," wrote *Variety*. Most critics praised it. Admittedly, its characters harked back to a past portrait of "gentle" film Negroes. But no one can deny its extraordinary power. It also marked a significant new depiction of the black family. Gone was the old matriarchal setup of such films as *Imitation of Life, Pinky*, even *A Raisin in the Sun*. Nor was the family in tendentious conflict with itself, as had been the case in *Anna Lucasta* and again *A Raisin in the Sun*—and as would later be the case with *Black Girl* and *The River Niger* (1976). In those dramas the tightness and congestion of the city (and the system) seemed to send members of the black family at one another's throats. And never before had audiences seen a black father and son talk in such personal and intimate terms. Much credit must go to Lonne Elder III's screenplay, which was nominated for an Academy Award, the first time a work by a black writer had ever been so honored. In 1976 a disappointing sequel, *Sounder, Part 2* (in which neither Tyson nor Winfield appeared) was released.

The heart of *Sounder* was its high-powered performances. Janet MacLachlan stood out in a supporting role as the teacher who aids the oldest son. Paul Winfield gave an Oscar-nominated performance, which, despite its acclaim, still seems underrated. One tends to forget how good and moving he was. Previously, having worked on television and in such films as *Brother John* and *Trouble Man*, Winfield was adept at portraying men whose blackness (their ethnic backgrounds) was apparent but never overstated. Often in the 1970s action films, the actors were all attitude, doing little more than striking a series of "street" poses and speaking in fake overdone "ethnic" rhythms. Winfield's mannerisms, speech patterns, the fluid body rhythms all flowed naturally.

Following *Sounder*, Winfield played leads in *Gordon's War, A Hero Ain't Nothin' But a Sandwich* (1978), and the controversial *White Dog* (1982). But too often this fine actor was stuck in supporting roles in such films as *Hustle* (1975), *Terminator*

Sparkle (1976), a low-budget film that became a cult favorite: with (bottom row) Dorian Harewood and Lonette McKee; (upper row) Dwan Smith, Philip M. Thomas, and Irene Cara.

Two of the decade's most powerful dramatic performances: Cicely Tyson as the resilient mother Rebecca in *Sounder* (1972); Paul Winfield (with Kevin Hooks) as the father Nathan, who while in prison struggles not only to hold his family together but to keep himself intact as well.

(1984), *Star Trek II: The Wrath of Khan* (1982), *Mike's Murder* (1984), *Death Before Dishonor* (1987), and *Presumed Innocent* (1990).

Sounder, of course, transformed Cicely Tyson into a national star, and for the black community, she became a luminous cultural icon. In such previous films as *A Man Called Adam, The Comedians*, and *The Heart is a Lonely Hunter* (1968), she had acquired a small but dedicated following. Always her characters were infused with a keen intelligence and a burning personal sense of integrity. She did not take herself lightly; neither did the audience. In *Sounder*, as Rebecca, the Louisiana sharecropper's wife, she was what critic Pauline Kael called "the first great black heroine on the screen." Kael added, "She is visually extraordinary. Her cry as she runs down the road toward her husband, returning from prison, is a phenomenon—something even the most fabled actresses might not have dared." Like Diana Ross in *Lady Sings the Blues*, Cicely Tyson won an Oscar nomination as Best Actress. In the black community, there was excitement over this historic event: two black women competing for the film industry's most valued prize. Liza Minnelli, however, won for *Cabaret*.

Afterwards the twists and turns and ultimate detours of Tyson's career were reminiscent of those of Ethel Waters. In 1974, she scored another major triumph with her Emmy-award-winning performance in the television film "The Autobiography of Miss Jane Pittman." Again Tyson portrayed a strong black woman whose survival instincts were sharply yet subtly honed. Her success was all the more remarkable because the fine-boned, slender Tyson did not physically fit the traditional image of the strong black woman, that of the large, physically overpowering mammy heroine. Tyson also became the first dark black woman in American films to play leading, serious, dramatic roles.

Yet like Ethel Waters, here soon was another great dramatic actress who found herself without great roles to play. Such films as *The Blue Bird* (1977), *The River Niger*, and *A Hero Ain't Nothin' But a Sandwich* were not strong enough to draw out her rich talent. Later in the Richard Pryor comedy *Bustin' Loose* (1981) she gave a sweetly romantic performance (one of her rare romantic roles). But her better roles in the late 1970s and 1980s came in television.

Sidney Strikes Again

One of the pleasant surprises of the early years, *Buck and the Preacher* (1972), was directed by Sidney Poitier and starred him with Harry Belafonte and Ruby Dee. Rousing, adventurous, nicely comic at times (often because of Belafonte's high-spirited performance), a sometimes uneven but level-headed popularization of black history, the movie was solid entertainment. It centered on the period following the Civil War when freed slaves were tracked down by bounty hunters and forced to return to unofficial slavery in the South. Poitier and Belafonte played an incongruous pair who outsmarted the bounty hunters.

Here Poitier attempted to re-establish his roots with the black community. In his 1980 autobiography *This Life*, Poitier has indicated that, aware of the criticism of his screen characters in the late 1960s, he sought to do a different type of movie. When Poitier, Belafonte, and sturdy Ruby Dee rode triumphantly across the plains, it seemed like a homecoming for the trio. Black audiences openly screamed out in joy and *Buck and the Preacher* emerged as a solid hit.

Afterwards, Poitier continued directing films pitched directly at the black audience: the romantic drama *A Warm December* (1973, with Poitier and Esther Anderson) and comedies in which he co-starred with Bill Cosby—*Uptown Saturday Night* (1974), *Let's Do It Again* (1975), and *A Piece of the Action* (1977).

At heart, these were escapist, nonthreatening, bourgeois yarns (black buddy movies) that sought to recapture the rich ethnic humor that had crept into such films as *Green Pastures*, *Cabin in the Sky*, and *Stormy Weather*. Despite the fact that the humor was stale and the pictures, in search of a comic sensibility, seemed too much like the dopey daydreams of an adolescent schoolboy, they did give black audiences of their day a sense of community (thanks to the actors and black writer Richard Wesley's scripts for the first two). They proved very popular with black audiences.

In all three, Poitier looked out of place, far too intelligent for all this nonsense. (Cosby, however, seems at home with this breezy, lightweight material.) A great disappointment for moviegoers was the fact that this fine dramatic actor still had not found a role worthy of his talents. His appearance in *The Wilby Conspiracy* (1975) seemed like a rehash of past exciting performances. In the 1980s, Poitier directed *Stir Crazy* (1980), *Hanky Panky* (1982), and *Fast Forward* (1985).

Superbadd, Supermama

By the mid-1970s, audiences also saw the arrival of the black superwoman, as personified by Tamara Dobson and Pam Grier in such rowdy action movies as *Cleopatra Jones* (1973), *Coffy* (1973), *Foxy Brown* (1974), and *Friday Foster* (1975). These macho goddesses answered a multitude of needs and were a hybrid of stereotypes, part buck/part mammy/part mulatto. On the one hand, each was a high-flung male fantasy: beautiful, alluring, glamourous voluptuaries, as ready and anxious for sex and mayhem as any man. They lived in fantasy worlds—of violence, blood, guns, and gore—which pleased, rather than threatened, male audiences. (Generally black women found it difficult to relate to Grier and Dobson.) Like the old-style mammies, they ran not simply a household but a universe unto itself. Often they were out to clean up the ghetto of drug pushers, protecting the black hearth and home from corrupt infiltrators. Dobson and Grier represented Woman as Protector, Nurturer, Communal Mother Surrogate.

Yet these women also had the look and manner of old-style mulattoes. They were also often perceived as being exotic sex objects (Grier's raw sexuality was always exploited)—yet with a twist. Although men manhandle them, Grier and Dobson also took liberties with men, at times using them as playful, comic toys.

Of the two, Dobson's career was the shorter. Except for appearances in *Norman, Is That You?* (1976) and later as the high-kicking inmate in *Chained Heat* (1983), she virtually disappeared after the 1970s.

Pam Grier's career proved more durable. Having first drawn attention in such women's prison dramas as *The Big Doll House* (1971), *The Big Bird Cage* (1972), and *Black Mama, White Mama* (1973, a female version of *The Defiant Ones*), she soon became the first black woman to rise to stardom through B movies, some of which were wacked-out revenge dramas. In *Coffy* she was out to catch up with the dope pushers who had hooked her kid sister on drugs. Then in the enjoyably perverse *Foxy Brown*, Grier had a sequence that few of her followers have forgotten. Her lover (Terry Carter), then her brother (Antonio Fargas), are killed by two drug kingpins, a corrupt white man and woman. First, Pam's Foxy catches up with the man. Pam has her boys unzip his pants. He is then castrated. Then Pam pays a visit to the man's ladyfriend—carrying a jar that contains the poor man's most valuable parts. The jar falls on the floor, its contents apparently rolling this way and that (mercifully, the audience doesn't see this; it's left to the imagination), all to the horror of the woman who, upon recognizing what is before her eyes, screams out the name of the man she has loved. It's her poor Steve! Audiences howled over this one!

Trash that Grier's movies were, her grit saved them. Some white feminists saw her as a heroine. Her picture even graced the cover of MS. But her studio, American International Pictures, failed to develop decent projects for her. The later less raunchy films *Sheba, Baby* (1975) and *Friday Foster* failed to do well. A subdued Grier appeared in *Greased Lighting* (1977). She was resilient enough to work into the 1980s in *Fort Apache: The Bronx* (1981), *Above the Law* (1988), and *The Package* (1989).

Sisters in Distress

If anything, these action heroines pointed up the sad state of affairs for black women in the movies. Very few films attempted to explore a black woman's tensions or aspirations or to examine the dynamics of sexual politics within the black community. The industry leaders might have us believe no one was interested in stories about black women. But when a film did emerge that touched on the life of a black woman, audiences, male as well as female, responded.

A film like the Maya Angelou-scripted *Georgia, Georgia* offered audiences the chance to see Diana Sands (not long before her death) as a driven pop singer on tour in Europe where, fatigued, weary, and adrift, she must contend with the demands of fans and followers—and with her own loneliness and alienation. Also featured was that underrated (and highly unusual) character actress Minnie Gentry as Sands's companion and tormenter—the maternal Mrs. Anderson, who strangles the young woman at the film's bizarre climax. Uneven and not fully developed, *Georgia, Georgia* nonetheless had riveting moments.

In the tawdry 1972 crime melodrama *Melinda*, audiences—particularly young black women—responded to the character created by Rosalind Cash. When her former boyfriend (Calvin Lockhart) is accused of having murdered a young woman named Melinda (Vonetta McGee), she sets out to help him unravel the mystery. Under the direction of black director Hugh Robertson and with a script by Lonne Elder III, Cash's character represented the bright, sensitive, perhaps difficult woman, who has been rejected by a man in favor of a more overtly sensual and perhaps manageable female. In classic terms of the woman's picture, Cash must compete (in this case with the dead woman) for her man. Though the movie never focuses on the inner workings of her character or the true nature of her anxieties and although the most that is known about her is her bond to this man, Cash herself—moody, smoky, troubled—creates a woman dissatisfied with the way things are. In fact, one feels that she does not even want to love this shallow man she's so attracted to.

In the film's most effective sequence, Cash, posing as the dead woman, goes to a bank where she hopes to retrieve the woman's safe-deposit box, which has information that will unlock the mystery. When the suspicious white bank official checks her references, Cash does a slow burn, building splendidly to a magnificent moment of explosive anger. "Is anything wrong?" the official asks her, to which she heatedly answers, "If I were a white woman I wouldn't have to go through half this shit." Her anger is not that of a love-obsessed female but that of a black woman repeatedly reminded of her place in a culture with racial-sexual signposts everywhere. It is one of those rare occasions in cinema when one sees black female rage—and when it looks as if the screen might not be able to contain it.

Cash also appeared in *The Omega Man* (1971), *Hickey and Boggs* (1972), *The Class of Miss McMichael* (1978), and *Wrong Is Right* (1982).

Claudine seemed to concentrate best on the issues and conflicts confronting a contemporary urban black woman. Directed by John Berry, this comedy-drama focused on a Harlem domestic worker, living on welfare with six children and no husband.

Claudine stands at the center of the children's universe. When she becomes involved with a sanitation worker (James Earl Jones)—a dirty, smelly, out-of-shape garbage man—the children don't want to lose their mother or see her hurt. Nor does Claudine want to be saddled with the same romantic mistakes she has made in the past.

Some things go haywire in *Claudine* (when the younger kids talk back to their mother, they strike one more as suburban youngsters than ghetto children), but much goes right. In one telling sequence, the oldest daughter (played expertly by Tamu) returns home late, intoxicated not only from drink but the idea of romance and sex. Claudine confronts the girl, who says that her boyfriend Abdullah was teaching her how to hold her liquor. Claudine snaps at the girl, hitting her stomach, as she asks, "Abdullah teach you anything about biology?" The two lash out at one another, then fall into each other's arms. Claudine desperately wants her daughter to avoid the pitfalls that she once fell into. This strikingly, often powerful moment dramatizes a type of emotional intimacy rarely seen between two black women. It becomes a special and charged moment to watch Diahann Carroll, the bronze Barbie Doll, pull deep inside herself to match Tamu's emotional peak. Vulnerable, intelligent, intense, Carroll—scrubbed clean of her glitter makeup and dressed plainly in a housedress—approaches her role with a simplicity and an earnest effort to please. For her performance, Diahann Carroll was nominated for an Oscar as Best Actress.

Mahogany, directed by Berry Gordy, Jr., and starring Diana Ross, centered on a young black woman's search for personal identity. This sudsy, romantic tale traces the rise of Chicago ghetto girl Tracy, who runs off to Rome where almost overnight she becomes an acclaimed model called "Mahogany." Often *Mahogany* was pure hokum, without the cunning wit and sense of style that sometimes distinguished this kind of picture in the past. Tracy must even make a choice between her career (decadent) and her man (a politico named Brian, played by Billy Dee Williams). Black audiences, however, seemed happy with this romance—and the fact that at least here the upwardly mobile young black woman was portrayed as having a *chance* to make a choice.

Mahogany's subtext also indicated shifts in social/political attitudes. As a heroine rising out of the ghetto to grab a piece of the pie, Tracy has no interest in tearing the system down. Nor does her beau Brian work outside the political system against the establishment. They represent the return of an old political philosophy: the idea is to go into the system and get what one can out of it. In the Rome sequences, Ross finds herself enveloped in a white world where white males (Tony Perkins and Jean-Pierre Aumont) fixate on her. Yet as eager as *Mahogany*'s central character is to move mainstream, she is determined to keep her personal racial identity intact. Black audiences felt comfortable with this new notion; so, too, did white ones.

Ross herself communicated the drive and energy of a woman who will not settle for the racial or gender dictates of her society. As Ross walked—with portfolio in hand—through the streets of Chicago's Southside, she was the type of ambitious and aggressive young black woman that the movies had never before observed. No one around Tracy quite understands her drive: she wants a life without tenements or restrictions. Of course, she is punished for independence and aggressiveness and made to return to what the film insists are her black roots *and* her man. It refuses to let her be both successful *and* black. Yet as politically lopsided and antifeminist as audiences today might find it, *Mahogany* nonetheless remains one of the few 1970s films to spotlight, even in a shallow manner, a young urban, career-oriented black woman, coping with a set of professional goals and a demanding private life.

Newcomer Lonette McKee also impressed audiences in *Sparkle* (1976). This low-budget film told the story of three sisters (McKee, Irene Cara, and Dwan Smith) who, growing up in the ghetto in the late 1950s, form a singing group (similar to The Supremes) and are off on their way to stardom. Early in the film, McKee's character, who is called Sister, becomes entangled in a messy, sadomasochistic relationship with a smooth, shadowy figure named Satin (Tony King, a good actor, cast here in a one-dimensional buck role). *Sparkle* then makes the mistake of killing her off. The second half focuses on the efforts of a ghetto lad named Stix (Philip M. Thomas) to turn the youngest sister, Sparkle, into a star.

While *Sparkle* has a cop-out ending and fails to be the hard-hitting examination of the music industry that is wanted, it nonetheless is often absorbing, in part because of the mood established by director Sam O'Steen and cinematographer Bruce Surtees. And the performances of Cara (for once fairly convincing), Dorian Harewood, Philip M. Thomas, Armelia McQueen, and Mary Alice (as the girls' mother) are all appealing. When Alice whispers to Sister that Satin will "drag you into the gutter" and adds, "I've lived in Harlem all my life and I do know a rat when I see one," the film resonates with her quiet but firm power.

But the real star is McKee, who gives the 1970s definitive portrayal of the likable, haughty, "hincty," high-yeller black girl who thinks she's got all the answers (and who usually has more than most). Her portrait of a black woman ready to take life on without fear or foolish constraints is similar to what past actresses such as Nina Mae McKinney, Fredi Washington, and Dorothy Dandridge attempted to present. She chews gum, shakes her hips, and talks trash with a forceful abandon. Ambition, drive, and survival are written all over this tall, curvy, jivey, sexy, hip sister. Why then does she succumb to a manipulative man? One feels she would tell Satin, "Later, for you, dude." Does this type of woman still seem too threatening to Hollywood? Because McKee is the lightest black actress in the cast, Sister's death also makes her look all the more like a past tragic mulatto. One wonders if McKee's Sister must, like Dandridge's important characters, be disposed of, as perhaps a kind of warning to other sexual, aggressive black women, whose very appearance challenges concepts about race. Of course, it cannot be overlooked that Hollywood's perennial color fixation turns up in *Sparkle* in other ways. The darkest sister, played by Dwan Smith, simply disappears. Although Joel Schumacher's botched script has her spout wooden political lines, the film has almost no interest in her. It is far happier to concentrate on the troubled high-yellers, McKee and Cara.

Other Films, Other Voices

Other unusual films met with varying degrees of success. Gillo Pontecorvo's *Burn!* (1970) remains a flawed but rousingly impressive neo-Marxist, revolutionary epic with an ingenious performance by Marlon Brando and a very intelligent one by Evaristo Marquez. The blatantly political *The Spook Who Sat by the Door* (1973), directed by Ivan Dixon and based on Sam Greenlee's novel about a black CIA-agent-turned-revolutionary, died an early death in theaters but was later revived on college campuses. Bill Gunn's moody, studied *Ganja & Hess* (1973) with Marlene Clark and Duane Jones, who had previously starred in the pop horror classic *Night of the Living Dead* (1968), acquired an art-house following and also, like *Sparkle* later, became a black cult film. So, too, did the Jamaican drama *The Harder They Come* (1973) with reggae star Jimmy Cliff. *Five on the Black Hand Side* (a 1973 release with a clever performance by Clarice Taylor and directed and written by Oscar Williams) and Mel Brooks's *Blazing Saddles* (1974) were comedies that proved popular. The latter presented audiences with a new-style coon: a coon with a double consciousness. Here in this uneven but wildly energetic spoof on Westerns, Cleavon Little plays a black man who shows up in a white (and hostile) Old West community. As the town's new sheriff, he knows the only way he'll survive is by playing the role of a *dumb black nigger*; he does precisely that and is able not only to survive but to triumph, too. Much of the manic and offbeat humor of this unpredictable comedy can be attributed to Richard Pryor, who was one of the scriptwriters and was also originally slated to star as the sheriff. Martin Ritt's *Conrack* (1974) introduced the gifted Madge Sinclair, who also worked in Sam Peckinpah's *Convoy* (1978). At the same time, black director Stan Lathan's *Amazing Grace* (1974, with a script by black writer Matt Robinson) gave everyone a chance to see the legendary Jackie "Moms" Mabley along with Rosalind Cash, Moses Gunn, and three showbiz veterans: Slappy White, Butterfly McQueen, and Stepin Fetchit. Unfortunately, the film was sluggish and so, too, were the veteran stars. Lathan and Robinson teamed again as director and writer for *Save the Children* (1973). Another more "serious" film was *The Education of Sonny Carson* (1974), which, uneven and underdeveloped as it was, had nonetheless the riveting performance of Rony Clanton, who years earlier (billed as Hampton Clanton) had been the young star of *The Cool World*. Then there was Ralph Bashki's *Coonskin* (1975), a part-animated, part-live action film that some black groups picketed against. Black director Gilbert Moses turned out *Willie Dynamite* (1973) with

Roscoe Orman and Diana Sands and *The Fish That Saved Pittsburgh* (1979). Another black director, Jamaa Fanaka, helmed *Emma Mae* (1976) and the first in his *Penitentiary* (1979) series. Actor Raymond St. Jacques directed *The Book of Numbers* (1973) with Philip M. Thomas and Freda Payne. And the films of Senegalese director Ousmane Sembène were also released in this country: *Borom Sarret* (1963), the cerebral *Mandabi* (1968), the master work of suicidal despair *Black Girl* (1966), and later *Xala* (1974) and *Ceddo* (1978).

Among the new personalities who were ballyhooed by the black press as part of the New Black Hollywood were Max Julien (star of *The Mack*), Vonetta McGee (one of the screen's great natural beauties), Denise Nicholas, the underrated Antonio Fargas, Robert Hooks, Calvin Lockhart—who briefly looked as if he would emerge as the era's most important black leading man in such films as *Joanna* (1968), *Halls of Anger* (1970), and *Leo the Last* (1970)—Brenda Sykes, Carol Speed, and Thalmus Rasulala.

Once black audiences had stopped supporting the cheaply made action movies, the black movie boom was over. Rather than attempting to produce other types of black films, the industry simply chose to produce fewer and fewer black-oriented pictures. Now it was believed that there was no longer a black audience for films. Thus came the emergence of the crossover film: if a film with blacks hoped to succeed, it had to have built-in devices to please white audiences. The first step towards making crossover movies was to strip the black film of any raw political content. The Poitier–Cosby comedies, because they were escapist fare that did not address racial issues, were early crossover hits.

So, too, was *The Bingo Long Traveling All-Stars and Motor Kings* (1976). Directed by John Badham, the film took a nostalgic, revisionist look at the all-black baseball teams that flourished in the 1930s and 1940s and nurtured such players as Satchel Paige and Josh Gibson. Here the colored baseball players—headed by Billy Dee Williams as Bingo Long—journey from one town to the next, playing for black crowds and often cooning it up for whites in the area. Always the idea is that the black athletes, in order to have a chance simply to play ball, must appear nonthreatening, congenial, and comic to the white world. The film, however, often seems too slick, too thought out, without enough heat or heart to it. It almost "gentrifies" the racism of the past. Yet the critics liked it and one cannot deny that the film has some memorable moments. The high-spirited cast included James Earl Jones, Mabel King, Tony Burton, and Richard Pryor. *The Bingo Long Traveling All-Stars and Motor Kings* was one of the last major predominantly black cast films made in the 1970s.

Finally, the late 1970s saw two unexpected developments: the rise of young black director Michael Schultz and the advent of Richard Pryor as a Movie Star.

Michael Schultz—the era's most productive black director—was also the director on whom most were then pinning their hopes for commercial films with an entertaining black point of view. *Honeybaby, Honeybaby* (1974) was an early film that failed. Then came the commercial hits: *Cooley High* (1975, a slick and mildly entertaining look at black teenagers coming of age in the 1960s) and *Car Wash* (1976, an affectionate although misconceived feature about a day in the life of workers at a West Coast car wash, featuring Franklyn Ajaye, The Pointer Sisters, Antonio Fargas, Richard Pryor, Bill Duke, and notably Tracy Reed and Ivan Dixon, who graces the film with moments of truth and a moral authority it otherwise lacks). Less successful was Schultz's *Sgt. Pepper's Lonely Hearts Club Band*, a 1978 homage to the Beatles. This film may have signaled the end of the critics' enchantment with Schultz. His later work on *Carbon Copy* (1981) and *Berry Gordy's The Last Dragon* (1985) was bland at best. *Krush Groove* (1985) was more interesting but disturbingly unfocused. *The Disorderlies* (1987) was an out and out embarrassment.

In retrospect, though, Schultz may have been most blessed, in having Richard Pryor as a star of three of his films: *Greased Lightning* (1977), *Which Way Is Up?* (1977), and *Car Wash*.

Richard Pryor: The Crazy Nigger as Conquering Hero

In the late 1970s, surely even Richard Pryor must have been surprised to find himself the most important black actor working in American motion pictures.

Pryor's route to movie stardom had been a long and circuitous one. Born in 1940 in Peoria, Illinois, he had grown up in a brothel run by his paternal grandmother. His mother also worked there as a prostitute. Pryor dropped out of high school, joined the army, and afterwards performed standup comedy at tiny clubs and bars. In the 1960s, he performed in Greenwich Village and later on the talk shows of Merv Griffin and Jack Paar. With his suits and ties, his neatly cut and groomed hair, and his rather soft-spoken manner, the young Pryor looked like a very bright but vulnerable kid with a wild mischievous streak. At this point in his career, Pryor, so he once said, patterned himself after his idol, Bill Cosby. But that soon changed.

In the 1970s, he developed a new persona: the ever-evolving, foul-mouthed, iconoclastic wild man, the Crazy Nigger, who spoke in the language and idiom of the streets. By doing so, Pryor seemed to be speaking in comic and frequently moving terms for a vast underclass of the disaffiliated and the disenfranchised in the ghettos of America. His was ethnic humor, infused with brilliant new insights, sometimes blistering with pain and pathos and trenchant comments on the social system.

Pryor first worked in films in the late 1960s in supporting (and sometimes forgettable) roles in *The Busy Body* (1967), the 1968 youth cult film *Wild in the*

Sidney Poitier turned to comedy as the star and director of such films as *Uptown Saturday Night* (1974) and (above) *Let's Do It Again* (1975) with co-star Bill Cosby.

To the surprise of many, Richard Pryor emerged as a major movie star. In *The Bingo Long Traveling All-Stars and Motor Kings* (1976), he played a black baseball player trying to "pass" as a Cuban. In a supporting role in *Silver Streak* (1976) with Gene Wilder, he walked away with the picture.

Streets, The Green Berets, The Phynx (1970), *You've Got to Walk It Like You Talk It or You'll Lose That Beat* (1971), and *Dynamite Chicken* (1972).

Then in *Lady Sings the Blues,* he proved he could intelligently play a warm and vulnerable character and steal scenes at the same time. Curiously, even Miss Ross, who on other occasions frequently acts as if there is no one else on screen but herself, appears so relaxed with him that the platonic relationship between Billie and Piano Man is wholly credible. In one scene when Pryor strolls with Ross on a West Coast beach while dressed in a beret and spiffy cardigan, black audiences screamed with laughter. They loved the notion that one of theirs—their dude Richie, *a brother—had* now *made it* (had *gone Hollywood*) without losing his sense of self. Such audience identification with Richard Pryor would remain strong throughout his career. With the exception of Dorothy Dandridge, it is doubtful if any other black film star, even Poitier or later Eddie Murphy, has ever connected to the black audience in quite the intense way that Pryor did.

Supporting roles followed in *Wattstax* (1973), *Hit!* (1973), *The Mack* (as a Los Angeles pimp), *Some Call It Loving* (1973), *Uptown Saturday Night,* and *Car Wash.* The closest he came to a star role was in the rather bizarre Western *Adios Amigo* (1975), under the direction of—of all people—Fred Williamson. Williamson's film set out to show Fred Williamson's infatuation with Fred Williamson. But even that master egotist must have realized by the mad gleam in Richard Pryor's eyes that when Pryor is on screen, the camera sees only Pryor. His performance—playful, prankish, boyish—is hardly a great one but it has a mad, zippy appeal nonetheless. The same was true of his appearance as the black baseball player who pretends to be Cuban in hopes of crashing the major leagues in *The Bingo Long Traveling All-Stars and Motor Kings.*

Silver Streak (1976), however, made him a star. Co-starring with Gene Wilder in this dull-witted crime caper, Pryor had to work against seemingly insurmountable odds. As set down by the scriptwriter Colin Higgins, Pryor's character Grover was little more than an old-style coon: the black man as comic petty thief and also as asexual sidekick for the hero.

But Richard Pryor, the actor, proved to be at least seventeen steps ahead of everybody else. In the film's most famous scene—a classic sequence in which Wilder and Pryor are in a train station on the run from the law—Pryor takes Wilder into the men's room. The only hope Wilder has of dodging the police, Pryor believes, is by pretending to be black. He has Wilder smear his face with dark shoe polish, then wear a bright purple jacket, a hat, and shades (dark glasses). "It'll never work," Wilder moans as he applies the shoe polish to his face. "What are you afraid of—that it won't come off?" Pryor responds. When the two are back in the station and about to board a train, Wilder—in blackface and bopping along in the most contortedly unrhythmic manner imaginable—says, "I don't think we'll make it pass the cops." Pryor replies, "We'll make it pass the cops. I just hope we don't see no Muslims."

Throughout, Pryor's timing is impeccable. He and Wilder have an extraordinary rapport, bouncing lines off one another in perfect coordination. But what elevates the material is Pryor's attitude. Like the great black screen performers of the past, he brazenly operates in a world all his own. No one knows where his Grover comes from or what he's all about. But this man seems inherently unphased by the whites he must deal with.

That's apparent in another sequence when Wilder and Jill Clayburg are held captive in a train compartment by the movie's villain, Patrick McGoohan. Dressed like a dining car attendant and carrying a breakfast tray, Pryor comes to the rescue. When McGoohan sarcastically comments on the train's excellent cuisine, a jivey Pryor says, "Oh, thank you, sir. I'll tell the boys in the kitchen. We aims to please." Here he mocks the type of humility black servants were always supposed to display (much as Robeson did in *The Emperor Jones*). A few minutes later, he turns raunchy. He looks at Clayburg, then asks Wilder, "Is that your lady, man?" Then he adds, "She's somethin' else. Stand up, mama. Let me get a look at you. Hum, hum, hum. *Have mercy!*" Here he's boldly and playfully sexy, naturally calling a lie to some of the script's notions about his character's supposed nonexistent sexuality. At one point, an indignant McGoohan screams in rage, "You ignorant nigger!" Whereupon Pryor's eyes flash as he whips out a gun and asks, "Who you calling nigger? You don't know me well enough to call me no nigger. I'll slap the taste out your mouth." Pryor's attitude seems to be that this-here white man has really gone bananas to think he can call him a nigger. It represents to Pryor the height of white stupidity. Racism does not intimidate or frighten him.

Richard Pryor's energy saved *Silver Streak*, turning it into a hit. Exuberant and inventive as his work is, Pryor may well have been able to reach the mass white audience partly because he is a sidekick and also because the movie promotes a very old theme: the huck-finn fixation. Once again, as in past films that showed a white and a black male who became friends, the white is a bit uptight; the black is freer emotionally. When Pryor teaches Wilder how to be black, he is also telling his white friend how to be looser, and not locked in by society's rules and regulations. In the late 1970s and the next decade, this huck-finn fixation—the theme of interracial male bonding—also wipes away any fears about tensions between black and white. The black-oriented films of the early 1970s stressed black in conflict with white and promoted a black separatist point of view and way of life. But by the end of the decade, the idea in films was that there was no such thing as true racial divisions. Many of the escapist films that starred Pryor represented a suppression of the race issue altogether.

Afterwards came the Pryor star roles in *Greased Lightning, Which Way Is Up?*, and *Blue Collar* (1978). Although he is quite good in them, none (with the exception of parts of *Which Way Is Up?*) fully touched base with his exuberant wildman spirit. Instead these films sought to domesticate him, to transform him into an acceptable, middle-class fellow whose aims and ambitions are simply for a good decent life. One has to wonder if the subtext of such films is the idea that the most imaginative spirit in the movies of the late 1970s must be contained, kept in its place with its rebellious threat and insights neutralized, its fires doused.

Pryor's other films, *The Wiz* (1978), *California Suite* (1978), and *The Muppet Movie* (1979), required nothing new of him. In fact, in *California Suite*, as he and Bill Cosby performed slapstick antics, their characters looked far too much like poorly defined coons. The material was frankly beneath them.

Fortunately, Pryor fully unleashed his rich talents in 1979 with *Richard Pryor Live In Concert*. For audiences it was a marvel to see this extraordinary mime and mimic in top form as he parodied the way blacks behave when walking in the woods; or created a scene in which a deer saw boxing champ Leon Spinks. He also played with the notion of a macho man. "If a dude comes after you with a knife," Pryor advised, "don't try to be macho. You run. And you teach your old lady how to run, too, so you don't have to go back for her." Here, too, he incorporated his personal experiences into his work. He dramatized the heart attack he had been stricken with, somehow bringing humor to the most painful of experiences. In complete control of his material, Pryor gave a virtuoso performance. Now his creation—the Crazy Nigger who used four-letter words to cut through shams and to attack taboos on sex and race—had taken center stage. *Richard Pryor Live In Concert*, a box-office hit and a crowning achievement in films of the 1970s, carried Pryor to full-fledged stardom.

The Wiz

The black movie to close the era—indeed the last such big-budget black film for many years to come and also, at $35 million, the most expensive movie musical then ever made—was *The Wiz* in 1978. Based on the highly successful all-black Broadway musical (which, in turn, was based on the L. Frank Baum book that had inspired the movie *The Wizard of Oz*), *The Wiz* starred Diana Ross as Dorothy, here a twenty-four-year-old Harlem schoolteacher so afraid of the world that she has never ventured below 125th Street. Of course, that changes when Dorothy and her dog Toto are swept up by a "snow cyclone" and carried to the land of Oz, which is Manhattan as a fantasy land.

Throughout, the viewer pulls for this film, hoping to see it spring to life. Director Sidney Lumet, a talented pro known for his tense urban dramas, proved all wrong, however, for an ethnic fantasy that should have been dripping with rich ethnic juices. Frequently, Lumet keeps his camera in long shots, so far away from the dancers and the movements that one wonders if he was scared off by this live-wire energy flow. All wrong, too, was scriptwriter Joel Schumacher, who knew nothing about black speech rhythms or colloquialisms or a black point of view.

It's a pity, of course, because the actors are anxious to put on a whale of a show. Nipsey Russell, Michael Jackson, Mabel King, Ted Ross—these people are entranced and in love with entertaining. But they seem to be working in a vacuum.

As for Ross, she was much too hip and sophisticated for the timid little dodo she's playing. Here is a woman who rose to fame during her days as the lead singer with The Supremes as well as in her first two films by having such drive and daring that she always looked as if she could do anything. When she turns weepy and whiny, you want to shake some sense into her. Audiences have always both loved and hated her aggressiveness. But a nonassertive Diana Ross is not Diana Ross at all.

Even Richard Pryor as The Wiz seems out of place, giving one of his least effective and least funny performances. Lena Horne, however, just about walks away with the picture when she shows up for one number, a replay of the song "Believe in Yourself." This was three years before her Broadway hit *Lena Horne: The Lady and Her Music.* The anger and deep sense of conviction she exhibited in that show are apparent in this number in *The Wiz.* This woman whom Hollywood had never given the chance to develop as the actress and musical star she hoped to be had learned to invest material with her own emotional commitment.

The Wiz was not well-received by the critics. *Newsweek*'s Jack Kroll wrote: "Lumet is too often ponderous and fuzzy." In *New York*, critic David Denby said: "In the hands of the screenwriter Joel Schumacher, the emotions of the story have grown thin, uneasy, synthetic." *The New Yorker*'s Pauline Kael wrote that "Lumet has worked for two years and employed the talents of hundreds of people to produce a film that looks rushed and cheap.... The whole film has a stagnant atmosphere; there's never a breath of air or a relaxed sense of space."

Once *The Wiz* proved a box-office disappointment, industry analysts told themselves that no one was interested in seeing black movies. Of course, this was absurd. The real point was that the black audience wanted a variety of decent, entertaining films just as any white audience did. Had *The Wiz* been a better picture, a larger audience, black and white, would have paid to see it. But it would be some years before audiences would see another major studio all-black feature.

And so the 1970s came to a close. The sad irony was that the decade, which had opened by revealing to the industry that there *was* a black audience, closed with the industry believing that the black film and black audience were both dead. Now the idea of the crossover film, which would star blacks with whites and consequently appeal (primarily) to whites, had firmly taken root.

9 THE 1980s: BLACK SUPERSTARS AND THE ERA OF TAN

Richard Pryor and Eddie Murphy soar to rarefied heights as authentic black box-office superstars. . . . Louis Gossett, Jr., takes the industry by surprise when he walks off with an Oscar for An Officer and a Gentleman. *. . . A* Soldier's Story *dramatizes internal frictions among black GIs on an army base during World War II. . . . Steven Spielberg directs the screen adaptation of Alice Walker's novel* The Color Purple, *amid controversy and outcries from sectors of the black community. . . . Whoopi Goldberg, flush with success, becomes the only black actress of the era to star in a lineup of screen comedies that ultimately fail and take her nowhere. . . . An independent film shot in Brooklyn called* She's Gotta Have It *becomes a hit, launching the career of its young director Spike Lee. . . . Denzel Washington wins an Oscar for his performance as a cynical soldier in* Glory.

And so in marched the 1980s: a mixed bag of a decade if ever there was one. It was the age of Reagan and the yuppie, of the New Right and Moral Majority, of scandals on Wall Street and of bands of the homeless wandering in cities around the country, of punk and funk in the world of music, of New Wave and neon, of campus protests against apartheid in South Africa, of the emergence of Third World powers, and of the rise of a new brand of political conservatism. For black Americans, it was a time to move fully into the system, rather than to remain outside it. Never was that social philosophy more apparent than in the candidacy of Jesse Jackson for president of the United States. The 1980s also was the era when the black superstar reigned supreme in the entertainment industry. Michael Jackson and Whitney Houston shot to the top of the music charts. "The Cosby Show" became the country's number one prime-time television program. Perhaps it was not surprising then that many Americans frequently lulled themselves into the assumption that the races were at peace with one another, that inner city blight and decay as well as social tension and racial inequities had ceased to exist, that indeed America's past history of racism had vanished. Consequently, when racial incidents sprang up in an area like Howard Beach in New York, many were jolted. Perhaps the nation had not changed so much after all.

At the movies, too, the attitude was that all was fine and dandy between the races. Many new films spotlighted teams of black and white buddies. Predictable comedies also assured the mass audience that blacks and whites could laugh together without fretting about social issues. For black performers, the 1980s was a two-way street. Most black performers found themselves playing supporting roles that sometimes looked like retreads from the 1930s or 1950s. Sadly, too, some of the directors and writers of the 1970s found little or no work in this era. An optimistic sign, however, was the success of certain independent black filmmakers and the full-fledged stardom of certain comedy stars. Yet the 1980s might be viewed as the age of the hybrid stereotype: a time when major stars played characters who were sometimes part coon/part buck, sometimes part coon/part mammy. Then, too, black men frequently found themselves desexed, rarely permitted romantic roles. Women had few major parts. But even more interesting, the 1980s might be called the Era of Tan, a time when films did all they could to make audiences forget the blackness of a black star. Often when a black performer appeared in a general release, he or she had no cultural identity. All ethnic edges had been sanded down, so that while they *looked* black, everything about them seemed expressed in a white cultural context; and in the long run, characters were neither black nor white but a tan blend. Even so, tan, like black, was often kept in the background.

Holding Up the Fort

The new practice of using black performers in supporting roles in big-budgeted, general white releases turned up at the very beginning of the new decade. Often these new characters were without tension or bite. The great subconscious goal of the 1980s may often have been to rid American films of the late 1960s/early 1970s rebellious figures. In actuality, the movies wanted audiences to believe that such figures no longer existed or, if they did, they could really be tamed, disposed of, or absorbed into the system. The menacing black characters in *American Gigolo* (1980, with Bill Duke as a poisonous pimp) and *Fort Apache: The Bronx* (with Pam Grier as a zonked-out terrorizing street walker; a metaphor, of course, for the random violence that lurks on city streets) were nastily killed off, often to audience applause.

Sometimes, as in *Seems Like Old Times* (1980), a black character (the eye-popping chauffeur played by T. K. Carter) was used simply for comic relief. Other times, as in Stanley Kubrick's *The Shining* (1980), a black character (Scatman Crothers as the cook Halloran) served as a noble, spiritual, childlike symbol.

On occasion, black characters were used, in varying degrees, to imbue a film with a certain social realism. Surely, in the Robert Redford film *Brubaker* (1980), the gritty natural look and intensity of Yaphet Kotto, Richard Ward, and Morgan Freeman made the world of this prison drama seem real, direct, more immediate. Watching them, one might also become distressed. An actor like Kotto had been in films for over a decade. As soon as audiences saw his tall, sturdy frame and heard his calmly controlled voice in a film like Ridley Scott's sci-fi thriller *Alien* (1979), they felt confident of Kotto's powers. As the characters on the doomed space expedition were killed off one by one, audiences had the mad hope that the traditions of horror films would now be completely reversed: both a woman (Sigourney Weaver) and a black would emerge as the only survivors. Maybe the space age would mark a new day for minorities. So strong and commanding a presence was Kotto that one felt he deserved to live. Consequently, it appeared as if *Alien*'s filmmakers almost had a failure of nerve by letting their black hero be killed by the space monster after all. Kotto also gave varied performances in *The Limit* (1972), which he also directed, *Man and Boy* (1972), *Live and Let Die* (1972), *Blue Collar, Report to the Commissioner* (1975), *The Shootist* (1976), and *Midnight Run* (1988). Always a subtly commanding presence, Kotto projected an assured yet never overstated brand of masculinity. Unlike some black actors of the 1970s, he didn't have to prove he was a *baad* brother. He was who he was. Quiet as it was kept, Yaphet Kotto often revealed himself a great actor, yet he was confined to supporting roles.

But certainly no early 1980s film so blatantly (and perhaps cruelly) reduced (and exploited) its black stars to mere background filler as did *The Blues Brothers* (1980). This lopsided musical calvacade, which starred John Belushi and Dan Aykroyd, featured such stellar black talents as Cab Calloway, Ray Charles, James Brown, and Lady Soul herself, Aretha Franklin. Of course, the black stars carried this clunky, ordinary picture on their shoulders. When Franklin delivers an astounding version of "Think," she's almost unbearably great, sending our senses soaring with one of the most blazingly energetic and felt sequences in American movie musical history. The movie never reaches that type of delirious, high artistic peak again. (Afterwards it has nowhere to go but down.) Nor is Aretha ever seen again. *The Blues Brothers* used its black stars—the true blues brothers and sisters of musical history and not some pallid, comic imitators—as walk-ons, there to provide flashy moments and some much needed rhythm.

Dramatic Possibilities

In the early 1980s there were some important dramatic performances by actors in supporting roles. Milos Forman's *Ragtime* (1981) featured Howard Rollins, Jr., as

Coalhouse Walker, the ragtime pianist who leads a band of black revolutionaries in a doomed takeover of the Morgan Library. The script drew a rather far-fetched character (one can never believe him as a man living in this particular time period, which is the early years of twentieth-century America; he seems too much an outgrowth of a 1960s political sensibility). Rollins nonetheless created an untyped hero: Thoughtful, intelligent, too full of self-respect and a sense of moral outrage to let himself be treated as less than a man. For his performance, Rollins won an Academy Award nomination as Best Supporting Actor.

Louis Gossett, Jr., also drew critical attention. This stage-trained New York actor had proved himself remarkably versatile in films: as the pompous prim suitor of Diana Sands in *A Raisin in the Sun*; as the broken husband in *The Landlord*; as the wily, slave con artist in *The Skin Game* (1971); as the flighty free spirit in George Cukor's *Travels with My Aunt* (1972) as well as in *White Dawn* (1974) and *The Deep* (1977, here miscast as a sinister islander—a symbol of dark and dangerous powers—who terrorizes a young white American couple in Bermuda).

Then, against the odds, he landed the role of Sergeant Foley in *An Officer and a Gentleman* (1982). Originally, Foley had not been written as a black character, which meant, of course, that a black actor would not even have a chance to audition for the part. But a determined Gossett persuaded the filmmakers he was right for the part. Afterwards he walked away with the picture.

For black audiences, there was a kind of crazy, perverse joy in seeing Gossett as Foley upset past movie traditions: here was a black sergeant taunting the white hero (whom he calls "boy") and the other recruits as he puts them through the rigors of military life. Gossett portrayed Foley as a black man, like millions of others in America, who works in a white environment/culture, operating there successfully without losing his own personal cultural identity. He graces the picture with a type of moral authority that its young hero (Richard Gere) never attains. For his work in *An Officer and a Gentleman*, Gossett made movie history by becoming the third black actor to win an Academy Award, as Best Supporting Actor of 1982.

Afterwards Gossett hardly found challenging roles. Instead he appeared in Richard Lester's *Finders Keepers* (1984), the atrocious *Jaws 3-D* (1983), the 1986 right-wing fantasy *Iron Eagle*, *Firewalker* (1986, as Chuck Norris's sidekick), and *The Principal* (1987). Under layers of hideous makeup, he played a lizardlike hermaphrodite in the science fiction drama *Enemy Mime* (1985). Midway in the film, he gives birth to a child, then dies. Critic Vincent Canby described Gossett's character as "unquestionably one of the most thankless roles in movie history." Here (despite the makeup) he obviously represented the black man as the Other, an alien creature with another way of life.

The year after Gossett's Oscar win, Alfre Woodard was nominated for Best Supporting Actress for her role as the servant Geechee in Martin Ritt's *Cross Creek* (1983). It was a bit dismaying, however, to see Woodard cast as the traditional faithful servant, who manages to endear herself to the white woman she works for. And the woman in turn even helps Geechee acquire a sense of responsibility and independence! Woodard managed to inject some intelligence into the part. Later she gave a rather bizarrely enjoyable but implausible performance in the overheated *Extremities* (1986).

Buddy Buddy

Without a doubt, the use of blacks as supporting players and background material was nowhere more apparent than in the interracial buddy pictures. Despite the nation's racial problems, for decades white audiences have responded to popular, seemingly well-adjusted and inseparable professional interracial buddies: Bing Crosby and Louis Armstrong, Will Rogers and Stepin Fetchit, Jack Benny and Eddie "Rochester" Anderson, and Frank Sinatra and Sammy Davis, Jr. In essence, all these teams have been wish-fulfillment fantasies for a nation that has repeatedly hoped to simplify its racial tensions. The movie relationships have usually been frauds, refusing to explore the complex and often contradictory dynamics of real interracial friendships. Such movie friendships have usually held to one dictum: namely, that interracial buddies can be such only when the white buddy is in charge.

In film after film of the 1980s, pairs of white and black men were depicted as the best of friends. Of course, more often than not, the black performer functioned as a sidekick or, as in past films, he blesses his white friend with a tender loyalty and imparts some comforting spiritual insight. In the 1980s, even one-time adversaries found themselves interracially bonded. The *Rocky* films illustrate that point best. In the 1979 *Rocky II* (as in *Rocky, The First*, in 1976), although Carl Weathers as Apollo Creed and Sylvester Stallone as Rocky were essentially opponents, they were also compatriots, respectful of one another and almost on equal footing. Of course, Apollo's presence served mainly to heighten Rocky's heroism and power. The fact that the Italian Stallion could defeat a man as skilled and bright as Creed made Rocky emerge as a true, even shrewd, undisputed champ. Carl Weathers's Apollo—with his flair and gift for showmanship and his shrewd intelligence and awareness that when clowning to hype a fight he is merely playing a role—seemed closely patterned on Muhammad Ali. For years, much of White America had resented Ali's brashness and bold confidence. Some boxing fans grumbled that the ring had been taken over, for too long, by a series of black boxers. Would there never again be a first-rate white fighter (that familiar great white hope figure) to defeat a loudmouth braggart and reclaim the throne? The *Rocky* movies may have succeeded as great unconscious national fantasies that rewrote boxing history: not only does Rocky eventually emerge as a successful white hope who defeats an Ali-surrogate, but he also is befriended by the former black champ.

Bonded buddies: the theme of interracial male bonding proved a major one throughout films of the 1980s. In *An Officer and a Gentleman* (1982), Louis Gossett, Jr.—as a tough drill sergeant—not only helps lead Richard Gere (left) on the road to maturity but he also walked off with an Oscar as Best Supporting Actor of 1982.

In the *Rocky* films, Carl Weathers (right) as Apollo Creed first fought, later befriended the young boxer (Sylvester Stallone).

In *Lethal Weapon* (1987), Mel Gibson, as an alienated suicidal cop, found *new meaning in life*, thanks to the sobering influence of a stable, middle-class black buddy, played by Danny Glover.

But in *Street Smart* (1987), Morgan Freeman as the pimp Fast Black lets Christopher Reeve know that tensions between black and white still exist. A buddy ain't always a buddy. Freeman's was one of the most powerful film performances of the decade.

Of course, the fantasy was taken in a new direction in *Rocky III* (1982) when the series introduces a garish buck figure, called Clubber Lang (played in true nightmarish fashion by Mr. T). Here you have a loudmouth muscular dolt, vicious, coarse, vulgar, an affront to middle-class American values, who not only attacks Rocky's manhood but comments on Rocky's wife, that beloved sweetie Adrian. More so than any other black screen character of the early 1980s, T's Lang touches on White American fears about strong, sexual black men. By now, Apollo had won audience approval and become an acceptable Negro. He aids Rocky for the fight against Lang, who Apollo, too, knows is an aberration that must be defeated. So manipulated is the audience into loathing T's Clubber that it cheers Lang's defeat. He's as repugnant as the pimp in *American Gigolo.* Both represent black men as perverted *street niggers* who must go! The movie ends with buddies Rocky and Apollo jubilant over the white champ's success. By the time of *Rocky IV* (1985), one has the queasy feeling that the once vigorous Apollo has gone from being a canny opponent to becoming such a diehard buddy that he's beginning to look a tad like the old-style self-sacrificing tom who seemingly would give up his very life for his white massa/friend. That feeling, shockingly enough, seemed to be verified when Apollo dies in the film! So heart-broken is Rocky that when he boxes the decadent Soviet champ, one knows he's not only fighting for truth, justice, and the American way, but for the sake of his dear departed Apollo. The subtext of the *Rocky* films takes audiences on an intriguing journey that flashes changing attitudes about blacks.

Other actors were improbably cast as the buddy/sidekick to white stars. Billy Dee Williams provided backup support for Sylvester Stallone in *Nighthawks* (1982) and the Star Wars gang in *The Empire Strikes Back* (1980) and *Return of the Jedi* (1983). Neither gave him much to do. Yet these supporting roles were the best the movies had to offer him. Star roles came in cheapies such as *Fear City* (1985) and *Deadly Illusion* (1987). Later, he appeared in *The Visit* (2000).

Broadway musical star Gregory Hines played supporting roles in *The History of the World, Part I* (1981), *Wolfen* (1981), and *Deal of the Century* (1983). Then he befriended Mikhail Baryshnikov in *White Nights* (1985), was the police partner of Billy Crystal in *Running Scared* (1986), and the military partner of Willem Dafoe in *Off Limits* (1988). Unlike other black actors of the period, Hines was granted a bit of a love life. But he was so mellow and laid back that perhaps he hardly seemed threatening; therefore it might not have mattered whether he had a woman or not.

Late in the decade, Richard Donner's popular action film *Lethal Weapon* (1987)—starring Danny Glover and Mel Gibson—provided interesting twists on the buddy theme. The two men are cops, partners. Gibson's character is hot-tempered, reckless, alienated, suicidal. Here the black man is a symbol of stability; he is a middle-aged, middle-class Cosbyesque family man. Gingerly, he offers his hand in friendship to the troubled Gibson, inviting the white man to his home. Glover's daughter (Traci Wolfe) even develops a crush on the cop. The movie reaches a bloody climax when the villain, played by Gary Busey, goes to Glover's home for revenge: here the traditional American household and family are in jeopardy, yet ironically, of course, a black family now represents an American ideal. Even Gibson feels this ideal must be defended. Yet the movie makes the black family acceptable for the mass white audience by carefully scrubbing it "clean" of too strong an ethnic identity. The family, of course, is a movie mix of colors with a dab of black here, a dab of white there, with the result a perfect composite tan.

Lethal Weapon says that there are no significant cultural gaps or distinctions for the two men to bridge. Never is one led to wonder what the black man's social life is like. Never is one led to think he finds his home a refuge from the white world in which he works. And true to the huck-finn fixation, the good black man brings to his white loner friend an element of calm control and a budding maturity. In some respects, the film was a retread of *Edge of the City*. With interracial male bonding, black men are a cross between toms and mammies: all-giving, all-knowing, all-sacrificing nurturers. (Never was the black-buddy-as-mammy-nurturer more apparent than with the chunky policeman who befriends, via a shortwave radio, the troubled Bruce Willis, in *Die Hard*, 1988.) But what does the white friend offer his black buddy?

Despite Danny Glover's critically well-received performances in *Places in the Heart* (1984), *Silverado* (1985), and *Witness* (1985), he did not become a star until he played the trusty friend in *Lethal Weapon*. Later he appeared in two *Lethal Weapon* sequels as well as *Bat 21* (1988), *Grand Canyon* (1991), *A Rage in Harlem* (1991), *Pure Luck* (1991), *Flight of the Intruder* (1991), *The Saint of Fort Washington* (1993), and *Bopha!* (1993).

Richard Pryor, Superstar: The Ups and Downs

Early in the 1980s, amidst all the interracial buddy shenanigans, Richard Pryor emerged as a full-fledged superstar and legendary pop hero. During this period, Pryor's private life was widely reported on. In 1980, he made headlines following an accident—a mysterious explosion—at his home in California. Pryor suffered third-degree burns over the entire upper half of his body: his hands, chest, abdomen, back, neck, and face. The chances of his survival were said to be one in three. Word circulated that the explosion had occurred while Pryor was free-basing cocaine. Afterwards as hospital bulletins daily announced his struggle for life, few stars in America, black or white, elicited the type of attention and sympathy that poured out for Pryor. (In some respects, the reactions to the stricken Pryor were similar to those following the news of Elizabeth Taylor's near fatal bout with pneumonia in 1961.) In the eyes of the public, the accident made him both more human (vulnerable to mortal wounds like all of us) and more mythic. Now this man, known as a hellion who had fought with wives, argued with coworkers, and lived (drinking and doping) self-destructively right on the edge, had seemingly looked death in the eye and walked away. During the years following the accident, Pryor's movie career peaked. The public could not seem to get enough of him.

Pryor's early appearances were inauspicious cameos in *In God We Trust* (1980) and *Wholly Moses* (1980). Then in the 1980 *Stir Crazy* he was reteamed with Gene Wilder. This Sidney Poitier-directed comedy centered on two out-of-work New Yorkers (Pryor and Wilder) who, falsely accused of a bank robbery, are thrown into jail where they tangle with a testy warden, hardened guards, and a range of stereotyped inmates. Curiously, *Stir Crazy* hardly utilized Pryor. Wilder was the real star, blessed with top billing and a leading lady; Pryor, the likable backup support. But Pryor is lively and funny, especially when he does his *gotta be badd* routine as he and Wilder walk through the prison.

Slow-witted and rambling, the film was panned by the critics. In *The New York Times*, Vincent Canby called it a "comedy of quite stunning humorlessness." But *Stir Crazy*, released not long after Pryor's accident, became the number three top money-making movie of 1981, and, as *Time* reported, was then the second most successful comedy in industry history. *Newsweek* reported that together *Stir Crazy* and *Silver Streak* grossed in the neighborhood of $200 million. And Pryor and Wilder were hailed as the screen's first successful interracial comedy team.

Bustin' Loose, which Pryor coproduced in 1981, was another hit. Based on a story idea by Pryor, this free-wheeling comedy cast him as a con man who drives a group of eight homeless orphans and their prim, fussy teacher (Cicely Tyson) from Philadelphia to Seattle. Although Pryor had some zingy moments in which he unleashed a mild version of his Crazy Nigger persona (the best was his unexpected encounter with the Klan), this congenial film, like several earlier ones, domesticates Pryor; it tames those uncontrollable spirits, those nasty urges, those foul imaginings in order to make one believe he's just like us, an ordinary, kind of wild but basically humble guy.

Pryor's first completed postaccident film—and also his best of this period—was *Richard Pryor Live on the Sunset Strip* (1982). At times nervous, edgy, and certainly vulnerable, Pryor tries stretching himself as an artist, to go beyond the audience's anticipations, to examine material, straight from his private torment, that has rarely been used as a source of comedy. He tells the audience of personal experiences: a trip to Africa, his relationship with his wife, the accident that almost wiped out his life. Often more touching than funny, it is one of the most intensely

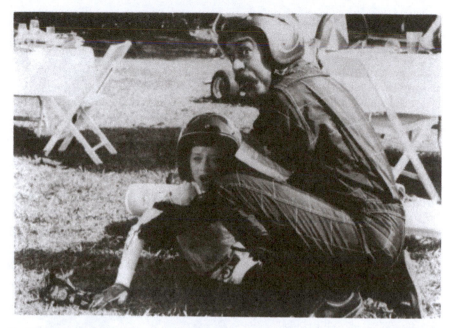

During the 1980s, Richard Pryor often found himself dogged by vapid scripts and lethargic directors, as in (above) *The Toy* (1982): here he played a black man who is literally bought as a companion/plaything for a spoiled white child (Scott Schwartz).

But in the concert film *Richard Pryor Live on the Sunset Strip* (1982), he was in better form, unhampered or constricted by having to play a dim-witted character.

Eddie Murphy in his most famous role as Axel Foley, the brash, streetwise hero of *Beverly Hills Cop* (1984).

Eddie Murphy, with Arsenio Hall, in *Coming To America* (1988), the first of Murphy's films to be geared towards pleasing the black mass movie audience, rather than the white one.

personal moments in the history of films. Although it lacks the full force of the first concert movie, *Richard Pryor Live on the Sunset Strip* remains—as does his third concert film *Richard Pryor Here and Now* (1983)—a rare glimpse of a remarkable talent not hampered by a lackluster script.

What became maddening for audiences to see was the appalling waste of Pryor's talents in his later features: *Some Kind of Hero* (1982); *The Toy* (1983, in which he plays an unemployed journalist hired to be a spoiled white child's plaything; here Pryor is sympathetic to dopey characters he would have satirized in the old days); and *Superman III* (1983). In the latter, when Superman flies through the air with Pryor by his side, Pryor's character is so jittery and scared that he looks suspiciously like a replay of a terr'fied Willie Best wandering through the haunted house with Bob Hope in *The Ghost Breakers*. No two ways about it, the part's old-style coon. Even Pryor could not save this picture.

Pryor, however, remained a major bankable star. In 1983, Columbia Pictures signed him to what was then one of the most lucrative deals in Hollywood history: an agreement to star in three films at the salary of $5 million each. Having achieved the kind of success no black star in Hollywood history had ever envisioned, he now stood at the pinnacle of his career. But such films as *Brewster's Millions* (1985), *Critical Condition* (1987), and *Moving* (1988) all proved disappointing. Moreover, it was also distressing for Pryor's fans to see the man who had once spoken for America's underclass now removed entirely from that class structure and often surrounded by white co-stars.

The failure of the autobiographical *Jo Jo Dancer, Your Life Is Calling* (1986) had to be a great setback. He directed, produced, cowrote (with Rocco Urbisci and black writer Paul Mooney), and starred in this tale about the life and times of comic Jo Jo Dancer—from a boyhood in a whorehouse to his rise to stardom to his literal burnout when the distraught Jo Jo sets himself on fire. Sadly, after this film, Pryor was no longer considered a significant box-office star.

In some of the worst of his films, he seemed at his most vulnerable. In *Moving*, the familiar nervous and darting eyes almost seemed to be pleading that someone understand what he was up against, that he was still an artist who wanted to make contact. Like many other fascinating American stars such as a Brando or Garbo or Taylor, as he moved through poor vehicles that could not match his talents, audiences wondered why he selected such trash. It was saddening to see his physical decline; he looked thin, haggard, enervated. Yet he remained such a major talent and cultural force that even at his least effective, he was a man who still had appeal. Audiences continued to hope that each new project would be the one to enable him to reclaim his throne. In him, the audience no doubt saw a part of itself, its faults and failings, its insecurities and doubts, and what it hoped were its brave efforts to keep afloat regardless. He remained one of the few great stars, black or white, of the era.

Trading Places: Eddie Murphy

While Pryor dominated American films in the early 1980s, Eddie Murphy's career took on a blazing rise from the middle to late years of the decade. Born in Brooklyn in 1962 and raised in Long Island in a middle-class black family, Eddie Murphy, as a teenager, formed a band with friends. Between the musical numbers, he told jokes to the audience. Not long afterward, he performed as a standup comic in Long Island nightclubs, earning between $25 and $50 a week. Upon graduating from high school, he fast-talked the managers of Manhattan's Comic Strip club into letting him perform. From there, he landed bookings at clubs along the East Coast. Then he spent four seasons on the television comedy series "Saturday Night Live." Afterwards he became the biggest crossover star of the 1980s.

Unlike Richard Pryor, who first won fame with black audiences and then eventually reached a broader following, Eddie Murphy had a large white constituency from the very beginning. While often raucous and rowdy and clearly influenced by Pryor, his comedy lacked the bite and anger of Pryor's. In 1983, Murphy told a reporter at *Newsweek*, "I'm not angry. I didn't learn this stuff hanging out with junkies on 158th Street. I never have been much of a fighter. If somebody white called me 'nigger' on the street, I just laughed." This statement indeed may touch on the basis of his appeal to the mass white audience. On one level, he represents the loose, jivey, close to vulgar black man, who does not threaten the white audience's feelings of superiority. Nor does he challenge (through insightful anger) racial attitudes. For Reagan-era audiences, his early screen characters may have represented a flight from serious confrontation with racial tensions. Murphy's movies paid lip service to racism (perhaps even exploited it) but took no stands at all. Fortunately, Murphy himself, through his unbridled confidence, presented a black man, quick-witted and sharp-tongued, undaunted and unconquerable.

His first movie, the Walter Hill action saga *48 Hrs* (1982), cast Murphy as Reggie Hammond, a convict, who is sprung from jail on a two-day pass to help a white cop named Jack Cates (Nick Nolte) catch up with a killer on the loose. When first seen, Murphy's Hammond sits in his prison cell, in an armchair, no less, wearing a hat, sun glasses, and a set of earphones. The character looks suspiciously like an old-style coon. Throughout the cop (a beefy, tough-minded cynic) and the convict (a bit of a profane free spirit) are at odds, repeatedly hurling hardball, macho insults at one another; often the cop's are racial. Not only does Nolte lavish onto Murphy such endearments as "asshole" and "shithead," but he also calls him "watermelon" and "an overdressed charcoal-colored loser."

Although black audiences often winced at such dialogue, they eventually brushed Nolte's comments aside because Murphy does not hesitate to talk back and is ever ready to play on the cop's stereotyped (racist) ideas about blacks. When Nolte takes a look at Reggie's snazzy European sports car, he says, "I didn't know you darker people went in for foreign jobs." Without missing a beat, Murphy responds, "Yeah, well, I had no choice. Some white asshole bought the last piece of shit skyblue Cadillac." When Nolte's Cates makes a crack about an expensive Giorgio Armani suit that Murphy wears, Reggie promptly pokes fun back at him, "I got a reputation for looking real nice with the ladies. Maybe when we get out, I can take you to a couple of spots. We can get you dressed up and I can take you on a pussy hunt." A few minutes later, Reggie asks, "You got a lady, Cates?" Cates answers, "Yeah." Reggie then counters with, "You know, the generosity of women never ceases to amaze me."

Throughout Murphy is revved up for action. For the black audience, Murphy seems to be playing a game of dozens, topping insult upon insult on an opponent. But the fact that Murphy's Reggie never becomes enraged or truly angry greatly neutralizes the inherent racism. The attitude of the scriptwriter is that America is now hip and sophisticated enough not to be bothered by racist remarks. It is the perfect casual just-shrug-your-shoulders-and-say-no-to-racist-remarks attitude for the Reagan 1980s. *48 Hrs* makes racist jokes acceptable. At least in a movie like *The Defiant Ones*, Poitier was able to respond to the racist remarks of Tony Curtis with a true and defined anger. But in *48 Hrs* Reggie has no true sense of moral outrage. Even in one of the movie's most famous scenes—when Reggie raises havoc in a redneck bar, telling the customers that he is their "worst fucking nightmare . . . a nigger with a badge"—he strikes one as merely playing a loudmouth role, that of the big, baad dude.

The film ends up as one more lopsided tale of brotherhood. Nolte explains to Murphy that when he called him "nigger" and "watermelon," he didn't "mean that stuff. I was just doing my job, keeping you down." Murphy responds, "Well, doing your job don't explain everything, Jack." That's a good piece of dialogue which, however, is quickly passed over as the movie moves on to another joke.

Interestingly enough, Murphy's Reggie usually has sex on his mind. Finally when he meets a young woman in a bar, he tells her almost immediately. "If I don't get some trim before the night is out, I'm going to bust." Despite the fact that it is known that Reggie's—well, horny—because he's been locked behind bars for too long, the script frequently plays on the idea of the oversexed black man. Never does the film establish a relationship for him with a woman. (The same thing happens in later Murphy films.) Throughout, the relationship that the white hero Cates has with actress Annette O'Toole adds another dimension to his character. Couldn't Reggie also have had a wife or girlfriend he had to leave behind? Might one not have known more about him if such were the case? One of the film's great shortcomings is that Reggie is seen almost exclusively from Cates's point of view without ever coming to know him in a full sense.

Yet Murphy, the actor, at the age of twenty, was in top form and in crisp control in *48 Hrs*, exuding a flair and confidence that set him apart from just about any other actor on screen at the time. He's a brash wiseguy loudmouth, with expert timing and a rapid-fire delivery, who next to the stocky and taller Nolte, is also a little guy underdog. Murphy's talent and style turned *48 Hrs* into a box-office bonanza.

A year later Murphy appeared in another box-office smash, John Landis's *Trading Places* (1983). Again he was costarred with a white actor, Dan Aykroyd. Here was a story of a nervy hustler (Murphy) and a preppy stock broker (Aykroyd) whose lives are turned topsy-turvy through the machinations of two billionaire brothers (Ralph Bellamy and Don Ameche). Having wagered a bet on the influence of environment versus heredity, the brothers set out to prove their points by reversing the fortunes of Murphy and Aykroyd. Murphy is ensconced in a mansion with an $80,000-a-year job; Aykroyd is framed as a thief and drug dealer and then dumped onto the streets.

When the audience first sees Murphy, he is posing as a blind, legless veteran who begs on the streets of Philadelphia. When the police get near him, he soon sprouts feet! Audiences howled at the sequence. But an old nagging question won't go away: why is Murphy cast in his first two films (and Pryor in some of his) as a black rip-off artist who must prove his worth? Do these films see the role of a clever petty thief (or criminal) the most plausible one for a black comic star?

Throughout, the film draws humor out of the highly "unlikely" spectacle of a black man who lives in high style. When Murphy first moves into his mansion, he invites his barroom friends over, most of whom (but not all) are black. As natural-born hell raisers, they dance, drink, strip, carouse. (You can take 'em out of the ghetto, but you can't take the ghetto out of 'em.) Murphy, however, is now on his way to becoming an "enlightened Negro." So, annoyed, he puts the trash out!

As the film traces the evolving friendship of Murphy and Aykroyd (yet another salute to interracial bonding), it becomes apparent that Hollywood, determined that this film have a built-in appeal to white audiences, has put Murphy into an acceptable cultural context. Lifted out of the black community, he is surrounded by white faces just as Pryor was in his 1980s features. Here Murphy is also sexually neutralized. Once again the white hero, Aykroyd, is granted a leading lady (Jamie Lee Curtis) while the film has no intention of setting up a relationship for Murphy. The movie uses him as a highfalutin supporting player—the rowdy coon—there for gritty laughs. Never is one to ask any pertinent questions about his life. Where does this man come from? Has he no set of past friends or relatives?

Murphy's next film, *Best Defense* (1984), in which he was cast as an American soldier in Kuwait, was a tepid comedy that failed at the box office.

But then came Martin Brest's *Beverly Hills Cop* (1984), which turned Murphy into a bonafide Movie Superstar. He's Detroit cop Axel Foley—a jivey keeper of the law—who zips off to Beverly Hills in search of the men who have murdered his best friend.

Beverly Hills Cop also tripped very lightly past the issue of race or racial distinctions. On one level, it too turns the very idea of racism into a joke. One of the best remembered scenes in *Beverly Hills Cop* occurs when Axel saunters into a posh Beverly Hills hotel, overhears the hotel receptionist tell someone on the phone that no rooms are available, and then proceeds to ask the woman if she has a reservation in his name. (Of course, he has made no such reservation.) When she says no, he launches into a loud, fast-talking pseudo-Crazy-Nigger routine. "Don't you think I realize what's going on here, Miss? Who do you think I am, huh? Don't you think I know that if I was some hotshot from out of town that pulled inside here and you guys made a reservation mistake, I'd be the first one to get a room? . . . I'm a small reporter from *Rolling Stone Magazine* that's in town to do an exclusive interview with Michael Jackson. . . . Now I think I just might as well call it 'Michael Jackson Can Sit on Top of the World Just as Long as he Doesn't Sit in the Palm Hotel Because There's No Niggers Allowed in There.'" At that point, the hotel manager, having overheard the exchange and no doubt anxious to calm down this embarrassing bigmouth lowlife, announces, "Excuse me, Sir. It seems we do have a last minute cancellation. There is a room available."

Here Murphy has used racism as a ploy to intimidate the whites at the hotel. This can be a disturbing scene, so indicative is it of certain attitudes about black outcries of racism. At this point in American history, some white Americans were complaining that blacks found racism in places where it did not exist. This scene, better than almost any other in American films of the 1980s, supports such attitudes. The black audience, however, feels that race is probably part of the issue. After all, Axel's ploy does get him the room. Yet because Axel is a bluffer and because the scene is played for quick laughter the idea of racism, in a sense, is suppressed altogether.

Throughout, the film uses Murphy's color as part of its running gag—about the contrast between the lowly black Detroit dude, in his jeans, sneakers, and sweatshirt, and the posh "high" Beverly Hills white world of wealth and privilege in which he finds himself—but also is determined that the audience forget the hero's color. Murphy is cut off almost completely from any semblance of a black community. The murdered best friend is white (actor James Russo). His newfound LA buddies, those dippy cops Billy Rosewood (Judge Reinhold) and Sergeant Taggart (John Ashton), are white as well. So, too, is the childhood friend from Detroit whom he meets up with in Beverly Hills, the art gallery director Jenny Summers (Lisa Eilbacher). For black audiences, all these white buddies were a bit puzzling. Would it not have been more realistic for this brother from Detroit to have grown up with black friends? Does Axel have any kind of family in Detroit?

Moreover, Murphy was also just about desexed. He may eye a pretty blonde in a convertible. But nothing comes of that. Originally, Sylvester Stallone was to have starred in *Beverly Hills Cop*; there is no way Stallone would not have had a movie romance with actress Lisa Eilbacher. One wonders if the creators of *Beverly Hills Cop* feared that Murphy's large white constituency might object to seeing him cast romantically opposite a white actress. If that were the case, why did the filmmakers not simply give Murphy a black actress in the Jenny Summers role? On a conscious or unconscious level, did the filmmakers fear Murphy's sexuality?

Beverly Hills Cop II, more a clamorous remake than a sequel, appeared in 1987. Again, too, Eddie Murphy's appeal led to a box-office smash. The same was true of the feeble *The Golden Child* (1986), in which Murphy journeys to Tibet in search of a magical child who can save the world.

In 1987, he signed an exclusive, five-picture contract with Paramount Pictures for a reported fee of $25 million. At this point, there was no star in America, with the possible exception of Sylvester Stallone, as powerful a box-office draw as Murphy. He had proved what the old movie moguls would never have imagined possible: that a black star could pull in the huge general audience. Yet liberal critics and black intellectuals wondered if he would ever use his great power to make a different type of movie. Would Murphy's future be a continuation of black/white buddy films? Would he continue playing essentially coon roles?

Murphy's first piece of more personal filmmaking was his concert film *Eddie Murphy Raw* (1987). Here he took off with wickedly accurate impersonations of Cosby and Pryor and a series of jokes and skits (some of which just dragged on without any particular insight) directed at macho Italian-Americans, homosexuals, and women. But rather than a display of the moving perceptiveness that had distinguished Pryor's concert films, what often emerged were signs of a mean-spiritedness and a mistrust and paranoia about women. Directed by Robert Townsend, *Eddie Murphy Raw* was a money-maker but in the years to come it may be viewed as Murphy's least gracious and possibly ugliest film.

As the decade neared its end, Murphy underwent a surprising image change in *Coming to America* (1988). Based on a story idea by Murphy, the movie focused on an African prince Akeem (from the mythical kingdom of Zamunda) who, balking at the prearranged marriage his parents the King and Queen have arranged for him, leaves with his aide-de-camp Semmi (Arsenio Hall) for America—in search of an independent young woman to marry. In New York, he courts and wins the daughter (Shari Headley) of his employer (John Amos) at a fast-food restaurant.

Old-fashioned and frequently sluggishly directed by John Landis, *Coming to America*'s fairy-tale view of a mythical African kingdom hardly seems to spring from a black sensibility. It is old-style Hollywood fakery. During an early lavish ceremonial sequence, the troupe of black dancers cavorting across the screen are reminiscent of the Ethiopian contingency in Cecil B. DeMille's 1956 *The Ten Commandments*. It is the use of blacks as high-style, far-fetched campy exotica. The bare-breasted black beauties who attend to Murphy during his morning bath also are used as sexy exotics, exploited to the hilt by the director. Once in New

York, Murphy's Prince Akeem encounters the expected movie ghettoites who steal his expensive luggage, then later try to sell his own items back to him. And the darker kid sister of Akeem's bride-to-be is turned into an overripe teen sex kitten.

Yet with that said and done, *Coming to America* often is charming and warm-hearted. Murphy's screen persona is softened and perhaps a tad sentimentalized. But what a pleasure to see him not only relate to other blacks but finally to have a romance with a black woman. When he walks home after his first date with his dreamgirl, he is so caught up in the evening's romantic aura that he bursts into song, performing Jackie Wilson's hit "To Be Loved." It is a deliriously romantic moment, the type rarely seen in black-oriented films. Murphy and Arsenio Hall, both heavily made up, also play cameo roles. Hall impersonates a barber, a raunchy minister, and a less than attractive young woman. Murphy is in high gear as a talky barber, an elderly Jewish man, and a long-haired singer with a group called Sexual Chocolate. Many of the other actors shine. Even that master of bombast James Earl Jones is hammily enjoyable. Madge Sinclair is regal and beautiful as the haughty queen. And John Amos shows his mean talent for comic toughness.

And so Eddie Murphy's movie career, while no doubt still hardly satisfying to the purists, seemed to be taking an interesting turn as the decade wound to a close. To his credit—whether his films were good, bad, or indifferent—he remained a cocky and frequently engaging talent, a young man whose self-assurance, energy, and unflagging determination to do things *his* way made him a distinctive hero, especially for the younger black audience of his era.

A Soldier's Story

One of the few films to offer a cast of promising black actors strong, vivid characters to play was Norman Jewison's *A Soldier's Story* (1984). Based on Charles Fuller's Pulitzer Prize–winning drama *A Soldier's Play* with a screenplay by Fuller, the film centered on the murder of a black army sergeant (played by Adolph Caesar) on a Louisiana military base in 1944. Through flashbacks, *A Soldier's Story* uncovers racial tensions within the barracks of the black soldiers. Never before had feature films entered into the psyche of a certain kind of black character; the dead Sergeant Waters, it is revealed, has been a foul-spirited man, torn and embittered by his own lofty self-hatred. *A Soldier's Story* succeeded as a detective story and also as an entertaining social document. For his screenplay, Fuller was nominated for the Academy Award.

Also nominated for an Oscar, as Best Supporting Actor of the Year, was Adolph Caesar. Sadly, Caesar died of a heart attack within two years of this triumph. Absorbing performances also came from Howard Rollins, Jr. (whose Poitier-like presence kept the film centered), newcomer Larry Riley (as the country boy tom figure the sergeant despises), Art Evans, David Alan Grier, and, perhaps best of all (and least heralded), Denzel Washington as the coolly intense Peterson. It's a nonflashy, perfectly controlled piece of work.

Say It with Music

By the mid-1980s, black musicals—or rather dramatic black-oriented films highlighted by musical numbers—also began appearing. Stan Lathan's *Beat Street* (1984) looked at the break dance phenomenon. The low-budget *Rappin'* (1985), featuring Mario Van Peebles, attempted to capitalize on the then popular rap music. So, too, did Michael Schultz's *Krush Groove*. Although half-heartedly directed, the film nonetheless featured such up-and-coming young music stars as Sheila E. (an interesting screen presence unfortunately mishandled here), Kurtis Blow, The Fat Boys, and Run-D. M. C. Schultz also directed *Berry Gordy's The Last Dragon*, more a kung-fu movie than a musical, which featured the music of Stevie Wonder, Smokey Robinson, The Temptations, and DeBarge. Strangely enough, this slight, almost amateurish film—which starred newcomers Taimak and Vanity— found a following, primarily among the urban young.

The most opulent (it reportedly cost around $50 million) and most disappointing black-oriented musical of the period was no doubt Francis Coppola's *The Cotton Club* (1984). Set in the famous Harlem club of the 1920s and 1930s, which had spotlighted such black performers as Duke Ellington, Ethel Waters, and the Nicholas Brothers, the movie raised hopes for an exploration of the tensions and triumphs of so many black entertainers just as they broke through to become major American stars. Coppola was successful at creating a jazzy, sensual world full of glamour and dark intrigue. Yet focusing primarily on Richard Gere (as a cornet player who becomes embroiled in the activities of the mob), the film failed to examine its black characters (particularly the dancing brothers played by Gregory and Maurice Hines). Repeatedly, the movie turns its back on its black cast. Lonette McKee appeared in a role that could have been perfect for her: she plays the light-skinned young black singer Lila who is so anxious for success that she passes for white while appearing at a swanky downtown "ofay" club. Unfortunately, McKee's singer is so sketchily developed in the script by Coppola and William Kennedy that the character emerges not as a flesh and blood woman but yet a continuation of the tragic mulatto stereotype. Still McKee has a sensational sequence when she sings "Ill Wind."

Surely the 1980s most successful black-oriented musical was *Purple Rain* (1984), starring that master of glitzy funk, his royal shortness himself, Prince. Rarely has any black star been so adored and worshiped in a film; the only rivals for this type of black star fixation are Otto Preminger's fascination with Dandridge in *Carmen Jones* or Berry Gordy's infatuation with Diana Ross in *Mahogany*. Here it is Prince's devotion to—who else but?—Prince! The film is mad for the boy and the boy seems mad for himself. *Purple Rain* represents the height of joyous narcissism. Its plot—hackneyed and tired—is a backstage tale, tracing the ups and downs of the Kid (Prince), a performer with a wild hunger for success and a burning desire to escape his tormented family situation. He is the product of a troubled interracial marriage. His father (black actor Clarence Williams III) is a self-destructive alcoholic and a failed musician turned wife beater. The mother (Greek actress Olga Kartalos) seems little more than a masochistic sad sack. The Kid must also contend with a slickster of a musical rival (Morris Day of the group The Time). And he woos, loses, then wins again a voluptuous beauty named Apollonia (Apollonia Kotero of the group Apollonia 6).

In many ways, the movie is terrible. Its women are treated like so much trash. One is even thrown into a dumpster, for comic effects. "In the Kid's world," wrote Ed Naha in *The New York Post*, "women are there to be worshipped, beaten or humiliated, not necessarily in that order."

Yet crazed and distorted as *Purple Rain* frequently is, each time a performer leaps into a musical number, audiences are willing to ignore the cliched, dopey story. The real surprise was newcomer Morris Day. When he goes into a backstage "Who's on first" routine (based on an old Abbott and Costello bit) with his companion Jerome (Jerome Benton), Day reveals himself to be a monster comic presence and arguably the film's real star. With his slicked-down processed hair, his wild-man eyes (his shamelessly enjoyable eye pops rival those of Mantan Moreland), the jivey, "cool breeze" delivery of his lines, his upfront simp vanity, and his pepped-up, sexy dude movements, he's old-time ethnic theater gone legit.

Prince's Kid was, of course, a lavish update of the old tragic mulatto. Not even Lonette McKee's Lila in *The Cotton Club* seemed as tormented and troubled, as restless and searching, as this poor racially mixed creature. Along with the other major characters, Prince was naturally more tan than black, which may explain some of the appeal of *Purple Rain* to the vast mass audience. Today it remains fascinating and funny to see what a lineup of influences went into the makeup of his androgynous, racially-fused screen persona: Prince as the Kid is part "misunderstood" James Dean, part motorcycle rebel Brando, part guitar-strumming Jimi Hendrix, part Little Richard (what with his modified pompadour), part Monroe (what with his "soft" vulnerable sexuality), and part Elizabeth Taylor (what with those heavily mascaraed brows and lashes). He pouts, broods, flirts, and struts like a 1950s screen siren: he's a coquette turned daredevil, who, during the musical segments, steams up the screen.

Purple Rain became an enormous hit, establishing Prince for a brief spell as a bankable movie star. Interestingly, *Purple Rain* was rarely discussed as a black film. The film has almost no sense whatsoever of its protagonist's black roots. Yet Prince was successful, more so than Pryor or Murphy at that point in their careers (1984), at creating a distinct screen persona he felt comfortable with. A dazzling tan sensibility now had full sway in American films. Prince's later vehicles *Under the Cherry Moon* (1986), *Graffiti Bridge* (1990), and the critically well-received concert film *Sign O' the Times* (1987) were commercial disappointments.

Different Directions

Other unusual or offbeat films appeared, some successful, some terrible failures. In *Leonard, Part 6* (1987), Bill Cosby starred as a spy out to exterminate an animal rights activist who has mind control of all the animals of the world! The movie failed. Walter Hill's *Crossroads* (1986) was an intriguing but misbegotten study of a blues musician (Joe Seneca) pursued and befriended by a young admirer (Ralph Macchio). Independent white filmmaker John Sayles came up with an interesting but overrated *The Brother from Another Planet* (1984). The 1986 remake of *Native Son* was pale and limpid. Carl Weathers attempted reviving the black action film with a tepid little number called *Action Jackson* (1988). *Soul Man* (1986)—the story of a white student who goes in blackface in order to qualify for a minority scholarship drew (deserved) criticism and some protests from the black community. The imports *Diva* (1982), the mournful *'Round Midnight* (1986), in which jazz musician Dexter Gordon gave an Oscar-nominated performance, and Euzhan Palcy's *Sugar Cane Alley* (1984), reached audiences weary of typical Hollywood fare. No doubt the strongest imported film—yet the least seen—was Australian filmmaker Fred Schepisi's *The Chant of Jimmie Blacksmith* (released in the United States in 1980), a searing examination of an aborigine who takes violent action against the white colonial system that has exploited his people. At the same time, whereas in the past, audiences had seen the myth of the noble, courageous white man conquering untamed forces in *savage* Africa, in such 1980s films as *Out of Africa* (1985) and *Gorillas in the Mist* there was a twist on the myth: now it was *the white woman* taming the wilds of *the dark continent*. Each woman was also attended to by a faithful black servant.

Women: As Exotics and Non-Racials

Sadly, in the 1980s, black women rarely had a chance for important roles. What with all the interracial male bonding, black women seemed to have disappeared. On those rare occasions when they found flashy roles, they often ended up playing exotics: Tina Turner, in metal-meshed minidress, as Aunty Entity in *Mad Max Beyond Thunderdome* (1985); Grace Jones, so intriguing and striking in photographs, simply a sepia Dragon Lady in such films as *Conan the Destroyer* (1984), *A View to a Kill* (1985, as the Amazonian villainess May Day, who battles James Bond on the Eiffel Tower), *Vamp* (1986), and *Siesta* (1987); and the young sex kitten, Lisa Bonet, used as the most exotic of tragic mulattoes in Alan Parker's *Angel Heart* (1987). Such women as Rae Dawn Chong and Jennifer Beals sometimes found themselves cast as nonblack heroines. In *Beat Street*, *The Color Purple*, and *Soul Man*, Chong played black characters. In such movies as *Quest for Fire* (1981), *Commando* (1985), and *American Flyers* (1985), Chong was cast as a "multinational": a woman who seems a mix but basically is colorless, with no one strongly defined racial/cultural identity. Beals, however, went without any racial identity whatsoever in her features. In *Flashdance* (1983)—a drama about a beautiful young welder in Pittsburgh, who aspires to be a dancer—Beals is clearly the tan Other. Next to nothing is known about her background. The film shrewdly graces her with a white mother surrogate, an older woman (Lilia Skala), who encourages Beals to pursue her dreams of being a dancer. When she becomes involved with a white married man, the subject of race never enters the picture. The film is a cheat. In the past, white actresses such as Jeanne Crain and Susan Kohner had played tragic mulattoes. Surely, a light black woman should be able to play any role. Had *Flashdance* fully established her as a white character—with a white family—one might have respected its courage. But Beals plays a woman cut off completely from any kind of roots. In *The Bride* (1985), a remake of *The Bride of Frankenstein*, Beals, as the creation of the mad Dr. Frankenstein (played by Sting), was again a woman coming out of nowhere with no cultural/racial links or traditions.

A Controversy about *Color*

The era's most talked-about black-oriented film was certainly Steven Spielberg's *The Color Purple* (1985). Based on the Pulitzer Prize-winning novel by black writer Alice Walker, the film's heroine is an uneducated, backwoods black Southern woman named Celie, whose life emerges as a shattering tale of horrors and abuses. At a young age, she is raped and twice impregnated by her stepfather (who sells her children to a barren couple). Later she is abused by her sadistic husband Mr.——, who separates her from her beloved sister Nettie. Gradually, she withdraws but is brought back to life through a friendship with her husband's mistress, the singer Shug Avery. *The Color Purple* ends on a triumphant, mock-transcendent note with the emergence of Celie as a confident woman (assured enough to confront the man who has emotionally imprisoned her) and with the reunion of Celie and her sister Nettie.

The Color Purple met with mixed reviews. Critic Rex Reed hailed it as "a noble, compelling, powerfully acted, magnificently photographed, richly textured film of heart-rending impact." But in *The New York Times*, Vincent Canby wrote: "It makes you laugh, it makes you cry and it makes you feel a little bit of a fool for having been taken in by its calculated, often phony effects." *Variety* said it was "overproduced, overly manipulative . . . saved by outstanding performances."

Within the black community, the reactions were heatedly mixed. The NAACP protested against the film's depiction of the black male characters. In *The New York Daily News*, black writer Earl Caldwell said that black men "saw red" over the film. *The Washington Post*'s black columnist Dorothy Gilliam, however, wrote about "the purity and depth of love" expressed in the movie. In newspaper articles around the country as well as on television programs as diverse as "The Today Show" and "Donahue," *The Color Purple* was discussed and debated.

The Color Purple's critics clearly had their points. The black males (played by Danny Glover, Willard Pugh, and Adolph Caesar) are indeed presented as caricatured pawns. Despite the decently defined performance of Danny Glover, Mr.—— seems little more than the familiar black brute, violent and oversexed. Never does one see the broader context in which any of the characters must live: the larger, dominant white culture that envelops—and certainly enslaves—them all. Worse than the fact that the pressures brought to bear on a black man in a white society are never dramatized, they are never even suggested. Moreover the men mainly unleash their violence on women, never on one another, and certainly never on whites. At the novel's conclusion, a warmth and love developed between Celie and Mr.——. He is the only one, she emphatically states, who understands some of her feelings. The novel was a fable ending on a note of reunion, not only between the sisters but symbolically also between black men and black women. In the film, Mr.—— undergoes a transformation. But one hardly understands it; one is merely puzzled by it.

Of course, what was missing most from *The Color Purple* was the very aspect that gave the novel such distinction: the voice of Celie. In it, readers saw life from the point of view of this poor, rejected black woman. The film, however, has the voice of Steven Spielberg. His sensibility informs almost every frame, turning an intimate tale into a large-scale, overblown Disneyesque Victorian melodrama, full of "big" moments and simplified characters (who can neatly be defined in terms of good and bad). Perhaps determined to make a family film, Spielberg also compromised the story by soft-pedaling its lesbian theme. In the novel, it was Celie's physical relationship with Shug that brought about her emotional awakening and set her on the road to fulfillment. In the film, the two have one tentative, ambiguous smiling-touching sequence; then any suggestion of a sexual relationship is dropped altogether.

Yet despite its failures, *The Color Purple* affected millions of viewers, black and white. No matter how much one might dismiss the film intellectually, it was often hard to reject it emotionally. What gave the movie its emotional power were the basic outline of the Walker story and the performances. Here in one of the few

Tan royalty: Prince, a masterly (and androgynous) fusion of black and white, in *Purple Rain* (1984), a film that reverberates to the tune of its star's glitzy narcissism.

Later Whoopi Goldberg emerged as the only black female star of the 1980s to work consistently in starring roles, although for the most part her films proved disappointing and wasted her talents.

Whoopi Goldberg and Margaret Avery in *The Color Purple* (1985), a controversial film which remains, however, one of the few movies of the era to focus on black women.

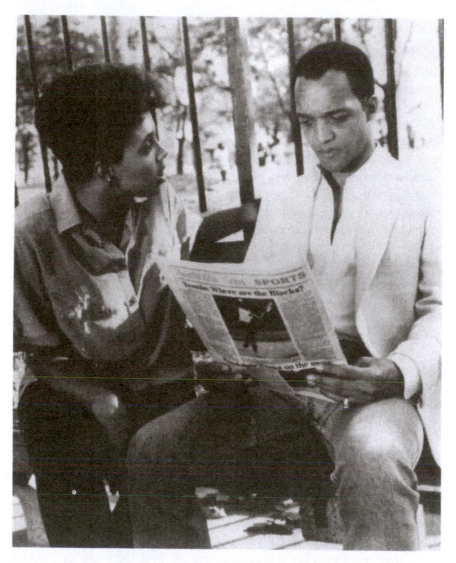

Spike Lee's *She's Gotta Have It* (1986), with Tracy Camila Johns and Tommy Redmond Hicks: a low-budget, independently produced "little" picture that became a surprise hit.

black-oriented dramatic films of the decade, the performers—Desreta Jackson (as the young Celie), Akosua Busia, Margaret Avery (as Shug), Oprah Winfrey (as hefty Sofia, a character precariously close to the mammy of old days), and Whoopi Goldberg (as the older Celie; sometimes too calculated, sometimes effective)— seemed to connect to their roles in an intensely personal way.

For her performance in *The Color Purple*, Whoopi Goldberg was nominated for an Oscar as Best Actress of the Year. Winfrey and Avery were each nominated as Best Supporting Actress. In total, *The Color Purple* earned eleven (including Best Picture) Academy Award nominations. Yet perhaps partly because of the controversy surrounding it and partly because of the industry's ambivalence toward Spielberg, *The Color Purple* won no Oscars whatsoever. Afterwards, none of the actresses went on to major dramatic film careers. One wondered if the industry still had no place for a serious dramatic black actress.

Whipping Whoopi

For a spell, Whoopi Goldberg's career took off. She became the only black woman of the late 1980s to star in Hollywood films. Yet few stars have been as thoroughly and embarrassingly trashed time and again in their features as was Goldberg.

Born Caryn Johnson in New York City (c. 1950), Goldberg had come to films after a long apprenticeship in theater, which had culminated with her critically acclaimed one-woman Broadway show *Whoopi Goldberg*. Her films, however, usually treated her as an oddity, never placing her within a cultural context with which a black audience could identify.

Goldberg's cultural rootlessness was immediately apparent in Penny Marshall's *Jumpin' Jack Flash* (1987). Cast as Terry Doolittle, Goldberg played a computer programmer, who, through a technological mix-up, receives messages from a British agent locked behind the Iron Curtain. Infatuated with the man, she sets out to save him. Thereafter begins a series of comic sequences, in one of which Goldberg is dragged through the streets of New York trapped inside a telephone booth. Here as she pops her eyes and screams like mad, she is not too different from the comically fearful Butterfly McQueen screaming that the Yankees is coming. Throughout, Goldberg's Terry remained a cultural/racial mystery. In her apartment, there are no cultural demarcations to suggest it as the home of a black woman. At her job, she is seen mainly with white coworkers. For a few minutes, she has a scene with that grand old stylized smoothie Roscoe Lee Browne. Audiences longed to watch these two skilled black performers riff and jam together, but Browne soon disappeared. As should now be expected, Goldberg is left romantically stranded in the picture. As a coworker, white actor Stephen Collins takes a friendly interest in her. But there is no way the film lets her get too close to this fair-haired

WASPy leading man. Their relationship is kept neatly platonic. At the conclusion when she has rescued the British agent (played by Jonathan Pryce), the two finally meet. But here in one of the most cynical scenes in Hollywood films of the 1980s, these would-be lovers are not permitted a hot, torrid, appropriate movie ending embrace.

It looked like Eddie Murphy's dilemma in *Beverly Hills Cop*. Again: did the filmmakers fear the mass white audience would be offended at seeing Goldberg in the arms of a white actor? Apparently so. That fact of life was borne home when Goldberg appeared in a love scene with white actor Sam Elliott in *Fatal Beauty* (1987). Preview audiences on the West Coast, however, objected to the scene. It was cut. The very idea of Whoopi Goldberg as a romantic film personality was unacceptable to certain audiences. Moreover, in such films as *Jumpin' Jack Flash* and *Fatal Beauty*, so unattractively and absurdly dressed was she in oversized clothes or sneakers that she seemed defeminized. The filmmakers seemed to view her as an asexual creature from another universe. Much of the same was true of her appearance in *Burglar* (1987).

By not casting her with other black characters, the comedies she starred in repeatedly kept Whoopi Goldberg removed from the black community. By throwing her into male-oriented action films, the industry prevented women from being able to identify fully with Goldberg. Three years after her *Color Purple* triumph, her career was in dismal shape. Reviewing the Goldberg film *The Telephone* (1988), Caryn James wrote in *The New York Times*: "The truest, most sanely existential lines spoken . . . came from the audience. . . . 'I want my money back,' one person yelled, which encouraged another to say, 'I hope the film breaks.'" Other critics reported such audience outcries. The audience had turned hostile towards Goldberg, no doubt intuitively aware that here was a rich talent being wasted. Of course, *she* was blamed for that waste, not the industry that treated her with such contempt. By 1988, Hollywood appeared to have Goldberg where it wanted: playing a maid in *Clara's Heart*. Here as a Jamaican domestic who works for a white family in Maryland and becomes attached to the young son, Goldberg gave a well-crafted, convincing performance. But the script desexed her character, presenting the black woman once again as a mighty nurturer—an updated mammy—without enough of a life of her own.

In most of her films, Goldberg must be credited with moments of dingbat originality. Underneath the brash, rough exterior is a vulnerable heroine, given to loneliness and feelings of isolation. Her humor serves as a veneer to shield a woman who may fear rejection, who is also blessed with a girlish warmth and a touching tenderness. No doubt audiences could have identified with her as a daffy, resilient outsider (not an oddity) who turns triumphant. But that rarely happened. Still, Goldberg held onto her career, and in the next decade, she would become a bigger—and more interesting—star.

Independents

Although black stars had appeared in hugely successful general films, many feared the commercial black film might be an anachronism, a relic of the 1970s and the earlier decades of race movies. Many, too, wondered if any new black directors would rise to prominence. The situation looked rather grim.

All that changed, however, with the appearance of a low-budget, independently produced movie called *She's Gotta Have It* (1986). Shot in twelve days in Brooklyn with a cast of unknowns on a budget of $175,000, it was the work of a young black director named Spike Lee. The film became a surprise hit.

She's Gotta Have It told a simple but offbeat story of a young black graphics artist, Nola Darling (Tracy Camila Johns), who must decide which of her three suitors suits her best. The men are a motley lot: there is Jamie (Tommy Redmond Hicks), somber, serious, dependable but mighty dull; Greer (John Canada Terrell), a gilded narcissist, who even at the point of making love, shows more interest in himself than Nola; and Mars Blackmon (played by Spike Lee), a loony, hopped-up, bespectacled sparkplug who talks, talks, talks, spinning out comic raps, often as a defense against a world that otherwise might not know he exists. Nola enjoys her relationships with all three. But it is the men who insist she make a choice. It is also the men—their vanities, follies, pretensions, and insecurities—which the film satirizes. Drawing its characters with affection, the film does not turn strident in letting audiences know these are black protagonists. Lee's great gift is to present contemporary urban black characters, who, in many respects, are no different from white ones caught up in a game of sexual politics. Yet their frame of reference and internal rhythms spring from a distinct black cultural tradition.

She's Gotta Have It was not a perfect film. Lee was criticized for his treatment of the lesbian character Opal (Raye Dowell), who is depicted as an odd-woman-out. In years to come, black women may even look at Nola in a different manner than did audiences in the 1980s. While free-spirited and unfettered by traditional assumptions about a woman's place, Nola is also a bit of a pretty blank, who serves as a backdrop for the story of the men. While they discuss politics, sports, and, in the case of Greer, his career, the script doesn't have Nola speak in such a way. The clippings on the wall of her apartment do suggest her possible social/political awareness. But viewers would prefer direct statements. When she is sexually violated in a disturbing sequence, the script again does not have her later fully comment on the incident. Still, Nola's determination to live by her own sexual/romantic rules say something, much as Dorothy Dandridge's Carmen does, about a woman operating on her own terms in what is considered a man's world.

But the director's style (and his refusal to make a formula picture) proved fresh and original. *She's Gotta Have It* was a true rarity: a black film with a black sensibility. Lee also wrote and edited the film, featured his sister Joie Lee in it, and hired his father, musician Bill Lee, to write the movie's score. The film was shot by black cinematographer Ernest Dickerson (who earlier had shot *The Brother from Another Planet*). *She's Gotta Have It*'s success with young black audiences and with some young white audiences seemed to indicate a new day for black films. Now there was hope that a black filmic sensibility (a black aesthetic) might also invigorate American movies, much as jazz and later the Motown sound had altered popular music—for blacks *and* whites.

Following *She's Gotta Have It*, Lee directed *School Daze* (1988). This satiric comedy focusing on life at a Southern black college may best be remembered for the categories in which Lee divided his students: the Wannabees, mainly those light-bright blacks fleeing their cultural roots, hoping like mad to get as close to a white ideal as possible; and the Jiggaboos, mainly those browner or darker students, shoved to the sidelines of social life at this black school. Despite the flaws—its canvas was so broad that it failed to cover any of its subjects with enough detail and as many women pointed out, its female characters were vapid, dimensionless sisters caught up mainly in *men*—*School Daze* nonetheless remained an uncompromising black film. It refused to make concessions to please a white audience. Indeed white critics seemed bewildered by it.

Another independent black film that reached a large audience during this period was Robert Townsend's *Hollywood Shuffle* (1987). Townsend had also raised his own financing—through the use of credit cards to cover the cost of raw film, wardrobe, and whatever else he needed. This limber, episodic film was a satiric sendup on the dilemmas confronting black actors and actresses in a Hollywood that offers them only stereotyped roles. Having acted in such films as *Streets of Fire* (1983), *A Soldier's Story*, *American Flyers*, and *Ratboy* (1986), Townsend knew the Hollywood system inside out. Uneven, and more a series of clever skits than a fully developed film, *Hollywood Shuffle* was carried along by its young director's spirit and enthusiasm. The film's greatest asset was Townsend, the actor. (He's a better actor than director.) In one sequence, he does what can only be described as a brilliant impersonation of Stepin Fetchit: it is a parody and a homage to Fetchit. Townsend sees clearly the timing and skill that went into Fetchit's work.

Spike Lee and Townsend brought to the forefront a new movement of independent black filmmakers who had been around for a time, some of them working on projects as far back as the late 1960s. St. Clair Bourne and Warrington Hudlin, for example, directed documentaries. Ayoka Chenzira, a young woman, turned out *Hair Piece* (1984), a clever and funny look at hair obsessions and fixations of the black community. Robert Gardner filmed *Clarence and Angel* (1975), a study of two restless students in New York's overcrowded school system. Haile Gerima directed *Child of Resistance* (1972), *Bush Mama* (1976), and *Harvest: 3000 Years* (1976). Charles Burnett directed the blistering *Killer of Sheep* (1977). Billy Woodberry directed the moving study of a black family, *Bless Their Little*

Hearts (1984). Julie Dash directed the short film *Illusions* (1983) with Lonette McKee. Also among this new group were Kathleen Collins, Ben Caldwell, Larry Clark, and Alile Sharon Larkin. The man considered the dean of the independents was William Greaves, who directed such documentaries as *From These Roots* (1974) and *Still A Brother: Inside the Black Middle Class* (1968), and later was the executive producer of *Bustin' Loose*. The work of the independents varied. But here were men and women making personal statements and taking film in a new direction. In the next decade, the independents would help lead to the rise of a new type of African American cinema.

Hollywood and the Race Theme

By the late 1980s, Hollywood also cast its eye on the race theme. Or it might be better to say that Hollywood flirted with the race theme but avoided a full examination of the subject with the films *Cry Freedom* (1987), *Mississippi Burning* (1988), *Bird* (1988), *A Dry White Season* (1989), *Glory*, and *Driving Miss Daisy* (1989).

Sir Richard Attenborough's highly touted *Cry Freedom*, which cast Denzel Washington as black South African anti-apartheid activist Steve Biko, was promoted as a provocative, courageous attempt to uncover the brutalities and injustices of apartheid. The truth of the matter, however, was that *Cry Freedom* was a mess. Rather than telling enough about Biko or his wife or the beautiful young activist black doctor we meet early in the film, director Attenborough focused on Biko's friendship with white South African journalist Donald Woods. For a while, it's another interracial buddy film. Then before it is half over, Biko dies. The rest of this tepid enterprise—centering on Woods's efforts to get his family out of the country—focused on these good, dear white people, suffering, suffering, suffering. (Another South African drama A *World Apart* [1988] took a similar approach but with more satisfying results.) Still Denzel Washington's impressive performance—controlled, intelligent, calm yet heated—won him an Oscar nomination as Best Supporting Actor.

Burning History: The White Man's Burden

Alan Parker's *Mississippi Burning* set out to dramatize a subject in American history that many yearned to see explored: the struggles of the Civil Rights Movement of the early 1960s.

Loosely based on a true story—the disappearance and murder of three civil rights workers (one Black Southerner, James Chaney; two white Northerners,

Michael Schwerner and Andrew Goodman) in Philadelphia, Mississippi, in 1964—
Mississippi Burning focuses on the efforts of two white FBI agents (Gene Hackman
and Willem Dafoe) to unlock the mystery and find the killers. What they encounter
in Mississippi is a war zone of terror and violence in which local law-enforcement
officers and members of the Klan are Storm Troopers determined to maintain
their racist status quo. Any sign of black resistance is promptly disposed of. Black
churches are bombed. Black homes are torched. And at every turn, in graphically
filmed scenes, the black residents are intimidated, beaten, or lynched.

On the surface, *Mississippi Burning* was a wrenching, high-voltage detective
thriller: fast-moving, dramatic, and hard-hitting, with some exciting performances.
"More than any other film I've seen," Roger Ebert wrote in the *New York Daily
News*, "this one gets inside the passion of race relations in America. . . . *Mississippi
Burning* is the best American film of 1988."

Yet under the film's slick surface were significant evasions and distortions.
Rather than examine American racism and violence (and the psyche from which
they spring), *Mississippi Burning* often appeared to exploit both with violence
so aestheticized (even the cross burnings were not so much horrifying as cruelly
fascinating) that it's a manipulative giddy turn-on that entranced rather than repelled
audiences. Worse, the violence often diverted attention from the fact that *Mississippi
Burning* had no real interest in dissecting the racial relations in the town. More
important, it did not care one iota about exploring the lives of the black residents.

For black moviegoers, the question was simple: How could Hollywood make a
film about the Civil Rights Movement without having any major black characters?
The film's few black characters were mainly depicted as rather sad-eyed, submissive
dolts, who just seem *tired, tired, tired* of what's going on but are too fearful of the
whites to make a decisive move.

In one sequence as the blacks solemnly stand while singing—one of those
familiar religious anthems of submission that Hollywood has always loved—it's
back to an image of inert Negroes who simply believe they must trust in the Lord.
What director Parker and screenwriter Chris Gerolmo do not understand is that
while black Americans believed in trusting in the Lord, they also believed the Lord
helps those who help themselves.

The most aggressive of the local blacks is a teenager (Darius McCrary), who in
a telling sequence seems eager to speak his mind to the white FBI agents while his
father stands by, looking as if afraid to open his mouth. Here the film's suggestion
of black assertion came not from an adult black male (or female) but from a nonthreatening black kid. Does *Mississippi Burning* fear black assertion?

Even this assertive teen was turned into a sacrificial lamb during a night
sequence when the Klan attacks a black church. The congregation flees. But little
Darius appears to just *hang around*, falling to his knees. One fears those nasty
white fellows will pound the kid if he doesn't get out of there. Sure enough they

wallop him. In a cheap shot, the director exploits him to unleash additional violence to shock us all the more.

Watching *Mississippi Burning*, one would never know that black Southerners, after all, propelled the fight for civil rights by organizing and joining the marches, the sit-ins, the boycotts, courageously putting their lives on the line. *Mississippi Burning* does not focus on one local black leader. Near the end, a black minister who preaches from a pulpit—letting us know his anger—seems almost like an afterthought. Also seen briefly was a poorly conceived black FBI agent who threatens a white character with castration. This is a total falsification of history. At this time, the FBI had no black FBI agents.

The true heroes—the real fighting activists—are the two marauding white FBI agents, who accept their responsibilities, the burden of being white men who must, in essence, defend and protect the Negro community nevertheless, to insure that America lives up to its promise of equal rights for all. (During this era, J. Edgar Hoover's FBI was hardly a champion for black civil rights.) It's a White Man's Burden movie, if ever there were one.

Mississippi Burning comes to a gritty climax shortly after a local white woman (Frances McDormand), the wife a Klan member involved in the murder of the three workers, heroically reveals the place where the men are buried. Afterwards she is brutally beaten by her husband and hospitalized. By then, so infuriated are the FBI agents that it is decided to toss out the rule book, to use any means to ensnare the culprits. Of course, what's happened here is that not only are we given another noble white character, but it is the violation of a white woman that rouses the heroes to effective action.

Director Parker's decision to focus on the white characters (to give the mass white audience people it can identify with) reveals Hollywood's cynicism about black subjects. Even when a film supposedly focuses on racism, it was believed best (here as in *Cry Freedom* and later to a certain extent in *Glory*) to explore that racism through white eyes.

The Bird Doesn't Fly

Clint Eastwood's *Bird* was a long-awaited dramatization of the life of black jazz musician—saxophonist—Charlie Parker. (In 1967, the film *Sweet Love, Bitter* had starred Dick Gregory as a tragic jazz musician based on Charlie Parker.) Known for years as a jazz enthusiast (who as a teenager heard Parker play in California), Eastwood sought to make a film that saluted Parker's innovative talents, recorded his personal struggles, and captured some flavor of the bebop era.

Screened at the Cannes Film Festival in the spring of 1988, *Bird* was well-received. Its star Forest Whitaker as Parker won the festival's Best Actor award.

Afterwards *Bird* was shown at the New York Film Festival. But while a laudable labor of love by Eastwood, *Bird* was also a significant disappointment.

The film's problems become apparent soon after it opens when an intense, troubled Charlie Parker walks into the bathroom of his New York apartment and attempts suicide by swallowing a bottle of iodine. This graphic, hyped-up beginning is meant to plunge us immediately into the pathos and pain of its hero. Afterwards the movie shifts (sometimes jumps and leaps) back and forth in time as it slowly and solemnly depicts a talented musician who seems at peace and in control only with his music. Otherwise he's a wreck who dopes himself up, drinks, carouses, broods, and destroys his personal relationships.

Bird has all the ingredients of movie melodrama, yet almost no dramatic spark. So committed is Eastwood to depicting Charlie Parker's life *sincerely* and *sensitively* that he does not dare to "cheapen" Parker's image by giving us a more traditional (and perhaps more enjoyable) type of movie biography that traces the highs and lows of its subject's life in a straightforward, resolutely dramatic fashion. One admires Eastwood for trying to approach Parker's life in a new manner. But in the long run, the life is not approached at all.

One gets no idea of the inner workings of the real Parker nor of the cultural setting that influenced his style. Born in 1920, Parker grew up in Kansas City, Missouri. At eleven, he was given an alto sax by his mother. A few years later, he dropped out of school and performed professionally. In 1939, he went to New York. Around 1941, he met Dizzy Gillespie; within a few years, they were known as partners/cofounders of bebop. Determined to stretch the intellectual boundaries of jazz, Parker was a master of improvisation, whose work demanded that the audience *listen* to discover in music a new sound and mood. Often his private life was a shambles: a series of wives; a string of breakdowns; and a heroin addiction that began when he was a teenager.

None of this is fully explored in *Bird*. You have no idea of the music that preceded him, what he reacted against. (Late in the film a completely misconceived sequence with Parker and a rhythm-and-blues star wants us to believe rhythm-and-blues was Parker's real enemy.) Nor is there any true sense of the glamorous, heated excitement of the jazz clubs on New York's 52nd Street and the evolving postwar mystique and perception of the jazz musician as a sexy, demanding, creative artist.

Bird has one significant female character, Parker's common-law wife Chan Richardson (played strongly by Diane Venora), who is depicted as bright, dependable, and fully aware of Parker's genius and his self-destructive edge. No one can criticize the fact that the Parker/Richardson relationship has been dramatized. But it is disturbing that the film fails to examine the presence of other women in Parker's life, especially such black women as Parker's mother and his first wife Rebecca Parker Davis (who makes some perceptive comments about their marriage and the man in the 1987 documentary *Celebrating Bird*). The subtext of *Bird*, however, suggests something terrible about black women, that they neither were a part of his life nor did they understand his genius. Black women are nonpeople.

The best thing about *Bird* is having the chance to hear Parker's music. But, of course, black men are almost absent from *Bird*, too. Instead of developing a sense of the camaraderie that existed between such musicians as Parker and Dizzy Gillespie, Eastwood's primary interest seems to be in the relationship of Parker and his white buddy Red Rodney. When Rodney tries drugs, Parker warns him of their terrible danger. He really cares for this here white boy. For the mass white audience *and* a segment of the white intellectual community, the Parker/Rodney scenes enable them to believe Charlie was one of theirs. But how is a black audience to respond? The movie nullifies any suspicions the real Parker may have had about whites. It also neutralizes the very real racism Charlie Parker lived with. Because it ignores the forces of family and society that shaped him as an artist and a man, the film's hero seems culturally adrift. And by not exploring the societal/professional tensions that made Parker want to withdraw into a drug-induced world (we get no sense of the animosity of some jazz critics toward him), *Bird* makes Parker look like just another bummed-out colored guy who cannot handle it. Is it any wonder large black audiences stayed away from the film?

Even Forest Whitaker's performance, which has some fine moments, becomes monotonous. Rather than depict Parker as a tragic figure, Whitaker lets the character become self-pitying and pathetic, which is all wrong. By the time *Bird* ends (it runs for two hours and forty minutes), the viewer is so worn out and left so uninformed about this man that it's almost a relief when he finally ODs; now you can go home—at last!

While the white male critical establishment went bananas over *Bird*, *The New Yorker*'s Pauline Kael blasted the film. The *New York Post* reported that Kael, speaking at the University of Pennsylvania, commented, "It's being called a 'consummate masterpiece' in *Time* and other magazines. And it's a stinker! It's a rat's nest of a movie." Kael added that many critics were fawning over the film because "although [Eastwood] is a perfectly atrocious director, they would like to be Clint Eastwood. It is basically as silly as that. I mean, he is tall and his stardom is very sexy and a lot of people on magazines who lead lives that are not very exciting imagine him to have a terrific time." Kael was one of the few critics who talked about the film with any sense.

Focusing on Apartheid

Another major release to focus on racism was black filmmaker Euzhan Palcy's South African drama *A Dry White Season*. Palcy's struggle to make the film had a

Euzhan Palcy, director of *Sugar Cane Alley* and *A Dry White Season*.

Morgan Freeman as the chauffeur Hoke with his employer Miss Daisy (Jessica Tandy) in the big hit of the Bush era, *Driving Miss Daisy*.

drama of its own. Having grown up in Martinique, one of six children of a pineapple factory manager, Palcy left for France in 1978. There she earned a degree in French literature at the Sorbonne and a film degree at the Vaugirard School in Paris. She also wrote, edited, and directed short films. Then she made her stunning French debut feature *Sugar Cane Alley*, the story of a young boy growing up in colonial Martinique during the 1930s. Afterwards she longed to do a film about South Africa. It took her some five years.

Warner Brothers showed interest when Palcy decided to film white South African Andre Brink's novel *A Dry White Season*. Its hero was a white Afrikaner who is politicized into action against the evils of apartheid. No doubt the studio felt such a hero was one the mass white audience could identify with.

When Warners later dropped the project, MGM picked it up. A committed Marlon Brando appeared in the film at scale salary, which came to $4,000. Susan Sarandon, Donald Sutherland, and Janet Suzman joined the cast as well as the black South African actors Zakes Mokae, Winston Ntshona, and John Kani.

Nonetheless, *A Dry White Season* proved disappointing. Working hard to inject life into a rather predictable story, Palcy's screenplay (cowritten with Colin Welland) attempted to make the black characters more pivotal to the story than simply as backdrops for the white hero's consciousness raising. Unlike the Brink novel, Palcy's film ended on a note of black resistance when the black character Stanley shoots and kills a malevolent white security police chief.

But in sequences that turned sluggish, too much attention was focused on the white Afrikaner schoolteacher Ben du Toit (Donald Sutherland), who ultimately pays a heavy price for his newfound political commitment. Dismissed from his job and rejected by his community, his wife walks out and, worse, his daughter turns informer on him. Once again, sympathies are to be extended to a violated good white man.

Still, with *A Dry White Season*, Palcy emerged as possibly the first black woman to direct a major studio production and also the first black director to shoot a mainstream production dramatizing the violence of South Africa's apartheid system.

Bringing History to Light: *Glory*

Directed by Edward Zwick (a creator of TV's "thirtysomething") with cinematography by Freddie Francis, *Glory* brought to popular attention a part of American history many were ignorant of: the story of the 54th Regiment, the first black infantry in the North during the Civil War. It also bore the mark of well-intentioned filmmakers who still felt the need for inbuilt safeguards and points of identification for a large white audience.

That was apparent early with *Glory*'s focus on its young white officer Robert Gould Shaw (Matthew Broderick), the Boston Brahmin who becomes the commander of the black regiment. (The film is based in part on the letters of the real Shaw.) So well-defined was Shaw within a specific cultural and psychological context away from the troops and battlefield (we see his abolitionist family background, his perspective and self-doubts) that *Glory* was as much about Shaw's maturation from insecure young twenty-five-year-old officer to full-fledged leader, as it was about anything else. His evolving awareness about race established him as a sensitive hero while it also sent out a reassuring message to the mainstream audience: Here is a good, decent man, who in important respects is removed from America's deplorable racial history. See, not all white people were bad!

Glory's rhythm and momentum changed once the black soldiers were introduced. Among them are Rawlins (Morgan Freeman), an older, philosophical grave digger; Thomas Searles (Andre Braugher), an educated young intellectual, who has been a social friend of Shaw in Boston; and Jupiter Sharts (Jihmi Kennedy), a good old country boy. For the recruits, who are underpaid and discriminated against, their training, more so than the war, becomes a testing ground.

Most interesting, perhaps because he best embodies contemporary attitudes, is the rebellious runaway slave Trip (Denzel Washington) who, having endured hardships none of the whites has ever experienced, sees racism most clearly and is eager to speak out.

Glory climaxes with the battle at Fort Wagner in Charleston harbor. Members of the regiment give their lives in the fight for a freedom they have never really had. Thus the movie ends on a note of heroism and *also* a note of defeat for the 54th Regiment. Granted, one might ask what else could be expected of a film based on a historical incident. But the African American audience might well have loved a historical film that ended with black heroes in living triumph.

Glory has stirring sequences. Who could forget Trip, having gone AWOL, returning to the military camp where he is whipped, only for us to learn that he has left to find shoes to wear? But one leaves the theater wanting to know more about the black soldiers, especially Trip and Rawlins. Why couldn't *Glory* have dramatized the lives of these men before they entered the war? Never do we see their families or the past events and forces that molded them and made them decide to fight this war, which might have made these soldiers even stronger and more vivid and also brought a new perspective to popular historical film.

Glory was distinguished primarily by the exciting, committed performances of its black actors, who (true to the tradition of African American performers in movies) seemed fired up with enthusiasm for bringing this piece of history to the screen.

As Rawlins, an experienced man aware of life's petty (and great) injustices, Morgan Freeman presented a shrewdly controlled pragmatist, in marked contrast to Washington's outspoken Trip. Their sequences together were sparked by a hot, fierce, brilliant glow and intensity. Here were two major African American actors; one never letting the other have a second more of screen time than required; yet each firmly remaining in character and never descending into the flamboyant type of grandstanding that lesser actors might have fallen victim to.

Generally, *Glory* received glowing reviews. In *The New York Times*, Vincent Canby hailed it as "beautifully acted" and "a good, moving, complicated film." But *New York*'s David Denby called *Glory* "a sturdily mediocre, sometimes moving spectacle film ... the roles are a series of stock characters borrowed from World War II platoon movies."

The film was nominated for five Academy Awards, including Best Picture. For Denzel Washington, *Glory* was a career milestone. He won an Academy Award as Best Supporting Actor.

Denzel Washington: On the Road to Stardom

By the time of *Glory*, Denzel Washington had been in films for almost ten years. The son of a minister and a mother who owned beauty shops, he grew up in Mount Vernon, New York, studied for a time at a private boarding school in New York, later graduated from Fordham University, and briefly attended the American Conservatory Theatre in San Francisco.

After theater roles, he made a surprisingly inauspicious movie debut (at age twenty-five) in Michael Schultz's *Carbon Copy*. But as Dr. Phillip Chandler in the TV series "St. Elsewhere," he acquired a following. In *A Soldier's Story*, he established the basics of his screen persona. Often his heroes have been cool, seemingly detached yet intense, intelligent, and free of affectations; his explosive moments (similar to Poitier's) are layered with an underlying calm control. The Washington character never loses himself in his anger.

Later he appeared in *Power* (1986), *Cry Freedom*, and the rarely seen British film *For Queen and Country* (1988). In the Caribbean murder mystery *The Mighty Quinn* (1989), he emerged as a true leading man: handsome, heroic, sexy, glamorous; precisely the qualities that struck filmmaker Spike Lee who, upon watching women in a swoon while Washington performed in the stage play *Checkmates*, signed him as the lead in his romantic jazz film *Mo' Better Blues* (1990). In the next decade, Denzel Washington became one of American movies strongest male leads.

Denzel Washington in his Oscar-winning role as Trip in *Glory*, with Jihmi Kennedy (left) and Morgan Freeman (right).

Denzel Washington on Oscar night.

Driving Miss Daisy: The Matter of Perspective

Glory's other important actor Morgan Freeman also starred in one of the era's most successful films, *Driving Miss Daisy*. Based on Alfred Uhry's Pulitzer Prize winning off-Broadway play and directed by Bruce Beresford, *Driving Miss Daisy* touched on issues of race and class as it dramatized the twenty-five-year-old relationship (from 1948 to 1973) of a Southern Jewish woman, Daisy Werthan, and her black chauffeur, Hoke Colburn. Along the way, it observed changing attitudes in the South, from the days of post-World War II conservatism through the Civil Rights era (the Black Power movement of the late 1960s doesn't seem to exist here).

As Daisy, veteran actress Jessica Tandy—appropriately demanding, stern, fussy—conveys the temperament of a woman who prides herself on being fair and open-minded, yet is unwilling to relinquish old habits and long-held customs and beliefs. Only when old age just about overtakes her, when the mind has grown so foggy that she is no longer locked in by past traditions and attitudes, does she feel free to show, finally, the feelings (and vulnerabilities) that run deepest. In a nursing home when her friend Hoke visits, Daisy says, "Hoke, you're my best friend."

Throughout, writer Uhry wisely (and skillfully) sticks to the character and cultural setting he knows best and is comfortable with. The film masterfully defines Daisy and her perspective through the lens of a network of relationships and emotions. Thus *Driving Miss Daisy* shows Daisy's home, her synagogue, her friends, her son, her daughter-in-law (with whom she does not get along), her fears and her concerns.

But *Driving Miss Daisy* faltered in its fundamental conception of Hoke. In the past, black Americans who worked as servants sometimes developed significant relationships with their employers. But often such servants were eager to communicate to friends and family their true feelings and insights about the people they worked for. At home, their tone, mood, and rhythm changed. None of this happens with Hoke. Left undramatized is his other life and world, his relationships and his perspective when away from Daisy's house, Daisy's car, Daisy's life. How exhilarating it might have been to hear him confide to a friend that he's *sick* of driving Miss Daisy! But *Driving Miss Daisy* no more presented Hoke's feelings away from Daisy's big house than *Gone with the Wind* fifty years earlier did with Hattie McDaniel's. For the black audience, that lack of perspective was the film's great shortcoming.

Indeed what *Driving Miss Daisy* does *not* tell may account for some of its extraordinary mainstream popularity. The film looks as if it could have been a problem picture from the late 1940s or 1950s, a gentler and kinder time no doubt when many were aware and mindful of their place.

What saved the character (and the picture) from being the familiar loyal retainer was Morgan Freeman, who invests Hoke with a sense of pride, a cool and sometimes cunning, manipulative intelligence, and an unfailing perceptiveness.

A black Southern working-class sophisticate, aware of the ways of his world (a time when the South's Jim Crow laws are still locked in place), and having learned to survive by saying the requisite "yessums," Freeman's Hoke retains a courtly deferential manner and demeanor. Yet he never sells himself cheap. Nor is he ever servile or meekly submissive. At times Hoke even seems to feel sorry (and a tad condescending) for this poor white woman who does not know how bad off she really is.

And when the script permits Hoke to express annoyance or speak his mind, Freeman goes to town. In one memorable sequence, during a long drive when he wants to stop the car, Daisy refuses to let him do so, until he firmly lets her know he is a man who intends to alleviate himself on the road, whether she likes it or not. He stops the car. And he takes the keys with him.

Freeman's work, which drew the black audience (especially an older one) to the character and the film, is a classic example of the way in which a performer can suggest another (an extratextural) life that the movie has little or no comprehension of. Aware of Hoke's nontextual history and other experiences, Freeman uses his observations of black men (and women) before him to capture and convey the speech patterns and rhythms—movements, gestures, postures—that remind us of African Americans of another generation.

Praised by the critics, *Driving Miss Daisy* won nine Academy Award nominations. Nominated for the Oscar as Best Actor, Freeman lost to Daniel Day-Lewis in *My Left Foot* (1989). But Tandy won as Best Actress and the film won as Best Picture.

Morgan Freeman: The Long Journey to Get There

Driving Miss Daisy catapulted Morgan Freeman to the ranks of stardom. But although many moviegoers were seeing him for the first time, Morgan Freeman, then fifty-two, had been meticulously honing his craft for years. His career looked like a series of dazzling starts, followed by some troubling dead ends.

Born in Memphis, Tennessee, in 1937, Freeman had been shifted about as a kid, growing up partly in Greenwood, Mississippi, partly in Chicago. In the early 1960s, after serving in the Air Force, this brash young man trotted off to Los Angeles, without any acting experience to speak of, in hopes of finding roles in movies. Freeman found that almost nothing happened.

Later he landed theater parts in *Can Can, Hello Dolly* (Broadway's 1967 black version starring Pearl Bailey), and *Purlie*. The very nature of his acting style—almost sternly realistic and uncompromising—seems at odds with these frothy musicals. But they proved an excellent training ground. He also played Easy Reader on the PBS children's series "The Electric Company."

When he won a Tony nomination and a Drama Desk Award in the late 1970s for his performance in Richard Wesley's play *The Mighty Gents*, his career seemed finally about to take off. He appeared on stage in *Coriolanus* and *Mother Courage* and in the films *Brubaker*, *Eyewitness* (1981), and African American director Woodie King's independent production *Death of a Prophet* (1981), in which Freeman, with goatee and glasses, played a revolutionary hero based on Malcolm X.

But by 1982, when he went to audition for the film *Harry and Son*, to be directed by Paul Newman, he had not worked in almost two years. So shocked was Newman that an actor as skilled as Freeman could be unemployed that, because the part he sought was already cast, Newman gave him another role in the movie.

Freeman found other work onstage and on television (including the daytime soap "Another World"). But he still had not played the big showy roles that can establish a career and put an actor into a whole other league.

Then came the modestly budgeted *Street Smart* (1987), which starred Christopher Reeve as a New York reporter who crosses paths with a pimp, called Fast Black, played by Freeman. Usually, the movie black pimp is all attitude, all phony posturing and posing. Rarely has he been depicted as a complex man in conflict with his culture and aware of its deceptions and injustices. Freeman changed that.

Freeman had a scene in *Street Smart* that yet sends shivers through viewers. When Fast Black believes a prostitute is about to betray him, he pushes her against a wall, pointing a pair of scissors at her eyes. "So it's your eyes need to be punished. I'm going to cut me out an eye," he says. "No, no," she pleads. "I'm gonna take one eye. You'll have to tell me which one. Right or left?" When he feels confident that he has taught her never to defy him, he relaxes. "Just foolin' around," he says.

Here Morgan Freeman created a wily, perceptive character who by turns could be cool, mean, or terrifying; a man who knew when to turn the charm on and when to suddenly—and effectively—turn it off. It remains one of the best dramatic film performances of the 1980s. And, fortunately, for Freeman, despite the fact that *Street Smart* was a box-office disappointment, his work did not go unnoticed. When reviewing the film, critic Pauline Kael asked the question, "Is Morgan Freeman the greatest American actor?" (Note: Kael did not say greatest *black* actor; she said actor *period*.) Many felt he was. He won an Academy Award nomination as Best Supporting Actor of 1987. He was about fifty.

Movie audiences did not see him again until he appeared in a small role, as a tough drug counselor, in *Clean and Sober* (1988) with Michael Keaton. With a face that was lean, lined, rugged, Freeman looked like a man who had lived through hard, demanding times. His voice—controlled, impassioned but no-nonsense—indicated he was a survivor who would not take any guff from anybody. It was a quietly powerful performance. Afterward came the stage version of *Driving Miss Daisy*, the film *Johnny Handsome* (1989), and as the controversial high school principal Joe Clark in *Lean on Me* (1989).

After *Driving Miss Daisy*, important supporting roles came in films good and bad: Brian de Palma's *Bonfire of the Vanities* (1990); *Robin Hood, Prince of Thieves* (1991, as the Moor Azeem); the South African drama *The Power of One* (1992, in which he somehow came away intact from a script that defined his character as yet another noble, one-man-support system for a young white hero), and Clint Eastwood's Western *Unforgiven* (1992, in which Freeman, as Eastwood's friend Ned Logan, was splendidly cast, despite the film's failure to create some kind of historical context/comment for the character). Later Freeman directed the South African drama *Bopha!* (1993).

Other Films

As the 1980s drew to a close, other films appeared. Gregory Hines starred in the romantic dance melodrama *Tap* (1989) with Suzzanne Douglas and a notable lineup of dancers: Sammy Davis, Jr. (his last movie role), Sandman Sims, Jimmy Slyde, Arthur Duncan, Pat Rico, Bunny Briggs, Savion Glover, and best, the great Harold Nicholas of the Nicholas Brothers.

Wes Craven's ambitious, atmospheric *The Serpent and the Rainbow* (1988, based on the book by Wade Davis) featured actors Paul Winfield, Zakes Mokae, Theresa Merritt, and Kathy Tyson (who starred in Neil Jordan's 1986 British film *Mona Lisa*) in a story about voodoo and magic in Haiti. The film, however, could not shake its view of its blacks as dark mysterious exotic Others.

Joining the ranks of filmmakers was Eddie Murphy who, in another attempt to update his image and connect to the black audience, not only starred in but also wrote, directed, and executive-produced *Harlem Nights* (1989). Despite the pleasure of seeing Murphy with such other black performers as Redd Foxx, Della Reese, Jasmine Guy, and Arsenio Hall, the film failed to evoke the atmosphere of 1930s Harlem. Nor could it successfully contextualize a basic formula piece with the African American cultural demarcations that might have given it some style or glimmers of originality. Then, too, its women seemed to spring from the imagination of a vindictive misogynist.

A very different type of film came from African American filmmaker Charles Lane. His *Sidewalk Stories* (1989) was a mostly silent, black-and-white, ninety-seven-minute comedy that marked the feature firm debut of thirty-five-year-old independent filmmaker Lane, who starred, wrote, directed, and produced. Shot in fifteen days on the streets of New York (during near zero weather) on a budget of $200,000, the film is a look at the plight of the homeless. Its hero is a plucky street artist (Lane), a Chaplinesque "little guy" dealing with the realities and cruelties of a sometimes impersonal city.

Mixing social comments with movie romance while conjuring up images from classic American silent comedies (the work of Chaplin and Keaton), *Sidewalk Stories* won the Prix du Publique at the Cannes Film Festival in 1989. Later it went into general release.

Sidney Returns

The late 1980s also marked the return to acting (after a ten year absence) of none other than Sidney Poitier. "It became more and more difficult to go back," he said of the years spent away from screen roles, "because the kind of material Hollywood was offering even to gifted American actors—Redford, Newman, Hoffman—was not becoming to their stature." He added, "I had had an extraordinary time as an actor. If I couldn't complement the work behind me, I would rather not work." Neither of Poitier's new films *Shoot to Kill* (1988) and *Little Nikita* (1988), both of which focused on the interracial bonding theme, had the impact of his earlier work. Yet in *Shoot to Kill*—in an unexpected way—it was a pleasure and also reassuring to see this veteran of almost forty years of cinema, who carried within him so much of the turbulent and contradictory history of blacks in films. Through all the vicissitudes, the uphill battles, the change in public tastes and outlooks, the demands of audiences, black and white, this talented man had survived. Poitier later appeared in *Sneakers* (1992) and *The Jackal* (1997).

Closing the Era on the Right Note

Finally, the decade closed with what remains its most controversial and provocative film by an African American filmmaker: Spike Lee's 1989 *Do the Right Thing*. No other black film drew as much attention or had as great a cultural impact as this drama, which examined a day in the life of black residents in Brooklyn's Bedford Stuyvesant section and culminated in a violent racial uprising.

After a much talked about screening at the 42nd Cannes International Film Festival, *Do the Right Thing* opened in the States where the press, amid much fanfare, greeted it with mixed reviews and, on occasion, outright indignation. In *The New York Times*, Vincent Canby raved, "*Do the Right Thing* is living, breathing, riveting proof of the arrival of an abundantly gifted new talent." In *New York*, however, David Denby criticized the film as "a demonstration of the pointlessness of violence that is also a celebration of violence. Confusing? *Do the Right Thing* is going to create an uproar—in part because Lee, a middle-class black hoping

Spike Lee as Mookie and Danny Aiello as Sal in the film that closed the decade on a note of controversy: *Do the Right Thing.*

to capture the anger of the underclass, is thoroughly mixed up about what he's saying."

But the reviews soon seemed almost irrelevant because *Do the Right Thing* became a media event that was written about as if something of a social phenomenon. Debate and discussions flourished on such programs as "Nightline" and "The Oprah Winfrey Show." Some white writers expressed fear that the movie might spark riots and even affect New York's mayoral elections. "If Lee does hook large black audiences, there's a good chance the message they take from the film will increase racial tensions in the city," Joe Klein wrote in *New York* magazine. "If they react violently—which can't be ruled out—the candidate with the most to lose will be David Dinkins."

The *Village Voice* also devoted pages to the film's pros and cons. Black writer Thulani Davis hailed it while black writer Stanley Crouch (under the headline "Do the Race Thing: Spike Lee's Afro-Fascist Chic") called the film the "sort of rancid fairy tale one expects of a racist." He labeled writer/director/producer Lee's aesthetic "fascist."

Despite the hullabaloo, the movie neither provoked riots nor had any effect on black mayoral candidate David Dinkins, who was elected to office. The controversy and coverage were reminiscent of all the noise that had enveloped *The Color Purple*. Black movies—particularly those popular ones with built-in commercial appeal—remain so few and far between that each new one is viewed almost as if it were the only black film ever made, as if it should satisfy all our needs, as if summed up in total black America's frame of mind.

Fortunately, *Do the Right Thing* itself was strong enough to carry the weight of all the attention. Much of it was the engrossing work of a talented filmmaker in control of the medium and blessed with a true filmic sense. Part of *Do the Right Thing* also seemed to go deliriously and compellingly haywire.

From the start, it moved at a masterly pace (with a *hip hop* sensibility, a *rap* drive) as the images and characters, on this hot summer day in Brooklyn, pleasurably whizzed by: dj Mister Senor Love Daddy (Samuel Jackson), who spins "da platters dat matter"; Da Mayor (Ossie Davis), a likable local drunk; Mother Sister (Ruby Dee), the sharp-eyed (and sharp-tongued) observer who, perched in her window, screens the activities of the day; Buggin Out (Giancarlo Esposito), a spike-haired, disgruntled young man; Smiley (Roger Guenveur Smith), inarticulate and desperate to communicate as he carries a photograph of Martin Luther King, Jr., and Malcolm X; Radio Raheem, who walks the streets with his radio blasting rap messages.

Then there are Jade (Joie Lee), a bright, pretty young woman, known mainly as the sister of Mookie (Spike Lee), a pizza deliveryman, who emerges as the film's central character; and Sal (Danny Aiello), the proprietor of Sal's Famous Pizzeria, which he has run for over twenty years, remaining in the area—with his two sons—long after the other whites moved out.

For the black audience, many of these character types (few were fully enough developed to be characters; even their names—Buggin Out, Mother Sister—were used to identify them as types) were immediately recognizable. The fact that they had almost never before appeared on the big screen simply intensified the audience excitement, connection, and giddy level of identification. Throughout, the language and humor were sharp and clever with a ring of authenticity. As Da Mayor eyed Mother Sister on her stoop, as she shushed him away, the camera angles, the editing, the spin that Davis and Dee put on their lines, created a rich, folkloric quality. So, too, did the dialogue of a trio of street-corner griots who boasted, fussed, and commented on the world around them.

But amidst the high spirits, the ethnic humor, the rush of sight and sound (the vibrant saturated colors of cinematographer Ernest Dickerson gave life to the pavements, the tenement walls, and the street garb—the sneakers, T-shirts, short skirts and tight blouses, all of which contributed to the film's cultural references), there pulsated an undercurrent of tension and anger, coming at unexpected times in unexpected places. Buggin Out, observing the photographs of Italian icons (Sinatra, Stallone, DeNiro) that line the walls of the pizza parlor, asks, "Hey, Sal, how come you ain't got no brothers up here?" Sal's oldest son Pino (John Turturro), a blatant racist, says he's sick of niggers and urges his father to get out of this neighborhood. The street corner philosophers debate the merits of the Koreans, who run a local produce stand. And at one point, facing the camera, a chorus of street characters, one ethnic group after another—Italians, Hispanics, Koreans, and African Americans—recites a litany of racial slurs and grievances.

Finally, *Do the Right Thing* climaxes with a confrontation and racial explosion that leaves Radio Raheem dead at the hands of the police and Sal's pizza parlor shooting up in flames as photos of Sinatra, Loren, and other Italian icons burn. Later Smiley's photo of Dr. King and Malcolm X is tacked to the wall. The film ends with words from King on nonviolence and words of Malcolm X on violence as a means of self-defense.

The climactic racial confrontation, powerfully filmed and edited, endowed the action with meaning and political power. It was also precisely what caused such a critical uproar. Because of so much real anger within African American urban centers about significant social/political issues, Buggin Out's rage struck some as displaced. Never was enough information given about him or the other characters for the audience to comprehend fully the real forces and the deeper field of oppression of American life that their justified anger springs from. For some, the riot seemed contrived. Without it, *Do the Right Thing* would have been simply a series of intriguing and enlightening vignettes.

Even the fact that Mookie helped spark the full explosion by throwing a trash can through the pizzeria's window seemed out of place and out of character because nothing about him suggested any deep-seated anger or strong convictions.

What's often been appealing about the Spike Lee screen persona here and in *School Daze* is that he's a laconic observer/outsider, withdrawn from heated commitments. Moreover, to indict Sal (a well-defined character) that audiences black and white often liked seemed too pat and evasive of identifying the real corruptive, oppressive powers in America.

Still, *Do the Right Thing* succeeded in other important ways. Better than any other film of the period, it touched on a great deal of the discontent and unexplained anger that was so much a part of urban life during the Reagan eighties. The movie says something that most Hollywood films then avoided: simply, that race relations in America remain abysmal; that racism and ethnic tensions underlie the facade of American life. At the same time, while Hollywood's tales of interracial male bonding present worlds in which significant cultural differences do not exist, *Do the Right Thing*, from the moment Public Enemy is heard blasting "Fight the Power," reverberates on African American cultural distinctions.

Lee wisely cast unusual and interesting performers. It is hard to recall when Ossie Davis, here using his personal warmth and generosity of spirit to turn Da Mayor into the film's true moral center, has been as much fun or as interesting. And Ruby Dee has rarely been able to unleash her gift for idiosyncratic comedy. Joie Lee (who layers her Jade with intelligence and charm), Robin Harris, John Turturro, Samuel Jackson, Rosie Perez, and Giancarlo Esposito give well-crafted, sometimes highly charged performances. As Sal, Danny Aiello won an Oscar nomination for Best Supporting Actor. Spike Lee also was nominated for Best Original Screenplay. But otherwise the film was wrongly overlooked by the Academy Awards.

Finally, Spike Lee's undeniable power to infuse his images with energy and insight and his determination to structure and direct a film in a style all his own—neither Hollywood slick nor European moody—set him apart and made *Do the Right Thing*, even when it may be most distressing, always fascinating, and surely one of the most distinct and invigorating movies of the decade. *Do the Right Thing* fittingly closed the Reagan/Bush decade. For it heralded the oncoming arrival of a new brand of African American commercial cinema in which the subjects of race, racism, cultural bearings, and social/political problems would move to the forefront.

10 THE 1990s: NEW STARS, NEW FILMMAKERS, AND A NEW AFRICAN AMERICAN CINEMA

Whoopi Goldberg nurtures a troubled white couple in Ghost *and wins an Academy Award as Best Supporting Actress. . . . New* Jack City, *directed by Mario Van Peebles, marks a return of the kind of tough black urban street drama not seen since the 1970s . . . Twenty-three-year-old John Singleton makes a highly touted debut as director of* Boyz N the Hood, . . . *Rappers Ice-T, Ice Cube, and Queen Latifah come to the movies, sometimes with, other times without, their music or their rap personas. . . . African American filmmakers such as Charles Burnett, Julie Dash, the Hughes Brothers, Carl Franklin, and Kasi Lemmons invigorate American films with a new perspective. . . . Spike Lee remains at the forefront of African American directors with a series of sometimes-controversial films:* Jungle Fever, Malcolm X, *and* Bamboozled. . . . *Whitney Houston and Angela Bassett star in* Waiting to Exhale *and help revive the black woman's film. . . . Wesley Snipes heats up the screen as a new kind of action hero while character actors Morgan Freeman and Samuel L. Jackson surprise the film industry by becoming bona fide stars with box-office appeal. . . . And Denzel Washington, in films as diverse as* The Pelican Brief, Philadelphia, *and* The Hurricane *emerges as the movies' most distinctive African American leading man since Sidney Poitier.*

It was the early 1990s, a vigorous period marked by a shift in political views, social drives, and the expected fare at movie theaters. From the start, the nation found itself preoccupied with an array of events and issues: a war in the Persian Gulf, a stagnant economy, big company layoffs, soaring unemployment statistics, a continuing AIDS health crisis, the issue of sexual harassment that grew out of the

Clarence Thomas–Anita Hill hearings, and throughout, complaints that the president—the first George Bush—was ineffectual in coping with massive problems. In the early 1990s, the nation was also compelled to confront the very type of festering racial tensions and divisions that had been carefully swept under the carpet during most of the previous decade.

No incident proved more disturbing or indicative of a country still beset by racial conflicts than that which occurred in Los Angeles on March 3, 1991, when black motorist Rodney King was stopped by the police and brutally beaten, allegedly for resisting arrest. Had the incident not been captured on videotape, it most likely would never have come to public attention. But television news programs ran repeated airings of the beating. A nation sat stunned. Then on April 29, 1992, immediately following the state trial of the four white policemen, who were accused of assaulting Rodney King and were found innocent on virtually all counts, outrage in Los Angeles's South Central section, touching on decades of anger and frustration, led to one of the worst civil disorders in American history. Los Angeles looked as if it were going up in flames. Some fifty-three were left dead. Property damage soared over $1 billion. The nation now came face to face with issues long apparent to black Americans: a judicial system that meted out justice differently to black and white; a social system in which basic inequities still persisted.

With the election of William Jefferson Clinton as President of the United States, the nation appeared to be on a course to reshape itself and redefine its destiny. Appointing an unprecedented number of minorities, including African Americans and women, to his cabinet, Clinton launched ambitious plans for a national health program and welfare reform. In time, Americans experienced an era of economic growth and prosperity. Then the country was rocked by a series of White House scandals that culminated with the impeachment of the president. Yet Bill Clinton remained in office and high in national opinion polls, especially among African Americans and other minorities.

Later generations could note that during the early years of the decade new interpretations of American history and culture also came to the fore. Traditional European achievements, cultural contributions, attitudes, and values were openly challenged, ironically in 1992, the five-hundredth anniversary of Christopher Columbus's "discovery" of America. Universities debated over Afrocentric versus Eurocentric perspective within the curriculum. A heightened awareness of the nation's social fabric, of its ethnic diversity, demanded a fresh view of America as a truly multicultural society—a view that had long been ignored in the history books and cultural studies.

African American popular culture veered in a new direction as it gave voice to social/racial concerns and issues. Rap music, often criticized for its sexism and violent imagery, nonetheless sent out messages through its language and themes about injustices, rebellion and dissent, cultural pride, and a new brand of black nationalism.

Film images of African Americans moved in two distinct directions in the early 1990s. Traditional Hollywood commercial cinema cast such black performers as Denzel Washington, Wesley Snipes, and Whoopi Goldberg in leading roles. Like Pryor and Murphy before them, some entered the ranks of superstar icons. Other performers also appeared in important supporting roles. Sometimes their presence invigorated old formulas. Other times, their presence in some films introduced surprising subtexts.

Most important, a movement of African American filmmakers also created a new kind of cinema, now becoming part of the commercial mainstream, in which African American cultural signs, signposts, and demarcations flew all over the place. American movies had a new look and sound. Often the new filmmakers (directors, writers, producers) made films (in the early stages) that reflected social problems or dilemmas. Later in the decade, ambitious historical dramas such as *Amistad* (1997) and *Beloved* (1998) would appear. Later in the decade too, some new African American filmmakers would move away from race or protest subjects to deal with more general themes. Sometimes coming-of-age dramas would appear. Other times moviegoers would see relationship dramas, focusing on the new black middle-class. But most significantly, from the early 1990s on, more African Americans would work in Hollywood than ever before in movie history.

The Good, the Bad, the Bonded, the Typed

As the era opened, it was often pleasurable for black moviegoers to see more black performers in some of the big blockbusters. *Die Hard 2* (1990), with John Amos and Art Evans, *The Fugitive* (1993), with L. Scott Caldwell, and *A Few Good Men* (1992), with Wolfgang Bodison as a marine accused of murder, offered African Americans roles suitable for any actor, black or white, and without the tricky kind of subtext that could make blacks feel uncomfortable and start twitching in their seats.

The interracial male bonding films continued. *Diggstown* (1992) starred Louis Gossett, Jr. (thankfully on leave from his *Iron Eagle* yarns) with James Woods. Cuba Gooding, Jr., and James Marshall played bonded boxers in *Gladiator* (1992). Forest Whitaker costarred with actor Anthony Edwards in the cop film *Downtown* (1990). Reteaming for *Lethal Weapon 3* (1992), Danny Glover and Mel Gibson were so chummy that by now they looked as if they would become *the* interracial movie couple of the decade. Also reunited were Richard Pryor and Gene Wilder, who, having appeared in the 1989 limp comedy *See No Evil, Hear No Evil*, costarred in yet another limp comedy *Another You* (1991). At least, audiences felt these two genuinely liked each other.

The results were different with Damon Wayans as the sidekick of Bruce Willis in *The Last Boy Scout* (1991). When poor Wayans looks (once too often) at Mr. Macho Willis and wants to know what they should do, most everyone probably felt Wayans should be satirizing this character rather than playing the part with such an earnest seriousness.

Other films showcased African Americans in more unusual ways. Cult director Abel Ferrara's *King of New York* (1990) delighted in the quirky rhythms of its black actors: Larry Fishburne, Wesley Snipes, Giancarlo Esposito, and Roger Guenveur Smith. As the leader of a drug ring, white star Christopher Walken's character sometimes looked as if he coveted the style and energy of his black cohorts. Unnoticed by the mass audience, the video release of *King of New York* found a following among young urban black viewers, who may have found it close in style to the attitudinizing and bravura of gangsta rap.

Other times the old types surfaced. The melodrama *Fried Green Tomatoes* (1991), partly set in the South in the 1920s/1930s, cast talented performers Cicely Tyson and Stan Shaw as almost shockingly familiar pliant, noble servants. No attempt at revisionist thinking about black household help here. So passive and good a tom-type was Shaw's character Big George that it's hard not to think of him as perhaps the great great great grandson of that noble giant Big Sam in *Gone with the Wind*.

Other accommodating servants or servant figures turned up elsewhere. In the hit *The Hand That Rocks the Cradle* (1992), Ernie Hudson played the mentally disabled handyman Solomon: he's a desexed, frightened, and childlike figure. It might be argued that such a description would apply to any actor who played this character. But at a time when black actors supposedly could be cast in any part, quiet as it was kept, they were often still considered only for certain kinds of seemingly colorless roles.

The same applied to Mike Nichols's *Regarding Henry* (1991), in which black actor Bill Nunn played the large and strong physical therapist Bradley, who befriends and nurtures—with an understated devotion—a lawyer (Harrison Ford) recovering from a gunshot wound to the head. One could not have asked for a more reassuring black-man-as-caretaker. But Bradley also eyed the ladies and was quick to comment, "I gotta get me some of that." Here the movie took pains not to present him as a milk-of-human-kindness desexed nurturer. Yet his comments fed into traditional distortions of African American male sexuality (here a gentle adolescent sexuality) and a brand of sexism that bordered on becoming truly disturbing.

But few characters called to mind the old stereotypes more so than did poor Cuba Gooding Jr.'s eye-rolling, childlike, mute sidekick to Australian Paul Hogan in *Lightning Jack* (1994) and even worse, Willard Pugh as—of all things—the mayor of Detroit in *RoboCop 2* (1990). The latter popped his eyes, grimaced, and mugged to the point that one questioned why the director encouraged or permitted this embarrassing performance. Pugh's antics did not go unnoticed. *People* called the movie "a vile insult to Detroit" with its black mayor character that "borders on racist." "He's so inarticulate, panicky and given to running away," wrote the reviewer, "that you half expect him to say, 'Feets, do yo' stuff.'" Well, at least comic master Mantan Moreland went through coon motions with style and ingenuity.

Other films were more subtle in the dubious ways in which they used black performers. Bruce Beresford's *Mister Johnson* (1991), based on a novel by Joyce Cary, attempted to deal in sensitive terms with the experiences of a black man in colonial Africa in the 1920s. But the film couldn't get inside the character's head to explain him culturally.

Some films distorted or glossed over history. In *Sandlot* (1993), James Earl Jones played a blind recluse who revealed to two suburban white boys his past as a baseball player who once played against Babe Ruth. He even showed a picture of himself with Ruth and Lou Gehrig. Of course, African Americans did not play in the major leagues until long after Ruth's heyday when Jackie Robinson broke baseball's color barrier in 1947. The movie has no interest in explaining that Jones's character, perhaps as a member of the Negro Leagues, might have played against Ruth in an off-season game, which sometimes occurred, when black players tested their skills against men from the major leagues. Not to explain this fact was a terrible disregard for history and a gloss-over of past racism in American sports.

Nonetheless in the early 1990s, black actors and actresses in mainstream cinema, much like those performers of the 1930s, played characters who were now incorporated into concepts of American life, or perhaps better to say, movie life.

Whoopi's Back

Nowhere was that incorporation more apparent than with the renewed rise of Whoopi Goldberg, whose work in mainstream cinema pointed out both the qualified glories and the pitfalls Hollywood proffered African American stars.

In early 1990, her career seemed yet stalled with another disaster: her misconceived, bewildering performance opposite Jim Belushi in *Homer and Eddie*. When television commercials for her film *Ghost* ran during the summer of 1990, most people no doubt felt poor Whoopi Goldberg had made another turkey.

But in *Ghost*, Goldberg's adroit and engaging performance surprised audiences and critics alike. Directed by Jerry Zucker with a screenplay by Bruce Joel Rubin, *Ghost* starred Patrick Swayze as a young investment banker who is killed during what appears to be a mugging. When he discovers himself a ghost, his efforts to communicate with his grieving girlfriend (Demi Moore) and also to track down his killer take wing once he finds a medium named Oda Mae Brown (Goldberg), who, before the picture's finale, has reunited the couple.

Throughout *Ghost*, Goldberg's character Oda traversed some familiar movie terrain. When Swayze's Sam first encounters her, Oda Mae, a fake medium dressed in a gold lame choir outfit and a long straight-haired wig, and attended by her two sisters (those terrific character actresses Armelia McQueen and Gail Boggs), is running a scam on a woman trying to reach a dead husband. Once Swayze's ghost character makes contact with her, Oda Mae, who can hear but not see him, is beside herself. Astonished and naturally scared silly, she widens her eyes, hops up, darts into another room, and slams the door behind her. She swears to the Lord never to cheat again. "I'll do anything, I'll do penance. Give me penance," she cries out. "But make that guy go away." But when Swayze's ghost speaks to her again, well, now fear just overpowers Oda, who screams, runs like mad, and literally knocks down the door trying to get away from dis here ole ghost.

It is a very funny sequence. But the truth of the matter is that while we might have hoped that blacks terrified of ghosts would now be consigned to the era when Willie Best popped his eyes as Bob Hope's servant sidekick in *The Ghost Breakers* in 1940, Oda Mae Brown is yet another readily excitable creature, often lit up with comic fear while operating in the realm of otherworldly spirits. Goldberg warmly modulates her reactions, giving them human dimensions. But an old set of stereotypical responses has simply been revamped for a new generation.

Goldberg soon finds herself playing a traditional seemingly nonsexual, feisty nurturer for Sam and girlfriend Molly. Never does she hesitate to bicker or fuss with Swayze's Sam. She doesn't want to be bothered with this ghost business. But she comes through for him. If she didn't, there would be no movie.

As Sam's last hope, she helps save the day by going to a bank where through prompting by Sam, Oda hilariously withdraws some $4 million. Of course, the humor is derived partly from the supremely prissy way she sashays around the bank while pulling off this scam (she's a pretty good scam artist too) and partly from the preposterous outfit she wears—she is dressed in a dark skirt flared at the bottom with a satiny red brocaded top and a red satiny hat with flowers, which seems to depict her further as an asexual oddball.

In a climactic sequence in the apartment of Sam's girlfriend Molly (Demi Moore), Oda performs her greatest nurturing act when Sam yearns to touch his girlfriend but knows it is impossible. Oda realizes she can help. Earlier when a woman came to Oda in hopes of communicating with her long lost Orlando, the ghost of the man, Orlando, entered Oda's body and spoke to the woman. The same can be done again. "You can use my body," Oda tells Sam. "Use your body?" "Just do it quick before I change my mind," she tells him as she sits down. Now Sam enters her body, able because of this black woman to communicate fully with the woman he loves. It is the film's most intense and romantic sequence.

Whoopi Goldberg in her Oscar-winning role as the nurturing medium Oda Mae Brown, with Patrick Swayze in *Ghost*.

But *Ghost* takes precautions not to disturb its mainstream audiences with any "unsettling thoughts." In the earlier sequence when Orlando's ghost entered her body, Goldberg, the actress, remained on screen as we heard the man's voice coming out of her.

Once Patrick Swayze's spirit moves into Goldberg's body, we first see Goldberg's dark hands touching Demi Moore's white ones. But soon Goldberg's image is replaced on screen by Swayze, who is seen softly touching and dancing with Moore.

We wonder what audience reactions would be had Goldberg played the scene with Demi Moore. While the filmmakers are obviously trying to give a romantic moment, are they not also precluding any suggestion of lesbianism that might arise with Goldberg and Moore dancing together? The scene with Swayze would go unquestioned had not the earlier Orlando sequence made such a point of keeping Goldberg on screen.

But Oda's nurturing does not end here. She soon becomes something of a grand protectress for Molly. When the two are pursued by the film's villain, Oda quickly directs Moore to head for a fire escape and once in another apartment, to a ladder that offers another escape. By the time Swayze's character has defeated the villain, he finds his lady love Moore held safely in the arms of Oda, who is sure not to let anything happen to the po' chile. As the film ends, Oda and Sam say their good-byes. And the audience has seen a very skillful presentation of another African American woman who has become heroic and endearing not only because of her comic fears but her sweet nurturing skills as well.

Goldberg was the real life in *Ghost*. So bland a yuppie pair were the attractive romantic leads that Goldberg's drive, push, and flamboyant antics mercifully enlivened the film and brought style to what might have been a dud. Shrewdly and perhaps intuitively, Goldberg used her African American cultural bearings (some might say misused) to give the character Oda definition. That was apparent in a scene when Swayze, having led Oda to Molly's apartment, is insistent that Oda tell Molly everything he says word for word. He instructs her to say, "Molly, you're in danger." "Now you just can't blurt it out like that," Oda says. "I'll just tell her in my own way." She pauses, then says, "Molly, you in danger, girl!"

Like Hattie McDaniel and other early black performers, Goldberg here uses certain cultural inflections (and language) to energize and ethnicize her character (and the film), yet without making it a caricature. Such cultural attitudes and expressions give Oda form. But because they are so lifted out of an African American cultural context (which would insure a deeper, complex definition), she often appears as the comic Other in Sam and Molly's white world.

Still, thanks to Goldberg, *Ghost* became a bona fide hit with *Variety* reporting a gross of over $200 million. For her performance, Goldberg also became the second African American woman to win the Oscar, as Best Supporting Actress. Now back on the map as a viable box-office attraction, Goldberg believed she could play any kind of role. But while her later characters might well have been played by white actresses, the casting of Goldberg still indicated that the industry preferred to use her as a trusty soul ready to provide a little nurturing here or there.

Even in *The Long Walk Home* (1990) which has her as a domestic who walks miles to work during the Montgomery bus boycott of 1955, Goldberg could not escape the covert nurturing theme. Instead of the film's simply telling her character's story, the domestic's plight serves to awaken (and humanize) her white employer (Sissy Spacek) to racial injustices.

Later the comedy *Soapdish* (1991) cast her as a soap opera writer who, aware that the soap's troubled leading lady (Sally Field) is down in the dumps, knows the perfect remedy. She takes the woman to a mall where she boosts Field's spirits by making sure all her fans recognize her. Field beams! And the audience knows she couldn't ask for a better friend than Whoopi!

The big hit *Sister Act* (1992) cast Goldberg as a Reno lounge singer named Deloris Van Cartier who, having witnessed a mob killing, hides out in a San Francisco convent where she pretends to be a nun called Sister Mary Clarence. Before the movie ends, the nuns grow close to this free spirit, who becomes their choirmaster and blesses them with some soul as she teaches them how to sing such rock and roll numbers as "My Guy" (now "My God") and "I Will Follow Him." She, too, grows close to them.

It is worth noting that race is a subject that *Sister Act* assumes is of no importance to its mainstream audience. Nothing is made of the fact that white actor Harvey Keitel plays Goldberg's boyfriend. Yet race-as-subtext rears its naughty head.

Noting that *Sister Act* originally was to have starred Bette Midler, *The New York Times* critic Janet Maslin commented on a scene in which Goldberg's Deloris "is scorned by the Mother Superior (Maggie Smith)." "Scenes that might have played as mere snobbery with Ms. Midler now have a hint of racism," Maslin wrote, "which might have been dispelled if the film had addressed it head on." Maslin added, "The fact that Deloris is the only black nun in the convent is not even mentioned descriptively. When a dozen nuns are loose in a gambling casino and Deloris is being frantically hunted among all the habits, no one thinks to cite her race as an identifying detail."

For the most part, Deloris is removed from other African Americans. Somehow the filmmakers assume that their black character does not need cultural references (other than occasional jokes about race) or a semblance of a black community to anchor her. By repeatedly denying a character this kind of cultural framework/ definition (as happened so often in the Murphy films as well as *Driving Miss Daisy* and earlier Goldberg movies), the movies say that a cultural base, indeed a culture from which these characters come, is nonexistent, invisible at best.

For African American audiences, the movies were also funny but possibly alienating. Goldberg herself endowed her characters with an ethnic definition, again through language, intonation, inflection, and attitude. Her look itself, especially when her hair is in dreadlocks, was a cultural sign. But it became frustrating that such cultural distinctions were often used only as points of derision in these films.

Interestingly, in the sequel *Sister Act 2* (1993), directed by African American Bill Duke, the Goldberg character, although still relating primarily to white characters in the convent, has a chance to interact with other black characters. Duke seems determined that Deloris not function in a total cultural vacuum. Also appearing in the film, in the role of a young student, was future hip hop diva Lauryn Hill.

Goldberg also appeared in Robert Altman's *The Player* (1992), *Sarafina* (1992, an interesting choice of roles, as a South African schoolteacher, but a less than inspired performance), and *Made in America* (1993), which costarred her with then real-life boyfriend, actor Ted Danson. But no matter what their relationship off-screen, on-screen precautions were taken not to scare away any patrons with too explicit an interracial couple. In the film, the audience is led to believe that Goldberg has had Danson's child through artificial insemination, certainly not any physical contact! Just when it appears that Goldberg and Danson will actually have a love scene, their romantic interlude turns into an unconsummated comic romp. As it turns out, Goldberg also learns that Danson has not fathered her child after all, not even through artificial insemination. Does the audience need any clearer statement that the races should not mix? Even the major ads for the film kept Goldberg and Danson apart; she stands on one side; he, on the other.

Goldberg's popularity continued. In December 1993, she told "Entertainment Tonight" that her salary for *Sister Act 2* (reportedly in the millions) made her "the highest paid woman in the history of film." She added, "For a little while, I was Queen Bee." Goldberg kept working almost nonstop in such films as *The Lion King* (1994), *Moonlight and Valentino* (1995), *Eddie* (1996), *Bogus* (1996), *The Associate* (1996), *An Alan Smithee Film: Burn Hollywood Burn* (1998), *The Deep End of the Ocean* (1999), *Girl, Interrupted* (1999), and *Monkeybone* (2001). Though she became part of the Hollywood establishment and hosted the Academy Awards ceremony in 1994, many within the entertainment industry, as well as moviegoers, questioned her projects. She "managed to bump into a few hits over the decade (like her *Sister Act* movies)," *Entertainment Weekly* reported in its November 1, 1996, issue, "but for the most part she's been utterly indiscriminate in her choices—and it shows." Having "churned out one flopped formula comedy after another," wrote the magazine, Goldberg had "squandered" her dramatic credibility.

To her credit, Goldberg attempted to do more varied work but with very mixed results. In *Corrina, Corrina* (1994), she appeared as Corrina Washington, a domestic/nanny who comforts a young girl who has lost her mother. She also comforts the girl's widowed father (Ray Liotta). Perhaps self-conscious about playing another maid, Goldberg reportedly insisted that Corrina not be your run-of-the-mill domestic. Thus Corrina is a smart, stylish, witty graduate of Fisk University who also is quite knowledgable about jazz. Though it's rather refreshing to see such characteristics, most moviegoers must have felt Corrina was overqualified for her job and still too much of a traditional nurturer in this white household. Worse, the film, which was set in 1959, hedged on fully defining what the interracial relationship between Goldberg and Liotta was *really* all about.

Another change of pace came with *Boys on the Side* (1995), in which she played a singer, Jane, traveling with two young white women (Drew Barrymore and Mary-Louise Parker). Jane is also a lesbian, which complicates her relationship with the other women—and also takes the film into unexpected emotional directions. "Jane's sexuality is never addressed directly," wrote Janet Maslin in *The New York Times*, "but still it shapes the story. She becomes the outsider whose presence casts new light on the ways the other two characters, both heterosexual, have behaved with men." The film does suggest, as Maslin pointed out, "that love can cross lines of sexuality, race and illness." Yet at the same time, Goldberg seemed stuck again in the role of the comforting friend.

Then in Rob Reiner's *Ghosts of Mississippi* (1996), she had what might have been a really challenging role as Myrlie Evers, the widow of real-life NAACP leader Medgar Evers, who had been killed by a white bigot in 1963 in Jackson, Mississippi. But rather than focusing on Myrlie Evers's tensions (telling *her* story—her efforts to reopen her husband's murder case after some twenty-five years), *Ghosts of Mississippi* mostly recorded the work of Bobby DeLaughter, the dedicated white prosecutor (Alec Baldwin), who finally got a conviction at the new trial in 1994. "When future generations turn to this era's movies for an account of the struggles for racial justice in America, they'll learn the surprising lesson that such battles were fought and won by square-jawed white Guys," wrote Godfrey Chesire in *Variety*. Myrlie Evers was never a strong enough presence in the movie.

Watching some of these films, moviegoers may have wondered where the old lively Goldberg had gone. Then she appeared as the best friend of Angela Bassett in *How Stella Got Her Groove Back* (1998) and proved to be a highlight of the film, enlivening this melodrama with her wisecracks and funny retorts. For many movie patrons, it was a pleasure to see Goldberg's talents displayed in this way; to see her contextualized as part of a community, as someone zany but sane and warm and not an oddity. It was one of her most engaging performances. She also appeared in the black-cast comedy *Kingdom Come* (2001).

In retrospect, though her films rarely matched her talents, Whoopi Goldberg never lost her comic timing and was at her best during those moments when she injected some down-to-earth common sense *attitude* into her dialogue. That was probably her most appealing quality: that ability to cut through the sham, and speak from the head and the heart. Goldberg also could still be convincing in those moments when her characters' loneliness or feelings of isolation surfaced. Her vulnerability made moviegoers think about her in a way that perhaps the films had not intended.

An Emerging New African American Cinema

At the same time that Goldberg's appearances in mainstream cinema proved successful, mainstream cinema itself underwent changes. Already the success of Spike Lee's films, particularly *Do the Right Thing*, revealed the presence of a large black audience eager for movies with specific African American cultural references, subjects, issues, and stars. When a segment of the general (white) mainstream audience responded to the films, it looked as if just as popular music by black artists had reached white music listeners, perhaps now so too would black movies that retained their cultural distinctions and definitions.

An early sign of the new-style black film's appeal came with newcomer director Reginald Hudlin's black teen picture *House Party* (1990), produced by his older brother Warrington. Starring the music duo Kid 'n Play, its story was simple and basic. A teenager, Kid (Christopher Reid), who has been grounded by his father because of problems at school, hankers to sneak out and hop over to the house of his buddy Play (Christopher Martin), whose parents are away. There are plans for some high-time, hard-driving partying.

House Party follows Kid's *After Hours-like* odyssey to and from Play's as he endures a series of nighttime adventures and dilemmas. Throughout, the audience is treated to the latest hip hop dance styles, hairstyles (including Kid's mile-high high-top fade), slang, music, and attitudes. And we see Kid trying to come to grips with the typical hassles of teen life: the demands of school, parents, and peers; also the pangs of first love.

Expanded from a short film Reginald Hudlin had directed while a student at Harvard, *House Party* had no great messages or social significance. Pleasant, agreeable, and paced at a fast clip with some bright, invigorating colors, it also had some likable performers—Robin Harris (as the father), Christopher Reid, Tisha Campbell, Martin Lawrence—and portrayed African American teenagers as they are rarely presented in films, simply as likable kids.

At times, *House Party* also expressed, sometimes simply through casting, traditional attitudes on women and class. Its black women are presented in color categories. The middle-class "good girl" Sidney (who Kid falls for) is played by the lighter Tisha Campbell. The browner A. J. Johnson plays the faster girl Sharanne from the projects. (In many early 1990s films by young black male filmmakers, dreamgirls were often lighter actresses.)

Sharanne's family in the projects is a crude batch, fit for the director's satire. We're to be comically appalled by these lowlifes! When fun is poked at the bourgeois—those older middle-class black Americans, however—it is done in more restrained, even deferential terms. In the *Village Voice*, writer Lisa Kennedy also commented on *House Party*'s "disquieting effects," mainly its homophobic jail-cell sequence when Kid—temporarily behind bars—wards off the hungry sexual eyes of his fellow inmates.

The critics, however, lavished the movie with praise. In *New York Newsday*, Wayne Robbins saluted the film's "relentless comic vitality." Made on a budget of $2.5 million, *House Party* went on to earn some $25 million. It spawned two uninspired sequels (neither directed by Hudlin) *House Party 2* (1991) and *House Party 3* (1994), both again starring Kid 'n Play, who also starred in another black youth-oriented picture *Class Act* (1992). Director Hudlin and his producer brother Warrington later were the executive producers of the animated film *Bebe's Kids* (1992). In 1992, Reginald Hudlin directed Eddie Murphy in *Boomerang*. He also directed *The Great White Hype* (1996) with Samuel L. Jackson, Damon Wayans, and Peter Berg, as well as *Ladies' Man* (2000) with "Saturday Night Live" star Tim Meadows.

Another African American filmmaker to reach a young audience was former child actor James Bond III who, at twenty-four, wrote, directed, produced, and appeared in *Def by Temptation* (1990), a sometimes sexy and stylish horror story (shot by cinematographer Ernest Dickerson) that was part satire, part parody.

Charles Burnett: A New Career Direction

In this emerging new movement of African American filmmakers was veteran Charles Burnett, whose career went in a new direction. Born in Vicksburg, Mississippi, Burnett grew up in South Central Los Angeles. He first studied electronics in college but switched to filmmaking, and made his first film *Several Friends* in 1969.

As a graduate student at UCLA, his highly praised thesis film, the 1977 *Killer of Sheep*, was well-known at film festivals and conferences, but not to general audiences. In this drama about a slaughterhouse worker in Los Angeles, Burnett focused on the emotionally disconnected character Stan who numbs himself (as a means of survival) to his work and his world: a place where men plot petty would-be hustles; where women look bruised and forlorn; where he is alienated from his wife, distanced from his children, and acutely aware of the absurdist, (racially) deterministic culture that offers him few options.

At times the action in *Killer of Sheep* appears to be both metaphor and all too cruelly real. Scenes of children playing in a cluttered lot are juxtaposed with images of sheep being led to slaughter. In one sequence, Stan journeys with a friend Bracy to the home of people down on their luck to buy a used engine for his car. Burnett's camera focuses on Stan and Bracy as they carefully carry the engine down the steps and outside. Once the engine is placed into his pickup truck, the two start to drive off only to have the engine fall out and crack the block. At another time when the men motor to the Santa Anita racetrack, confident of a tip on a winning horse, their car breaks down. There is no spare tire. There is no way.

Powerful and haunting, *Killer of Sheep* won the Critics Prize at the Berlin International Film Festival in 1981. Later Burnett wrote and directed *My Brother's Wedding* (1984). He was also the writer and director of photography on independent filmmaker Billy Woodberry's *Bless Their Little Hearts*.

In 1990, *To Sleep with Anger*, which lacked the mythic power of *Killer of Sheep*, its mood and tone far more relaxed, nonetheless brought Burnett critical attention.

Its opening credits well set the stage for the action to follow. A man sits on a chair, facing the camera, next to a table with a bowl of fruit. Behind him is a portrait of a woman. In the midst of this beautifully composed still life, flames suddenly lick the fruit. Then flames dart on the man's shoes, his vest. Beneath the arresting calm surface are fiery secrets and poetic passions.

Essentially a family drama, *To Sleep with Anger* centered on an older black couple, Gideon and Susie (Paul Butler and Mary Alice), originally from the South, now living in Los Angeles where they have raised two grown sons, Junior and Babe Brother, who could not be more different or distant. Babe Brother (Richard Brooks) and his realtor wife (Sheryl Lee Ralph) are Buppies, cut off from the family and traditions.

But a change in tone and the household comes about with the arrival of an old friend from the South, Harry Mention (Danny Glover), who en route to Oakland, visits Gideon and Susie and ends up a house guest who won't go away. He rummages through the couple's photographs and drawers, even their sugar bowl. His movements are governed by charms and superstitions. There seems no relief from Harry, not even after he finally dies. Burnett's tone then becomes playful, even absurdist. It almost seems like a different movie. Throughout Burnett pays attention to the cultural bearings. With a vegetable garden and chickens in the backyard, Gideon and Susie have brought their patch of the South to South Central. With blues and spirituals on the soundtrack, with Harry's charms and superstitions, Burnett casually sets the characters in a rich cultural tradition.

Harry himself is the Trickster of African American folklore, who stirs things up. His presence jolts the family's old patterns and emotional evasions; the long-buried secrets and tensions surface to be resolved. Even the title plays on the familiar black saying, "Never go to bed angry."

The winner of a Special Jury Prize at the 1990 Sundance United States Film Festival, *To Sleep with Anger* picked up a major distributor but did not find a large audience. Burnett believed the distributor did not know how to handle the film, how to make a black audience aware of its uniqueness in a market in which black films were pitched mainly for a young audience. Later Burnett directed *The Glass Shield* (1995) as well as the television dramas "Nightjohn" and "The Wedding."

Also screened at the 1990 Sundance Festival where it was awarded the grand prize for independent films was Wendell Harris's *Chameleon Street* (1991). Based on a true story that writer/director/star Harris had read about in a 1983 newspaper account, *Chameleon Street* dramatizes the experiences of impersonator William Douglas Street who, having barely graduated from a Detroit high school, posed as a reporter, an exchange student at an Ivy League university, a lawyer, and a doctor (successfully performing twenty-three operations). Harris was determined to bring Street's story to the screen. It took him seven years.

His film emerged as a study in both identity and alienation. In one scene, a prison doctor says that Street (played by Harris) intuits what other people need and then becomes that person. Not only is it a way of making contact with other human beings but also of establishing identity for a man who seems lost without a public pose. Lonely and adrift, he is cynically and contemptuously aware that he lives in a culture that has no place for him unless he is able to assume a socially acceptable role. The fact that he is a black male makes the question of identity and role assumption all the more affecting.

Chameleon Street was not widely distributed, although its subject was intriguing enough that a major studio hoped to buy the rights to Harris's film, then remake it as a popular work, possibly starring Arsenio Hall. Its failure to reach a significant black audience may have had as much to do in part to its structure, tone, and distant protagonist as with its lack of theater dates. (Its women are not well-defined either.) But like *To Sleep with Anger*, *Chameleon Street* attempted to explore new subject matter and structure.

A Breakthrough Year

But for the new crop of African American filmmakers, 1991 was a banner year. "Blacks Taking the Helm," read the title of a front-page article in the March 18, 1991, issue of *Variety*. "Black directors are making an unprecedented number of pies this year, pies that distribs hope to sell—like the rap and Motown many are scored to—in the mall as well as the inner city," the article reported. Thirteen films directed by African Americans were scheduled for release that year; twenty others starring black actors were scheduled for release. By now, with estimates that some twenty-five percent of the movie going public was African American, there was great optimism about the future of black films.

Among the early films of the year (but not a great hit) was Robert Townsend's *The Five Heartbeats*. Its subject touched on an African American pop archetype: it told the story of a 1960s rhythm-and-blues singing group, whose five members fall victim to the pressures of the music industry as well as their own foibles.

While *The Five Heartbeats* had its admirers, the film was dramatically disappointing. Struggling to cover too many subjects—the Mob in the music industry, racism, exploitation, drugs, familial tensions, even religious redemption—it seemed unable to focus long enough on any topic. One subject in need of exploration was the film's narrow understanding of its female characters, not a one of whom is sensitively defined.

Throughout, the musical sequences had some energy and drive. But only in later episodes did *The Five Heartbeats* build so that some semblance of a coherent, poignant story emerged, thanks mostly to its actors: Leon, Michael Wright (who appeared in Robert Altman's 1983 *Streamers* and later *Sugar Hill*, 1994), Diahann Carroll, Chuck Patterson, and Harold Nicholas.

The early 1990s was not the best of times for director Townsend, whose 1993 *The Meteor Man* was also a critical and commercial disappointment. He also directed *B*A*P*S* (1997).

New Jack Movies

Perhaps no film heralded the full-fledged arrival of the new filmmakers quite as flamboyantly as *New Jack City* (1991), directed by Mario Van Peebles, son of filmmaker Melvin Van Peebles. Mario Van Peebles came to directing after serving an apprenticeship as an actor. When a teenager, he played the young Sweetback in his father's *Sweet Sweetback's Baadasssss Song*.

Later after earning a degree in economics from Columbia University, he worked as a model and also as an actor in such films as *The Cotton Club*, *Exterminator II* (1984, in which he does a fairly gritty job as a villainous, punk-style, Messianic leader called X), *Rappin'* (1985, an early attempt to reach the rap audience), *The Delivery Boys* (1986), *Heartbreak Ridge* (1986), and *Jaws: The Revenge*. He also appeared briefly in the television series "LA Law" and as the star of the series "Sonny Spoon."

As an actor, under that glamorous glacial surface (he had the striking looks of a star), he lacked any suggestion of tension (which may account for his success as a model) or the ingredients essential for a movie star—power and threat.

In 1990, he was the star and writer of *Identity Crisis*, a film directed by his father. Then came *New Jack City*. Fast-moving, gritty, pulsating with tension and threat from its opening aerial view of a tight New York City while Queen Latifah briefly raps on the soundtrack, and propelled in great part by the highly kinetic, charismatic performance of Wesley Snipes, this hypnotic urban potboiler charted the rise and fall of quick-witted, ruthless drug kingpin Nino Brown, caught up in a maddening pursuit of power and money. Here, so the script said, was the American notion of success at any cost. Here too is the ultimate degenerate American capitalist.

In some ways, *New Jack City* seems to have sprung from the hip of *Super Fly* with some help from gangsta rap. Both films seemed awed by the sheer drive and macho power of their businessmen dope dealers, who are able not only to survive on mean streets but also to live in high style. Neither film had much regard for defining its female characters. But while *Super Fly*, released in an era more casual about the drug experience, made no moral judgments on its pusher protagonist Priest, *New Jack City* arrived when African American leaders were expressing outrage about the proliferation of drugs in the black community. Consequently, the film, after celebrating its hero, felt compelled to punish him—but not without first affording him the opportunity to deliver a self-serving statement ("It's bigger than Nino Brown," he tells a packed courtroom. "It's big business. It's the American Way") that on one level justifies his acts. Nonetheless, when Nino is blown away by an older community resident, *New Jack City* sought to alleviate any guilt feelings a new age might have had about enjoying Nino so much.

With its focus on crack and capitalism, violence and vengeance, and the efforts of a law enforcement officer to trap Nino, *New Jack City* (like a 1930s Warner Brothers gangster saga) looked as if it leaped out of the headlines. Its gangster motif also appealed to the young enthusiasts of gangsta rap; so, too, did its stars. Portraying the cop out to get Nino was none other than rap singer Ice-T (a true irony, given Ice-T's attitudes, expressed later in his *Body Count* album, on the police force). Also in the cast were Allen Payne, Vanessa Williams, Mario Van Peebles himself, and Judd Nelson.

Sad to see was Tracy Camila Johns, whose performance as Nola Darling in *She's Gotta Have It* helped launch the idea of a new kind of black screen heroine. In *New Jack City*, she seems almost debased in a role that is little more than the conventional black ho'.

New Jack City emerged as a solid hit with the moviegoing young. Shot on a budget of $8.5 million, the film, within weeks of its release, grossed, according to *Variety*, over $44 million. Its success clearly made the industry aware of the new audience for black films as well as the unique (lucrative) perspective African American artists could bring to such movies. Mario Van Peebles later directed the black western *Posse* (1993), and in 1995 he directed and co-produced, along with his father Melvin Van Peebles, *Panther*, which the elder Van Peebles also scripted.

A Black New Wave

Other films quickly followed. In this black new wave was a heady brew of creative talents. Bill Duke, who had directed for television and acted in *Car Wash* and *Bird on a Wire* (1990), directed a stylized version of Chester Himes's novel *A Rage in Harlem* (1991, with an all star cast: Gregory Hines, Forest Whitaker, Robin Givens). Later, Duke directed a perhaps overly stylish *Deep Cover* (1992); a gun-for-hire-like *Sister Act 2;* the nonblack *Cemetery Club* (1992); and *Hoodlum* (1997). Tony Brown's *The White Girl* (1990), a drama about cocaine addiction, was more widely distributed at this time. Following *Sidewalk Stories*, Charles Lane directed, with less success, Disney's $16 million *True Identity* (1991). Joseph Vasquez directed *Hangin' with the Homeboys* (1991). Seasoned filmmaker Michael Schultz directed the satiric comedy *Livin' Large* (1991). And nineteen-year-old Matty Rich directed *Straight Out of Brooklyn* (1991), which dramatized the disintegration of an African American family in Brooklyn's Red Hook section. Rich later directed *The Inkwell* (1994).

With all this activity, mainstream cinema had not had so many black artists working behind the cameras since the 1970s. Along with the directors were other African American creative artists: a cinematographer like Ernest Dickerson; an editor like Sam Pollard; a set designer like Wynn Thomas; a costume designer like Ruth Carter; a casting director like Robi Reed; a sound wizard like Russell Williams who won Oscars for Best Achievement in Sound for *Glory* and *Dances with Wolves* (1990); and a musician like Terence Blanchard.

John Singleton's South Central

Among the most successful new films was *Boyz N the Hood* (1991) by writer/ director John Singleton, a graduate of the University of Southern California Filmic Writing Program. Here he turned his camera to a coming-of-age story in South Central Los Angeles.

Prophetic as well as indicative of a fundamental malaise in urban centers during the Reagan era (and the Bush years to follow), Singleton's film opened in 1984 as young Tre Styles and friends, en route to school, discuss the gunshots they heard the night before. In a straightforward manner, Singleton coolly immerses us in a violent world in which such children have few options; and in which Tre struggles to survive and to hold onto his hopes—and his humanity.

Boyz N the Hood follows as Tre's mother (Angela Bassett) sends him to live with his father, her estranged husband Furious Styles (Larry Fishburne). "It's like you told me. I can't teach him how to be a man. That's your job," she says. The father's firm but sensitive discipline leads Tre on the road to manhood. But for Tre's friends, the half-brothers Ricky (a star athlete) and Doughboy (struggling in a society without any concerns about him), the future is bleak. Both end up bloody and dead on the streets.

Like a first novelist, Singleton appeared so eager to express so many pent-up feelings and observations that *Boyz N the Hood* suffered from an overload of subjects and issues: unwanted pregnancies, the use of condoms, AIDS, gentrification, racism.

Then, too, while the film idealized Furious and stressed the role of African American fathers, it rarely drew its women with much insight or sympathy. "And you ain't shit. You're just like your daddy," Doughboy's mother Mrs. Baker (Tyra Ferrell) is heard telling him just at the moment she is introduced in the film. Tough and foul-mouthed, she, like the neighbor on the block who lets her little girl wander out into the street, is indicted as an insensitive, irresponsible mother. Even Tre's educated, ambitious mother is made to seem inadequate at rearing a son. Singleton does not seem willing to consider the pressures with which these women live.

Still, *Boyz N the Hood* remains moving and often powerful. Scenes of children walking through mean streets where they might encounter a hostile group or stumble across a dead body are infused with an intense brooding melancholia. The very opening statement that. "One out of every twenty-one black American males will be murdered in their lifetime" is chilling. So too is the comment, "Most will die at the hands of another black male." Throughout he uses sound effectively: out of nowhere come indiscriminate gunshot pops as well as the buzzing whirl of helicopters hovering above this tight, insulated world.

The playful banter and the fierce male camaraderie reveals Singleton's belief that this type of African American male bonding preserves the men but also can lead to their destruction. Their language, clothes, and attitudes enable them to maintain their cultural identity and connections.

Interestingly, when the young males refer to one another as bitch (a sign of their evaluation of women as weak and powerless), the language is *authentic* in reflecting their distrust, suspicion, or dislike of women. Yet Singleton and other filmmakers seemed unwilling to challenge such perspectives.

Wisely, he cast the drama with fine performers: Fishburne; Tyra Ferrell; Cuba Gooding, Jr. (as the older Tre); and rap star Ice Cube (formerly of the group N.W.A.), who compellingly captures Doughboy's alienation and sensitivity. Later Ice Cube, along with Ice-T, took his gangsta rap persona to Walter Hill's *Trespass* (1992).

"There are subtler, more polite movies around, but none made out of such a heart-stopping sense of urgency," David Ansen wrote in *Newsweek*. Other critics concurred. In *New York*, David Denby wrote that Singleton presented "a coherent picture of a tragic way of life." When violence broke out at some movie theaters showing *Boyz N the Hood* (similar to the violence that broke out at showings of *New Jack City*), both Ansen and Denby again wrote about the film, stressing that rather than promoting violence, *Boys N the Hood* was an eloquent plea for such violence to end.

For *Boys N the Hood*, John Singleton became the first African American nominated for an Oscar as Best Director as well as the youngest directorial nominee ever. The film emerged as the most successful black genre film in movie history at that time. A reason for its appeal to the general white audience may be that *Boyz N the Hood*, rather than focusing exclusively on white racism directed at African Americans, instead addressed violence and conflict within the black community. The white audience may have felt it was let off the hook.

Singleton's next film *Poetic Justice* (1993)—which focused on a young beauty parlor worker and poet, Justice (pop star Janet Jackson), on an odyssey as she travels with a friend (the vivid Regina King) and two young men (rapper Tupac Shakur and Joe Torry) from Los Angeles to Oakland in a mail van—did not fare well yet had some oddly perceptive and moody sequences. Afterwards he directed *Higher Learning* (1995). Certainly, Singleton must have been disappointed by the lukewarm response to his film *Rosewood* (1997). Here he dramatized a long-lost episode in American history: the murder of an unknown number of African Americans and the annihilation of a nearly all-black town in Rosewood, Florida, in the early 1920s by an angry white mob from a neighboring community. The devastation is sparked by the false accusation of a young white woman, who claims that she has been brutally raped and beaten by a black man. In actuality, the rapist/ attacker is her white lover. Generally, the critics complained that the film failed to create convincing, realistic characters and that even its powerful theme was reduced to the stuff of melodrama. Still, with a cast that included Don Cheadle, Ving Rhames, Jon Voight, and Esther Rolle, Singleton captured some of the paranoia and hysteria as well as the unbridled racism that can erupt from a lie. He then turned to a more commercial vehicle with his 2000 remake of *Shaft* starring Samuel L. Jackson. That in turn was followed in 2001 by *Baby Boy*, in which Singleton returned to the South Central setting of *Boyz N the Hood*.

Still more films followed. In the early 1990s, a number of these new movies had a set of distinguishing characteristics (and limitations), which were reminiscent of black films of the early 1970s. Most focused on young African American males coming of age in tough urban settings, their lives often defined by the racial dynamics and racism of the dominant culture. Most were also eager to address harsh urban realities: drugs, crime, violence, death on the streets. Women were rarely developed characters, sometimes treated like little more than disposable items. Unlike films of the blaxploitation era, however, which often closed on a mood of triumphant fantasy, the new films often ended on a grim, nihilistic, yet realistic note. Many films also were shot on low budgets, which meant the major studios financing them minimized their risks. The films that were successful like *New Jack City* turned over great profits. For the most part, the films of this new *home-boy cinema* were infused with a hip hop/rap aesthetic and sensibility, and were made to appeal to the young.

Unfortunately, the films (in general) failed to create a diversity of images, settings, themes. For the new African American cinema to be vital, it had to extend

Surviving in the "hood": Cuba Gooding, Jr., and Laurence Fishburne as Tre and Furious Styles in *Boyz N the Hood*.

its perspective, to move beyond the "hood" to include other, varied aspects of black life, goals, tensions, and dreams. If the new cinema continued to fail to do so, it could easily stop midstream and go the route (to oblivion) of the black cinema of the early 1970s.

Rising from the Dust

The new African American cinema's form and style as well as its depiction of women took a wholly different and unexpected turn with independent writer/director/producer Julie Dash's *Daughters of the Dust* (1990). Having studied film at New York's City College and later the American Film Institute and UCLA, Dash had been making short films since the 1970s: *Diary of an African Nun* (1977, based on an Alice Walker story), *Four Women* (1978), and *Illusions*. For ten years she struggled to finance, shoot, and complete *Daughters of the Dust*. It proved to be a stunning piece of work.

Set on the Sea Islands off the South Carolina coast in the summer of 1902, *Daughters of the Dust* looked at the experiences of a family of Gullah women on the eve before they leave for life on the mainland. Foremost is the family's matriarch—eighty-eight-year-old Nana Peazant (Cora Lee Day)—who is aware that the women risk losing their cultural roots, customs, rituals, beliefs, history, and identities by going North.

Telling her story in a highly visual style (with breathtaking cinematography by Arthur Jafa) and a nonlinear narrative (part of the story is told by an unborn child; it's almost as if a griot were recounting the events), Dash creates a rich, absorbing tableau in which the landscape itself is a presence and a character; and in which were cast African American actresses of various colors (Barbara 0, Alva Rogers, Kaycee Moore) and perspectives who helped break the mold in which black women have traditionally been portrayed.

Another African American woman, Leslie Harris, directed a feature, *Just Another Girl on the IRT* (1993), focusing on a young woman coming of age in New York.

More by Spike

During this period no African American filmmaker received more attention than Spike Lee, who directed a trio of films that were among the most discussed and debated of the early 1990s: *Mo' Better Blues* in 1990, *Jungle Fever* in 1991, and *Malcolm X* in 1992.

With *Mo' Better Blues*, Lee set out to make a jazz film with an African American cultural context through which to view the jazz artist and his struggle to create.

Julie Dash's *Daughters of the Dust*: a portrait of African American women at the turn of the century.

Rather than focusing on some doomed and drugged-out hero whose life is one long drawn out study of torment and self-despair, Lee presented an almost ordinary but talented young middle-class musician, trumpet player Bleek Gilliam (Denzel Washington), whose life is traced from his childhood in Brooklyn to his early success with a quintet. Ambitious, confident, controlled, and dedicated to his art, but also often insensitive and blind to the needs of those closest to him—be it the members of his quintet or the two young women who vie for his attentions—Bleek eventually has to make a choice or commitment. Ultimately, he leaves his art to accept his role as patriarch of a rather mundane middle-class lifestyle.

Many critics found *Mo' Better Blues* disappointing. "From characters to camera angles, this story of a self-absorbed jazz trumpeter is one long cliché, the kind that might make his most loyal admirers wince and wonder, 'Spike, what happened?'" wrote Caryn James in *The New York Times*.

Mo' Better Blues was not without its weaknesses. Its female characters seemed categorized into the standard nurturing (browner) Good Woman (Joie Lee) versus the career-driven, sexier (lighter) Bad Woman (Cynda Williams). Its ending was also perplexing. Why must Bleek give up his art? Some wondered if *Mo' Better Blues* might be a wish-fulfillment for Spike Lee, the son of musician Bill Lee, who might here finally be telling Pop he should have given it up and spent more time at home with the family! Pop psychology, yes! But *Mo' Better Blues* lends itself to various interpretations.

Yet despite its unevenness, *Mo' Better Blues* remains on many levels an impressive, beautifully shot, dreamily romantic movie. Black cinematographer Ernest Dickerson's camera captures the warm interiors of a Brooklyn brownstone, the shafts of light in Bleek's loft, the splendor and burnished sexy glamour of the club Beneath the Underdog, the brilliant romanticism of Bleek at night on the Brooklyn Bridge. Unlike *Bird* in which the black performers were sometimes atrociously lit, the rich colors of such actors as Washington, Wesley Snipes, Joie Lee, Cynda Williams, and Giancarlo Esposito are on vivid display.

Throughout as Bleek and his quintet joke and "sound" on one another, Lee, rather than presenting a black/white bonded tale as did *Sweet Love Bitter*, *Bird*, and *'Round Midnight*, establishes the camaraderie of black jazz artists, whose cultural experiences, language, and attitudes are unique points of group identification. These men who work with one another are inside each other's heads and minds too.

Summoning up urban rhythms and the lush glamour of show business, *Mo' Better Blues* may be Spike Lee's most old-style movie-movie. If *School Daze* is Spike Lee's attempt to look back (at his experiences at a black college), then *Mo' Better Blues* could be an attempt to examine his life after his success; it's his 1990 here-and-now film. Throughout its subtext is about show business, success, glamour, beauty, the struggle for artistic expression amid the pressures of a demanding career.

Movie romance, movie triangle: Denzel Washington with Cynda Williams (LEFT) and Denzel Washington with Joie Lee in *Mo' Better Blues*.

With *Jungle Fever*, Lee dramatized an affair between an African American man (an upwardly mobile architect, Flipper Purify who lives in Harlem with wife Drew and their daughter) and a young white woman (his secretary Angie Tucci who lives with her working-class father and brothers in New York's predominantly Italian-American Bensonhurst) whose lives and communities could not be culturally more different or divergent. With explicit romantic/sexual sequences and stingingly realistic culture collisions, *Jungle Fever* went further than earlier film explorations of interracial romance. It also had a second story, that of Flipper's crackhead brother Gator.

Jungle Fever revealed Spike Lee's strengths and flaws. Throughout he proves himself a master at writing rich, clever, funny, dramatic dialogue, yet the film (like others of Lee) was in need of a stronger developed story line and characters. Lee was quick to say that the film was about two people caught up in the sexual mythology of one another's races. Yet The Flipper/Angie relationship cried out for elaboration and definition. At the same time the story of Gator, which climaxed with a crack house sequence and then a killing, was compelling. But the script never convincingly tied the two narratives together.

What distinguished the film was the imaginative, original direction. Lee brought real power to highly charged scenes (some overblown, some overextended) that revealed the manner in which relationships can thrive or perish because of cultural attitudes and clashes. The sequences when Flipper and Angie dine with his parents, when Angie is brutally beaten by her father (upon his discovery of the affair), when Flipper searches for Gator in a crack house (set to Stevie Wonder music), even in a hokey war council scene when Drew and her African American women friends discuss black men (and the lure of white women), all resonate rhythmically as Lee's unusual angles, his ever-moving camera, and his vigorous edits pumped up the scenes to match the dramatic force of the talented performers.

Ultimately, he was able to get close to basic mass African American attitudes and arrive at a certain truth without necessarily explaining it. The film expressed (thanks also to the exciting performances of Samuel L. Jackson, Lonette McKee, Ossie Davis, Ruby Dee, and Annabella Sciorra) then contemporary urban rhythms, energies, tensions, taboos.

Surely, one of the most talked-about movies black or white of the period was Spike Lee's *Malcolm X*. Now some twenty-seven years since Malcolm X's assassination, a renewed interest in Malcolm X swept through the black community and elevated him to the status of *mass* political/cultural icon. For the young sporting hats with the X insignia and T-shirts proclaiming "By Any Means Necessary," Malcolm X once again represented rebellion against a racist system. For an older 1960s generation, he was a farsighted, uncompromising hero whose words were as relevant in 1992 as in 1962. As Malcolm's meaning was personalized, just about everyone felt his/her view of Malcolm was sacrosanct. Some of the interest among the young may well have been sparked by Lee, who had mentioned the slain leader in previous films.

Even before one frame was shot, a controversy arose about Spike Lee's right to dramatize Malcolm X's story. Poet Amiri Baraka, spokesman for the United Front to Preserve the Legacy of Malcolm X, was quoted in *Newsweek* (August 21, 1991) as saying, "We will not let Malcolm X's life be trashed to make middle-class Negroes sleep easier." He added, "I'm horrified of seeing Spike Lee make Malcolm X. I think Eddie Murphy's films are better."

Controversy continued through filming and post-production. *Newsweek*'s November 16, 1992, issue chronicled Lee's budget problems: "Lee wanted $33 million; Warner Bros. agreed to put up only $20 million." When the film "went $5 million over budget, the bond company that insured it took financial control of the production." Finally, Lee enlisted financial support from such wealthy African Americans as Bill Cosby, Michael Jordan, Oprah Winfrey, Prince, Janet Jackson, and others. "They saved *Malcolm X*," Lee said. Warners also hassled Lee over the film's length. Lee would not budge. Its final running time was three hours and twenty-one minutes.

Based on *The Autobiography of Malcolm X* by Malcolm X and Alex Haley and working with a screenplay begun by James Baldwin and Arnold Perl, Lee's *Malcolm X* opened with a spell-binding credit sequence. As the words of Malcolm are heard, images of a burning American flag are intercut with sequences from the videotape of Rodney King being beaten by members of the Los Angeles police force.

Thereafter *Malcolm X* dramatized the pivotal events in the leader's life: his Nebraska family terrorized by the Klan; his mother (Lonette McKee), following his father's death, left emotionally shattered; his early adulthood as a hustler in Boston; his years of imprisonment where he undergoes a political/religious awakening through the Nation of Islam; his tumultuous years in New York as a nationally known leader; to his 1965 assassination at age thirty-nine in New York's Audubon Ballroom. The film ended with Ossie Davis's eulogy and a hymn of praise to Malcolm, featuring among others Nelson Mandela.

Ironically, in a film focusing on a fiery unconventional leader, Spike Lee, the movie industry's born rebel, made his most conventional film, which, as a piece of popular filmmaking intended to reach a large audience (by using traditional movie devices), often succeeded on these terms. From the beginning, as Ernest Dickerson's camera glides through the early Boston sequences in a dazzling virtuoso manner, the streets and the vast ballroom where a zoot-suited Malcolm joins dancing revelers look like a movie set with imaginatively choreographed, stylized action. For Lee's critics, such early movie-ish scenes were without the type of docurealism they might have expected or wanted. These may well be the film's most striking flaws. (So too may be the fact that Lee appeared as the character Shorty, which temporarily dispelled the audience's willing suspension of disbelief.) But obviously Lee wanted

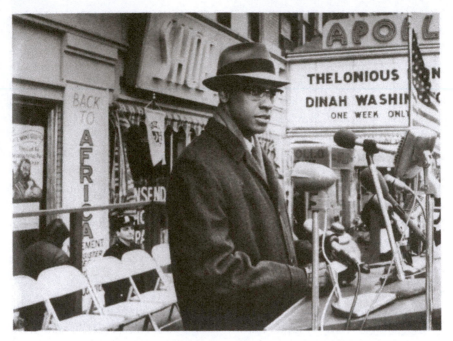

Taking a political icon mainstream for a new audience: Denzel Washington in one of his best performances in Spike Lee's *Malcolm X*.

Denzel Washington as Malcolm X and Angela Bassett as his wife Betty Shabazz in *Malcolm X*.

the early sections to entertain as they summon up some of the energy and optimism of the black community and Malcolm during the years of World War II.

The action, tone, mood, perspective, and characterizations as well as the look of the film, change dramatically in—sometimes austere, sometimes stately—later sequences; all paralleling Malcolm X's psychological and political transformations. Throughout, as Lee handled large crowd scenes as well as the intensely private, lonely moments of Malcolm X, the director's growth was impressive. The climactic sequence the night before and the day of Malcolm's death, as he stoically moves toward his unavoidable fate, are handled adroitly with a restrained but chilling dramatic intensity.

Much of the film's strength lay in the performance of Denzel Washington, who enabled us to see Malcolm *think*, making his conversion and straight-arrow drive altogether convincing and heroic. Washington was also able to compete with an audience's awareness of Malcolm the legend and not to be dwarfed by comparisons with the real man's charisma, look, and speech patterns. Washington brings perfect intonations to Malcolm's speeches.

The casting of Washington (who had played Malcolm X in the play *When the Chickens Come Home to Roost*) also helped make the man acceptable to the mainstream audience. Unlike Malcolm who had a rugged, less conventionally handsome look and who, while possessing charm, also (because of his revolutionary politics) frightened people black and white, Washington's quick and ready smile, smooth handsome face, and indisputable charm make it hard *not* to like him or to agree with his politics. Larry Fishburne might have made an interesting scrappier Malcolm, but it is questionable if the mass audience would have gravitated to him as it did to Washington. In no way is this meant to fault Washington's near flawless performance. But it points out that his star power added to the movie's appeal to a new audience.

The film has other fascinating performances: Al Freeman, Jr. (who endowed his Elijah Muhammad with a soft, whispery, and appropriate scary strength); Delroy Lindo (as West Indian Archie); Lonette McKee; Ernest Thomas; and Albert Hall, as the fellow prisoner who converts Malcolm to the Nation of Islam. (In real life, Malcolm was converted through his brothers and a sister, which might have added another perspective to this mostly male-driven drama.) Mainly because of the script, Angela Bassett's Betty Shabazz, however, remains a puzzle. There is more to this woman than the film says.

Malcolm X garnered mainly good reviews. Lee's detractors (black as well as white) criticized him for failing to make a political film. True, the film simplifies the details of Malcolm's political stance and also wipes clean from the record some of his more controversial comments and positions. But never does the film distort his politics. Remaining true to what he believes are Malcolm's convictions and commitments, Lee has focused on a human drama with a political figure at its center.

During this period, it was also interesting to watch the shifting responses to Spike Lee's career. With *She's Gotta Have It*, he was the critic's darling: a little, unknown independent working outside the established film community. Yet once Lee was perceived as a successful, *commercial* filmmaker, once he made TV commercials and music videos, and emerged as possibly, next to Steven Spielberg, the most famous film director in America, Spike Lee found himself faced with critical backlash, partly from segments of the African American community.

His critics, however, failed to understand the nerve Lee touched; the very nature of serious popular work. In *Cineaste*, African American writer Jacquie Jones, then editor of *Black Film Review*, perceptively wrote that Lee's critics suffered from elemental delusions about Hollywood and "some pretty off-base assumptions about contemporary African-American popular culture." Were the point of *Malcolm X*, she explained, "to capture faithfully the meaning and the resilient spirit of Malcolm in a manner that would satisfy the needs of every person of African descent in the United States, it would have remained as unmade as it has been for the past two decades." She added, "Instead *Malcolm X* communicates loyally the tide of new Black Nationalism that is as American as the Afrocentrism to which it lays claim."

Come Oscar time, the epic film, certainly Academy Award material, won only two Oscar nominations: Denzel Washington for Best Actor and Ruth Carter for Best Costume Design. Spike Lee's outspokenness not only about the racism in the industry but about racism in America did not win him many friends in Hollywood. His films were denied the recognition they deserved and the type of honors that would enable them to reach larger audiences. Although Lee's movies were clearly open to criticism (for his treatment of women, his sometimes jumbled political comments, and his weak development of character and stories), they remained among the most vital American films of the early 1990s.

During the mid-to-second half of the era, Lee's films often still received a drubbing from the critics and, generally, were less successful commercially. Yet as the director ventured into new territory, his films became all the more interesting. His 1994 feature *Crooklyn*, based on a script by Lee, his sister Joie Susannah Lee, and his brother Cinque Lee, provided a nostalgic look at a Brooklyn family of four rambunctious brothers and one little sister (much like the Lee family) in the 1970s. Though he still had a problem pulling together the dramatic elements to create a satisfying storyline (there really is not much of a story at all), *Crooklyn* remains his most tender-hearted film, enhanced by a woman's point of view. As the mother, Alfre Woodard gave a vivid performance—despite the fact that her character's motivations sometimes seem in desperate need of explanation. As the often-unemployed father, Delroy Lindo revealed the wide range of his great talent. Whoever would have thought that the actor best known as West Indian Archie in *Malcolm X* could play such a sensitive, warm-spirited musician.

There followed other features that broke new ground: *Clockers* (1995), a nervy, tense drama based on the novel by Richard Price, which focuses on a white cop's determination to find a killer in a drug-infested Brooklyn neighborhood and that was stunningly shot by Malik Hassan Sayeed, with powerful performances by the great Delroy Lindo, Regina Taylor, Harvey Keitel, Isaiah Washington, and newcomer Mekhi Phifer; an uneven *Girl 6* (1996), based on a script by playwright Suzan-Lori Parks and starring Theresa Randle as a frustrated actress who takes a job as a phone-sex operator (and that included cameo appearances by Naomi Campbell, Madonna, and Halle Berry); *Four Little Girls* (1997), a moving documentary about the four black children who were killed in the 1963 bombing of the Sixteenth Street Baptist Church in Birmingham—a tragedy that roused the civil rights movement; and the somber, reflective *He Got Game* (1998), the story of a convict who—while temporarily released from prison to persuade his talented athletic son (portrayed by real-life NBA player Ray Allen) to play basketball for the governor's favorite college team—tries to reach the young man he loves so much but feels he's failed. With this latter film, Lee achieved a new maturity, drawing commanding performances and creating some of his emotionally most affecting sequences.

Surprisingly, the 1996 *Get on the Bus* proved to be one of Spike Lee's most entertaining films. Here he focused on a group of African American males who board a bus in South Central Los Angeles that will take them to the historic Million Man March in Washington, D.C. Among this group, which represents a cross section of male attitudes within the African American community, there are: a biracial cop (Roger Guenveur Smith) whose father has been killed by a black man; a former gang member (Gabriel Casseus), now a Muslim; a gay former Marine (Isaiah Washington) and his straight-arrow lover (Harry Lennix); an egotistical, homophobic actor (played in rousing high style by Andre Braugher); a young UCLA film student (Hill Harper); and the oldest man in the group (Ossie Davis) who, though jovial and warm, reveals his lifelong frustrations and disappointments in a stirring monologue. There is also a conservative black Republican (Wendell Pierce) who so annoys the other men that they do what audiences no doubt yearned for them to do—they simply kick the deluded brother off the bus. Throughout, screenwriter Reggie Rock Bythewood's combustible, in-your-face dialogue takes the audience through a series of ideological debates and confrontations as each man tries to explain himself. *Get on the Bus* wanted its audience to understand the diversity and the divisions as well as the ties that existed within the African American community; also to see the way these black men have been shaped by religion, politics, or personal ethics and their cultural experiences.

Shot in Super 16 mm in three weeks on a budget of $2.5 million with financing from the African American community (among the investors were Lee and screenwriter Bythewood as well as Robert Guillaume, Wesley Snipes, Johnnie Cochran, Jr., and Will Smith), Lee worked wonders with what was essentially a one-set setting, his camera always on the move, always searching and fluid. One can even accept some of the idiosyncrasies of his style, namely his rapid jump cuts that can otherwise be disconcerting. At turns funny, solemn, and serious, *Get on the Bus* was perhaps over-explained, even a tad didactic (and at times like a position paper), yet it was also often emotionally searing and always fascinating.

Marking a bold departure for Lee was *Summer of Sam* (1999), in which he worked with a large nonblack cast that included Ben Gazzara, Anthony LaPaglia, Patti LuPone, Jennifer Esposito, and Michael Badalucco. Written by Lee with Victor Colicchio and actor Michael Imperioli (one of the stars of the hit HBO series "The Sopranos") and shot by cinematographer Ellen Kuras, *Summer of Sam* was set in a working-class Italian-American neighborhood in the Bronx during the summer of 1977 when the serial killer David Berkowitz, known as the Son of Sam, seemed to hold New York City hostage. Rather than focusing on the killings, Lee instead explored the way the killing spree affects the city, feeding the fears and paranoia of a group of people already in the midst of social/cultural change; for this is the time, after all, when New Yorkers not only sought escape and the promise of sexual freedom (as well as drugs) in clubs like Plato's Retreat and Studio 54 but also endured a brutal heat wave, a citywide electrical blackout, and city riots. Near the center of the action was the character Ritchie (Adrien Brody) who returns from England where he's acquired a taste for punk music and punk regalia (most noticeable in his spiked hair)—and also a phony cockney accent. Ill at ease with the old group, he moonlights as a stripper at a gay club and also hustles gay johns on the side. There is also the couple Vinny (John Leguizamo) and Dionna (Mira Sorvino) who must deal with the state of their sexually unfulfilled marriage—and his non-stop philandering.

Though some critics argued that Lee was insensitive to Italian-Americans, and though others accused the filmmaker of insensitivity to the families of the victims of the serial killer—while other critics dismissed the film—*Summer of Sam* appears destined to appeal to later generations as a film that encapsulates some of the moods, passions, and trends of a distinct period in American social history.

Later, Lee directed the raw and ribald comedy *The Original Kings of Comedy* (2000). A filmed record of a comedy concert performed at the Charlotte Coliseum in North Carolina, *The Original Kings of Comedy* featured such comedy stars as Steve Harvey, Cedric "the Entertainer," and D. L. Hughley—who, as stars appearing on black sitcoms, were popular with black audiences—and the wildly unpredictable Bernie Mac. (As you laugh your head off at Mac's profane routines, you may also feel that he's unleashing humor you're likely to feel guilty about. Political correctness is an idea Mac appears to know nothing about. But he probably gets at some ugly truths about family life—and the appeal of a term like *mother fucker*.) During their long tour with this concert, these four comics drew in huge black crowds and grossed $37 million nationwide. Yet mainstream America seemed to know nothing about these standup stars—and their brand of humor. Made especially for African American audiences (to let those who only heard about the concert see what all the fuss was about), *The Original Kings of Comedy* also pulled in younger white moviegoers.

Afterwards Lee directed his most daring film, the scalding satire on American popular culture, *Bamboozled* (2000). Centering on a Harvard-educated television writer Pierre Delacroix (Damon Wayans)—the only writer of color on the network's staff—who is pressured by his white network boss (Michael Rapaport) to come up with a hit black series, *Bamboozled* chronicled an African American man's road to abject compromise and self-loathing. Delacroix comes up with the idea for a show that he believes is so racist that even his boss, who professes to know blacks even better than they know themselves, will be repelled by. But he is surprised when the executive *and* TV viewers love the program, called "Mantan: The New Millennium Minstrel Show," in which two homeless street performers (Tommy Davidson and dancer Savion Glover) are enlisted to play—in blackface— two brazenly coon characters called Mantan and Sleep 'N' Eat. Also in the show are an array of past degrading images and racist iconography: watermelons and chickens alongside the "characters" Aunt Jemima, Rastus, Jungle Bunny, and Sambo.

Here Lee took a swipe at some of the black sitcoms then popular on such television networks as the WB and UPN, which had been fiercely criticized within the African American community for exploiting the needs of black viewers for black entertainment. He also appeared to call into question the appeal and critical success of an earlier TV program like *In Living Color*, which ironically had starred Damon Wayans. Weren't these shows trading on stereotypical images of African Americans? But *Bamboozled* didn't stop there. A revolutionary Afrocentric political Hip Hop group that calls itself the Mau Maus—and is led by Big Black (rapper Mos Def)—declares war on the show. Yet Lee revealed the way that Hip Hop imagery also caricatured African Americans. With his insider's portrait of the way network-TV life works (the conference rooms where the faces are mainly white), Lee looks at those who control black images on television, whether it be an executive or the consultant/advisers or even the critical establishment that can sanction programming that is fundamentally insulting or degrading. Shot by Ellen Kuras on digital video, *Bamboozled* reverberated on a set of shocking visuals. No one is likely to forget a sequence that re-created the very way in which performers of the past prepared burnt cork for their blackface makeup. Unforgettable too was the sight of Mantan and Sleep 'N' Eat appearing on stage by stepping out of a huge painted backdrop of a minstrel's face—with a grotesque gaping mouth.

Not without its flaws, *Bamboozled* often veered in far too many directions without the cohesive narrative that might have made the characters stronger. Unanswered questions about black humor itself arose when one saw the nightclub routine performed by Delacroix's father (Paul Mooney), who was a standup comic. Appearing as the socially conscious assistant of Delacroix was Jada Pinkett Smith, who ultimately represented the film's moral conscience. At the climax when she sets out to kill Delacroix for betraying his people (and himself), it looks like too neat a way to pull some of the loose ends together. You have to ask why she doesn't attempt to wipe out the white TV executive who after all is in the power seat that has led to Delacroix's compromise and corruption.

Then, too, some audience members, with a sense of movie history, may wonder why the character for the show is called Mantan. Obviously making a reference to Mantan Moreland, the film overlooks an important aspect of his career: namely, that as the star of race movies, including *Mantan Runs for Mayor* (1946) and *Mantan Messes Up* (1946), Moreland clearly had a black following that didn't see him as a sellout. *Bamboozled* never quite gets at the fact that black audiences responded to black performers, despite whatever stereotyped roles they played, because of those performers' rich talents and the covert (cultural) messages they sent out. One scene acknowledges the talent of the early comedy star and pantomimist Bert Williams. In another dazzling sequence in *Bamboozled* the great dancer Savion Glover's character, free of the racist imagery in which he's been imprisoned, briefly performs brilliantly. We clearly see what's been under the mask. Maybe the audience has seen the same thing all along. But this great paradox of black entertainment history is never fully enough explored and examined.

Bamboozled's title was derived from a quote by Malcolm X: "You've been hookwinked. You've been had. You've been took. You've been led astray and amok. You've been bamboozled." Obviously influenced by Elia Kazan's *A Face in the Crowd* (1957) and Sidney Lumet's *Network* (1976), *Bamboozled* also seemed to be influenced by the 1994 David Clark Johnson-directed tale of corporate racism, *Drop Squad*, which centered on an advertising executive, played by Eriq LaSalle who, eager for success, creates an outlandish, insulting advertising campaign. The Drop Squad—a group that re-programs those blacks who have committed black-on-black crimes against the community—sets out to bring the brother to his roots and his senses. The cast included Paula Kelly, Vanessa Williams, Vondie Curtis-Hall, Charnelle Brown, and Ving Rhames. Spike Lee, who also makes a brief appearance, executive-produced the film.

Still, *Bamboozled* remains a rich, provocative, challenging film that raises many issues and closes with a scathing montage of racist imagery in movie history, including clips from cartoons and footage of some of the screen's great white icons in blackface: from Al Jolson, Fred Astaire, Mickey Rooney and Judy Garland to Shirley Temple *and* Bugs Bunny. In the end, *Bamboozled* makes audiences question who has created these images—and also reveals the institutionalized racist images present in American popular culture through much of the twentieth century.

Other New Directors and Films

Other feature directors emerged throughout the era, including an unexpected one: William Greaves, the former actor and documentary filmmaker who in 1967, had shot *Symbiopsychotaxiplasm: Take One*, an experimental movie about the making of a movie. It lay buried until unearthed for a 1991 retrospective of Greaves's films at the Brooklyn Museum. *Symbiopsychotaxiplasm: Take One* was a bold experiment: an exploration of film, film technique, and the film-making process (the role of the director as well as actors and crew). It acquired a new following for Greaves.

A disturbing and powerful film, ingeniously shot by cinematographer Lisa Rinzler, was Allen and Albert Hughes's (twenty-one-year-old twins) *Menace II Society* (1993). From the opening with the killing of two Korean grocers by a Watts teenager, to its violent, bloody shootout, *Menace II Society* was a harrowing, graphic nihilistic depiction of stunted teenage lives. Influenced by directors such as Martin Scorsese and Brian De Palma, the Hughes brothers created an innovative film: a fast free-flowing stream of surprising camera angles, voice-overs, rapid edits, and naturalistic performances. Later the Hughes brothers filmed *Dead Presidents* (1995), a well-directed, often gripping drama tracing the life of a young African American man (Larenz Tate) from his youth in the Bronx in the 1960s through his experiences in Vietnam to his return to the States—and what he then sees as an existence that leads him nowhere, which in turn leads him to bank heist. Michael Henry Brown's screenplay veered toward the obvious and sometimes the heavy-handed. But no one could fault the film's direction—or the actors Tate and N' Bushe Wright. Afterwards, the Hughes brothers directed the documentary *American Pimp* (2000) and the feature *From Hell* (2001) starring Johnny Depp.

Other films by new directors included cinematographer Ernest Dickerson's urban drama *Juice* (1992)—which featured such new young actors as Tupac Shakur and Omar Epps—and *Surviving the Game* (1994) with Ice-T; Haile Gerima's allegorical *Sankofa* (1993); television director and producer Thomas Carter's Nazi-era drama *Swing Kids* (1993), his Eddie Murphy-starrer *Metro* (1997), and later his surprise hit *Save the Last Dance* (2001); Rusty Cundieff's rap-world sendup *Fear of a Black Hat* (1994) and later the disappointing comedy *Sprung* (1997). Television star Tim Reid's deeply felt coming of age story, *Once upon a Time When We Were Colored* (1996), was set in the Mississippi Delta from 1946 to the 1960s with such stars as Al Freeman, Jr. (who gives a stellar performance), Richard Roundtree, Phylicia Rashad, and Paula Kelly. A former child actor, Kevin Hooks directed the comedy *Strictly Business* (1991) and the Wesley Snipes action film *Passenger 57* (1992), which unlike *Predator II* (1992) with Danny Glover did not deracialize its black hero. (Nor significantly did the 1991 *Ricochet* deracialize Denzel Washington's character.) Hooks also directed a jumbled replay of *The Defiant Ones* called *Fled* (1996) with Laurence Fishburne and Stephen Baldwin.

Director F. Gary Gray surprised everyone with his 1995 comedy *Friday*, a raw and raucous look at life for the young in L.A.'s South Central. With a cast that included Ice Cube (who also co-wrote and co-produced), Johnny Witherspoon, Chris Tucker, Nia Long, Tiny Lister, Jr., Anna Maria Horsford, LaWanda Page, Bernie Mac, and Regina King, *Friday* delighted in its bathroom humor and was about as low-down trashy and coarse as you can get. One particularly *memorable* scene featured the perversely engaging Witherspoon actually seated on a toilet—in action—as he laid down the law to his son.

For the most part, the film, lacking any kind of sustained story-line, didn't seem to be going anywhere. Still, like it or not, *Friday* was funny. Mostly younger audiences flocked to see it, no doubt viewing its puerile antics as a sign of youthful rebellion. Yet in an odd unpleasant way, *Friday* also may have appealed to the dopey slob in some older patrons too, even though, upon leaving the theater, they may have felt that they wanted to head for a shower to cleanse themselves. Too much of this kind of thing was like too much alcohol: good for the time but afterwards leaving you with a lot of dead brain cells. Later a sequel *Next Friday* (2000)—directed by Steven Carr with a script by Ice Cube and mainly populated by sexually hungry or vengeful women and a rowdy batch of roustabout men—tried but fortunately failed at re-creating the previous crude magic. Nonetheless, the original *Friday*'s success afforded director Gray the chance to work on other projects like the film *Set It Off* (1996). And *Friday*'s star Ice Cube (born O'Shea Jackson and previously best known to moviegoers as a star of *Boyz N the Hood*) later directed *The Player's Club* (1998), and appeared in the films *Anaconda* (1997), *Dangerous Ground* (1997), and *Three Kings* (1999).

Other directors appeared later in the decade. Targeting a young hip hop audience, former video director Michael Martin directed rap star/producer Master P, along with Ice Cube, Helen Martin, and Snoop Doggy Dogg, in the comedy *I Got the Hook Up* (1998). Another video director, Hype Williams, directed the gangsta tale *Belly* (1998). Christopher Scott Cherot wrote, directed, and edited the offbeat comedy *Hav Plenty* (1998). And Antoine Fuqua's *Replacement Killers* (1998) marked the American debut of Chinese action star Chow Yun-Fat. Though the film received lukewarm reviews, *The Replacement Killers* indicated a new direction for a black filmmaker. Not only was Fuqua hoping to reach a large general American audience (rather than a specific African American one) but also to tap the huge international market. He later directed Denzel Washington in *Training Day* (2001).

Also arriving on the directorial scene was Malcolm Lee (the younger cousin of Spike Lee), who directed the new-generation-style battle-of-the-sexes comedy *The Best Man* (1999). Featuring such actors as Morris Chesnut, Taye Diggs, Nia Long, Sanaa Lathan, and the actor who walks away with the picture, Terrence Howard, *The Best Man* tapped a young, educated audience by focusing on young black professionals. Most of the characters have dream jobs. One is a professional athlete. Another is a television producer. Another is a writer whose novel has just been published. Fifteen years earlier, these characters might have seemed implausible for a popular black film. But Lee's characters, faced here with personal problems rather than gnawing racial ones, clearly reflect a change in American society and the makeup of the new black bourgeoisie. In the late 1990s, their professions are wholly believable—and often refreshing. *The Best Man* was a box-office hit that opened as the nation's number-one film, quite an achievement for a first-time feature director. There also appeared such other young black relationship comedy/ dramas as Rick Famuyiwa's *The Wood* (1999), Kwyn Bader's *Loving Jezebel* (2000), and Gary Hardwick's *The Brothers* (2001). But perhaps the great surprise for the industry was Keenen Ivory Wayans *Scary Movie* (2000), a spoof of youth-oriented horror films that starred Shawn and Marlon Wayans. Though technically not a black film and promoted to publicize its "multicultural cast," *Scary Movie* grossed $150 million, becoming the most successful movie ever directed by an African American filmmaker. (Poitier's *Stir Crazy*, having grossed $101 million, previously held that position.) Wayans then filmed a sequel *Scary Movie 2* (2001).

Throughout the decade, white filmmakers also worked with the race theme with varying results. Steve Anderson's lugubrious *South Central* (1992) had little to recommend it other than Glenn Plummer's performance. Newcomer Anthony Drazen's overrated *Zebrahead* (1992) and Jonathan Kaplan's *Love Field* (1992), with Michelle Pfeiffer and Dennis Haysbert, focused on interracial relationships. *Cool Runnings* (1993) was a relaxed look at a Jamaican bobsled team, directed by Jon Turtel Taub, and starring Doug E. Doug. Also trying for a light touch but with dismal offensive results was the sports "comedy" set in Africa *The Air up There* (1993). Tamra Davis directed the gangsta rap satire *CB4* (1993) with Chris Rock while MTV's Ed Lover and Dr. Dre appeared with Queen Latifah and Kriss Kross in Ted Demme's bumbling *Who's the Man* (1993). Damon Wayans starred in, wrote, and executive-produced the excruciatingly dim comedy *Mo' Money* (1992), directed by Peter Macdonald. Based on John Guare's play (inspired by a true story), Fred Schiespi's *Six Degrees of Separation* (1993) told the story of a young man (Will Smith) who cons an affluent white New York couple into believing he is the son of Sidney Poitier. Jeff Pollack's basketball drama *Above the Rim* (1994) starred Duane Martin, Tupac Shukur, and Tonya Pinkins, with a script by Barry Michael Cooper. Boaz Yakin's disturbing *Fresh* (1994) featured Sean Nelson as a 12-year-old school kid who is also a drug runner. Neil Jordan's *The Crying Game* (1992) also explored the question of identity and gender with the seductive character Dil (Jaye Davidson), but avoided any examination of the character's cultural bearings. Marc Levin's lopsided *Slam* (1998) celebrated the beauty and restorative power of (black) poetry.

The same might be said of artist Julian Schnabel's *Basquiat* (1996), a partly fictionalized dramatization of the life of young black artist Jean-Michel Basquiat. Growing up in Brooklyn (the son of a Haitian father and a Puerto Rican mother), Basquiat began his career as a graffiti artist known as Samo. Later he switched to oil on canvas (as well as windows and doors) to become a highly praised and glittering presence on the New York art scene in the 1980s. But his meteoric rise ended in a tragic death at age twenty-seven from a heroin overdose in 1988. Starring Jeffrey Wright as Basquiat and with David Bowie as an appropriately pale Andy Warhol, *Basquiat* succeeded best in its evocation of the New York art scene. The drives and demons of the restless, complicated Basquiat remained a mystery.

British director Mike Leigh's *Secrets and Lies* (1996) focused on a white middle-aged working-class woman (the terrific Brenda Blethyn) who is reunited with the adult daughter that she had given up for adoption years earlier. The young woman was fathered by a black man. Audiences responded to Leigh's great feeling for his characters, and Blethyn was hard to resist as a woman coming to grips with her past—and her family. But *Secrets and Lies* doesn't offer much insight into the daughter's life. When mother and daughter meet, you wait for some knockout perceptive comment on race and culture. That doesn't happen. For her performance as the daughter, Marianne Jean-Baptiste nonetheless won a Best Supporting Oscar nomination.

On the other hand, James Toback's *Black and White* (1999) was *all* about race and culture. Here the director of *Fingers*, who had been so drawn to Jim Brown in the early 1970s, turns his camera to the fascination of young white America with African American culture, in this case hip hop. His cast included professional actors like Joe Pantoliano, Jared Leto, Brooke Shields, and Robert Downey, Jr., as well as such nonprofessionals as basketball star Allan Houston, music star Power of Wu-Tang Clan, Method Man, and Mike Tyson. Nothing was satisfactorily worked out. Toback still viewed black males through a distorted lens: as super-powerful and sexual, violent supermen. Yet the film was often compelling, especially a scene in which Robert Downey, Jr.'s, gay character makes a pass at Tyson. "I had a dream about you," says Downey. The mayhem that follows was apparently *not* scripted. It's a classic high point for the film. Race relations also were explored in David Gordon Green's *George Washington* (2000). Both *Black and White* and *George Washington* offered far more challenging thoughts on race than the standard buddy films like *Finding Forrester* (2000) or the anachronistic *The Legend of Bagger Vance* (2000).

As one of the decade's most publicized films, Steven Spielberg's $75 million dollar production *Amistad* in 1997 drew some heated criticism and controversy. Based on the true story of the 1839 rebellion of 53 West Africans on the Spanish slave ship *La Amistad* (which ironically means *Friendship*) and the trial of the Africans that went to the Supreme Court, Spielberg's drama was an earnest, well-intentioned attempt at exploring some of the brutalities of slavery (there is a horrifying slave-ship sequence)—and also the political as well as moral issues of the case. *Amistad's* controversy swirled from black writer Barbara Chase-Riboud's claim that the film plagiarized her 1989 historical novel *Echoes of Lions. Amistad's* criticism came mostly because of its point of view. Rather than focus on the slaves themselves, the film was quick to record the valiant efforts of a white attorney (Matthew McConaughey, bespectacled and miscast) as well as those of former president of the United States, John Quincy Adams (Anthony Hopkins), to free the men. Though Morgan Freeman played a free-thinking abolitionist, the film gave him little to do. Too often he just seemed to be hanging around. As the leader of the revolt Cinque (whose African name was Sengbe Pieh), Djimon Hounsou was a striking presence: strong, virile, quick to take action. But David Franzoni's script never reveals the depth of torment of this Sierre Leone rice farmer—a husband and a father—who had been kidnapped and thrown into chains. In its attempt at a bonding theme, even here in the supposed re-creation of a real historical drama, a meeting occurs between Hopkins's Adams and Hounsou's Cinque. There is no historical evidence that any such meeting ever transpired. Though one may applaud Spielberg for making the film (clearly, the studios were not going to finance such a multimillion dollar production for an African American filmmaker), *Amistad* lacked drama and excitement.

Carl Franklin: Film Noir from Another Point of View

Of the new directors of the mid- and later-1990s, Carl Franklin proved to be one of the most interesting and perhaps most stylish. Early in the decade, he impressed the critics with his independently produced *One False Move* (1992). The movie came at a crucial time in the director's life. The son of a brick mason who died just before Franklin was born, and a mother who worked as a cleaning woman until she was partially blinded by a laundry solution, he had spent his formative years in Richmond, California, some twelve miles from San Francisco. In the 1960s, he studied at the University of California at Berkeley with plans to become a teacher or lawyer. But after a teacher persuaded him to appear in a production of August Strindberg's *Miss Julie*, Franklin decided to become an actor. In 1971 he moved to New York, where he appeared in minor roles in *Cymbeline* and *Timon of Athens* in Joseph Papp's Shakespeare in the Park series, as well as in plays at Lincoln Center and the Arena Stage in Washington, D.C.

Once back in California, he found work in such television series as "The A-Team," "Caribe," "Fantastic Journey," and "McClain's Law." By the mid-1980s, he felt he was at loose ends. His acting career hadn't gone where he wanted. He was the father of two children. His first marriage had ended in divorce. A second marriage was headed in the same direction. In 1986, he applied to the American Film Institute to study writing and directing. Though he directed a film for low-budget producer Roger Corman, Franklin preferred never to discuss the film in interviews. (Could the experience—or the film—have been *that* bad?) The thriller *One False Move*, however, won the attention that enabled him to continue his directing career.

Then came his big 1995 Hollywood feature *Devil in a Blue Dress*, based on a 1990 novel by African American writer Walter Mosley. Set in black Los Angeles in 1948, *Devil in a Blue Dress* starred Denzel Washington as Easy Rawlins, a veteran of World War II, who has moved from Texas to Los Angeles. There he works as an aircraft mechanic and settles into a nice little home, thanks to the G.I. Bill. But after losing his job and fearful he won't be able to make his mortgage payments, Easy accepts an offer by a white man named DeWitt Albright (Tom Sizemore) to track down—for the fee of $100—the white socialite girlfriend of a local politician. The woman, Daphne Monet, is known to prefer the company of black men. Easy realizes he has been hired mainly because he is black and therefore has an entree into a world his employer does not. But because he's not a professional investigator and is unfamiliar with the various psychological back alleys that must be traversed, he has to learn on the job, and we can see his fears and his courage as he is drawn into a web of intrigue, blackmail, scandal, and betrayal.

Part old-style film noir—with the paranoia, corruption, and complicated story line that one anticipates in films of the 1940s as well as the novels of James M. Cain and Raymond Chandler—*Devil in a Blue Dress* had a distinct new twist: this time everything comes from the point of view of an African American man. In a very offhand way, Easy is aware of racial politics at every turn, just as most African Americans of this period were, so much so that he doesn't have to discuss it: or be surprised by it. A cautious man when around whites, Easy understands that the helpful and solicitous DeWitt Albright—if displeased about anything—can withdraw his "tolerance" and turn nasty and brutal while comfortably receding into an ugly protective whiteness. Even the secret that the mysterious Daphne Monet hides is something Easy can comprehend: she is not a white woman at all but a black woman who is passing for white.

In some respects, *Devil in a Blue Dress* spins a tale of the old-type tragic mulatto. Yet director Franklin, who also wrote the script, attempts to explain why Daphne has chosen the path that leads her across the color line. As played by Jennifer Beals (so appealing in *Flashdance*), Daphne, however, lacks fire and a genuine mysterious allure. Surprisingly, in their big scene together, Washington and Beals don't set sparks flying. It's rather tepid and glaringly unsexy. Because the characters don't become sexually involved (as they do in the novel), the movie lacks a key ingredient that might have given it the kind of dangerous sensual kick of so many past *noir* dramas. Author Walter Mosley told *The New York Times* (on September 9, 1995), that when he learned that the browner Washington could not kiss the lighter-skinned Beals because of the studio's fear that the picture would then "lose Alabama," he simply thought, "Maybe Denzel could *think* about kissing her. He's a good actor." But even such thoughts don't appear to be on the actor's mind.

Devil in a Blue Dress succeeded though as taut, evocative, stylish storytelling. Director Franklin told *The New York Post* (on September 25, 1995) that he sought "a fusion of film noir and social realism." The backdrop for the story—a vivid re-creation of post-War Los Angeles—is as memorable as the story itself. No Jim Crow signs appear. But Franklin never lets his audience forget this is still a segregated city. Nor does he let go unnoticed the vitality of the hub of Black L.A. in the 1930s and 1940s, Central Avenue: that throbbing street with its clubs, nightspots, and shops that rivaled Harlem's; the street that signaled a whole separate cultural identity for African Americans on the West Coast. Shot by cinematographer Tak Fujimoto with a score by Elmer Bernstein, this is L.A. at a time of high energy and optimism, a city that's a far cry from the despairing, burnt-out images of South Central of later decades. In this setting, Denzel Washington gave one of his strongest performances. We can see his mind at work, and we really do observe the world from his point of view. Also on hand was Don Cheadle as Easy's trigger-happy Texas buddy Mouse.

Though praised by the critics, *Devil in a Blue Dress* was not a great box-office success, leading some industry observers to the conclusion that audiences were not interested in period dramas—or black films with more serious themes. Actually, *Devil in a Blue Dress* might have benefited from a different type of promotional campaign. Perhaps its studio should have opened the film "small" at a select group of theaters—and then let word of mouth lead a broader audience eventually to "find" the picture. Nonetheless, *Devil in a Blue Dress* remains in a class by itself as one of the more unusual and absorbing black films of the 1990s. Afterwards, Carl Franklin directed the family drama *One True Thing* (1998) with a white cast that included Meryl Streep, William Hurt, and Renee Zellweger. At this point in his career, Franklin may have realized that a key to survival for black filmmakers—in a Hollywood not eager for more adult black films—was to be known as capable of handling any kind of production. (No doubt Antoine Fuqua felt the same way.) White directors—for decades—had been free to direct black films; so black directors should be considered eligible to helm non-black productions as well.

Actresses in Search of Roles

For African American actresses, the era, like most of the 1980s, was not the best of times. Among the new actresses were Joie Lee (unusual, underrated and underused),

Tisha Campbell (*House Party; Boomerang; Another 48 Hrs*, 1990); Robin Givens (who gave great suggestions of movie queen hauteur in *A Rage in Harlem*, 1991; and *Boomerang*); Sheryl Lee Ralph (*Mistress; The Distinguished Gentleman*, 1992; *To Sleep with Anger*); Theresa Randle (*King of New York; The Five Heartbeats; Malcolm X; Sugar Hill; Beverly Hills Cop III*, 1994); Cynda Williams (glamorous and larger than life in *Mo' Better Blues* and *One False Move*); Thandie Newton (*Jefferson in Paris*, 1995, as Sally Hemings; *Besieged*, 1998; *Gridlook'd*, 1997; and Tom Cruise's leading lady in *Mission: Impossible 2*, 2000); and Tyra Ferrell (who played women of various ages, classes, and moods in *Jungle Fever, Boyz N the Hood*, and *Poetic Justice*). Younger actresses such as Nia Long (*Boiler Room*, 2000; *The Broken Hearts Club—A Romantic Comedy*, 2000; *Big Momma's House*, 2000; and *The Best Man*, 1999) and Regina King (*Enemy of the State*, 1998, and *Down to Earth*, 2001) appeared in important films. Vanessa Williams—who became known as Vanessa L. Williams—also costarred in *Eraser* (1996), *Hoodlum*, and the remake of *Shaft*. Newcomer singing star/actress Aaliyah—the female lead in *Romeo Must Die* (2000) and signed to appear in *The Matrix* sequels—looked as if she were destined for stardom until her death at age 22 in an airplane crash in 2001. Halle Berry appeared in *Boomerang, Strictly Business, Jungle Fever* (as the spaced-out-junkie), *The Flinstones* (1994), *Losing Isaiah* (1995), *The Rich Man's Wife* (1996), *B*A*P*S*, and *X-Men* (2000). Her topless scene in *Swordfish* (2001) drew outcries that she had permitted herself to be exploited. Though she garnered great media coverage, few believed she possessed true *movie star* power. Then came the controversial *Monster's Ball* in 2001. Many Black moviegoers found the film's images disturbing. But Berry gave a fine and moving performance—as an emotionally adrift woman who has lost her husband and son.

For a spell, the actress taken most seriously by the critics was Alfre Woodard. Woodard had grown up the youngest of three children in Tulsa, Oklahoma. At fifteen, she decided to become an actress. After graduating from Boston University, she moved to Los Angeles. Spotted by director Robert Altman in a production of *for colored girls who have considered suicide when the rainbow is enuf*, she appeared in the Altman-directed *Health* (1979) and the Altman-produced *Remember My Name* (1978).

After her Oscar nomination for *Cross Creek* and her appearance in *Extremities*, film work came in bits and drabs: *Scrooged* (1988), *Miss Firecracker* (1989), *Grand Canyon, Rich in Love* (1992), *Bopha!*, and *Heart and Souls* (1993).

Although sometimes compared to Cicely Tyson (perhaps mainly because both were dark black women who played dramatic roles), Woodard's characters were without the mythic power or bravura intensity of Tyson's important heroines. Often there was something mildly offbeat or vaguely out-of-kilter about Woodard's women, perhaps because of her voice, her manner, and her unusual line readings. Nonetheless it was refreshing to see Woodard (her basic look was a statement unto itself) even if one was not always sure what she was trying to do with a character.

An important role came in John Sayle's *Passion Fish* (1992). In this story, a white soap opera actress May-Alice (Mary McDonnell) returns to her deserted family home in Louisiana after an accident has left her paralyzed. Woodard plays the nurse Chantelle, who must contend with the woman's heavy drinking and sharp tongue. It is a test of wills that unsurprisingly ends with the women developing a friendship.

Although *Passion Fish* was one of the few movies to reflect on the lives of women (which accounts for the fact that many people liked it), the film did not venture far from traditional images of African Americans. Why does such a fantasy—black women as nurturing, caretaking marvels at helping poor white women untangle the knots in their lives—linger on, even in the mind of a contemporary independent filmmaker?

When it is revealed that the black woman is a former drug addict (whose young daughter who has been in the custody of Chantelle's rigid father in Chicago), we also ask: why couldn't she have had another problem, besides the old drug-addict routine? (It's almost enough to drive you to drink!) Then too the black male characters are not developed with much thought or insight. When Chantelle's former lover from Chicago has a talk with May-Alice, it is an unnecessary and gratuitously "threatening" sequence. Even Chantelle's Louisiana love interest, a black cowboy named Sugar LeDoux (Vondie Curtis-Hall), is depicted as a ladies' man with an assortment of children. Both characters carry with them the *suggestion* of African American male irresponsibility.

One scene, however, is surprising. Among a group of May-Alice's soap opera friends who visit Louisiana is a black actress, played by Angela Bassett. When she has a few private moments with Chantelle, we fear the worst, that these two "sisters" will be antagonists.

But Sayles brings warmth to their meeting. Seeing Bassett and Woodard together (Bassett is far better in these few minutes than in some of her larger roles), one knows that *Passion Fish* might really have been daring and an unusual comment on race and class had the story been about these black women rather than Chantelle and the white lady in the Big House.

Woodard also appeared in *Blue Chips* (1994) and *Crooklyn*. She scored well later when she starred in the Maya Angelou-directed *Down in the Delta*. Here she gave a spirited performance as a single mother coming to know herself on a trip South.

Waiting to Exhale: Reaching the Black Female Audience

Briefly, a shift in the tide for African American actresses came with the 1995 release of *Waiting to Exhale*. Based on African American writer Terry McMillan's 1992 best-selling novel and directed by Forest Whitaker from a script by McMillan and Ronald Bass (who had scripted *Rain Man*, 1988, and *The Joy Luck Club*, 1993), *Waiting to Exhale* centered on the lives and romantic tensions of four young African American women. There is Savannah (Whitney Houston) who while searching for Mr. Right is advised by her mother that the best thing to do is to wait for her married lover to get his divorce (some advice!). There is Bernadine (Angela Bassett) whose husband tells her on New Year's Eve that he's leaving her for another woman; as it turns out, the other woman is white. (That doesn't sit too well with Bernadine.) There is the full-figured hairdresser Gloria (Loretta Devine), who while rearing her teenage son hopes for a reconciliation with her former husband. But she gives up all such hopes when she learns that he is gay. There is the voluptuous Robin (Lela Rochon), so man-hungry that she leads herself into a series of humiliating situations. Each is holding her breath, hoping for a dramatic change in her life when love will work out and men won't be such heels. But whereas the novel reverberated on some earthy dialogue and throughout grounded its women with the signs and symbols of modern-day life (the music they listen to, the movies and television they view, the celebrities they refer to) so that the reader understood, at least in pop terms, the social dynamics and the culture under which the women lived, the film often seemed locked inside something of a cultural vacuum. (In the novel, readers also had a better sense of the characters as working women.) Featured on the soundtrack by Kenneth (Babyface) Edmonds were such recording artists as Houston, Chaka Kahn, Toni Braxton, and the great Aretha Franklin (singing "It Hurts like Hell"), which may have added to the film's appeal. Forest Whitaker's direction, however, was, at best, bland.

Having previously directed the 1993 HBO drama "Strapped" with a feral grittiness, Whitaker seemed to do everything here in a laid-back L.A. style. Rather than smoothly pulling together the individual stories into a coherent flowing narrative, *Waiting to Exhale* remained a series of vignettes. Missing was an awareness of what really drove the women individually—and what held them together as friends. Too many of the scenes just *sat* without much really dramatic ever happening. For too long, audiences (those who had not read the book and perhaps even many who had) may have wondered when the movie would really get started. Even the Phoenix setting didn't have anything distinct about it. For some unfathomable reason, Whitaker, because of this film, acquired a reputation as being a woman's picture director (in the tradition of George Cukor). But such talk seemed grossly inflated, at the least. Ultimately, what Whitaker may have done best was to create a relaxed, sensitized working environment (on the set) that helped the actresses develop interesting and sometimes vivid characterizations. He did, however, follow up *Waiting to Exhale* with *Hope Floats* (1998), a nonblack film starring Sandra Bullock that had some pleasant moments.

Waiting to Exhale, which marked a return of the popular black woman's film, with Loretta Devine, Whitney Houston, Angela Bassett, and Lela Rochon.

The actresses, however, gave *Waiting to Exhale* some style and vitality and at odd moments a sweet sensitivity. Investing her character Bernadine with anger and a sense of true outrage at her husband's betrayal, Angela Bassett, at one point, empties his closet, throws all his clothes into his sparkling BMW, and then triumphantly sets it afire. It was no doubt the film's most memorable scene—and perhaps its most inauthentic. The sequence is sheer theater. Yet because Bassett's tough assurance—in her eyes and her walk—snapped audiences to attention, the sequence lent the picture some semblance of structure and dramatic mood.

As Gloria, Loretta Devine worked wonders with what could easily have been an old-style stereotype: the hefty, brown-skinned nurturing black woman. But Devine moves as far away as possible from the mammy figure. Much like Ethel Waters in her cabaret sequence in *Cabin in the Sky*—when she kicked up her legs and shook her hips and struck a pose like those of her blues singing days when she was called Sweet Mama Stringbean—Devine showed there was life in those broad hips. In a sequence when she walks away from Gregory Hines (whom she hopes will become a new man in her life), she swings her backside with both abandon and control. Like Waters again in that cabaret sequence, Devine called a lie to the notion that a heavier, dark woman can't be sexy. She also expressed a vulnerability that darker women in the movies generally weren't supposed to have.

In such past films as *Harlem Nights* and *Boomerang*, Lela Rochon had seemed so much a fantasy come-on, so much a dreamy sex kitten, without much else going on, that audiences may have felt she was a dizzy broad and nothing more. They also may have felt she was being exploited. But her Robin—still sexy and *realistically* dreamy—was at times poignant and emotionally affecting. When she finds herself on a date with a heavyset fellow who doesn't seem fit to even be in her presence, she's desperate to please even at the expense of her self-respect. During such moments, as we sense the yearning and some of the possible torment inside, Rochon is reminiscent of the characters that Marilyn Monroe struggled to create.

As the most famous of all the actresses, pop star Whitney Houston might have easily overshadowed the other women and the film itself simply because of her star power and the audience's knowledge of her. (*Or* she might have been upstaged by those more experienced actresses with a long list of credits behind them.) But Houston scaled herself down without losing her identity to work well within this ensemble group. She appears to respect the talents of her co-stars. She also appears not to want to make any mistakes. The cool distance she maintains works well for her character Savannah. And like Rochon and Devine, she has a vulnerability that is never far from the surface. Though she doesn't fully give into that vulnerability, you see it, and it makes her an interesting screen presence.

Most reviewers didn't like the film. In *The New Yorker*, Anthony Lane noted, "Some of the performances aren't bad—Whitney Houston calms the camera down with her dreamy, just-waked up look and Wesley Snipes puts in a solid (and uncredited) appearance as one of the movie's many errant husbands—but the film has no basic rhythm they can hook up to." Yet Lane, like other critics, saw something else, which proved more important: *the audience*, which disregarded the critics and turned *Waiting to Exhale* into a hit. "I saw *Waiting to Exhale* in a full theater," wrote Lane. "Their pleasure was full-throated and sincere, and it threw me. I am used to reading movies wrong, but with this one I felt for the first time that I was speaking another language altogether. What I saw as dumb visual grammar and blatant emotional rhetoric was part of someone else's lingua franca. If the divide were purely racial—if the movie were fencing off different areas of sensibility for whites and blacks, with each side baffled by the other's reacting—then we would have something to worry about. But the disagreement is rather more entertaining than that: a lot of women, black and white, seem to love this picture."

Even *love* might be an understatement. Despite the fact that it was based on a huge best-selling novel, the film had been shot on a relatively small budget of $14 million because the studio had doubts about its box-office appeal. Those studio executives were proved wrong. *Waiting to Exhale* became something of a cultural phenomenon. The media reported on the large turnout of African American women who saw the film with friends—and who saw the film several times, turning the viewings into uninhibited pop communal experiences. Often they spoke back to the action on screen, so much so that, as Rebecca Ascher-Walsh reported in the January 19, 1996, issue of *Entertainment Weekly*, "At some showings, it's amazing they can hear any of it." *Exhale* producer Deborah Schindler told the magazine, "I've heard from several theater managers that people are going back because they couldn't hear all the dialogue." Whether it really answered audience needs or simply touched on them, *Waiting to Exhale*'s success nonetheless clearly indicated there was an audience for the black woman's film; something that at least acknowledged the concerns and conflicts of African American women—just as movies such as *Lady Sings the Blues* and *Mahogany* had done in the 1970s and *The Color Purple* in the 1980s, although the issue of *contemporary* relationships with men was now boldly placed front and center. "This audience, for the first time in history," wrote *Entertainment Weekly*, "is African-American women, who, after years of seeing downbeat hood films, have welcomed a glossy portrait of their middle-and upper-middle-class lives (and have enjoyed some pot-shots at the men who make their days difficult)."

Though *Waiting to Exhale* opened as the number-one movie in the country and went on to gross over $70 million, the actresses who brought the movie to life found that afterwards their film careers had mixed results. Loretta Devine worked in supporting roles in such films as *The Preacher's Wife* (1996), *What Women Want* (2000), and *Kingdom Come*. No doubt Lela Rochon had hopes that her role in *The Chamber* (1996) might give her career another boost. But the film failed at the box office, and Rochon seemed miscast. Later in Oliver Stone's *Any Given Sunday*

(1999), she turned in an affecting performance as the love interest of a professional football player; a woman who finds herself too often relegated to the sidelines of this life.

Angela Bassett: Still Holding Her Breath

Most audiences assumed that Angela Bassett's career would now be on solid footing. Bassett had grown up in St. Petersburg, Florida. "Single-parent family, welfare, same song, second verse," she told *The New York Times* on January 29, 2000, indicating that she had discussed the matter perhaps too many times before and didn't feel compelled to discuss it further. After graduating from the Yale Drama School, she said that when performing at the Hartford Stage Company she was cast as "every woman in the Bible: Mary, Eve, Noah's wife opposite five guys." In New York City, she played Antigone off-Broadway and later appeared on Broadway in August Wilson's *Joe Turner's Come and Gone*. She also began working in television and films.

Angela Bassett fared well with her portrayals of the real-life women Betty Shabazz (in *Malcolm X*), Katherine Jackson (on TV's "The Jacksons"), and most importantly, Tina Turner in *What's Love Got to Do with It* (1993). With Bassett as his star, director Brian Gibson turned *What's Love Got to Do with It*—based on Tina Turner's autobiography *I, Tina*—into a surprisingly rousing, postfeminist woman's picture (which males enjoyed too) that centered on a once-battered woman who picks up the pieces and triumphs. *What's Love Got to Do with It* ended with a blazing appearance by the real Tina Turner, which made the script's inadequacies—in explaining the character's passivity and drives—seem almost irrelevant: patrons left the theater on an emotional high. As Turner, Bassett won a Golden Globe Award and an Oscar nomination as Best Actress by accomplishing a difficult task: she established her own screen identity while playing a woman known to millions.

Following her performance in *What's Love Got to Do with It*, she co-starred with Eddie Murphy in Wes Craven's rather flat *Vampire in Brooklyn* (1995). In Kathryn Bigelow's futuristic drama *Strange Days* (1995), Bassett proved to be supremely confident and assertive opposite British actor Ralph Fiennes. Though the depiction of the interracial Bassett/Fiennes relationship wasn't as emotionally detached as that of Dorothy Dandridge and John Justin in *Island in the Sun*, *Strange Days* still didn't appear at ease in defining what drew the two together. But African American viewers probably preferred seeing her in that picture, in which she at least had a starring role, than in *Contact* (1997) in which she had a supporting one.

In some respects, Bassett's screen persona was strangely reminiscent of Joan Crawford's (during Crawford's middle years): even when she tried to play it soft and vulnerable, she still had hard edges; basically, she seemed like a tough cookie who couldn't be trifled with. Like Crawford, Bassett at times also seemed too intense, overworking her eyes and her mouth, becoming a tad too broad and theatrical and *actressy*, at times almost too *dramatic*. Like Crawford, Bassett also had an underlayer of anger, which could be read as the result of a restlessness that sprang from her awareness of her position in the industry; the fact that she may have felt she still had to prove herself and had to fight ten times harder than anybody else just to stay in place in Hollywood. (Actress Nia Long had a similar kind of anger. But hers wasn't on the mature, womanly scale of Bassett's.) Actresses such as Devine and Rochon were able, when the movie roles didn't come, to work well in television. But though Bassett also appeared on television, she often seemed too big for the tube, too strong, too charismatic, too *movie-starish*, too explosive a presence.

Later Bassett had a plum role as the star of the movie version of another Terry McMillan novel, *How Stella Got Her Groove Back* (1998), directed by Kevin Rodney Sullivan. As a successful 40-year-old divorced stockbroker in San Francisco, with a son to rear and without romance in her life, Bassett's Stella goes with a friend (Whoopi Goldberg) to Jamaica. There she has a love affair with a young medical student (Taye Diggs) who is half her age. Afterwards, as she deals with the reactions of family and friends, she must decide if she will dismiss the relationship as just a holiday fling or if she will let the young man become a part of her life. Though this kind of story had been told before in mainstream movies with white actresses, it was new for African American women to see a black woman in a film making such a choice. Bassett appeared in such other films as *Music of the Heart* (1999, in a supporting role), the sci-fi *Supernova* (2000), the adaptation of South African playwright Athol Fugard's 1969 drama *Boesman and Lena* (2000) opposite Danny Glover, and *The Score* (2001) with Robert DeNiro and Marlon Brando. But she still had to search for roles. Nothing came easy for her in Hollywood.

Whitney Houston: Pop Goddess Turned Movie Star

Of all the *Exhale* actresses, Whitney Houston's film career looked the most promising. Ironically, Houston was already the woman Hollywood believed might become *the* important black dramatic actress, despite the fact that Houston was primarily not an actress but still a major pop star. But the explanation was simple. Her film *The Bodyguard* (1992), a thriller/melodrama with a romance between a black pop star (Houston) and her white bodyguard (Kevin Costner), grossed over $122 million in the United States and $247 million abroad.

Rollin': Laurence Fishburne and Angela Bassett as Ike and Tina Turner in *What's Love Got to Do with It.*

The Bodyguard also lured audiences into theaters with the idea of an interracial romance, yet the subject of race is never discussed in the film. Neither it nor significant cultural differences seem to exist. *The Bodyguard* was really an ideal white male fantasy. Costner is the strong, sensitive fellow always in control, able to protect her when no one else can. When the film has Houston and her sister (Michele Lamar Richards) vying for the bodyguard's attentions—two black women competing for a wannabe white hunk!—one may feel the fantasy has really gotten out of hand.

Houston herself, surprisingly, did a credible job. Wisely, the director, Mick Jackson, understood that in her debut film the pop goddess has to be convincing not as a character but as a personality (something the great cinema stars had always done and not as easy as it sounds). Whether or not she could sustain a credible star persona in future films was open to question. But Houston's glamour and beauty, along with her high-voltage rendition of mega-hit pop tunes on the highly successful soundtrack, helped *The Bodyguard* to soar not only in the States but also in the European market as well.

Because of the international success of *The Bodyguard*, the studios greatly attributed the success of *Waiting to Exhale* to Houston's box-office clout. Though many might argue that point, the industry has always had its own way of evaluating the appeal of a film. Following *Waiting to Exhale*, Houston began work opposite Denzel Washington on *The Preacher's Wife*, a remake of the 1947 film *The Bishop's Wife*, which had starred Loretta Young, Cary Grant, and David Niven. She also signed a major contract with Disney. Whitney Houston looked as if she could do no wrong. Her recording career continued to soar. Her face adorned the covers of magazines. She also found herself, then and in the years to come, the subject of countless sometimes mean-spirited tabloid stories: rumors swirled about her marriage to performer Bobby Brown; about her other relationships; about her possible drug abuse; about her extravagant spending sprees and her huge entourage. Yet initially, none of these stories appeared to hurt her as a film actress. If anything, the rumors, the stories, the catty innuendoes simply indicated, from an industry perspective, that Houston was an old-style classic kind of star, along the lines of an Elizabeth Taylor *or* a Dorothy Dandridge: a dazzling, larger-than-life goddess, about whom the public seems fascinated.

In the midst of all this attention, Houston, having secured the rights to a new biography of Dorothy Dandridge, announced that she would play the troubled actress in a major movie. This was *the* role that almost all of Hollywood's black actresses wanted to play, everyone from Janet Jackson to Vanessa L. Williams, Lela Rochon, and Halle Berry. A new generation considered Dandridge the one true black female movie star of Hollywood's past; its one great haunting tragic African American star with a story as gripping and powerful as that of Marilyn Monroe, even more so, for while Monroe battled her personal demons as well as the

An interracial romance that made a mint at the box office but avoided any discussion of the issue of race: *The Bodyguard* with the goddess of pop, Whitney Houston, and Kevin Costner.

industry's blatant sexism, Dandridge had to fight the same battles as well as the industry's inherent racism. Houston's detractors felt she was all wrong for the Dandridge role. The griping was similar to that which flared up when it had first been announced that Diana Ross would star as Billie Holiday in *Lady Sings the Blues*. Yet no matter what Houston's critics thought, she had the glamorous presence and the sensuality to pull the part off. Most importantly, as evident from her music, Whitney Houston had the emotional depth the role required. This proved to be an important moment in her career—and in the history of Hollywood. No other African American actress before Houston, not even Whoopi Goldberg during her brief period as the highest paid woman in films, was viewed by the studios as a genuine box-office mega-star. In the mid- and late-1990s, Whitney Houston was the only African American actress whom the studios were willing to create movies around; to finance almost anything in which she appeared.

But then the situation changed. Directed by Penny Marshall, *The Preacher's Wife*—a fantasy about an angel (Washington) who comes into the lives of a minister and his wife (Houston)—opened to mixed reviews and a sluggish box office. Houston suffered through a series of personal traumas, including a highly publicized miscarriage. She also appeared to vacillate about portraying Dandridge. Was she insecure now about playing so dramatically challenging a role? Eventually, Halle Berry starred in the HBO production "Introducing Dorothy Dandridge." Though the TV film met with success, despite its shortcomings, the fact remained that Dandridge's story should have been told on the big screen. And while the industry did numerous dramatizations of Monroe's life, it evidently believed one Dandridge drama was enough. An announcement also was issued that Houston would star in a big-screen version of the 1970s TV series "Get Christie Love" and also a comedy with Will Smith. But those films never materialized. In the end, she may have stayed off the screen for far too long. Even during the last years of the twentieth century, a film actress still had to make the best of her early years, and once an actress was in her late thirties or early forties, it remained hard for her to maintain film stardom. Houston focused again on her singing career amid an onslaught of new, now often damaging, stories about her in the tabloids. But a great opportunity had been lost—for Houston *and* the movies.

Post-*Exhale* Women

Following *Waiting to Exhale*'s success, one might have expected a steady lineup of films about African American women. Generally, Hollywood operated in cycles. If one type of film pulled in a huge audience, ten more versions of that same type were bound to be produced. That didn't happen. Yet there appeared a scattering of interesting films—some under the direction of African American filmmakers—that centered on African American women.

Friday's director F. Gary Gray came up with another unexpected hit, *Set It Off*. This heist drama focused on a quartet of young African American women who have grown up together in a Los Angeles project. Each finds herself a victim of the system. Frankie (Vivica A. Fox), a bank employee, has unfairly lost her job. The sad-eyed Stony (Jada Pinkett) mourns the death of her law-abiding brother who has been killed by policemen in a case of mistaken identity. The fragile Tisean (Kimberly Elise)—a single parent—loses her son to the child-welfare system. And the rowdy pot-smoking lesbian Cleo (Queen Latifah) has been fighting, so we believe, the system all her life. Feeling trapped yet refusing to let themselves be written off as victims and determined to turn their lives around, these emotionally bruised women—seeing money as the way out and up—successfully pull off a bank robbery. Afterwards, intoxicated by this brand of audacious self-assertion, the women continue on a bank robbing spree that ultimately leads to tragedy for all but one.

Within what was traditionally considered a male genre, *Set It Off*'s writers Takashi Bufford (*House Party 3*) and Kate Lanier (*What's Love Got to Do with It*) managed to incorporate a woman's-picture theme. Sometimes the attempts to recontextualize the story from a woman's viewpoint fall flat. A subplot centering on a romance between Stony and a Harvard-educated buppie lawyer (Blair Underwood) seemed fake and merely slowed down the story. The sequences intended to dramatize Tisean's motherhood woes lacked fire and resonance. And throughout, the film's heavy-handed efforts to make us sympathetic to the women were almost shamelessly sentimental and hokey. So much about the film was obvious and overstated that it reminded one of certain blaxploitation-era films.

But Gray at least moved the action along at a brisk pace, and he showed respect for his actresses's talents, aware that nothing would work without their commitment to the material. Though Vivica A. Fox proved often—during the decade—to be an actress in need of a director to tell her when to tone it down (when to quit the over-ethnicizing bit) here she seemed on target, capturing the rhythms and the heated anger of a woman fighting to liberate herself. Jada Pinkett also shed her homegrown homegirl persona to create a rather somber heroine who occasionally seemed to spring from the pages of a Joan Didion novel. "*I know what 'nothing' means, and keep on playing.*" The performance is one of Pinkett's better ones, leading the way to her engaging portrayal of Eddie Murphy's love interest in *The Nutty Professor* (1996) and as the conscience-stricken network employee in *Bamboozled*. Pinkett, however, later became better known as the wife of Will Smith and was also later billed as Jada Pinkett Smith.

But the real surprise was Queen Latifah. This hip hop goddess, whose CDs *All Hail the Queen* and *Black Reign* climbed the charts, had previously worked in small or supporting roles. As a waitress who speaks her mind to Wesley Snipes's character about his interracial dating habits in *Jungle Fever*, she no doubt struck audiences as a budding actress yearning to let loose and announce herself on screen. In *Set It Off*, she played Cleo without inhibitions or any fear. Another kind of actress might have held back, concerned that audiences would identify her too closely with her character. Too accurate a portrayal of the lesbian Cleo might cost an actress a chance at other roles or even her career. But Latifah unleashed her vitality and bold sexuality, making her butch Cleo boldly funny and resilient; a take-charge sister who isn't afraid of anything. Though different in style and persona, Latifah's fierce energy resembled that of Rosalind Cash. So did her refusal to tone down her character for fear that the audience might see something ugly or unappealing. Later Latifah appeared in *Living out Loud* (1998) and *The Bone Collector* (1999).

Though hardly complicated or challenging, *Set It Off* touched on the need for films about African American women and became a box-office success that appealed to female *and* male moviegoers. It also put Gray firmly on the director's map. He later directed Samuel L. Jackson in another heated melodrama, *The Negotiator* (1998).

Another film with vivid roles for black actresses was 28-year-old writer/director George Tillman's *Soul Food* (1997). Inspired by childhood Sunday afternoons in Milwaukee where he watched his grandmother, mother, and aunts gossip as they prepared meals, Tillman created a well-textured drama that focused on a large middle-class family that is held together by a strong-willed matriarch (Irma P. Hall). At weekly gatherings over elaborately prepared meals, she watches her three daughters—Vanessa L. Williams, Vivica A. Fox, and Nia Long—wrestle with problems with the men in their lives and with one another. Funny and dramatic by turns, *Soul Food* had a wonderful feel for its characters, especially the young son of one sister, played by Brandon Hammond. Clearly a surrogate for the director, the character observes the tensions, rivalries, and love of the women around him. He also experiences the pain of losing the grandmother who had understood all her children and their conflicts.

The son of a father who was a Chrysler plant worker and a mother who was a nurse, director Tillman had studied at Columbia College in Chicago. His first film—the thirty-minute-long *Paula*—centered on teenaged mothers. Afterwards, his second film *Scenes for the Soul*—three different stories all set in Milwaukee— was not released. Later he struggled to find a studio to produce *Soul Food*. His agent sent the script to singer/songwriter/producer Kenneth (Babyface) Edmonds in hopes that Edmonds might agree to do a soundtrack that in turn might prove helpful in getting the movie financed. Edmonds and his wife Tracey, however, liked the script so much that they put their production company behind it. "But we got turned down everywhere we went," Kenneth Edmonds told *The Los Angeles Times* in their June 14, 1998, edition. Tracey Edmonds recalled that the studios "kept (left to right) Jada Pinkett, Kimberly Elise, Queen Latifah, and Vivica A. Fox in *Set It Off*, a surprise hit that struck a chord with younger audiences.

Soul Food's battling three sisters: Vivica A. Fox, Vanessa L. Williams, and Nia Long.

saying, 'Who's going to go see it?'" Finally, Laura Ziskin, who headed 20th Century-Fox's division Fox 2000, decided to take a chance on it. What clinched the deal was a very low $6.5-million budget and Kenneth Edmonds's agreement, indeed, to produce the soundtrack. By this time, a hot soundtrack had become a powerful marketing tool for films, especially a black one.

Soul Food grossed $43 million on its initial release. Ultimately, it proved successful with the same female audience that Babyface had attracted with his music. "Pop and R&B have always been female driven and that's true back to the days of Motown," said Kenneth Edmonds. "The same women who buy that music are the ones who went to see *Waiting to Exhale* and *Soul Food*." Yet some believed *Soul Food* could have done even better—and reached a larger audience—had its promotion and release been handled in another way. After the film was released, Fox's Ziskin recalled that if the studio had anything to do differently, "it would have been to create TV spots directed at a white audience. The important thing about *Soul Food* wasn't that it was about an African American family, but that it was about a family." When the film was screened for specially selected white audiences, it scored well. Yet, said Ziskin, "We failed to cross over with this movie." Another problem in the late 1990s for a potential black crossover film like *Soul Food* was the narrow range of theaters in which it was booked. "*First Wives Club* was released in 2,000 theaters," Kenneth Edmonds recalled. "But most African American films usually don't play in more than 1,100. So even if Oprah recommends a film, some of the [white] women can't go out to see it because it's not playing in their neighborhood, but some place on the other side of town where they're less likely to go. That's why it's hard for black films to get the big [$100 million] numbers."

Still, *Soul Food* established George Tillman as a mainstream director. Yet a few years later when he was set to direct Cuba Gooding, Jr., in *Men of Honor* (2000)—which told the story of Carl Brashear, the first black diver in the Navy—it, too, had problems finding a studio. Only after Bill Cosby signed on as the executive producer—and was able to get the script to Robert De Niro—did a studio back *Men of Honor*. Interestingly, the completed film not only told Brashear's story but also focused on his relationship with a tough white Navy officer played by De Niro. Apparently, the studio felt Brashear's story would have more appeal if once again the white audience had a major white character with which to identify.

Another feature film with the woman's audience in mind was *Eve's Bayou* (1997), directed by Kasi Lemmons, formerly an actress in such films as *The Silence of the Lambs* (1991), *Fear of a Black Hat*, and *Drop Squad*. Rather than focusing on urban violence, poverty, or discrimination, all themes usually associated with African American filmmakers, Lemmons chose to examine in *Eve's Bayou* a sophisticated, upper-middle-class African American family in the Louisiana bayou in the 1960s. On the surface, the Batiste family seems to live an ideal life. The father is a well-liked doctor (played to perfection by Samuel L. Jackson, who also co-produced the film); the mother (Lynn Whitfield), an attractive and socially adroit hostess. The three children—two daughters and a son—have the expected sibling squabbles and rivalries. But beneath the hanging moss and lush sensual muddy waters of the setting, discontent brews within the family. "Memory is a selection of images," the youngest daughter, Eve, says—in voiceover—at the opening. "Some elusive, others printed indelibly on the brain. . . . We lived in a town named after a slave. It's said that when General Jean-Paul Batiste was stricken with cholera, his life was saved by . . . an African slave called Eve. . . . We are the descendants of Eve." It's a startlingly mysterious moment. Eve also says, "The summer I killed my father, I was ten years old."

The drama unfolds to reveal that the father is a hopeless womanizer; the mother, a tight, distant woman. The older 14-year-old daughter Cisely (Meagan Good) finds herself in a complex and disturbing relationship with her father. And Eve herself (Jurnee Smollett) is so disillusioned by her father's indiscretions that she seeks the help of a conjure woman (Diahann Carroll made up in ghostly white face). Ultimately, the story ends in tragedy.

Part coming-of-age story, part portrait of a family's secrets and evasions, and part melodrama with magical and mystical overtones, *Eve's Bayou* never fully created the complicated characters and situations that would have made it, as one feels at its opening, a bit of a more accessible *Daughters of the Dust*: an intense, poetic portrait of women examining their lives and a film that explores the way culture (and a landscape and setting) can shape one's very sense of self, if not one's destiny. The film can't take us close enough to the doctor for us to understand him. And it never adequately explores what we might believe is partly the reason for his philandering: the marriage to a woman who can't open herself up to him emotionally—or perhaps sexually too. Rather than being glamorously mysterious, the wife is simply a glamorous blank. Instead our attention goes elsewhere, namely to Debbi Morgan's enjoyably energetic and idiosyncratic performance as the physician's sister Mozelle who, having lost three husbands, turns to psychic readings to find answers to the perplexing riddles of other women's lives. Still, *Eve's Bayou* was beautifully shot on location by cinematographer Amy Vincent (with a striking computer-enhanced black-and-white dream sequence), and director Lemmons had the power to cast a spell over her audience. *Eve's Bayou* was the kind of film you might want to view more than once to luxuriate in its *dreamy romanticism* and psychic portents—and, oddly enough, to become pleasurably lost in the film's inability (and struggle) to articulate the mystery of familial ties and disappointments that you yearn for it to uncover. Later Lemmons directed *The Caveman's Valentine* (2001), also starring and co-executive produced by Samuel L. Jackson.

Women were also prominently featured in Gregory Nava's *Why Do Fools Fall in Love* (1998), which purportedly dramatized the life of 1950s music star Frankie

Lymon (played by Larenz Tate). The experiences of the troubled and drug-addicted Lymon (who died in 1968 from a drug overdose), however, served as a backdrop for the comic trials and tribulations of a trio of his wives (Vivica A. Fox, Halle Berry, Lela Rochon), who battle over his estate and each of whom, in *Rashomon* style, recalls the Lymon she knew. Unfortunately, the script by African American writer and former actress Tina Andrews never says enough about Lymon. No one would have any idea that at the time of Lymon's hit song "Why Do Fools Fall in Love," which he recorded with his group The Teenagers, he was only thirteen-years old; nor that his career was over by the age of eighteen; nor that he was twenty-six when he died.

Still, as *Why Do Fools Fall in Love* delights in the antics and dilemmas of the women (with a tone and point of view that owe much to 1996's *The First Wives Club*), it was often enough more entertaining than it had a right to be and more so than the critics gave it credit for. Actor Tate and the three actresses gave spirited performances. Looking terrific in her period-style makeup and costumes, Halle Berry had rarely been so animated. The women were far more engaging than those found in such sex comedies as the pathetic *Booty Call* (1997) and *Def Jam's How to Be a Player* (1997)—and certainly not offensive like the psychotic female judge and the overripe, older mother in a movie like *The Brothers*. In the end though, *Why Do Fools Fall in Love* was a commercial disaster. Female audiences apparently didn't buy its pop homage to the idea of sisterhood. Repercussions of this failure were felt within the industry. The assumption was that there was no audience for films about African American women. Plans for a movie version of the Michael Bennett-choreographed Broadway hit of the 1980s, *Dreamgirls*, were shelved.

Oprah's Opus: *Beloved*

Also appearing late in the decade was Jonathan Demme's 1998 adaptation of Toni Morrison's Pulitzer Prize winning novel *Beloved*. Or it might be more appropriate to say Oprah Winfrey's adaptation. By now, Oprah Winfrey had become one of the most famous women in America—and a true cultural phenomenon who was written about and discussed continually. Her syndicated talk show had soared in the ratings. So had her mini-series "The Women of Brewster Place." Having formed her own production company, she also produced films for television throughout the 1990s. Yet Winfrey still had not conquered the movies. No doubt she believed *Beloved* would change that. Having worked some ten years to bring the 1987 book to the screen, Winfrey was the film's co-producer and star. From the beginning, the studio—Disney's Touchstone Pictures—understood that *Beloved* hardly told the kind of story that audiences would flock to see on a Friday night. Like Spielberg's *Amistad*, *Beloved* was a historical drama that recounted some of the terrors and brutalities of slavery. At its opening, a former slave, Sethe (Winfrey), lives in a home outside Cincinnati that seems haunted. Floorboards shake. Grunts and cries are heard. Corridors turn red. It is, as Morrison wrote in her novel, "a house peopled by the living activity of the dead." Through flashbacks (with Lisa Gay Hamiton playing Sethe as a young woman), Sethe's horrifying past is revealed: as a slave at the Sweet Home farm in Kentucky, she witnessed a series of devastating human atrocities as slaves were sold, tortured and killed. She had seen her own mother hanged. Sethe had escaped but at a high emotional cost. (Her husband—having been driven mad—had not survived.) While trying to cross the river from Kentucky to Ohio, she had given birth to her youngest daughter Denver—with the help of a crazed white girl—in a canoe. And later when Sethe had found refuge in Ohio, her former master came to take her back. And desperate Sethe had attempted to kill her children rather than see them returned to a life of slavery. She did indeed murder her oldest daughter.

But now years later in 1873 Sethe, living with Denver after having been abandoned by her sons, finally is confronted by her past: first when an old friend from the Kentucky plantation, Paul D (Danny Glover), arrives at her home; and later when a young woman (Thandie Newton), dressed in black as if in mourning, appears in front of her home in a trancelike state. The young woman calls herself Beloved. Is Beloved inhabited by the spirit of Sethe's dead child?

Shot on a budget of $53 million with an estimated $30 million spent for marketing, *Beloved* proved to be the most expensive film then ever made about the African American experience. (Because of its integrated cast, *Amistad* technically was not considered a black film.) It opened with great fanfare as Winfrey launched a heavy promotion campaign, turning up on talk shows while her face peered out from the covers of magazines as diverse as *Time*, *In Style*, and *Vogue*. In its October 13, 1998, edition, *The New York Times* reported that *Beloved* was "viewed in Hollywood as almost a test case of whether studios will continue to finance the handful of serious films each year on black themes. The thinking is that if this film, given its pedigree, blanket marketing campaign and potential attraction to women, can't make it, how many can?"

Running almost three hours (the first 25 minutes of the film covered the first 20 pages of the novel), *Beloved* met with mixed reviews as well as mixed reactions from those movie-goers who actually saw it. *New York Times* critic Janet Maslin called *Beloved* a "transfixing, deeply felt adaptation" that "accelerates into a gripping, wildly imaginative film that's not quite like any other." In the *New York Post*, however, critic Rod Dreher said that the film was "slack and meandering" and that it failed "to deliver the healing catharsis the material calls for. It's a noble disappointment." In theaters, only those patrons who had read the novel appeared to understand the story. Otherwise audiences were openly baffled as well as impatient with the pacing. By November 9, 1998, *The New York Times* reported that several industry executives believed *Beloved* had little appeal for black audiences, especially young black movie-goers. "One distribution executive," reported the *Times*, "said that in its second week, the film dropped sharply among African Americans, a big disappointment to Disney. He said that the film was now playing in mostly upscale theaters, catering to white as well as black audiences, and was performing poorly at suburban malls." In the end, *Beloved* proved to be a box-office failure. For many within the industry, *Beloved*, as well as *Amistad*, spelled the end of Hollywood's periodic attempts to do more serious films about the black experience in America. Like *Why Do Fools Fall in Love*, *Beloved*'s failure also seemed to spell the death of the black woman's film.

Yet though one can only wonder what a director such as Julie Dash or Charles Burnett might have brought to the material, *Beloved* had some fine moments with sometimes startling portraits of African American women. *The New Yorker*'s critic David Denby, who found the film "blindly tedious" and "a trial to sit through," believed nonetheless that "the images of women at least give us something to hold on to." Winfrey had stripped herself of many of the mannerisms and gestures that her television viewers were so familiar with. Not an easy feat. Though not the kind of larger-than-life mythic performance you might want, Winfrey nevertheless provided audiences with the unexpected sight of a world-famous woman giving herself over to a project she believes is of extraordinary importance. Hers is a felt and convincing performance. Kimberly Elise, who had seemed so spacey and unformed an actress in *Set It Off*, created a stunning Denver: awkward and petulant at times, and then, at the conclusion of the film, as she goes off to make a new life for herself, mature and beautifully assured, a ray of hope for a new day for black America. Perhaps the less said about Thandie Newton's misconceived performance, the better. The *New York Post*'s critic wrote that the character "seems not quite human. In fact, she's almost a cartoon freak. As she jarringly plays her, Beloved gawks and drools and yammers and carries on like a 'Cosby' show version of Linda Blair in *The Exorcist*—which alas, is funny. This is not supposed to be a funny movie." Why Demme didn't rein this actress in or guide her to another interpretation for the character are great unanswered questions.

Most striking though was the performance of Beah Richards, whom critic David Denby pointed out, "as Sethe's mother-in-law, the inspired amateur Baby Suggs, is almost redemption itself. Richards, bending and shaking, and lifting her great cracked voice, is so completely alive that she seems to gather up all of black experience in the body of one very unghostly old lady." By the time of *Beloved*, Richards had been an actress for over fifty years. The daughter of a Baptist minister and a seamstress, Richards had been born in Vicksburg, Mississippi, where—she recounted later—white children had insulted and stoned her on her way to school. "I suffered every day in my life in that town," she recalled in an article in *The New York Times* on September 16, 2000. After studying at Dillard University in New

Orleans, Richards began her career at the Old Globe Theater in San Diego. In New York, she worked off-Broadway in Louis Peterson's *Take a Giant Step* and repeated her role as the grandmother in the film version. Later, she appeared on Broadway in *The Miracle Worker* and in James Baldwin's *Amen Corner* (as Sister Margaret, the pastor of a storefront church). When she understudied the part of the mother in the Broadway version of *A Raisin in the Sun*, cast members such as Ivan Dixon and Ruby Dee would recall—for years to come—the power of her unusual interpretation of the role. She also performed in a one-woman show, *A Black Woman Speaks*.

In films, Richards played supporting roles: from her days in *Hurry Sundown* and *Guess Who's Coming to Dinner* (which had won her a Best Supporting Actress Oscar nomination) to *The Great White Hope* and *In the Heat of the Night* to *Drugstore Cowboy* (1989). More important opportunities came in numerous television programs, including "Frank's Place" (which won her an Emmy in 1988), "Roots: The Next Generations," "The Bill Cosby Show," and "ER." When the material failed to match her talents, Richards infused her characters with a soulful resiliency and an emotional intensity that made almost all her performances memorable. Her own belief in her talents and her commitment to her art kept her going for decades. What she once said of the theater—which she related to her childhood experiences as the daughter of a minister—could also apply to her work in films. "I always relate theater to the church," she commented. "There is the sharpness of image, the poetry. And like the church, the theater must always be an exploration for truth." Her appearance in *Beloved* should have earned her a Best Supporting Actress Oscar. But Richards was not even nominated for the award. She won a second Emmy for her guest appearance on the TV series "The Practice," but *Beloved* marked her last important role. Beah Richards died in 2000.

Movies for the Smart Young Hip Crowd: *love jones* and *Love and Basketball*

Appealing to a young college and post-grad-age generation was Theodore Witcher's *love jones* (1997). In this modern-day black romance, Nia Long and Larenz Tate were cast as the young artists and lovers, Nina and Darius, who juggle their love for one another with the demands of their art and their own self-absorption. Theirs is a world of dark jazzy clubs—places where intellectuals gather to reveal their passions and their pretensions. These are also places where love blooms and dies. The antithesis of the type of black film the studios usually preferred to release, *love jones*—neither a crude sex comedy nor a black action flick—prided itself on its intelligence and its cool sophistication. On the night they meet at a poetry club in Chicago, Darius goes to the mike where he dedicates a poem to Nina. "Who am I?"

he says. "It's not important. But they call me Brother to the Night. And right now I'm the blues in your left thigh, trying to become the funk in your right." Not a bad way to flirt. The soundtrack itself featured the music of Duke Ellington, John Coltrane, Lauryn Hill, Cassandra Wilson, and Maxwell.

At times *love jones* seemed too infatuated with its own hipness, its characters too eager to showcase how cultivated they are as references to Mozart, playwright Bernard Shaw, and Gordon Parks fly all over the place. Once Nina and Darius have finally slept together, she awakens the next morning to see her buffed beau preparing breakfast for her. He's both a hunk and a sensitive guy. A principal setting is an apartment that looks like a set designer's dream. It can all become heady in just the way you don't want it to be. But Witcher wants to articulate the sensibility of a segment of the black audience that's always been ignored by the movies. Moody, pouty, and personal, *love jones* was in a class all its own, the type of film its small but dedicated audience would remember fondly and, perhaps depending on whom you first saw it with, bittersweetly in the years to come; a film that captures some of the youthful passions and yearnings of a segment of the black audience of the late 1990s.

Gina Prince-Bythewood's *Love and Basketball* (2000) also appealed to a similar young black audience. Bythewood had struggled to get the film financed. Finally, Spike Lee came on board as a producer along with Sam Kitt. Its unusual story was of a black girl, Monica (Sanaa Lathan), and a black boy, Quincy (Omar Epps), who grew up together in middle-class black Los Angeles, bound by their affection for one another and their love for the game of basketball. As the film follows the two through high school and college and young adulthood, *Love and Basketball* solemnly recounts their relations with their parents. Monica's mother, played by Alfre Woodard, doesn't see any future in basketball for Monica. Quincy is disillusioned when he discovers that the father he idolized (Dennis Haysbeth) is a womanizer. Throughout, the often troubled and moody Monica and Quincy seem perfect for one another, but, of course, it takes time for them to realize that.

Prince-Bythewood understands her characters and makes it easy for the audience to identify with them. Yet, ironically, too often the dramatic effectiveness of *Love and Basketball* was weakened by the film's rhythm. Too many scenes—the important as well as the transitional ones—were directed at the same pace and in the same tone and seemingly at the same length so that when the big moments came, they didn't have much of an emotional wallop because there was nothing to distinguish them from the less important sequences. Too often there seemed to be a directorial emotional distancing, as if Bythewood didn't want to be accused of making an *emotional* woman's picture. In his early scenes, Omar Epps did little more than strike a hip modern male pose. He's just Omar Epps trying to look cool and sexy. Fortunately, by the last third of the film, he finally begins to play the character, creating a portrait of a vulnerable young man.

Sanaa Lathan, however, connected beautifully to her character, and Prince-Bythewood sensitively tapped Lathan's painful youthful yearnings. Often appearing to be a surrogate for the director, Lathan emerged as the film's oddly languid emotional base. For an African American actress, hers was a highly distinct characterization. She displayed none of the tragic grandeur of a Dandridge (even when Dandridge, in *Malaga*, seems languid and lost, one still feels the idea of tragic destiny hovering over her). Nor does she have the stateliness of a Cicely Tyson; nor any of the giddy narcissism of a Diana Ross; nor the steely determination of an Angela Bassett. Yet something seemed achingly real and natural about her—and appealing. The daughter of film/TV director Stan Lathan, Sanaa Lathan also appeared in *The Wood*, *Blade* (1997), *Life* (1999), and *The Best Man*.

New Actors

Unlike the actresses, African American male stars still found the male-dominated industry more receptive to their talents. That was as true in the 1990s as it had been in the 1950s and 1960s when Sidney Poitier rose to stardom. Audiences took note of talented actors such as Giancarlo Esposito, Roger Guenveur Smith, Mykelti Williamson (who played the tender-hearted Bubba in *Forrest Gump*, 1994) and the underrated Larenz Tate. Forest Whitaker, who had previously worked in *Fast Times at Ridgemont High* (1982); *The Color of Money* (1986); *Good Morning, Vietnam*; and *Bird* appeared in the 1990s in *The Crying Game*; *A Rage in Harlem*; *Downtown*; *Article 99* (1992); *Diary of a Hitman* (1992); *Bank Robber* (1993); and *Ghost Dog* (2000). After his impressive performance in Oliver Stone's *Any Given Sunday*, comedian Jamie Foxx made a bid for movie stardom in such films as *Bait* (2000) and *Held Up* (2000). Rapper Tupac Shakur, who became a cult figure after being shot to death at age 25 in 1996, had appeared in such films as *Juice*, *Poetic Justice*, and *Gridlock'd* (1997). Marlon Wayans appeared in *Don't Be a Menace to South Central while Drinking Your Juice in the Hood* (1996), *Senseless* (1998), and *Requiem for a Dream* (2000). Rap star/impresario Sean "Puffy" (P. Diddy) Combs appeared in *Made* (2001) and *Monster's Ball* (2001). A startling new group of actors also performed in some of the era's most talked-about films: Don Cheadle in films as diverse as *Devil in a Blue Dress*, *Out of Sight* (1998), *Mission to Mars* (2000), *The Family Man* (2000), and *Traffic* (2000); Isaiah Washington in *Clockers*, *Girl 6*, *Get on the Bus*, *True Crime* (1999), and *Romeo Must Die*; Ving Rhames in *Striptease* (1996), *Mission: Impossible*, *Pulp Fiction* (1994), *Bringing out the Dead* (1999), and *Mission: Impossible 2* (2000); and Delroy Lindo in *Clockers*, *Get Shorty* (1995), *Ransom* (1996), *Red Arrow* (1996), and *Cider House Rules* (1999).

A new generation of actors such as Will Smith, Martin Lawrence, Chris Tucker, and Cuba Gooding, Jr., emerged as stars. Whether their careers would have longevity remained an unanswered question. Using his TV series "Fresh Prince of Bel-Air" as a springboard to movie work, Will Smith had turned in a rather likable performance in *Made in America* and a tentative one in *Six Degrees of Separation.* Audiences, however, saw no signs of any big-screen size persona. Then came the Don Simpson/Jerry Bruckheimer-produced hit *Bad Boys* (1995), a familiar action picture cop yarn made appealing mainly by Smith's work with co-stars Martin Lawrence and Téa Leoni. There followed the sci-fi mega-hits *Independence Day* (1996) and *Men in Black* (1997), which had been driven by special effects rather than any particular star power.

Curiously, though Smith had been able to escape typing in his films, moviegoers may have found him rather bland and without much of an edge. At times, he also seemed almost too boyish, looking like an overgrown kid with a big goofy smile.

Not until the Tony Scott thriller *Enemy of the State* (1998) did Smith actually carry a film and reveal a relatively interesting screen persona. Cast as a Washington, D.C., lawyer whose reputation is ruined by renegade executives at the National Security Agency, he had some convincing scenes with Regain King as his wife— and with the sweetly wistful Lisa Bonet as an old girlfriend. For the first time in his movie career, Will Smith seemed like an adult. Race appeared to play no part whatsoever in the film. A few cultural references here or there might have helped. But *Enemy of the State* was a big hit. Afterwards, Hollywood anointed Smith the Black Star du Jour. A program like "Entertainment Tonight" chronicled his every appearance at this opening or that. The media was quick to publicize his marriage to actress Jada Pinkett. Talk circulated that he would replace Denzel Washington as the top African American actor in the movie colony. And, of course, his salary soared to the $20 million a picture range. But once Smith reverted to rather bland form in the clinker *Wild Wild West* (1999), the industry seemed to have second thoughts. Plans to star Smith in a biopic of the life of boxer Muhammad Ali, to be filmed by *Men in Black* and *Wild Wild West* director Barry Sonnenfeld, were dropped. But eventually the film, *Ali* (2001), was made with a new director, Michael Mann. For a spell, though, audiences seemed to like Smith's rather light touch and easygoing manner. Smith also appeared (distressingly) in *The Legend of Bagger Vance.*

A stand-up comic, Martin Lawrence worked his way to stardom in supporting roles in such films as *Do the Right Thing, Boomerang*, then his hit TV series "Martin," and movies such as *Bad Boys* and *Nothing to Lose* (1997). When Lawrence starred, co-wrote, executive-produced, and directed *A Thin Line Between Love and Hate* (1996), the results were numbing—for him as an actor and a filmmaker. Centering on a ladies' man (Lawrence) and a former love (Lynn Whitfield) who won't let go of their relationship (it looked as if everyone connected with this film had seen the 1987 *Fatal Attraction* too many times), *A Thin Line Between Love and Hate* was a misogynistic, hateful mess that trashed its leading lady. Yet it proved to

Buffed and ready for action: Will Smith (RIGHT) and Chris Tucker (BELOW).

be a box-office success. Usually Lawrence relied on his manic screen persona to get him through his films. Not until the feature *Life*, perhaps because of the challenge of working with Eddie Murphy, did Martin Lawrence actually create a character with some shading and nuances.

Then came the big hits *Blue Streak* (1999) and *Big Momma's House*. Pure star vehicles, the films had little to recommend them other than Lawrence, who reveled in his gifts for far-flung comic exaggeration. When he shows up in *Blue Streak* with extensions that make him look like a cracked-out Buckwheat, the questions are: Why is he doing this to himself? And isn't there a way to be funny without turning yourself into such a blatant caricature? For years, actors such as Poitier and Bill Cosby had been determined *not* to let this kind of thing be a part of their work.

In *Big Momma's House*, Lawrence plays an undercover cop who poses as a heavyset woman known to family and friends as Big Momma. The real Big Momma, played by Ella Mitchell, is treated mercilessly by the camera, especially in a bathroom sequence in which she is partially nude. What could be funnier, the sequence says, than the sight of a large, grotesquely overweight woman with layers of fat around her waist, hips, and backside? Under padding, makeup, and a wig, Lawrence as the pretend Big Momma was something of a mammy figure: quick to nurture and protect and obviously without any kind of alluring sexuality. (There is a scene with an older man in a pant and in bed awaiting the pretend Big Momma. It too is done in the name of Comedy of the Grotesque.) Audiences accepted the old-style typing mainly because they knew that underneath all the padding was their guy Martin. Still, Lawrence, often funny and even strangely touching, was mesmerizing for a few minutes in a church sequence as he sang and danced. You marvel at his skills. Surprisingly, playing the character freed Lawrence in key moments to express a sweetness and vulnerability. He was far more interesting as Big Momma than he was as the cop Malcolm in the film. Maybe even Martin Lawrence enjoyed those times on screen when he could be somebody other than Martin Lawrence. This relatively low-budget film drew a huge profit, becoming a surprise summer hit. Afterwards, though, Lawrence co-starred with Danny De Vito, in 2001, in the disappointing *What's the Worst That Could Happen?* (*This movie* is what some of the critics said.)

Chris Tucker also rose to stardom through caricature. With a high, screechy hysterical voice and enough eye pops and facial muggings to make Mantan Moreland blush, this lanky comic sometimes looked as if he belonged in a Hollywood film of the 1930s. But perhaps his anachronistic behavior made him seem modern and fresh to a new generation without much sense of movie history. After brief appearances in *House Party 3* and *Panther*, Tucker used his retro style to comically dominate his scenes in *Friday*. He also had funny roles in *Dead Presidents* and *Jackie Brown*. Perhaps the most charitable thing to be said about his performance as a cross-dressing radio star in Luc Besson's 1997 futuristic *The Fifth Element* (set in the twenty-third century) is that it was *out there*. Neither the director nor actor seems to have thought this character out. As he sashayed about in his Jean-Paul Gaultier designer outfits with his hair (at one point) dyed blond and styled with a phallic cone jutting out above his forehead, Tucker—grating and even embarrassing—seemed to be doing little more than giving a crude sendup of a drag queen, lacking the smooth polish and know-how of the real thing, a performer like the mighty Ru Paul.

But Tucker moved up the ranks quickly, first opposite Charlie Sheen in the hit *Money Talks* (1997) and then with Asian martial arts master Jackie Chan in the mega hit *Rush Hour* (1998). Intended as a clash and blend of cultures, *Rush Hour*'s script sometimes had anti-Asian aspects, all in the name of humor, of course. Much was made over the fact that *Rush Hour*, which cost $35 million and grossed $241 million worldwide, performed so well abroad. Chris Rock's manager, Michael Rotenberg, informed *The New York Times* magazine (September 3, 2000) that the foreign market was a problem for black stars. "Denzel is flat," explained Rotenberg. "Eddie is not strong overseas. Will Smith works, but he usually teams with a white actor, and he does action films. Every day I hear from the studios that you cannot sell black stars internationally. And you can't really blame the studios. There is so much racism in these countries. They don't want black pictures." Though part of the foreign success of *Rush Hour* could be attributed to Jackie Chan's popularity, Tucker was perceived within the film industry as a comic who could appeal to international audiences.

With the exception of *Friday*, Tucker's important films also were not considered *black* films because they weren't set within an African American context. Unlike a number of African American performers who, as they became bigger crossover stars, were concerned about maintaining and not alienating their core black following, Tucker was quick to tell *The New York Times* magazine, "I want everyone to relate to what I am doing. And that's been easy, because in my career I haven't experienced any racism." He also commented, "From the beginning, people seemed to like what I did. I was a regular person who was funny. That's what the audience is looking for. They want regular, and they want funny." What Tucker didn't seem to understand was that, whether he liked it or not, he would be viewed by most audiences, black and white, as a black star, and that, fair or not, his work would often be interpreted in racial terms, whether as part of the text or subtext. Nevertheless *Rush Hour*'s success immediately put Tucker in the stratosphere of the $20-million-a-picture deal, making him one of the highest paid African American actors then working in the movies. In 2001, he reteamed with Jackie Chan in the sequel *Rush Hour 2*.

Another standup comic, Chris Rock, worked his way up from supporting roles in *New Jack City* and *Boomerang* and as the star of the low-budget *CB4* (which he co-wrote) to more important parts in such films as *Lethal Weapon 4* (1998), *Dogma* (2000), *Nurse Betty* (2000), and then the lead in *Down to Earth*. But by the end of the twentieth century and the start of a new millennium, Rock, having become a favorite of the intelligentsia (black and white) for his irreverent and sometimes-pointed political humor on his Emmy-winning HBO series "The Chris Rock Show," still hadn't attained full-fledged movie stardom.

Of this new generation, none was more honored than Cuba Gooding, Jr., who walked off with an Oscar as Best Supporting Actor of 1996 for his near-over-the-top performance as the hyper-kinetic, show-me-the-money football player in *Jerry Maguire*. Having already appeared in such films as *Boyz N the Hood* and *A Few Good Men*, Gooding acquired a whole new status in the industry, becoming known to everyone, especially after his Oscar acceptance speech when he literally did a flip on stage. Afterwards, he worked opposite Anthony Hopkins in *Instinct* (1999) (and didn't do badly) and also appeared in *What Dreams May Come* (1998) and *As Good as It Gets* (1997). But those films failed to do much for his career. The same was true of *The Chill Factor* (1999). His performance was "quite a comedown from the heights of *Jerry Maguire*," wrote the critic for *The New York Times*. "His scared-witless ice-cream delivery man belongs to the same category of wisecracking characters as LL Cool J's indestructible, scared-witless chef in *Deep Blue Sea*." (Watching LL Cool J in that film, audiences found it hard to believe this was the same person who was so *cool* and in control when he performed his rap music.)

Not until the 2000 *Men of Honor* did Gooding have a lead role he could really work with. Like Will Smith, Gooding usually projected a boyish brand of masculinity, similar to that of Tom Cruise and Ben Affleck. During this era, some critics believed the traditional adult manly kind of screen hero—represented in the past by a Clark Gable, Spencer Tracy, or John Wayne—was passé. Yet surprisingly, black actors such as Denzel Washington, Samuel L. Jackson, Morgan Freeman, and Laurence Fishburne were closer to the traditional masculine stance of past movies. Gooding also appeared as real-life World War II hero Dorie Miller in *Pearl Harbor* (2001), and he appeared with Whoopi Goldberg in *Rat Race* (2001), an idea from *It's a Mad, Mad, Mad, Mad World*. But at the start of the new century, his Oscar win, like that of that dazzler Louis Gossett, Jr., in the 1980s, had not yet led him to major movie stardom.

Even in the final years of the twentieth century, African American actors, more so than filmmakers, occupied unique positions of some influence and power within the industry. And, of the decade's actors, six remained at the forefront of American films for various reasons and with varying degrees of success: Eddie Murphy, Wesley Snipes, Laurence Fishburne, Morgan Freeman, Samuel L. Jackson, and Denzel Washington.

Martin Lawrence strikes a pose—looking like a buck-toothed, zonked-out version of Buckwheat—in *Blue Streak*.

Show Him the Money: Cuba Gooding, Jr., in his Best Supporting Oscar-winning role as the football star in *Jerry Maguire.*

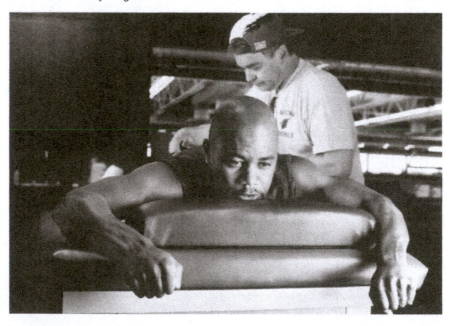

Eddie Murphy: All Grown Up, Looking for a Place to Go

During the early 1990s, Eddie Murphy remained a well-publicized, visible star. But no longer were his films the blockbuster hits that had kept his studio Paramount Pictures so happy in the politically conservative 1980s. Perhaps hoping to recapture some of the old audience, Murphy reteamed at the start of the decade with Nick Nolte in the sequel *Another 48 Hrs.* They reprised their roles as the con Reggie Hammond and the cop Cates.

But like *Lethal Weapon 2*, the film failed to take its central characters and their relationship to any new direction. Far be it for *Another 48 Hrs* to depict a more mature Hammond, who might have picked up a book in the prison library and learned something about the system that's incarcerated him. How different this might have been had Hammond been politicized and come out a firebrand. Maybe it would have made for a new kind of entertainment that could bring Murphy into the 1990s, instead of keeping him locked in a Reagan-era time warp.

No doubt he hoped his role as a womanizing marketing executive who has gender roles switched on him in *Boomerang* would touch base with the young new Nationalist-style African American audience. Despite its all-star cast (including Martin Lawrence and David Alan Grier) and engaging performances by Robin Givens and Halle Berry, the movie met with mixed reviews and was also criticized for its female characters (notably those played by Grace Jones and Eartha Kitt; actually, some of the male characters needed shaping up too). Yet Murphy, as he reworked his timing and pacing to accommodate this comedy's less physical and less exaggerated tone, was indeed disarming in a transitional more mature role. But the critics did not seem to notice.

His 1992 appearance in *The Distinguished Gentleman* did not generate a roar at the box office either. By 1994, still in search of that elusive big-time hit, Murphy returned to his most famous role as Axel Foley in *Beverly Hills Cop III* but with tepid results. Nor did *Vampire in Brooklyn* do anything for his career. Would he be able to meet the expectations—or the needs—of a new generation of moviegoers?

The answer came when he appeared in a remake of the 1963 Jerry Lewis film *The Nutty Professor* in 1996. Murphy was cast as Sherman Klump, a brilliant science professor who is also obese—and (literally) the butt of endless fat jokes. Shy, insecure, and always an outsider, Sherman lives at home with his mother, father, grandmother, and brother. When Klump develops a crush on a young colleague (Jada Pinkett), he experiments with DNA restructuring and—presto!—is transformed into Buddy Love, a slender, loud-mouth braggart and ladies' man with an insatiable libido. In this comic Dr. Jekyll/Mr. Hyde update, Sherman must fight to defeat the obnoxious Buddy and get back to being his sweet-tempered self, no matter how heavy he is. An otherwise routine picture was transformed by Murphy's

Eddie Murphy and Nick Nolte reteam in the disappointing sequel *Another 48 Hrs.*

highly imaginative performance (or rather performances) into a very funny one. With makeup by Rick Baker, Murphy played the other family members so cleverly that had audiences not known in advance of his multiple characters, it's doubtful anyone would have guessed. His raunchy grandmother seems to be inspired by Moms Mabley. Most impressive was Murphy's interpretation of Sherman. Buried under fake jowls and body padding, he created a very sensitive, vulnerable *character.* Perhaps for the first time in his career, Eddie Murphy was not playing Eddie Murphy. Ironically, as Buddy Love, Murphy was like the comic that audiences had been seeing for years. But this time around, his funky cockiness—Eddie, the Loud-Mouth—struck audiences as obnoxious—and hard to identify with. Nonetheless, *The Nutty Professor* was a blazing triumph for Murphy as he put his talents on brilliant display. The film was a hit.

When Murphy returned to his fundamentally flip brash persona in films such as Thomas Carter's *Metro* (1997) and Frank Oz's *Bowfinger* (1999), the box office results were disappointing. (Playing two roles in the latter film, he was actually quite good as the pampered, paranoid movie star. Here Murphy may have revealed more than he intended.) The Sherman role had softened the Murphy persona and taken his career in a new direction, indicating a new generation wanted a Murphy hero that was less rowdy and outspoken. This was clear by the whopping success of Murphy's remake of the 1967 musical *Doctor Dolittle.* The original, which had starred Rex Harrison, who discovers that animals can talk to him, had been a box-office bomb, which had almost ruined its studio. The only memorable thing was its hit Oscar-winning song "Talk to the Animals," sung by Sammy Davis, Jr. Why do it again? Yet, though Murphy's *Doctor Dolittle* in 1998—with voices of the animals recorded by such stars as Chris Rock, Ellen DeGeneres, and Julie Kavner—was not much better than its predecessor, it proved to be a hit, mainly with younger audiences, marking the full domestication of Murphy. Now cast as a family man in what amounted to a family movie, he had managed to re-invent himself. Afterwards, he reprised his Sherman role in a sequel, *The Nutty Professor 2: The Klumps* (2000), followed by the sequel *Doctor Dolittle 2* (2001). He also co-starred with Martin Lawrence in the prison comedy *Life* and supplied his voice for characters (actually, rather loud ones) in the animated features *Mulan* (1998), and the huge summer hit *Shrek* (2001).

Laurence Fishburne: From Child Actor to Leading Man

The career of Laurence Fishburne (once billed Laurence Fishburne 3rd and then Larry Fishburne) was clearly on the upswing during the early years of the period.

Born in Augusta, Georgia, and reared in Brooklyn, the son of a corrections officer father and a schoolteacher mother, Fishburne acted as a child on the TV soap "One Life to Live," the film *Cornbread, Earl and Me* and, at fourteen, in *Apocalypse Now* (1979; *Apocalypse Now Redux*, 2001).

Afterwards he played supporting roles in films that his later fans may have been unaware of: *Red Heat* (1988), *Gardens of Stone*, *The Cotton Club*, *Rumble Fish* (1983), *A Nightmare on Elm Street III* (1987), *Quicksilver* (1986), *Band of the Hand* (1986), *Willie and Phil* (1980), and most chillingly as the unforgettable Cutter in *Death Wish II* (1982). He also appeared on the TV show "Peewee's Playhouse." Later came other supporting roles in *Cadence* (1991), *King of New York*, and *Class Action* (1991, in which he played to smooth perfection an attorney). His role in *Searching for Bobby Fischer* (1993), that of a street hustler chess whiz who befriends the young hero, was now a familiar type. A more interesting (and perhaps challenging) role would have been as the demanding chess teacher played by Ben Kingsley.

It seemed, however, as if he would be relegated to a lifetime of supporting roles, mainly because, as Spike Lee told *The New York Times* (August 8, 1993) in reference to Fishburne, "There's the thing about what the leading man should look like, and then there's the matter of race." Fishburne hardly had the looks of the traditional leading man. But Lee cast Fishburne as a lead—the committed student activist Dap—in *School Daze*. His performance indicated his range and gift for playing intelligent, shrewd, seemingly ordinary, downhome men, perceptive of the people and events around them.

Finally, in a trio of other lead roles, Fishburne displayed his talents to great effect. As Furious in *Boys N the Hood*, he expressed the maturity and seriousness (coupled with genuine tension) of a figure that might have been a polemic rather than a character. When he meets his former wife at an upscale restaurant, he also subtly suggests an underlying resentment of her success and upward mobility. Here he gets at an emotional truth of *certain* African American males, uneasy with a successful educated black woman. It's all the more a remarkable performance when one realizes that Fishburne was then in his late twenties. Later he starred as the loner undercover cop in *Deep Cover*.

But the star signature role that perhaps drew most of his resources was as Ike Turner, the Svengali who creates and sets out to demolish Tina Turner (Angela Bassett), in the popular Tina Turner film biography *What's Love Got to Do with It*. Because the script cannot fathom the forces that shape, propel, and torment the character, the coked-out Ike, who berates, belittles, and beats Turner, had shades of the old brutal Buck. But Fishburne worked wonders. "He saved Ike. Salvaged it. Lifted it. We had to add so much," co-star Angela Bassett told *The New York Times* (August 8, 1993). "He brought out Ike's dignity."

His very funny, affecting performance captured Ike's hot temper, shrewd insights, wildman talents, irrationality, assured masculinity (which no doubt drew the actual Turner to him), and surprising charm. As he stormed about in a series of hairdos (a straight-haired short pageboy; a fluffy Afro) and costumes (bell bottoms, chains, even hot pants that are a scream!), Fishburne's performance won him an Oscar nomination as Best Actor.

But the early and mid-1990s may be viewed by later generations as a highpoint of Fishburne's film career. The performances that followed were always carefully measured but without great impact. One might have assumed Fishburne would give a towering performance when, in 1995, he became the first African American actor to play the title role in a film version of *Othello*. But in a movie that was far too studied and stilted, Fishburne appeared a few steps removed from the character. Too often he looked as if he were so concerned about proving he could actually do Shakespeare—and do it with dignity—that Othello's passion was missing as well as that instinctive let-it-bleed quality that had made Paul Robeson's Othello so memorable for theatergoers of an earlier time.

There was initial interest in *Bad Company* (1995), a film noir thriller in which Fishburne and Ellen Barkin performed some fairly dicey sexual escapades. Yet the two—panting and groping—often look as if they were mainly going through the motions for the camera. The film itself lost its heat and became predictable fare. The same was true of *Just Cause* (1995) and the Kevin Hooks's-directed *Fled*. Bill Duke's *Hoodlum* starred Fishburne as the real-life king of the black numbers racket, Ellsworth "Bumpy" Johnson (a character he had played briefly years earlier in *The Cotton Club*). Though part of the film's appeal was its enjoyably highflung, old-fashioned gangster style melodrama, audiences may have considered it *too* old-fashioned and stayed away. *Hoodlum*'s most entertaining performance was Cicely Tyson's as the French-speaking *grande dame* of the rackets trade, Stephanie St. Clair. Fishburne also starred in the sci-fi drama *Event Horizon* (1997). By the time he appeared in a supporting role in another sci-fi adventure, the hugely successful *Matrix* (1999), a mannered Fishburne was so busy *intoning* as he spoke that he seemed (like Andre Braugher on certain occasions) to be enchanted by the sound of his own voice. Otherwise he was rather elegant background material and indeed provided this action film with some class and intelligent sophistication. It was rather funny—and ironic—however, to see Fishburne as the shrewd counselor to the young white savior (Keanu Reeves) of the world. Fishburne also wrote and directed the film *Once in the Life* (2000), which was adapted from his play *Riff Raff*.

Wesley Snipes: Action Hero

In another age, Wesley Snipes's striking looks—the perfect layer of dark skin, high cheek bones, chiseled jaw and chin lines, sculpted full lips—might have consigned him to supporting roles. But the new Afrocentricized audience saw Snipes play a series of dynamic leads. The Bronx-bred actor who studied at New York's High School for the Performing Arts and New York's State University College in Purchase had the taut, wiry body and graceful agile movements of a dancer (which he once wanted to be) fused with a quick-witted athleticism.

That athleticism shone through in Snipes's early roles: as a boxer in *Streets of Gold* (1986); a football player in *Wildcats* (1986); the baseball player Willie Mays Hays in *Major League* (1989); and the street tough in the Michael Jackson video "Bad."

The path to stardom came with important roles in *Mo' Better Blues* and *Jungle Fever*. Ironically, in the latter, Snipes strikes a hollow pose; the character Flipper Purify doesn't seem to draw on his rich resources as an actor. You're not sure if he believes in the character or if he feels uncomfortable playing a middle-class man so locked in the system.

Other roles (particularly the outsider renegades) revealed Snipes's range and daring: another tough in *King of New York*; the drug kingpin in *New Jack City*; the basketball hustler in *White Men Can't Jump* (1992); the paraplegic Raymond in *Water Dance* (1992); the security expert John Cutter in *Passenger 57*; the treasury agent in *Boiling Point* (1993); the Los Angeles police detective Web Smith in *Rising Sun* (1993); the cartoonlike villain in *Demolition Man* (1993). Even in the underwritten role of drug lord Roemello in *Sugar Hill* (more a stunning, over-estheticized visual meditation than a movie), he brings out the character's stoic withdrawal. Snipes also appeared as a U.S. marshal in *Drop Zone* (1996).

Some characters had shades of the old buck. Certainly, Nino in *New Jack City* is callous, ruthless, brutal, highly sexual. But Snipes projects the restless intelligence of someone aware of the demands of the corrupt world in which he operates. Throughout he is vibrantly alive, a kinetic mass of movement and energy ready to strike at any moment ("I used the image of the panther as the paradigm for my character," he told *The New York Times* on March 27, 1991) as he holds onto the belief that his energy can save him.

In *Rising Sun*, Snipes played a character that was originally white in the Michael Crichton novel on which the film was based. Director Philip Kaufman may have believed he was bringing a liberal slant (minority input) to a project that was criticized as being anti-Japanese. But because the black character Web seemed befuddled through much of the action, Kaufman's liberalism may have backfired by adding a racial subtext to the film. Only in a misconceived South Central Los Angeles episode (not found in the novel) with a crew of movie-style black hoods did Snipes seem in control. Otherwise, he's little more than a sidekick to Sean Connery's very knowing, very shrewd, very in-charge white-man hero.

Surely, old-style buckdom lay at the base of his blond-haired, one-green-eyed, one-blue-eyed "brutal savage" Simon Phoenix in the futuristic action film *Demolition Man*. Here again the casting of a black actor—as the city's most vicious criminal who must be defeated to keep the streets safe—opened the film to certain interpretations.

Throughout the period, Snipes, however, was fascinating to observe as he brought a new vigor and cultural demarcation to standard action films, elevating them to another level, infusing them with a new aesthetic. Audiences often liked what his color and attitude *suggested* as much as what Snipes did. Even in *Demolition Man*, Snipes was in giddy, malevolent form, reeling in being able to bop Sylvester Stallone about—and also outwit him (not such a difficult chore, really). Perhaps his most daring role was as one of three drag queens (the other two played by Patrick Swayze and John Leguizamo) en route to Hollywood in the comedy *To Wong Foo: Thanks for Everything, Julie Newmar* (1995). When their car breaks down, the trio is stalled in a small town where, as might be expected in such a movie, they eventually endear themselves to the locals. The film stretched credulity: there was no way that anyone could have mistaken Snipes or Swayze for women. But Snipes didn't inhibit himself in creating the character. At times, he even seemed relieved not to have to be such a take-charge macho-man hero. An oddly touching moment occurs when Snipes sits with an elderly white woman of the town who warmly recalls the career of Dorothy Dandridge. Though the scene comes out of nowhere (you're totally unprepared for it), it worked well as one of the 1990s homages to the 1950s star now being rediscovered. In 1995, Snipes also teamed again with Woody Harrelson in *The Money Train*. Tony Scott's *The Fan* (1996) starred him as a pro-baseball player stalked by an overzealous fan (Robert De Niro).

Snipes's later films were less successful. *Murder at 1600* (1997) proved to be a standard and rather bland thriller, distinguished only by the fact that now a black actor was playing the lead in this nonrace-specific feature. He played a homicide detective investigating the murder of a twenty-five-year-old blond in the White House. Here there was no race problem. Here he was provided with a white sidekick (Dennis Miller). Here he was assisted in the investigation by an attractive, tough Secret Service agent (Diane Lane). Who could ask for a better case of color-blind casting? But, ironically, that may not have been enough for audiences in the late 1990s. The funny—and entertaining aspect—of a Snipes nonrace-theme film like *Passenger 57* had been those unexpected moments when the subtext of race comically raised its head. None of that popped up in *Murder at 1600*. Audiences may have wanted some telling African American cultural references so that they might better understand—or even enjoy—this black hero. Yet race appeared to be on the minds of the filmmakers as they made sure certain lines were not crossed. "My father was a history buff, so I guess it kind of rubbed off on me," Snipes's character, Harlan Regis, tells Diane Lane's character, Nina Chance. Thereafter he shows her a scale replica of Washington, D.C., around 1861. The two are in his home as they converse. "That's about as close to romance as *Murder at 1600* is

A new kind of action hero? Or the buck returns! Wesley Snipes in *Demolition Man*.

willing to go," wrote *New York Times* critic Janet Maslin. Obviously, the filmmakers wanted to steer clear of an interracial relationship. Though Snipes was provided a girlfriend in the 1998 *U.S. Marshals*—also rather standard fare but with a bit more verve—African American audiences still may have felt they weren't being told much about the character's cultural identity.

Nowhere was that more sorely missing than in Mike Figgis's *One Night Stand* (1997). You might say its theme was cultural/ethnic evasion. Yet the film didn't seem to acknowledge that cultural/ethnic/racial distinctions even existed. *One Night Stand* centered on a director of television commercials, Max (Snipes), who, while on a trip to New York from Los Angeles, encounters—in a hotel elevator—a European (we assume that from her accent) rocket scientist named Karen (*yes*, a rocket scientist, played by Nastassja Kinski). When she notices that his leaky pen is staining his shirt (*yes*, they meet, thanks to a leaky pen), she coyly tells him he has a *black* heart. (No one connected with the scene, neither director nor stars, appears to understand that this line of dialogue could have *another* meaning for the audience.) She lets him come to her room to change his shirt. Later, after he misses his flight to L.A., the two attend a performance of the Juilliard String Quartet. Following a pleasant dinner, they are mugged as they leave the restaurant. She's shaken and Max tries to comfort her. He ends up in her hotel room where they have a moody night of lovemaking. To the credit of the director and the stars, the scenes are far more sensual than those overblown pyrotechnics of Fishburne and Barkin in *Bad Company*.

One Night Stand tries to dramatize the change that now comes about in Max's life. When he arrives back in Los Angeles, even Max's dog—who sniffs him suspiciously—is aware that something has happened. Max soon becomes aware of his alienation from his Asian-American wife (Ming-Na Wen) Mimi who, unlike the demure Karen, "crudely" talks and talks while they make love. He also grows weary of his wife's sophisticated friends. The entire world Max lives in seems shallow and false, and you know he's got to get out, that indeed Karen has awakened something pure and good and decent within him. (You also know—that with the contrast between Karen and Mimi—you are beginning to hate what the director does to the Asian-American character.) But there's little else about the film that seems right. A subplot centers on Max's friendship with a young man (Robert Downey, Jr.) who is dying of AIDS.

Figgis, who had previously directed the painfully moving *Leaving Las Vegas* (1995), brought great style and mood to *One Night Stand*. Beautifully shot by cinematographer Declan Quinn, *One Night Stand* had a lulling rhythm that could draw the viewer in (or put the viewer to sleep, depending on your point of view). But for all Mike Figgis's talent, he failed to create a realistic story. Clearly, *One Night Stand* was not written with an African American character in mind. No one can complain about Figgis's decision to cast Snipes. Nor can anybody gripe about

Snipes's decision to accept the role. But at the end of the twentieth century, audiences no doubt believed that race/culture still played some part in everyone's life, and while Figgis certainly didn't have to turn *One Night Stand* into a race-theme picture, some basic changes in the script might have explained the way this flow of cultural experiences/distinctions (African American, European, Asian-American) affected the characters' lives. Snipes walked off with a Best Actor Award at the Venice Film Festival. But while he's mysteriously interesting, the film doesn't call for him to do much, and he can't give the story much of a subtext. What might have been a fascinating character study seems almost a perfunctory performance. Max, Karen, and Mimi remain tantalizing ciphers.

"As an actor for hire," Wesley Snipes told *The New York Times* on August 21, 1998, "your job and influence are finished once you leave the set." Aware of the importance of controlling his image and also aware that Hollywood was a town in which black stars, rather than black directors and producers, now had some clout, he formed the production company, Amen Ra Films (Afrakhan Minds Engaged N Royal Affairs), and set out to do a variety of projects. One of his most successful films was that year's *Blade*. Based on a Marvel Comics character that had first appeared in *Tomb of Dracula* in 1973, *Blade* recounted the adventures of a half-human, half-vampire hero who sets out to save the world from the domination of a new radical fringe of vampires. You may feel the film's too disjointed and character-impaired to be coherent. But *Blade* opened as the number-one movie in America, and it became a favorite of young audiences. Snipes's production company also made the Maya Angelou directed *Down in the Delta*, in which he gave a very subdued, engaging performance. Here, as in his cameo appearance in *Waiting to Exhale*, moviegoers saw Snipes playing a sensitive, rather ordinary character that was far removed from the action heroes that made Snipes a star and which he continued to play in a disappointing film like *The Art of War* (2000).

Character Actors Turned Stars: Morgan Freeman and Samuel L. Jackson

Other actors such as Morgan Freeman and Samuel L. Jackson—basically considered character actors—may have been surprised to see themselves emerge as full-fledged stars with a real box-office appeal that enabled them to command multimillion dollar salaries. Both men were formidable actors with forceful personalities. Within the industry itself, Freeman was perceived as someone that could not be messed with. (Curiously enough, the same was true of Bill Cosby.)

The Freeman persona was a smooth-malted blend of intelligence, assurance, and a keen self-awareness. By turns, depending on the requirements of the role, he could be cunning, perceptive, shrewd, resourceful, ruthless yet always endowed with a no-nonsense straightforwardness. Morgan Freeman had the air of a self-sufficient man who you believed was capable of doing almost anything, even building a house singlehandedly, from the ground up. He didn't need anybody (certainly not Miss Daisy in the late 1980s). That lay at the heart of his performance in Frank Darabont's adaptation of the Stephen King prison drama *The Shawshank Redemption* (1994). Here, Freeman played a long-term inmate who in time strikes up a friendship with a white prisoner (Tim Robbins). Even while audiences might reject the hokey bonding theme—even while asking why Freeman's character, Red, isn't depicted as having any real alliance with another black prisoner—Freeman's voice-over narration throughout the film framed it beautifully with a sense of moral gravity. And late in the film, when the character sits before a parole board, Freeman plays Red as a man who will ask nothing of anyone, not even his release from prison. "The files say you've served forty years of a life sentence," the young white man on the parole board informs Red. "Do you feel you've been rehabilitated?" Freeman's Red responds, "Rehabilitated? Well, now let me see. You know I don't have any idea what that means." The young man tells him, "It means you're ready to rejoin society." "I know what you think it means, sonny," says Freeman. "To me, it's just a made-up word. A politician's word. So young fellows like yourself can wear suits and ties. And have a job. What do you really want to know? Am I sorry for what I did?" Freeman continues, "There's not a day goes by I don't feel regret. Not because I'm in here. And you think I should be. I look back on the way I was then. A young stupid kid who committed that terrible crime. I want to talk to him. I want to try to talk some sense to him. Tell him the way things are. But I can't. That kid's long gone. This old man is all that's left. I got to live with that. *Rehabilitated* is just a word. So you go on and stamp your forms, sonny, and stop wasting my time. Cause to tell you the truth, I don't give a damn." It's a tour-de-force moment in the film, and you may feel it has strong ties to Juano Hernandez's often unacknowledged great performance in *Intruder in the Dust.* Afterwards the character Red is paroled.

In David Fincher's *Se7en* (1995)—a suspense drama about the hunt for a serial killer who murders his victims for committing one or the other of the Seven Deadly Sins—Freeman might easily have been little more than a by-the-numbers sidekick, who is there mainly to make the hero look good. Audiences learned almost nothing about his detective character—other than the fact that he's about to retire and is breaking in a new partner (Brad Pitt)—while the script lavished attention on Pitt's detective, cuing us to his relationship with his newlywed wife (Gwyneth Paltrow), which ultimately becomes an important plot device. Freeman, however, brought a weighty maturity and seriousness to *Se7en*, making it next to impossible for Pitt to control any of the scenes in which they appear together. Fortunately, Brad Pitt, aware (and one might say respectful) of the power of his co-star, wisely never attempted to upstage Freeman and seemed eager just to remain on the same footing with him.

Freeman's fundamental weight also distinguished his characters in such run-of-the-mill films as *Outbreak* (1995), *Chain Reaction* (1996), *Moll Flanders* (1996), and *Hard Rain* (1998). The producers and directors of those films seemed to understand that the young stars, like a Keanu Reeves or a Christian Slater, needed the sure, steady presence of Freeman to anchor the films with a degree of realism. In her August 13, 1996, *Village Voice* review of *Chain Reaction*, critic Amy Taubin wrote that Freeman "steals the show. With eyes colder than a Midwest winter glinting behind his hornrims, Freeman radiates power and intelligence from every pore. Unlike [Keanu] Reeves, who hurls himself pell-mell into play-acting, Freeman exerts Machiavellian control by seeming to do nothing at all." Yet, ironically, not even Freeman could do much with his role in Steven Spielberg's *Amistad*. Cast as an abolitionist (modeled, so audiences may have been hoping, on Frederick Douglass), Freeman's role looked like sheer tokenism.

When he played the President of the United States in the disaster film *Deep Impact* (1998)—the tale of humankind's preparation for a comet heading toward the earth that will destroy the planet—he was so confident and in control that moviegoers may have felt this was the kind of man who in the future *should* be in office. In the 1990s, critics loved to talk about those black actors who managed to "transcend" race. (This was said of Thandie Newton's appearance as Tom Cruise's leading lady in *Mission: Impossible 2*.) Yet those same critics never seemed to comment on white actors transcending *their* race in films. Interestingly enough, Freeman really may have "transcended" the *idea* of race in this film, the human race, that is. It's doubtful if audiences ever questioned the fact that an African American was the most powerful ruler in the world. Freeman seemed born for the job, to lead puny humankind through its last days when it finally realizes that love, courage, and self-dignity are about the only things that are important.

When Freeman finally was cast in a bona fide lead role—as the forensics psychologist Alex Cross in the movie adaptation of James Patterson's novel *Kiss the Girls* (1997)—Hollywood seemed almost shockingly cautious in the way it treated him. In this thriller, Cross heads from Washington, D.C., to North Carolina to find his young niece who has disappeared. He believes she's been kidnapped by a serial killer known as Casanova. After a young doctor (Ashley Judd), who has also been kidnapped by the Casanova killer, escapes, Cross seeks her help in rescuing his niece—and trapping the kidnapper. The two strike up a respectful father–daughter type of relationship. In Patterson's novel, however, the characters have a love affair. Despite the love scenes in *Bad Company* and in the 1997 *One Night Stand*, Hollywood, so the press noted, still backed off from relationships between black men and white women. "Gays can kiss. White men can kiss black women," reported the *New York Post* (October 2, 1997). "But a black man smooching with a white woman is still a Tinseltown taboo. What are they afraid of?"

But even more significant was the industry's initial attitude about casting the character Cross, who in the Patterson novel was black. "One studio who talked about the rights wanted to make Alex Cross white," white author James Patterson told the *New York Post*. "This is [the] first time Morgan has had a lead solo. It's the first time that one of the best actors in the world has had a leading role in which he's not playing the sidekick.... I think that's where the real problem lies in Hollywood." Once Freeman was cast, the industry did not have great hopes for *Kiss the Girls*. The *Hollywood Reporter* predicted the picture would "likely translate into moderate rather than killer business." But *Kiss the Girls* opened as the number-one film in the country and remained in first place the second week. Whether or not the country was ready for Freeman to be involved in an interracial affair on screen is open to debate. *But* the audience *was* ready for Freeman as a lead. A sequel, *Along Came a Spider*, with Freeman reprising his Cross role, appeared in 2001.

As an actor, Morgan Freeman was known to audiences as never making a false move. Even when cast as a heavy in Neil LaBute's *Nurse Betty*—a character who scalps and murders a man—Freeman did the seemingly impossible (as he'd done years ago in *Street Smart*): he invests a familiar, scary type of black character with an unexpected intelligence and even a stateliness.

When Samuel L. Jackson arrived at stardom in the late 1990s, audiences probably were unaware how long they had been watching him in movies (and on television). Born in 1948 in Chattanooga, Tennessee, Jackson once said the L in his name stood for Lucky (actually, it stood for Leroy). At Morehouse College, Jackson was known as something of a campus rebel who reportedly was temporarily expelled in 1968 for holding trustees hostage to protest for the creation of a Black Studies Program. While still a student, he also met his future wife, actress Latanya Richardson. Once the couple moved to New York City in the mid-1970s, Jackson worked in theater, and over the years played a variety of movie roles in which he stretched his talents and honed his craft: from his early appearance as a gang member in *Ragtime*; as Eddie Murphy's uncle in *Raw*; as a hold-up man in *Coming to America*; as the DJ Mister Senor Love in *Do the Right Thing*; to roles in *Def by Temptation*, *Juice*, *GoodFellas* (1990), and *Strictly Business*; to his breakthrough performance as Gator in *Jungle Fever*; to *Jurassic Park* (1993), *Amos and Andrew* (1993), *National Lampoon's Loaded Weapon* (1993), and *True Romance* (1993); to other important supporting roles in *Fresh* and *Losing Isaiah*, and later as the master violin restorer in *The Red Violin* (1999) as well as the disillusioned high-school teacher in *187* (1997, which he said had been his most challenging role). An exceptionally versatile actor, able

A character actor who may have been surprised to become a bona fide star: Morgan Freeman with Brad Pitt in *Se7en*. Freeman's sturdy presence and moral gravity brought weight and power to the film.

Samuel L. Jackson, who earlier in his career hoped he could become a *working* character actor *like* Morgan Freeman. Jackson also emerged as a full-fledged star with a surprising following among the young, black and white.

to play straight-arrow characters or brothers of the street, Jackson once said his ambition was to develop into a solid working character actor like Morgan Freeman. Stardom didn't seem to be on his mind. What usually distinguished his performances was his ability to give each part an ethnic marker and also to inject humor and irony into characters that might otherwise be forgettable or old-style types.

That was certainly true when Jackson played *against* the script in movies such as the 1996 *A Time to Kill* and *Die Hard with a Vengeance* (1995). In the former, he plays a Mississippi mill worker named Carl Lee Hailey, whose 10-year-old daughter is raped by two white thugs. Because he believes the men will be acquitted of the crime by an all-white Southern jury, Jackson's Hailey takes the law into his own hands and shoots them in the courthouse. Afterwards, he solicits the help of a young white attorney (Matthew McConaughey) to save him from the gas chamber. Influenced by such films as *Intruder in the Dust* and *To Kill a Mockingbird*, Joel Schumacher's *A Time to Kill*, which was based on the first novel of best-selling author John Grisham, was set in the 1990s but had the look and feel of a movie from the late 1940s or 1950s. It's like a Negro Problem Picture that makes a big deal over the fact that (even at this late date) the white attorney has to inform the white jury of its own racism. And throughout, we're to feel for the poor white attorney's welfare and that of his family because he's *so* heroic in defending this black man.

You might expect Jackson to play the role tentatively, as a man who—in hopes of saving his life by appealing to the compassion of everyone around him—is meek and soft-spoken. But Jackson's character was tough and even abrasive as he gave orders to McConaughey. In the latter part of the film (in a sequence that doesn't always ring true), he bitingly accuses the attorney of being racist himself. While McConaughey, who looks like a model for *GQ*, is there to set hearts apatter (although, frankly, he gives a credible performance), Jackson energizes *A Time to Kill* with his intensity and his star power. You get the sense that he's a man who won't compromise himself—even though he knows he's at the mercy of a not-so-friendly white community. (Jackson, like Morgan Freeman, may have seen the great Juano Hernandez in *Intruder in the Dust*; if so, then he clearly understood what a skilled actor can do with such material.)

In John McTiernan's action film *Die Hard with a Vengeance*, which centered on the attempts to thwart a terrorist madman (Jeremy Irons) who threatens to blow up New York City, Jackson's character Zeus—a Harlem storekeeper—was called upon frequently to appear nervous and scared. Despite his strong early scenes, he soon has to follow the lead of the star, Bruce Willis. While the two yap and yell at each other like a bickering married couple, Jackson's humor—and the sanity that underlies it—makes Zeus fun to watch as he shrewdly maneuvers his way around the dialogue and situations. And he knows how to highlight lines that express his character's intelligence. (The same is true of his work in *The Long Kiss Goodnight*, 1996, in which the filmmakers make sure that—despite a kiss—as close as he gets to leading lady Geena Davis, he doesn't get *too* close.)

But none of his roles veered closer to familiar types than those in Quentin Tarantino's *Pulp Fiction* and *Jackie Brown*. Ironically, Jackson gave two of his most adroit performances in the films. The dark, postmodern *Pulp Fiction*—winner of the Palme d'Or at the 1994 Cannes Film Festival—cast Jackson and John Travolta as hit men for a local crime kingpin (Ving Rhames). They are capable of acts of shocking violence and brutality. But Tarantino is less interested in the violence than in the behavior of the men before and after their brutal acts, which, ironically, they view merely as work. At one point, they've even dressed in dark suits and ties as they go about the job—to blast somebody away. During the course of a day, the two shoot the breeze—they might be commenting on the fact that the Dutch use mayonnaise on their french fries; or they might be engaged in a philosophical debate. Jackson's character, Jules Winnfield, even quotes from the Scriptures as he's about to execute his victims. What people actually do during their workday apparently has nothing to do otherwise with their sense of morality or their code of ethics.

With its disjointed time scheme and nonlinear narrative (it tells three overlapping, interlocking stories), *Pulp Fiction* presented a bizarre demimonde of small-time hoods, drugs, killings, betrayals, blood, and gore—all the lurid details *and* the types of pulp, similar to what could be found in 1930s and 1940s crime magazines like *Black Mask*. Ving Rhames's character, Marsellus, was almost pure buck: menacing, violent, cruel, and still hot for white women. (Uma Thurman plays his wife.) But Jackson cleverly works around the buck territory. His character Jules—perhaps because Tarantino has written such achingly funny dialogue for him—seemed one step removed from his deeds. And in the film's most unexpected sequence—and the aspect that in some ways elevates the story—Jules finds pop redemption. Part street-corner evangelist and part hood out to fleece somebody, he's more complicated than we think, and Jackson suggests a complexity—a real moral drive—that really is not in the script. Jackson received a Best Supporting Actor Oscar nomination for his performance. Within the industry, it was rumored that Jackson was upset by the decision of Miramax (which had released *Pulp Fiction*) to campaign for his nomination in the supporting category rather than lead (despite the fact that he had a co-starring role) in order that John Travolta might have a better chance at a Best Actor Oscar. Travolta won the nomination but not the award. (Something similar had occurred a few years earlier when the producers of the 1993 *Philadelphia* had wanted to campaign for Denzel Washington in the Oscar's Best Supporting Actor category, so that Tom Hanks might have a better chance at winning the Best Actor Oscar. Aware that he was as much a star of the film as Hanks, Washington reportedly balked at being put in such a category and was not nominated. In the end, Hanks did win the Best Actor Academy Award.)

Based on Elmore Leonard's best-selling 1995 novel *Rum Punch*, *Jackie Brown* was another Tarantino tale of a bizarre underworld—and also a homage to blaxploitation cinema of the 1970s. At its center was that raunchy icon of that earlier era, Pam Grier, as flight attendant Jackie Brown, who is caught smuggling $500,000 into the country. She's working for Ordell Robbie (Jackson), a slick but tough arms dealer living with his perpetually stoned girlfriend (Bridget Fonda) in Hermosa Beach. If Jackie doesn't cooperate with the feds, she knows they will send her off to prison for a very *long* time. If she does turn in evidence against Ordell, Jackie knows she may end up dead. Shrewdly, Jackie plays the authorities and Ordell off one another. Often meandering and way too long, yet cleverly using its 1970 soul-and-funk soundtrack (that features the Delfonics, the Brothers Johnson, Bobby Womack, and Bill Withers), and making excellent use of its actors, *Jackie Brown* was fairly entertaining with the trademark Tarantino mix of jolting violence and outrageous humor; a juxtapositioning of the shocking and the mundane. Again, much of the fun comes from the banality of the characters' lives. In this brutal world, where death can come at any moment, there is a lot of small talk and long drives, and trips to the mall, and songs heard on car radios. Do people caught in the grip of explosive situations really act like, well, everybody else? Tarantino thinks so.

Unlike much blaxploitation cinema, *Jackie Brown*, however, was not a pop declaration of war between black and white. For the characters, race is no big deal. A solidly middle-class bail bondsman (Robert Forster) even falls hard for Grier, and audiences no doubt wanted to see this saving grace of a relationship work out for her. (That hardly would have happened in black popular cinema of the 1970s.) And Ordell uses the n-word almost at every other turn, *judiciously* applying it to characters black and white. (So often was the word heard that Spike Lee complained. It's one thing when a black filmmaker uses it as part of his in-group lexicon. It's another matter when an outsider feels he has the right to bandy the word about.)

Older and still a sight to behold (even though she's not always filmed in the most flattering manner), Pam Grier seemed delighted to be back on-screen in a leading role—and in a major Hollywood film in which her co-stars were such performers as Jackson and Robert De Niro. Although the heroine in the book was white, blond and fortyish, Tarantino wanted Grier, whom he had originally auditioned for *Pulp Fiction*. "I don't consider the little Hollywood gene pool that everyone else uses," he told *The New York Times* on December 21, 1997. "I knew I needed a great-looking 44-year-old who looks like she can handle anything but is actually very vulnerable. Sounds like Pam Grier to me." Not as gritty and raunchy as in her earlier period and with an acting range that seemed even narrower, she

She's back and she's still *baad*: Pam Grier off-screen (LEFT) and as the frazzled but resilient heroine in *Jackie Brown.*

managed (at age forty-eight) to bring out Jackie's carefully honed survival skills and her very real fears. Of course, when the moment comes that everybody's been waiting for—when she finally turns up decked out in a sexy red number that showcases her wares, she no doubt elicits the same response from a new generation of horny teenage boys as she did two decades earlier. But the film's affection for her is sweet-tempered, and Tarantino lets the actress control the action.

Tarantino also gave Jackson free reign to strut about as if he owned the screen. With a ponytail and pointy goatee, Jackson's Ordell has just the right look and attitude; just the right menace and cruelty coupled with an unexpected nonchalance and, again, humor. When an employee, Beaumont Livingston (Chris Tucker), proves troublesome, Ordell first persuades him to lie down in the trunk of a stolen car, then eliminates him. Upon seeing the corpse, another character asks, "Who's that?" Ordell tells him, "That's Beaumont." "Who's Beaumont?" "An employee I had to let go," answers Ordell. Hyper, restless, quick-tempered, and on occasion disarming, he's all extrovertism, a character that looks as if it sprang from the hip of the old-style buck. But Jackson (much like Morgan Freeman in *Street Smart*) enlivens and individualizes Jules, making him shrewd and daring.

During the end of the decade and into the twenty-first century, Samuel L. Jackson worked in such films as *Sphere* (1998), *The Negotiator, Deep Blue Sea* (1999), and *Rules of Engagement* (2000). In a film like George Lukas's *Star Wars: Episode I—The Phantom Menace* (1999), he had so little to do that it almost looked as if he were being used as a contrast to the caricatured antics of Jar Jar Binks. (Like Freeman in *Amistad*, this seemed another case of tokenism.) But Jackson had such presence and assurance that you would have thought he was the film's star. The same was true of his chilling performance (in a very disturbing role as an asexual madman who commits mass murders) in M. Night Shyamalan's *Unbreakable* (2000). Perhaps the real testament to his skills could be seen in John Singleton's remake of *Shaft*. Navigating his way through a soggy script that didn't give him a real character to play, he performed the role of John Shaft mainly as a series of angry poses and postures. He also had to overcome the fact that he was basically miscast. Yet his great rapport with the audience turned the remake into a hit. Soon afterwards, one of Hollywood's best-kept secrets was revealed. Whereas stars such as John Travolta and Kevin Costner received salaries in the $20 million range for films that were huge bombs, Jackson, who then averaged about $7 or $10 million a picture, really could pull in audiences. Samuel L. Jackson had become an authentic movie star (the kind of actor audiences were really glad to see make it) with a large young following, black and white, as well as some middle-aged folks who had been seeing him since his early days. His other films included *Sea of Love* (1989), *The Return of Super Fly* (1990), *Mo' Better Blues, Betsy's Wedding* (1990), *The Exorcist III* (1990), *Kiss of Death* (1993), Reginald Hudlin's *The Great White Hype* (1996) and *Out of Sight* (uncredited).

Denzel Washington: Leading Man, Occasional Romantic Hero, Enduring Superstar

Certainly no African American actor proved more successful during this period than Denzel Washington. In Hollywood, his credentials were impeccable. Not only did he project the requisite sex appeal and glamour that Hollywood expects and admires in its stars but, lo and behold, the guy could act. Ultimately, he embodied but also—as a black actor—reconfigured (as had Dorothy Dandridge) the concept of classic movie stardom.

For the most part, his movie choices—from *Malcolm X* to *Much Ado about Nothing* (1993)—were sound, diverse, challenging. His one bad movie was the offensive black/white buddy movie *Heart Condition* (1990). As the romantic lead in *Mo' Better Blues* and also in Indian director Mira Nair's informed study of culture clashes between blacks and the East Indian community in *Mississippi Masala* (1992), he generated the appropriate sexual heat in love scenes but never let his sexuality dominate his characters.

Two very successful films cast him in roles originally created with white actors in mind. In the thriller *The Pelican Brief* (1993) he gave an adroit, wonderfully assured performance as a journalist who befriends an endangered Julia Roberts. In the John Grisham novel on which the film was based, the reporter and young woman ended up in one another's arms. But even with its most prized black actor, Hollywood still took precautions not to fiddle with mainstream sensibilities. The film kept the Washington/Roberts relationship as chaste as that of Sidney Poitier and Katharine Houghton in *Guess Who's Coming To Dinner*.

Jonathan Demme's *Philadelphia* (1993), the first Hollywood film to focus on the subject of AIDS, cast Washington as a homophobic lawyer who defends another lawyer (Tom Hanks), who has been fired after his law firm learns he has contracted the disease. Other actors might have heavy-handedly huffed their way through or sentimentalized the homophobic lawyer's emerging sensitization. But with humor, earthiness, and the appropriate suggestion of *casual* everyday bigotry, Washington charted the character's newfound awareness with a very realistic touch. The film also did a decent job of establishing a familial/cultural context for the character.

For the rest of the decade, Washington gave backbone to one film after another with taut, controlled, and often remarkable performances. In some respects, he reminded audiences of some Sidney Poitier heroes from the 1950s and 1960s. Both Poitier and Washington represented thoughtful, committed, honest men, almost paragons of decency and virtue without a possibly threatening or aggressive sexuality. But whereas the Poitier hero often had to prove himself ready for integration, Washington's heroes, at least on the surface, were supposedly living testaments to a free and open society—symbols of an African American male operating in color-free worlds. Tony Scott's old-style cold war drama *Crimson Tide* (1995) cast Washington as a lieutenant in a face-off with his commander (Gene Hackman) on a nuclear submarine. Theirs is a battleground of perspectives without any racial fireworks. Ultimately, his intelligent moral force prevents a war with Russia. In Edward Zwick's *Courage under Fire* (1996), he portrayed a troubled lieutenant colonel, investigating the death of a young female captain (Meg Ryan) who is being considered for a Medal of Honor. As he pieces together the facts of her life, he broods over his own past when he was responsible for the death, by friendly fire, of members of his platoon. Audiences almost always waited for that key moment in a Washington film (here again similar to Poitier) when he exploded in anger and righteous indignation. He did less of a slow burn than Poitier. But both were able to handle such scenes without resorting to histrionics or melodramatics. Race was almost an afterthought in these Washington films, although African American audiences often saw a racial subtext. He also played an FBI agent dealing with a New York City terrorist attack in *The Siege* (1998).

Watching Spike Lee's *He Got Game*, audiences saw Washington break away from the expected role. As the convict trying to reach his son (Ray Allen), he's a man aching inside. A part of him has withdrawn and still mourns the death of his wife (which he accidentally caused) and his son's alienation from him. The weariness, the exasperation, the sadness come across in his eyes and his voice in every frame. Though *He Got Game* didn't win Washington any big awards, it was one of the strongest male performances, black or white, of the decade.

One senses that same withdrawal and that same suppressed anger as well as a controlled restlessness in another of the finest performances of the 1990s: Washington as real-life boxer Rubin (Hurricane) Carter in *The Hurricane* (1999), directed by Norman Jewison. In 1966, Carter—a middleweight contender—had been wrongly convicted (along with another innocent man) of murdering three people in Paterson, New Jersey. After nineteen years, he was released from prison due to the efforts of a black teenager, Lesra Martin (who had read Carter's autobiography), and a group of Canadians. In recounting Carter's story, *The Hurricane* was far from being an impressive film. So thoughtful and virtuous a lot were the three liberal white Canadians—with whom the teenage Lesra (Vicellous Reon Shannon) lives (they've informally adopted him and taught him how to read)—that sometimes we feel we're supposed to think as much of them as heroes as we do the real hero, Carter. Truth be told, in the film they're props—and boring props at that—once again noble white faces that the mainstream audience is supposed to identify with in order to feel that it, too, would have been as perceptive and morally driven as these people to fight for Carter's freedom. (The three in the film were also a composite of the real nine commune members who lobbied for Carter's release. No credit was given in the film to the journalists and lawyers who

They get close but not too close: Denzel Washington and Julia Roberts in *The Pelican Brief.*

BELOW: The performance that should have won him a second Oscar: Denzel Washington, with Vicellous Reon Shannon (LEFT), in *The Hurricane.*

also worked on the case.) *The Hurricane* also created a racist white cop who—long out to *get* Carter—in essence frames him. But, as Allison Samuels and David Ansen commented in the January 10, 2000, issue of *Newsweek*, "by putting the onus on one evil white man, it diminishes the systemic racism that kept Carter behind bars.... It would be nice if *The Hurricane* trusted the audience to swallow a less simplistic view of reality."

Although one can fault the weak, sorry script of *The Hurricane*, no one could fault Denzel Washington's performance. Having lost forty-four pounds and having done strenuous workouts in preparation for the role, he created an emotionally hardened man, so despairing and disillusioned that while in prison he refuses to see his wife and daughter; a man who has lost his faith in just about everything, even in proving his innocence. (The movie avoids any significant comment on Carter's relationship with his family. After Debbi Morgan establishes such an interesting portrait of his wife, she just about disappears from the movie.) Yet in Washington's hands, another part of Carter remains vitally alive, refusing to back down from his beliefs. "It's a moving, fiercely compacted performance that invites us to marvel at the resilience of the spirit," wrote *Newsweek*.

For his performance, Washington won a Golden Globe Award as Best Actor in a Drama. He was also nominated for the Academy Award. Had he won, it would have been a truly historic event: the first black actor to win two Oscars and the first since Poitier to walk off with a Best Actor Oscar. But then there was a backlash against the picture itself. Families of the real-life murder victims denounced *The Hurricane* for making "a hero out of a cold-blooded killer," the *New York Post* reported on February 10, 2000. Carter's lawyers countered that the families had been misled by authorities who refused to admit that they had made a mistake. In the end, Kevin Spacey won the Best Actor Oscar for his performance in *American Beauty* (1999). Afterwards, *The New York Times* reported in its March 26, 2000, edition: "Many were wondering whether Mr. Spacey's victory over Denzel Washington, the early Oscar favorite for his critically praised performance in Norman Jewison's *The Hurricane*, had resulted partly from the uproar over the accuracy of the film based on the life of the boxer Hurricane Carter." Some within the industry believed that there had been a concerted effort to ensure that Washington did *not* win.

Another Washington film at the end of the decade was less controversial but hugely profitable. *The Bone Collector* opened as a number-one movie, indicating Washington's box-office clout. In the thriller *The Bone Collector*, he played a forensics detective who, following an accident while on a case, has been left a paraplegic. Often depressed and suffering from epileptic seizures (that could leave him in a vegetative state), he wants to end his life. Yet from his apartment, he can still solve crimes by use of voice commands and one finger that can operate the computers that surround his bed. Assisting him on solving a particularly gruesome series of killings is a young police officer and former model (Angelina Jolie). Yet while Washington and the sensual Jolie appear to give each other some knowing glances, Washington was kept chaste. "One finger, shoulders, and brain. That's all I have," Washington says at one point. Audiences need not fret that the two might fall into one another's arms—even though that one finger could prove problematic.

Reviewers commented on the lack of romance in such Washington's films as the cyberspace thriller *Virtuosity* (1995) and in the supernatural thriller *Fallen* (1998). *New York Times* critic Janet Maslin referred to the latter as "another of the star's platonic pictures." Washington was said to feel uncomfortable playing love scenes. Interestingly enough, when he had such a scene with white actress Milla Jovovic in *He Got Game*, black women were said to have booed the action on-screen, not wanting to see their dreamboat involved with a white woman. The same had happened years earlier with preview audiences who saw the love scene between Washington and Mimi Rogers in *The Mighty Quinn*. The scene was cut from the film. "I know that a large part of my audience is black women," Washington told *Newsweek* in its January 10, 2000, issue. "I also know there aren't many black love stories they can see on the big screen—and that's an issue." Washington's female following, however, did not object to his romantic scenes with black actresses in *Mo' Better Blues* (even though they may have despised some of his characters' attitudes about women), and frankly, a few sexy sparks between the characters played by Washington and Whitney Houston in *The Preacher's Wife* might have enlivened the picture and even turned it into a hit. But Washington's romantic appeal was never tapped deeply enough.

By the end of the millennium and the start of a new era, Washington, with a solid body of work behind him, had become, as *Newsweek* commented, "the preeminent black actor of the '90s."

Throwbacks to the Past

Even during the supposedly new liberal Hollywood of the late 1990s—the age of mega-black stardom and mega-black salaries—Hollywood remained a town where certain color lines were still drawn—where there remained *acceptable* roles for African American performers. Black moviegoers were often surprised to see distressing images—obvious throwbacks to the past—in such films as *Bulworth* (1998) and *The Green Mile* (1999).

The group of naive, almost childlike black characters in Warren Beatty's political satire *Bulworth* seemed capable of doing little more than celebrating their great white father figure (the politician Bulworth) as a savior—for telling them the very things that should have been obvious to them.

But by far, the most egregious use of these familiar images could be found in *The Green Mile*. Frank Darabont's Great Depression-era tale *Green Mile*, based on a story by Stephen King, cast black actor Michael Clarke Duncan as a prisoner on death row in Louisiana. Accused of having raped and murdered two nine-year-old white girls, Duncan's character, John Coffey, is a huge man who towers above everyone else. Coffey turns out to be a gentle giant, who is afraid of the dark and refers to his prison guards as *boss*. He also has magical healing powers. In fact, Coffey was what came to be known as a *magical Negro*: really an outgrowth of the noble tom. Ready to help whites, the magical Negro works wonders for the white folks around him. Not only does he cure a prison guard, played by Tom Hanks, of a bladder infection—and in doing so helps restore the Hanks character's sexual relations with his wife—but he also breathes life into the then-dying wife of the prison's warden. It doesn't take long to realize that John Coffey's initials, JC, might also stand for Jesus Christ. A black Jesus? How progressive for the movies? Actually, how retro. You soon realize that what makes him truly *noble* in the eyes of the filmmakers are his self-sacrificial heroics, which are performed for the benefit of these white strangers in his life.

Many African American moviegoers, even those who liked the film, found the character something of an embarrassment. No one knows where this black man in this white community has come from. Nor do we know anything about *his* loved ones. Even at the climax when the identity of the real rapist/killer (who is white) is revealed, Coffey is not permitted (by the screenplay) to speak out for himself. Why does he let himself be thought of as one more black rapist who *deserves* to be put to death? Here *The Green Mile* really makes no sense. The character's "capacity for self-sacrifice has its inadvertently racist overtones," Janet Maslin wrote in *The New York Times*. And later, on March 19, 2000, *The New York Times*'s Elvis Mitchell commented that *The Green Mile* pushed "across the boundary between a movie about racism and a vaguely racist movie." Despite the criticism, Duncan walked off with an Oscar nomination as Best Supporting Actor.

What a way for one century to end—and another to begin!

But of course, in the 1990s there had been another part of the story of which moviegoers, black and white, were aware. The established stardom of actors Denzel Washington, Morgan Freeman, Wesley Snipes, Samuel L. Jackson, and Eddie Murphy—despite the built-in paradoxes and complications of their careers that had long plagued African American actors in the movies—really did signal a change in American films at the tail end of the twentieth century and at the start of the new millennium. So too did the drive of an Angela Bassett to keep working to reach audiences in a new way. So too did the emergence of performers such as Delroy Lindo, Don Cheadle, Tyra Ferrell, Ving Rhames, Terrence Howard, and, yes, even the often-maligned Whitney Houston. And, quite significantly, so did the presence on the scene of such directors as Spike Lee, John Singleton, Charles

Burnett, Julie Dash, the Hughes Brothers, Carl Franklin, and late-1990s newcomers such as George Tillman and Kasi Lemmons, all of whom offered new directorial visions, all of whom were aware that in the movies it is always important for the audience, black and white, to understand who is telling the story, whose point of view those screen images are coming from, what is being told, and what is not being said in feature films. In the last decade of the twentieth century, more African American filmmakers had worked in mainstream cinema than ever before in American movie history. That in itself was quite a feat that should never go underestimated. And that clearly was a sign of hope for the future: filmmakers who go against the odds to get their work on the silver screen.

11 THE NEW CENTURY, THE NEW MILLENNIUM: OLD TYPES, NEW STARS, NEW FILMMAKERS, RE-EXAMINATIONS OF THE PAST

Denzel Washington gives an Academy Award-winning performance as a rogue cop but the film sets off a wave of controversy. . . . Halle Berry walks off with an Oscar but also draws criticism for her role as an emotionally displaced widow who falls into the arms and home of the man who led her husband to his death. . . . A trio of young Black singers—played by Jennifer Hudson, Beyoncé Knowles, and Anika Noni Rose— makes hits and endures heartaches in Dreamgirls. *. . . Will Smith as a homeless father caring for his young son and as a hero saving the world in epic adventures emerges all the more as a huge international box office star. . . . Outside the Hollywood system, Tyler Perry, a man who was once homeless, begins writing and starring in his own dramas on stage, then makes movies and comes up with money-makers that surprise the industry and enrage the critics . . . Terrence Howard is a pimp with three hos by his side as he sets off for a career in rap/crunk. . . . An Old South plantation drama set in Louisiana and another climaxing in Mississippi alter film history with images of brutality and cruelty. . . . Other films place history front and center as they tell the stories of the march on Selma, Alabama; of the life of a White House butler; of a young Black man killed at a transit station in San Francisco. . . . Morgan Freeman, Jamie Foxx, Forest Whitaker, Jennifer Hudson, and Mo'Nique and others walk off with Oscars or Oscar nominations.*

And so it was a new century, indeed a new millennium, with a brave new world of technological developments and advancements as well as a new world of domestic and international horrors. On September 11, 2001, a tragedy occurred that shook and shocked the nation and the world. Terrorists high-jacked and then crashed two planes into New York's World Trade Center. A third high-jacked plane crashed into the Pentagon just outside Washington, D.C. A fourth on which passengers fought the terrorist high-jackers crashed onto an open field in Pennsylvania. Over three thousand people were killed, including police and firefighters, and almost 10,000 were treated for injuries. President George W. Bush sought to comfort and then rouse the nation. The Department of Homeland Security was established. Airports, train and bus stations, public buildings and national landmarks were closely guarded and monitored. Afterward there also came a controversial war in Iraq.

Politics and social change ultimately loomed large over the early decades of the new millennium. The nation witnessed another historic event but of a far different kind as it watched an exciting Democratic primary campaign between two unprecedented Presidential candidates—a woman, Hillary Rodham Clinton and an African American, Barack Obama. In November 2008, Barack Obama, the son of a white American mother and a Kenyan father, defeated the Republican Senator John McCain to become the first African American President of the United States. Optimism swept through parts of the country, especially in the African American community. But soon the nation was faced with domestic issues of staggering unemployment numbers and then a great recession. Talk of a post-racial nation—the idea that racial inequities and divisions no longer existed—vanished as racial tensions re-emerged, notably with the treatment of victims of Hurricane Katrina in New Orleans in 2005. In time, protests sprang up in American cities, often enough centered on conflicts between police forces and African American men.

At the same time, the nation was transformed by the technological advances, be it the iPod, the iPhone, the iPad, the indispensability of the Internet, email, bloggers, and also other wonders: the Kindle, the Nook, Blu Ray, HD TV, Facebook, Twitter, Instagram, texting, sexting, and who knows what. Concurrent with the splendors of the new technology—the new social media—was a steady decline in the old forms of communication and media, the traditional ways of gathering information and better understanding the world. Readership of newspapers and magazines sank to new lows, many folding up shop. Even traditional television—viewing shows on that box that sat in the living room—was altered as more programs were watched on the new devices. At the movies, it wasn't just the old word of mouth that could make or break a film. Soon it was average moviegoers taking to Twitter or Facebook or a blog to voice their opinions. The same would be true of protest groups around the world. All these changes would be commonplace to later generations. But the start of the new millennium marked societal shifts that could not have been predicted or anticipated.

Some movies reflected the social/political shifts in national attitudes and outlooks; others were seemingly oblivious to the rising tide of change. More African American directors, male and female, veterans as well as newcomers—from Spike Lee and Antoine Fuqua to Ava DuVernay and Lee Daniels—would find work. In some instances, black filmmakers such as Tim Story and F. Gary Gray would direct such popular non-black features as the action film *Fantastic Four* and the enjoyably slick and breezy *Italian Job*. During the new decade and into the next, there also would be more significant roles for African American women in mainstream cinema.

Such actresses and actors as Jennifer Hudson, Anthony Mackie, Paula Patton, Nate Parker, Sophie Okonedo, Gugu Mbatha-Raw, Laz Alonso, Jeffrey Wright, Vin Diesel, Tyrese Gibson, Aunjanue Ellis, Tasha Smith, Cedric the Entertainer, and Tika Sumpter showed up on the scene while such other performers as Don Cheadle, Kimberly Elise, Nia Long, Regina King, Thandie Newton, Megan Good, Morris Chestnut, Loretta Devine, Regina Hall, and that crafty master Samuel L. Jackson, who had been working since the previous decade, held onto their screen careers. Among the performers who emerged as stars in this era were: Queen Latifah, Bernie Mac, Taraji P. Henson, Terrence Howard, Viola Davis, Octavia Spencer, Lupita Nyong'o, Idris Elba, and Kevin Hart. Other black superstars such as Denzel Washington and Will Smith continued to have extraordinary success in popular mainstream movies. For African Americans in cinema, the era would be very active with some remarkable achievements.

Yet along with the significant changes were the familiar images that had so long been embedded in American movies.

Seems Like Old Times, Old Types

Shortly after the start of the decade, the old types and familiar distortions reared their heads to reveal they were still thriving and infecting American motion pictures, in such well-made and seemingly forward-looking movies as *The Patriot* (2000), *Traffic* (2000), and *The Legend of Bagger Vance* (2000). In the colonial South Carolina of 1776 that was depicted in the Revolutionary War drama *The Patriot*, much was done to depict the brutality of this war. Yet nothing even remotely suggested the inhumanity of slavery. "The charitable will perhaps overlook one dreadful mistake—the happy slaves on the plantations," commented David Denby in *The New Yorker*. Though *The Patriot* made a gesture toward historical accuracy depicting blacks who fought in the War, you're bound to agree with *Newsweek*'s David Ansen that this was "civics-lesson condescension."

Even Steven Soderbergh's much-lauded *Traffic* fell into the trap of old images. In this drama about the drug trade, the fair-haired daughter of an American antidrug czar (Michael Douglas) becomes hooked on drugs. In search of a fix, she wanders into a black neighborhood (the old ghetto of the 1970s-style films) where she ends up in a room with a naked, muscular young black man, who's ready to shoot her up—and also take her sexually. The scene is meant to send shivers up the spines of the mainstream audience. What worse thing could happen to this poor misguided lass—on a seedy path of self-humiliation and degradation—than to be taken advantage of by a character who is dangerously close to a new-style/old-style buck figure. Interestingly, in another sequence the young woman's father breaks into a room where she is holed up with an older white man, also ready to take advantage of her. But he is fully clothed and hardly menacing.

Whereas a film of the previous decade such as *The Green Mile* at least acknowledged racism, the Robert Redford-directed *The Legend of Bagger Vance* seemed oblivious to the topic. Set in the South between 1917 and 1931, the film stars Matt Damon as a onetime golf champ Rannulph Junuh, who, having witnessed the horrors of War World I, returns to his native Georgia disillusioned and reclusive, unable to live a normal life and unable to play golf. When his old flame, Adele Invergordon (Charlize Theron) is desperate for money to save the golf resort that her father built before the Depression, Junuh is enlisted to play in a big celebrity match. Still a riddle of insecurities and fears, he is, however, unable to get his swing back; that is, until one evening when a black man, Bagger Vance (Will Smith), mysteriously appears and offers to caddie for the young man for $5. (It appears he wouldn't dream of asking for the standard 10 percent that most caddies received.) Thereafter Bagger is often by Junuh's side, cleaning the crud off Junuh's shoes and encouraging him while seeking to boost his spirits—and doing so while speaking in an old-style/movie-style dialect. "The sight of one of Hollywood's biggest black stars playing a caddie—and delivering worthy lines like 'sho is some storm-a-brewing'—is not a little depressing," noted *New York Post* critic Jonathan Foreman. But Bagger is a magical Negro who ends by working wonders, indeed enabling Junuh to get his swing back—and along the way to reunite him romantically with Adele. Like Coffey in *The Green Mile*, Bagger has helped the white man regain his manhood, his very sexuality. Here is another black angelic or Krishna-like or Christ-like figure out to help white characters solve their problems.

Poor deluded Bagger seemed part noble tom, part adoring nurturing mammy, and most times downright laughable. *Newsweek*'s David Ansen described Vance as "a cross between Krishnamurti and Uncle Remus." One only wonders why the black Bagger is not prone to giving a helping hand to any black people with their problems, especially since this is the apartheid South of the Great Depression era.

Will Smith as the "kindly" Bagger Vance who helps Matt Damon get his "swing" back in *The Legend of Bagger Vance.*

You cannot help but agree with *The Washington Post*'s Rita Kempley who wrote that "nobody connected with this sap-oozing fantasy seems to have taken the time or the place into consideration ... director Robert Redford plays possum when it comes to racism." Kempley also referred to "the degrading aspects of Smith's role," adding, "Isn't it time to put Stepin Fetchit to rest?" Like the character in *The Green Mile*, Vance might not have been meant to be taken as a real person "but a spiritual emanation," wrote *The New York Times*'s A. O. Scott. "But supernatural is not much better than subhuman: Hollywood is still, in the year 2000, disinclined to let black actors play human beings."

Nowhere were the complaints and controversies more apparent than in 2001 with the Oscar winning roles of Denzel Washington in *Training Day* and Halle Berry in *Monster's Ball*.

Denzel Washington: Still at the Top Despite a Rogue Cop

Early in the decade—in 2000—Denzel Washington showed his box-office clout with the profitable, entertaining film *Remember the Titans* which opened as the number one movie. Set in the early 1970s the film is really an old-style integrationist sports drama that keeps its focus on the relations of high school football players at a recently integrated school. When Washington's character is signed to replace the school's white coach, naturally, everyone has to learn to get along together. Much like George Tillman Jr.'s *Men of Honor*, which opened the same year, *Remember the Titans* was another drama that could have starred Sidney Poitier in an earlier era. Though the film provided Washington with a wife (Nicole Ari Parker) and family, little was seen of Washington's family life. No love scenes turned up either. Its success indicated a relaxed mood among moviegoers who seemed to prefer race-relations pictures that were subdued and predictable and comfortably set in the past, with the subtext that America had overcome its race problems. Nonetheless, *Remember the Titans* was a well-acted, entertaining film.

But during this decade, none of Washington's roles drew as much attention *or* controversy as his rogue cop in Antoine Fuqua's 2001 *Training Day*. Tracing one day in the lives of two police officers, the film focuses on a rookie Jake Hoyt (Ethan Hawke) learning the ropes from an experienced old-hand narcotics detective Alonzo Harris (Washington), who is cynical, corrupt, and foul, out to make a quick buck and neither troubled nor guilt-ridden by his own seething corruption. To say that Alonzo had shades of the old-style buck would be an understatement. Here was a highly sexual man, violent and brutal to the core, preying on his own community. No serious attempts were made in David Ayer's cold-blooded—and bloody—script to explain his pathology. Not only is Alonzo a perversion of law enforcement but a perversion of fundamental morality. *Training Day* brought to mind other images of brutal, monstrous black men who deserved to be stomped out, shot down, obliterated from the face of the earth. That had been the case with the pimp in *Magnum Force* (1973) who pours drain cleaner liquid down the throat of a prostitute who has broken his rules; of Jim Brown's character Dreems in *Fingers* (1978); of Morgan Freeman's pimp in *Street Smart* (1987) who holds scissors to the eye of a prostitute who has also broken his rules. One only wonders what these shocking (and shockingly powerful) images do in forming perceptions. These black men have been presented as a blight on society, a poison that must be eradicated.

Still, Washington's performance was riveting. Clearly in search of a role to extend his talents and refusing to let himself get stuck in the groove of the fundamentally decent characters of his established screen persona, he had traveled a route that Poitier had not dared. Of course, Poitier had come of screen age at a time when he believed it crucial to provide a positive, uplifting image; for that, he has to be commended. But Washington was taking chances. He gets inside Alonzo's head, although we the audience may not understand what he's found to motivate or delineate the character. Every move he makes is an artistically honest one. For his tour de force performance, he won his second Academy Award, this time as Best Actor of 2001, an award that had so long eluded him. The evening he accepted his Oscar proved to be a historic Oscar ceremony. That very evening, Sidney Poitier, now a grand old master who had survived changing attitudes without sacrificing his elemental dignity, was awarded a special Oscar for his trailblazing career. And that same evening, Halle Berry walked off with her Best Actress Oscar for *Monster's Ball*, becoming the first African American woman to do so.

Afterward Washington continued to stretch himself. Basically, these were good years for him when he worked non-stop and earned as much as $20 million a movie. Whether good or bad, many of the Washington vehicles had unusual storylines and characters.

In the 2002 *John Q*, he portrayed John Quincy Archibald, a factory worker—also at heart a paragon of decency and honesty—who is at his wit's end because his insurance carrier will not cover the medical expenses for his young son who is in need of a heart transplant. There are other mounting problems. His company has reduced him to part time, his car has been repossessed, and he cannot find a second job. His desperation leads him to take hostages at the very hospital where his son is a patient. Attention must be paid to his son's plight and that of his fellow Americans, battling rising medical costs, unscrupulous insurance providers, and widespread unemployment. Washington's performance wasn't as layered as many of his earlier ones. But then it didn't have to be. The characterization came straight from the gut—and from the heart. He believes in the movie's message. Cast as Washington's

Denzel Washington giving a riveting performance as the corrupt cop in the controversial film that brought him a second Oscar, *Training Day*.

wife was the talented Kimberly Elise. Surely, Washington had approved this casting, which he could be commended for. Elise was hardly the standard cookie cutter cutie that might have shown up in such a film. Instead she gave an effective performance as a pained woman, unsure of the future of her son and her husband. Later she worked opposite Washington again in *The Manchurian Candidate* (2004). Though it was not much of a movie and though its hostage characters were little more than urban stereotypes, *John Q*, like old Warner Bros. movies, sought to deal with some then very pressing social issues. *John Q* opened as the number-one movie in the country, and audiences frequently cheered Washington's character.

Washington also turned his hand to directing in 2002 with *Antwone Fisher* and in 2007 with *The Great Debaters*. Based on a true story by its scriptwriter Antwone Fisher, *Antwone Fisher* told the story of an angry young Navy seaman—played by twenty-eight-year-old Derek Luke—who suffers psychic wounds incurred during his troubled childhood. He undergoes psychiatric treatment from a sympathetic doctor, played by Washington. In some respects, the film was similar to *Good Will Hunting* (1997) with Matt Damon and Robin Williams. But for audiences with a sense of movie history, it may have reminded them of the traumatized black soldier in the 1949 *Home of the Brave*.

The Great Debaters was also based on a true story. In 1935, the African American poet/professor Melvin Tolson had coached the debate team at the black Wiley College in Texas, to a national championship in which it defeated the debate team at the University of Southern California. In the film, it is Harvard. Why such a change was made is anyone's guess. The film also omitted the fact that Wiley could not call itself victorious because it did not belong to a debate society. Blacks were not admitted to the debate society until after World War II. But Washington's direction of *The Great Debaters*, which was produced by Oprah Winfrey, was straightforward, earnest, admiring of the characters. Newcomer Nate Parker was impressive with his calm, sturdy anchored presence. Parker went on to appear in such films as *The Secret Life of Bees* (2008), *Non-Stop* (2014), and *Beyond the Lights* (2014). Some might see *The Great Debaters* as old-fashioned bourgeois family entertainment. The film took viewers back to an earlier time when those pioneering black trail blazers were truly heroic and inspiring, and it was refreshing to see a film that focused on a dedicated teacher.

Sometimes it was surprising to see the way some of Washington's films were constructed to once again comfort mainstream audiences by making Washington such a "safe" star. Nowhere was this more apparent than in the Tony Scott directed *Man on Fire* (2004). Here he played a tough but disillusioned former government operative/assassin, now consumed with both guilt—and one too many Jack Daniels. An old buddy (Christopher Walken) persuades him to become a bodyguard for a fair-haired young daughter (Dakota Fanning) of a wealthy businessman (played by singer Marc Anthony) and his wife in Mexico City. For

Washington's character John Creasy, to protect the girl from kidnappers, it's all just a job. But the little girl's charms and vulnerabilities soon open him up, make him *feel* again. Before you know it, he's her swim coach and her school tutor, totally devoted to her and able to communicate with her in a way that her parents cannot. As the story progresses, you may feel you've seen this kind of bond before but you may be surprised where you've seen it. For a film that seems so contemporary with its jump cuts, its booming sound effects, and its strange changes in color and naturally with its delight in violence, the relationship of its primary characters is reminiscent of Bill Robinson and little Shirley Temple in movies like *The Little Colonel* and *The Littlest Rebel*, both from 1935. Here the sunny optimism of Robinson's Bojangles has been replaced by Washington's glum cynicism. At the end of the film, his character is ready to sacrifice himself for the girl in a hailstorm of bullets. Of course, Washington and Fanning are such accomplished actors that as much as we felt with Robinson and Temple, we begrudgingly half-way believe in their relationship.

In this decade and into the next, Washington took on the challenge of starring in remakes of classic thrillers: *The Manchurian Candidate* (2004, working again with *Philadelphia* director Jonathan Demme) and *The Taking of Pelham 123* (2009, again working with director Tony Scott; he also worked with Scott opposite Paula Patton in the 2006 time-travel suspense yarn *Deja Vu*). Neither *The Manchurian Candidate* nor *The Taking of Pelham 123* matched the original on which it was based, and Washington appeared to be playing rather routine leads. In *The Taking of Pelham 123*, his co-star John Travolta had the meatier, flashier role. At this point, a weariness was creeping into Washington's characters, his basic screen persona. Looking older and a bit heavier in *The Taking of Pelham 123*, he wasn't showing that slow burn burst of energy that had added to the intensity of some of his earlier performances. The weariness had shown at times in *Hurricane* (1999) but it worked well for the characterization. Now though audiences may have asked if acting still excited Washington, if indeed during these years of his mega-stardom, was a disillusionment setting in? Was he searching for more challenging roles?

Perhaps that explains his decision to star in Ridley Scott's 2007 *American Gangster*, in which he again went against his established persona to play the real-life drug kingpin Frank Lucas. In the 1970s, Lucas presided over a New York crime empire. But as the film dramatizes, Lucas is not your typical drug criminal. In his private life, he does almost nothing to draw attention to himself. He dresses conservatively in suits and ties, marries a lovely young Latina, and is such a family man that he brings his five brothers and his mother from North Carolina to live in New Jersey. His brothers are brought into his business. His mother (Ruby Dee) resides in a palatial home where there are Sunday night family dinners. In his business dealings, Washington's Lucas can of course be ruthless and shockingly violent. In one sequence, early in the film, he throws a lighted match onto a man who has been doused with gasoline and then as the man is in flames, shoots him. A shrewd businessman, who cuts the mob out of his dope deals, he travels to Thailand where he buys his own heroin, then has it shipped back to the States in military planes. Then he sells his top grade heroin at half the price that the mob would charge. But *American Gangster* also tells the story of an earnest, relentlessly honest cop Richie Roberts, played by Russell Crowe, who eventually brings Lucas down. Director Scott cuts between the contrasting lifestyles and stories of Roberts and Lucas.

In some respects, *American Gangster* picks up on the heroes or anti-heroes of *Super Fly* and *New Jack City* but does it, thanks to Scott's direction, with style and texture. Like its predecessors, the film wants us to see its hero as an emblem of Black American capitalism. The film also wants us to admire him. Lucas gives out turkeys to the Harlem community at Thanksgiving. Thinking about *that*, we may want to say: Big deal! This is the community he's already sacked, exploited, and poisoned. With all these films, there is a moral ambiguity that is true of many gangster films. We are dazzled by the black gangster's fundamental masculinity and his self-assertion, especially in the light of a racist culture that's cut him out of another kind of success. And we are impressed with his imagination, the deals he makes, the way he outsmarts others around him. Despite our mixed feelings about the hero in *Super Fly*, we cheer his successful strategies to outwit the white men who control the drug business—*and* his success in leaving the drug trade. In *New Jack City*, we are relieved to see him die at the hands of the community he's betrayed. Here Lucas is apprehended and turns in evidence. The audience, however, may leave the theater still in awe of Lucas, never really questioning his morality, which is a major flaw of *American Gangster*.

The actors brought their characters to life. Crowe wisely underplays his cop while with Washington we see the juices flowing. He comes alive in the role, relishing the opportunity to once again stretch his talents. Cuba Gooding, Jr., as the flashy Nicky Barnes (another real life figure), and Josh Brolin (as a corrupt cop), have their moments. But the real surprise was Ruby Dee. When we first see her, we may wonder if she understands the world her son has brought her into; if she questions his violence and his criminality. Then there is a sequence when she lets him have it and slaps him. It is powerful and all-involving. Watching her, one may recall her fine Oscar worthy but Oscar overlooked performances in such movies as *The Tall Target* (1951) and *Edge of the City*. One could only rejoice in 2000 when the Screen Actors Guild gave its Lifetime Achievement Award to Dee and her husband Ossie Davis, who had worked tirelessly for decades, earning good notices but rarely receiving the kind of industry acknowledgment that went to far less talented figures. With *American Gangster*, Dee finally won an Oscar nomination as Best Supporting Actress.

Washington also proved eager to work with African American filmmakers such as Carl Franklin in *Devil in a Blue Dress* and *Out of Time* (2003). He worked again with Spike Lee in *Inside Man* (2006), a taut, immensely enjoyable bank heist thriller. In the next decade, he brought a gravitas and that now familiar weariness (that was appropriate to his character) to The Hughes Brothers post-apocalyptic drama *The Book of Eli* (2010). He also worked with Antoine Fuqua again in *The Equalizer* (2014).

Washington, now growing older, took on the mature persona of a kind of a wise counselor to younger actors: in *Unstoppable* (2010) to Chris Pine; in *Safe House* (2012), to Ryan Reynolds; in *2 Guns* (2013), to Mark Walhberg; and in *The Equalizer*, to actress Chloë Grace Moretz. Sometimes it appeared as if his characters were replays of the huck-finn fixation: the outsider Black man who endows a younger white with wisdom and a soulfulness.

Perhaps his most interesting role of this period was the pilot in Robert Zemeckis' *Flight* (2012) which also indicates something about the mechanics and maneuvers of mass movie-making. Those who green light movies—enabling them to go into production—generally do not want a movie to be too *black*. A film may have a black star but always—stretching back to the late 1970s and 1980s with such crossover stars as Richard Pryor and Eddie Murphy—the star is put into a white cultural context. Other white actors are cast in important roles, and the setting is generally not in the African American community. But while the black star may appeal to the African American audience in personal terms, the movies tend to deny or distort African American culture, often rendering such a culture invisible. How do you make a movie that appeals to that large white audience yet also speaks in personal terms with African American cultural markers to the black audience? *Flight* manages to reach both audiences without offending African Americans. Here Washington portrays an alcoholic, self-destructive yet excellent commercial pilot. When his airplane has mechanical problems that lead to an in-flight catastrophe and the loss of lives, he's able nonetheless to bring the flight to a safe landing and save other passengers. But during an investigation that follows, his alcoholism is probed, and the pilot must come to terms with his life, his family, and himself. It's a moving film with a theme that is significant to all audiences. But what the film also does is to bring in cultural markers, bearings, and signposts for the pilot. (The same was true in his earlier film *Ricochet*.) The depiction of the family provides some of that; so does the script's reference to the pilot's father—a Tuskegee Airman. Washington received another well-deserved Best Actor Oscar nomination for his performance.

As the new millennium's second decade began, Washington had reaffirmed his stature in the movie industry and within the consciousness of American moviegoers that no other black actor before, except Poitier, had attained. He had won two Academy Awards. Audiences had also watched him as he went from exciting young actor in such films as *A Soldier's Story* to mature star in *Malcolm X* to older hero/character actor in *The Equalizer*. He had lived a life in film.

Halle Berry Comes of Age

Perhaps most surprising in the early years was the career momentum of Halle Berry. By 2000, she had worked in films for over a decade, known mainly as a sweet-tempered leading lady. Born in 1966 in Cleveland, Ohio, the younger of two biracial daughters of a black father, who had been a hospital attendant, and a white mother, who had been a psychiatric nurse, Berry recalled being told by her mother at an early age that she must learn to see herself as the world would: as an African American woman. In some respects, she would be more open and outspoken about matters of race in her Hollywood career than some of her contemporaries. With a career that began in beauty pageants, including being named the first runner-up in the Miss USA Pageant, she took the leap and headed to Los Angeles in search of roles. There she appeared in the television series "Living Dolls" and "Knots Landing" as well as in guest shots on such programs as "Amen" and "A Different World." In the tradition of Lena Horne and Dorothy Dandridge, she was physically the mulatto, what was once known as *café au lait* beauty with light brown skin, keen features, and straight hair. Her looks opened some doors for her but that was not what took her eventually to movie stardom.

In her movie debut as a crack addict in Spike Lee's explosive *Jungle Fever*, she worked hard at portraying a grungy, troubled young woman, but truth be told, she never seemed inside the character. The externals were there: the jittery, anxious movements. But the soul of the character seemed dormant or missing. Yet oddly enough she held the screen in her scenes opposite Samuel L. Jackson, who clearly was inside *his* character. Though hardly glamorized here, perhaps it still was her beauty that enabled her not to become lost in space. In such films as *Boomerang* and *The Flintstones*, she seemed in her element: these were charming, intelligent portraits. But when a more challenging role came along such as the young former crack-addicted mother trying to keep custody of her child in *Losing Isaiah*, she was hardly effective and was clearly out-acted by her co-star Jessica Lange. What seemed missing in that film (and others to come) was both an inner focus and an inner fire (the very things that had made her idol Dorothy Dandridge so compelling in *Carmen Jones*). Surprisingly, signs of such fire flared up excitely in her character in *Why Do Fools Fall in Love*, one of her best but least acknowledged performances.

Still, there was the question if she would ever become more than a lovely face. What gave Berry's career its first great lift was her starring role in the 1999 HBO movie "Introducing Dorothy Dandridge." Not as magnetic nor as complex as the real life Dandridge (an actress whose "subtexts" in her performances always elevated her characters to another level), Berry nonetheless gave a heartfelt, committed performance that won her both a Golden Globe and an Emmy. One just regretted that the script and director had not put together a more challenging dissection of Hollywood and its attitude to a great African American star.

Shrewdly, Berry underwent a major shift in her screen image that put her on the road to stardom. In 2000, she appeared as the character Storm in *X-Men*—and such sequels as *X-Men 2* (2003) and *X-Men: The Last Stand* (2006)—all part of a super-heated sci-fi action series based on the characters created by Stan Lee and Jack Kirby for Marvel Comics. No great performances here but she was seen by a younger audience—and a larger mainstream one—in a successful film franchise. (In 2016, Alexandra Shipp played Storm in *X-Men: Apocalypse*.) Then came another commercial hit, the Dominic Sena-directed *Swordfish* (2001) that cast her opposite John Travolta and Hugh Jackman. Here Berry projected a more sexualized image. Much to-do was made over a scene in which she went topless. It's a purely gratuitous sexy sequence in which while reading a book, she puts the tome down so we can see the Berry boobs. Stories circulated that she was paid an extra $500,000 for giving moviegoers the chance to look her over, indeed to objectify her. At the same time, no significant cultural context was established for her character Ginger. As the girlfriend of Travolta, she's just *there* without enough backstory. The more sexualized image, however, worked well in raising Berry's profile and further broadening her audience. It would have been wonderful if she could have attained stardom by staying on the path of the sexy, ladylike, Audrey Hepburn-style characters of her films *Boomerang* and *The Flintstones*. But it didn't happen. What *did* happen was *Monster's Ball* in 2001 in which she played another more sexualized character, Leticia Musgrove, in a tale of white male redemption.

After her convict husband (Sean Combs) has been led to his execution by an emotionally detached prison guard Hank Grotowski (Billy Bob Thornton), Leticia, forced to put together the pieces of her life, must cope with her loneliness, her dire financial situation, and her obese young son. Not much seems to go right for her—her son is killed in a car accident and she is evicted from her home—until she meets the very guard who led her husband to his death. Hank's saddled with problems of his own: an openly racist father; his alienated adult son (played superbly by Heath Ledger) who commits suicide. On a day when he sits in the restaurant where Leticia works, he's immediately drawn to her.

In a graphic key scene, she pleads, actually begs, that he make love to her. Or to be more precise, as she groans and gyrates while undressing, she implores him: "Fuck me." Considering the obvious fact that he's physically rather wasted and hardly in his prime and that she is luscious and at the peak of her beauty/sexual appeal, it seems rather odd that this black woman has to *ask* this white man to take her in his arms. He's lucky that she even gives him the time of day. Is this a familiar rewriting of history: it's not the white man who brutalizes and takes advantage of an African American woman (as those slave masters did in the slave quarters they visited so frequently) but rather that she's *asking* and desperately wants the white

Monster's Ball, a tale of white male redemption with Oscar Winner Halle Berry and Billy Bob Thornton.

man to take (rather than violate) her! Of course, he answers her request, and ultimately, we find her living in his home. Setting out to redeem himself, he carts off his aging bigoted father to a nursing home. He even befriends a black neighbor (Mos Def) and his family. That neighbor is one of the few black people we see in the film which is set in Georgia. But mainly it's the fact that Billy Bob's come to her rescue—her white knight in shining armor—that we're supposed to be impressed by. Directed by German-Swiss Marc Forster, *Monster's Ball* has no interest in creating a cultural context for Leticia. One might even question if Forster understood that the character needed one. The most obvious question for African American viewers is: Doesn't she have some family—relatives somewhere—or black friends in the community (or a nearby one) that she can go to for help when she's evicted? This apparently never crosses the mind of the director or writer. Here we have a familiar lack of a strong backstory and context for an important African American character. Interestingly enough, one of the producers of the film was African American Lee Daniels who later directed *Precious* (2009).

But perhaps most disturbing was the ending of *Monster's Ball*. Leticia stumbles across information in Hank's home that reveals his involvement in her husband's execution. Yet instead of confronting him, she is seen at the film's conclusion seated next to him on the steps of his home. All is all right with her—as if there is nothing to be resolved, nothing to be questioned. Even if the film intended to show an interracial couple that has surmounted societal or personal issues to have a functioning balanced relationship, at least give the audience some sense of Leticia grappling with this situation and coming to terms with her relationship. But the film has no interest in that. Basically, *Monster's Ball* was a tale about the rehabilitation of a troubled white man, who's forgiven by a black woman and set on the path of making himself whole again!

Monster's Ball met with mixed reviews. Within the African American community, bloggers criticized the film. In the July 1, 2002 issue of *Newsweek*, actress Angela Bassett spoke out to interviewer Allison Samuels about the film's "graphic, tortured" affair. Bassett said she had turned down the role, although producer Lee Daniels reportedly said she was never actually offered the part. "It's about *character*, darling," said Bassett. "I wasn't going to be a prostitute on film. I couldn't do that because it's such a stereotype about black women and sexuality." The character actually was not a prostitute. But, still, you get the gist of the point Bassett was making. Bassett wanted it clear that she wasn't "criticizing Berry—just the way Hollywood views women in general and black women in particular," said Samuels. Said Bassett: "It's about putting something out there you can be proud of 10 years later. I mean, Meryl Streep won Oscars without all that." In that same interview, she elaborated further on Hollywood's treatment of African American women. After her Oscar nomination for *What's Love Got To Do With It*, Bassett recalled thinking: "This is great! This is the beginning of something big for me." But little happened.

"I didn't work again for another year and a half. I guess I was pretty naive to think it would be different—that it was just about the talent—particularly for someone who looks like me. You forget that sometimes." Here she was referring to Hollywood's long-standing color caste system. She also related her experience when actor Sean Connery was excited about the prospect of having her as his leading lady in the 1999 *Entrapment*. "It's mine," she recalled thinking of the role. "But a few weeks later, they cast a lesser-known actress at the time [Catherine Zeta Jones]. I guess Hollywood wasn't as progressive as Connery thought."

Nonetheless, with the release of *Monster's Ball*, Halle Berry was taken seriously as a film actress. When she has her big scene—pleading for him to take her—she's near over-the-top. Otherwise she's sensitive, sympathetic, and oddly touching, delicately etching a moving portrait of a lost soul, some might say of a victim. Perhaps what made her performance work was that for the first time her basic passivity fit into the conception of the character. For her performance, she became the first African American woman to win a Best Actress Academy Award. Her highly emotional acceptance speech acknowledged women who came before such as Dandridge, Lena Horne, and Diahann Carroll as well as her contemporaries Angela Bassett and Jada Pinkett Smith. It was a great moment in Academy Award history.

After the Oscar win, Berry struggled to find her footing. An appearance in the James Bond *Die Another Day* (2002), which was filmed before the Oscar, was yet another more overtly sexualized role which better suited an actress trying to make a name for herself rather than an established star. Her big star turn in the creepy *Gothika* (2003) had seemed promising, at least before anyone actually saw the film. Then it failed to excite moviegoers. Then came her turn as Patience Phillips in *Catwoman*, opposite Benjamin Bratt. She tried to pull out the sexual fireworks, but the performance, especially compared to that of Michelle Pfeiffer as Catwoman in *Batman Returns* (1992) or Eartha Kitt's campy interpretation of the character on the old "Batman" TV series of the late 1960s, lacked wit and bite. As the movie tanked, it had to be a great disappointment for her, all the more so because it meant the loss of a possible franchise series.

Other lackluster movies such as the 2007 *Perfect Stranger*, opposite Bruce Willis, followed. As a widow in *Things We Lost in the Fire* (2007), she pulled out the mopey mood of *Monster's Ball*. Again the filmmakers showed a lack of respect for its black character by failing to establish some kind of cultural context for her. Her performance as a schizophrenic stripper in *Frankie & Alice* (2010) had an interesting twist and earned her a Golden Globe nomination but ultimately was ignored by mainstream moviegoers. In the all-star *New Year's Eve* (2011), she was one of the crowd that included Michelle Pfeiffer, Robert De Niro, Zac Efron, and Common. *Cloud Atlas* (2012)—directed by Tom Tykwer and Andy and Lana Wachowski—gave her a chance at more ambitious multi-characterizations. But she was done in by the pretentious jumbled narrative. It must have been frustrating for her that neither great films nor great roles had come her way. A pleasant irony was that she had a success in the high-grade B-movie *The Call* (2013) in which she played a 911 dispatcher, trying to save a young girl's life. She also had some success in the 2005 television adaptation of Zora Neale Hurston's classic novel "Their Eyes Were Watching God."

Off-screen, she was a dazzling figure on the red carpet, shimmering, glittery, and elegant as she arrived at industry functions, every inch an attention-getting star. Her private life also drew press coverage with her plea of no contest to a misdemeanor charge of leaving the scene of a traffic accident in 2000. Her marriages and divorces from baseball star David Justice and singer Eric Benét also garnered media attention as did her relationship with the male model Gabriel Aubry. Afterward the couple engaged in a custody battle for their daughter Nahla in 2008. Then came a marriage to actor Olivier Martinez and the birth of another child. Off-screen dilemmas or tensions of great movie stars of the past were often a part of their legend. But Berry's personal problems, like those of many new stars of the era, were hardly larger than life, hardly mythic in the mass imagination.

Berry turned to television in the series "Extant" in 2013.

Royalty's Rocky Reign: Queen Latifah

The early years of the decade also saw rap empress Queen Latifah rise to movie stardom. Born Dana Owens in 1970 in East Orange, New Jersey, she succeeded in the mostly male world of rap/hip hop with her songs about female self-empowerment. On stage, she was known for wearing her power turbans. Highly ambitious, far more so than she may have appeared, she worked in small roles to get her foot in the door in such films as *Jungle Fever*, *House Party 2*, and *Juice*. Her best training ground may have been her starring role as Khadijah James in the TV series "Living Single" from 1993 to 1998. Her most exciting performance during the 1990s, and some might say during her career, was in *Set It Off*. But then it was back to smaller or supporting roles in such films as *Hoodlum*, *Living Out Loud* (1998), *Bone Collector*, and *Brown Sugar* (2002).

The prize came when she reportedly beat out such stars as Whoopi Goldberg, Kathy Bates, Bette Midler, Rosie O'Donnell, and Liza Minnelli for the role of the prison matron in Rob Marshall's screen adaptation of the Bob Fosse–John Kander–Fred Ebb Broadway musical *Chicago* (2002). Most surprising was her self-confidence, best seen as she sauntered as she sang, "When You're Good To Mama." Here was a woman who knew what she was doing; who understood the demands of the camera; who also knew how not to get lost in a cast that included such seasoned pros as Catherine Zeta Jones, Richard Gere, and Renée Zellweger. All those years in those smaller roles had been spent wisely. Significantly, she was a full-figured young woman who was comfortable with herself and understood how to make use of her height (she was 5'10"), her weight, and her posture. She really does have the stature and composure of a queen. Though the dramatic demands were not great and though her performance here (as well as in other films) is less a case of in-depth acting than it is of convincing *non-acting*, her assured presence caught the critics and the industry off-guard, and she walked off with an Academy Award nomination as Best Supporting Actress. *Chicago* itself ended up with a Best Picture Oscar and Catherine Zeta-Jones won for Supporting Actress.

The question was: Where does Latifah go from here? Unfortunately, it was to a familiar type in the 2003 hit *Bringing Down the House*. Listed as an executive producer of the film, she played Charlene, an escaped convict who has been in communication via emails with a white tax attorney (Steve Martin). In those emails, Charlene has passed herself off as a white Ivy League educated lawyer. He's impressed. But when she shows up at his door, he's confronted with the reality of this ghetto gal who wants him to help her prove herself innocent of the bank robbery charge that she's been put in the clinker for. He protests but before he knows it, she's moved into his house and into his life.

True to the attitude of this period (stretching back now to the rise of Eddie Murphy in movies of the 1980s), *Bringing Down the House* sees racism as a fit subject for humor. A neighbor of Martin's (Betty White) is a nosy, blatant racist at whom the movie delights in laughing. One of his clients is another old-school bigot: a wealthy elderly eccentric (played by the great Joan Plowright) who has a nostalgia for what the old days must have been—*before* the Emancipation Proclamation! She sings *a capella* a little ditty in which a slave asks if Massa Gonna Sell Me Tomorrow? Regrettably, her rendition is funny! Divorced, Martin lives with his young son and teenage daughter. Charlene's soon concerned about those children and about his way of life. You couldn't ask for a more lopsidedly maternal figure.

Queen Latifah said that the first draft of the script "was a wreck and offensive . . . but it was funny, too. The question was, Can we make it what it needs to be?"

She helps teach Martin's young son to read. She rescues his daughter from a possible rapist. (We're thankful he's not black!) She fights Martin's snobbish sister-in-law and demonstrates to the witch who's toughest. In an embarrassing scene, Martin reveals he's got some newly acquired soul when he talks jive! In an equally embarrassing scene, she teaches the uptight Waspy Martin character a few things about sex. She also helps reunite him with his wife. In some respects, she gives the white hero his sexuality back, his very manhood—similar to what the magical Negro character (played by Michael Clarke Duncan) did for Tom Hanks in *The Green Mile*. She also finds that his friend (well played by Eugene Levy) has fallen for her. By the end of the movie, she's cleared up things for the major characters, gotten their lives back on track, and she's mighty happy to have done so.

Queen Latifah with Steve Martin (left) and Eugene Levy in *Bringing Down the House.*

Her sexuality may make Latifah's character seem rounded. But in the context of the film, it's a comic sexuality. Otherwise Charlene seems to be a clear example of an updated mammy. Latifah herself is funny, full of attitude, and so sure of herself that she makes the other characters look weak and indecisive. Fortunately, that persona carries much of the film, even saves it. *Bringing Down the House* opened as the number-one movie in the country and stayed in that position for the following two weeks.

The films that followed produced mixed results: *Scary Movie 3* (2003), *Barbershop 2: Back in Business* (2004), *The Cookout* (2004), *Taxi* (2004, a boring mess of a picture that teamed her with Jimmy Fallon), *Beauty Shop* (2005), *Mad Money* (2008, co-starring Diane Keaton and Katie Holmes in what must have looked promising), and *What Happens in Vegas* (2008). Most were routine films in which it looked as if she was working just to be working. But at least she was now recognized by the industry as a star who might have some clout at the box-office. That Oscar nomination had not hurt her either.

Her most interesting films of the period were *Last Holiday* (2006), *Hairspray* (2007), and *The Secret Life of Bees* (2008). That doesn't mean they were great projects. But Latifah was clearly seeking more diverse characters to play. Based on the British film of 1950 that starred Alec Guinness, *Last Holiday*, directed by Wayne Wang, starred her as a shy department store clerk in pre-Katrina New Orleans, who is (mis)diagnosed with an incurable, fatal illness. Realizing her life has been spent living by the rules, she cashes in her retirement accounts and heads to Karlovy Vary in the Czech Republic for a gourmet vacation. There she takes up residence at the posh Grand Hotel where of course she interacts with a group of diverse characters, including French actor Gérard Depardieu as well as the muscular hunk LL Cool J. The movie sought to give her the kind of romantic, melancholic, dreamy role which is seldom reserved for a full-figure actress. Though moviegoers may have preferred a livelier Latifah, she pulled it off.

In the 2007 musical *Hairspray*, she co-starred with John Travolta, Michelle Pfeiffer, Christopher Walken, and newcomer Nikki Blonsky. Based on the Broadway musical which in turn was based on the John Waters 1988 movie of the same name, *Hairspray* prided itself on being an entertaining film that had social comments as it sought to break the retro rules of race and gender. Directed and choreographed by Adam Shankman and set in Baltimore in the 1960s, it cast John Travolta as the mother (a role originated by the actor Divine in the earlier movie version) of young Tracy Turnblad, a heavyset teenager who longs to perform on the afternoon teen dance program "The Corny Collins Show." But neither overweight kids nor blacks kids are welcomed there. There is, however, a once monthly Negro Day on the program. Tracy leagues herself with black teenagers in her area, who teach her how to dance—and also something about race relations. Her best friend even falls for the black teenager Seaweed, played wonderfully by actor Elijah Kelley. As the loud blond Motormouth Maybelle, who is the dj on Negro day, Latifah tries her best to move the character away from a comic stereotype. But neither the racial/social commentary nor the casting of Travolta as the mother proved particularly ground-breaking, and the film wasn't as much fun as the original.

She worked hard too in *The Secret Life of Bees*, based on the novel by Sue Monk Kidd and directed and scripted by African American Gina Prince-Bythewood with Will Smith as one of its producers. You yearned to see what these creative forces would make of material set in the South in the Civil Rights era. Well-intentioned, the movie, however, was stuck in an old concept. It follows the journey of a 14-year-old girl Lily (Dakota Fanning) who, having been daily abused by her tyrannical father, runs away from home, along with the family's housekeeper Rosaleen (Jennifer Hudson). Rosaleen has also been abused: when she tried to register to vote, she was beaten and thrown into jail.

For part of the film, Lily and Rosaleen are re-workings of Huck and Jim as they set off to find a better place in life. They arrive at the pink home of three sisters who are beekeepers. There is the rather militant June (Alicia Keys), the sadly delicate May (Sophie Okonedo), and the matriarch of the house August Boatwright (Queen Latifah),who is blessed with a type of folk wisdom and great insights. Much like Tracy Turnblad in *Hairspray*, little Lily learns from her new black friends, who obviously are there not so much for their own stories but to help bring the girl to a new awareness and a budding maturity. Lily even falls for a black teenager. In a scene that seems false, Lily and her black boyfriend go together to a movie theatre—where they are assaulted. Yes, they would be assaulted if they were foolish enough to go to a "white" theater together. But it's questionable that such an interracial movie-going experience would have happened in such a time period. Or that the two would not have been firmly aware of the risk they were taking.

Though *The Secret Life of Bees* seeks to spotlight the independent black characters played by Alicia Keys and Nate Parker (as her boyfriend) and though Queen Latifah has a warm, majestic quality, the movie is still caught up in the concept of good black people who are noble and decent because of what they will do for whites. In *Entertainment Weekly*, critic Owen Gleiberman asked: "In an age when Will Smith is the world's most popular movie star and Barack Obama could well be elected president, it's fair to ask: Isn't it time that Hollywood took a sabbatical—maybe a permanent one—from movies in which black characters exist primarily to save the souls of white ones?" In *The New York Times*, A. O. Scott called the film "a tired fable of black selflessness, in which African-Americans take time out from their struggle against oppression to lift the battered self-esteem of white people who have the good sense not to be snarling bigots."

In 2010, Queen Latifah appeared with rapper Common, Paula Patton, Phylicia Rashad, and by now, screen veteran Pam Grier, in the Debra Martin Chase-produced and the Sanaa Hamri-directed *Just Wright*. Cast as a warm and rather

Dakota Fanning (far right) as a troubled runaway who finds refuge with black women Queen Latifah, Sophie Okonedo, Jennifer Hudson, and Alicia Keys in *The Secret Life of Bees*.

low-key, level-headed physical therapist, she nurses an injured basketball player and at the same time nurses her own crush on him. It was good to see her in another romantic role and also projecting an intelligence and maturity.

As this tall, large young woman went from one role to another and developed a real following, her rise in film had a clear significance. Though she later became a pitchwoman in television commercials for a weight reduction program, she appeared to do so for health reasons and, successful as she was in losing weight, she was never bone thin. Always she looked as if she was proud of her physicality. When *Vogue* ran photographs of a lush Latifah and as she was seen in advertisements for *Cover Girl* makeup, she may well have made audiences rethink their notions about beauty standards just as Cicely Tyson, in another way, had done in the past.

Chris Rock Trying to Rock the Boat

During the decade, moviegoers also witnessed the uneven movie career of comedian Chris Rock. Born in Andrews, South Carolina, in 1965, one of eight children, and growing up mainly in Brooklyn, Chris Rock had been on the movie scene perhaps longer than most remembered, since the 1980s when he appeared in small or supporting roles in such films as *I'm Gonna Git You Sucka, Hangin' with the Homeboys, Beverly Hills Cop II, New Jack City, CB4, Boomerang, Panther, Beverly Hills Ninja* (1997), and *Pootie Tang* (2001). He was also a cast member on television's "Saturday Night Live" and "In Living Color" and did guest shots on such sitcoms as "Fresh Prince of Bel-Air" and "Martin." Despite all this activity, he looked as if he wasn't getting very far, at least not to a level of big time stardom. But he hit his stride with his HBO comedy concerts that included the Emmy-winner "Bring the Pain" in 1996 and "Bigger & Blacker" in 1999. Audiences enjoyed the seemingly audacious way in which he brought race into his standup monologues. Comparisons shot up of Rock and Pryor. "I like Chris Rock," Pryor himself was quoted in the August, 1998 issue of *Vanity Fair* as saying. "Does he remind me of me? I'm afraid so." But no one was the innovator that Pryor had been. Nor had anyone possessed his comic timing and his extraordinary skills at mime and mimic. Dave Chappelle was the closest to Pryor in spirit, imagination, and sheer exuberance. Still, Rock had an impact on a new generation.

As the 1990s ended and the new decade began, Rock made a more serious push at becoming a movie star. Wisely, he accepted supporting roles in the offbeat films *Dogma* (1999) with Matt Damon and Ben Affleck and in Neil Labute's *Nurse Betty* with René Zellweger and Morgan Freeman. Both films received a fair amount of critical attention, though Rock's work was hardly earth-shattering. Standing next to Freeman, Rock looked puny and a tad insecure (which worked well for the character he was playing) as if aware he was no match for Freeman's weighty screen presence and his mighty talent.

Rock went on to the starring role in Chris and Paul Weitz's 2001 *Down to Earth*, a remake of the Warren Beatty 1978 hit *Heaven Can Wait*, which in turn had been a remake of the 1941 hit *Here Comes Mr. Jordan* with Robert Montgomery. In this new millennium, remakes ran rampant. The film industry seemed woefully lacking in new ideas—and also fearful of taking chances on original work. Remakes (and sequels or prequels) were based on projects that had already proven successful; so the risks *appeared* minimal. There were even remakes of television shows like *I Spy* (2002) with Eddie Murphy and Owen Wilson and *The Honeymooners* (2005) with Cedric the Entertainer and Mike Epps. Yet remakes often proved disappointing or outright bombs.

Rock co-wrote the script for *Down to Earth* with three writers (Lance Crouther, Ali LeRoi, and Louis CK) from his HBO series "The Chris Rock Show." Here he played a comic who is prematurely whisked off to heaven by a too eager angel. In heaven—depicted as a swanky nightclub—Rock's character protests his early arrival and is granted a chance to return to earth and life but in another guise—in the body of a deceased white businessman who is basically loathed by everyone who knows him. There are the expected laughs when the white man whose body Rock inhabits acts jivey *black* while listening to music or dancing! But you couldn't help asking: Haven't we gone beyond this kind of trite humor. Gene Wilder, with the help of Richard Pryor, had already done it brilliantly in *Silver Streak*. By the time Steve Martin tried it in *Bringing Down the House*, however, it had become stale. Usually, Rock himself is seen in those scenes in which he's the white character. But those scenes don't work. We cannot accept the reactions to him from the other characters. We know we're seeing a black man even if they don't. The film did team him with Regina King, always a pleasure to see, and with Wanda Sykes, then still something of a newcomer. Otherwise *Down to Earth* just didn't cut it.

But Hollywood was willing to give Rock another chance. He co-starred with Anthony Hopkins in the flat thriller *Bad Company* (2002). Then Rock directed and co-wrote (with Ali LeRoi) the comedy *Head of State* in which he played a committed alderman in Washington, D.C. who, incredible as it seemed in 2003, becomes a serious candidate for President of the United States! At first, his style—casual shirts and sneakers—is that of a common man of the people. But then he loosens up and gets jiggy with it, decking himself out in sweat suits and Kangol hats. When his down-with-it brother (Bernie Mac) becomes his running mate, the people gravitate to these "real" brothers. Considering what transpired later in American history with the campaign and presidency of Barack Obama, one sees that kind of jivey, even stereotyped image is certainly not what the people wanted. Though *Head of State* had little impact, it was a forward looking fantasy. Rock continued working—*and* directing.

Apparently drawn to French cinema, he directed (and co-wrote and co-produced) a remake of French director Eric Rohmer's 1972 *Chloe in the Afternoon*, which became *I Think I Love My Wife* (2007). It was not a good fit. Here Rock played a suburban husband and father who informs the audience in voice-over that his wife (Gina Torres) will not have sex with him. He ends up having sexy uncommitted afternoons with a very willing hot young woman (Kerry Washington). Rohmer's film was about a man discovering some pleasure in the fact that he can't have sex with a very desirable woman. For Rock, it's simply about his maddening frustration. It was hard to understand what he saw in the material that made him so determined to do an Americanized version. Where Rohmer was known for his pensive, subtle, quietly nuanced style, what audiences loved about Rock was that everything was upfront and out in the open. Also evident were his limitations as an actor (not only here but in his other films as well). Rock had about three stock facial expressions, and the voice—commanding in his comedy concerts—couldn't convey different moods and attitudes in dialogue. Mainly, he sounded whiney. Whereas comedians Pryor and Martin Lawrence were able to bring out vulnerabilities of their characters, Rock was just a blank. In the end, *I Think I Love My Wife* was a commercial and artistic disappointment. Still, the fact that Rock had been given the greenlight to direct films was a sign of his acceptance in the industry, although Rock later had insightful comments on the people who generally get to greenlight movies. Usually, the critics, even when not excited about Rock's films, were respectful in their discussions.

Another sign of his acceptance was that he hosted the Oscar ceremonies in 2005. But Rock the iconoclastic rebel proved too acerbic, and he also revealed a surprising lack of insight into what the ceremony meant. There was something mean-spirited about his comments on actor Jude Law. There also was not that appropriate blend of poking fun at Hollywood without offending it. As many an Oscar host has noted, the audience at the Academy Awards is probably the toughest to play.

Rock kept working, doing voice-overs for the animated films *Madagascar* (2005) and *Bee Movie* (2007) and appearing in supporting roles in such Adam Sandler movies as the remake of *The Longest Yard* (2005) and later *Grown Ups* (2010) and *Grown Ups 2* (2013). His most successful film may have been his most controversial, the documentary-style *Good Hair* (2009), directed by Jeff Stilson and co-written by Rock. Through interviews and some fascinating footage, Rock examined the styles and treatments that African American women used to coif their hair: straighteners, relaxers, perms, extensions, weaves, wigs. Often the film concentrated on the treatment extremes, which were becoming commonplace. In the past, there had been a relaxer which contained sodium hydroxide. It could eat away a soda can in two hours! Actresses Nia Long and Eve spoke about their hair experiences. Some wigs worn by African Americans came from the hair of women

Writer/director/star Chris Rock with Kerry Washington and Gina Torres in *I Think I Love My Wife*, a replay of the French film *Chloe in the Afternoon*.

in India who had cut it during religious ceremonies. Fascinating as the film was, there was criticism that this was "insider" information that might be misinterpreted by mainstream culture. Though Rock made a crack about the hair of Prince at one point, some complained about so heavy a focus on the hair of African American women. Rock himself had chemicals in his hair in *New Jack City*. Still, the statements of some men interviewed by Rock, especially some of the chatter in a barber shop, were outright sexist and/or worthless. Yet Rock can't bring himself to seriously challenge some of the comments. No doubt, the best and most insightful analysis was that of A'Lelia Bundles (great, great granddaughter of the black woman who created an empire through her hair and beauty products for black women, Madame C. J. Walker) and interior designer Sheila Bridges who suffered from the auto-immune disorder alopecia which caused her to lose her hair. Here the film was examining significant issues.

From 2005 to 2009, he was the co-creator with Ali LeRoi and executive producer of the TV series "Everybody Hates Chris" about a black kid growing up in Brooklyn in the 1980s. In 2014, he wrote and directed the comedy *Top Five*, the story of a comedy star (Rock) who wants an image change. He hopes to succeed as a "serious" actor in a new film he's made. He's also preparing for his wedding to a TV reality star (Gabrielle Union). Here Rock cast a gallery of performers, many doing cameos: Rosario Dawson; Tracy Morgan; Kevin Hart; Cedric the Entertainer; J. B. Smoove; Ben Vereen; Tichina Arnold; Miriam Colon; Taraji P. Henson; Gabourey Sidibe; Whoopi Goldberg; Adam Sandler; DMX; and Jerry Seinfeld. This ambitious undertaking was Rock commenting perhaps on his own film career. Many reviews were glowing. "Pulsating with the rhythm of his great stand-up, Chris Rock's *Top Five* takes things to the next level, reveling in the high and the low, and blending a star-studded comedic romp with an irresistible romance. *Top Five* digs under the surface of show business, politics, rap, and the exigencies of being black and famous today—holding it all up to the light in the way only Chris rock can," wrote the critic for Rotten Tomatoes. "Rock has finally found a big screen vehicle for himself that comes close to capturing the electric wit, shrewd social observations and deeply autobiographical vein of his standup comedy," wrote Scott Foundas in *Variety*. "At once personal in its sensibilities yet made with an eye towards reaching a broad, mainstream audience." Yet *Top Five* failed to ignite fires at the box-office. Within the industry, the word was: Maybe audiences just don't want to see Chris Rock in a movie. That may have been true. It may have indicated that sometimes big stars in one arena cannot have the same magic and power in the world of movies. That certainly was true of many important music performers who did not have comparable important careers as film stars. Maybe Rock still had not found the right film role for his talents.

Rock himself had some trenchant and insightful comments about the industry (and the people who decide which movies should get a green light) in an essay in the December 12, 2014 issue of *The Hollywood Reporter*. He expressed his belief that Hollywood executives still did not understand what African American audiences wanted to see and that the industry still denied many African American men (surprisingly, rather than African American women) the opportunity to work within the studio system and perhaps change it.

Crash and *Hustle & Flow*

Two films released in 2005 garnered much critical attention: Paul Haggis's *Crash* and Craig Brewer's *Hustle & Flow*. With an ensemble cast that included Don Cheadle, Matt Dillon, Thandie Newton, Terrence Howard, Larenz Tate, Sandra Bullock, Beverly Todd, and Michael Peña, *Crash* was a Robert Altman-style drama with overlapping characters, encounters, and incidents as it recorded events in the lives of a group of residents in Los Angeles. Most significant was its view of race, ethnicity, and class as driving and divisive forces in its characters' lives—and in the life of Los Angeles itself. The incidents cover a range of experiences: an upper-middle-class white couple (Bullock and Brendan Fraser) are carjacked at gunpoint; on an expressway as he searches for the high-jacked car, a racist cop (Dillon) humiliates a black TV director (Howard) and gropes the man's wife (Newton); a likeable pair of young black men (Tate and rapper Chris "Ludacris" Bridges) converse about the racial situation, then are revealed to be carjackers themselves; an Iranian shopkeeper (Shaun Toub), fearful for his safety, purchases a gun for self-protection but is insulted by the owner of the gun store who calls him "Osama," in turn, the shopkeeper, upon finding his shop broken into and trashed, blames the Hispanic locksmith (Michael Peña) for not properly insuring the security of the place; that same locksmith is suspected by the woman originally carjacked as being a Hispanic gang member who has kept duplicates of her keys; she also berates her Hispanic maid.

Reversals in the film are meant to show us the "other side" of characters, albeit in an unsuccessful attempt to depict them as complex. That very racist cop who stopped the black couple is depicted as being loving to his incapacitated father. The cop also recuses a woman from a car about to explode. Indeed she is the very woman he had earlier sexually humiliated. To the credit of director Haggis and his co-script writer Bobby Moresco, scenes can be powerful, and there is an admirable attempt to comment on then contemporary urban dilemmas and ills. But ultimately, in spite of deeply felt performances, too much of *Crash* was a series of implausible coincidences; too much was excessively grim and manipulative. Greatly distressing was Thandie Newton's character which was written as a snappish harpy who unrealistically does not understand the pain her husband experiences at his treatment by the white cops. Los Angeles, known as the City of Angels, has become a city of Hell. Perhaps the only decent, tender sign is the portrait of Michael Peña as a loving father with his daughter; yet even that might seem sentimentalized.

Still, *Crash*, an independently produced film that was shown at the Toronto Film Festival where it was picked up for distribution by Lions Gate, went on to win the Best Picture Oscar, beating out a film that more subtly and brilliantly examined another kind of bigotry and its effects, Ang Lee's *Brokeback Mountain* (2005).

In many respects, writer/director Craig Brewer's *Hustle & Flow* was a rather sentimental old-style movie about a man with a dream—who overcomes adversities to see that dream fulfilled. The film, however, looked contemporary and perhaps daring to a young audience because its hero was a dreamy-eyed pimp, living in a crumbling home in Memphis with three of his "hos" and no air-conditioning. He yearns for a career as a rapper. Here it's southern style rap known as crunk. "You know what they say, everybody got a dream," are the words of the pimp DJay, played by Terrence Howard, who struggles to land a record deal. Of course, DJay, for all his grungy drive, is naive and must endure a trail of tribulations before he finally gets a deal.

Hustle & Flow captured the sad drift of its characters' lives—and their efforts for change. Music is clearly a way out but to what it will lead is never really asked nor examined. Perhaps most distressing is the way it romanticizes DJay. He's hardly a tough, cutthroat pimp. Except for a scene in which he kicks one of his women—and her young child—out of his home, he's a relatively gentle soul. We're to think of him as a victim of circumstance, and Brewer, influenced by Blaxploitation cinema, does all he can to make us admire rather than question the character. Why does this pimp fascinate the filmmaker? Without the performance of Terrence Howard, the character might well have been simply an old-style buck. Here he's a modified one.

The actresses are all excellent. But their characters are written without much thought or insight. As the loyal, pregnant Shug, Taraji P. Henson is sweet-tempered and likable but she's playing a sap who we're supposed to like because she doesn't put up much of a fuss and stands by her man. When she sings, "It's hard out here for a pimp," you may like the melody and the beat, but you also may want to puke. The blond prostitute Nola, played by Taryn Manning, also stands by DJay. But as the only white woman in his trio, she is ironically depicted as perhaps the most ambitious and intelligent. The woman who does cause problems is Lexus, played as directed in an appropriately coarse hateful way by Paula Jai Parker. There may be some sympathy when she's shown the door by DJay but not much. The real sympathy is for the child. And you may be stunned that writer/director Brewer doesn't do more with this scene, to say something about his protagonist. Nor is there any feeling that the women, like DJay, may have dreams. The "women, if they behave themselves, are allowed to sing backup," commented A. O. Scott in *The New York Times*. "This disdain for women is not incidental to the

Terrence Howard as the pimp DJay with three of his "co-workers": (left to right) Taraji P. Henson, Paula Jai Parker, and Taryn Manning—in *Hustle & Flow*.

film; it is integral to the fantasy Mr. Brewer is selling, which is that pimping is not as hard as it looks."

Regardless, *Hustle & Flow* proved successful. At the Sundance Film Festival, it won an audience award and picked up a big distributer. On board as producers were John Singleton and Stephanie Allain which no doubt helped the film acquire some street cred for its white director/writer. But the best thing going for it was really its leading man Terrence Howard. *Hustle & Flow* needed a star if it was going to work, and Howard was precisely that. Having appeared in such films as *Mr. Holland's Opus* (1995), *Hart's War* (2002), *Big Momma's House* (2000), *Idlewild* (2006), and (sometimes billed as Terrence Dashon Howard) on such TV shows as "Living Single," "Coach," "New York Undercover," and "Law and Order," Howard proved himself a fine dramatic actor. But he was wickedly funny at other times, especially in a film like *The Best Man*—and later its sequel *Best Man Holiday* (2013). In *Hustle & Flow*, his sex appeal, his charisma, his relaxed masculinity, and his ability to invest his character with an underlying vulnerability all were used to bring life to DJay. He won an Oscar nomination for Best Actor which gave his career a jolt upward. Later he appeared in such films as *Iron Man* (2008), *Red Tails* (2012), *Winnie Mandela* (2011, as Nelson Mandela), and *Lee Daniels' The Butler* (2013). Interestingly, his greatest success may well have been in the TV series "Empire" in 2015.

Ironically, "It's Hard Out Here for a Pimp"—written by the group Three 6 Mafia and Cedric Coleman—won the Oscar as Best Original Song, and Three 6 Mafia would be the first hip hop group to perform at an Oscar ceremony.

Music Stars In Pursuit of Movie Stardom

During the decade, more hip hop stars, musicians, even a music producer, and certainly video directors, worked in films. No matter how big the star, they were still lured by the hope for another type of iconic stardom, to make it in Hollywood, still a part of the quintessential American Dream. Many were also no doubt hopeful that the extraordinary gains in music—behind the scenes as moguls as well as in front of the mic—would extend to films. The results were mixed. In 2002, music mogul Damon Dash had appeared in the violent, bloody, black gangsta drama *State Property*, directed by Abdul Malik Abbott. In 2005, he not only starred in the sequel *State Property 2*, but also directed it. Sadly, in both films the old buck was alive but decidedly not well.

Under the direction of video auteur Bryan Barber, performers André Benjamin and Antwan A. Patton, both of the group OutKast, joined Patti LaBelle, Ben Vereen, and others in the Prohibition era musical *Idlewild*—along with Cicely Tyson, Ving Rhames, and Paula Jai Parker. Barber professed his admiration for *Cabin in the Sky*, perhaps hoping to recapture the charm of long-ago life in the South expressed in the Vincent Minnelli feature. But *Idlewild*, jerky and over-edited, moved too quickly without enough time or forethought to establish any real sense of character, place or story. The film fell also into another long-standing familiar trap: its dream girl Angel was the lighter Paula Patton. André Benjamin, however, who also appeared in John Singleton's *Four Brothers* in 2005, didn't give up on the movies. Later he played Jimi Hendrix in John Ridley's *Jimi: All Is By My Side* (2013).

That skilled, innovative, introspective rapper Mos Def (born Dante Terrell Smith in Brooklyn in 1973 and also known as Yasiin Bey) showed his versatility with performances in *Monster's Ball*; in Rick Famuyiwa's ode to hip hop *Brown Sugar* (2002, with Sanaa Lathan, Taye Diggs, Queen Latifah, and Nicole Ari Parker); in F. Gary Gray's *The Italian Job*; in *The Woodsman* (2004); and in *The Hitchhiker's Guide to the Galaxy* (2005). In the much-publicized *16 Blocks* (2006), he was cast as a hood being transported by NYPD detective Bruce Willis to testify before a grand jury. It was a rather familiar tale of interracial male bonding. Later he gave an enjoyable performance as rock-and-roller Chuck Berry in Darnell Martin's *Cadillac Records* (2008), the story of Chess Records, home to such stars as Etta James, Howlin' Wolf, and Muddy Waters. Ja Rule turned up in *Assault on Precinct 13* (2005).

Midway in the decade, the skating rink suddenly became fashionable. Bow Wow—once known to music fans as Lil Bow Wow—starred in Malcolm D. Lee's roller skating drama *Roll Bounce* (2005). A year later, Tip "T.I." Harris starred in video director Chis Robinson's skating drama *ATL* (2006), co-produced by Will Smith. OutKast's Big Boi—Antwan Patton—also appeared, along with Lonette McKee, Mykelti Williamson, and Keith David.

Born Curtis Jackson, music superstar 50 (pronounced Fitty) Cent starred in the biographical gangsta-turned-rapper tale *Get Rich or Die Tryin'* (2005). Despite the excitement of rap fans, Fitty's music power didn't translate to the big screen. Irish born director Jim Sheridan, who had helmed the powerful *My Left Foot* (1989) and *In the Name of the Father* (1993), seemed out of his element. So did Fitty as an actor. "On the basis of his underwhelming performance as a version of himself," wrote critic Lou Luminick in the *New York Post*, "rapper 50 Cent shouldn't plan on giving up his day job just yet." His love interest was played by Joy Bryant. The best performance in the film was probably Terrence Howard as Fitty's prison buddy.

The irrepressible rapper Snoop Dogg (no longer Snoop Doggy Dogg) kept working, often entertainingly in such films that misfired as *The Wash* (2001), *The Tenants* (2005), and New York-born Dominican director Jessy Terrero's hip hop comedy of stereotypes *Soul Plane* (2004). His most notable performance was as Huggy Bear in director Todd Phillips *Starsky & Hutch*, the 2004 movie version of the TV series from the 1970s. His was not so much acting as it was amusing non-acting that worked exceedingly well. (Of course, the same was sometimes true of Queen Latifah and almost always true of the most idiosyncratic music star of all,

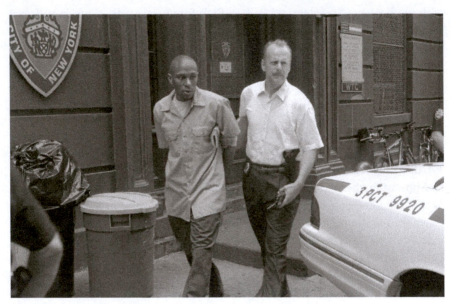

One of the music stars making a bid for movie stardom: the multi-talented Mos Def with Bruce Willis in *16 Blocks*, a familiar theme of interracial male bonding.

the sublime Macy Gray.) He also had such unexpected screen presence that it was hard to watch anyone else. Other music stars aspiring to make it in the movies might take a tip from him.

Mary J. Blige worked in such films as *I Can Do Bad By Myself* (2009), *Rock of Ages* (2012), and *Black Nativity* (2013). LL Cool J (the Ladies Love Cool James) appeared in Renny Harlin's *Mindhunters* (2004). Later he starred in TV's hit series "NCIS: Los Angeles." He was born James Todd Smith in 1968.

Outsiders Coming In: T. D. Jakes and Tyler Perry

Bishop T. D. Jakes and Tyler Perry, who both first successfully worked outside the movies, came to films—and brought their followings with them. Each had an unexpected impact and were able to do something that many African American independents still struggled to do, namely to make movies for black audiences that seemed grateful for them. The critics felt otherwise.

Born Thomas Dexter Jakes in 1957 in South Charleston, West Virginia, T. D. Jakes was a hugely popular pastor/evangelist at the non-denominational Potter's House in Dallas where he preached to a congregation of some 30,000. His message of self-help often appeared to speak directly to women. Also a playwright and an actor, Jakes in time was the author of over thirty books, a number of which were best-sellers. He also launched a religious record label, Dexterity Sounds. In the new millennium, he clearly saw the power of the movies to preach his message of redemption and self-advancement.

Two of his faith based novels—tales of women attempting to turn their lives around—were adapted for the screen. Produced by Jakes and based on his novel and directed by 1970s veteran Michael Schultz, *Woman Thou Art Loosed* (2004) starred Kimberly Elise as a woman struggling to come to grips with herself. Having been raped as a girl by her mother's boyfriend, she had drifted into prostitution. While imprisoned, she is visited by Jakes (playing a wise adviser) who gently guides her to self-awareness of her faults and her strengths. Though most critics lambasted the film as little more than warmed over clichés, *Woman Thou Art Loosed* had a sincerity and earnestness that affected black female moviegoers. Shot by Schultz in twelve days on a budget of $2 million, the film, reported Allison Samuels in the October 25, 2004 issue of *Newsweek*, quickly earned back twice that amount. Five years later, another Jakes novel *Not Easily Broken* was adapted for the screen, starring Taraji P. Henson and Morris Chestnut as a couple working their way through their troubled marriage. Its director Bill Duke was, like Schultz, a veteran from an earlier period.

In the next decade, *Woman Thou Art Loosed: On The 7th Day* (2012) was released, starring Blair Underwood, Sharon Leal, and Nicole Beharie and directed by yet another veteran Neema Barnette.

Jakes was a producer on several films, including *Jumping the Broom* (2011), the 2012 remake of *Sparkle* with Whitney Houston, and Kasi Lemmons' *Black Nativity*. The movies were different from his sermons which could raise righteous indignation. There were quiet moments with a solemn painfulness. But like those sermons, the films had a moral didacticism that could not be ignored—and which could be hard to take. But most significant, Jakes was touching on the needs primarily of a segment of the African American female audience that otherwise was ignored or dismissed by Hollywood. The same was true of Tyler Perry.

Much to the dismay of many critics, both black and white, African American movies of the new decade could not be discussed without acknowledging the work of Perry. Much like his early life, Perry's movies reverberated on a series of often overblown set of trials and tribulations. Born Emmitt Perry, Jr., in 1969 in New Orleans, he grew up in a home with a religious church-going mother and a fierce, frightening physically abusive father. Once his father whipped him with an electrical cord, he told *Entertainment Weekly* in its October 16, 2009 issue, "until the skin was coming off my back." As a child, he was sexually abused by a female friend of his mother and also by three males. In time, he legally changed his name to Tyler Perry. In 1990, he moved to Atlanta and was basically at loose ends. An episode of "The Oprah Winfrey Show," however, marked a turning point in his life. The therapeutic power of writing was discussed. Thereafter Perry wrote letters about his life—*to himself*. He turned those letters into his first play *I Know I've Been Changed*, a musical drama about struggle, faith, and redemption which was produced at an Atlanta community theater and was financed out of his $12,000 life savings. The play bombed. At one point, he was homeless, living in his car.

Undaunted, he revised the play but still without any success. Finally, in 1998, he struck gold when the play opened at Atlanta's House of Blues and its Fox Theater. By then, he had mastered the technique of promoting his productions, reaching out to church and community groups. Thereafter he continued writing dramas—again with themes of struggle, the power of faith, and personal triumph. Shrewdly, he built an empire. Performing on what was known as the "chitlin circuit" or later as the "urban theater circuit," he reached out to African American audiences—a large percentage of which was black women—with a hunger for entertainment that seemed to speak directly to them with African American cultural references, signs, and signposts. Renting the theaters where his plays were performed, he reaped the profits for himself. Eventually, he also had a newsletter that was said to reach some 400,000 people, and he sold videotapes of his productions at theaters where new productions were performed. Along the way, he created a character named Madea whom he believed represented black matriarchs determined to hold their families together and to right past wrongs. Her name was a term of endearment, a way of saying "Ma Dear' (or "Mother Dear"), used by a segment of the African American community. By 2005, according to *Forbes* magazine, Perry had sold "more than $100 million in tickets" and "an estimated $20 million in merchandise." Having turned his sights to producing films based on his theater work, he was not deterred by the Hollywood studio executives who couldn't see an audience for his work. Finally, Perry got backing—a $5.5 million budget—to do *Diary of A Mad Black Woman* (2005), directed by Darren Grant.

Diary of A Mad Black Woman told the story of a passive, gentle woman named Helen (Kimberly Elise) who is dumped by her upwardly mobile attorney husband (Steve Harris) after eighteen years. It's not a case where he calmly tells her that they have differences too great to overcome. No such quiet or even subtle moments occur in this melodrama. Instead the buck-like husband literally drags her out of his luxurious house. It's a shocking sequence of physical abuse and emotionally cruelty. He's also installing his mistress—the mother of his two children—onto the premises. Without making an issue of it, the film comments in a sly way on the color caste system within the African American community. His mistress is far lighter than the brown-skinned Elise; the mistress also struts about as if privileged because of her complexion. The script doesn't have to elaborate on such color distinctions: it's intentionally planted there in the casting, and the black audience knows it.

Vulnerable, weepy, fragile Helen finds herself unsure what to do until rescued by her grandmother, Madea, played by Perry in full dress, wig, and makeup, a 6'4" figure of massive physical might and power. Refusing to let Helen wallow in self-pity, the feisty, no-nonsense Madea arrives at Helen's home—equipped with a gun—and goes into action. Fuming and fusing, she literally chainsaws the property of the couple in half. The message is loud and clear: Don't Mess With Madea or Her Kin. She soon has Helen on the road to emotional and spiritual recovery. Throughout there is the suggestion that Helen, with her materialistic lawyer husband, has been torn away from her roots. She has to reclaim her soul and sense of identity. Creeping into this film and other Perry films that follow is the issue of class within the African American community. Educated, upwardly mobile young black women such as Helen are often in for a hard time and are brought down a few pegs as they navigate their way through life. By the film's end, Elise's Helen has been rewarded with a dream prince (handsome Shemar Moore): kind, sensitive, good-looking, and ready to attend church with her. The idea of the black dream prince (and also a light-skinned one) would turn up in other Perry films. Part domestic drama, part morality tale, part revenge fantasy, and part movie-style romance, *Diary of A Mad Black Woman* was also a parable of sorts that its church-going audience connected to.

Tyler Perry as the much debated Madea.

Madea herself was in so many ways the old-style mammy—big, bossy, desexed, controlling—who, true to form, is all-knowing, all-hearing, all-seeing, basically all-understanding; a kind of godlike heroine close to the spirit of the Old Testament. She clearly believes an eye for an eye. But as a mammy Madea is primarily concerned about *her* community, not Miss Ann up on the hill. Yet, the film clearly operated on old types. The same was true of later Perry films in which an actress like Tasha Smith often came across as *an angry black woman*: seemingly irrational and overdone in her dissatisfaction with just about everything. But much like all-black films of the past, there was some semblance of a community in Perry's movies—with some semblance perhaps of different images. Included in the cast was Cicely Tyson. Perry also plays Madea's trifling brother Joe and her upright educated nephew Brian. With the way he's written Madea—without nuances or any sense of complexity—Perry succeeds by will, drive, determination, and a belief in his own powers that parallel the way he overcame adversities in his own life.

To the surprise of most, except perhaps Perry himself, *Diary of A Mad Black Woman* opened as the number-one movie of the week and eventually grossed $50 million. In 2006, his second film. *Madea's Family Reunion*, opened also in the number-one spot. This time around, and in the films that followed, Tyler Perry wrote, produced, and *directed*: such films as *Daddy's Little Girls* (2007, also known as *Tyler Perry's Daddy's Little Girls* with Idris Elba and Gabrielle Union but no Madea); *Why Did I Get Married?* (2007, with Perry playing a jilted husband); *Meet the Browns* (2008, with Madea and Joe briefly back on screen); *The Family That Preys* (2008, with Perry as Ben); the outrageous *Madea Goes to Jail* (2009, yes *outrageous* even for Perry; in one sequence which audiences loved, Madea demolished the car of a rude, obnoxious white woman who has foolishly and arrogantly taken Madea's parking spot); *I Can Do Bad All By Myself* (2009, with Taraji P. Henson as yet another wayward woman who must examine herself and put her life back in order); *Why Did I Get Married Too?* (2010); *Madea's Big Happy Family* (2011); and *Madea's Witness Protection* (2012). Actors and actresses were eager to work for him: Alfre Woodard, Janet Jackson, Jill Scott, and others. After all, Hollywood wasn't pounding down their doors with offers.

Criticism within the African American community was strong, especially when Perry turned to television with the series "Meet the Browns" and "House of Payne," which clearly were a collection of rigid, embarrassing types. At first supportive but later very critical, Spike Lee lambasted the coon antics.

Perry sought to broaden his audience. With the movie *The Family That Preys*, he cast Oscar winner Kathy Bates. He also adapted for the screen Ntozake Shange's play *for colored girls who've considered suicide/when the rainbow is enuf*, now simply called *For Colored Girls* (2010) with Thandie Newton, Kimberly Elise, Phylicia Rashad, Janet Jackson, Whoopi Goldberg, Tessa Thompson, Omari

A movie seeking to reach the black female audience, Tyler Perry's *Why Did I Get Married?*, with Jill Scott, Janet Jackson, Tasha Smith, and Sharon Leal.

Hardwick, Anika Noni Rose, Hill Harper, Kerry Washington, and the ever oddly fascinating Macy Gray. Perhaps a courageous effort and perhaps Perry's most obvious attempt to speak to African American women, the movie, however, literalized Shange's "choreopoem." Its poignant and powerful monologues were either chopped up or placed at strange moments in what otherwise was a routine melodrama. The actresses, however, seemed committed to the material.

As an actor, Perry also tried to stretch, dropping the Madea drag to star in *Good Deeds* (2012) as Wesley Deeds, a successful corporate man who tries to help a homeless woman (Thandie Newton) who works in his office. He also starred in *Alex Cross* (2012), playing the role of the tough, gritty police forensics expert that had been originated by Morgan Freeman in the 1997 *Kiss the Girls*. For those with memories of Freeman's performance, Perry was out of his element. It was wonderful though to see Cicely Tyson playing his mother. Perry was later, however, quite convincing as an attorney in David Fincher's *Gone Girl* (2014).

In spite of his critics, Tyler Perry tenaciously emerged as the era's most prolific and most discussed African American filmmaker. Having boldly challenged the Hollywood system, he also had made audiences aware of the way African American women, especially African American leading female characters, had too often been invisible in American cinema. From Thandie Newton to Jill Scott to Taraji P. Henson, to the great Cicely Tyson, Perry's actresses may not have had truly challenging roles, but they challenged themselves to make something out of those roles. Perry later created television shows for Oprah Winfrey's network OWN. Through his movies, in an unexpected way, he may have helped lead to the new starring roles that were created for African American women in such television shows as "Scandal," "How to Get Away with Murder," and "Empire."

Inter-Ethnic Casting

A number of biracial actors and actresses came to the fore: Daniel Sunjata, Rashida Jones (daughter of Quincy Jones and actress Peggy Lipton), Wentworth Miller, Paula Patton, Dwayne "The Rock" Johnson, Maya Rudolph, Jesse Williams, Vin Diesel. Generally, they had the opportunity to play a variety of characters, some not written specifically as African American. This was not entirely new. During the silent period, light-skinned actor Noble Johnson had played black characters and also diverse ethnic characters. Johnson, however, yearned for leading black characters and black films, and thus by helping to establish the Lincoln Motion Picture Company, he was able to play strong-minded, heroic African American leading roles in race movies. But playing other ethnics helped keep his Hollywood career alive. But he was able to do so because mainstream moviegoers knew little, if anything, about him or his racial background.

In the Hollywood of the 1930s and 1940s, actress Fredi Washington (not biracial; instead the daughter of two light-skinned African Americans) found her career stunted because the studios had almost no significant black characters for her to perform. Nor was she given a chance to play just "any" kind of character. At the time she appeared in the original 1934 *Imitation of Life*, she was known as being a Negro actress. In the 1950s, there was Frank Silvera. Born in Jamaica and raised in Boston, the son of a Spanish-Jewish father and a Jamaican mother, Silvera was cast as the Italian father of Ben Gazzara and Anthony Franciosa in the acclaimed 1955 Broadway production *A Hatful of Rain*. But when the drama became a film, white actor Lloyd Nolan played the father. Still, Silvera played all types of roles, with moviegoers and television viewers often unaware of his racial identity. He made two films for Stanley Kubrick: *Fear and Desire* (1953) and *Killer's Kiss* (1955). Other films included *Viva Zapata!* In 1952 (as Victoriano Huerta), *Mutiny on the Bounty* (1962, as a Polynesian); *The Greatest Story Ever Told* (1965, as one of the Biblical Magi), *The Appaloosa* (1966, as Ramos), and *Hombre* (1967, as a Mexican bandit). Indeed often enough he played Mexicans. But in *Uptight* he was a black political leader. Silvera always considered himself black, and in 1964, he was a co-founder of Los Angeles's Theatre of Being, which sought to provide black actors and actresses with non-stereotyped roles. But like Noble Johnson, Silvera was an exception to the way roles for black performers were generally cast.

In this new era, the situation had changed somewhat, although when biracial or very light actors or actresses were cast, they often played racially "vague" parts. Sometimes it didn't matter if nothing was said about the character's ethnicity. It was good to see such actors and actresses get unusual roles that in the past would have been blocked for them. Rashida Jones played a character who was fundamentally not African American in *The Social Network* (2010). Because she clearly looked like a light-skinned African American, Paula Patton played black characters in movies like *Déjà Vu* (2006) and *Just Wright*. In *Mission Impossible: Ghost Protocol* (2011), however, she was one of the Mission team without a racial demarcation, which was fine. The African American audience which always saw her as being African American was happy to see her have a chance at such a role in a big commercial film. Interestingly enough, Cruise's romantic leading lady in the earlier *Mission: Impossible II* (2000) was Thandie Newton. In that instance, some kind of backstory with some comment on her ethnic identity was sorely needed— mainly to make a better-developed and richer character. A performer's racial identification would always be important to the black audience.

When Hollywood returned to the "passing" theme in Robert Benton's adaptation of Philip Roth's novel *The Human Stain* (2003), eyebrows were raised at the casting of Anthony Hopkins as Coleman Silk, an African American college professor who has hidden his racial identity for years. Watching him, African American audiences found it hard to connect or identify with his plight because nothing about him suggested that his character came from an African American experience. Instead, audiences were always aware that on screen they were seeing Anthony Hopkins.

But *The Human Stain* was indeed affecting in its sections focusing on Coleman Silk as a young man when he made the decision to cross the color line. In flashbacks, we see that he is the son of a solidly black middle-class family. His father (Harry Lennix) has high standards and a refined bearing with an underlying resentment and bitterness. We understand why when we see that he goes to work looking as if heading to an office. Instead he is a porter on the railway. The mother (played superbly by Anna Deavere Smith) is a very light-skinned woman also with high standards but she is warm, loving, and understanding of the way that race restricts the lives of the entire family. Once her son Coleman has left home—and left his identity behind—she meets him in a public setting where she can never reveal their relationship. The pain is etched into her face. These were fascinating, sometimes heartbreaking sequences. But most involving was the startling performance of newcomer Wentworth Miller as the young Coleman Silk. Introspective and moody, everything about him—from the way he spoke so tentatively to the way he moved to the way he boxed in a sequence, to the way he looked at other characters— suggested someone with heart-rending secrets, with repressed conflicts, with an aching awareness that the path he had taken to fulfillment had, in the end, left him wholly unfulfilled and wholly alone. Handsome and engaging, Miller was like a young Montgomery Clift, an actor with a riddle of doubts and a piercing sensitivity. Those black audiences unaware of Miller's racial identity may have had the feeling that he *had* to be black.

Born in Chipping Norton, Oxfordshire, England in 1972 of an African American lawyer father and a white special education teacher mother, Miller moved with his family to Park Slope, Brooklyn, when he was a year old. After graduating from Princeton with a degree in English Literature, the 6'1" Miller took up residence in Los Angeles where he worked for a production company, then pursued acting jobs without much luck at first. The issue of how to cast this very light-skinned actor must have been on the minds of casting directors. Eventually, he landed roles on TV in "ER," "Buffy the Vampire Slayer," and "Dinotopia." After *The Human Stain*, he didn't work for about two years. Interestingly, he landed a lead role as Michael Scofield on TV's hit series "Prison Break." Essentially, he was playing a white character. This type of casting was unthinkable in past decades, although it appeared to be less publicized at this time that Miller was indeed black. He found other work in such films as *Resident Evil Afterlife* (2011) and perhaps most newsworthy in a Mariah Carey video. He also returned to England where he wrote the screenplay for *Stoker* (2013), starring Nicole Kidman. But Wentworth Miller didn't emerge as the film star he should have been. And there is always the nagging question if race cut short that kind of stardom with challenging roles—sad to say because Wentworth Miller was one of the most interesting and exciting new actors to come on the screen. So in some ways, Hollywood's casting procedures had not changed.

Also on the scene was Daniel Sunjata, hardly as intense as Miller but very skilled with a relaxed yet commanding screen presence. Born Daniel Sunjata Condon in 1971 in Illinois and described as being multi-racial (part African American, Irish, and German), he studied at Florida A & M University and later earned an MFA from New York University's Tisch School of the Arts. Appearing on Broadway in *Take Me Out*, he starred later as Langston Hughes in writer/director Rodney Evans's *Brother to Brother* (2004), which dramatized the dilemma of a young black gay man (played by Anthony Mackie) struggling to understand himself. In a homeless shelter in New York, he meets an older black gay writer. Through the older man come stories about leading figures of the Harlem Renaissance—Langston Hughes, Zora Neale Hurston, and poet Bruce Nugent—which eventually lead to a new awareness by the young man of himself. Though miscast as Hughes, Sunjata gave an engaging performance. Afterward he sometimes played African American characters. Sometimes he didn't. He did guest spots on such television shows as "Sex and the City." On the series "Rescue Me," he played the role of the Latino character Franco Rivera. He also had a recurring role on "Grey's Anatomy" as the love interest of Chandra Wilson and a starring role—a character written as white until Sunjata persuaded the casting director otherwise—on "Graceland." In the movies, he proved himself especially adroit as the designer James Holt in *The Devil Wears Prada* (2006). Race was not a part of his character's definition. The same was true of his roles in such films as *One for the Money* (2012) and *The Dark Knight Rises* (2012). In *Ghosts of Girlfriends Past* (2009), he played second male lead. The primary male lead was played by Matthew McConaughey as a womanizer who discovers late in the film that he loves Jennifer Garner. In turn, she has become attracted to Sunjata who plays a character named Brad. He's supposed to be second fiddle. The audience knows that Garner will end up with McConaughey. But Sunjata is so appealing that he hardly seems like second fiddle. Though the role is underwritten, Sunjata is a viable rival for McConaughey, and his presence almost throws the film out of kilter. No cultural context or suggestion of a racial identity, however, is established, and in this instance, Sunjata needs more than the script gives him. But better than most actors faced with his casting predicament, Sunjata understood how Hollywood sometimes operated in the new millennium. "As an ambiguously non-white actor," Sunjata said during a panel discussion at the Langham Hotel in Pasadena on January 7, 2013, "I've been able to play light-skinned African American guys, Latinos, and I don't think that I've ever had to play some kind of ethnic stereotype or something was typed specifically for a person of color."

Of these biracial actors and actresses, the most successful, although not the best, was for a time Vin Diesel. Interestingly, he was known to rarely discuss his racial

Inter/multi-ethnic heroes: Vin Diesel and Dwayne "The Rock" Johnson with Paul Walker (right) in one of the films in *The Fast and the Furious* franchise; Wentworth Miller as the tormented young man who decides to pass for white in *The Human Stain*; and Daniel Sunjata who looks ready to wed Jennifer Garner—until Matthew McConaughey intervenes—in the comedy *Ghosts of Girlfriends Past*.

background. "There are things Vin Diesel doesn't want you to know about Vin Diesel," wrote Benjamin Svetkey in his cover story on Diesel for the August 2, 2002 issue of *Entertainment Weekly*. "His real name, for one (that would be Mark Sinclair). His ethnic background, for another (half African-American, half Italian-American, or so we hear)." He also did not appear eager to discuss his age. Born in New York City in 1967, Diesel and his fraternal twin brother Paul (who later became a film editor) had grown up in a subsidized building for artists in New York's Greenwich Village. His mother was an astrologist; his adoptive step-father, Irving Vincent, a director of an off-off Broadway repertory company where young Mark Vincent worked for a time. Of his biological father who he said he had never met (nor apparently had any desire to meet), he commented: "That's all I need, some Darth Vader knocking on my door." For a time, he studied at Hunter College but dropped out, worked as a bouncer at New York clubs, changed his name to Vin Diesel, and briefly went to Hollywood, hoping to make it as an actor. After a year, he returned to New York. But the Hollywood experience gave him material for a short film he wrote *Multi-Facial* (1995), in which he played an actor who at various auditions changes his racial identity in hopes of getting work. It was a very clever premise that hit home for Diesel himself.

Diesel's fortunes changed after Steven Spielberg cast him in his World War II film *Saving Private Ryan* (1998) Those who criticized Spielberg for not including black soldiers had not been aware of Diesel's background. But he played an Italian character, Private Adrian Caparzo. From there, he went on to roles in the 1999 animated film *The Iron Giant* (his voice was heard as the Iron Giant); *Boiler Room* (2000); and *Pitch Black* (2000), in which he played the tough as nails Richard B. Riddick who fights off horrifying creatures on another planet. For some reason, the Riddick role resonated with younger audiences, and later Diesel found himself with a franchise character which he reprised in *The Chronicles of Riddick* (2003), the animated *The Chronicles of Riddick: Dark Fury* (2004), and *Riddick* (2013).

But he hit the jackpot in the action film *The Fast and the Furious* (2001). In many respects an old-style B-movie (in temperament rather than budget) produced for the youth market, it featured Diesel as part of a multi-ethnic cast that included Michelle Rodriguez, Rick Yune, and rapper Ja Rule. Originally, the blond, blue-eyed Paul Walker was to be the real star of this enterprise, playing an undercover cop who infiltrates a gang of street car racers. But as the tough and cool leader of the pack Dominic Toretto Diesel somehow commandeered this racing sideshow. Yet in this multi-racial/ethnic cast, his ethnicity was vague, if anything. Playing his sister was white actress Jordana Brewster. *The Fast and The Furious* became a big hit. A year later, Diesel played Xander Cage in *xXx* (2002), which he also co-executed-produced. Yet when John Singleton directed the sequel *2 Fast 2 Furious* (2003), cast member Paul Walker was back for the ride, along with black actors Tyrese Gibson, Chris "Ludacris" Bridges, Michael Ealy, and Latina actress Eva Mendes in a story about the car team helping the FBI capture a Miami drug dealer. Vin Diesel, however, was nowhere in sight. The next time around none of the previous ensemble cast was onboard for the 2006 *The Fast and the Furious: Tokyo Drift*—none ironically *except* Diesel who made a cameo appearance as Dominic Toretto. When the film grossed a seriously disappointing $62.5 million, it looked as if the bloom was off the *Furious* rose—*permanently*. But unwilling to give up on the franchise, the studio went back to basics with the original cast, added Laz Alonso, gave Diesel billing over Walker, and released the 2009 *Fast & Furious* which opened to a $71 million gross and went on to be a box-office bonanza. In 2011, *Fast Five* made its way to theaters with the original ensemble plus Gibson and Ludacris. It grossed $210 million domestically and $626.1 million worldwide. *Fast and Furious 6* followed in 2013 and became another big hit. By 2015 when Diesel starred in *Furious 7*, the film opened at number one and wouldn't quit. By its second weekend, its total box-office gross was $252.5 million, and that kept growing. The film series was a box-office phenomenon.

In all the *Furious* films, Diesel—with his head shaven and his hooded eyes—looked rather reptilian. His acting was a series of scowls and sharp commands to his crew. Even his athleticism could look hokey, as if his exploits could be attributed more to rapid fire editing than to any great innate athletic prowess. Later generations may wonder how Diesel ever rose to stardom. He did, however, have a strong enough screen presence not to be overshadowed by the other actors, and he was playing a rebel which no doubt helped draw the young (or perhaps best stated, young adolescent males) to him.

Interestingly, in number six of the *Furious* franchise, Diesel worked with Dwayne "The Rock" Johnson. Born in Canada, Johnson's father was black; his mother, Samoan. Standing 6'5", Johnson played football at the University of Miami and later became a professional wrestler—known as The Rock—following in the footsteps of both his father and grandfather. As Daniel Sunjata said of himself, perhaps The Rock or Johnson could also be described as an "ambiguously non-white actor." He was also open about his ethnic background. What made him engaging perhaps was his sense of humor and the fact that he didn't take himself too seriously.

The people behind the *Furious* movies, as well as the publicists, worked overtime to pump up interest in Diesel and trumpeted the idea that he appealed to all groups. "Hollywood has seen the future of the action hero, and it's multi-ethnic," wrote *Time* magazine in its August 5, 2002 issue. "In the past, John Wayne and Jimmy Stewart were the face of America," said Santiago Pozo of Arenas Entertainment which specialized in reaching the Latin market in the United States. "Today it's The Rock or Vin Diesel."

Time made an interesting cultural point. In the James Bond and *Batman* series, the hero was indeed a white sophisticate—at ease in elegant settings with stylish, glamorous women and often conniving, shrewd villains. Bond and Batman could wear splendidly tailored suits, shirts, and ties. Always moviegoers could sense that the minds of these men were at work. A hero like Superman could also wear a suit well enough (when he was Clark Kent) as he projected a healthy, wholesome traditional white all-Americanism—despite the fact that he was from another planet. No one ever thought about the ethnicity of these heroes because they had none. In the *Furious* series, the only white hero was the outsider cop, played by Paul Walker, who comes to identify with the ethnics who surround him. Interestingly, the ethnicity was visible in the casting, not necessarily in the way the characters were written. In the case of Vin Diesel, he *seemed* ethnic because of his complexion and his features and perhaps (and this is a strong *perhaps*) in his speech rhythms and intonations.

"By stripping away all identifying marks, presenting himself as a blank slate—particularly when it comes to his racial background—he's found a way to market himself to the broadest possible audience," commented *Entertainment Weekly* in its August 2, 2002 issue. "He's selling himself as a multiethnic Everyman, a movie star virtually every demographic can claim as its own." Maybe. Maybe not.

"If you're Hispanic, you look at Vin and see an Hispanic. If you're Italian, you see an Italian," Rob Cohen, director of *The Fast and the Furious*, told *Entertainment Weekly*. "If you're African American, you see an African American." Again: Maybe. Again: Maybe not. Frankly, it was doubtful that African American audiences felt that kind of identification with him. Ludacris and Tyrese Gibson and Dwayne "The Rock" Johnson were more relatable in that respect for black moviegoers. The ethnic/racial identity of stars like Denzel Washington, Samuel L. Jackson, and Morgan Freeman clearly were known to audiences and appreciated. They had become huge stars not by running away from nor stripping down their ethnic backgrounds nor by overplaying them but by simply carrying it within them in a casual way.

If anything, Diesel was indeed, as the magazine stated, a blank slate. Yet what exactly was projected onto him by an audience? It's like watching a comic strip character that is not real in any way. Instead the audience could accept him on the most superficial of levels. With African American performers, a subtext in their movies can make them more complicated and complex, even more compelling, certainly as perceptive audiences watched them. But with Diesel he got the job done through adroit editing and digitized effects—and again significantly enough through his weighted presence. But you could leave the movie without ever thinking twice about him and what the picture *might* mean.

Interestingly, Diesel succeeded primarily as "the face of America" in action films, not so much in human dramas (as was the case with James Stewart and with

John Wayne) where the audience responded to the person rather than the action. Diesel may have seemed simply like an effective tool or pawn in the action games, in the realm of one-dimensional comic strip heroes. Usually, he was a video game in human form. That may be more of a compliment than it sounds.

He attempted to broaden his range in such films as F. Gary Gray's *A Man Apart* (2003) and *The Pacifier* (2005, a comedy in which he played a rugged Navy Seal trying to manage five rambunctious kids). Surprisingly, director Sidney Lumet cast him as Jack DiNorscio, a real life gangster who represents himself while on trial, in *Find Me Guilty* (2006). "At last he plays a real character instead of a swaggering cartoon of testosterone on the rampage," wrote Stephen Holden in *The New York Times*. "Mr. Diesel also succeeds in making a dangerous thug almost lovable with his sensational performance." He also was a shrewd negotiator. On *Find Me Guilty*, Diesel also had a producing credit.

Nonetheless, his success as well as that of actors like Johnson, Sunjata, and Miller did mark a shift in casting for some African American performers. It wasn't so much multi-ethnic casting as it was inter-ethnic casting for light-skinned actors. How other ethnic actors may have felt about some of such casting was another matter altogether.

Oscar Time

A significant sign of change in mainstream cinema came with the cherished and coveted Oscars as a lineup of performers and some filmmakers either won the award or were nominated, more than ever before in Hollywood history. Some might dismiss the award. But as Federico Fellini said upon winning his fourth Foreign Film Oscar with *Amarcord* (1974): "In the mythology of the cinema, the Oscar is the supreme prize." It was a formal recognition, the highest Hollywood could confer. Not only did it mark talent but on occasion, it indicated the industry's political and social attitudes. Too many skilled and imaginative black performers had been overlooked in the past; so the award carried great historical weight.

Long overdue for the award and one of the most film talented actors, black or white—and a previous nominee—was Morgan Freeman who walked off with the 2004 Best Supporting Actor award for his performance as Eddie Scrap-Iron Dupris in Clint Eastwood's *Million Dollar Baby*. As often happened in Oscar history, actors sometimes might not win for their best performances. Instead they are awarded compensation Oscars which might be the case with Freeman— although frankly he was so good in *Million Dollar Baby* that you'd be hard-pressed to think of anyone else that year in that category who was better. A master at projecting a moral gravitas (in *Bruce Almighty* (2003) and the 2007 *Evan Almighty*, he was actually cast as God), Freeman now was playing rather saintly characters: sturdy, adjuncts to white leads, standing sometimes as a conscience or a soulful advisor. Yes, right back to the huck-finn fixation. In this story of a young woman (Hillary Swank) in pursuit of a boxing career, she seeks help from a reluctant Eastwood to manage her. Freeman is there to remind Eastwood of choices he's made in the past. He's also Eastwood's only friend. Having worked together previously in *Unforgiven*, Freeman and Eastwood had a compelling chemistry. They are perfectly in sync in balancing or counter-balancing one another's attitudes and rhythms. *Million Dollar Baby* won Oscars that year also for Best Picture, for Eastwood as Best Director, and for Hillary Swank as Best Actress. Afterward Freeman worked in film and after film: *Batman Begins* (2005); *The Bucket List* (2008, well-teamed with Jack Nicholson and Beverly Todd); *Red* (2010); *Oblivion* (2013); and opposite Diane Keaton in *5 Flights Up* (2014). He was nominated for a 2009 Best Actor Oscar for his performance as Nelson Mandela in *Invictus*.

But Freeman was not the only African American winner that year; so was one of his competitors in the Supporting Actor category: Jamie Foxx, who was nominated for Michael Mann's *Collateral* with Tom Cruise and Jada Pinkett Smith (all three at their best) and also for Best Actor for his performance as Ray Charles in Taylor Hackford's biopic *Ray*. This was truly historic: a black actor nominated in two categories in one year. Interestingly enough, that same year Don Cheadle was also nominated for Best Actor and Sophie Okonedo for Best Supporting Actress in director Terry George's harrowing drama *Hotel Rwanda* which focused on the real-life genocide of a million Tutsis in Rwanda in 1994. In the end, Foxx won for *Ray*. Portraying the great musical star without slipping into impersonation, Foxx dug deep inside to come up with a complicated character. Foxx revealed a talent that one might not have expected by his rather haphazard work on "The Jamie Foxx Show." Many films followed: Michael Mann's film version of the TV series *Miami Vice* (2006, with a miscast Foxx); *The Soloist* (2009); *Law Abiding Citizen* (2009); *Django Unchained* (2012); and *White House Down* (2013).

Former model Djimon Hounsou, who was born in Benin, West Africa, was nominated for his performance as a Nigerian painter living in a tenement in New York's Hell's Kitchen in Jim Sheridan's *In America* (2002). Reclusive and angry, yet also gentle, Hounsou's character is stricken with AIDS. Throughout the era, he appeared in such films as *Gladiator* (2000, his towering assured fighter bringing to mind William Marshall in the 1954 spectacle *Demetrius and the Gladiators*), *Beauty Shop* (2005), *Blood Diamond* (2006), and those huge hits *Guardians of the Galaxy* (2014) and *Furious Seven*.

During the period, both James Earl Jones and Harry Belafonte were awarded honorary Lifetime Achievement Oscars. Some other big names also got nods (as nominees or winners) from Oscar.

Will Smith: Oscar Nominee, Megastar, Movie Disappointments

The Legend of Bagger Vance had to be a disappointment for Will Smith. But it wasn't his only one. Throughout the new millennium's first decade and into the next, Smith starred in a series both of extraordinary hits and surprising dismal misses. Certainly a challenge and a highlight of his acting career was Michael Mann's *Ali* (2001) in which Smith played the embattled Muhammad Ali during a ten-year period (1964 to 1974) of turmoil. Slow, uneven, and never fully capturing the turbulence or excitement of these years, especially of "The Rumble in the Jungle" boxing match, the film also rarely examined Ali, the man, in a significant or eye-opening way. Working with such co-stars as Jamie Foxx, Jon Voight, Jeffrey Wright, and his wife Jada Pinkett Smith, Smith himself, however, managed to capture Ali's braggadocio and some of his spirit. Clearly, his performance was an acting stretch that marked a new maturity for him. One only wishes there had been more sequences when we saw an emotionally torn or troubled Ali. But in the scene in which he does get a chance to show a mixture of anger and confusion, Smith's compelling. It won him his first Academy Award nomination as Best Actor of the Year. But *Ali* failed to reach a large audience which may have made Smith wary of taking chances.

Playing it safe, Smith promptly returned to formulaic movies, appearing in the routine sequels *Men in Black II* (2002)—and later *Men in Black 3* (2012)—a continuation of the buddy cop saga about a search by Smith and co-star Tommy Lee Jones to find aliens hiding on earth. He also teamed up again with Martin Lawrence for the cop actioner sequel *Bad Boys II* (2003). "I got scared and started choosing incorrectly," Smith told *Entertainment Weekly* in its December 2, 2007 issue. "I did *Bad Boys II* and *Men in Black II* out of fear. That was a bad time for me psychologically because I wasn't thinking the right way about filmmaking." But he soon rebounded in super heroic mode in the futuristic *I, Robot* (2004). Set in the year 2035, the film starred Smith as a character who knows something is afoul with the army of robots designed to perform as servants in a technologically advanced society. Directed by Alex Proyas and drawn from Isaac Asimov's stories, *I, Robot* admittedly had a good premise. But there were false starts and frequent stalls, to the point where the film eventually descended into an unrelieved tedium. Smith, however, somehow carried it, looking as if he could single-handedly save the world. He performed in a similar way in the then post-apocalyptic *I Am Legend* (2007). Here, after a plague has destroyed most of humankind, Smith alone searches for an antidote. In both films, the tall, muscular, confident Smith was a frazzled but likeable take-charge guy who didn't understand the concept of defeat or failure. In both, he projected such confidence surprisingly with a light touch and without a heavy-handed attitude. That was part of the power and magnetism of his brand of heroic stardom. These two films were clearly geared toward a large mainstream audience; to do so, the filmmakers assumed that the films had to be devoid of African American cultural markers and signs. There is a reference to Bob Marley in *I Am Legend*. Smith also has a family that he has lost. His daughter Willow Smith makes an appearance. But both *I, Robot* and *I Am Legend* appear to feel embarrassed by presenting him culturally as a black character—as if that might turn off the mainstream audience, as if that might remind moviegoers they were watching and cheering for a black star.

Another box-office hit for Smith was the comedy *Hitch* (2005). He played a "love doctor" coaching a client (Kevin James) on dating a woman; he's also trying to keep his own life romantically afloat. There was some discussion about the fact that Smith had not chosen an African American actress as his leading lady; he had the box office clout to do so. She wasn't a white one either. It was the stunning Latina actress Eva Mendes. Smith's African American following hoped he would show some sign of a cultural consciousness, whether subtle or not, in his mainstream hits.

Smith moved in a different direction in *The Pursuit of Happyness* (2006), based on the book about the financial and psychological downs and ups of the real life Chris Garner. Smith as Garner loses his wife (Thandie Newton), struggles to provide for his five-year-old son (played by his real life son billed as Jaden Christopher Syre Smith), ends up homeless, then climbs his way back up. *The New York Times* critic Manohla Dargis called it a "fairy-tale in realist drag ... the kind of entertainment that goes down smoothly until it gets stuck in your throat." Dargis added: "It's the same old bootstraps story, an American dream artfully told, skillfully sold. To that calculated end, the filmmaking is seamless, unadorned, transparent, the better to serve Mr. Smith's warm expressiveness." *The Pursuit of Happyness* drew out of him a vulnerability and sensitivity (in those scenes with his real life son)—and also a near desperation. For one of the rare times in a Will Smith movie, the audience may have wanted to comfort *him*. Indeed, here he gave one of his most-felt performances which in turn earned him a second Academy Award nomination as Best Actor of the Year.

The films that followed met with varying degrees of success. Occasionally, he experimented again with a different type of role. But calculation seemed to govern his choices. The offbeat *Seven Pounds* (2008) seemed vague and bewildering to audiences. *Hancock* (2008), in which he played a disheveled, grungy bum of a guy with super human powers, was probably just as vague and bewildering, but it put him back in heroic mode, and once again he was a box-office champ. On July 7, 2008, the *New York Post* reported: "Will Smith, showing what star power is all about, overcame some of the worst reviews of his career to top the weekend box

Will Smith, back in heroic mode in *I Am Legend*, looking like he can save the world.

office with *Hancock*—scoring a superheroic $66 million. Smith, who has been using July 4th as his personal ATM ever since *Independence Day* in 1996, had his third-best July opening when adjusted to inflation." But following *Hancock's* success, the going got rough.

Another futuristic drama, *After Earth* (2013), which cast him with his son Jaden, Sophie Okonedo, and Zoë Kravitz, was one of his least successful films. Previously, Smith and his wife Jada Pinkett Smith had been among the producers of a successful remake of *The Karate Kid* (2010) which had starred their son. But this time around, audiences stayed away. Attempting to reinvent himself, Smith played a smooth conman opposite sexy, blonde Margot Robbie in the caper *Focus* (2015), which also proved critically and commercially disappointing. So much of Smith's career had entailed proficient calculation. So much seemed targeted at bringing a huge audience into theaters without enough personal statements (other than that of the calculation, of course). Yet Smith showed—at surprising moments—that he was willing to take risks. That certainly was the case when he appeared as the dedicated forensic pathologist in *Concussion* (2015).

2006: Forest Whitaker, A Big Year

Another big Oscar win occurred when Forest Whitaker walked off with the Best Actor award for his performance as Ugandan dictator (and madman) General Idi Amin in Kevin Macdonald's *The Last King of Scotland* (2006). The film also featured James McAvoy, Gillian Anderson and future stars Kerry Washington and David Oyelowo. Much of the movie focused on McAvoy as a Scottish doctor who is first charmed by Amin, then betrayed and brutalized by him. It's asking our sympathies for him more than the other characters. Amin's atrocities and horrors are here. But there's no real attempt to figure him out. Maybe that's not possible. But it would be worth the effort to see the filmmakers try. Whitaker's strong, galvanizing performance, however, captures the insanity and some of the frightening perverse humor of Amin. But because it also was never clear how Amin came to power, moviegoers may have left the theater feeling they had seen a horror show rather than an incisive political drama. After Whitaker's Oscar win, there were no equally mesmerizing performances or roles. His later films included *Powder Blue* (2009), *Hurricane Season* (2009), *Our Family Wedding* (2010), *The Last Stand* (2013), and *Taken 3* (2014). In *Black Nativity*, he and Angela Bassett as the parents of an estranged adult daughter did project a warm glow; both were sweetly relaxed, giving just the right touch to roles that otherwise did not require much from them.

The new millennium brings more Academy Award recognition for African American performers. (TOP) Forest Whitaker wins the Best Actor Award for his performance as Idi Amin in the disjointed drama *The Last King of Scotland*. (MIDDLE) Jamie Foxx wins for his performance as singer Ray Charles in *Ray*. (BOTTOM) Finally, an Oscar for Morgan Freeman as Clint Eastwood's reliable, thoughtful buddy in *Million Dollar Baby*.

Big Dreams: Dreamgirls

Possibly the most emotionally charged Oscar win of the decade came with a newcomer—Jennifer Hudson—in one of the era's important films focusing on young African American women, Bill Condon's *Dreamgirls* (2006). Based on Michael Bennett's groundbreaking production of the Tom Eyen/Henry Krieger Broadway musical of 1981, *Dreamgirls*—much like the 1976 version of *Sparkle*—was inspired by the extraordinary singing group The Supremes, which in the 1960s took its record company Motown to the top of the charts. The Supremes crossed over with white record buyers in a way that few black groups had done. With Mary Wilson and Florence Ballard backing her up, the lead singer was the ambitious and unstoppable Diana Ross. Culturally, The Supremes was probably the most significant girl group of the past century: three ghetto girls from the Detroit projects whose success personified the American Dream. But the group was marked by tragedy when Florence Ballard left The Supremes or rather (so most believed) was pushed out. She returned home to Detroit. Though she tried for musical comebacks, Ballard found herself applying for welfare and then died of cardiac arrest at the age of thirty-two. It was one of popular music's great tragedies.

Dreamgirls pretty much followed the real life story but also added its own dramatic points. Here the three young woman—Beyoncé Knowles (as Deena, the Diana Ross figure), Anika Noni Rose, and Jennifer Hudson (as Effie, the Ballard surrogate)—find themselves under the control of an aggressive and ultimately ruthless record producer Curtis Taylor (Jamie Foxx), inspired by Motown chief Berry Gordy, Jr. Hudson's tempestuous relationship with the producer—as well as her realization that he will replace her as lead singer with Deena—all lead to her downfall. Once Effie is out of the group, Foxx's character not only marries Deena but also does all he can to prevent Effie from having a successful solo career. *Dreamgirls* sought to uncover the unsavory and unethical practices of the music industry. It also attempted to chart changing musical tastes during the nation's Civil Rights movement and then its Black Power era in the late 1960s. Some of it didn't jell, especially those sequences that tried to reveal social/political changes. There was a black Cleopatra sequence that fell flat and simply looked irrelevant. What were they thinking?

But *Dreamgirls* told a good story, and where it worked best was with Hudson's character Effie. Heavier than the other two women and browner than Deena, she's not, however, some selfless, nurturing mammy figure. She is outspoken yet vulnerable. Whenever Hudson was on screen, audiences sat riveted. Whenever she was off-screen, the picture slowed and lost some of its momentum. Hudson/Effie's big number "And I am Telling You I'm Not Going" (originally performed on Broadway by Jennifer Holliday) pulls out all stops. Director

Inspired by the real life singing trio The Supremes, *Dreamgirls* starred Anika Noni Rose, Beyoncé Knowles, and Jennifer Hudson—who walked off with the picture and a Best Supporting Actress Oscar.

Condon shoots from different angles that are splendidly edited together. The lyrics of the song are frankly on the pathetic side. How can she possibly make Curtis love her—and why bother since he's such a heel? Yet the number is exciting, perhaps mostly because Hudson pitches everything at such a high emotional level that as the song progresses one wonders if she can pull it all together. And she does. It's a triumphant sequence for her—and for the film. So were her beautifully calibrated dramatic scenes. In many ways, Effie echoed the real Hudson who had been a contestant for several weeks on TV's "American Idol." But after the critical comments of one of the judges, she seemed to lose her confidence. Always her vulnerability was apparent as well as her personal struggle to make something of herself. In the end, she was booted from the show. Most might have assumed that would be it for her. But somehow she won the Effie role. Condon understood that mixture of sass and fear within her, and he helped her use it perfectly for the character.

Also strong as the James Brown-style singer James "Thunder" Early was Eddie Murphy. The movie indicates that Early is too ethnic, too old-style *colored* to cross over. In a sequence when his character performs in his traditional style—saying the hell with crossover dreams—Murphy is sensational. Though he won an Oscar nomination as Best Supporting Actor, his chance at winning seemed wrecked by an odd turn of events. Not long after the release of *Dreamgirls*, Murphy's film *Norbit* (2007) appeared. His portrayal of an obnoxious female character who was large, dominating, vulgar, and vindictive was criticized as a hateful caricature. In the end, many felt that *Norbit* alienated moviegoers *and* Academy voters. Alan Arkin won the award for *Little Miss Sunshine* (2006).

Originally, *Dreamgirls* looked as if it might be Beyoncé Knowles's picture. This talented singer who had performed with the group Destiny's Child had already inherited the glam goddess throne once held by Diana Ross, although Ross occupied such a unique position in music/cultural history that she could never be surpassed. But Beyoncé's Deena was not an especially sympathetic character, much as the script softens her. Nor does the script fully develop the character. One aspect Beyoncé brought to the later scenes—when the successful Deena has endured the machinations of her music mogul husband—was an awareness of the personal toll a major career can take. A disillusionment and a hardness slip into her characterization that work exceptionally well. If only the script had understood Deena the way Knowles does. Already Beyoncé had appeared in such movies as *Austin Powers in Goldmember* (2002, playing Foxxy Cleopatra), *The Fighting Temptations* (2003), and the Steve Martin version of *Pink Panther* (2006). In 2009, she co-starred with Idris Elba in the domestic thriller *Obsessed*.

The rest of the cast—Anika Noni Rose, Sharon Leal, Danny Glover, and of course, Foxx—were all in top form. Rose went on to provide the voice in Disney's

The *Princess and the Frog* (2009) which was criticized for its depiction of Disney's first black animated heroine. Sharen Davis, who had been nominated for an Oscar for her costumes in *Ray*, won another nomination for her costumes in *Dreamgirls*.

But *Dreamgirls* was Hudson's movie. She won the Golden Globe and then the Academy Award as Best Supporting Actress of 2006. It was quite an Oscar ceremony as both she and Forest Whitaker walked off with big awards.

Women on the Rise: New Roles

As *Dreamgirls* and, yes, even Tyler Perry's movies indicated, the era provided more roles for African American women but obviously with varying degrees of success. In some popular films like *Monster-in-Law* (2005) and *Sex and the City* (2008), the new "assistants" to the white stars were variants on the sassy or nurturing maid roles of the past. In *Monster-in-Law*, Jane Fonda's assistant Ruby, played by Wanda Sykes, delivers one expertly delivered wisecrack after another much like Hattie McDaniel's outspoken maids. But Ruby has a life that primarily revolves around the woman she works for and certainly likes. In *Sex and the City*, the assistant Louise (Jennifer Hudson) puts the life of the character Carrie Bradshaw (Sarah Jessica Parker) in order and is so devoted that even on Louise's wedding day, she has to check in on the woman she cares so much about. In *The Other Woman* (2014), Nicki Minaj sits in the office of her co-worker Cameron Diaz, eager to dispense advice on men and what Diaz must do with her life. Curiously, Minaj projects such a gilded narcissism that sometimes her advice, while sound, also seems like so much chatter; Nicki Minaj always seems far too interested in Nicki Minaj to care but so much about anyone else.

Women figured prominently in such movies as *Something New* (2006) and *Jumping the Broom*, each of which touched on the theme of class within the African American community. In both, the Black Bourgeoisie has to be taken down a peg or two. In *Something New*, the issue of class was used as a twist on the theme of interracial love. A young African American professional (Sanaa Lathan) finds herself successful at her corporate offices but unsuccessful in finding love—until a handsome white landscaper (Simon Baker) works at her home. In older films, it would have been the white family objecting to such a union. Here it is Lathan's middle-class family. Her mother, played by Alfre Woodward, doesn't approve. Her brother, played by Donald Faison, can't believe she's hooking up with "the help." Directed by Sanaa Hamri, written by Kriss Turner, and produced by Stephanie Allain, *Something New* was an entertaining romance with engaging performances and a sharp-eyed portrait of a contemporary educated African

A twist on interracial love amid class warfare—*Something New* with Simon Baker and Sanaa Lathan.

American woman opposing racial and class attitudes within her own community. And it was significant to see three black women (Morocco-born director Hamri, Turner, and Allain) examining a theme and characters they felt connected to. Also in the cast were Taraji P. Henson, Wendy Raquel Robinson, Mike Epps, Henry Simmons, and Blair Underwood. But sad to say, *Something New* was surprisingly not a big hit.

Class issues were also present in Salim Akil's *Jumping the Broom* (2011). It told the story of a properly raised young black woman (Paula Patton) about to marry a young professional (Laz Alonso) from a working class background. Playing the mother of the bride was Angela Bassett. Playing the mother of the groom was Loretta Devine. *Jumping the Broom* had a warm glow that was a welcome relief from some of the other black comedies in which characters come and go, argue, make amends, and then resolve their differences without ever taking time to look closely into the lives and minds of the characters. Reflective moments in many of those comedies were rare and sorely needed.

Akil also directed the remake of *Sparkle* with a script by his wife Mara Brock Ali, based on the Joel Schumacher story from the 1976 original. Produced by Debra Martin Chase, the new *Sparkle* starred Jordin Sparks, Carmen Ejogo, Mike Epps, Derek Luke, Tika Sumpter, Terrence Jenkins, and CeeLo Green. Its story was fundamentally the same as the original but told with a contemporary beat and perspective. As the "fast" Sister, who believes she has answers to everything but is sadly disillusioned, Carmen Ejogo had the energy and insights to pull the role off. Much like Lonette McKee in the original, Ejogo's performance gives the film much of its drive. But of greatest interest and certainly the most moving aspect of the remake was the appearance of Whitney Houston as the mother of the young women in pursuit of careers in music. Older, warmly vulnerable, and seemingly more assured than in her earlier performances (she doesn't appear to be fearful of acting itself or so it seems; you can't say for sure), her character is aware of life's pitfalls and doesn't want to see her daughters stumble into them. As one views the film and is aware that Houston died not long after completing the role, you have a sadness about what has been lost.

A Long Time In the Making

Some actresses garnered well-deserved attention. Both Taraji P. Henson and Viola Davis won Oscar nominations in the 2008 Best Supporting Actress category. In David Fincher's affecting fable *The Curious Case of Benjamin Button* (adapted from a story by F. Scott Fitzgerald), an infant is born old and wizened in New Orleans in 1918, and as the film progresses he (Brad Pitt) ages in reverse, going from old-age to middle-age, youth, and childhood until his death. Playing a loving woman named Queenie who took care of Benjamin Button at one point in his life—and who cared deeply for him—was Henson. In some respects, the role was written as yet another archetypal portrait of a nurturing wise black woman. But it was hard not to be moved by some of Henson's scenes with Pitt. Though we the audience may not know enough about Queenie, Henson does, making her character strong and kindly. It's like watching the kindly deluded soul in both versions of *Imitation of Life* (1934 and 1959). Intellectually, you may reject the character (as written), but you cannot reject it emotionally because of the actress's performance.

The Curious Case of Benjamin Button was a career boost for Henson. Born in 1970 in Washington, D.C. and a graduate of Howard University, she had come to Hollywood in the late 1990s. She worked steadily in such TV shows as "Sister, Sister," "ER," "Saved by the Bell," "Felicity" and such films as *The Adventures of Rocky & Bullwinkle* (2000), *Baby Boy* (2001), *Four Brothers* (2005), *Something New*, Kasi Lemmons' *Talk to Me* (2007); and, of course, as the placid pregnant girlfriend in *Hustle & Flow*, as well as others. Clearly, Henson had been around the acting block, and her versatility was apparent even when audiences might remember her face but not her name. After the Oscar nomination, she worked Tyler Perry's *I Can Do Bad All by Myself*, *Date Night* (2010), the remake of *The Karate Kid*, (as the mother of Jaden Smith), the comedies *Think Like A Man* (2012) and *Think Like A Man Too* (2014), and as the resilient wife in the ho-hum woman-in-distress thriller *No Good Deed* (2014). Many of her later films did not offer her much to work with, but Henson never walked through a role. There was something both earthy *and* actressy about her which enlivened her characters. Ironically, the character that brought her to full-fledged (and much deserved) stardom was as the indomitable, morally questionable, *and* hugely enjoyable Cookie on the TV series "Empire" in 2015.

Count Ms Davis In

Viola Davis had also been on the scene for years. Born in 1965 in St Matthews, South Carolina, Davis had grown up under harsh conditions with five siblings in Rhode Island. Her father groomed horses for Rhode Island's Narragansett Park. Her mother worked in a candy factor. The family was so poor, she told *Entertainment Weekly* in its February 27, 20015 issue, that: "People would look at me and go 'Oh, I know she's poor.' I would think, 'Just give me some food and I could take care of the rest.'" She also recalled unending racist taunts. "Constantly being called 'black ugly nigger'—those words together," she said in Bill Duke's 2011 documentary *Dark Girls*. Through this turmoil, she stayed focused and soon pursued an acting career. After graduating from Rhode Island College, she later spent four years studying at Juilliard. Her early television work included such shows as "NYPD Blue," "New York Undercover," "Judging Amy," and "City of Angels." In movies, she appeared in the Steven Soderbergh films *Out of Sight* (1998), *Traffic* (2000), and *Solaris* (2002) as well as in Denzel Washington's *Antwone Fisher*. Her performance in Todd Haynes's *Far From Heaven* (2002) was singled out by the critics.

But the film *Doubt* (2008) turned her career around. In *Doubt*, set in a Bronx parish in 1964, Davis played the mother of a boy (the first black student at his high school) who may have been molested by a priest. In a pivotal sequence, she meets with the principal of the school, a formidable nun (Meryl Streep) who is determined to find the priest guilty. The sequence is startling in part because of a revelation by Davis and in part of course because of the actresses igniting one another's fires. Davis matches Streep in intensity and in power. Morose and troubled, Davis confesses to Streep's character, that at heart whether her son was molested or not, the priest had helped the boy find his way in life. The performance was riveting—with perhaps one false overly dramatic note when she doesn't try to wipe away the tears or runny nose during the big scene. It's almost as if she wants to impress us with her depth of feeling. Ironically, she does. Her compelling performance rightly won her a Best Supporting Actress nomination.

One of Davis' great supporters was indeed Meryl Streep who, upon winning a Golden Globe for her performance in *Doubt*, cited Davis in her acceptance speech and let it be known that somebody should give this woman a movie! Roles in films featuring major stars followed: *Law Abiding Citizen* (2009), starring Jamie Foxx; *Knight and Day* (2010), starring Tom Cruise; and *Eat Pray Love* (2010), starring Julia Roberts. But none of the films offered her a substantial part. Davis was one of the few actresses to speak honestly about the situation confronting her: a Hollywood that had little interest in older, browner African American women.

"I always got the phone call that said: 'I have a great project for you. You're going to be with, hypothetically, Vanessa Redgrave, Julianne Moore, Annette Bening,'" she told *The New York Times* in the September 14, 2014 edition. "Then I get the script, and I have a role that lasts for a page or two." She added: "I have been given a lot of roles that are downtrodden, mammy-ish." She further commented on her roles: "A lot of lawyers or doctors who have names but absolutely no lives. You're going to get your three or four scenes, you're not going to be able to show what you can do. You're going to get your little bitty paycheck, and then you're going to be hungry for your next role, which is going to be absolutely the same. That's the truth."

Precious and Lee Daniels' Gothic Cinema of Excess

As the decade neared its end, striking performances were delivered by newcomer Gabourey Sidibe and by now veteran Mo'Nique in the controversial 2009 Lee Daniels-directed film *Precious: Based on the Novel 'Push' by Sapphire*. Yes, that was the complete title. Set in 1987, it told the story of an obese teenage girl called Precious, emotionally isolated and shockingly abused by her parents. So numbed is she by her experiences that she sees no way out of her hellish life. Raped by her father, Precious is twice impregnated by him. Her first child, born when Precious was twelve, suffers from Down Syndrome. Repeatedly harangued and physically *and* sexually abused by her psychotic mother (ironically named Mary and played by Mo'Nique), the dark-skinned, sullen Precious is something of an invisible girl as she walks the streets of Harlem. Her constant dream is one in which she is considered a beauty and is courted by a light-skinned young African American man. Her life changes once an attractive light-skinned teacher (Paula Patton) takes an interest in her. So do a welfare counselor (a deglamorized Mariah Carey) and a nurse (Lenny Kravitz). By the end of the film, you feel that somehow Precious will pull through her torment and begin a new life. Coming on board as executive producers were Oprah Winfrey and Tyler Perry.

"It's a potent and moving experience," wrote Owen Gleiberman in *Entertainment Weekly*. Other critics praised the film. Others, however, felt differently. "The elements of *Precious* are powerful and shocking, but the movie is programmed," David Edelstein commented in *New York* magazine. "It is its own study guide." The comments of both critics were valid. Lee Daniels skillfully directs sequences that are hard to watch and hard to forget. The performances by Sidibe and Mo'Nique give the film its poignancy and its terror. But *Precious* suffered from its own excesses. The mother's cruelties are overwritten. The fact that she uses Precious and the child of Precious as her meal ticket to collect from welfare is probably the least of her abuses. Throughout, one humiliation—one ugly insult—after another was directed at this helpless victim of a girl. In a climactic sequence when the mother hurls a television at her daughter, moviegoers may have felt the film had gone way too far. You already have gotten its important point. Though the film attempts to say something about the mother's jealousy of her daughter, *Precious* fails to provide any insight into the mother. The other horrors facing Precious are also overwritten. When the father rapes Precious, he is one more faceless, basically nameless violent black man, a terrifying buck straddling his defenseless daughter. When you learn that he has AIDS, which you feel will be transmitted to Precious, you may want to yell: "When will it end!" and run the heck

Gabourey Sidibe with Academy Award winner Mo'Nique as her vengeful, sadistic, monstrous mother in *Precious*.

out of the theater. What might have been a serious domestic drama has become a Gothic horror movie. Talented as director Daniels is, he didn't seem to know when to pull back. Oddly enough, the few admirable characters who help Precious— Patton's lesbian teacher, Carey's social worker, Kravitz's friendly nursing assistant— are all light-skinned. How did this type of casting come about? Is *Precious* suggesting that perhaps skin color has sensitized and even ennobled them? It almost looks as the casting people have fantasies similar to those of Precious herself.

With all that said and done, *Precious* succeeded in making perhaps its most significant point. Gabourey Sidibe's character is indeed the face of someone moviegoers might see on city streets, then turn away from, preferring not to think about the woman who has passed them. But after watching the film, a viewer will not be able to *not* think about such a young woman. Sidibe makes Precious a breathing, living soul who is unforgettable.

Precious marked a career milestone for Mo'Nique. A one-time standup comedienne who had been born Mo'Nique Imes in 1967 in Woodlawn, Maryland, she hit her stride as the feisty (and often love-lorn) mother Nikki on the enjoyable TV series "The Parkers," which ran from 1999 to 2004. Warm, lively, often enough outspoken, she also made guest appearances on such series as "The Hughleys," "The Bernie Mac Show," "Nip/Tuck," "The Game," "The Boondocks," and "Ugly Betty." She appeared in such movies as *Baby Boy*, *Two Can Play that Game* (2001), *Soul Plane* (2004), and *Phat Girlz* (2006). But none of her earlier performances could have prepared audiences for the fierce dramatic power of her role in *Precious*, a mean, sadistic, unrelentingly cruel characterization that can be arguably compared to Bette Davis' ferocious (and enjoyably campy) character Jane in *What Ever Happened to Baby Jane?* (1962).

Precious itself was Oscar nominated as Best Picture; Lee Daniels, nominated as Best Director; Sidibe, nominated as Best Actress, a real coup for an actress making her movie debut. Mo'Nique won the Best Supporting Actress Oscar, and Geoffrey Fletcher became the first African American screenwriter to win an Academy Award for the Best Screenplay (adapted from another source).

Afterward Mo'Nique hosted the TV talk program "The Mo'Nique Show." But there were few movie roles. Director Daniels said she had not learned to play the game by Hollywood's rules. Reportedly, she had balked about personal appearances to promote *Precious*. In 2014, she starred in *Blackbird*. Her best and most publicized post-*Precious* performance was as blues singer Ma Rainey in the 2015 HBO movie "Bessie," starring Queen Latifah as blues singer Bessie Smith.

Lee Daniels, however, remained confidently and exuberantly present on the Hollywood scene. Born in Philadelphia in 1959, Daniels had first-hand experience with surviving a difficult childhood. He was the son of a police officer who objected strenuously to his son's sexuality. After graduating from Lindenwood University in Missouri, Daniels moved to Los Angles. For a time, he had a nursing agency. Later he was a casting director and talent manager. He then became involved in film production, serving as a producer on *Monster's Ball*. Afterward he produced *The Woodsman*, a 2004 film that starred Kevin Bacon as a pedophile attempting to turn his life around. Daniels' directorial debut came with *Shadowboxer* (2005) which starred Helen Mirren as a hit woman and Cuba Gooding, Jr., as her partner in crime (they had a surprising chemistry). Also in the cast were Joseph Gordon-Levitt and both Mo'Nique (playing a character ironically named Precious) and Macy Gray. In 2008, he produced *Tennessee* in which Mariah Carey appeared.

In the next decade, Daniels directed the wildly trashy and tawdry but perversely fascinating *The Paperboy* (2012). Set in a sexy overheated Florida in 1969, *The Paperboy* was another example of Gothic excess which starred Matthew McConaughey, Zac Efron, Nicole Kidman, David Oyelowo, John Cusack, and Macy Gray. It was said that Daniels originally wanted Oprah Winfrey for the role that Gray played. But in one scene when moviegoers saw Gray lying on the floor as she masturbated, they could understand why Winfrey may not have accepted the part. Ostensibly a murder mystery in which McConaughey investigated the killing of a local sheriff, the film was brazenly gory, meandering, disjointed. Yet it had an undeniable strange intensity that often (but not always) made it hard to stop watching. On Daniels' own terms, *The Paperboy*, like *Precious*, was personal filmmaking in which the director gives into his kooky obsessions and excesses—and manages to draw idiosyncratic performances from Kidman, McConaughey, and Cusack. He also delights in showing his young hero Efron shirtless. Once moviegoers are hip to Daniels' perspective, parts of the movie can be compelling and hilarious.

Daniels was able not only to keep working in the next decade but to assemble impressive casts. With his all-star *Lee Daniels' The Butler* (2013), he *did* sign Oprah, along with Forest Whitaker, Vanessa Redgrave, Jane Fonda, Cuba Gooding, Jr. (giving a very adroit performance), Lenny Kravitz, Clarence Williams III and David Oyelowo. His great success in the following decade came, however, with the creation (with writer Danny Strong) of the trashy and vastly entertaining super hit television series "Empire," starring Taraji P. Henson and Terrence Howard.

Directors, Veterans and Newcomers

Directors continued to push and pull to get their films financed and distributed. Those who directed studio films, even though the studio system that reigned supreme into the 1950s no longer really existed, still struggled to get the green light to make their movies with deals from the big movie companies—and often found themselves saddled with concessions in order to do so. Those who were independents still faced the problems of having their films distributed, publicized, and exhibited in theaters. The systemic problems in the industry were well-described by Chris Rock in an essay he wrote for the December 12, 2014 issue of *The Hollywood Reporter*. "It's a white industry. Just as the NBA is a black industry. I'm not even saying it's a bad thing. It just is. And the black people they do hire tend to be the same person. That person tends to be female and that person tends to be Ivy League. And there's nothing wrong with that. As a matter of fact, that's what I want for my daughters. But something tells me that the life my privileged daughters are leading right now might not make them the best candidates to run the black division of anything. And the person who runs the black division of a studio should probably have worked with black people at some point in their life." He added: "But how many black men have you met working in Hollywood? They don't really hire black men. A black man with bass in his voice and maybe a little hint of facial hair? Not going to happen." Considering what Rock stated, it was ironic that from the 1970s into the new millennium, most black films financed by the studios starred African American men rather than African American women.

Now a grand master of black cinema, Spike Lee directed such films as the documentary *A Huey P. Newton Story* (2001), *The 25th Hour* (2002), *She Hate Me* (2004, starring Anthony Mackie), *Miracle at St. Anna* (2008), *Passing Strange* (2009), and *Red Hook Summer* (2012). One of Lee's best films of the era was the masterful *Inside Man* (2006), essentially a studio film produced by Brian Grazer. In this bank heist drama, he showed his powers at pacing as well as his ability to work with such top notch actors as Denzel Washington, Clive Owen, Jodie Foster, and Christopher Plummer. Quite significant was that he revealed that he indeed could direct a popular mainstream film—and to do so with clever cultural markers. There was talk of a sequel but for whatever reasons, that didn't happen. Lee also directed the surprising *Oldboy* (2013) which was a remake of Chan-wook Park's Korean film, now starring Josh Brolin, Samuel L. Jackson, Elizabeth Olsen, and Michael Imperioli. Lee's new millennium films, however, lacked the impact of his earlier ones. Lee had a critical success with his 2006 HBO documentary "When the Levees Broke: A Requiem in Four Acts," which focused on the devastating effects of Hurricane Katrina in New Orleans. In time, Lee went to the online fund-raising Kickstarter to acquire financing for *Da Sweet Blood of Jesus* (2014), his re-working of Bill Gunn's *Ganja & Hess*. He also found financing from Amazon for his film *Chi-Raq* (2015), starring Samuel L. Jackson, Jennifer Hudson, Angela Bassett, Common, Dave Chappelle, and Wesley Snipes in a contemporary reworking of *Lysistrata*, set in Chicago. For Snipes, it was an important film after his career had been side-tracked by tax problems that led to a prison term.

Another veteran John Singleton opened the decade with his remake of *Shaft* (2000), starring a miscast Samuel L. Jackson, Vanessa Williams, Christian Bale, Jeffrey Wright, Lynne Thigpen, Busta Rhymes, and Toni Collette. Best of all were the cameos by original *Shaft* director Gordan Parks, Sr., and the original (most would say the *only*) Shaft, Richard Roundtree. Singleton also directed: *Baby Boy*, *2 Fast 2 Furious*, *Four Brothers*, and *Abduction* (2011).

Making a name for himself in the new era was Tim Story, who directed the hit *Barbershop* (2002) with Ice Cube, Cedric the Entertainer, Eve, Troy Garity, Anthony Anderson, and Michael Ealy. A sequel *Barbershop 2: Back in Business* (2004) was directed by Kevin Rooney Sullivan. Story also directed the misbegotten *Taxi*. But he ventured into new territory—that proved to be franchise gold—with his non-black action film hits *Fantastic Four* (2005) and *4: Rise of the Silver Surfer* (2007). It was good to see an African American director have the opportunity to work on such popular mainstream movies. Story was also the director of *Think Like A Man* and *Think Like A Man Too*, which grew out of the best-selling self-help book *Act Like A Lady, Think Like A Man* by comedian Steve Harvey. Both movies were ensemble pieces full of energy yet perhaps dubious social value. Such actors as Taraji P. Henson, Megan Good, Gabrielle Union, Sherri Shephard, Michael Ealy, Jenifer Lewis, Romany Malco, and Terrence Jenkins were primed for action, looking excited (as had been the case with black-cast films of the past) to be working. Interesting always was Regina Hall who filmmakers rarely seemed to know how to use to the actress's best advantage. Hall's intelligence and vulnerability were fused with an edgy assertiveness that largely went unexplored. In both films, Story can also be credited with helping to engineer the breakout movie career of comedian Kevin Hart. Brash, frenetic, over-confident, and often over the top, Hart had already appeared in such movies as *Not Easily Broken*, and *Little Fockers* (2010) but then rode the wave of popularity in Story's *Ride Along* (2014) with Ice Cube. Later Hart appeared with Will Ferrell in the fairly wretched *Get Hard* (2015), directed by Etan Cohen. Story also co-directed with Leslie Small the concert film *Kevin Hart: Let Me Explain* (2013).

Interestingly enough, the movies *Ride Along* and the earlier *Are We There Yet?* (2005) and *Are We Done Yet?* (2007) marked an image change for Ice Cube. Having begun his career as a rebel in the rap group N.W.A. and having moved audiences with his deeply-felt portrayal in *Boyz N the Hood*, Ice Cube had now often become the star of family friendly films. *Are We Done Yet?* was even a remake of the classic *Mr. Blandings Builds His Dream House*, which had starred Cary Grant, Myrna Loy, *and* least we forget, Louise Beavers as the maid who comes up with the advertising slogan that enables Grant to keep his job! Who could have forecast such an image change for Mr. Cube? But he appeared to want (as he grew older) to play other types of roles; in the long run, by doing so, he held onto his career with a new generation of moviegoers.

Director Charles Stone III's *Drumline* (2002) also proved to be a family/teen friendly coming of age story about a wiseguy teenage drummer—from the big city, New York—who learns the importance both of humility and of working together with fellow marching band members at a college in Georgia. Stone directed comedian Bernie Mac during Mac's brief heady days of stardom in the baseball film *Mr. 3000* (2004). One of the best comedians of the era, Mac appeared in such films as *Ocean's Eleven* (2001), *Ocean's Twelve* (2004), *Bad Santa* (2003), and the dim-witted *Guess Who* (2005) with Ashton Kutcher and Zoe Saldana, a clunky misconceived replay of *Guess Who's Coming to Dinner*. His best work was probably as the frazzled father on the TV series "The Bernie Mac Show." Nevertheless, the film and television community was shocked when Mac died at age fifty in 2008.

After his great success with the TV comedy show "In Living Color" and other television productions, Keenen Ivory Wayans directed such films as *Scary Movie* (2000), *Scary Movie 2* (2001), *White Chicks* (2004), and *Littleman* (2006).

Phil Bertelsen's *Rock the Paint* (2005) also had a coming of age theme but with different racial politics. Bertelsen also directed documentaries for PBS. A satirical rewrite of American history was dramatized in Kevin Willmott's *C.S.A.: Confederate States of America* (2004), a tense and frightening portrait of America had the South won the Civil War. Theater director George C. Wolfe directed Richard Gere and Diane Lane in *Nights in Rodanthe* (2008). Another new director was Barry Jenkins who helmed the independent romantic tale *Medicine for Melancholy* (2008).

George Tillman, Jr., continued a directing career that had first caught the eye of moviegoers with his *Soul Food*, which later became a successful cable TV series. In the new decade, he directed such films as *Men of Honor* (2000); the movie biography of rapper Biggie Smalls *Notorious* (2009); and the film that heralded the stardom, whether permanent or short-lived, of the young hunk Scott Eastwood (son of Clint Eastwood), *The Longest Ride* (2015). During this decade, the Detroit-born twin brothers Allen and Albert Hughes directed *The Book of Eli*. On his own, Allen directed *Broken City* (2013), starring Mark Wahlberg, Russell Crowe, Catherine Zeta Jones, and Jeffrey Wright.

Also still very much on the scene was F. Gary Gray who directed such disparate films as *A Man Apart*, the expert *The Italian Job*, and *Law Abiding Citizen*. Gray also helmed the huge 2015 box-office hit *Straight Outta Compton* which chronicled the origin and rise in the late 1980s of the iconic rap group N.W.A. *Straight Outta Compton* highlighted the tensions and conflicts between the youthful members of N.W.A. with hostile police in Los Angeles—which led to one of the group's most famous raps: "F _ _ _ tha Police." It also made them heroes for the young, past and present. In the new millennium when the Black Lives Matter movement often protested police confrontations and brutality against African Americans, *Straight Outta Compton* proved timely. In other respects, the film, however, was a rather conventional biopic—characters that were not fully developed and with backstories that were minimal. The performances were often good. The role of Ice Cube (born O'Shea Jackson) was played convincingly by the rapper's son O'Shea Jackson, Jr., while Corey Hawkins portrayed a low-key rather somber Dr. Dre (née Andre Young). Perhaps the most interesting characterization was that of Jason Mitchell as the more complicated Eazy-E (born Eric Wright). The two other members of the group DJ Yella (née Antoine Carraby) and MC Ren (née Lorenzo Patterson) at times seemed missing in action in the movie, appearing almost like an afterthought of the screenwriter. The roles of the women were sadly mostly walk-ons. More definition to Eazy-E's wife but not much more. Some attention was paid to the violent Suge Knight character, well-played by R. Marcos Taylor. Still, unlike the dramatization of the life of rapper Biggie Smalls in *Notorious* in which its conventional narrative style undercut the force and meaning of Smalls' life and music, *Straight Outta Compton* worked well by skillfully using the music of the group to provide an edgy tone and perspective—and some fast-moving energy. Indeed, the music and director Gray's rather frenetic style carried the film, making it a real audience pleaser.

Mainstream reviewers gave *Straight Outta Compton* both good and mixed reviews. If anything, it was the vast social media coverage that got people rushing into theaters. Social media clearly now was the new word of mouth. But social media could be a double-edged sword. On Facebook and Twitter, there were outcries because of what was not included in the story: namely the misogyny and homophobia that was embedded in the lyrics of many raps—*and* the way women had been treated during the heady days of rap. Though the film has a scene that touches on the group's misogyny—a young woman is locked out of a hotel room, standing half-naked and alone in a hallway—it's treated almost comically and in no way reveals some of the disturbing incidents with women. In 1991, there had been a well-known attack by Dr. Dre on the female hip hop journalist Denise "Dee" Barnes. He had "objected" to comments she had made. At the time, Dee Barnes said that he viciously beat her; he punched her and slammed "her face and the right side of her body repeatedly against a wall." Ultimately, Dre was charged with assault and battery. He pled no contest, was fined $2500, sentenced to community service and probation, and "ordered to make a domestic violence P.S.A.; a civil suit was settled out of court," reported *The New York Times* on August 15, 2015. None of this turned up in the film, although director Gray said an early draft of the script had referred to the attack which apparently had to be cut because of time factors. Most people weren't buying that explanation.

Straight Outta Compton, a biopic about the rise of rap group N.W.A.: (TOP ROW) the group's original stars Ice Cube (left) and Dr. Dre (right) with the film's director F. Gary Gray and their movie counter-parts (LOWER ROW) O'Shea Jackson Jr. as Ice Cube, Jason Mitchell as Eazy-E, and Corey Hawkins as Dr. Dre.

Eventually, in *The New York Times*'s front-page August 15, 2015 story, Dr. Dre issued an apology: "Twenty-five years ago I was a young man drinking too much and in over my head with no real structure in my life. However, none of this is an excuse for what I did."

In retrospect, the movie and the Dre character would have been far more complex had the film examined the attack not only on Dee but reportedly other women—had it been willing to seriously comment on the conflicting nature of the powerful, groundbreaking music and performers of N.W.A. Oddly enough, the social media commentary may well have begun the job the movie backed away from.

With *Best Man Holiday* (2013), director Malcolm D. Lee returned to the characters of his 1999 debut feature film *The Best Man*. Fourteen years later, moviegoers were still interested in the tangled relationships and emotional dilemmas of these now middle-aged urban professionals. The film was a bona fide hit. In the two *Best Man* films, Lee's eye for casting the right actors and actresses served him well. He understood their quirks and most important, how to use their personas to shape his characters. Few directors understood better than Lee how to put to splendid use Taye Diggs' narcissism and egotism; or Morris Chesnut's ability to project decency beneath his macho exterior; or Terrence Howard's agreeable cad qualities. In the second film, he seemed to have lost interest in Sanaa Lathan. But he gave Regina Hall some lively and moving moments. Lee directed *Undercover Brother* (2002) with comic Eddie Griffin, Dave Chappelle, Aunjanue Ellis, Robert Townsend, *and* that romantic heartthrob of the 1970s, Billy Dee Williams. Based on an Internet series by John Ridley, the film's screenplay was written by Ridley and Michael McCullers. Among Lee's other films were *Roll Bounce* (2005); *Soul Men* (2008) with Bernie Mac and Samuel L. Jackson as reunited singing partners off on a road trip to perform at Harlem's Apollo Theater; *Welcome Home, Roscoe Jenkins* (2008) with Martin Lawrence, Margaret Avery, Joy Bryant, Mo'Nique, and Mike Epps; *Scary Movie 5* (2013); and *Barbershop 3* (2016).

During this period, Antoine Fuqua cut out a place for himself with his gritty, controversial *Training Day*. Just by the fact that he had directed Denzel Washington in an Oscar-winning role was enough to make the studios take notice. Fuqua created tough, violent existential male worlds. In *King Arthur* (2004), he reworked the age-old tale into yet another violent, more realistic rendering. By the time he directed Washington in *The Equalizer*, Fuqua had taut but slow sequences where a disturbing sadism was apparent—but which seemed to be true, however, to the horrific situations he was depicting. Humor was rarely part of his violent landscape as it was in the violent, bloody films of Quentin Tarantino. Fuqua also directed such films as *Tears of the Sun* (2003) starring Bruce Willis and Eamonn Walker; *Brooklyn's Finest* (2009), starring Don Cheadle, Richard Gere, Wesley Snipes, and

Terrence Howard, Nia Long, and Eddie Cibrian who must deal with friendship and, quiet as it is kept, the perils of approaching middle-age in *Best Man Holiday*, director Malcolm Lee's sequel to his popular *The Best Man*.

Ethan Hawke; *Olympus Has Fallen* (2013) with Morgan Freeman, Angela Bassett, Gerard Butler, and Dylan McDermott; and the boxing drama *Southpaw* (2015) with Jake Gyllenhaal, Forest Whitaker, Curtis "50 Cent" Jackson, Naomie Harris, and Rachel McAdams.

Many directors wrote their films. Many also worked in television. In the new millennium, television was increasingly more appealing to filmmakers because of the unusual projects that the medium, especially cable, could offer.

Within the ranks of feature film directors, more women came to the fore, ushering in a new sensibility and perspective. They also directed traditional narratives that centered on male protagonists. Kasi Lemmons directed *Talk to Me* and the warm hearted *Black Nativity*, based on Langston Hughes' play. In the latter film, a troubled teen named Langston brings about a reconciliation between his mother and her parents. Liberian-born Cheryl Dunye, who had directed *Watermelon Woman* in 1996, brought *My Baby's Daddy* (2004) and *Mommy Is Coming* (2012) to the screen. Moroccan Sanaa Hamri directed the underrated comedy *Something New* and *Just Wright*. Following *The Secret Life of Bees*, Gina Prince-Bythewood directed *Beyond the Lights* (2014), the story of a biracial pop star (Gugu Mbatha-Raw), wrestling not only with the pressures of her profession and fame but also with questions of personal identity—and with conflicting feelings about her white mother who loves but doesn't fully understand her daughter. Here was an attempt to lift the old-style mulatto figure out of the realm of types. Back on the scene was director Neema Barnett with such films as *Civil Brand* (2002) and *Woman Thou Art Loosed: On The 7th Day*. Bronx-born Sarah Lawrence-graduate Darnell Martin directed *Cadillac Records*, an ambitious look at the Chicago-based Chess Records.

Also examining the question of self-identity was writer/director Dee Rees, who made an impressive feature film debut with *Pariah* (2011), a longer version of her 2007 short *Pariah*. When Rees was in the graduate film program at New York University's Tisch School of the Arts, she studied with Spike Lee who recognized her talent and later served as the Executive Producer of the feature version of *Pariah*. The film's heroine (Adepero Oduye) searches to define herself as she is coming of age—and also coming out. With her parents unable to accept that she is gay, she lives a whole other life away from her family. Black lesbian (or bisexual) characters had appeared in *The Color Purple* (1985) and *She's Gotta Have It* (1986), but here the subject matter was explored in a wholly different, more personalized and incisive manner. In 2015, Rees directed the HBO movie "Bessie."

Another newcomer Tanya Hamilton wrote and directed *Night Catches Us* (2010). Set in Philadelphia in 1976, the film starred Anthony Mackie as a restless and conflicted former Black Panther returning home where he is suspected of being responsible in part for the death of a former comrade. Befriending him is

Kerry Washington. Thoughtful and meditative, *Night Catches Us*'s images of Philadelphia neighborhoods stick with the viewer long after the film has ended. Also important in bringing the perspectives of African American women to the screen were such producers as Debra Martin Chase and Stephanie Allain.

Another Decade: Re-examining the Past

Significantly, in the second decade, a number of films re-examined the historical past. Perhaps such an investigation into the nation's racial history, even the not so distant past, was an outgrowth of the Obama presidency. Filmmakers appeared to have a heightened awareness that the turbulent history that had preceded Obama needed re-telling, whether it be in *The Help* (2011), *Lee Daniels' The Butler*, *42* (2013), Ava DuVernay's *Selma* (2014), *Django Unchained* (2012), *12 Years A Slave* (2013), *Lincoln* (2012), *Belle* (2013) or *Fruitvale Station* (2013). Much like the Negro Problem Pictures of 1949 and the films of Spike Lee, race was front and center in these films. As the era moved on, what with renewed social protests and outrage over the deaths of African American men during conflicts with law enforcement, some of the films had an immediate urgency and relevancy.

Director Tate Taylor's adaptation of Kathryn Stockett's novel *The Help* dramatized the experiences of African American maids in the South (Mississippi) in the early 1960s as the Civil Rights movement was growing. Actually, it might be more accurate to say that the movie dramatized the experiences of a young white Southern woman named Skeeter (Emma Stone) who, having left home to study in school, returns to her community and is stunned by the indignities and insults the black domestic workers endure. Deciding to write about the women's experiences, she interviews a group of maids and in a sense spurs them to action. The primary women interviewed are Abileen (Viola Davis), who is devoted to the young white child she cares for while she also grieves the loss of her adult son; and Minny (Octavia Spencer) who, humiliated by the white woman she works for exacts her own brand of revenge with a pie she has baked for her employer with a decidedly distasteful ingredient. Minny is also physically abused by her husband. Later she comes to care for another employer, a younger white woman (Jessica Chastain) from the wrong side of the tracks. There is also Constantine (Cicely Tyson), the older, faithful black woman who realizes late the debasing racial attitudes of the family she has served so well.

Hardly progressive, *The Help* was a fundamentally a comedy with laughs that come frequently. That in itself seems often to undercut the message of the film—and of the history it wants to explore and bring to light. The film also is similar to *Precious* in that Minny's abusive husband, who we never see, is one more threatening, nameless, faceless black man out there. Nor does *The Help* even tell us what has happened to the father of Abileen's departed son. At heart, the women are still nurturers with no glimmers of mature sexual lives.

Nor is there enough exploration of their lives away from their white employers. There is a sequence in a black church, which is fine, and once Skeeter has set a plan in motion, we do see them gathered together. But the movie has no textured acknowledgment of the way the forces of family and community strengthen the women and bring joy into their lives. When Aibileen is fired from her job at the end of the film, she is saddened that she must leave the little girl she loves deeply—who daily she has tried to endow with self-pride. In most respects, the culture of the South will be ready to provide the girl with such pride. It would have been far more interesting if we saw Aibileen working to instill such self-pride in a little black girl. In an unexpected way, this film, which was a bona fide box office success, seems to remind its mainstream audience of a seemingly less complicated time when people still knew their place—and just needed to be treated a little better. The mainstream audience is reassured that those maids most certainly did care about the "kind" white folks they worked for; it was simply the villainous employers who wrecked things for a social system that was otherwise fine.

With all that said and done—and here's the kicker—*The Help* was entertaining with solid performances by its entire cast. It is yet one of those ironies of popular films (the same was true of *The Blind Side* (2009))—that audiences can have such conflicting reactions (that are not necessarily sorted out) about something they enjoy. The actresses do the work that the script does not, much as talented performers did in the past. A prime example is Octavia Spencer. Having worked in films and television since the late 1990s—in *A Time to Kill* (1996), *Being John Malkovich* (1999), *Blue Streak*, *Big Momma's House*, *Bad Santa*, *Beauty Shop* (2005), *Miss Congeniality 2: Armed and Fabulous* (2005)—the Montgomery, Alabama-born Spencer may have wondered if she would ever have a part that put her on the map. *The Help* did precisely that, and it was her spirited performance as Minny—a character it was hard not to feel for—that gave the film some dimension. With impeccable timing and subtle double-takes and sometimes not so subtle *attitude*, her performance won her the Oscar as Best Supporting Actress of 2011. Afterward Octavia Spencer appeared in such films as *Fruitvale Station* (another excellent performance as a mother hoping to reach and save her son), *Get On Up* (2014), *Black or White* (2014), *Insurgent* (2015), *Fathers and Daughters* (2015), and as the star of the short-lived TV series "Red Band Society."

Viola Davis scored a second Oscar nomination for her performance in *The Help*, this time for Best Actress. But the award went to her great ally Meryl Streep for *The Iron Lady* (2011). Afterward when she appeared in such films as *Extremely Loud & Incredibly Close* (2011) with Tom Hanks and Sandra Bullock and *Prisoners* (2013) with Hugh Jackman, she may have wondered if anything had changed—about appearing in big pictures with big stars but without having much to do in

Octavia Spencer and Viola Davis give strong performances as the seemingly radicalized yet still nurturing maids of an earlier era in *The Help*.

such films. Interestingly, when she worked again for director Tate Taylor in his James Brown biopic *Get On Up*, she was cast as the singer's crazed mother. Here she ventured into new creative territory and gave a strange, jolting, enjoyably idiosyncratic and perplexing performance. The movie failed to give her character enough of a backstory. The movie had other failures as well. Brown's sympathetically depicted father disappears without enough explanation of why we don't see him again. But significantly, Davis had crafted her own backstory for her character. We just may not have been sure what it was, but we believed in her character. In the past, there was a *sameness* in some of her performances. Though compelling to watch, she seemed glum without a variety of moods. Maybe she felt unchallenged. In *Get On Up*, it was terrific to see her enlivened and emboldened. Not long afterward, Davis broke completely free when she starred as Annalise Keating on the hit TV series "How To Get Away With Murder." Here she was, in Hollywood terms, an "older" brown-skinned woman who is smart, sexual, energetic, and treacherous when necessary! Television had given Davis a chance at the kind of role that the movies missed out on. Interestingly enough in the new millennium, other African American actresses found compelling characters *and* stardom on television: Kerry Washington in "Scandal" and Taraji P. Henson in "Empire."

History, Slavery, and Plantation Dramas

An important period in America's racial history was dramatized in Steven Spielberg's *Lincoln*, a stately, rather formal film with the strong production values usually associated with dramas aiming for Oscar gold. Starring Daniel Day-Lewis as Lincoln, the film looked at the last four months of the president's life as he attempts to get through Congress the Thirteenth Amendment that abolished slavery. *Lincoln* was partly an absorbing character study with a fine performance by Lewis that ultimately won him his third Best Actor Academy Award. It was also partly a political drama. But it was hardly a drama that said enough about its black characters. Most of the images of African Americans were soft: a glimpse of black soldiers; a dutiful seamstress and a confidant Elizabeth Keckley (Gloria Reuben) to Mrs. Lincoln (Sally Field) who has a harsh backstory that reveals slavery's horrors; a warm-hearted manservant (Stephen McKinley Henderson) to the President; and the black mistress (S. Epatha Merkerson) of Thaddeus Stevens. One hopes for some view of abolitionists like Frederick Douglass who stayed on the President to change history. The slave population doesn't seem vital or present enough. Still, *Lincoln* was impressive and highly lauded by the critics.

Lincoln's polar opposites were two films that re-examined history in very different ways with their depictions of plantation life in the days of slavery: Quentin Tarantino's *Django Unchained* and Steve McQueen's *12 Years A Slave*. Influenced by

Blaxploitation cinema and Italian "spaghetti westerns" (mainly Sergio Corbucci's original *Django* that starred Franco Nero, who makes a cameo appearance in this film), writer/director Tarantino's comedy/drama rewrites history—much as the filmmaker had done with the Nazi reign in *Inglourious Basterds* (2009). Opening in Texas in 1858 (two years before the Civil War), *Django Unchained* traces the journey of a freed slave Django (Jamie Foxx) and a German bounty hunter Schultz (Christoph Waltz) to the Mississippi plantation where the black man's wife Broomhilda (Kerry Washington) is enslaved. Along the way, they encounter racism in its most blatant and its bloodiest forms. Foremost are the vicious slave owners the Brittle Brothers, who are promptly disposed of, just blown away. There is also a hooded Ku Klux Klan-like group (actually the Klan had not yet been organized in 1858). The Klansmen are depicted as inept comic fools. Here *Django Unchained* is a sendup of D.W. Griffith's "heroic" figures in *The Birth of A Nation*. The film never backs off from the violence of the period and the brutalities of the slave system. In a sequence that is hard to watch, savage dogs are unleashed on a black man.

Upon arriving at the Mississippi plantation—called Candieland—Schultz and Django contend with its sly, seemingly affable owner, Calvin J. Candie, played by Leonardo DiCaprio. Beneath his Southern "charm" is the heart and soul of an unrelentingly cruel sadist who enjoys watching Mandingo fighters battle to the grisly death in his plush drawing room. Here Tarantino is paying a kind of homage to the shocking Blaxploitation film *Mandingo* (1975). Much of *Django Unchained* is cringe-worthy—to the point where a moviegoer may feel uncomfortable about being so engrossed in the steady blood bath. But indeed much of *Django Unchained* keeps a moviegoer on the edge of his/her seat. "Tarantino's intent may have been to showcase the horrors of slavery," wrote Dana Stevens in *Slate*, "but there's something about his directorial delectation in all these acts of racial violence that left me not just physically but morally queasy. His fascination with repeated acts of graphic retribution puts the viewer in the position of Calvin J. Candie, watching with a cigarette hold and a coconut drink in hand as the mandingoes fight it out." "It is digressive, jokey, giddily brutal and ferociously profane," wrote A. O. Scott in *The New York Times*. "But it is also a troubling and important movie about slavery and racism."

Throughout, Candie's devoted tom servant Stephen, played by Samuel L. Jackson, makes sure the massa is happy. Theirs is a complex relationship with possible homo-erotic undertones. One striking sequence shows the two men alone together sipping brandy in Candie's drawing room. You might mistake them for lopsided equals.

At Candieland, Django—most intent in saving Broomhilda—curiously has no apparent connection to the other slaves, who mostly seem like passive frightened automatons without a thought in their heads of resistance or rebellion. Fear dictates their every move. Even once Django has led the charge to demolish Candieland, there is no trace of an insurrection among the others. Tarantino buys into the idea that slavery marked men and women as childlike dolts. History, of course, tells us otherwise.

Ultimately, *Django Unchained* reaches the point where the blood bursts become cartoonish as is some of the climactic violence. Throughout, there is also an over-use of the n-word for which Spike Lee (once again) and others criticized Tarantino. TV's "Roots" also used the n-word generously. But viewers didn't feel it was used gratuitously or with some perverse delight as is sometimes the case with *Django Unchained*. Tarantino believes he's a *brother* entitled to use the word whenever he wants. He can't seem to fathom why some African Americans like the film *but* object to his frequent usage of the word. But what did Mr. T once say: "I pity the fool."

Nonetheless, *Django Unchained* has admittedly, shall we say, its entertainment value. Tarantino casts such actors as Don Stroud, Bruce Dern, Michael Parks, Russ Tamblyn, Tom Wopat, Robert Carradine, and James Russo in cameos that movie buffs enjoy because some of these performers had not been on screen in some time. They bring back movie and TV memories. Best of the lot is Don Johnson in the Klan sequence. He's got a clever glint in his eyes.

Django Unchained was a hit. Tarantino won the Best Original Screenplay Oscar. Christoph Waltz's clever performance won him the Best Supporting Actor Oscar. (He had previously won that Supporting Actor Oscar for *Inglourious Basterds*, a performance not that different from this one.) But it was the brilliant often underrated performances of DiCaprio and Jackson that jolt moviegoers in odd, inexplicable ways. Jackson completely reconfigured the tom type, making the character intelligent, canny, shrewd, observant, mean as they come, and able to run the plantation, striking fear into the heads of the other slaves, whether Candie was present or not. But ultimately he remained a tom who will preserve Candie's supremacy even if he has to sacrifice himself to do so. He had certainly sacrificed his own humanity and sense of self-worth. It was one of Jackson's best performances. Throughout the new era, Jackson was always fun to watch in such movies as *Black Snake Moan* (2006), *Lakeview Terrace* (2008), *Oldboy*, and playing Nick Fury in *Captain America: The First Avenger* (2011), *The Avengers* (2012), *Captain America: The Winter Soldier* (2014), and *Avengers: Age of Ultron* (2015) as well as the FBI agent in the over-hyped nonsensical *Snakes on a Plane* (2006). In 2015, he also starred in Tarantino's *The Hateful Eight*.

Afro-British director Steve McQueen's *12 Years A Slave* traveled a different route in its dramatization of the plantation experience. Based on a once famous book of the same title published originally in 1853, the film told the true story of free black man Solomon Northup (Chiwetel Ejiofor), a talented violinist from Saratoga, New York. In 1841, Northup is tricked by two musicians into traveling to Washington,

D.C. for a performance. Thereafter he is kidnapped and sold into slavery. He ends up in Louisiana where he is the property of a "benevolent" slave holder, played by Benedict Cumberbatch (if such a word as "benevolent" can be used to describe a slave holder), then sold to a brutal, violent psychopath (Michael Fassbender). Throughout, horrific scenes detail the devastating realities of life during slavery: a young black woman (Adepero Oduye) cries out in agony as her children are torn from her, to be sold elsewhere; a household of slaves is awakened in the middle of the night by their crazed master who insists that they dance for him; out of nowhere an object is thrown by that slaveholder's wife (Sarah Paulson) at the young slave woman Patsey (Lupita Nyong'o) whom her husband is attracted to, indeed has raped. Strung from a tree with a noose around his neck, Solomon Northup himself does a delicate dance to stay alive because his feet barely touch the ground. Northup is also forced by the plantation master to whip Patsey. The educated, once-free Northup can never let it be known that he can read and write for fear of brutal repraisals. The lives of the slave population are unrelieved humiliation, debasement, and physical agony.

The unflinching *12 Years A Slave* also rewrote movie history. All those past films with images of contented or happy go lucky slaves are shattered—in both a similar and different way from *Django Unchained*. In 1984, Gordon Parks, Sr., had directed a sensitive television version of Solomon Northup's story, titled "Solomon Northup's Odyssey" that starred Avery Brooks. Here McQueen strives for a naturalistic approach. Yet at times, the film may strike viewers as a bit over-aestheticized with its perfectly composed frames of a group of slaves standing as they bathe themselves before their journey to be sold. It's engrossing to watch yet there is something almost too artful about the sequence. Other scenes have a similar look. Viewers may long for a change in tone or mood. "For a while, the movie becomes a redundant moral and physical struggle between a noble, forbearing African-American and a white madman," wrote David Denby in *The New Yorker*. A fascinating shift, however, occurs with the appearance of Alfre Woodard as the wife of a white slave owner—who seems to live on the plantation as a free woman. But director McQueen doesn't elaborate on this character or her situation. Still, its power is undiminished. McQueen had previously directed the films *Hunger* (2008) and *Shame* (2011).

The performances were also powerful. Without much dialogue, Chitwetel Ejiofor uses his expressive eyes to convey his terror, confusion, and intelligence. Born in England of Nigerian parents, Ejiofor had already appeared in such films as *Dirty Pretty Things* (2002), *She Hate Me, Kinky Boots* (2005), *Inside Man, Children of Men* (2006), *Talk to Me, American Gangster* and *Salt* (2010). Always the performances were thoughtful, reflective, and eye-catching. No matter how much or little screen time he had, you knew he was there. *12 Years A Slave*, however, gave him the opportunity for a career-defining role. "It's Ejiofor's extraordinary performance that holds *12 Years A Slave*. He gives Solomon a deep inner strength, yet he never softens the nightmare of his existence," wrote Owen Gleiberman in *Entertainment Weekly*. Ejiofor was nominated as Best Actor in the Oscar race. The award, however, went to Matthew McConaughey for his fine performance in *Dallas Buyers Club* (2013).

Also nominated in the Supporting Actor category was Michael Fassbender. For thirty-year-old actress Lupita Nyong'o, born in Mexico City of Kenyan parents and raised in Nairobi, Kenya, *12 Years A Slave* marked her movie debut. While still a student at the Yale Drama School, she learned she had been cast in the role of Patsey. Hers was a heartbreaking performance that won her the Best Supporting Actress Oscar. Much media attention was showered on this stunning beauty who was featured on the covers of *Vogue, People* (which cited her as the world's most beautiful woman), *New York*, and other magazines. For a dark black actress, such attention was significant, perhaps a sign (as was the case with Viola Davis on television) that the industry *might* forgo its color caste system. Then it might not. Most seemed to forget that the equally stunning Cicely Tyson had broken through such color barriers decades earlier. Yet never did Tyson win the number of lead roles she should have, and it would be interesting to chart the course of Nyong'o's career in the future. Nyong'o also appeared in a small role in *Non-Stop* (2014). After the Oscar, she was cast in *Star Wars: The Force Awakens* (2015).

Though McQueen was nominated as Best Director, the award went to Alfonso Cuarón for his direction of *Gravity*. Cuarón was the first Mexican director to win the award. African American writer John Ridley, however, was awarded the Oscar for Best Screenplay. *12 Years A Slave* also walked away with the big Oscar as Best Picture of the Year.

The British import *Belle* (2013) took yet another approach to the history of slavery. Directed by Amma Asante and suggested by a true story, it followed a young mulatto/biracial woman Dido (Gugu Mbatha-Raw). The "illegitimate" daughter of an eighteenth-century Royal Navy admiral, she is raised in the home of her white aristocratic uncle in England. Considered a member of the family, she and her cousin bond as sisters. Hers is a life of privilege. Yet she endures the subtle and not so subtle racism of her family and the society. On special occasions with guests at her uncle's home, she is not permitted to dine at the family table. Upon the death of her father, Dido becomes an heiress, which presents problems. There is the question about whom Dido will wed. Ultimate enlightenment comes as she grows aware of the issue of the British slave trade and also aware of herself as a black woman. Not wholly satisfying nor thematically as cohesive as it should be—and ending with a fairy-tale like relationship for Dido—*Belle* was nonetheless often absorbing.

Other Films: Other Re-examinations

Other films focused on other aspects of American history. *Lee Daniels' The Butler* honed in on the life and experiences of a black man (Forest Whitaker) who grows up on a Georgia cotton field and works his way to the White House where he is a butler observing up close American Presidents and their families as they come and go. *The Butler* also looks at his private life: a disenchanted but ultimately loyal wife (Oprah Winfrey); a militant son (David Oyelowo) who fails to understand the perspective of his hard-working, proud father; and the friends of the butler both in and outside the White House. With an all-star cast that included Vanessa Redgrave, Jane Fonda, Cuba Gooding Jr., Lenny Kravitz, Liev Schreiber, and John Cusack and inspired by the real-life experiences of Eugene Allen who had served at the White House from the Truman to the Reagan administrations, the film, while entertaining, never managed to take the audience into the head of the title character. In many ways, he remains, despite the intentions of Daniels, Whitaker and screenwriter Danny Strong, a blank tom-like protagonist. Audiences may feel a little like the =son in the film: the father is far too passionate. This might have been a complex character who represented past historical attitudes. But the script does not delineate the man in historical or personal terms. *The Butler*, however, had an epic feel to it and was distinguished by its strong and vivid performances, including an off-beat one by Oprah Winfrey. The problem for Winfrey, however, was that she was so famous as being Oprah that audiences may not have detected the thought she brings to her characterization.

The 2012 *Red Tails* focused on the all-black Tuskegee Airmen whose heroic exploits during World War II became the stuff of legend. Directed by Anthony Hemingway and executive-produced by George Lucas, *Red Tails* was a rather standard old-style war movie. Its cast included Nate Parker, Elijah Kelley, Cuba Gooding, Jr., Terrence Howard, and Gerald McRaney.

42 dramatized the early career of baseball pioneer Jackie Robinson when he integrated the Brooklyn Dodgers in 1947. Directed by British filmmaker Brian Helgeland, the film records the racism that Robinson endured on the baseball diamond—from hostile spectators and opposing teams as well as tensions Robinson had with some of his teammates. Sometimes there was a self-congratulatory tone, as if the nation could pat itself on the back for ultimately accepting Robinson. Newcomer Chadwick Boseman brought a steely dignity to his character. And Nicole Beharie was appealing as Robinson's wife Rachel, one of those unsung heroines who in real life fought long and hard to insure that her husband would not be forgotten. One might still prefer the earnest version in 1950—*The Jackie Robinson Story*—when Robinson played himself and when actors playing his mother (Louise Beavers) and brother (Joel Fluellen) added another dimension to the Robinson character. *42* was successful, and for a new generation, it indeed re-introduced the athlete. A graduate of Howard University and the British American Dramatic Academy in Oxford, England, Boseman also appeared in *Draft Day* (2014) and *Message from the King* (2016). He also played funk-master James Brown in the Brown biopic *Get On Up*.

Newcomer African American director/writer Ryan Coogler reflected on more recent history in his independent film *Fruitvale Station*. The film told the true story of 22-year-old Oscar Grant (Michael B. Jordan) who on January 1, 2009, had been detained—and then shot and killed—by a transit officer in Oakland. The film earnestly looked at the young man's efforts to sort out his troubled life before the night the fatal shot was fired. Playing his mother was Octavia Spencer. In the wake of another real life case of an unarmed African American teenager Trayvon Martin who had been killed in Florida in 2012, *Fruitvale Station* had an immediacy that audiences responded to. Its writer/director Coogler went on to direct and write *Creed* (2015), a continuation of the Rocky Balboa saga starring Sylvester Stallone and, as the son of boxer Apollo Creed, Michael B. Jordan. During this period, other shootings and killings of African American men often at the hands of law enforcement officers led to renewed social activism and a steady stream of protests in such cities as Cleveland, New York, Ferguson (Missouri), and later Baltimore. In time, film and television images were affected by the changing social atmosphere.

During the time of such renewed protests, Ava DuVernay's *Selma* was released. The film had been long in the making. British screenwriter David Webb's script was written in 2007. But no one stepped forward to finance such a production even though such filmmakers as Spike Lee, Lee Daniels, and Michael Mann expressed interest in the project. Finally, Ava DuVernay got the film into production. A former publicist (who had worked on promoting *The Help*), DuVernay had directed the independent films *I Will Follow* (2010) and *Middle of Nowhere* (2012). Reportedly, she rewrote part of the script for *Selma*. Eventually, Pathe UK put up financing along with Brad Pitt's Plan B production company and with Paramount as distributer. Pitt's Plan B was also a prime mover in the production of *12 Years A Slave*.

Selma focused on the historic battles of Martin Luther King, Jr., and others to secure passage of the Voting Rights Act of 1965. For King, those battles were both inside the White House with President Lyndon Johnson (Tom Wilkinson) and outside with such African American leaders as James Foreman (Trai Byers). The film culminated with the Selma/Montgomery, Alabama march. Though some historians such as Johnson biographer Robert Caro disputed the portrayal of Johnson, the film still managed to record the tensions, terrors, and political maneuvering of the time. Among its cast were Oprah Winfrey who played the activist Annie Lee Cooper and Carmen Ejogo who portrayed Coretta Scott King. British actor David Oyelowo's performance as King was a bold triumph: without missing a beat, he captured King's speech intonations and rhythms in an uncanny way. Yet his King was never a collection of mannered outer-trappings. Though praised for his work, Oyelowo did not win an Oscar nomination. Nor did director DuVernay. But Oyelowo did

David Oyelowo (second from left) as Martin Luther King, Jr., leads the march in *Selma*.

win a Golden Globe nomination as Best Actor in a Drama, and significantly, DuVernay did become the first African American woman to be nominated for a Golden Globe directorial award. The film was nominated for a Golden Globe Best Picture award. *Selma* was also nominated as Best Picture by the Academy of Motion Picture Arts and Sciences, and John Legend and Common walked off with an Oscar for their song "Glory" which was featured in the film.

So many of these films seemed to point, even if only temporarily, to a new phase of African American film history: more thoughtful and reflective movies no matter how well or disappointingly done. Other films tackled other issues and subjects. The film *Mandela: Long Walk to Freedom* (2013) traced the experiences of the great South African leader with Idris Elba and Naomie Harris as Nelson and Winnie Mandela. *Winnie Mandela* focused on Mandela's wife, played by Jennifer Hudson with Terrence Howard as the leader himself. Directed by Benh Zeitlin, *Beasts of the Southern Wild* (2012) featured Quvenzhané Wallis as resilient, independent six-year-old Hushpuppy, forced to survive on her own during a hurricane that sweeps through her bayou in Southern Louisiana. Born in 2003, Wallis became the youngest actress ever nominated for an Oscar—as Best Actress. She later played the title role in a remake of the musical *Annie* (2014). Also released was Paul Greengrass's *Captain Phillips* (2013) which chronicled the real-life 2009 capture of the cargo ship *Maersk* by four Somali pirates. The ship's captain, played by Tom Hanks, is taken hostage. Convincingly playing one of the hijackers was Somali newcomer Barkhad Abdi who was Oscar nominated as Best Supporting Actor of the Year. Appearing a year later was the smart Justin Simien/Adriana Serrano directed *Dear White People* (2014) which provided an insider's view of "casual" racism on the nation's college campuses and of the tensions within the black student population to combat it. Here the story revolved around four African American students at an Ivy League school.

Several of the new films at the start of the second decade were hopeful signs for the future. Different types of film stories had been told. Different types of performers had a chance to work. One could only hope this was not a temporary phase. Yet after those initial historic Oscar wins and nominations in the new millennium, there were no African American nominations in the twenty Oscar acting categories for the years 2014 and 2015, which led to controversy and outcries —and to continued questions about diversity and recognition in Hollywood.

And so in the early decades of the twenty-first century, American cinema found itself undergoing yet another transformation because of the presence and contributions of some remarkable African American talents. Despite stumbling blocks and despite those old images that continued to pop up, the movies did look as if they could head in a wholly new direction. Maybe now alternative cinema—the idea behind the early independent race movies—might fully emerge as mainstream cinema, altering American popular culture, invigorating it with new rhythms,

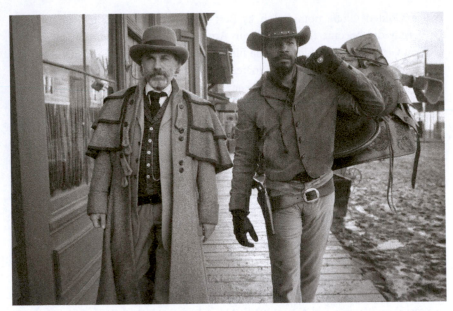

Re-writing movie depictions of slavery: Christoph Waltz and Jamie Foxx in Quentin Tarantino's *Django Unchained* [ABOVE] and Michael Fassbender, Oscar winner Lupita Nyong'o, and Chiwetel Ejiofor in the Oscar-winning film *12 Years A Slave* [BELOW].

insights, perspectives, and a new aesthetic. Of course, the new talents, both in front of and behind the camera, joined a lineup of past dazzling African American men and women who had worked wonders. Those early actors turned roles inside out to come up with personal statements that moved and affected audiences in ways we still cannot always explain. Too often the African American experience in American films has been given short shrift by insensitive directors, producers, and writers who chose an easy route out by settling for old formulas and types. But the talents of individual black artists have buoyed hopes and far-fetched dreams—whether it be Hattie McDaniel, rowdy and fiercely aggressive; or Eddie "Rochester" Anderson, assured and confident; or Robeson, towering and brave in the face of adversities on screen and off; or Cicely Tyson and Paul Winfield, as they revealed characters refusing to relinquish their integrity or pride; or Diana Ross and Billy Dee Williams, as they proved crafty Oscar Micheaux right, that a little star power can go a long way; or Pyror, as he moved one and all with his personal pain and transcendent talent; or Spike Lee, as he proved a low-budget movie coupled with a lot of ingenuity can carry one a great distance; or Dandridge, haunting and magnetic, as she sent hopes flying for a new type of leading lady in a new kind of cinema; or Denzel Washington challenging himself and us as he took on a variety of roles; or Viola Davis, turning a few minutes of screen time into dramatic gold.

And so now, having viewed African American film history in over a hundred year span, one might ask exactly what goes into the making of a decent, humane, forward-looking black film. Exactly, what should the new black artists give to their audiences? There are, of course, no definite outlines of what should be done, but from knowledge of the past, one does have an idea of the possibilities, the potentialities, of a new black cinema. If there are to be significant African American films, the black actors and actresses, the directors, the writers, the producers, and the technicians who are now being given a chance to work must articulate the contemporary African American's mind, his/her perspectives, aspirations, and goals. The black filmmaker must come to terms with the world in which he or she lives. African American films can liberate audiences from illusions, black and white, and in doing so, can give all of us vision and truth. It is a tremendous responsibility, in some cases perhaps greater than that placed on ordinary white moviemakers. But the dignity of the African American man and woman has traditionally lain in his or her ability to face reality no matter how senseless it may seem and if lucky, to alter that reality. Politics and history. Romance and adventure. Love and hope. The subjects are limitless. And now one can only hope that new dazzling black lights will continue to emerge on the screen—and behind it—to capture and extend one's imagination as good performers, good filmmakers, and good movies should, to both entertain and enlighten us.

Yesterday may not have been great. But the talents of some extraordinary past black film artists make us believe that tomorrow has to be better.

INDEX

Page numbers in *italic* refer to illustrations, those in **bold** indicate major discussions.